John
Sean Johnson

Sams **Teach Yourself**

iPhone™
Application
Development

in **24**
Hours

800 East 96th Street, Indianapolis, Indiana, 46240 USA

Sams Teach Yourself iPhone Application Development in 24 Hours

Copyright © 2010 by Sams Publishing

All rights reserved. No part of this book shall be reproduced, stored in a retrieval system, or transmitted by any means, electronic, mechanical, photocopying, recording, or otherwise, without written permission from the publisher. No patent liability is assumed with respect to the use of the information contained herein. Although every precaution has been taken in the preparation of this book, the publisher and author assume no responsibility for errors or omissions. Nor is any liability assumed for damages resulting from the use of the information contained herein.

ISBN-13: 978-0-672-33084-1

ISBN-10: 0-672-33084-9

Library of Congress Cataloging-in-Publication Data is on file.

Printed in the United States of America

First Printing October 2009

Trademarks

All terms mentioned in this book that are known to be trademarks or service marks have been appropriately capitalized. Sams Publishing cannot attest to the accuracy of this information. Use of a term in this book should not be regarded as affecting the validity of any trademark or service mark.

Warning and Disclaimer

Every effort has been made to make this book as complete and as accurate as possible, but no warranty or fitness is implied. The information provided is on an "as is" basis. The authors and the publisher shall have neither liability nor responsibility to any person or entity with respect to any loss or damages arising from the information contained in this book.

Bulk Sales

Sams Publishing offers excellent discounts on this book when ordered in quantity for bulk purchases or special sales. For more information, please contact

U.S. Corporate and Government Sales

1-800-382-3419

corpsales@pearsontechgroup.com

For sales outside of the U.S., please contact

International Sales

international@pearson.com

Associate Publisher
Greg Wiegand

Acquisitions Editor
Laura Norman

Development and Copy Editor
Keith Cline

Managing Editor
Patrick Kanouse

Indexer
Tim Wright

Proofreader
Debbie Williams

Technical Editor
Matthew David

Publishing Coordinator
Cindy J. Teeters

Designer
Gary Adair

Compositor
Bronkella Publishing LLC

Contents at a Glance

Table of Contents

Sams Teach Yourself iPhone™ Application Development in 24 Hours

About the Author

John Ray is currently serving as a senior business analyst and development team manager for The Ohio State University Research Foundation. He has written numerous books for Macmillan/Sams/Que, including *Special Edition Using TCP/IP*, *Teach Yourself Dreamweaver MX in 21 Days*, *Mac OS X Unleashed*, and *Macromedia All-In-One*. As a Macintosh user since 1984, he strives to ensure that each project presents the Macintosh with the equality and depth it deserves. Even technical titles such as *Special Edition Using TCP/IP* contain extensive information on the Macintosh and its applications and have garnered numerous positive reviews for its straightforward approach and accessibility to beginning and intermediate users.

Sean Johnson is a long-time Mac developer with more than 15 years of product development experience in the world of micro-ISVs, start-ups, and enterprise software vendors such as IBM. He writes a column on product design for the Mac Developer Network, and he's written articles for IBM's developerWorks and various magazines. Sean runs a product development consultancy, Snooty Monkey, LLC, which hand crafts extraordinary web, Mac, and iPhone applications. He lives with his wife and two children in the beautiful town of Chapel Hill, North Carolina.

Dedication

John Ray's dedication:

[thisBook setDedication: @"You!"]

Sean Johnson's dedication:

To my wife and best friend, Michelle, and to my wonderful children, Samantha and Scott, may you never again have to hear, "No, I'm working on the book."

Acknowledgments

John Ray's acknowledgements:

Many thanks to the group at Sams Publishing: Laura Norman, Patrick Kanouse, Keith Cline, Matthew David—for keeping the project under control and making sure that my words make sense! As always, many thanks go to my friends and family for dealing with me as I worked on the project, and my lawn for being patient about the mowing.

Most of all, thanks to you, the reader, for being interested in learning about iPhone development. I can't wait to see your apps on the App Store!

Sean Johnson's acknowledgments:

This book wouldn't have been possible without my beautiful and hard-working wife, Michelle. Thank you, Michelle, for doing the million things that needed done while I sat behind the computer and the hours turned into days and weeks and months.

I'm honored to be working with my experienced and talented co-author, John Ray. Thank you, John. I would also like to thank the fantastic editorial, technical, and production professionals at Pearson. This book is truly a team effort, and I was fortunate to have a great team.

I also want to acknowledge the companionship of my rats, Carolina and Savannah, who were by my side in my office as every word was written. No author has ever had companions that were more respectful of the writing process.

Thank you to Steve Jobs, Jonathan Ives, and the hundreds of engineers and designers at Apple who created the iPhone. It is a joy to use, to develop applications for, and to write about. It has inspired me and countless others, and it reminds me why I love developing software. I couldn't possibly ask more of any product. Well done.

Lastly, thank you to "America's Most Livable Small City," Chapel Hill, North Carolina, for providing me a great place to live and be inspired.

We Want to Hear from You!

As the reader of this book, *you* are our most important critic and commentator. We value your opinion and want to know what we're doing right, what we could do better, what areas you'd like to see us publish in, and any other words of wisdom you're willing to pass our way.

You can email or write me directly to let me know what you did or didn't like about this book—as well as what we can do to make our books stronger.

Please note that I cannot help you with technical problems related to the topic of this book, and that due to the high volume of mail I receive, I might not be able to reply to every message.

When you write, please be sure to include this book's title and author as well as your name and phone or email address. I will carefully review your comments and share them with the author and editors who worked on the book.

E-mail: consumer@samspublishing.com

Mail: Greg Wiegand
            Associate Publisher
            Sams Publishing
            800 East 96th Street
            Indianapolis, IN 46240 USA

Reader Services

Visit our website and register this book at informit.com/register for convenient access to any updates, downloads, or errata that might be available for this book.

Introduction

Over the past 2 years, Apple has moved from a nonplayer in the world of handheld computing to a dominating force. The iPhone and iPod Touch platform has changed the way that we, the public, think about our mobile computing devices. With full-featured applications and an interface architecture that demonstrates that small screens can be effective workspaces, the iPhone has become the smartphone of choice for users and developers alike.

Part of what makes the iPhone such a success is the combination of an amazing interface and an effective software distribution method. The iPhone operating system was designed to be controlled with your fingers, rather than with a stylus or keypad. The applications are "natural" and fun to use, instead of looking and behaving like a clumsy port of a desktop app. (We're looking at you, Windows Mobile!)

Through the App Store, Apple has created the ultimate digital distribution system for developers. Programmers of any age or affiliation can submit their applications to the App Store for only the cost of a modest yearly developer membership fee. In 2008, simple sound effects applications made profits of thousands of dollars per day. Experiential applications such as Koi Pond have sold hundreds of thousands of copies. No matter what the content, with a user base as large as the iPhone, there is an audience.

In mid-2009, Apple added a wide range of new features to the iPhone platform through the release of the iPhone OS 3.0 and iPhone 3GS platform. This advancement offers developers the tools to continue building unique and creative games, utilities, and applications.

Our hope is that this book will bring iPhone development to a new generation of developers. *Teach Yourself iPhone Development in 24 Hours* provides a clear natural progression of skills development—from installing developer tools and registering with Apple, to submitting an application to the App Store. It's everything you need to get started in 24 1-hour lessons.

Who Can Become an iPhone Developer?

If you have an interest in learning, time to invest in exploring and practicing with Apple's developer tools, and an Intel Macintosh computer, you have everything you need to begin developing for the iPhone.

Developing an application for the iPhone won't happen overnight, but with dedication and practice, you can be writing your first applications in a matter of days. The more time you spend working with the Apple developer tools, the more opportunities you'll discover for creating new and exciting projects.

You should approach iPhone application development as creating software that *you* want to use, not what you think others want. If you're solely interested in getting rich quick, you're likely to be disappointed. (The App Store is a crowded marketplace—albeit one with a lot of room—and competition for top sales is fierce.) However, if you focus on building apps that are useful and unique, you're much more likely to find an appreciative audience.

Who Should Use This Book?

This book targets individuals who are new to development for the iPhone and have experience using the Macintosh platform. No previous experience with Objective-C, Cocoa, or the Apple developer tools is required. Of course, if you do have development experience, some of the tools and techniques may be easier to master, but the authors do not assume that you've coded before.

That said, we do expect some things from you, the reader. Specifically, you must be willing to invest in the learning process. If you just read each hour's lesson without working through the tutorials, you will likely miss some fundamental concepts. In addition, you need to spend time reading the Apple developer documentation and researching the topics we present in the book. There is a vast amount of information on iPhone development available, and only a limited space in this book. We'll cover what you need to forge your own path forward.

What Is (and Isn't) in This Book?

We have specifically targeted iPhone OS release 3.0 with this book. Much of what you'll be learning is common to all the iPhone OS releases, but we also cover several important advances in 3.0, such as accessibility, A/V library access, map integration, and more!

Unfortunately, this is not a complete reference for the iPhone application programming interfaces (APIs). Some topics require much more space than the format of this book allows. Thankfully, the Apple developer documentation is available directly within the free tools you'll be downloading in Hour 1, "Preparing Your System and iPhone for Development." In many lessons, we've included a section titled "Further Exploration." This will guide you toward additional related topics of interest. Again, a willingness to explore will be an important quality in becoming a successful iPhone developer!

Each coding lesson is accompanied by project files that include everything you need to compile and test an example or, preferably, follow along and build the application yourself. Be sure to download the project files from the book's website at http://iphonein24hours.com.

Conventions Used in This Book

This book uses several design elements and conventions to help you prioritize and reference the information it contains:

▶ When you are asked to type or enter text in a block of code, that text appears in bold.

▶ Menu options are separated by a comma. For example, when you should open the File menu and choose the New Project menu option, the text says "Select File, New Project."

▶ A special monospace font is used on programming-related terms, language, and code. Wherever possible, we've used the default Xcode color scheme.

▶ Some code statements presented in this book are too long to appear on a single line. In these cases, we've attempted to wrap the lines in logical locations. Sometimes, however, line-continuation characters are used to indicate that the following line is a continuation of the current statement.

HOUR 1

Preparing Your System and iPhone for Development

What You'll Learn in This Hour:

- ▶ What makes an iPhone an iPhone
- ▶ Where to get the tools you need to develop for the iPhone
- ▶ How to join the iPhone Developer Program
- ▶ The need for (and use of) iPhone provisioning profiles
- ▶ What to expect during the first few hours of this book

The iPhone opens up a whole new world for developers—a multitouch interface, always-on Internet access, video, and a whole range of built-in sensors can be used to create everything from games to serious productivity applications. Believe it or not, as a new developer, you have an advantage. You will be starting fresh, free from any preconceived notions of what is possible in a handheld application. Your next big idea may well become the next big thing on Apple's App Store.

This hour will get you prepared for iPhone development. You're about to embark on the road to becoming an iPhone developer, but there's a bit of prep work before you start coding.

Welcome to the iPhone Platform

If you're reading this book, you already have an iPhone, and that means you already understand what it means to own and use the system. A unique and responsive interface, crisp graphics, multitouch, and hundreds of apps—this just begins to scratch the surface. As a developer, however, you'll need to get accustomed to dealing with a platform that, to borrow a phrase from Apple, forces you to "think different."

Display and Graphics

The iPhone screen is 320x480 pixels—giving you a limited amount of space to present your application's content and interface (see Figure 1.1). iPhone applications also eliminate the notion of multiple windows. You will have one window to work in. You can change the content within that window, but the desktop and multiwindow application metaphors are gone.

FIGURE 1.1
The iPhone has a screen resolution of 320x480.

The screen limits aren't a bad thing. As you'll learn, the iPhone development tools give you plenty of opportunities to create applications with just as much depth as your desktop software—albeit with a more structured and efficient interface design.

The graphics that you display on your screen can include complex animated 2D and 3D displays thanks to the OpenGL ES implementation available on all iPhone models. OpenGL is an industry standard for defining and manipulating graphic images that is widely used when creating games. The iPhone 3GS improves these capabilities with an updated 3D chipset and more advanced version of OpenGL (v. 2.0), but all the models have very respectable imaging abilities.

Application Resource Constraints

Like the high-definition displays on our desktops and laptops, we've grown accustomed to processors that can work faster than we can click. The iPhone employs a 412MHz ARM in the early models, and a 600MHz version in the 3GS—both underclocked to preserve battery life. This is a far stretch from your MacBook Pro, but still quite capable of handling everyday productivity apps and games.

Apple has gone to great lengths to keep the iPhone responsive, no matter what you're doing. Unfortunately, this has contributed to one of the biggest limitations placed on the platform—only a single *third-party* application can run at a time. This means that your program must provide the features users need without forcing them to jump into other apps. It also means that your application must remain active to communicate with the user. With iPhone OS 3.0, Apple has provided a means of "pushing" notifications to the user, but no actual processing can take place when your application has exited.

Another constraint that you need to be mindful of is the available memory. In the original and iPhone 3G devices, there is 128MB of RAM available for *the entire system, including your application*. There is no virtual memory, so you must carefully manage the objects that your application creates. In the iPhone 3GS, Apple has graciously provided 256MB, but keep in mind that there are no RAM upgrades for earlier models!

> Throughout the book, you'll see reminders to "release" memory when you're done using it. Even though you may get tired of seeing it, this is a very important process to get used to.

By the Way

Connectivity

Connectivity is one of the areas where the iPhone truly shines. Unlike our current Mac laptops, the iPhone has the ability to always be connected via a cellular provider (such as AT&T in the United States). Each successive generation of the iPhone has improved these capabilities—from the relatively low-speed EDGE to HSDPA 7.2 in the current incarnation of the device.

This wide-area access is supplemented with built-in WiFi and Bluetooth. WiFi can provide desktop-like speeds within the range of a wireless hot spot. BlueTooth, on the other hand, can now (with iPhone OS 3.0) be used to connect a variety of peripheral devices to your phone.

As a developer, you can make use of the always-connected Internet access to update the content in your application, display web pages, or create multiplayer games. The only drawback is that the more cellular bandwidth you consume, the greater the chance your application will be rejected from the App Store. At present, there is a poorly defined limit as to what you can and can't do on the AT&T network, something that has plagued developers large and small.

Input and Feedback

The iPhone shines when it comes to input and feedback mechanisms and your ability to work with them. You can read the input values from the capacitive multitouch (four-finger!) screen, sense motion and tilt via the accelerometer, determine where you are using the GPS (3G/3GS), which way you're facing with the digital compass (3GS), and how the phone is being used with the proximity and light sensors. The phone itself can provide so much data to your application about how and where it is being used that the device itself truly becomes a controller of sorts—much like the Nintendo Wii.

The iPhone also supports capturing pictures and video (3GS) directly into your applications, opening a realm of possibilities for interacting with the real world. Already applications are available that identify objects you've taken pictures of and finds references to them online.

Finally, for each action your user takes in interacting with your application, you can provide feedback. This, obviously, can be visible feedback on the screen, or it can be high-quality audio and force feedback via vibration. As a developer, you can access all of these capabilities, and you'll use them in this book!

That wraps up our quick tour of the iPhone platform. Never before has a single device defined and provided so many capabilities for a developer. As long as you think through the resource limitations and plan accordingly, a wealth of development opportunities awaits you.

Although this book targets the iPhone specifically, almost all the information carries over to development for the iPod Touch. These systems differ in capabilities, such as support for a camera and GPS, but the development techniques are otherwise identical.

Becoming an iPhone Developer

Obviously there is more to being an iPhone developer than just sitting down and writing a program. You need a modern Intel Macintosh desktop or laptop running a recent version of Leopard or Snow Leopard, and at least 6GB of free space on your hard drive. The more screen space you have on your development system, the easier it will be to switch between the coding, design, simulation, and reference tools that you'll need to be using. That said, I've worked perfectly happily on a 13" MacBook Pro, so an ultra-HD multimonitor setup certainly isn't necessary.

So, assuming you already have a Mac, what else do you need? The good news is that there isn't *much* more, and it won't cost you a cent to write your first iPhone application.

Joining the Apple Developer Program

Despite somewhat confusing messages on the Apple website, there really is no fee associated with joining the Apple Developer Program, downloading the SDK (Software Development Kit), writing iPhone applications, and running them on Apple's iPhone Simulator.

There are limitations, however, to what you can do for free. If you want to have early access to beta versions of the iPhone OS and SDK, you'll need to be a paid member. If you want to load the applications you write on a physical iPhone device or distribute them on the App Store, you'll also need to pay the membership fee. Most of the applications in this book will work just fine on the simulator provided with the free tools, so the decision on how to proceed is up to you.

> **Did you Know?**
>
> If you aren't yet sure if the paid program is right for you, you can upgrade at any time. I recommend starting out with the free program and upgrading after you've had a chance to write a few sample applications and run them in the simulator.
>
> Obviously, things such as vibration and sensor input can't be accurately presented in the simulator, but these are special cases and won't be needed until later in the book.

If you choose to pay, the paid Developer Program offers two levels: a standard program ($99) for those who will be creating applications that they want to distribute on the App Store, or an enterprise program ($299) for larger companies wanting to develop and distribute applications in-house but *not* through the App Store. Chances are, the standard program is what you want.

> **By the Way**
>
> The standard ($99) program is available for both companies and individuals. If you want to publish to the App Store with a business name, you'll be given the option of choosing a standard "individual" or "company" program during the registration.

Registering as a Developer

Big or small, free or paid, your venture into iPhone development begins on Apple's website. To start, visit the Apple iPhone Dev Center (http://developer.apple.com/iphone/), shown in Figure 1.2.

If you already have an Apple ID from using iTunes or other Apple services, congratulations, you're almost done! Use the Log In link to access your account, agree to Apple's developer terms, and provide a few pieces of additional information for your developer profile. You'll immediately be granted access to the free iPhone developer resources!

FIGURE 1.2
Visit the iPhone Dev Center to log in or start the enrollment process.

If you don't yet have an Apple ID, click the Register link and choose Create an Apple ID in the first step, as shown in Figure 1.3.

The registration process walks you through the process of creating a new Apple ID, and collects information about your development interests and experience, as shown in Figure 1.4.

After the registration is complete, Apple will verify your email address by sending you a clickable link to activate your account.

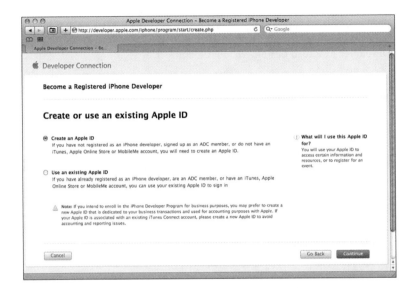

FIGURE 1.3
You'll use an Apple ID to access all the developer resources.

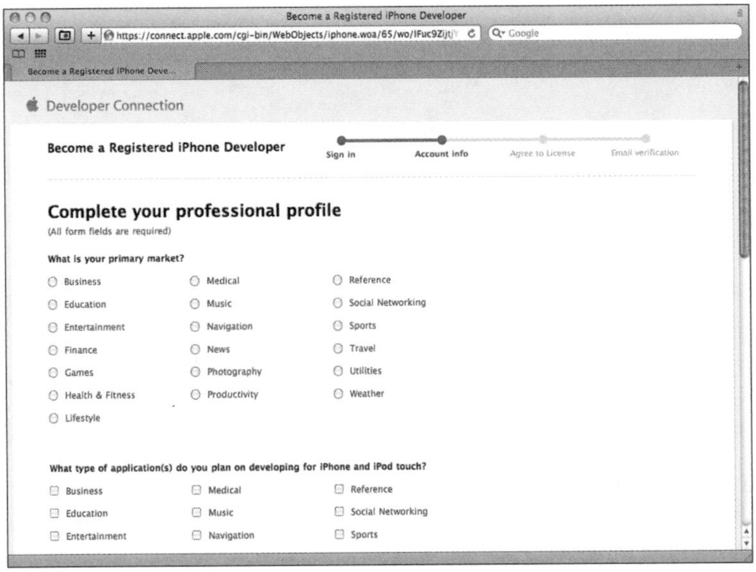

FIGURE 1.4
The multistep registration process collects a variety of information about your development experience.

Joining a Paid Developer Program

Once you have a registered and activated Apple ID, you can make the decision to join a paid program, or continue using the free resources. If you choose to join a paid program, again point your browser to the iPhone Dev Center (http://developer.apple.com/iphone) and click the Register button. Choose Use an Existing Apple ID for the Developer Program option, visible in Figure 1.3.

The registration tool will now guide you through applying for the paid programs, including choosing between the standard and company options, as shown in Figure 1.5.

FIGURE 1.5
Choose the paid program that you want to apply for.

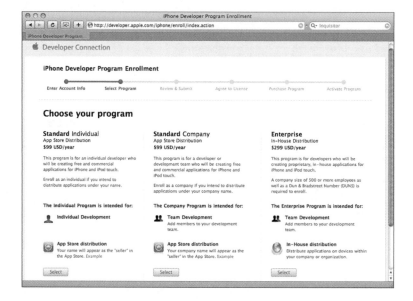

Unlike the free Developer Membership, the paid Developer Program does not take effect immediately. When the App Store first launched, it took months for new developers to join and be approved into the program. Today, it may take hours or a few days—just be patient. You can check your current status at any time by logging in to the iPhone Dev Center and following the Check Your Enrollment Status Now link.

Use the Register link to create a new free Developer Membership, or follow the links in the iPhone Developer Program section (currently http://developer.apple.com/iphone/program/) to join a paid program.

Installing the iPhone Developer Tools

After you've registered your Apple ID, you can immediately download the current release version of the iPhone developer tools directly from the iPhone Dev Center (http://developer.apple.com/iphone/). Just click the Download link and sit back while your Mac downloads the massive (~3GB) SDK disk image.

If you have the free Developer Membership, you'll likely only see a single SDK to download—the current release version of the development tools. If you've become a paid program member, you may see additional links for different versions of the SDK (2.2, 3.0, and so on). The examples in this book are based on the 3.x series of SDKs, so be sure to choose that option if presented.

Did you Know?

When the download completes, open the resulting disk image, and double click the iPhone SDK icon. This will launch the Mac OS X installer application and assist you in the installation. There is no need to change any of the defaults for the installer, so just read and agree to the software license and click Continue to proceed through the steps.

Unlike most applications, the Apple developer tools will be installed in a folder called Developer located at the root of your hard drive. Inside the Developer folder are dozens of files and folders containing developer frameworks, source code files, examples, and of course, the developer applications themselves. Nearly all of your work in this book will start with the application Xcode, located in the Developer/Applications folder (see Figure 1.6).

FIGURE 1.6
Most of your work with the developer tools will start in the Developer/Applications folder.

Although we won't get into real development for a few more hours, we *will* be configuring a few options in Xcode in the next section, so don't forget where it is!

Creating a Development Provisioning Profile

Even after you've obtained an Apple Developer Membership, joined a paid Developer Program, and downloaded and installed the iPhone development tools, you *still* won't have the ability to run applications that you write on your own iPhone! The reason for this is that you haven't created a development provisioning profile.

In many iPhone development guides, this step isn't covered until after development begins. In my mind, once you've written an application, you're going to want to immediately run it on the iPhone. Why? Because it's just cool to see your own code running on your own phone!

What Is a Development Provisioning Profile?

When Apple opened the iPhone up to developers, they wanted to make absolutely certain that the development process is controlled and that groups couldn't just distribute software to anyone they pleased. The result is a rather confusing process that ties together information about you, any development team members, and your application into a "provisioning profile."

A development provisioning profile identifies the developer who may install an application, an ID for the application being developed, and the "unique device identifiers" for each iPhone that will run the application. This is *only* for the development process. When you are ready to distribute an application on the App Store or via ad hoc means, you'll need to create a separate "distribution" profile. Because we're just starting out, this isn't something you'll need right away. We talk more about distribution profiles in Hour 24, "Distributing Applications Through the App Store."

Generating and Installing a Development Provisioning Profile

One of the biggest complaints from early entrants into the iPhone Developer Program was that the process of creating a provisioning profile was cumbersome and, frankly, sometimes just didn't seem to work. Apple has streamlined the process tremendously in an online provisioning assistant, but we'll still need to jump through some hoops. Let's bite the bullet and get through this!

Getting Your iPhone Unique Device Identifier

To run your application on a real iPhone, you'll need the ID that uniquely identifies your iPhone from the tens of millions of other iPhones. To find this, first make sure that your iPhone is connected to your computer, and then launch Xcode from the Developer, Applications folder. When Xcode first launches, immediately choose Window, Organizer from the menu. The Organizer utility slightly resembles iTunes in its layout. You should see your phone listed in the leftmost column of the Organizer under the Devices section. Click your phone to select it. Your screen should now resemble Figure 1.7.

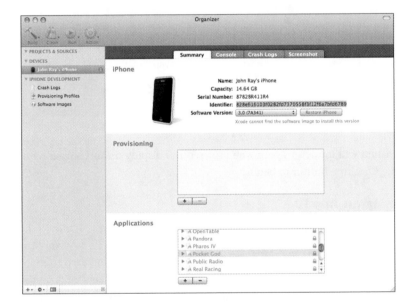

FIGURE 1.7
First, grab the ID of your iPhone.

The Identifier field is the unique device ID that we're looking for. Go ahead and copy it to the Clipboard. You'll need to paste it into the provisioning assistant shortly.

Starting the Provisioning Assistant

Next, head to the Apple website and the iPhone Dev Center (http://developer.apple.com/iphone). Make sure that you've logged in to the site, and then click the iPhone Developer Program Portal link, currently located in the upper-right side of the page. The Developer Program Portal is designed to give you access to the tools you need to create provisioning and distribution profiles. It also includes the Development Provisioning Assistant, which is the web utility that will make our lives much easier. Click the Launch Assistant button (see Figure 1.8).

FIGURE 1.8
Head to the
Developer
Program Portal,
and then launch
the
Development
Provisioning
Assistant.

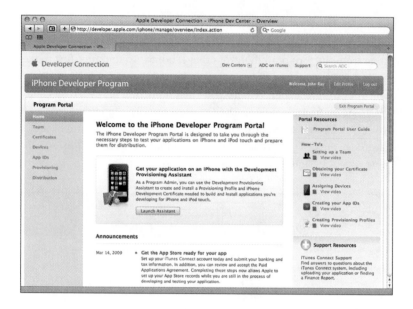

The assistant will launch in your web browser and display a short splash screen.
Click the Continue button to begin.

Choosing an App ID

Your first step will be choosing an App ID. This is an ID that will identify a shared
portion of the keychain that your application will have access to. Say what? The
keychain is a secure information store on the iPhone that can be used to save pass-
words and other critical information. Most apps don't share a keychain space (and
therefore can't share protected information). If you use the same App ID for multiple applications, however, they *can* share keychain data.

For the purposes of this book, there's no reason the tutorial apps can't share a single
App ID, so create a new ID named anything you'd like. If you have already created
App IDs in the past, you'll be given the option to choose an existing ID. I'm creating
a new App ID, Tutorials, as shown in Figure 1.9. Enter the ID and click Continue to
move on.

Assigning a Development Device

Next you are asked to assign a development device, as shown in Figure 1.10. This is
the device ID that identifies which iPhone will be allowed to run the applications
you create. Enter a meaningful description for the device (Joe Smith's iPhone, for
example), and then paste the string you copied from the Xcode organizer into the
Device ID field. Click Continue to move on.

FIGURE 1.9
An App ID can
be used for a
single applica-
tion or group of
applications.

FIGURE 1.10
Assign a device
that can run
your application.

Note that as with the App IDs, if you've already used a device ID in the past, you will be given the option of simply selecting it from a drop-down list.

Generating a Certificate Signing Request

Now things are getting fun. The next step of the process takes place outside of your browser. Leaving the Development Provisioning Assistant open, go to the Applications, Utilities folder on your hard drive and open the Keychain Access utility. Next, choose Keychain Access, Certificate Assistant, Request a Certificate from a Certificate Authority from the menu (see Figure 1.11).

FIGURE 1.11
In this step, you create a certificate request that is uploaded to Apple.

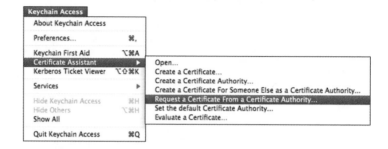

The Keychain Access Certificate Assistant will start. Thankfully, this is a pretty short process. You simply need to enter your email address, name, and highlight the Saved to Disk option, as shown in Figure 1.12.

FIGURE 1.12
Enter the information needed for the certificate request. You can leave the CA Email Address field empty.

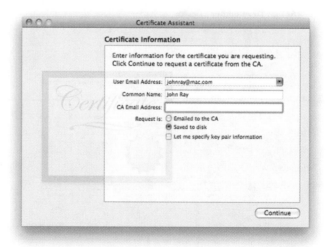

Click Continue to save the certificate to your disk. Make sure you make a note of where you save the certificate, because you're going to be uploading it to Apple back in the Development Provisioning Assistant. Once saved, you can close the Certificate Assistant window.

Uploading the Certificate Signing Request

Return to the Development Provisioning Assistant in your web browser. Click continue until you are prompted to submit the certificate signing request that you just generated (see Figure 1.13). Use the Choose File button to select the request file, and then click Continue to upload it.

FIGURE 1.13
Upload the certificate signing request to Apple.

Naming and Generating the Provisioning Profile

We're almost done! After uploading the request, you'll be prompted to name the provisioning profile (see Figure 1.14). Because this profile contains information that can potentially identify individual phones and applications, you should choose something relevant to how you intend to use it. In this case, I'm only interested in using it as a generic development profile for all of my apps, so I'm naming it Development Profile. Not very creative, but it works.

Click the Generate button to create your provisioning profile. This may take 20 to 60 seconds, so be patient. The screen will eventually refresh to show the final profile information, as shown in Figure 1.15.

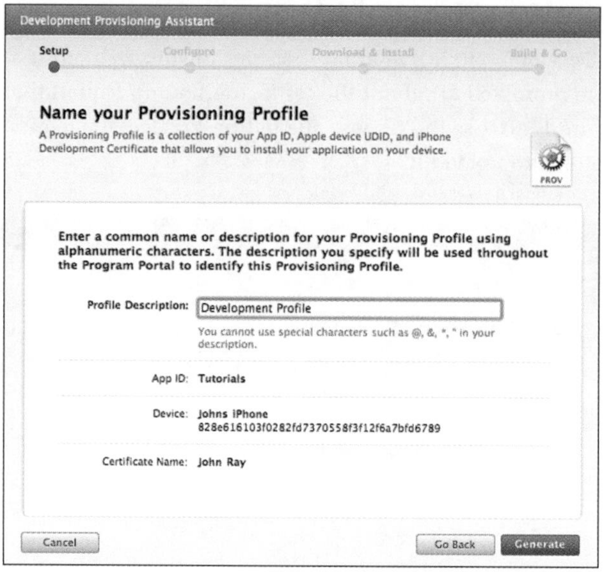

FIGURE 1.14
Name the pro-
file to reflect
how you intend
to use it.

FIGURE 1.15
After several
seconds, the
profile is gener-
ated.

Our final steps will be downloading and installing the profile, and downloading and installing a security certificate that will be associated with the profile.

Downloading the Development Provisioning Profile and Certificate

At this point, your profile has been generated, along with a security certificate that can be used to uniquely associate your applications with that profile. All that remains is downloading and installing them. Click the Continue button to access the provisioning profile download screen, as seen in Figure 1.16. Click the Download Now button to save the profile to your Downloads folder (file extension .mobileprovision).

FIGURE 1.16
Download the provisioning profile.

As much as I hate to say it, the next thing to do is to ignore the onscreen instructions—the installation process that Apple describes in the assistant isn't the most efficient route. Instead, click the Continue button until you are given the option of downloading the development certificate, as shown in Figure 1.17.

Click the Download Now button to download the certificate file (file extension .cer) to your Downloads folder. You are now finished with the provisioning assistant and can safely exit.

FIGURE 1.17
Download the
development
certificate.

Installing the Development Provisioning Profile and Certificate

To install the profile and certificate, we'll just need that very useful skill—double-clicking. First, install the development certificate by double-clicking it. This will open Keychain Access and prompt you for the keychain where the certificate should be installed. Choose the login keychain, and then click OK, as demonstrated in Figure 1.18.

FIGURE 1.18
Choose the
login keychain
to hold your
development
certificate.

After adding the certificate, you should be able to browse through your login keychain for a key labeled with your name that contains the certificate.

To install the development profile, double-click the downloaded .mobileprovision file. Xcode will launch—if it isn't already running—and silently install the profile. You can verify that it has been successfully installed by launching the Organizer within Xcode (Window, Organizer), and then clicking the Provisioning Profiles item within the iPhone Development section, as shown in Figure 1.19.

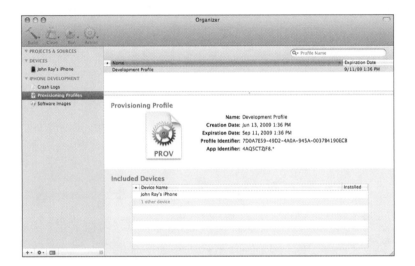

FIGURE 1.19
If the profile has been successfully installed, it should be listed in the Xcode Organizer.

But Wait... I Have More Than One iPhone!

The Development Provisioning Assistant helps you create a provisioning profile for a single iPhone or iPod Touch device—but what if you have multiple devices that you want to install onto? No problem. You'll need to head back to the iPhone Developer Program Portal and click the Devices link listed on the left side of the page. From there, you can add additional devices that will be available to your profile.

Next, click the Provisioning link, also on the left side of the page, and use the Edit link to modify your existing profile to include another iPhone or iPod Touch, as demonstrated in Figure 1.20.

Finally, you'll need to use the download link to redownload the modified profile and then import it into Xcode so that the additional device is available.

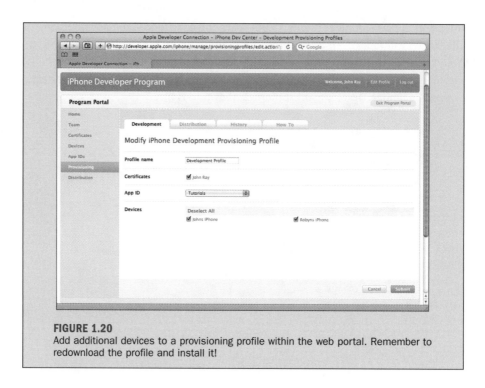

FIGURE 1.20
Add additional devices to a provisioning profile within the web portal. Remember to redownload the profile and install it!

Testing the Profile with an iPhone App

It seems wrong to go through all of that work without some payoff, right? For a real-world test of your efforts, let's actually try to run an application on your iPhone. If you haven't downloaded the project files to your computer, now would be a good time to visit http://iphonein24hours.com and download the archives.

Within the Hour 1 Projects folder, open the Welcome folder. Double-click the Welcome.xcodeproj to open a very simple application in Xcode. After the project opens, your display should be very similar to Figure 1.21.

Next, make sure that your phone is plugged into your computer. Using the menu in the upper-left corner of the Xcode window, choose iPhone Device 3.0 (Base SDK). This will tell Xcode that when the project is built, it should be installed on your iPhone. Finally, click Build and Run.

After a few seconds, the application should be installed and launched on your iPhone, as you can see in Figure 1.22.

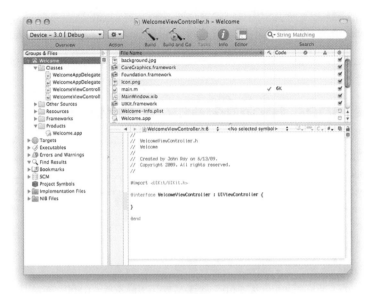

FIGURE 1.21
Open the
Welcome.xcode-
proj in Xcode.

FIGURE 1.22
Congratulations,
you've just
installed your
first home-
grown iPhone
application!

You can now exit Xcode and quit the Welcome application on your phone.

> When you clicked Build and Run, the Welcome application was installed and started on your phone. It will remain there until you remove it manually. Just press and hold the Welcome icon and delete it as you would any other application.

Developer Technology Overview

Over the course of the next few hours, you will be introduced to the technologies that you'll be using to create iPhone applications. Our goal is to get you up to speed on the tools and technology, and then start actively developing. This means you're still a few hours away from writing your first app, but when you start coding, you'll have the necessary background skills and knowledge to successfully create a wide variety of applications.

The Apple Developer Suite

In this chapter, you downloaded and worked with the Xcode application. This is just one piece (albeit a very important piece) of the developer suite that you will be using throughout the book. Xcode, coupled with Interface Builder and the iPhone Simulator, will make up your development environment. These three applications are so critical, in fact, that we've devoted two hours (2 and 4) to covering them.

It's worth mentioning that every iPhone application and (almost) every Macintosh application you run, whether created by a single developer at home or a huge company, is built using the Apple developer tools. This means that you have everything you need to create software as powerful as any you've ever run.

Later in the book, you'll be introduced to additional tools in the suite that can help you debug and optimize your application.

Objective-C

Objective-C is the language that you'll be using to write your applications. It will provide the structure for our applications, and be used to control the logic and decision making that goes on when an application is running.

If you've never worked with a programming language before, don't worry; we cover everything you need to get started in Hour 3, "Discovering Objective-C." Developing for the iPhone in Objective-C is a unique experience. The language is unobtrusive and structured in a way that makes it easy to follow. After your first few projects, Objective-C will fade into the background, letting you concentrate on the specifics of your application.

Cocoa Touch

While Objective-C defines the structure for iPhone applications, Cocoa Touch defines the functional building blocks, called *classes*, that can make the iPhone do certain things. Cocoa Touch isn't a "thing," per se, but a collection of interface elements, data storage elements, and other handy tools that you can access from your applications.

As you'll learn in Hour 4, "Inside Cocoa Touch," there are literally hundreds of different Cocoa Touch classes that you can access and thousands of things you can do with them. We cover quite a bit of the most useful classes in this book, and give you the pointers you need to explore even more on your own.

Model-View-Controller

The iPhone and Macintosh use a development approach called Model-View-Controller (MVC) to structure applications. Understanding why MVC is used and the benefits it provides will help you make good decisions in structuring your most complex applications. Despite the potentially complicated-sounding name, MVC is really just a way to keep your application projects arranged so that you can easily update and extend them in the future. We look more at MVC in Hour 6, "Model-View-Controller Application Design."

Summary

This hour introduced you to the iPhone platform, its capabilities, and its limitations. You learned about the iPhone's graphic features, RAM size, and the array of sensors that can be used in your applications to create uniquely "aware" experiences. We also discussed the Apple iPhone developer tools, how to download and install them, and the differences between the varying pay-for Developer Programs. To prepare you for actual on-phone development, you explored the process of creating and installing a development provisioning profile in Xcode and even installed an application on your phone.

The hour wrapped up with a quick discussion of the development technologies that will make up the first part of the book and form the basis for all the iPhone development you'll be doing.

Q&A

Q: *I thought the iPhone had at least 8GB of RAM and 32GB in the iPhone 3GS. Doesn't it?*

A: The "memory" capabilities for the iPhone that are advertised to the public are the storage sizes available for applications, songs, and so forth. It is separate from the RAM that can be used for executing programs. If the iPhone implemented virtual memory, it is possible that the larger storage could be used for that purpose, but Apple has not made any indication that this is, or could be, a future feature.

Q: *What platform should I target for development?*

A: That depends on your goals. If you want to reach the largest audience, make sure that your application runs equally well on the newest and oldest iPhones and iPod Touches. If you want to make use of the latest hardware, you can certainly target the unique capabilities of the iPhone 3GS and beyond, but you will potentially be limiting the size of your customer base.

Q: *Why isn't the iPhone platform open?*

A: Great question. Apple has long sought to control the user experience so that it remains "positive" regardless of how users have set up their device, be it a Mac or an iPhone. By ensuring that applications can be tied to a developer and enforcing an approval process, they can limit the potential for a harmful application to cause damage to data or otherwise negatively impact the user. Whether this is an appropriate approach, however, is open to debate.

Workshop

Quiz

1. What is the resolution of the iPhone 3GS screen?

2. What is the cost of joining an individual iPhone Developer Program?

3. What is the language that you will use when creating iPhone applications?

Answers

1. 320x480. The iPhone screen resolutions are identical across the platform variants.

2. The Developer Program costs $99 a year for the individual option.

3. Objective-C will be used for iPhone development.

Activities

1. Establish an Apple Developer Membership and download and install the developer tools. This is an important activity that, if you didn't follow along in the course of the hour, should be completed before starting the next hour's lesson.

2. Review the resources available in the iPhone Dev Center. Apple has published several introductory videos and tutorials that can act as a helpful supplement to this book.

HOUR 2

Introduction to Xcode and the iPhone Simulator

What You'll Learn in This Hour:

- ▶ How to create new projects in Xcode
- ▶ Code editing and navigation features
- ▶ Where to add classes and resources to a project
- ▶ How to modify project properties
- ▶ Compiling for iPhone devices and the iPhone Simulator
- ▶ How to interpret error messages
- ▶ Features and limitations of the iPhone Simulator

The core of your work in the Apple Developer Suite will be spent in three applications: Xcode, Interface Builder, and the iPhone Simulator. This trio of apps provide all the tools that you need to design, program, and test applications for the iPhone. And, unlike other platforms, the Apple Developer Suite is entirely free!

This hour will walk you through the basics you need to work within two of the three components—Xcode and the iPhone Simulator—and you'll get some hands-on practice working with each. We cover the third piece, Interface Builder, in Hour 5, "Exploring Interface Builder."

Using Xcode

When you think of coding—actually typing the statements that will make your iPhone work magic—think Xcode. Xcode is the IDE, or integrated development environment, that manages your application's resources and lets you edit the code that ties the different pieces together.

In your reading, you're likely to see *Xcode* used to refer to the entire Developer Suite as well as the like-named application. When we use the term *Xcode* in this book, we mean the application.

After you install the developer tools, as described in Hour 1, "Preparing Your System and iPhone for Development," you should be able to find Xcode in the /Developer/Applications folder located at the root level of your hard drive. We'll be walking through the day-to-day use of Xcode in this hour, so if you haven't installed the tools yet, do so now!

Launch Xcode from the /Developer/Applications folder. After a few moments, the Welcome to Xcode screen will display, as shown in Figure 2.1.

FIGURE 2.1
Explore Apple's developer resources, right from the Xcode Welcome screen.

You can choose to disable this screen by unchecking the Show at Launch check box, but it does provide a convenient "jumping off" point for most sample code and documentation. In Hour 4, "Inside Cocoa Touch," we'll take a detailed look at the documentation system included in Xcode, which is quite extensive.

Creating and Managing Projects

Most of your iPhone work will start with an Xcode project. A project is a collection of all the files that are associated with an application, along with the settings that are needed to "build" a working piece of software from the files. This includes images, source code, and a file that describes the appearance and objects that make up the interface.

Choosing a Project Type

To create a new project, choose File, New Project (Shift+Command+N) from the Xcode menu. Do this now. Xcode will prompt you to choose a template for your application, as shown in Figure 2.2. The Xcode templates contain the files you need to quickly start on a new development effort. Although it is possible to build an application completely from scratch, the time saved by using a template is pretty significant. We'll use several templates throughout the book, depending on what type of application we're building.

FIGURE 2.2
To create a new project, start by choosing an appropriate template.

Along the left side of the Template window are the categories of templates you can choose from. Our focus will be on the iPhone OS Application category, so be sure that it is selected. On the right side of the display are the templates within the category, with a description of the currently highlighted template. For this tutorial, click the Window-Based Application template, then click the Choose button.

After choosing the template, you'll be prompted for a location and a name to use when saving the project. Name the test project for this hour **HelloXcode** and click Save. Xcode will automatically create a folder with the name of the project and place all the associated files within that folder.

Within your project folder, you'll find a file with the extension .xcodeproj. This is
the file you'll need to open to return to your project workspace after exiting Xcode.

Project Groups

After you've created or opened a project in Xcode, the interface displays an iTunes-
like window for navigating the project's files. On the left side of the window, the
Groups and Files list contains a logical grouping of the files within your project.
Clicking the top group, called the "project group" (and named after the project),
updates the list to the right and shows all the files associated with the application,
as shown in Figure 2.3.

FIGURE 2.3
Use the Groups
and Files list to
navigate
through your
project
resources.

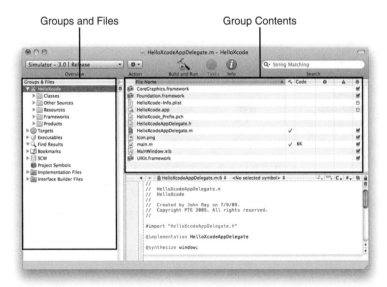

By the Way

Keep in mind that these are logical groupings. You won't find all of these files in
your project directory, nor will you find the same folder structure. The Xcode layout
is designed to help you find what you're looking for easily—not to mirror a file system structure.

Within the project group are five subgroups that you may find useful:

Classes: As you'll learn in the next hour, classes group together application
features that complement one another. Most of your development will be
within a class file.

Other Sources: These are any other source code files that are associated with
the application. You'll rarely need to touch these files.

Resources: The Resources group contains the files that define the user interface, application properties, and any images, sounds, or other media files that you want to make use of within the project.

Frameworks: Frameworks are the core code libraries that give your application a certain level of functionality. By default, Xcode includes the basic frameworks for you, but if you want to add special features, such as sound or vibration, you may need an additional framework. We'll walk through the process of adding frameworks in Hour 11, "Getting the User's Attention."

Products: Anything produced by Xcode is included here (typically, the executable application).

Outside of the project group are additional groups, most of which you won't need to touch for the purposes of learning iPhone development—but a few can come in handy. The Errors and Warnings group, for example, contains any error or warning messages that are generated when you try to build your application. The Bookmarks group enables you to mark specific lines in your code and quickly jump to them. Finally, two smart groups (denoted by the violet folder with the gear icon) are defined by default: Implementation Files and NIB Files. Smart groups cluster together files of a particular type from throughout a project. These groups, in particular, provide quick access to the files where you'll be adding your application logic (known as *implementation files*), and the files which define your interface (NIB "now known as XIB" files).

Didn't You Just Say My Work Would Be with the Class Files? What's This About Implementation Files?!

As you'll learn in the next hour, classes are made up of two files: a header file that describes the features a class will provide, and an implementation file that actually contains the logic that makes those features work. When we say "implementation file," we're just referring to one of the two files in a class.

If you find that you want additional logical groupings of files, you can define your own smart groups via Project, New Smart Group.

Did you Know?

Adding New Code Files to a Project

Even though the Apple iPhone templates do give you a great starting point for your development, you'll find, especially in more advanced projects, that you need to add additional code classes or interface files to supplement the base project. To add a new file to a project, choose File, New. In an interface very similar to the project templates, Xcode will prompt you, as shown in Figure 2.4, for the category and type of file that you want to add to the project. We'll be guiding you throughout the book, so don't worry if the options in the figure look alien.

FIGURE 2.4
Use Xcode to add new files to a project.

Can't I Add Empty Files Manually?

Yes, you could drag your own files into one of the Xcode group folders and copy them into the project. However, just as a project template gives you a head start on implementation, Xcode's file templates do the same thing. They frequently include an outline for the different features that you'll need to implement to make the code functional.

Adding Existing Resources to a Project

Many applications will require sound or image files that you'll be integrating into your development. Obviously Xcode can't help you "create" these files, so you'll need to add them by hand. To do this, just click and drag the file from its location into the Resources group in Xcode. You will be prompted to copy the files. Always make sure the "copy" check box is selected so that Xcode can put the files where they need to go within your project directory.

In the downloadable project folder that corresponds with what you're building this hour, an Images folder contains a file named Icon.png. Drag this file from the Finder into to the Xcode Resources folder. Choose to copy if needed, as shown in Figure 2.5.

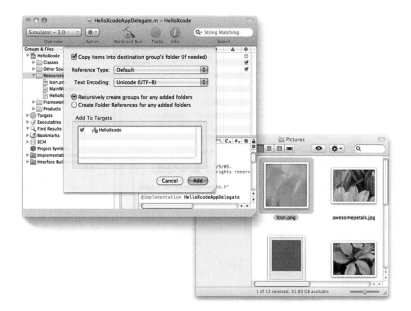

FIGURE 2.5
Drag the icon.png file into the Resources folder and choose to copy if needed.

This file will ultimately serve as the icon for the HelloXcode app.

Removing Files and Resources

If you've added something to Xcode that you decide you don't want, you can delete it easily. To remove a file or resource from your project, simply select it within one of the Xcode groups where it appears, and then press the Delete key. Xcode gives you the option to delete any references to the file from the project and move the file to the trash or just to delete the references (see Figure 2.6).

If you choose to delete references, the file itself will remain, but will no longer be visible in the project.

If Xcode can't find a file that it expects to be part of a project, that file will be highlighted in red in the Xcode interface. This might happen if you accidentally delete a file from the project folder within the Finder. It also occurs when Xcode knows that an application file will be created by a project, but the application hasn't been generated yet. In this case, you can safely ignore the red .app file within the Xcode groups.

By the Way

FIGURE 2.6
Deleting a file's references leaves the actual file untouched.

Editing and Navigating Code

To edit code in Xcode, just click the group that contains the file, and then click the filename. The editable contents of the file are shown in the lower-right pane of the Xcode interface (see Figure 2.7).

FIGURE 2.7
Choose the group, then the file, then edit!

Selected file

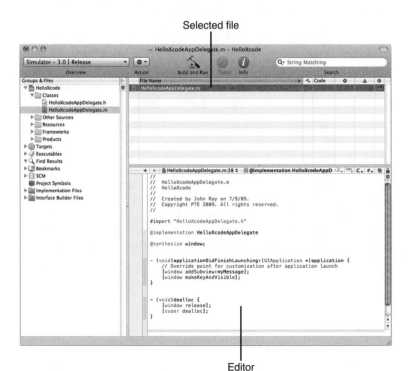

Editor

The Xcode editor works just like any text editor, with a few nice additions. To get a feel for how it works, click the Classes group within the HelloXcode project, then HelloXcodeAppDelegate.m to begin editing the source code.

For this project, we're going to use an interface element called a *label* to display the text Hello Xcode on the iPhone screen. This application, like most that you write, will use a method to show our greeting. A method is just a block of code that executes when something needs to happen. In this sample, we'll use an existing method called applicationDidFinishLaunching that runs as soon as the iPhone application starts.

Jumping to Methods with the Symbol Menu

The easiest way to find a method or property within a source code file is to use the symbol pop-up menu, located above the editing pane. This menu, shown in Figure 2.8, will automatically show all the methods and properties available in the current file, and enables you to jump between them by selecting them.

FIGURE 2.8
The symbol pop-up menu is a quick way to jump between methods and properties.

Find and select applicationDidFinishLaunching from the pop-up menu. Xcode will select the line where the method begins. Click the *next* line, and let's start coding!

Code Completion

Using the Xcode editor, type the following text to implement the
applicationDidFinishLaunching method. You should only need to enter the bold-
ed code lines:

```
- (void)applicationDidFinishLaunching:(UIApplication *)application {
    // Override point for customization after application launch
    UILabel *myMessage;
    UILabel *myUnusedMessage;
    myMessage=[[UILabel alloc] initWithFrame:CGRectMake(25,225,300,50,50)];
    myMessage.text=@"Hello Xcode";
    myMessage.font=[UIFont systemFontOfSize:48];
    [window addSubview:myMessage];
    [window makeKeyAndVisible];
}
```

As you type, you should notice something interesting happening. As soon as you get
to a point in each line where Xcode thinks it knows what you intend to type, it displays an autocompleted version of the code, as demonstrated in Figure 2.9.

FIGURE 2.9
Xcode automati-
cally completes
the code as you
type!

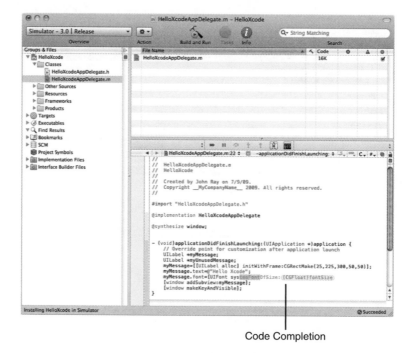

Code Completion

To accept an autocompletion suggestion, just press Tab, and the code will be inserted,
just as if you typed the whole thing. Xcode will try to complete method names, variables
that you've defined, and anything else related to the project that it might recognize.

After you've made your changes, you can save the file by choosing File, Save.

It's not important to understand exactly what this code does—we just want to make sure you get experience in the Xcode editor. The "short and sweet" description of this fragment, however, is that it creates a label object roughly in the center of the iPhone screen, sets the label's text, font, and size, and then adds it to the application's window.

By the Way

Using Snapshots

If you're planning to make many changes to your code and you're not quite sure you'll like the outcome, you may want to take advantage of the "snapshot" feature. A code snapshot is, in essence, a copy of all your source code at a particular moment in time. If you don't like changes you've made, you can revert to an earlier snapshot. Snapshots are also helpful because they show what has changed between multiple versions of an application.

To take a snapshot, choose File, Make Snapshot. That's all there is to it!

To view the available snapshots, choose File, Snapshots. The snapshot viewer displays available snapshots in the leftmost column, a list of changed files to the right, and, if a file is selected, the changes that were made between the selected snapshot and the preceding one. Figure 2.10 shows all of these elements.

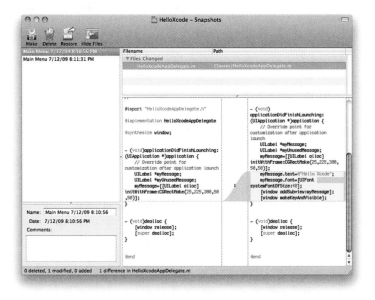

FIGURE 2.10
Use a snapshot to figure out what changes you've made between different versions of your application.

To restore to a specific snapshot, select it in the list, and then click the Restore button.

You can also use the Name and Comments fields at the lower left of the snapshot viewer to provide a meaningful name and relevant comments for any snapshot in the list.

Adding Bookmarks and Pragma Marks

Earlier in the hour, we mentioned the Bookmarks group that displays bookmarks within your project and allows for simple navigation within and between files. To create a new bookmark, position your cursor in whatever portion of a file you want to mark, and then choose Add to Bookmarks from the Action menu in the toolbar (see Figure 2.11).

FIGURE 2.11
Create your own code book-marks.

You'll be prompted for a title for the bookmark, just like in Safari. Once you've saved your bookmark, you can access it from the Bookmarks group in the Groups and Files list.

By the Way

Not only are the bookmarks Safari-like, but you'll also notice a History pop-up menu beside the symbol jump-to menu, and, to the left of that, forward and back-ward arrows to take you back and forward in the history.

Another way to mark points in your code is by adding a #pragma mark directive. Pragma marks do not add any features to your application, but they can be used to create sections within your code that are displayed within the symbol menu. There are two types of pragma marks:

```
#pragma mark -
```

and

```
#pragma mark <label name>
```

The first inserts a horizontal line in the symbol menu, while the second inserts an arbitrary label name. You can use both together to add a section heading to your code. For example, to add a section called "Methods that update the display" followed by a horizontal line, you could type the following:

```
#pragma mark Methods that update the display
#pragma mark -
```

Once the pragma mark is added to your code and saved, the symbol menu will update appropriately.

Building Applications

After you've completed your source code, it's time to build the application. The build process encompasses several different steps, including compiling and linking. Compiling translates the instructions you type into something that the iPhone understands. Linking combines your code with the necessary frameworks the application needs to run. During these steps, Xcode displays any errors that it might find.

Before building an application, you must first choose what it is being built to run on: the iPhone Simulator or a physical iPhone.

Configuring the Build Output

To choose how your code will be built, use the Overview pop-up menu at the upper left of the Xcode window. There are two main settings within this menu that you may want to change: the Active SDK and the Active Configuration, visible in Figure 2.12.

Use the Active SDK setting to choose between the iPhone Device SDK and the iPhone Simulator (which we'll be exploring shortly). For most day-to-day development, you'll want to use the simulator—it is faster than transferring an application to the iPhone each time you make a simple change.

By default, you have two configurations to choose from: Release and Debug. The Debug configuration adds additional debugging code to your project to help in the debugging process; we take a closer look at this in Hour 23, "Application Debugging and Optimization." The Release configuration leaves debugging code out and is what you eventually submit to the App Store.

FIGURE 2.12
Change the
active SDK and
configuration
before building.

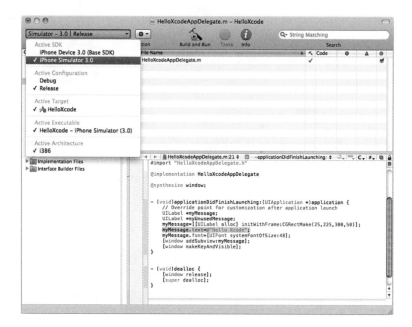

For most development, you can set the SDK to the iPhone Simulator and the Active
Configuration to Debug unless you want to try real-world performance testing.
Choose these options in Xcode now.

Building and Executing the Application

To build and run the application, click the Build and Run button from the Xcode
toolbar (Command+R). Depending on the speed of your computer, this may take a
minute or two for the process to complete. Once done, the application will be transferred to your iPhone and started (if selected in the build configuration and connected) or started in the iPhone Simulator.

To just build without running the application (useful for checking for errors), choose
the Build button from the Build menu. To run the application without building,
choose Run from the Run menu.

Quite a few intermediate files are generated during the build process. These take
up space and aren't needed for the project itself. To clean out these files, choose
Clean All Targets from the Build menu.

The HelloXcode application is shown running in the iPhone Simulator in Figure
2.13. Try building and running your version of the application now.

FIGURE 2.13
The iPhone Simulator is a quick and easy way to test your code.

If you've been following along your application should... *not* work! There are two problems with the code we asked you to type in earlier. Let's see what they are.

Correcting Errors and Warnings

You may receive two types of feedback from Xcode when you build an application: errors and warnings. Warnings are potential problems that may cause your application to misbehave; they are displayed as yellow caution signs. Errors, on the other hand, are complete showstoppers. You can't run your application if you have an error. The symbol for an error, appropriately enough, is a stop sign. A count of the warnings and errors is displayed in the lower-right corner of the Xcode window after the build completes.

If you are viewing the code that contains the error or warning, the error message is visible directly after the line that caused the problem. If you're in another file, you can quickly jump to a list of the errors (with links to the source code in which they occurred) by clicking the error or warning count in the Xcode window. Figure 2.14 shows an error and a warning you should be receiving in the HelloXcode app.

The warning points out that we have an unused variable, myUnusedMessage, in the code. Remember, this is just a helpful warning, not necessarily a problem. If we choose to remove the variable, the message will go away; but even if we don't, the application will still run. Go ahead and delete the line that reads UILabel *myUnusedMessage; in HelloXcodeAppDelegate.m. This fixes the warning, but there's still an error to correct.

FIGURE 2.14
You should be experiencing an error and a warning in HelloXcode.

Warning

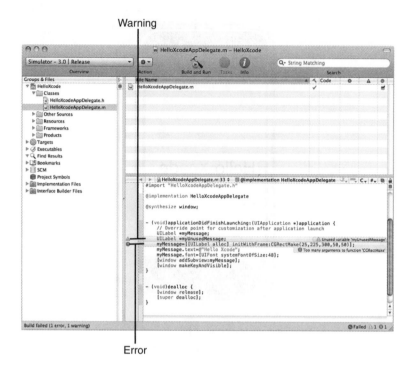

Error

The error message reads "too many arguments to function 'CGRectMake'." The reason for this is that the function takes four numbers and uses them to make a rectangle for the label—we've typed in five numbers. Delete the fifth number and preceding comma from the CGRectMake function.

Click Build and Run. HelloXcode should now start in the iPhone Simulator, just like what we saw in Figure 2.12.

Project Properties

Before finishing our brief tour of the Xcode interface, quickly turn your attention to a specific project component—the Info property list resource. This file, found in the Xcode Resources folder, is created automatically when you create a new project, is prefixed with the project name, and ends in info.plist. This file contains settings that, while you won't need right away, will be necessary for deploying an application to the App Store and configuring some functionality in later hours. Click the HelloXcode-Info.plist file in Xcode now. Your display should resemble Figure 2.15.

To change a property value, double-click the right column and type your changes.

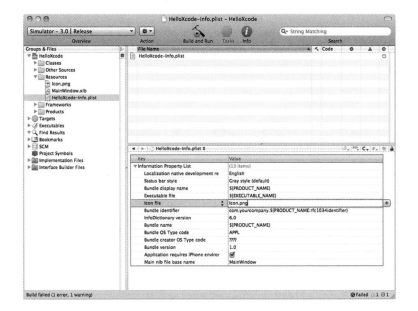

FIGURE 2.15
Project proper-
ties control a
few important
settings for your
application.

Setting an Application Icon

If you look closely at the Info properties for your project, you'll notice an Icon File property that is completely blank. To set the property to the icon that you added to the project earlier this hour, double-click the right side to enter edit mode, and then type in **Icon.png**. Ta da! You've just set the icon for your iPhone application.

We've included icon files with many of the projects in this book. You're welcome to use ours, or create new icons on your own. iPhone icons should be 57x57 PNG images with no special rounding or effects applied. The "iPhone look" will automatically be applied to the icons for you!

Setting a Project ID

Another property that you'll want to keep in the back of your mind is the Bundle Identifier. This unique ID becomes critical when publishing to the iTunes App Store. We'll talk more about this process in Hour 24, "Distributing Applications Through the App Store."

Setting the Status Bar

Two final interesting properties that we'll mention here relate to display of the status bar (the thin line with the signal and battery status at the top of the iPhone display). By default, neither of these properties are present in the Info.plist file. To add a new item to the list, right-click one of the existing lines and choose Add Row.

Once a new row has appeared, click the leftmost column to display all the available properties. You'll notice that Status Bar Is Initially Hidden is an option. If selected, this property adds a check box in the rightmost column that, if checked, automatically hides the iPhone status bar for your application. Another status bar option, Status Bar Style, enables you to choose between the default gray status bar and opaque and black versions.

That's it for Xcode! There's plenty more that you'll find as you work with the software, but these should be the foundational skills you need to develop apps for your phone. We'll round out this hour by looking at the next best thing to your real iPhone: the Apple iPhone Simulator.

By the Way

> Note that although we haven't covered it here, Xcode includes a wonderful documentation system. We'll look at this in depth as we start to get our feet wet with the Cocoa framework in Hour 4.

Using the iPhone Simulator

In Hour 1, we told you that you didn't even need an iPhone to start developing for the platform. The reason for this is the iPhone simulator included with the Apple developer tools. The simulator behaves as a stripped-down version of an iPhone, with the Safari, Contacts, Settings, and Photos apps available for integration testing, as shown in Figure 2.16.

FIGURE 2.16
The iPhone Simulator includes a stripped-down version of the iPhone apps.

Targeting the simulator for the early stages of your development can save you a great deal of time; you won't need to wait for apps to be installed on your physical device before seeing the effects of changes in your code. In addition, you don't need to buy and install a developer certificate to run code in the simulator.

The simulator, however, is not a *perfect* iPhone. It can't display OpenGL graphics, vibrate, simulate complex multitouch events, or provide readings from the majority of the iPhone sensors (GPS, proximity, camera/video, and so on). The closest it comes on these counts is the ability to rotate to test landscape interfaces and a simple "shake" motion simulation. That said, for most apps, it has enough features to be a valuable part of your development process.

Watch Out!

One thing that you absolutely *cannot* count on in the simulator is that your simulated app performance will resemble your real app performance. The simulator tends to run silky smooth, whereas real apps may have more limited resources and not behave as nicely. Be sure to occasionally test on a physical device so that you know your expectations are in line with reality.

Launching Applications in the Simulator

To launch an application in the simulator, open the project in Xcode, make sure that the active SDK is set to iPhone Simulator, and then click Build and Run. After a few seconds, the simulator will launch and the application will be displayed. You can test this using the HelloSimulator project included in this hour's Projects folder.

Once up and running, the HelloSimulator app should display a simple line of text (see Figure 2.17).

Once an application is running, you can interact with it using your mouse as if it were your fingertip. Click buttons, drag sliders, and so on. If you click into a field where input is expected, the iPhone keyboard will display. You can "type" using your Mac keyboard, or click the keyboard's buttons onscreen. The iPhone OS 3.0's Copy and Paste services are also simulated by clicking and holding on text until the familiar loupe magnifier appears.

Clicking the virtual Home button, or choosing Hardware, Home from the menu, exits the application.

Did you Know?

Launching an application in the simulator *installs* it in the simulator, just like installing an app on the iPhone. When you exit the app, it will still be present on the simulator until you manually delete it.

To remove an installed application from the iPhone Simulator, click and hold the icon until it starts "wiggling," and then click the X that appears in the upper-left corner. In other words, remove apps from the simulator in the exact same way you would remove them from a physical iPhone!

FIGURE 2.17
Click Build and
Run in Xcode to
launch and run
your application
in the simulator.

Generating Multitouch Events

Even though you have only a single mouse, simple multitouch events, such as two-finger pulls and pinches, can be simulated by holding down Option when your cursor is over the iPhone Simulator "screen." Two circles, representing fingertips, will be drawn and can be controlled with the mouse. To simulate a touch event, click and drag while continuing to hold down Option. Figure 2.18 shows the "pinch" gesture.

Try this using the HelloSimulator app. You should be able to use the simulator's multitouch capabilities to shrink or expand the onscreen text.

Rotating the iPhone

To simulate a rotation on the iPhone, choose Rotate Right or Rotate Left from the menu (see Figure 2.19). You can use this to rotate the simulator window through all four possible orientations and view the results onscreen.

FIGURE 2.18
Simulate simple multitouch with the Option key.

FIGURE 2.19
Rotate the interface through the possible orientations.

Again, test this with HelloSimulator. The app will react to the rotation events and orient the text properly.

Simulating Other Conditions

You will want to test against a few other esoteric conditions in the simulator. Using the Hardware menu, you can access these additional features:

Version: Check to see how your app will behave on earlier versions of the iPhone OS. This option enables you to choose from many of the recent versions of the operating system.

Shake Gesture: Simulate a quick shake of the iPhone.

Lock: Simulates the condition of a locked iPhone. Because a user can lock an iPhone while an application is running, some developers choose to have their programs react uniquely to this situation.

Simulate Memory Warning: Triggers an application's low-memory event. Useful for testing to make sure your application exits gracefully if resources run low.

Toggle In-Call Status Bar: When a call is active and an application is started, an additional line appears at the top of the screen ("Touch to return to call"). This option will simulate that line.

Test a few of these out on the HelloSimulator application. Figure 2.20 shows the application's reaction to a simulated memory warning.

FIGURE 2.20
The iPhone Simulator can test for application handling in several unique conditions.

Summary

This hour introduced you to the Xcode development environment and the core set of tools that you'll be using to create your applications. You learned how to create projects using Apple's iPhone templates and how to supplement those templates with new files and resources. You also explored the editing and navigation capabilities of Xcode that you'll come to depend on every day. To illustrate the concepts, you wrote and built your first iPhone application—and even corrected a few errors that we added to try to trip you up!

We finished up this hour by walking through the use of the iPhone Simulator. This tool will save wear and tear on your iPhone (and your patience) as it provides a quick and easy way to test code without having to install applications on your phone.

Q&A

Q. *What is Interface Builder, and how does it fit in?*

A. Interface Builder is a very important tool that gets its own lesson in Hour 5. As the name implies, Interface Builder is mostly about creating the user interface for your applications. It is an important part of the development suite, but your interactions with it will be very different from those in Xcode.

Q. *Do I have to worry about constantly saving if I'm switching between files and making lots of changes in Xcode?*

A. No. If you switch between files in the Xcode editor, you won't lose your changes. Xcode will even prompt you to save, listing all the changed project files, if you attempt to close the application.

Q. *I notice that there are Mac OS X templates that I can access when creating a project. Can I create a Mac application?*

A. Almost all the coding skills you learn in this book can be transferred to Mac development. The iPhone, however, is a somewhat different piece of hardware than the Mac, so you'll need to learn the Mac model for windowing, UI, and so on.

Q. *Can I run commercial applications on the iPhone Simulator?*

A. No. You can only run apps that you have built within Xcode.

Workshop

Quiz

1. How do you add an image resource to an iPhone project?

2. Is there a facility in Xcode for easily tracking multiple versions of your project?

3. Can the iPhone Simulator be used to test your application on older versions of the iPhone OS?

Answers

1. You can add resources, including images, to an iPhone project by dragging from the Finder into the project's Resources group.

2. Yes. Using the snapshot feature you can create different copies of your project at specific points in time and even compare the changes.

3. Yes. The Hardware, Versions menu can be used to choose earlier versions of the iPhone OS for testing.

Activities

1. Practice creating projects and navigating the Xcode editor. Try out some of the common editor features that were not covered in this lesson, such as Find and Replace. Test the use of pragma marks for creating helpful jump-to points within your source code.

2. Return to the Apple iPhone Dev Center and download a sample application. Using the techniques described in this hour's lesson, build and test the application in the iPhone Simulator.

Further Exploration

You're not quite at the stage yet where we can ask you to go off and read some code-related tutorials, but if you're interested, you may want to take some time to look into more of the features offered in Xcode. Our introduction was limited to roughly a dozen pages, but entire volumes can (and have) been written about this unique tool. Anything else you need will be covered in the lessons in this book, but we still recommend reviewing Apple's *Xcode Workspace Guide*. You can find this document by choosing Help, Xcode Workspace Guide from the menu while in the Xcode application.

HOUR 3

Discovering Objective-C: The Language of Apple Platforms

What You'll Learn in This Hour:

▶ How Objective-C will be used in your projects
▶ The basics of object-oriented programming
▶ Simple Objective-C syntax
▶ Common data types
▶ How to manage memory

This hour's lesson marks the midpoint in our exploration of the Apple iPhone development platform. It will give us a chance to sit back, catch our breath, and get a better idea of what it means to "code" for the iPhone. Both the Macintosh and the iPhone share a common development environment and, with them, a common development language: Objective-C.

Objective-C provides the syntax and structure for creating applications on Apple platforms. For many, learning Objective-C can be daunting, but with patience, it may quickly become the favorite choice for any development project. This hour takes you through the steps you need to know to be comfortable with Objective-C and starts you down the path to mastering this unique and powerful language.

Object-Oriented Programming and Objective-C

To better understand the scope of this hour, take a few minutes to search for Objective-C or object-oriented programming in your favorite online bookstore. You will find quite a few books—lengthy books—on these topics. In this book, we have roughly 20 pages to cover what these books teach in hundreds. While it's not possible to fully cover Objective-C and object-oriented development in this single hour, we can make sure that you understand enough to develop fairly complex apps.

To provide you with the information you need to be successful in iPhone development, we concentrate on fundamentals—the core concepts that will be used repeatedly throughout the examples and tutorials in this book. Our approach in this hour's lesson is to introduce you to a programming topic in general terms—then look at how it will be performed when you sit down to write your application. Before we begin, let's learn a bit more about Objective-C and object-oriented programming.

What Is Object-Oriented Programming?

Most people have an idea of what programming is and have even written a simple program. Everything from setting your TiVo to record a show to configuring a cooking cycle for your microwave is a type of programming. You use data (such as times) and instructions (like "record") to tell your devices to complete a specific task. This certainly is a long way from developing for the iPhone, but in a way the biggest difference is in the amount of data you can provide and manipulate and the number of different instructions available to you.

Imperative Development

There are two primary development paradigms. First, imperative programming (sometimes called procedural programming) implements a sequence of commands that should be performed. The application follows the sequence and carries out activities as directed. Although there may be branches in the sequence or movement back and forth between some of the steps, the flow is from a starting condition to an ending condition with all the logic to make things "work" sitting in the middle.

The problem with imperative programming is that it lends itself to growing, without structure, into an amorphous blob. Applications gain features when developers tack on bits of code here and there. Frequently, instructions that implement a piece of functionality are repeated over and over wherever something needs to take place. On the other hand, imperative development is something that many people can pick up and do with very little planning.

The Object-Oriented Approach

The other development approach, and what we use in this book, is object-oriented programming (OOP). OOP uses the same types of instructions as imperative development, but structures them in a way that makes your applications easy to maintain and promotes code reuse whenever possible. In OOP, you will create objects that hold the data that describes something along with the instructions to manipulate that data. Perhaps an example is in order.

Consider a program that enables you to track reminders. With each reminder, you want to store information about the event that will be taking place—a name, a time to sound an alarm, a location, and any additional miscellaneous notes that you may want to store. In addition, you need to be able to reschedule a reminder's alarm time, or completely cancel an alarm.

In the imperative approach, you have to write the steps necessary to track all the reminders, all the data in the reminders, check every reminder to see whether an alarm should sound, and so on. It's certainly possible, but just trying to wrap your mind around everything that the application needs to do could cause some serious headaches. An object-oriented approach brings some sanity to the situation.

In an object-oriented model, you could implement a reminder as a single object. The reminder object would know how to store the properties such as the name, location, and so on. It would implement just enough functionality to sound its own alarm and reschedule or cancel its alarm. Writing the code, in fact, would be very similar to writing an imperative program that only has to manage a single reminder. By encapsulating this functionality into an object, however, we can then create multiple copies of the object within an application and have them each fully capable of handling separate reminders. No fuss and no messy code!

> Most of the tutorials in this book make use of one or two objects, so don't worry about being overwhelmed with OOP. You'll see enough to get accustomed to the idea—but we're not going to go overboard!

By the Way

Another important facet of OOP is *inheritance*. Suppose you want to create a special type of reminder for birthdays that includes a list of birthday presents that a person has requested. Rather than tacking this onto the reminder object, you could create an entirely new "birthday reminder" that inherits all of the features and properties of a reminder, and then adds in the list of presents and anything else specific to birthdays.

The Terminology of Object-Oriented Development

OOP brings with it a whole range of terminology that you need to get accustomed to seeing in this book (and in Apple's documentation). The more familiar you are with these terms, the easier it will be to look for solutions to problems and interact with other iPhone developers. Let's establish some basic vocabulary now:

Class: The code, usually consisting of a header and implementation file, which defines an object and what it can do.

Subclass: A class that builds upon another class, adding additional features. Almost everything you use in iPhone development will be a subclass of something else, inheriting all of the properties and capabilities of its parent class.

Superclass/parent class: The class that another class inherits from.

Object/instance: A class that has been invoked and is active in your code. Classes are the code that makes an object work, while an object is the actual class "in action." This is also known as an "instance" of a class.

Instantiation: The process of creating an active object from a class.

Instance method: A basic piece of functionality, implemented in a class. For the reminder class, this might be something like `setAlarm` to set the alarm for a given reminder.

Class method: Similar to an instance method, but applicable to *all* the objects created from a class. The reminder class, for example, might implement a method called `countReminders` that provides a count of all the reminder objects that have been created.

Message: When you want to use a method in an object, you send the object a message (the name of the method). This process is also referred to as "calling the method."

Instance variable: A storage place for a piece of information specific to a class. The name of a reminder, for example, might be stored in an instance variable. All variables in Objective-C have a specific "type" that describes the contents of what they will be holding.

Variable: A storage location for a piece of information. Unlike instance variables, a "normal" variable is only accessible in the method where it is defined.

Parameter: A piece of information that is provided to a method when it is messaged. If you were to send a reminder object the "set alarm" method, you would presumably need to include the time to set. The time, in this case, would be a parameter used with the `setAlarm` method.

Property: An instance variable that has been configured using special directives to provide easy access from your code.

Did you Know?

You may be wondering, if almost everything in iPhone development is a subclass of something else, is there some sort of master class that "starts" this tree of inheritance? The answer is yes—the NSObject class serves as the starting point for most of the classes you'll be using on the iPhone. This isn't something you'll really need to worry about in the book—just a piece of trivia to think about.

It's important to know that when you develop on the iPhone, you're going to be taking advantage of hundreds of classes that Apple has already written for you! Everything from creating onscreen buttons to manipulating dates and writing files is covered by prebuilt classes. You'll occasionally want to customize some of the functionality in those classes, but you'll be starting out with a toolbar that is already overflowing with functionality.

Did you Know?

Confused? Don't worry! We introduce these concepts slowly, and you'll quickly get a feel for how they apply to your projects as we work through several tutorials in the upcoming hours.

What Is Objective-C?

A few years ago, I would have answered this question with "one of the strangest looking languages I've ever seen." Today, I love it (and so will you!). Objective-C was created in the 1980s and is an extension of the C language. It adds many additional features to C and, most important, an OOP structure. Objective-C is primarily used for developing Mac OS X and iPhone applications, which has attracted a devoted group of followers who appreciate its capabilities and syntax.

Objective-C statements are easier to read than other programming languages and often can be deciphered just by looking at them. For example, consider the following line that compares whether the contents of a variable called myName is equal to John:

```
[myName isEqualToString:@"John"]
```

It doesn't take a very large mental leap to see what is going on in the code snippet. In traditional C, this might be written as follows:

```
strcmp(myName,"John")
```

The C statement is a bit shorter, but does little to convey what the code is actually doing.

Because Objective-C is implemented as a layer on top of C, it is still fully compatible with code that is written entirely in C. For the most part, this isn't something that you should concern yourself with, but unfortunately, Apple has left a bit of "cruft" in their iPhone SDK that relies on C-language syntax. You'll encounter this infrequently and it isn't difficult to code with when it occurs, but it does take away from the elegance of Objective-C just a little.

Now that you have an idea of what OOP and Objective-C are, let's take a look at how you'll be using them over the course of this book.

Exploring the Objective-C File Structure

In the last hour, you learned how to use Xcode to create projects and navigate their files. As we mentioned then, the vast majority of your time will be spent in the Classes folder of Xcode, shown in Figure 3.1. You'll be adding methods to class files that Xcode creates for you when you start a project, or occasionally, creating your own class files to implement entirely new functionality in your application.

FIGURE 3.1
Most of your coding will occur within the files in the Classes folder.

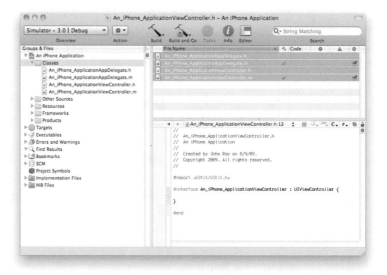

Okay, sounds simple enough, but *where* will the coding take place? If you create a project and look in the Classes folder, you'll see quite a few different files staring back at you.

Header/Interface Files

Creating a class creates two different files: a header or interface file (.h) and an implementation file (.m). The header/interface file is used to define a list of all of the methods and properties that your class will be using. This is useful for other pieces of code, including Interface Builder (which you'll learn about in Hour 5, "Exploring Interface Builder"), to determine how to access information and features in your class.

The implementation file, on the other hand, is where you'll go to write the code that makes everything defined in the header file work. Let's review the structure of a very short, and entirely made-up, interface file:

```
 1: #import <UIKit/UIKit.h>
 2:
 3: @interface myClass : myParent <myProtocol> {
 4:   NSString *myString;
 5:   IBOutlet UILabel *myLabel;
 6: }
 7:
 8: +(NSString)myClassMethod:(NSString)aString;
 9:
10: -(NSDate)myInstanceMethod:(NSString)aString anotherParameter:(NSURL)aURL;
11:
12: @property (nonatomic, retain) UILabel *myLabel;
13:
14: @end
```

The #import Directive

```
1: #import <UIKit/UIKit.h>
```

First, in line 1, the header file uses the #import directive to include any other interface files that our application will need to access. The string <UIKit/UIKit.h> designates the specific file (in this case, UIKit, which gives us access to a vast majority of the iPhone classes). If we need to import a file, we'll be explaining how and why in the text. The UIKit example will be included by default when Xcode sets up your classes and covers most of what you'll need for this book's examples.

Wait a Sec, What's a "Directive?"

Directives are commands that are added to your files that help Xcode and its associated tools build your application. They don't implement the logic that makes your app work, but they are necessary for providing information on how your applications are structured so that Xcode knows how to deal with them.

The @interface **Directive and Instance Variables**

Line 3 uses the @interface directive to begin a set of lines (enclosed in {} braces) to describe all the instance variables that your class will be providing:

```
3: @interface myClass : myParent <myProtocol> {
4:    NSString *myString;
5:    IBOutlet UILabel *myLabel;
6: }
```

In this example, a variable that contains an object of type NSString named myString is declared, along with an object of type UILabel that will be referenced by the variable myLabel. An additional keyword IBOutlet is added to the front of the UILabel declaration to indicate that this is an object that will be defined in Interface Builder. You'll learn more about IBOutlet in Hour 5.

**Watch
Out!**

All instance variables, method declaration lines, and property declarations must end with a semicolon (;).

Notice that line 3 includes a few additional items after the @interface directive: myClass : myParent <myProtocol>. The first of these is the name that we're giving the class that we're working on. Here, we've decided the class will be called myClass. The class name is then followed by a colon (:) and a list of the classes that this class is inheriting from (that is, the "parent" classes). Finally, the parent classes are followed by a list of "protocols" enclosed within angle brackets <>.

**By the
Way**

The implementation and interface files for a class will usually share the name of the class. Here, the interface file would be named myClass.h and the implementation file myClass.m.

Protocols? What's a Protocol?

Protocols are a unique feature of Objective-C that sound complicated, but really aren't. Sometimes you will come across features that require you to write methods to support their use—such as providing a list of items to be displayed in a table. The methods that you need to write are grouped together under a common name—this is known as a "protocol."

Some protocol methods are required, others are optional—it just depends on the features you need. A class that implements a protocol is said to "conform" to that protocol.

Defining Methods

Lines 8 and 10 declare two methods that need to be implemented in the class:

```
8: +(NSString)myClassMethod:(NSString)aString;
9:
10: -(NSDate)myInstanceMethod:(NSString)aString anotherParameter:(NSURL)aURL;
```

Method declarations follow a simple structure. They begin with a + or -; the + denotes a class method, while - indicates an instance method. Next, the type of information the method returns is provided in parenthesis, followed by the name of the method itself. If the method takes a parameter, the name is followed by a colon, the type of information the method is expecting, and the variable name that the method will use to refer to that information. If multiple parameters are needed, a short descriptive label is added, followed by another colon, data type, and variable name. This pattern can repeat for as many parameters as needed.

In the example file, line 8 defines a class method named myClassMethod that returns an NSString object and accepts an NSString object as a parameter. The input parameter is made available in a variable called aString.

Line 10 defines an instance method named myInstanceMethod that returns a NSDate object, also takes an NSString as a parameter, and includes a second parameter of the type NSURL that will be available to the method via the variable aURL.

You'll learn more about NSString, NSDate, and NSURL in Hour 4, "Inside Cocoa Touch," but as you might guess, these are objects for storing and manipulating strings, dates, and URLs, respectively.

By the Way

Very frequently you will see methods that accept or return objects of the type id. This is a special type in Objective-C that can reference *any* kind of object and is useful if you don't know exactly what you'll be passing to a method, or if you want to be able to return different types of objects from a single method.

Another popular return type for methods is void. When you see void used, it means that the method returns *nothing*.

Did you Know?

The @property Directive

The final functional piece of the interface file is the addition of @property directives, demonstrated in line 12:

```
12: @property (nonatomic, retain) UILabel *myLabel;
```

The @property directive is used in conjunction with another command called syn-thesize in the implementation file to simplify how you interact with the instance variables that you've defined in your interface.

Traditionally, to interact with the objects in your instance variables, you have to use methods called *getters* and *setters* (or accessors and mutators, if you want to sound a bit more exotic). These methods, as their names suggest, get and set values in your instance variable objects. For example, a UILabel object, like what we're referencing with the myLabel instance variable in line 12, represents an onscreen text label that a user can see. The object, internally, has a variety of instance variables itself, such as color, font, and the text that is displayed. To set the text, you might write something like this:

```
[myLabel setText:@"Hello World"];
```

And to retrieve the text currently displayed, you'd use the following:

```
theCurrentLabel=[myLabel getText];
```

Not too tough, but it's not as easy as it could be. If we use @property and synthe-size to define these as properties, we can simplify the code so that it looks like this:

```
myLabel.text=@"Hello World";
theCurrentLabel=myLabel.text;
```

We'll make use of this feature nearly everywhere that we need easy access to instance variables. After we've given this treatment to an instance variable, we can refer to it as a property. Because of this, you'll typically see things referred to as "properties" rather than instance variables.

By the Way

Technically, you can use @property and synthesize to create a property that references an instance variable via another name. This is hardly ever used in practice and has little real value beyond serving as a point of confusion.

Did you Know?

The attributes (nonatomic, retain) that are provided to the @property directive tell Xcode how to treat the property it creates. The first, nonatomic, informs the system that it doesn't need to worry about different parts of the application using the property at the same time, while retain makes sure that the object the property refers to will be kept around. These are the attributes you should use in nearly all circumstances, so get used to typing them!

Ending the interface File

To end the interface file, add @end on its own line. This can be seen on line 14 of our example file:

```
14: @end
```

That's it for the interface! Although that might seem like quite a bit to digest, it covers almost everything you'll see in an interface/header file. Now let's look at the file where the actual work gets done: the implementation file.

Implementation Files

After you've defined your instance variables (or properties!) and methods in your interface file, you need to do the work of writing code to implement the logic of your application. The implementation file (.m) holds all of the "stuff" that makes your class work. Let's take a look at a sample skeleton file myClass.m that corresponds to the interface file we've been reviewing:

```
 1: #import "myClass.h"
 2:
 3: @implementation myClass
 4:
 5: @synthesize myLabel;
 6:
 7: +(NSString)myClassMethod:(NSString)aString {
 8:     // Implement the Class Method Here!
 9: }
10:
11: -(NSString)myInstanceMethod:(NSString)aString anotherParameter:(NSURL)aURL {
12:     // Implement the Instance Method Here!
13: }
14:
15: @end
```

The #import Directive

The #import directive kicks things off in line 1 by importing the interface file associated with the class:

```
1: #import "myClass.h"
```

When you create your projects and classes in Xcode, this will automatically be added to the code for you. If any additional interface files need to be imported, you should add them to the top of your interface file rather than here.

The @implementation **Directive**

The implementation directive, shown in line 3, tells Xcode what class the file is going to be implementing. In this case, the file should contain the code to implement myClass:

```
3: @implementation myClass
```

The @synthesize **Directive**

In line 5, we use the @synthesize directive to, behind the scenes, generate the code for the getters and setters of an instance variable:

```
5: @synthesize myLabel;
```

Used along with the @property directive, this ensures that we have a straightforward way to access and modify the contents of our instance variables as described earlier.

Method Implementation

To provide an area to write your code, the implementation file must restate the method definitions, but, rather than ending them with a semicolon (;), a set of curly braces {} is added at the end, as shown in lines 7–9 and 11–13. All the magic of your programming will take place between these braces:

```
 7: +(NSString)myClassMethod:(NSString)aString {
 8:    // Implement the Class Method Here!
 9: }
10:
11: -(NSString)myInstanceMethod:(NSString)aString anotherParameter:(NSURL)aURL {
12:    // Implement the Instance Method Here!
13: }
```

> You can add a text comment on any line within your class files by prefixing the line with the // characters. If you'd like to create a comment that spans multiple lines, you can begin the comment with the characters /* and end with */.

Ending the Interface File

To end the implementation file, add @end on its own line just like the interface file. This can be seen on line 15 of our example:

```
15: @end
```

Structure for Free

Even though we've just spent quite a bit of time going through the structure of the interface and implementation files, you're rarely (if ever) going to need to type it all out by hand. Whenever you add a new class to your Xcode project, the structure of the file will be set up for you. Of course, you'll still need to define your variables and methods, but the `@interface` and `@implementation` directives and overall file structure will be in place before you write a single line of code.

Objective-C Programming Basics

We've explored the notion of classes, methods, and instance variables, but we still don't have a real idea of how to go about making a program do something. In this section of our lesson, we'll review several key programming tasks that you'll be using to implement your methods:

▶ Declaring variables

▶ Allocating and initializing objects

▶ Using an object's instance methods

▶ Making decisions with expressions

▶ Branching and looping

Declaring Variables

Earlier we documented what instance variables in your interface file will look like, but we didn't really get into the process of *how* you declare (or "define") them (or use them!). Instance variables are also only a small subset of the variables you'll use in your projects. Instance variables store information that is available across all the methods in your class—but they're not really appropriate for small temporary storage tasks, such as formatting a line of text to output to a user. Most commonly, you'll be declaring several variables at the start of your methods, using them for various calculations, then getting rid of them when you're done with them.

Whatever the purpose, you'll declare your variables using this syntax:

```
<Type> <Variable Name>;
```

The type is either a primitive data type, or the name of a class that you want to instantiate and use.

Primitive Data Types

Primitive data types are defined in the C language and are used to hold very basic values. Common types you'll encounter include the following:

`int`	Integers (whole numbers such as 1, 0, and -99)
`float`	Floating-point numbers (numbers with decimal points in them)
`double`	Highly precise floating-point numbers that can handle a large number of digits

For example, to declare an integer variable that will hold a user's age, you might enter the following:

```
int userAge;
```

After a primitive data type is declared, the variable can be used for assignments and mathematical operations. The following code, for example, declares two variables, `userAge` and `userAgeInDays`, and then assigns a value to one and calculates the other:

```
int userAge;
int userAgeInDays;
userAge=30;
userAgeInDays=userAge*365;
```

Pretty easy, don't you think? Primitive data types, however, will make up only a very small number of the variable types that you use. Most variables you declare will be used to store objects.

Object Data Types and Pointers

Just about everything that you'll be working with in your iPhone applications will be an object. Text strings, for example, will be instances of the class `NSString`. Buttons that you display on the iPhone screen are objects of the class `UIButton`. You'll learn about several of the common data types in the next hour's lesson. Apple has literally provided hundreds of different classes that you can use to store and manipulate data.

Unfortunately for us, for a computer to work with an object, it can't just store it like a primitive data type. Objects have associated instance variables and methods, making them far more complex. To declare a variable as an object of a specific class, we must declare the variable as a *pointer* to an object. A pointer references the place in memory where the object is stored, rather than a value. To declare a variable as a pointer, prefix the name of the variable with an asterisk. For example, to declare a variable of type NSString with the intention of holding a user's name, we might type this:

```
NSString *userName;
```

Once declared, you can use the variable without the asterisk. It is only used in the declaration to identify the variable as a pointer to the object.

> **By the Way**
>
> When a variable is a pointer to an object, it is said to *reference* or *point to* the object. This is in contrast to a variable of a primitive data type, which is said to *store* the data.

Even after a variable has been declared as a pointer to an object, it still isn't ready to be used. Xcode, at this point, only knows what object you intend the variable to reference. Before the object actually exists, you must manually prepare the memory it will use and perform any initial setup required. This is handled via the processes of allocation and initialization—which we review next.

Allocating, Initializing, and Releasing Objects

Before an object can be used, memory must be allocated and the contents of the object initialized. This is handled by sending an alloc message to the class that you're going to be using, followed by an init message to what is returned by alloc. The syntax you'll use is this:

```
[[<class name> alloc] init];
```

For example, to declare and create a new instance of UILabel class, you could use the following code:

```
UILabel *myLabel;
myLabel=[[UILabel alloc] init];
```

Once allocated and initialized, the object is ready to use.

> **By the Way**
>
> We haven't covered the method messaging syntax in Objective-C, but we'll be doing so shortly. For now, it's just important to know the pattern for creating objects.

Convenience Methods

When we initialized the UILabel instance, we *did* create a *usable* object, but it doesn't yet have any of the additional information that makes it *useful*. Properties such as what the label should say, or where it should be shown on the screen, have yet to be set. We would need to use several of the object's other methods to really make use of the object.

Sometimes, these configuration steps are a necessary evil, but Apple's classes often provide a special initialization method called a *convenience method*. These methods can be invoked to set up an object with a basic set of properties so that it can be used almost immediately.

For example, the NSURL class, which you'll be using later on to work with web addresses, defines a convenience method called initWithString.

To declare and initialize an NSURL object that points to the website http://www.iphonein24hours.com/, we might type the following:

```
NSURL *iphoneURL;
iphoneURL=[[NSURL alloc] initWithString:@"http://www.iphonein24hours.com/"];
```

Without any additional work, we've allocated and initialized a URL with an actual web address in a single line of code.

> In this example, we actually created *another* object, too: an NSString. By typing the @ symbol followed by characters in quotes, you allocate and initialize a string. This feature exists because strings are so commonly used that having to allocate and initialize them each time you need one would make development quite cumbersome.

Using Methods and Messaging

You've already seen the methods used to allocate and initialize objects, but this is only a tiny picture of the methods you'll be using in your apps. Let's start by reviewing the syntax of methods and messaging.

Messaging Syntax

To send an object a message, give the name of the variable that is referencing the object followed by the name of the method—all within square brackets. If you're using a class method, just provide the name of the class rather than a variable name:

```
[<object variable or class name> <method name>];
```

Things start to look a little more complicated when the method has parameters. A single parameter method call looks like this:

```
[<object variable> <method name>:<parameter value>];
```

Multiple parameters look even more bizarre:

```
[<object variable> <method name>:<parameter value>
additionalParameter:<parameter value>];
```

An actual example of using a multiple parameter method looks like this:

```
[userName compare:@"John" options:NSCaseInsensitive];
```

Here an object userName (presumably an NSString) uses the compare:options method to compare itself to the string "John" in a non-case-sensitive manner. The result of this particular method is a Boolean value (true or false), which could be used as part of an expression to make a decision in your application. (We'll review expressions and decision making next!)

Throughout the lessons, we refer to methods by name. If the name includes a colon (:), this indicates a required parameter. This is a convention that Apple has used in their documentation and that we've adopted for this book.

Did you Know?

A useful predefined value in Objective-C is nil. The nil value indicates a *lack* of any value at all. You'll use nil in some methods that call for a parameter that you don't have available. A method that receives nil in place of an object can actually pass messages to nil without creating an error—nil simply returns another nil as the result.

We'll use this a few times later in the book, which should give you a better picture of why this behavior is something we'd actually *want* to happen!

Did you Know?

Nested Messaging

Something that you'll see when looking at Objective-C code is that the result of a method is sometimes used directly as a parameter within another method. In some cases, if the result of a method is an object, a developer will send a message directly to that result.

In both of these cases, using the results directly avoids the need to create a variable to hold the results. Want an example that puts all of this together? We've got one for you!

Assume you have two NSString variables, userFirstName and userLastName, that you want to capitalize and concatenate, storing the results in another NSString called finalString. The NSString instance method capitalizedString returns a capitalized string, while stringByAppendingString takes a second string as a parameter and concatenates it onto the string invoking the message. Putting this together (disregarding the variable declarations), the code looks like this:

```
tempCapitalizedFirstName=[userFirstName capitalizedString];
tempCapitalizedSecondName=[userLastName capitalizedString];
finalString=[tempCapitalizedFirstName
stringByAppendingString:tempCapitalizedSecondName];
```

Instead of using these temporary variables, however, you could just substitute the method calls into a single combined line:

```
finalString=[[userFirstName capitalizedString]
stringByAppendingString:[userLastName capitalizedString]];
```

This can be a very powerful means of structuring your code, but can also lead to long and rather confusing statements. Do what makes you comfortable—both approaches are equally valid and have the same outcome.

> A confession. I have a difficult time referring to using a method as sending a "message to an object." Although this is the preferred terminology for OOP, all we're really doing is executing an object's method by providing the name of the object and the name of the method.

Expressions and Decision Making

For an application to react to user input and process information, it must be capable of making decisions. Every decision in an app boils down to a "yes" or "no" result based on evaluating a set of tests. These can be as simple as comparing two values, to something as complex as checking the results of a complicated mathematical calculation. The combination of tests used to make a decision is called an *expression*.

Using Expressions

If you recall your high-school algebra, you'll be right at home with expressions. An expression can combine arithmetic, comparison, and logical operations.

A simple numeric comparison checking to see whether a variable userAge is greater than 30 could be written as follows:

```
userAge>30
```

When working with objects, we need to use properties within the object and values returned from methods to create expressions. To check to see if a string stored in an object userName is equal to "John", we could use this:

```
[userName compare:@"John"]
```

Expressions aren't limited to the evaluation of a single condition. We could easily combine the previous two expressions to find a user that is over 30 and named John:

```
userAge>30 && [userName compare:@"John"]
```

Common Expression Syntax

( )   Groups expressions together, forcing evaluation of the innermost group first

==   Tests to see if two values are equal (e.g., userAge==30)

!=   Tests to see if two values are not equal (e.g., userAge!=30)

&&   Implements a logical "AND" condition (e.g., userAge>30 && userAge<40)

¦¦   Implements a logical OR condition (e.g., userAge>30 ¦¦ userAge<10)

!   Negates the result of an expression, returning the opposite of the original result (e.g., !(userAge==30) is the same as userAge!=30)

For a complete list of C expression syntax, you may want to refer to https://www.cs.drexel.edu/~rweaver/COURSES/ISTC-2/TOPICS/expr.html.

As we've said repeatedly, you're going to be spending lots of time working with complex objects and using the methods within the objects. You can't make direct comparisons between objects as you can with simple primitive data types. To successfully create expressions for the myriad objects you'll be using, you'll need to review each object's methods and properties.

Making Decisions with if-then-else and switch Statements

Typically, depending on the outcome of the evaluated expression, different code statements are executed. The most common way of defining these different execution paths is with an if-then-else statement:

```
if (<expression>) {
  // do this, the expression is true.
} else {
  // the expression isn't true, do this instead!

}
```

For example, consider the comparison we used earlier to check a userName NSString variable to see whether its contents were set to a specific name. If we want to react to that comparison, we might write the following:

```
If ([userName compare:@"John"]) {
  userMessage=@"I like your name";
```

```
} else {
  userMessage=@"Your name isn't John, but I still like it!";
}
```

Another approach to implementing different code paths when there are potentially many different outcomes to an expression is to use a switch statement. A switch statement checks a variable for a value, and then executes different blocks of code depending on the value that is found:

```
switch (<numeric value>) {
  case <numeric option 1>:
    // The value matches this option
    break;
  case <numeric option 2>:
    // The value matches this option
    break;
  default:
    // None of the options match the number.
}
```

Applying this to a situation where we might want to check a user's age (stored in userAge) for some key milestones and then set an appropriate userMessage string if they are found, the result might look like this:

```
switch (userAge) {
  case 18:
    userMessage=@"Congratulations, you're an adult!";
    break;
  case 21:
    userMessage=@"Congratulations, you can drink champagne!";
    break;
  case 50:
    userMessage=@"You're half a century old!";
    break;
  default:
    userMessage=@"Sorry, there's nothing special about your age.";
}:
```

Repetition with Loops

Sometimes you'll have a situation where you need to repeat several instructions over and over in your code. Instead of typing the lines repeatedly, you can, instead, *loop* over them. A loop defines the start and end of several lines of code. As long as the loop is running, the program executes the lines from top to bottom, and then restarts again from the top. The loops you'll use are of two types: count based and condition based.

In a count-based loop, the statements are repeated a certain number of times. In a condition-based loop, an expression determines whether a loop should occur.

The count-based loop you'll be using is called a `for` loop, with this syntax:

```
for (<initialization>;<test condition>;<count update>) {
  // Do this, over and over!
}
```

The three "unknowns" in the `for` statement syntax are a statement to initialize a counter to track the number of times the loop has executed, a condition to check to see if the loop should continue, and finally, an increment for the counter. An example of a loop that uses the integer variable `count` to loop 50 times could be written as follows:

```
int count;
for (count=0;count<50;count=count+1) {
  // Do this, 50 times!
}
```

The `for` loop starts by setting the `count` variable to 0. The loop then starts and continues as long as the condition of `count<50` remains true. When the loop hits the bottom curly brace (}) and starts over, the increment operation is carried out and `count` is increased by 1.

> In C and Objective-C, integers are usually incremented by using ++ at the end of the variable name. In other words, rather than using count=count+1, most frequently you'll encounter count++, which does the same thing. Decrementing works the same way, but with - -.

Did you Know?

In a condition-based loop, the loop continues while an expression remains true. There are two variables of this loop type that you'll encounter, `while` and `do-while`:

```
while (<expression>) {
  // Do this, over and over, while the expression is true!
}
```

and

```
do {
  // Do this, over and over, while the expression is true!
} while (<expression>);
```

The only difference between these two loops is when the expression is evaluated. In a standard `while` loop, the check is done at the beginning of the loop. In the `do-while` loop, however, the expression is evaluated at the end of every loop.

For example, suppose you are asking users to input their name and you want to keep prompting them until they type John, you might format a do-while loop like this:

```
do {
    // Get the user's input in this part of the loop
} while (![userName compare:@"John"]);
```

The assumption is that the name is stored in a string object called userName. Because you wouldn't have requested the user's input when the loop first starts, you would use a do-while loop to put the test condition at the end. Also, the value returned by the string compare method has to been negated with the ! operator, because you want to continue looping as long as the comparison of the userName to John *isn't* true.

Loops are a very useful part of programming, and, along with the decision statements, will form the basis for structuring the code within your object methods. They allow code to branch and extend beyond a linear flow.

While we can't paint an all-encompassing picture of programming, this should give you some sense of what to expect in the rest of the book. We'll close out the hour with a topic that causes quite a bit of confusion for beginning developers: memory management.

Memory Management

In the first hour of this book, you learned a bit about the limitations of the iPhone as a platform. One of the biggies, unfortunately, is the amount of memory that your programs have available to them. Because of this, you must be extremely judicious in how you manage memory.

The iPhone doesn't clean up memory for you. Instead, you must keep track of your memory usage manually. This is such an important notion, in fact, that we've broken it out into its own section.

Releasing Objects

Each time you allocate memory for an object, you're using up memory on the iPhone. If you allocate too many objects, you run out of memory and your application crashes or is forced to quit. To avoid a memory problem, you should only keep objects around long enough to use them, and then get rid of them. When you are finished using an object, you can send the release message (or "call the release method" if you prefer that semantic), like this:

```
[<variable> release];
```

Consider the earlier example of allocating an instance of NSURL:

```
NSURL *iphoneURL;
iphoneURL=[[NSURL alloc] initWithString:@"http://www.iphonein24hours.com/"];
```

Suppose that after you allocate and initialize the URL, you use it to load a web page. Once the page is loaded, there's no sense in having the URL sitting around taking up memory. To tell Xcode that you no longer have a need for it, you can use the following:

```
[iphoneURL release];
```

Using the autorelease Method

In some instances, you may allocate an object, and then have to pass that object off to another method to use as it pleases. In a case like this, you can't directly release the object, because you are no longer in control of it. If you find yourself in a position where an object is "out of your hands," so to speak, you can still indicate that you are done with it and absolve yourself of the responsibility of releasing it. To do this, use the autorelease method:

```
[<variable> autorelease];
```

The autorelease method shouldn't be used unless release can't be. Objects that are autoreleased are added to a pool of objects that are *occasionally* automatically released by the iPhone system. This isn't nearly as efficient as taking care of it yourself.

Retaining Objects

On some occasions, you may not be directly responsible for creating an object. (It may be returned from another method, for example.) Depending on the situation, you may actually need to be worried about it being released before you're done using it. To tell the system that an object is still needed, you can use its retain method:

```
[<variable> retain];
```

Again, you'll want to release the object when you've completed using it.

> **Retain and Release, Behind the Scenes**
>
> Behind the scenes, the iPhone maintains a "retain" count to determine when it can get rid of an object. For example, when an object is first allocated, the "retain" count is incremented. Any use of the `retain` message on the object also increases the count.
>
> The `release` message, on the other hand, decrements the count. As long as the retain count remains above zero, the object will not be removed from memory. When the count reaches zero, the object is considered unused and is removed.

Releasing Instance Methods in `dealloc`

Instance variables are unique in that they usually stick around for as long as an object exists—so, when do they get released? To release instance variables, you add the appropriate release lines to a method called `dealloc` that will exist in each of your classes. By default, this method has a single line that calls its parent class's `dealloc` method. You should add your release messages prior to this. An implementation of `dealloc` that releases an instance variable called `myLabel` would read as follows:

```
- (void)dealloc {
  [myLabel release];
  [super dealloc];
}
```

Because managing memory is such a critical piece of creating an efficient and usable iPhone application, we make a point of indicating when you should release objects throughout the text—both for variables you use in your methods and instance variables that are defined for your classes.

Rules for Releasing

If you find yourself looking at your code wondering what you should release and what you shouldn't, there are a few simple rules that can help:

- ▶ Variables that hold primitive data types do not need to be released.

- ▶ If you allocate an object, you are responsible for releasing it.

- ▶ If you use `retain` to keep an object around, you need to send a `release` when you're done with it.

- ▶ If you use a method that allocates and returns an object on its own, you are not responsible for releasing it.

- ▶ You are not responsible for releasing strings that are created with the `@"text string"` syntax.

As with everything, practice makes perfect and you'll have plenty of opportunities for applying what you've learned in the book's tutorials.

Keep in mind that a typical book would spend multiple chapters on these topics, so our goal has been to give you a starting point that future hours will build on, not to define everything you'll ever need to know about Objective-C and OOP.

Summary

In this hour, you learned about object-oriented development and the Objective-C language. Objective-C will form the structure of your applications and give you tools to collect and react to user input and other changes. After reading this hour's lesson, you should understand how to make classes, instantiate objects, call methods, and use decision and looping statements to create code that implements more complex logic than a simple top-to-bottom workflow. You should also have an understanding of memory management on the iPhone and how to free memory used by objects that you have instantiated.

Much of the functionality that you'll be using in your applications will come from the hundreds of built-in classes that Apple provides within the iPhone SDK, which we'll delve into in Hour 4.

Q&A

Q. *Is Objective-C on the iPhone the same as on Mac OS X?*

A. For the most part, yes. One of the big differences, however, is that Mac OS X implements automatic garbage collection, meaning that much of the memory management is handled for you, rather than the manual process used on the iPhone.

Q. *Can an `if-then-else` statement be extended beyond evaluating and acting on a single expression?*

A. Yes. The `if-then-else` statement can be extended by adding another `if` statement after the `else`:

```
if (<expression>) {
  // do this, the expression is true.
} else if (<expression>) {
  // the expression isn't true, do this instead.
} else {
  // Neither of the expressions are true, do this anyway!
}
```

You can continue expanding the statement with as many `else-if`s as you need.

Q. *Why are primitive data types used at all? Why aren't there objects for everything?*

A. Primitive data types take up much less memory than objects, and are much easier to manipulate than objects. Implementing a simple integer within an object would add a layer of complexity and inefficiency that just isn't needed.

Q. *Why do I have to release objects that exist for the entire lifetime of my application? Won't they just go away when it quits?*

A. It's good practice. Even if your application is quitting, it is still responsible for cleaning up after itself.

Workshop

Quiz

1. When creating a subclass, do you have to rewrite all of the methods in it from the parent class?

2. What is the basic syntax for allocating and initializing an object?

3. What does the `release` message do?

Answers

1. No. The subclass inherits all of the methods of the parent class.

2. To allocate and initialize an object, use the syntax `[[<class name> alloc] init]`.

3. Sending the `release` message to an object decrements the object's retain count. When the count is zero, the object is removed from memory.

Activities

1. Start Xcode and create a new project using the iPhone View-Based Application template. Review the contents of the classes in the Xcode Classes folder. With the information you've read in this hour, you should now be able to read and navigate the structure of these files.

2. Return to the Apple iPhone Dev Center (http://developer.apple.com/iphone/library/) and begin reviewing the "Learning Objective-C: A Primer" tutorial.

Further Exploration

Although you can be successful in learning iPhone programming without spending hours and hours learning more Objective-C, you will find it easier to create complex applications if you become more comfortable with the language. Objective-C, as we've said, is not something that can be described in a single hour. It has a far-reaching feature set that makes it a powerful and elegant development platform.

To learn more about Objective-C, we recommend *Programming in Objective-C 2.0*, Second Edition (Addison-Wesley Professional, 2009), *Mac OS X Advanced Development Techniques* (Sams, 2003), and *Xcode 3 Unleashed* (Sams, 2008).

Of course, Apple has its own Objective-C documentation that you can access directly from within the Xcode documentation tool. (You'll learn more about this in the next hour.) I recommend the following documents provided by Apple:

> Learning Objective-C: A Primer
>
> Object-Oriented Programming with Objective-C
>
> The Objective-C 2.0 Programming Language

You can read these within Xcode, or via the online Apple iPhone Reference Library at http://developer.apple.com/iphone/library/. One quick warning: These documents total several hundred pages in length, so you may want to continue your Objective-C education in parallel with the iPhone lessons in this book.

HOUR 4

Inside Cocoa Touch

What You'll Learn in This Hour:

▶ What is Cocoa Touch and what makes it unique

▶ The technology layers that make up the iPhone OS

▶ A basic iPhone application life cycle

▶ Common classes and development techniques you'll be using

▶ How to find help using the Apple developer documentation

When computers first started to appear in households almost 30 years ago, applications rarely shared common interface elements. It took an instruction manual just to figure out the key sequence to exit from a piece of software. Today, user interfaces have been standardized so that moving from application to application doesn't require starting from scratch.

What has made this possible? Not faster processors or better graphics, but frameworks that enforce consistent implementation of the features provided by the device they're running on. In this hour, we'll take a look at the frameworks you'll be using in your iPhone applications.

What Is Cocoa Touch?

In the last hour, you learned about the Objective-C language, the basic syntax, and what it looks like. Objective-C will form the functional skeleton of your iPhone applications. It will help you structure your applications, make logical decisions during the life cycle of your application, and enable you to control how and when events will take place. What Objective-C doesn't provide, however, is a way to access what makes your iPhone an iPhone.

Consider the following "Hello World" application:

```
int main(int argc, char *argv[]) {
        printf("Hello World");
}
```

This code is typical of a beginner "Hello World" application written in C. It will compile and execute on the iPhone, but because the iPhone relies on Cocoa Touch for creating interfaces and handling user input and output, this version of "Hello World" is quite meaningless. Cocoa Touch is the collection of software frameworks that is used to build iPhone applications, and the runtime that those applications are executed within. Cocoa Touch includes hundreds of classes for managing everything from buttons to URLs.

By the Way

> Cocoa Touch is the highest of several "layers" of services in the iPhone OS, and isn't necessarily the *only* layer that you'll be developing in. That said, there really isn't a need to worry too much about where Cocoa Touch begins and ends—the development will be the same, regardless. We'll give an overview of complete OS service layers later in the chapter.

Returning to the "Hello World" example, if we had defined a text label object named `iphoneOutput` within a project, we could set it to read "Hello World" using Objective-C and the appropriate Cocoa Touch class property like this:

```
[iphoneOutput.text=@"Hello World"];
```

Seems simple enough, as long as we know that the `UILabel` object has a `text` property, right?

Keeping Your Cool in the Face of Overwhelming Functionality

The questions that should be coming to most beginners right about now include "I know there are *many* different features provided through iPhone applications, how in the world will this book document all of them? How will I ever find what I need to use for my own applications?"

These are great questions, and probably some of the biggest concerns that I've heard from individuals who want to program the iPhone, but have no idea where to start.

The bad news is that we can't document everything. We can cover the fundamentals that you need to start building, but even in a multivolume set of "teach yourself" books, there is so much depth to what is provided by Cocoa Touch that it isn't feasible to document a complete how-to reference.

The good news is that Cocoa Touch and the Apple developer tools encourage exploration. In Hour 6, "Understanding the Model-View-Controller Approach," you'll start building interfaces visually using the Interface Builder application. As you drag objects (buttons, text fields, and so on) to your interface, you will be creating instances of Cocoa Touch classes. The more you "play," the quicker you will begin to recognize class names and properties and the role they play in development. Even better, Xcode's developer documentation provides a complete reference to Cocoa Touch—allowing you to search across all available classes, methods, properties, and so on. We'll take a look at the documentation tool later this hour.

Young, Yet Mature

One of the most compelling advantages to programming using Cocoa Touch versus platforms such as Android or the Palm Pre is that while the iPhone is a "young" platform for Apple, the Cocoa frameworks are quite mature. Cocoa was borne out of the NeXTSTEP platform—the environment that was used by NeXT computers in the mid-1980s. In the early 90s, NeXTSTEP evolved into the cross-platform OpenStep. Finally, in 1996, Apple purchased NeXT Computer, and over the next decade the NeXTSTEP/OpenStep framework became the de facto standard for Macintosh development and was renamed Cocoa. You'll notice that there are still signs of Cocoa's origins in class names that begin with *NS*.

What Is the Difference Between Cocoa and Cocoa Touch?

Cocoa is the development framework used for most native Mac OS X applications. The iPhone, although based on many of the foundational technologies of Mac OS X, isn't quite the same. Cocoa Touch is heavily customized for a touch interface and working within the constraints of a handheld system. Desktop application components that would traditionally require extensive screen real estate have been replaced by simpler multiple-view components, mouse clicks with "touch up" and "touch down" events.

The good news is that if you decide to make the transition from iPhone developer to Mac developer, you'll follow many of the same development patterns on both platforms—it won't be like starting from scratch.

Exploring the iPhone Technology Layers

Apple describes the technologies implemented within the iPhone operating system as a series of layers, with each layer being made up of different frameworks that can be used in your applications. As you might expect, the Cocoa Touch layer is at the top (see Figure 4.1).

FIGURE 4.1
The technology layers that make up the iPhone OS.

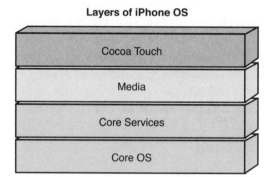

Let's review some of the most important frameworks that make up each of the layers.

Apple has included three important frameworks in every iPhone application template. These frameworks are all that is needed for simple iPhone applications, and will cover most of what you do in this book. When additional frameworks are needed, we describe how to include them in your projects.

The Cocoa Touch Layer

The Cocoa Touch layer is made up of several frameworks that will provide the core functionality for your applications. Of these, UIKit could be described as the "rock star"—delivering much more than the *UI* in its name implies.

UIKit

UIKit covers a wide range of functionality. It is responsible for application launching and termination, controlling the interface and multitouch events, and providing access to common views of data (including web pages and Word and Excel documents, among others).

UIKit is also responsible for many intra-iPhone integration features. Accessing the camera, Photo library, and accelerometer is also accomplished using the classes and methods within UIKit.

Map Kit

The Map Kit framework enables developers to add Google Map views to any application, including annotation, location, and event-handling features. Prior to the iPhone 3.0 release, developers were forced to implement web views that displayed Google or Microsoft map services, leading to a less-than-native feel.

Game Kit

Also new in iPhone OS 3.0, the Game Kit framework adds new levels of interactivity to iPhone applications. Game Kit supplies mechanisms for creating and using peer-to-peer networks, including session discovery, mediation, and voice chat. These features can be added to any application, game or not!

Message UI/Address Book UI

Apple is sensitive to the need for integration between iPhone applications. The Message UI and Address Book UI frameworks can be used to enable email composition and contact access from any application you develop.

The Media Layer

When Apple makes a computing device, you'd better believe that they put some thought into the media capabilities. The iPhone can create complex graphics, play back audio and video, and even generate real-time three-dimensional graphics. The Media layer's frameworks handle it all.

Audio Toolbox

The Audio Toolbox framework exposes methods for handling the playback and recording of audio on the iPhone. It also includes System Sound Services, which can be used for playing alert sounds or generating short vibrations.

OpenGL ES

OpenGL ES is a subset of the popular OpenGL framework for embedded systems (ES). OpenGL ES can be used to create 2D and 3D animation on the iPhone. Using OpenGL requires additional development experience beyond Objective-C, but can generate amazing scenes for a handheld device. The iPhone 3GS supports an enhanced version of OpenGL (OpenGL ES 2.0), which is capable of effects similar to popular game consoles.

Media Player

The Media Player framework provides you, the developer, with an easy way to play back movies with typical onscreen controls. The player can be invoked directly from your application.

Core Graphics

Use the Core Graphics framework to add 2D drawing and compositing features to your applications. Although most of this book will use existing interface classes and images in its applications, you can use core graphics to programmatically manipulate the iPhone's view.

Quartz Core

The Quartz Core framework is used to create animations that will take advantage of the hardware capabilities of your iPhone. This includes the feature set known as Core Animation.

The Core Services Layer

The Core Services layer is used to access lower-level operating system services, such as file access, networking, and many common data object types. You'll make use of core services frequently by way of the Foundation framework.

Foundation

The Foundation framework provides an Objective-C wrapper around features in Core Foundation. Manipulation of strings, arrays, and dictionaries is handled through the Foundation framework, as are other fundamental application necessities, including managing application preferences, threads, and internationalization.

Core Foundation

Core Foundation provides much of the same functionality of the Foundation framework, but is a procedural C framework, and therefore requires a different development approach that is, arguably, less efficient than Objective-C's OO model. You should probably avoid Core Foundation unless you absolutely need it.

Core Location

The Core Location framework can be used to obtain latitude and longitude information from the iPhone's GPS (or the cell/WiFi-based location service introduced with the original iPhone) along with a measurement of precision.

Core Data

The Core Data framework can be used to create the data model of iPhone applications. Core Data provides a relational data model based on SQLite, and can be used to bind data to interface objects to eliminate the need for complex data manipulations in code.

Store Kit

New in iPhone OS 3.0, the Store Kit framework enables developers to create in-application transactions for purchasing content without exiting the software. All interactions take place through the App Store, so no financial data is requested or transmitted through the Store Kit methods.

System Configuration

Use the System Configuration framework to determine the current state of the iPhone network configuration—what network it is connected to (if any), and what devices are reachable.

The Core OS Layer

The Core OS layer, as you'd expect, is made up of the lowest-level services in the iPhone operating system. These features include threads, hardware accessories, network services, and cryptography. You should only need to access these frameworks in very rare circumstances.

CFNetwork

The CFNetwork provides access to BSD sockets, HTTP and FTP protocol requests, and Bonjour discovery.

External Accessory

The External Accessory framework is used to develop interfaces to accessories connected via the dock connector or Bluetooth.

Security

The Security framework provides functions for performing cryptographic functions (encrypting/decrypting data). This includes interacting with the iPhone keychain to add, delete, and modify items.

System

The System framework gives developers access to a subset of the typical tools they would find in an unrestricted UNIX development environment.

Tracing the iPhone Application Life Cycle

To help you get a sense for where your "work" in developing an iPhone application fits in, it helps to look at the iPhone application life cycle. Apple's simplified diagram of the life cycle is pictured in Figure 4.2.

FIGURE 4.2
The life cycle of a typical iPhone application.

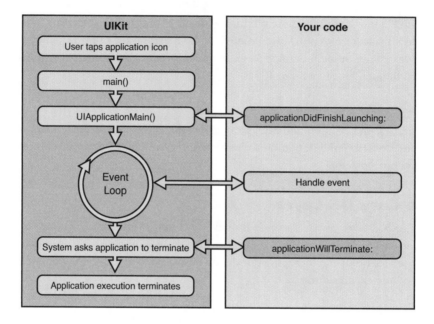

Let's try to put some context around what you're looking at, starting on the left side of the diagram. As you've learned, UIKit is a component of the Cocoa Touch that provides much of the foundation of iPhone applications—user interface management, event management, and overall application execution management. When you create an iPhone application, UIKit handles the setup of the application object via the main and UIApplicationMain functions—neither of which you should need to touch.

Once the application is started, an event loop begins. This loop receives the events such as screen touches, and then hands them off to your own methods. The loop continues until the application is asked to terminate (usually through the user pushing the iPhone's Home button).

Your code comes into play on the right side of the diagram. Xcode will automatically set up your iPhone projects to include an application delegate class. This class can implement the methods applicationDidFinishLaunching and `applicationWillTerminate` (among others) so that your program can execute its own custom code once the application launches and when it is exiting.

After an application finishes launching, the delegate object typically creates a view controller object and view, and adds them to the iPhone "window." We'll learn more about these concepts in the next hour, but for now, think of a view as what is being displayed on the iPhone screen, and the view controller as an object that can be programmed to respond when it receives an event notification from the event loop.

The majority of your work will take place within the view controller. You'll receive events from the Cocoa Touch interface and react to them by writing Objective-C code that manipulates other objects within the view. Of course, things can get a bit more complex than a single view and a single view controller, but the same basic approach can be applied in most cases.

Now that we have a better picture of the iPhone service layers and application life cycle, let's take a look at some of the classes that you'll be seeing throughout this book.

Cocoa Fundamentals

Hundreds of classes are available in the iPhone SDK, but most of your applications will be using a small set of classes to implement 90% of their features. To get you familiarized with the classes and their purposes, let's review some of the names you're going to be seeing *very, very* frequently over the next few hours. Before we begin, there are a few key points to keep in mind:

▶ Apple sets up much of the structure of your application for you in Xcode. This means that even though you need some of these classes, you won't have to lift a finger to use them. Just create a new Xcode project and they're added for you.

▶ You'll be adding instances of many of these objects to your projects just by dragging icons in the Interface Builder application. Again, no coding needed!

▶ When a class is used, we'll tell you why it is needed, what it does, and how it is used in the project. We don't want you to have to jump around digging for references in the book, so focus on the concepts, not memorization.

▶ In the next section of this hour's lesson, you'll learn about the Apple documentation tools. These helpful utilities will enable you to find all the class, property, and method information that you could ever hope for. If it's gritty details you want, you'll have them at your fingertips!

Core Application Classes

When you create a new application with even the most basic user interaction, you'll be taking advantage of a collection of common core classes. Many of these you won't be touching, but they still perform an important role. Let's review several of these classes now.

The Root Class (NSObject)

As you learned in Hour 3, "Discovering Objective-C: The Language of Apple Platforms," the power of object-oriented programming is that when you create a subclass of an object, you inherit that object's functionality. The root class, from which almost all Objective-C classes inherit, is NSObject. This object defines methods common to all classes, such as alloc, dealloc, and init. You will not need to create NSObject instances manually in this book, but you will use methods inherited from this class to create and manage new objects.

The Application Object (UIApplication)

Every application on the iPhone implements a subclass of UIApplication. This class handles events, such as notification of when an application has finished loading, as well as application configuration, such as controlling the status bar and setting badges (the little red numbers that can appear on application icons). Like NSObject, you won't need to create this yourself; just be aware it exists.

Window Objects (UIWindow)

The UIWindow class provides a container for the management and display of views. In iPhone-speak, a view is more like a typical desktop application "window," whereas an instance of UIWindow is just a container that holds the view. You will be using only a single UIWindow instance in this book, and it will be created automatically in the project templates that Xcode provides for us.

Views (UIView)

The UIView class defines a rectangular area and manages all the onscreen display within that region—what we will refer to as a view. Most of your applications will start by adding a view to an instance of UIWindow.

Views can be nested to form a hierarchy; they rarely exist as a single object. A top-level view, for example, may contain a button and field. These controls would be referred to as subviews and the containing view as the superview. Multiple levels of views can be nested, creating a complex hierarchy of subviews and superviews. You'll be creating almost all of your views visually in Interface Builder, so don't worry: Complex doesn't mean difficult!

Responders (`UIResponder`)

The `UIResponder` class provides a means for classes that inherit from it to respond to the touch events produced by the iPhone. `UIControl`, the superclass for virtually all onscreen controls, inherits from `UIView`, and subsequently, `UIResponder`. An instance of `UIResponder` is simply called a responder.

Because there can be multiple objects that could potentially respond to an event, the iPhone will pass events up what is referred to as a chain of responders. The responder instance that can handle the event is given the designation first responder. When you're editing a field, for example, the field has first responder status because it is actively handling user input. When you leave the field, it "resigns" first responder status. For most of your iPhone work, you won't be directly managing responders in code.

Onscreen Controls (`UIControl`)

The `UIControl` class inherits from `UIView` and is used as the superclass for almost all onscreen controls, such as buttons, fields, and sliders. This class is responsible for handling the triggering of actions based on touch events, such as "pressing" a button.

As you'll learn in the next hour, a button defines a handful of events that you can respond to; Interface Builder gives you a means of tying those events to actions that you've coded. `UIControl` is responsible for implementing this behavior behind the scenes.

View Controllers (`UIViewController`)

You'll be using the `UIViewController` class in almost all the application projects throughout this book to manage the contents of your views. You'll use a `UIViewController` subclass, for example, to determine what to do when a user taps a button. Make a sound? Display an image? However you choose to react, the code you use to carry out your action will be implemented as part of a view controller instance. You'll learn much more about view controllers over the next 2 hours.

Data Type Classes

An object can potentially hold data. In fact, most of the classes we'll be using contain a number of properties that store information about an object. There are, however, a set of Foundation classes that you'll be using throughout this book for the sole purpose of storing and manipulating information.

By the Way

> If you've used C/C++ before, you may find that these data type objects are similar to data types already defined outside of Apple's frameworks. By using the Foundation framework implementations, you gain access to a wide range of methods and features that go well beyond the C/C++ data types. You will also be able to work with the objects in Objective-C using the same development patterns as any other object.

Strings (NSString/NSMutableString)

Strings are collections of characters—numbers, letters, and symbols. You'll be using strings to collect user input and to create and format user output frequently throughout the book.

As with many of the data type objects you'll be using, there are two string classes: NSString and NSMutableString. The difference, as the name describes, is that one of the classes can be used to create strings that can be changed (mutable). An NSString instance remains static once it is initialized, whereas an NSMutableString can be changed (lengthened, shortened, replaced, and so on).

Strings are used so frequently in Cocoa Touch applications that you can create and initialize an NSString using the notation @"<my string value>". For example, if you needed to set the text property of an object called myLabel to a new string that reads "Hello World!", you could use the following:

```
myLabel.text=@"Hello World!"
```

Strings can also be initialized with the values of other variables, such as integers, floating-point numbers, and so on.

Arrays (NSArray/NSMutableArray)

A useful category of data type is a collection. Collections enable your applications to store multiple pieces of information in a single object. An NSArray is an example of a collection data type that can hold multiple objects, accessed by a numeric index.

You might, for instance, create an array that contains all the user feedback strings you want to display in an application:

```
myMessages = [[NSArray alloc] initWithObjects: @"Good Job!",@"Bad job!",nil]
```

Nil is always used to end the list of objects when initializing an array. To access the strings, you use the index value. This is the number that represents its position in the list, starting with 0. To return the "Bad job!" message, we would use the objectAtIndex method:

```
[myMessages objectAtIndex: 1]
```

As with strings, there is a mutable `NSMutableArray` class that creates an array capable of being changed after it has been created.

Dictionaries (`NSDictionary`/`NSMutableDictionary`)

Like arrays, dictionaries are another collection data type, but with an important difference. Whereas the objects in an array are accessed by a numeric index, dictionaries store information as object/key pairs. The key is an arbitrary string, whereas the object can be anything you want, such as a string. If the previous array were to be created as an `NSDictionary` instead, it might look like this:

```
myMessages = [[NSDictionary alloc] initwithObjectsAndKeys:@"Good
Job!",@"positive",@"Bad Job!",@"negative",nil];
```

Now, instead of accessing the strings by a numeric index, they can be accessed by the keys `"positive"` and `"negative"` with the `objectForKey` method, as follows:

```
[myMessages objectForKey:@"negative"]
```

Dictionaries are useful because they let you store and access data in abstract ways rather than in a strict numeric order. Once again, the mutable form of the dictionaries, `NSMutableDictionary`, can be modified after it has been created.

Numbers (`NSNumber`/`NSDecimalNumber`)

We can store strings and collections of objects, but what about numbers? Working with numbers is a bit different. In general, if you need to work with an integer, you'll use the C data type `int`, and for floating-point numbers, `float`. You won't need to worry about classes and methods and object-oriented programming at all.

So, what about the classes that refer to numbers? The purpose of the `NSNumber` class is to take a numeric C data type and store it as an `NSNumber` object. The following line creates a number object with the value 100:

```
myNumberObject = [NSNumber alloc]numberWithInt: 100]
```

You can then work with the number as an object—adding it to arrays, dictionaries, and so on. `NSDecimalNumber`, a subclass of `NSNumber`, can be used to perform decimal arithmetic on very large numbers, but will only be needed in special cases.

Dates (`NSDate`)

If you've ever tried to work with a date manually (interpreting a date string in a program, or even just doing date arithmetic by hand), you know it can be a great cause of headaches. How many days were there in September? Was this a leap year? And so on. The `NSDate` class provides a convenient way to work with dates as an object.

For example, assume you have a user-provided date (`userDate`) and you want to use it for a calculation, but only if it is earlier than the current date, in which case, you want to use *that* date. Typically, this would be a bunch of nasty comparisons and assignments. With `NSDate`, you would create a date object with the current date in it (provided automatically by the `init` method):

```
myDate=[NSDate alloc] init]
```

And then grab the earlier of the two dates using the `earlierDate` method:

```
[myDate earlierDate: userDate]
```

Obviously, you can perform many other operations, but you can avoid much of the ugliness of data and time manipulation using `NSDate` objects.

URLs (`NSURL`)

URLs are certainly a different type of data from what we're accustomed to thinking about, but on an Internet-connected device like the iPhone, you'll find that the ability to manipulate URLs comes in very handy. The `NSURL` class will enable you to manage URLs with ease. For example, suppose you have the URL http://www.floraphotographs.com/index.html and want to get *just* the machine name out of the string? You could create an `NSURL` object:

```
MyURL=[[NSURL alloc] initWithString:
@"http://www.floraphotographs.com/index.html"]
```

Then use the `host` method to automatically parse and grab www.floraphotographs.com:

```
[MyURL host]
```

This will come in very handy as you start to create Internet-enabled applications. Of course, many more data type objects are available, and as we mentioned earlier, some objects store their own data, so you won't, for example, need to maintain a separate string object to correspond to the text in labels that you have onscreen.

Speaking of labels, let's round out our introduction to common classes with a quick look at some of the UI elements that you'll be adding to your applications.

Interface Classes

Part of what makes the iPhone such an enjoyable device to use are the onscreen touch interfaces that you can create. As we explore Interface Builder in the next hour, you'll get your first hands-on experience with some of these interface classes. Something to keep in the back of your head as you read through this section is that many UI objects can take on very different visual appearance based on how they are configured—so there is quite a bit of flexibility in your presentation

Labels (UILabel)

You'll be adding labels to your applications both to present static text onscreen (as a typical label) and as a controllable block of text that can be changed as needed by your program (see Figure 4.3).

FIGURE 4.3
Labels add text to your application views.

Buttons (UIButton)

Buttons are one of the simplest user input methods that you'll be using. Buttons can respond to a variety of touch events and give your users an easy way to make onscreen choices (see Figure 4.4).

FIGURE 4.4
Buttons provide a simple form of user input/interaction.

Switches (UISwitch)

A switch object can be used to collect "on" and "off" responses from a user. It is displayed as a simple toggle and is frequently used to activate or deactivate application features (see Figure 4.5).

FIGURE 4.5
A switch moves between on and off states.

Segmented Control (UISegmentedControl)

A segmented control creates an elongated touchable bar with multiple named selections (Category 1, Category 2, and so on). Touching a selection will activate it and can trigger your application to perform an action, such as updating the screen to hide or show other controls (see Figure 4.6).

FIGURE 4.6
Segmented con-
trols can be
used to choose
one item out of
a set and react
accordingly.

Sliders (`UISlider`)

A slider provides the user with a draggable bobble for the purpose of choosing a value from across a range. Sliders, for example, are used to control volume, screen brightness, and other inputs that should be presented in an "analog" fashion (see Figure 4.7).

FIGURE 4.7
Sliders offer a
visual means of
entering a value
within a range.

Text Fields (`UITextField`/`UITextView`)

Text fields are used to collect user input through the iPhone's onscreen keyboard. The `UITextField` is a single-line field, similar to what you'd see on a web page order form. The `UITextView` class, on the other hand, creates a larger multiline text entry block for more lengthy compositions (see Figure 4.8).

FIGURE 4.8
Collect user
input through
text fields.

A Text Field (UITextField)

Pickers (`UIDatePicker`/`UIPicker`)

A picker is a unique interface element that resembles a slot machine display. By letting the user change each segment on the wheel, it can be used to enter a combination of several different values. Apple has implemented one complete picker for you: the `UIDatePicker` class. With this object, a user can quickly enter dates and times. You can also implement your own arbitrary pickers with the `UIPicker` class (see Figure 4.9).

These are only a sample of the classes that you can use in your applications. We'll be exploring these and many others in the hours to come.

FIGURE 4.9
Pickers enable
users to choose
a combination
of several
options.

Exploring the iPhone Frameworks with Xcode

So far in this hour, you've learned about dozens of frameworks and classes. Each framework could be made up of dozens of classes, and each class with hundreds of methods, and so on—in other words, there's a ridiculous amount of information available about the iPhone frameworks.

One of the most efficient ways to learn more is to pick an object or framework you're interested in and then turn to the Xcode documentation system. Xcode provides an interface to the immense Apple development library in both a searchable browser-like interface as well as a context-sensitive Research Assistant. Let's take a look at both of these features now so that you can start using them immediately.

Xcode Documentation

To open the Xcode documentation application, choose Help, Documentation from the menu bar. The help system will launch, as shown in Figure 4.10.

Find information by typing into the search field. You can enter specific class, method, or property names, or just type in a concept that you're interested in. As you type, Xcode will start returning results.

Navigating Content

The documentation window is divided into two parts. The left column contains the information that matches your search – divided into groups based on whether the results were found in the API (programming) documentation, tutorial files, and so on. On the right, the content of the selected is displayed, as seen in Figure 4.11.

FIGURE 4.10
Search through
the documenta-
tion to find tuto-
rial articles and
programming
information.

FIGURE 4.11
Navigate
through the
available docu-
mentation using
the web-like
search, results,
and navigation
features.

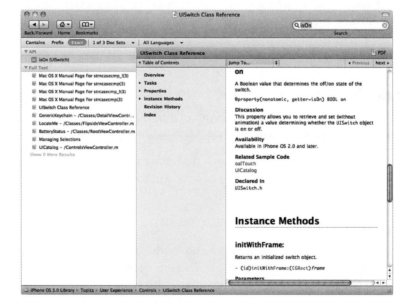

When you've arrived at a document that you're interested in, you can read and navigate within the document using the blue links—just like a web page. It's so much like a web page, in fact, that you can add a bookmark to the current document by clicking the + button in the lower-left corner of the window. You can also navigate forward and backward using the arrow buttons directly above the content view, and access a history of documents you've visited using the history menu to the right of the arrows. Finally, to the right of the history is another drop-down menu that will let you jump to specific references within an individual document.

The Xcode documentation tool makes it easy (even fun!) to find and developer documents, but Apple offers an even better tool for locating information when you're in the middle of coding.

Limiting the Search

If you know exactly what you want to find, you can limit the search results using the button bar that appears directly underneath the toolbar. If you want only exact matches, for example, you can click the Exact button. You can also use the Languages button in the toolbar to limit your search to a specific implementation language, such as Objective-C or C.

Managing Document Sets

Document sets are broad categories of documents that cover development for specific Mac OS X versions, Xcode itself, and the iPhone OS releases. To download and automatically receive updates to a documentation set, open the Xcode preferences (Xcode, Preferences) and click the Documentation icon in the preference pane list.

In the Documentation pane, click the "Check for and install updates automatically" checkbox. Xcode will connect to Apple's servers and automatically update your local documentation. You'll also notice that additional documentation sets may be listed. Click the "Get" button beside any of the listed items to download and automatically include it in any future updates.

You can force a manual update of the documentation using the "Check and Install Now" button.

Quick Help

One of the easiest and fastest ways to get help while coding is through the Xcode Quick Help assistant. To open the assistant, hold down Option and double-click a symbol in Xcode (for example, a class name or method name) or choose Help,

Quick Help. A small window opens with basic information about the symbol, as well as links to other documentation resources.

Using Quick Help

Consider the following line that allocates and initializes a string with the contents of an integer variable:

```
myString=[[NSString alloc] initWithFormat:@"%d",myValue]
```

In this sample, there is a class (NSString), and two methods (alloc and initWithFormat). To get information about the initWithFormat: method, hold down Option, then double-click initWithFormat:. Quick Help window appears, as demonstrated in Figure 4.12.

To open the full Xcode documentation for the symbol, click the "book" icon in the upper-right corner. You can also click any of the hyperlinks in Quick Help results to jump to a specific piece of documentation or code.

By default, Quick Help will close itself when you click off of the selected symbol. To keep Quick Help open, just click add drag the assistant window outside of the Xcode window. While open, its contents will automatically update as you click on other symbols in your code. It will even update as you *type* new symbols – providing documentation on the fly!

Quick Help will remain open until you click the "X" close box in the upper-left corner.

Interpreting Quick Help Results

Quick Help displays information related to your code in up to seven different sections.

Documents—Documents that define the selected symbol, such as method references, class references, and header files

Declaration—The structure of a method or definition of a data type

Abstract—A description of the feature that the class, method, or other symbol provides

Availability—The versions of the operating system where the feature is available

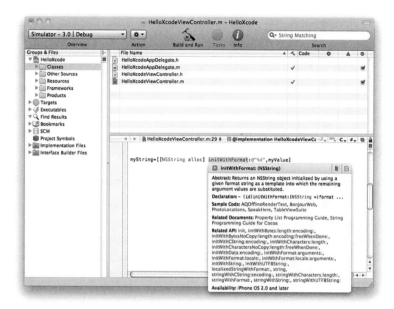

FIGURE 4.12
Quick Help
updates as you
type.

Related API—Other methods within the same class as your selected method

Related Documents—Additional documentation that references the selected symbol

Sample Code—Sample code files that include examples of class/method/property use

Quick Help simplifies the process of finding the right method to use with an object. Instead of trying to memorize dozens of instance methods, you can learn the basics and let Quick Help act as an on-demand reference of all an object's exposed methods.

Summary

In this hour, you explored the layers that make up the iPhone OS: Cocoa Touch, Media, Core Services, and Core OS. You learned the structure of a basic application—what objects it uses, and how the iPhone manages its life cycle. We also reviewed the common classes that you'll encounter as you begin to work with Cocoa, including data types and UI controls.

To give you the tools you need to find class and method references on your own, we introduced you to two features in Xcode. The first, the Xcode documentation window, offers a browser-like interface to the complete iPhone documentation. The second, Quick Help, finds help for the class or method you are working with, automatically, as you type. Ultimately, it will be these tools that help you dive deeper into the Apple development environment.

Q&A

Q: Why are the operating system services layered? Doesn't that add complexity?

A: Using the upper-level frameworks reduces the complexity of your code. By providing multiple levels of abstraction, Apple has given developers the tools they need to easily use iPhone features as well as the flexibility to highly customize their application's behavior by using lower-level services more closely tied to the OS.

Q: What do I do if I can't find an interface object I want?

A: Chances are, if you're writing a "normal" iPhone application, Apple has provided a UI class to fill your need. If you find that you'd like to do things differently, you can always subclass an existing control and modify its behavior as you see fit—or create a completely new control!

Workshop

Quiz

1. How many layers are there in the simplified Apple iPhone OS architecture?

2. How frequently will you be manually creating the UIApplication object in your applications?

3. What helpful feature can watch your typing and show relevant help articles?

Answers

1. Four. Cocoa Touch, Media, Core Services, and Core OS.

2. If you're building using Apple's iPhone application templates, the initial setup of the UIApplication object is automatic. You don't need to do a thing!

3. Quick Help offers interactive help as you code.

Activities

1. Using the Apple Xcode Documentation utility, explore the NSString class and instance methods. Identify the methods you'd use to compare strings, create a string from a number, and change a string to upper- and lowercase.

2. Open Xcode and create a new window-based application on your desktop. Expand the Classes folder and click the file that ends in AppDelegate.m. When the contents of the file appear, open Quick Help by holding Option and double-clicking inside the class name UIApplication. Review the results. Try clicking other symbols in the Xcode class file and see what happens!

HOUR 5

Exploring Interface Builder

What You'll Learn in This Hour:

▶ What Interface Builder does, and what makes it special
▶ How to create user interfaces using the Library
▶ Common attributes that can be used to customize your interface
▶ Ways to make your interface accessible to the visually impaired
▶ How to connect interfaces to code with outlets and actions

Over the past few hours, you've become familiar with the core iPhone technologies and the Xcode and iPhone Simulator applications. While these are certainly important skills for becoming a successful developer, there's nothing quite like building your first iPhone application interface and seeing it come alive on the iPhone screen.

In this hour, we introduce the third (and flashiest) component of the Apple Developer Suite: Interface Builder. Interface Builder provides a visual approach to application interface design, but, behind the scenes, does much, much more.

Understanding Interface Builder

Let's get it out of the way up front: Yes, Interface Builder (or IB for short) does help you create interfaces for your iPhone applications, but it isn't a just a drawing tool for GUIs; it helps you symbolically build application functionality without writing code. This translates to fewer bugs, less development time, and easier-to-maintain projects!

Although IB is a standalone application, it is dependent on Xcode and, to some extent, the iPhone Simulator. In this hour, we focus on navigating through Interface Builder, but will return in Hour 6, "Model-View-Controller Application Design," to combine all three pieces of the Apple Developer Suite for the first time.

The Interface Builder Approach

Using Xcode and the Cocoa toolset, you can program iPhone interfaces by hand—instantiating interface objects, defining where they appear on the screen, setting any attributes for the object, and, finally, making them visible. For example, in Hour 2, "Introduction to Xcode and the iPhone Simulator," you entered this listing into Xcode to make your iPhone display the text Hello Xcode in the middle of the screen:

```
UILabel *myMessage;
UILabel *myUnusedMessage;
myMessage=[[UILabel alloc] initWithFrame:CGRectMake(25,225,300,50)];
myMessage.text=@"Hello Xcode";
[window addSubview:myMessage];
```

Imagine how long it would take to build interfaces with text, buttons, images, and dozens of other controls—and think of all the code you'd need to wade through just to make small changes!

Over the years, there have been many different approaches to graphical interface builders. One of the most common implementations is to enable the user to "draw" an interface, but, behind the scenes, create the code that generates that interface. Any tweaks require the code to be edited by hand—hardly an acceptable situation.

Another tactic is to maintain the interface definition symbolically, but to attach the code that implements functionality directly to interface elements. This, unfortunately, means that if you want to change your interface, or swap functionality from one UI element to another, you have to move the code as well.

Interface Builder works differently. Rather than autogenerating interface code or tying source listings directly to interface elements, IB builds live objects that connect to your application code through simple links called *connections*. Want to change how a feature of your app is triggered? Just change the connection. As you'll learn a bit later, changing how your application works with the objects you create in Interface Builder is, quite literally, a matter of connecting or reconnecting the dots as you see fit.

The Anatomy of an Interface Builder XIB File

Your work in Interface Builder results in an XML file called an XIB or (for legacy reasons) NIB file, containing a hierarchy of objects. The objects could be interface elements—buttons, toggle switches, and so forth—but might also be other noninterface objects that you need to use in your app. When the XIB file is loaded by your application, the objects described in it are instantiated and can be accessed by your code.

By the Way

Instantiation, just as a quick refresher, is the process of creating an instance of an object that you can work with in your program. An instantiated object gains all the functionality described by its class. Buttons, for example, automatically highlight when clicked, content views scroll, and so on.

The Document Window

What do XIB files look like in IB? Open the Hour 5 Projects folder and double-click the file EmptyView.xib to open Interface Builder and display a barebones XIB file. The contents of the file are shown in the IB "document" window (see Figure 5.1).

FIGURE 5.1
An XIB file's objects are represented by icons.

By the Way

If you do not see a window with icons when opening the XIB file, choose Windows, Document to ensure that the document window is active and visible on your screen.

In this sample file, there are three icons initially visible: File's Owner, first responder, and view. The first two are special icons used to represent unique objects in our application; these will be present in all XIB files that you work with:

File's Owner: The File's Owner icon denotes the object that loads the XIB file in your running application. This is the object that effectively instantiates all the other objects described in the XIB file. For example, you may have an interface defined in myInterface.xib, which is loaded by an object you've written called `myInterfaceController`. In this case, the File's Owner would represent the `myInterfaceController` object. You'll learn more about the relationship between interfaces and code in Hour 6.

First responder: The first responder icon stands for the object that the user is currently interacting with. When a user works with an iPhone application, there are multiple objects that could potentially respond to the various gestures or keystrokes that the user creates. The first responder is the object currently in control and interacting with the user. A text field that the user is typing into, for example, would be the first responder until the user moves to another field or control.

View: The view icon is an instance of the object `UIView` and represents the visual layout that will be loaded and displayed on the iPhone screen. You can double-click view icons to open and edit them with the IB tools, as shown in Figure 5.2.

FIGURE 5.2
Double-click the view icon to open and edit the iPhone application's GUI.

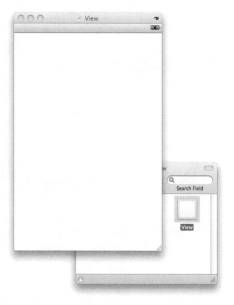

Views are hierarchical in nature. This means that as you add controls to your interface, they will be contained *within* the view. You can even add views within views to cluster controls or create visual elements that can be shown or hidden as a group. Because a view can contain many other objects, we recommend using the list or column view of the document window to make sure that you can view the full hierarchy of objects you've created in an XIB file. To change the document view, click the view mode icon in the document window toolbar (see Figure 5.3).

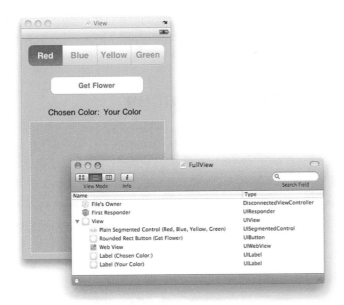

FIGURE 5.3
Using the list view mode ensures that you can see all of the objects in your XIB files. Here an XIB with a full interface and view hierarchy is displayed.

At its most basic level, a view (UIView) is a rectangular region that can contain content and respond to user events (touches and so forth). All the controls (buttons, fields, and so on) that you'll add to a view are, in fact, subclasses of UIView. This isn't necessarily something you need to be worried about, except that you'll be encountering documentation that refers to buttons and other interface elements referred to as *subviews* and the views that contain them as *superviews*.

Just keep in the back of your mind that pretty much everything you see on your iPhone screen can be considered a "view" and the terminology will seem a little less alien.

Did you Know?

Working with the Document Icons

The document window shows icons for objects in your application, but what good are they? Aside from presenting a nice list, do the document window icons provide any functionality?

Absolutely! These icons give you a visual means of referring to the objects they represent. You will interact with the icons by dragging to and from them to create the connections that drive your application's features.

Consider an onscreen control, such as a button, that needs to be able to trigger an action in your code. By dragging from the button to the File's Owner icon, you can create a connection from the GUI element you've drawn to a method you've written in the object that loaded the XIB file.

We'll go through a hands-on example later this hour so that you can get a feel for how this works. Before we do that, however, let's take a look at how you go about turning a blank view into an interface masterpiece.

Creating User Interfaces

In Figures 5.2 and 5.3, you've seen an empty view and a fully fleshed-out iPhone interface—but how do we get from one to the other? In this section, we explore how interfaces are created with Interface Builder. In other words, it's time for the fun stuff!

If you haven't already, open the EmptyView.xib file included in this hour's Projects folder. Use the document window to open the empty view and prepare for adding content.

The Objects Library

Everything that you add to a view comes from the IB Objects Library, shown in Figure 5.4. The Library can be opened from the menu bar by choosing Tools, Library (Command+Shift+L). When you click an object in the Library, the bottom of the window refreshes to show a description of how the element can be used in the interface.

> Using the action (gear) menu at the bottom of the Library, you can change the Library to show just the icons, icons and names, or icons and full descriptions for each object. You can even group items based on their purpose. When starting out, using the icons and descriptions option may prove useful in getting your bearings.

To add a object to the view, just click and drag from the Library to the view. For example, find the label object (UILabel) in the Library and drag it into the center of the view window. The label should appear in your view and read Text. Double-click the Text and type **Hello**. The text will update, as shown in Figure 5.5, just as you would expect.

With that simple action, you've almost entirely replicated the functionality implemented by the code fragment earlier in the lesson. Try dragging other objects from the Library into the view—buttons, text fields, and so on. With few exceptions, the objects should appear and behave just the way you'd expect.

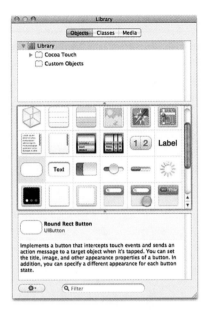

FIGURE 5.4
The Library provides a palette of objects that can be added to your views.

FIGURE 5.5
If an object contains text, in many cases, just double-click to edit it.

To remove an object from the view, click to select it, then press the Delete key. You may also use the options under the edit menu to copy and paste between views, or duplicate an element several times within a view.

Layout Tools

Instead of relying on your visual acuity to position objects in a view, Apple has included some useful tools for fine-tuning your layout. If you've ever used a drawing program like OmniGraffle or Adobe Illustrator, many of these will be familiar.

Guides

As you drag objects in a view, you'll notice guides (shown in Figure 5.6) appearing to help with the layout. These blue dotted lines will be displayed to align objects along the margins of the view, to the centers of other objects in the view, and to the baseline of the fonts used in the labels and object titles.

FIGURE 5.6
Guides help position your objects within a view.

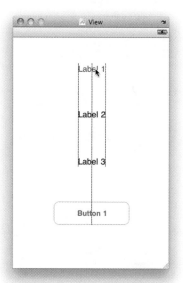

As an added bonus, guides will automatically appear to indicate the approximate spacing requirements of Apple's interface guidelines. If you're not sure why it's showing you a particular margin guide, it's likely that your object is in a position that Interface Builder considers "appropriate" for something of that type and size.

You can manually add your own guides by choosing Layout, Add Horizontal Guide or by choosing Layout, Add Vertical Guide.

Selection Handles

In addition to the layout guides, most objects include selection handles to stretch an object either horizontally, vertically, or both. Using the small boxes that appear alongside an object when it is selected, just click and drag to change its size, as demonstrated using a button in Figure 5.7.

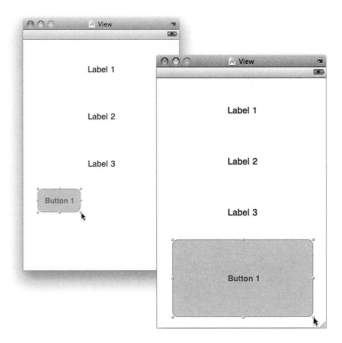

FIGURE 5.7
Use the resize handles around the perimeter of an object to change its size.

Note that some objects will constrain how you can resize them; this preserves a level of consistency within iPhone application interfaces.

Alignment

To quickly align several objects within a view, select them by clicking and dragging a selection rectangle around them or by holding down the Shift key, and then choose Layout, Alignment and an appropriate alignment type from the menu.

For example, try dragging several buttons into your view, placing them in a variety of different positions. To align them based on their horizontal center (a line that runs vertically through each button's center) select the buttons, and then choose Layout, Alignment, Align Horizontal Centers. Figure 5.8 shows the before and after results.

FIGURE 5.8
Use the
Alignment menu
to quickly align
a group of items
to an edge or
center.

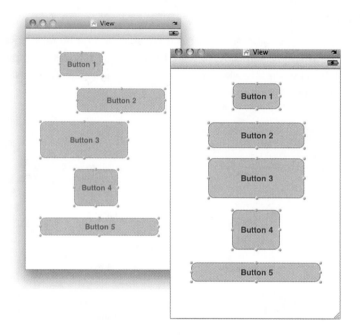

**Did you
know?** To fine-tune an object's position within a view, select it, and then use the arrow
keys to position it left, right, up, or down, one pixel at a time.

The Size Inspector

Another tool that you may want to use for controlling your layout is the Size
Inspector. Interface Builder has a number of "inspectors" for examining the attributes of an object. As the name implies, the Size Inspector provides information
about sizes, but also position and alignment. To open the Size Inspector, first select
the object (or objects) that you want to work with, and then press Command+1 or
choose Layout, Size Inspector (see Figure 5.9).

Using the fields at the top of the inspector, you can view or change the size and
position of the object by changing the coordinates in the H/W and X/Y fields. You
can also view the coordinates of a specific portion of an object by clicking one of the
black dots in the size and grid to indicate where the reading should come from.

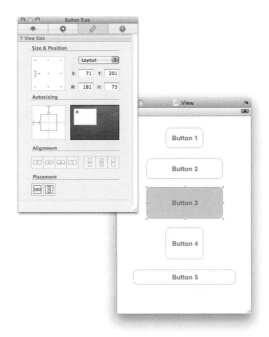

FIGURE 5.9
The Size Inspector enables you to adjust the size and position of one or more objects.

Within the Size and Position settings, you'll notice a drop-down menu where you can choose between Frame and Layout. These two settings will usually be very similar, but there is a slight difference. The frame values represent the exact area an object occupies onscreen, whereas the layout values take into account spacing around the object.

By the Way

The Autosizing settings of the Size Inspector determine how controls resize/reposition themselves when the iPhone changes rotation. You'll learn more about these in Hour 17, "Building Rotatable and Resizable User Interfaces."

Finally, the same controls found under Layout, Alignment can be accessed as clickable icons at the bottom of the inspector. Choose your objects, and then click one of the icons to align according to the red line.

Customizing Interface Appearance

How your interface appears to the end user isn't just a combination of control sizes and positions. For many kinds of objects, there are literally dozens of different attributes that can be adjusted. While you could certainly configure things such as colors and fonts in your code, it's easier to just use the tools included in Interface Builder.

Using the Attributes Inspector

The most common place you'll tweak the way your interface objects appear is through the Attributes Inspector, available by choosing Tools, Attributes Inspector or by pressing Command+1 in IB. Let's run through a quick example to see how this works.

Make sure that the EmptyView.xib file is still open and that you've added a text label to the view. Select the label, and then press Command+1 to open the Attributes Inspector, shown in Figure 5.10.

FIGURE 5.10
To change how an object looks and behaves, select it and then open the Attributes Inspector.

The top portion of the Attributes Inspector will contain attributes for the specific object. In the case of the text object, this includes things such as font, size, color, and alignment—everything you'd expect to find for editing text.

In the lower portion of the inspector are additional inherited attributes. Remember that onscreen elements are a subclass of a view? This means that all the standard view attributes are also available for the object and for your tinkering enjoyment. In many cases, you'll want to leave these alone, but settings such as background and transparency can come in handy.

Did you Know?

Don't get hung up on trying to memorize every attribute for every control now—we'll cover interesting and important attributes when they are needed throughout the book.

You should feel free to explore the many different options available in the Attributes Inspector, and to see what can be configured for different types of objects. There is a surprising amount of flexibility to be found within the tool.

Did you Know?

The attributes you change in Interface Builder are simply properties of the objects themselves. To help identify what an attribute does, use the documentation tool in Xcode, to look up the object's class and review the descriptions of its properties.

Setting Accessibility Attributes

For many years, the "appearance" of an interface meant *just* how it looks visually. Today, the technology is available for an interface to vocally describe itself to the visually impaired. New to iPhone OS 3.0 and the iPhone 3GS is Voiceover—a combination of speech synthesis and a change to how nonsighted users can navigate an onscreen interface.

Using Voiceover, a user can touch interface elements and hear a short description of what they do and how they can be used. While you gain much of this functionality "for free" (the iPhone software will read button labels, for example), you can provide quite a bit of additional assistance by configuring the accessibility attributes in Interface Builder.

To access the Accessibility settings, you'll need to open the Identity Inspector by choosing Tools, Identity Inspector or pressing Command+4. The Accessibility options have their own section within the Identity Inspector, as shown in Figure 5.11.

There are four sets of attributes that you can configure within this area:

Accessibility: If enabled, the object is considered accessible. If you create any custom controls that *must* be seen to be used, this setting should be disabled.

Label: A simple word or two that serves as the label for an item. A text field that collects the user's name might use "your name," for example.

Hint: A short description, if needed, on how to use the control. This is needed only if the label doesn't provide enough information on its own.

Traits: This set of check boxes is used to describe the features of the object—what it does, and what its current state is.

FIGURE 5.11
Use the
Accessibility
section in the
Identity
Inspector to
configure how
the iPhone's
accessibility
software inter-
acts with your
application.

For an application to be available to the largest possible audience, you should take advantage of accessibility tools whenever possible. Even objects like the text labels you've used in this lesson should have their traits configured to indicated that they are static text. This helps a potential user know that he or she can't interact with them.

Simulating the Interface

At any point in time during the construction of your iPhone interface, you can test the controls in the iPhone Simulator. To test the interface, choose File, Simulate Interface (Command+R). After a few seconds, the iPhone Simulator will start and display your interface design. You can use all of the same gestures and controls that you learned about in Hour 2.

Watch Out!

> When you use the Simulate Interface command, *only* the interface code is being run. Nothing that you may have written in Xcode is included. This means that you can simulate interfaces even if you haven't written a single line of supporting code or if your code has errors. However, it also means that if your code modifies the display in any way, you won't see those changes onscreen.
>
> To compile and run your code along with the interface, switch to Xcode and click Build and Run, or, as a shortcut, choose File, Build and Run in Xcode from the IB menu (Command+Shift+R).

Enabling the Accessibility Inspector

If you are building accessible interfaces, you may want to enable the Accessibility Inspector in the iPhone Simulator. To do this, start the simulator and click the Home button to return to the main (simulated) iPhone screen. Click the Settings application and navigate to General, Accessibility, and then use the toggle button to turn the Accessibility Inspector on, as shown in Figure 5.12.

FIGURE 5.12
Toggle the Accessibility Inspector on.

The Accessibility Inspector adds an overlay to the simulator workspace that displays the label, hints, and traits that you've configured for your interface elements, as demonstrated in Figure 5.13. Note that navigating the iPhone interface is *very* different when operating in accessibility mode.

Using the X button in the upper-left corner of the inspector, you can toggle it on and off. When off, the inspector collapses to a small bar, and the iPhone simulator will behave normally. Clicking the X button again turns it back on. To disable the Accessibility Inspector altogether, just revisit the Accessibility setting in the Settings application.

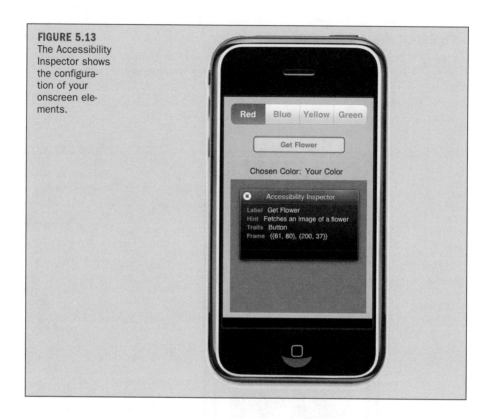

FIGURE 5.13
The Accessibility Inspector shows the configuration of your onscreen elements.

Connecting to Code

You know how to make an interface, but how do you make it *do* something? Throughout this hour, we've been alluding to the idea that connecting an interface to the code you write is just a matter of "connecting the dots." In this last part of the hour, we'll do just that: take an interface and connect it to the code that makes it into a functional application.

Launching Interface Builder from Xcode

To get started, we'll use the project Disconnected contained within this hour's Projects folder. Open the folder and double-click the Disconnected.xcodeproj file. This will open the project in Xcode, as shown in Figure 5.14. Almost all of your work in Interface Builder will start from inside of Xcode, so we might as well get used to using it as our launching point for IB.

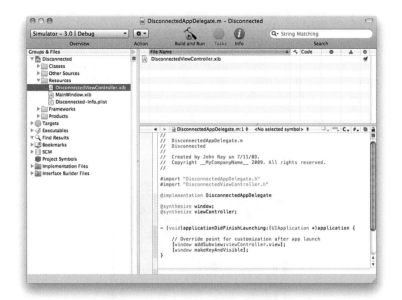

FIGURE 5.14
Almost all of your work in Interface Builder will start in Xcode.

Once the project is loaded, expand the Resources file group, and double-click the DisconnectedViewController.xib file. This XIB file contains the view that this application displays as its interface. After a few seconds, IB will launch and display the interface document window as well as the view, as shown in Figure 5.15.

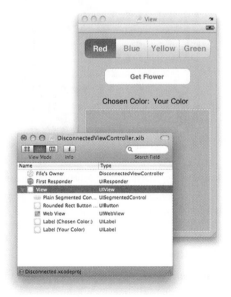

FIGURE 5.15
After launching, Interface Builder will show the document window and view from the XIB file.

Implementation Overview

The interface contains four interactive elements: a button bar (called a *segmented control*), a push button, an output label, and a web view (an integrated web browser component). Together, these controls will interface with application code to enable a user to choose a flower color, click the Get Flower button, and then display the chosen color in a text label along with a random flower fetched from the site www.floraphotographs.com that matches their choice. The final result is demonstrated in Figure 5.16.

FIGURE 5.16
The finished application will enable a user to choose a color and have a flower image returned that matches that color.

Unfortunately, right now the application does nothing. The interface isn't connected to any application code, so it is hardly more than a pretty picture. To make it work, we'll be creating *connections* to outlets and actions that have been defined in Xcode.

Outlets and Actions

An outlet is nothing more than a variable by which an object can be referenced. For example, if you had created a field in Interface Builder intending that it would be used to collect a user's name, you might want to create an outlet for it in your code called userName. Using this outlet, you could then access or change the contents of the field.

An action, on the other hand, is a method within your code that is called when an event takes place. Certain objects, such as buttons and switches, can trigger actions when a user interacts with them through an event—such as touching the screen. By defining actions in your code, Interface Builder can make them available to the onscreen objects.

Joining an element in Interface Builder to an outlet or action creates what is generically termed a *connection*.

For the Disconnected app to function, we need to create connections to these outlets and actions:

colorChoice   An outlet created for the button bar to access the color the user has selected

getFlower   An action that retrieves a flower from the web, displays it, and updates the label with the chosen color

chosenColor   An outlet for the label that will be updated by getFlower to show the name of the chosen color

flowerView   An outlet for the web view that will be updated by getFlower to show the image

Let's make the connections now.

Creating Connections to Outlets

To create a connection from an interface item to an outlet, Control-drag from the File's Owner icon either to the visual representation of the object in the view or to its icon in the document window of Interface Builder.

Try this with the button bar (segmented control). Click and drag from the File's Owner icon in the document window to either the onscreen image of the bar or its icon in the document window. A line will appear as you drag, enabling you to easily point to the object that you want to use for the connect. When you release the mouse button, the available connections will be shown in a pop-up menu (see Figure 5.17).

FIGURE 5.17
Choose from the outlets that are available for that object.

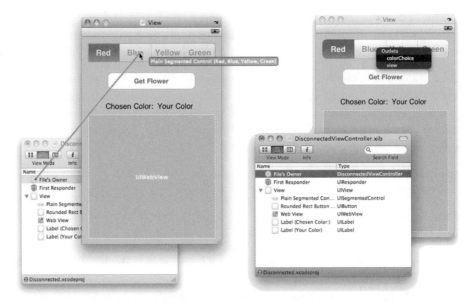

By the Way

Interface Builder knows what type of object is allowed to connect to a given outlet, so it will only display the outlets that are appropriate for the connection you're trying to make.

Repeat this process for the label with the text Your Color, connecting it to the chosenColor outlet, and the web view, connecting to flowerView.

Creating Connections to Actions

Connecting to actions is a bit different; an object's events trigger actions in your code. So, the connection direction reverses; you connect from the object to the File's Owner icon. Although it is possible to Control-drag and create a connection in the same manner you did with outlets, this isn't recommended because you don't get to specify which event triggers it. Does the user have to touch the button? Swipe across the button?

Actions can be triggered by *many* different events, so you need to make sure that you're picking exactly the right one, instead of leaving it up to Interface Builder. To do this, select the object that will be calling the action and open the Connections Inspector by choosing Tools, Connections Inspector (or by pressing Command+2).

The Connections Inspector, in Figure 5.18, shows a list of the events that the object supports—in this case, a button. Beside each event is an open circle. To connect an event to an action in your code, click and drag from one of these circles to the File's Owner icon.

FIGURE 5.18
The Connections Inspector shows all the connections you've made to and from an object.

For example, to connect the Get Flower button to the `getFlower` method, select the button, and then open the Connections Inspector (Command+2). Drag from the circle beside the Touch Up Inside event to the File's Owner icon and release. When prompted, choose the `getFlower` action, as demonstrated in Figure 5.19.

FIGURE 5.19
Drag from the event to the File's Owner Icon, and then choose the action you want to use.

After a connection has been made, the inspector will update to show the event and the action that it calls, as shown in Figure 5.20. If you click other objects, you'll notice that the Connections Inspector shows connections to outlets as well as actions.

FIGURE 5.20
The
Connections
Inspector
updates to
show the
actions and out-
lets that an
object refer-
ences.

> ## Connections Without Code!
>
> Although most of your connections in Interface Builder will be between objects and outlets and actions you've defined in your code, there are actually some built-in actions that certain objects implement without you writing a single line of code.
>
> The web view, for example, implements actions, including goForward and goBack. Using these actions, you could add basic navigation functionality to the view by dragging from a button's Touch Up Inside event directly to the web view object (rather than the File's Owner). As described previously, you'll be prompted for the action to connect to, but this time, it isn't an action you had to code yourself!

Well done! You've just linked an interface to the code that supports it. Switch to Xcode and choose Build and Run to run and test the application in the iPhone Simulator.

Object Identity

As we finish up our introduction to Interface Builder, we'd be remiss if we didn't introduce one more feature: the Identity Inspector. You've already accessed this tool to view the accessibility attributes for interface objects, but there is another reason why we'll need to use the inspector in the future—setting class identities.

As you drag objects into the interface, you're creating instances of classes that already exist (buttons, labels, and so on). Throughout this book, however, we're going to be building custom subclasses that we'll also need to be able to reference in Interface Builder. In these cases, we'll need to tell Interface Builder exactly what class an object should be so that the right kind of object is created when the XIB file is loaded.

For example, suppose we created a subclass of the standard button class (UIButton) that we named ourFancyButtonClass. We might drag a button into Interface Builder to represent our fancy button, but it would just be the same UIButton that got created when the XIB file loaded.

To fix the problem, we could select the button we've added to the view, open the Identity Inspector by choosing Tools, Identity Inspector (Command+4), and then use the drop-down menu/field to enter the class that we really want instantiated when the interface is loaded at runtime (see Figure 5.21).

FIGURE 5.21
If you're using a custom class, you'll need to manually set the identity of your objects in Interface Builder.

This is something we'll cover on an as-needed basis, so if it seems confusing, don't worry. We'll come back to it later in the book.

Summary

In this hour, you explored Interface Builder and the tools it provides for building rich graphical interfaces for your iPhone applications. You learned how to navigate the IB document window and access the GUI elements from the Objects Library. Using the various inspector tools within Interface Builder, you customized the look and feel of the onscreen controls and how they can be made accessible to the visually impaired.

More than just a pretty picture, an IB-created interface uses simple outlets and actions to connect to functionality in your code. You used Interface Builder's connection tools to turn a nonfunctioning interface into a complete application. By maintaining a separation between the code you write and what is displayed to the user, you can revise your interface to look however you want, without breaking your application. In Hour 6, you'll examine how to create outlets and actions from scratch in Xcode (and thus gain a full toolset to get started developing).

Q&A

Q. *Why do I keep seeing things referred to as NIB files?*

A. The origins of Interface Builder trace back to the NeXT Computer, which made use of NIB files. These files, in fact, still bore the same name when Mac OS X was released. In recent years, however, Apple has renamed the files to have the XIB extension—unfortunately, documentation hasn't quite caught up yet.

Q. *Some of the objects in the Interface Builder Library can't be added to my view. What gives?*

A. Not all of the Library objects are interface objects. Some represent objects that provide functionality to your application. In the next hour, we'll look at the first object that does this (a view controller).

Q. *I've seen controls in applications that aren't available here. Where are they?*

A. While some developers choose to make their own UI objects, many of the controls you see in the Library can morph dramatically depending on how their attributes are configured.

Workshop

Quiz

1. Simulating an interface from IB also compiles the project's code in Xcode. True or false?

2. What tool can you use within the iPhone Simulator to help review accessibility of objects in your apps?

3. How is Interface Builder typically launched?

Answers

1. False. Simulating the interface does not use the project code at all. As a result, the interface will not perform any actions that may be assigned.

2. The Accessibility Inspector makes it possible to view the accessibility attributes configured within Interface Builder.

3. Although Interface Builder is a standalone application, it is typically launched by opening an XIB file from within Xcode.

Activities

1. Practice using the interface layout tools on the EmptyView.xib file. Add each available interface object to your view, and then review the Attributes Inspector for that object. If an attribute doesn't make sense, remember that you can review documentation for the class to identify the role of each of its properties.

2. Revise the Disconnected project to design as accessible an interface as possible. Review the finished design using the Accessibility Inspector in the iPhone Simulator.

Further Exploration

Interface Builder gives you the opportunity to experiment with many of the different GUI objects you've seen in iPhone applications and read about in the previous hours. In the next hour, Xcode and Interface Builder will finally come together for your first full project, from start to finish.

To learn even more about what you can do in Interface Builder, I suggest reading through the following three Apple publications:

> *Interface Builder User Guide*: Accessed by choosing Help, Interface Builder Help from the IB menu, this is more than a simple help document. Apple's user guide walks you through all of the intricacies of IB and covers some advanced topics that will be important as your development experience increases.

> *iPhone Human Interface Guidelines*: Accessible through the Xcode documentation system, the Apple iPhone HIG document provides a clear set of rules for building usable interfaces on the iPhone. This document describes when you should use controls and how they should be displayed, helping you to create more polished, professional-quality applications.

> *Accessibility Programming Guide for iPhone OS* (accessible through the Xcode documentation system): If you're serious about creating accessible apps, this is a mandatory read. The *Accessibility Programming Guide* describes the accessibility features mentioned in this hour's lesson as well as ways to improve accessibility programmatically and methods of testing accessibility beyond the tips given in this hour.

As a general note, from here on, you'll be doing quite a bit of coding in each lesson, so now would be a great time to review the previous hours if you have any questions.

HOUR 6

Model-View-Controller Application Design

What You'll Learn in This Hour:

▶ What the Model-View-Controller design pattern means

▶ Ways in which the Apple Developer Suite implements MVC

▶ Design of a basic view

▶ Implementation of a corresponding view controller

You've come a long way in the past few hours—you've provisioned a developer profile for your phone, learned the basics of the Objective-C language, explored Cocoa Touch, and gotten a feel for Xcode and Interface Builder. Although you've already used a few prebuilt projects, you have yet to build one from scratch. That's about to change!

In this hour, you will learn about the application design pattern known as Model-View-Controller and create a single application from start to finish.

Understanding the Model-View-Controller Paradigm

When you start programming, you'll quickly come to the conclusion that there is more than one "correct" way to do just about everything. Part of the joy of programming is that it is a creative process that allows you to be as clever as your imagination allows. This doesn't mean, however, that adding structure to the development process is a bad idea. Having a defined and documented structure means that other developers will be able to work with your code, projects large and small will be easy to navigate, and you'll be able to reuse your best work in multiple applications.

The application design approach that you'll be using on the iPhone is known as Model-View-Controller (MVC), and will guide you in creating clean, efficient applications.

In Hour 3, "Discovering Objective-C" you learned about object-oriented programming and the reusability that it can provide. OO programs, however, can still be poorly structured—thus the need to define an overall application architecture that can guide the object-oriented implementation.

Making Spaghetti

Before we get into MVC, let's first talk about the development practice that we want to avoid, and why. When creating an application that interacts with a user, several things must be taken into account. First, the user interface. You must present *something* that the user interacts with: buttons, fields, and so on. Second, handling and reacting to the user input. Finally, the application must store the information necessary to correctly react to the user—frequently in the form of a database.

One approach to incorporating all of these pieces is to combine them into a single class. The code that displays the interface is mixed with the code that implements the logic and the code that handles data. This can be a very straightforward development methodology, but it limits the developer in several ways:

▶ When code is mixed together, it is difficult for multiple developers to work together because there is no clear division between any of the functional units.

▶ The interface, application logic, and data are unlikely to be reusable in other applications because the combination of the three is too specific to the current project to be useful elsewhere.

▶ The application is difficult to extend. Adding features requires working around existing code. The developer must work around the existing code to include new features, even if they are unrelated.

In short, mixing code, logic, and data leads to a mess! This is known as "spaghetti code" and is the exact opposite of what we want for our iPhone applications. Model-View-Controller to the rescue!

Structured Application Design with MVC

MVC defines a clean separation between the critical components of our apps. As implied by the name, MVC defines three parts of an application:

▶ A **model** provides the underlying data and methods that provide information to the rest of the application. The model does not define how the application will look or how it will act.

▶ One or more **views** make up the user interface. A view consists of the different onscreen widgets (buttons, fields, switches, and so forth) that a user can interact with.

▶ A **controller** is typically paired with a view. The controller is responsible for receiving the user's input and acting accordingly. Controllers may access and update a view using information from the model and update the model using the results of user interactions in the view. In short, it bridges the MVC components.

The logical isolation created between the functional parts of an application, illustrated in Figure 6.1, means the code becomes more easily maintainable, reusable, and extendable—the exact opposite of spaghetti code.

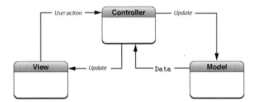

FIGURE 6.1
MVC design isolates the functional components of an app.

Unfortunately, MVC comes as an afterthought in many application development environments. A frequent question that I am asked when suggesting MVC design is, "How do I do that?" This isn't indicative of a misunderstanding of what MVC is or how it works, but a lack of a clear means of implementing it.

In the Apple Development Suite, MVC design is natural. As you create new projects and start coding, you'll be guided into using MVC design patterns automatically. It actually becomes more difficult to program poorly than it does to build a well-structured app.

How Xcode and Interface Builder Implement MVC

Over the past few hours, you've learned about Xcode and Interface Builder and have gotten a sense for what the two applications do. In Hour 5, "Exploring Interface Builder," you even connected objects in an XIB file to the code in an application. Although we didn't go into the nitty-gritty details at the time, what you were doing was binding a view to a controller.

Views

Views, although possible to create programmatically, will most frequently be designed visually in Interface Builder. Views can consist of many different interface elements—the most common of which we covered in Hour 4, "Inside Objective-C and Cocoa Touch: Where the Rubber Meets the Road." When loaded at runtime, views create any number of objects that can implement a basic level of interactivity on their own (such as a text field opening a keyboard when touched). Even so, a view is entirely independent of any application logic. This clear separation is one of the core principles of the MVC design approach.

For the objects in a view to interact with application logic, they require a connection point to be defined. These connections come in two varieties: outlets and actions. An outlet defines a path between the code and the view that can be used to read and write values. Second, an action defines a method in your application that can be triggered via an event within a view, such as a touch or swipe.

So, how do outlets and actions connect to code? In the preceding hour, you learned to control-drag in Interface Builder to create a connection, but Interface Builder "knew" what connections were valid. It certainly can't "guess" where in your code you want to create a connection; instead, you must define the outlets and actions in the code that implement the view's logic (that is, the controller).

View Controllers

A controller, known in Xcode as a view controller, handles the interactions with a view, and establishes the connection points for outlets and actions. To accomplish this, two special directives, IBAction and IBOutlet, will be added to your project's code. Specifically, you add these directives to the header files of your view controller. IBAction and IBOutlet are markers that Interface Builder recognizes; they serve no other purpose within Objective-C.

> View controllers can hold application logic, but we don't mean to imply that all your code should be within a view controller. Although this is largely the convention for the tutorials in this book, as you create your own apps, you can certainly define additional classes to abstract your application logic as you see fit.

Using `IBOutlet`

An `IBOutlet` is used to enable your code to talk to objects within views. For example, consider a text label (`UILabel`) that you've added to a view. If you want to access the label under the name `myLabel` within your view controller, you would declare it like this in the header file:

```
IBOutlet UILabel *myLabel;
```

Once declared, Interface Builder enables you to visually connect the view's label object to the `myLabel` variable. Your code can then fully interact with the label object—changing its properties, calling its methods, and so on.

Easy Access with `property` and `synthesize`

In Hour 3, you learned about the Objective-C `@property` and `@synthesize` directives, but you're about to start seeing them frequently, so we think a refresher is in order.

The `@property` directive declares elements in a class that should be exposed via "getters" and "setters" (or accessors and mutators, if you prefer). Properties are defined with a series of attributes, most frequently `nonatomic` and `retain` on the iPhone.

The `@synthesize` directive creates simplified getters and setters, making retrieving and setting values of an object very simple.

Returning to the example of a `UILabel` instance called `myLabel`, I would initially declare it as a property in the header file of my view controller:

```
@property (retain, nonatomic) NSString *myLabel;
```

And then use `@synthesize` in the implementation file to create simplified getters and setters:

```
@synthesize myLabel;
```

Once those lines are added, the current `MyLabel` value could be retrieved from `UILabel`'s text property using `theCurrentLabel=myLabel.text` (the getter) or set to something new with `myLabel.text=@"My New Label"` (the setter).

Using `IBAction`

An `IBAction` is used to "advertise" a method in your code that should be called when a certain event takes place. For instance, if a button is pushed, or a field updated, you will probably want your application to take action and react appropriately. When you've written a method that implements your event-driven logic, you can declare it with `IBAction` in the header file, which subsequently will expose it to Interface Builder.

For instance, a method `doCalculation` might be declared like this:

```
-(IBAction)doCalculation:(id)sender;
```

Notice that the declaration includes a `sender` parameter with the type of `id`. This is a generic type that can be used when you don't know (or need to know) the type of object you'll be working with. By using `id`, you can write code that doesn't tie itself to a specific class, making it easier to adapt to different situations.

When creating a method that will be used as an action (like our `doCalculation` example), you can identify and interact with the object that invoked the action through the `sender` variable (or whatever you decide to call it in your code). This will be handy if you decide to design a method that handles multiple different events, such as button presses from several different buttons.

Data Models

Let me get right to the point. For many of the exercises we'll be doing in this book, a separate data model is not needed; the data requirements are handled within the controller. This is one of the trade-offs of small projects like the one you'll be working through in a few minutes. Although it would be ideal to represent a complete MVC application architecture, sometimes it just isn't possible in the space and time available. In your own projects, you'll need to decide whether to implement a stand-alone model. In the case of small utility apps, you may find that you rarely need to consider a data model beyond the logic you code into the controller.

As you grow more experienced with the iPhone Software Development Kit (SDK) and start building data-rich applications, you'll want to begin exploring Core Data. Core Data abstracts the interactions between your application and an underlying data-store. It also includes a modeling tool, like Interface Builder, that helps you design your application, but rather than visually laying out interfaces, you can use it to visually map a data structure, as shown in Figure 6.2.

For our beginning tutorials, using Core Data would be like using a sledgehammer to drive a thumbtack. We'll take a closer look at its capabilities in Hour 16, "Reading and Writing Data." Right now, let's get started building your first app with a view and a view controller!

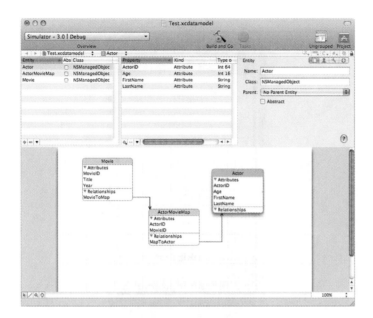

FIGURE 6.2
Once you become more familiar with iPhone development, you'll want to explore the Core Data tools for managing your data model.

Using the View-Based Application Template

The easiest way to see how Xcode and Interface Builder manage to separate logic from display is to build an application that follows this approach. Apple has included a useful application template in Xcode that quickly sets up an empty view and an associated view controller. This View-Based Application template will be the starting point for many of your projects, so we'll spend the rest of this chapter getting accustomed to using it.

Implementation Overview

The project we'll be building is simple: Instead of just writing the typical "Hello World" app, we want to be a bit more flexible. The program will present the user with a field (UITextField) for typing and a button (UIButton). When the user types into the field and presses the button, the display will update an onscreen label (UILabel) so that "Hello" is seen, followed by the user's input. The completed HelloNoun, as we've chosen to call this project, is shown in Figure 6.3.

FIGURE 6.3
The app will
accept input
and update the
display based
on what the
user types.

Although this won't be a masterpiece of development, it does contain almost all the different elements we discuss in this hour: a view, a controller, outlets, and actions. Because this is the first full development cycle that we've worked through, we'll pay close attention to how all the pieces come together and why things work the way they do.

Setting Up the Project

First we want to create the project, which we'll call HelloNoun, in Xcode:

1. Launch Xcode from the Developer/Applications folder.

2. Choose File, New Project.

3. You'll be prompted to choose a project type and a template. On the left side of the New Project window, make sure that Application is selected under the iPhone OS project type. Next find and select the View-Based Application option from the list on the right, as shown in Figure 6.4, and then click Choose.

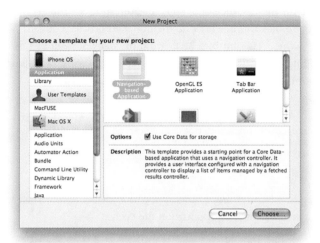

FIGURE 6.4
Choose the
View-Based
Application tem-
plate.

This will create a simple application structure consisting of an application delegate,
a window, a view, and a view controller. After a few seconds, your project window
will open (see Figure 6.5).

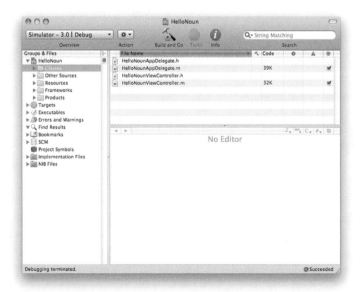

FIGURE 6.5
Your new project
is open and
ready for cod-
ing.

Classes

Click the Classes folder and review the contents. You should see four files (visible in
Figure 6.5). The HelloNounAppDelegate.h and HelloNounAppDelegate.m files make

up the delegate for the instance of UIApplication that our project will create. In other words, these files can be edited to include methods that govern how the application behaves when it is running. By default, the delegate will be responsible for one thing: adding a view to a window and making that window visible. This occurs in the aptly named applicationDidFinishLaunching method in HelloNounAppDelegate.m:

```
- (void)applicationDidFinishLaunching:(UIApplication *)application {
    // Override point for customization after app launch
    [window addSubview:viewController.view];
    [window makeKeyAndVisible];
}
```

You won't need to edit anything in the application delegate, but keep in mind the role that it plays in the overall application life cycle.

The second set of files, HelloNounViewController.h and HelloNounViewController.m, will implement the class that contains the logic for controlling our view—a view controller (UIViewController). These files are largely empty to begin, with just a basic structure in place to ensure that we can build and run the project from the outset. In fact, feel free to click the Build and Run button at the top of the window. The application will compile and launch, but there won't be anything to do!

By the Way

Notice that when we create a project, Xcode automatically names the classes and resources based on the project name.

To impart some functionality to our app, we need to work on the two areas we discussed previously: the view and the view controller.

XIB Files

After looking through the classes, click the Resources folder to show the XIB files that are part of the template. You should see MainWindow.xib and HelloNounViewController.xib files. Recall that these files are used to hold instances of objects that we can add visually to a project. These objects are automatically instantiated when the XIB loads. Open the MainWindow.xib file by double-clicking it in Xcode. Interface Builder should launch and load the file. Within Interface Builder, choose Window, Document to show the components of the file.

The MainWindow XIB, shown in Figure 6.6, contains icons for the File's Owner (UIApplication), the First Responder (an instance of UIResponder), the HelloNoun App Delegate (HelloNounAppDelegate), the Hello Noun View Controller (HelloNounViewController), and our application's Window (UIWindow).

As a result, when the application launches, MainWindow XIB is loaded, a window is created, along with an instance of the HelloNounViewController class. In turn, the HelloNounViewController defines its view within the second XIB file, HelloNounViewController.xib—this is where we'll visually build our interface.

FIGURE 6.6
The MainWindow.xib file handles creating the application's window and instantiating our view controller.

Any reasonable person is probably scratching his head right now wondering a few things. First, why does MainWindow.xib get loaded at all? Where is the code to tell the application to do this?

The MainWindow.xib file is defined in the HelloNoun-Info.plist file as the Main NIB File Base Name property value. You can see this yourself by clicking the Resources folder and then clicking the plist file to show the contents (see Figure 6.7).

Second, what about the HelloNounViewController.xib tells the application that it contains the view we want to use for our user interface? The answer lies in the MainWindow XIB file. Return to the MainWindow.xib document window in Interface Builder.

Click once on Hello Noun View Controller to select it in the list, and then press Command+1 or choose Attributes Inspector from the Tools menu. A small window will appear, as shown in Figure 6.8. Expand the View Controller section and you should see that the NIB Name field is set to HelloNounViewController. This means that the view controller loads its view from that XIB file.

FIGURE 6.7
The project's plist file defines the XIB loaded when the application starts.

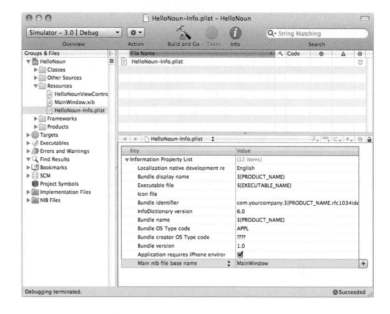

FIGURE 6.8
After the MainWindow.xib instantiates the view controller, it loads its view from HelloNounView Controller.xib.

In short, the application is configured to load MainWindow.xib, which creates an instance of our view controller class (`HelloNounViewController`), which subsequently loads its view from the HelloNounViewController.xib. If that still doesn't make sense, don't fret; we'll guide you through this every step of the way.

Preparing the View Controller Outlets and Actions

A view is connected to its view controller class through outlets and actions. These must be present in our code files before Interface Builder will have a clue where to connect our user interface elements, so let's work through adding those connection points now.

For this simple project, we're going to need to interact with three different objects:

- ▶ A label (UILabel)
- ▶ A text field (UITextField)
- ▶ A button (UIButton)

The first two provide an output area and an input area for the user. The third triggers an action in our code to set the contents of the label to the contents of the text field. Based on what we now know, we can define the following outlets:

```
IBOutlet UILabel *userOutput;
IBOutlet UITextField *userInput;
```

And this action:

```
-(IBAction)setOutput:(id)sender;
```

Open the HelloNounViewController.h file in Xcode and add the IBOutlet and IBAction lines. Remember that the outlet directives fall inside the @interface block, and the action should be added immediately following it. Your header file should now resemble this:

```
#import <UIKit/UIKit.h>

@interface HelloNounViewController : UIViewController {
    IBOutlet UILabel *userOutput;
    IBOutlet UITextField *userInput;
}

-(IBAction)setOutput:(id)sender;

@end
```

Congratulations! You've just built the connection points that you'll need for Interface Builder to connect to your code. Save the file and get ready to create a user interface!

Creating the View

Interface Builder makes designing a user interface (UI) as much fun as playing around in your favorite graphics application. That said, our emphasis will be on the fundamentals of the development process and the objects we have at our disposal. Where it isn't critical, we move quickly through the interface creation.

Adding the Objects

The interface for our HelloNoun application is quite simple—it must provide a space for output, a field for input, and a button to set the output to the same thing as the input. Follow these steps to create the UI:

1. Open HelloNounViewController.xib by double-clicking it within the Xcode Resources folder.

2. If it isn't already running, Interface Builder will launch and open the XIB file, displaying the document window for the XIB file (see Figure 6.9). If you don't see the window, choose Window, Document from the menu.

FIGURE 6.9
The HelloNounView Controller.xib file's view will contain all of the UI objects for the application.

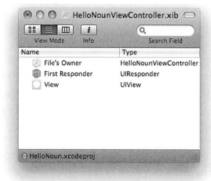

3. Double-click the icon for the instance of the view (UIView). The view itself, currently empty, will display. Open the Library by choosing Tools, Library. Make sure that the Objects button is selected within the Library—this displays all the components that we can drag into the view. Your workspace should now resemble Figure 6.10.

4. Add two labels to the view by clicking and dragging the label (UILabel) object from the Library into the view.

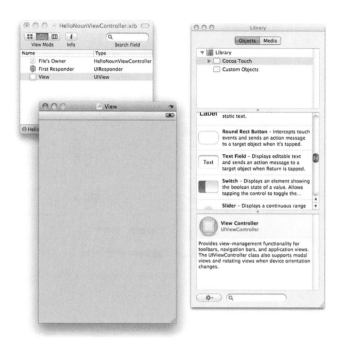

FIGURE 6.10
Open the view
and the object
Library to begin
creating the
interface.

5. The first label will simply be static text that says Hello. Double-click the
default text that reads Label to edit it and change the content to read **Hello**.
Position the second label underneath it; this will act as the output area.

For this example, I changed the text of the second label to read <Noun Goes
Here!>. This will serve as a default value until the user provides a new string.
You may need to expand the text labels by clicking and dragging their han-
dles to create enough room for them to display.

I also chose to set my labels to align their text in the center. If you want to do
the same, select the label within the view by clicking it, and then press
Command+1 or choose Tools, Attributes Inspector from the menu. This opens
the Attributes Inspector for the label, as demonstrated in Figure 6.11.

The Alignment setting within the layout section will give you the option of
aligning to the center. You may also explore the other attributes to see the
effect on the text, such as size, color, and so on. Your view should now resemble Figure 6.12.

FIGURE 6.11
Use the
Attributes
Inspector to set
the label to
align in the mid-
dle.

FIGURE 6.12
Add two labels,
one static, one
to use for out-
put, into the
view.

6. Once you're happy with the results, it's time to add the elements that the user will be interacting with: the text field and button. For the field, find the Text Field object (UITextField) within the Library and click and drag it under your two labels. Using the handles on the label, stretch it so that it matches the length of your output label.

7. Click-drag a Round Rect button (UIButton) from the Library into the view, positioning it right below the text field. Double-click in the center of the button to add a title to the button, such as Set Label. Resize the button to fit the label appropriately.

Figure 6.13 shows our version of this view.

FIGURE 6.13
Your interface should include two labels, a field, and button—just like this!

Connecting Outlets and Actions

Our work in Interface Builder is almost complete. The last remaining step is to connect the view to the view controller. Because we already created the outlet and action connection points in the HelloNounViewController.h file, this will be a piece of cake!

Make sure that you can see both the document window and the view you just created. You're going to be dragging from the objects in the view to the File's Owner icon in the document window. Why File's Owner? Because, as you learned earlier, the XIB is "owned" by the HelloNounViewController object, which is responsible for loading it.

1. Control-drag from the File's Owner icon to the label that you've established for output (titled <Noun Goes Here!> in the example), and then release the mouse button. You can use either the visual representation of the label in the view or the listing of the label object within the document window.

2. When you release the mouse button, you'll be prompted to choose the appropriate outlet. Pick userOutput from the list that appears (see Figure 6.14).

FIGURE 6.14
Connect the
label that will
display output
to the
userOutput out-
let.

3. Repeat the process for the text field, this time choosing userInput as the outlet. The link between the input and output view objects and the view controller is now established.

4. To finish the view, we still need to connect the button to the setOutput action. Although you *could* do this by Control-dragging, it isn't recommended. Objects that can trigger actions can have dozens of different events that can be used as a trigger. To make sure that you're using the right event, you must select the object in the view, and then press Command+3 or choose Tools, Connections Inspector. This opens the Connections Inspector, which shows all the possible events for the object.

5. For a button object, the event that you're most likely to want to use is Touch Up Inside, meaning that the user had a finger on the button, and then released the finger while it was still inside the button.

   To do this for the button in our view, select the button, and then open the Connections Inspector. Drag from the circle beside Touch Up Inside to the File's Owner icon. When prompted for an action, choose setOutput (it should be the only option). The Connections Inspector should update to show the completed connection, as shown in Figure 6.15.

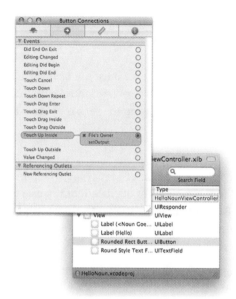

FIGURE 6.15
Use the
Connections
Inspector to
create a link
from the event
to the action it
should trigger.

Your view is now complete! You can safely exit Interface Builder, saving your changes.

Implementing the View Controller Logic

With the view complete and the connection to the view controller in place, the only task left is to fill in the view controller logic. Let's turn our attention back toward the HelloNounViewController.h and HelloNounViewController.m files. Why do we need to revisit the header? Because we'll need to easily access the userOutput and userInput variables, and to do that, we'll have to define these as properties, like this:

```
@property (retain, nonatomic) UITextField *userInput;
@property (retain, nonatomic) UILabel *userOutput;
```

Edit HelloNounViewController.h to include these lines after the @interface block. The finished file will read as follows:

```
#import <UIKit/UIKit.h>

@interface HelloNounViewController : UIViewController {
    IBOutlet UILabel *userOutput;
    IBOutlet UITextField *userInput;
}

@property (retain, nonatomic) UITextField *userInput;
@property (retain, nonatomic) UILabel *userOutput;
```

```
-(IBAction)setOutput:(id)sender;
```

```
@end
```

To access these properties conveniently, we must use `@synthesize` to create the get-ters/settings for each. Open the HelloNounViewController.m implementation file and add these lines immediately following the `@implementation` directive:

```
@synthesize userInput;
@synthesize userOutput;
```

This leaves us with the implementation of `setOutput`. The purpose of this method is to set the output label to the contents of the field that the user edited. How do we get these values? Simple! Both `UILabel` and `UITextField` have a property called `text` that contains their contents. By reading and writing to these properties, we can set `userInput` to `userOutput` in one easy step.

Edit HelloNounViewController.m to include this method definition, following the `@synthesize` directives:

```
-(IBAction) setOutput:(id)sender {
        userOutput.text=userInput.text;
}
```

It all boils down to a single line! Thanks to our getters and setters, this single assign-ment statement does everything we need.

By the Way

> Had we not used `@synthesize` to create the accessors, we could have implement-ed the `setOutput` logic like this:
>
> `[userOutput setText: [userInput getText]];`
>
> Either way is fine technically, but you should always code for readability and ease of maintenance.

Freeing up Memory

Whenever we've used an object and are done with it, we need to release it so that the memory can be freed and reused. Even though this application needs the label and text field objects (`userOutput`, and `userInput`), as long as it is running, it is still good practice to release them in the `dealloc` method of the view controller. The release method is called like this:

```
[<my Object> release]
```

Edit the HelloNounViewController.m file's `dealloc` method to release both `userOutput` and `userInput`. The result should look like this:

```
- (void)dealloc {
    [userInput release];
    [userOutput release];
    [super dealloc];
}
```

Well done! You've written your first iPhone application!

Building the Application

The app is ready to build and test. If you'd like to deploy to your iPhone, be sure it is docked and ready to go, and then choose iPhone Device from the drop-down menu in the upper left of the Xcode window. Otherwise, choose Simulator. Click Build and Run.

After a few seconds, the application will start on your iPhone or within the simulator window, as shown in Figure 6.16.

FIGURE 6.16
Your finished application makes use of a view to handle the UI, and a view controller to implement the functional logic.

Summary

In this hour, you learned about the MVC design pattern and how it separates the display (view), logic (controller), and data (model) components of an application. You also explored how Apple implements this design within Xcode through the use Core Data, views, and view controllers. This approach will guide your applications through much of this book and in your own real-world application design, so learning the basics now will pay off later.

To reinforce the lesson, we worked through a simple application using the View-Based Application template. This included creating outlets and actions that linked a view and view controller via Xcode and Interface Builder. While not the most complex app you'll write, it included the elements of a fully interactive user experience: input, output, and (very simple) logic.

Q&A

Q: *Is it possible to have multiple views or view controllers?*

A: Yes, absolutely. In Hour 13, "Using Tab Bars to Manage Multiview Interfaces," you'll create an application that uses several view controllers, each with an independent view.

Q: *Why do I drag from the File's Owner to the Object in Interface Builder, rather than the other way around?*

A: Think of the File's Owner as the code that you're going to be writing. Your code needs to reference the Interface Builder object (through an outlet), not the other way around.

Workshop

Quiz

1. What event do you use to detect a button tap?

2. What purpose does the @synthesize directive accomplish?

3. Which Apple project template creates a simple view/view controller application?

Answers

1. The Touch Up Inside event is most commonly used to trigger actions based on a button press.

2. The `@synthesize` directive creates the simplified getters and setters for a property. In the case of the label and field we used in the tutorial, it enabled us to access the `text` property by using `<variable name>.text`.

3. The View-Based Application template sets up a view and a view controller.

Activities

1. Explore the attributes of the interface objects that you added to the tutorial project in Interface Builder. Try setting different fonts, colors, and layouts. Use these tools to customize the view beyond the simple layout created this hour.

2. Review the Apple Xcode documentation for the Core Data features of Cocoa. Although you won't be using this technology in this book's tutorials, it is an important tool that you'll ultimately want to become more familiar with for advanced data-driven applications.

Further Exploration

Before moving on to subsequent hours, you may want to learn more about how Apple has implemented the MVC design versus other development environments that you may have used. An excellent document, titled "Cocoa Design Patterns," provides an in-depth discussion of MVC as applied to Cocoa. You can find and read this introduction by searching for the title in the Xcode documentation system, which we discussed in Hour 4, "Inside Cocoa Touch."

You may also want to take a breather and use the finished HelloNoun application as a playground for experimentation. We discussed only a few of the different Interface Builder attributes that can be set for labels, but there are dozens more that can customize the way that fields and buttons are displayed. The flexibility of the view creation in Interface Builder goes well beyond what can fit in one book, so exploration *will* be necessary to take full advantage of the tools. This is an excellent opportunity to play around in the tools and see the results—before we move into more complex (and easy to break!) applications.

HOUR 7

Working with Text, Keyboards, and Buttons

What You'll Learn in This Hour:

▶ How to use text fields
▶ Input and output in scrollable text views
▶ How to enable data detectors
▶ A way to spruce up the standard iPhone buttons

In the last hour, you explored views and view controllers and created a simple application that accepted user input and generated output when a button was pushed. These are the basic building blocks that we expand on in this hour. We'll be creating an application that uses multiple different input and output techniques. You'll learn how to implement and use editable text fields, text views, graphical buttons, and configure the onscreen keyboard.

This is quite a bit of material to be covering in an hour, but the concepts are very similar, and you'll quickly get the hang of these new elements.

Basic User Input and Output

The iPhone gives us many different ways of displaying information to a user and collecting feedback. There are so many ways, in fact, that we're going to be spending the next several hours working through the tools that the iPhone SDK provides for interacting with your users—starting with the basics.

Buttons

One of the most common interactions you'll have with your users is detecting and reacting to the touch of a button (UIButton). Buttons, as you may recall, are elements of a view that respond to an event that the user triggers in the interface, usually a "Touch Up Inside" event to indicate that the user's finger was on a button and then released it. Once an event is detected, it can trigger an action (IBAction) within a corresponding view controller.

Buttons are used for everything from providing preset answers to questions to triggering motions within a game. Although we've used only a single Rounded Rect button up to this point, they can take on many different forms through the use of images. Figure 7.1 shows an example of a fancy button.

FIGURE 7.1
Buttons can be simple, fancy (like this one), or set to any arbitrary image.

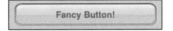

Text Fields and Views

Another common input mechanism is a text field. Text fields (UITextField) give users space to enter any information they'd like into a single line in the application—these are similar to the form fields in a web form. When users enter data into a field, you can constrain their input to numbers or text by using different iPhone keyboards, something we'll do later this hour. Text fields, like buttons, can respond to events, but frequently are implemented as passive interface elements, meaning that their contents (provided through the text property) can be read at any time by the view controller.

Similar to the text field is the text view (UITextView). The difference is a text view can present a scrollable and editable block of text for the user to either read or modify. These should be used in cases where more than a few words of input are required. Figure 7.2 shows examples of a text field and text view.

FIGURE 7.2
Text fields and text views provide a means for entering text using the iPhone's virtual keyboard.

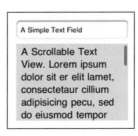

Labels

The final interface feature that we're going to be using here and throughout this book is the label (`UILabel`). Labels are used to display strings within a view by setting their `text` property.

The text within a label can be controlled via a wide range of label attributes, such as font and text size, alignment, and color. As you'll see, labels are useful both for static text in a view and for presenting dynamic output that you generate in your code.

Now that you have basic insight into the input and output tools we'll be using in this hour, let's go ahead and get started with our project: a simple substitution-style story generator.

Using Text Fields, Text Views, and Buttons

Despite what *some* people may think, I enjoy entering text on the iPhone. The virtual keyboard is responsive and simple to navigate. What's more, the input process can be altered to constrain the user's input to only numbers, only letters, or other variations. You can have the iPhone automatically correct simple misspellings or capitalize letters. This project will review many aspects of the text input process.

Implementation Overview

In this project, we'll be creating a Mad Libs–style story creator. We'll enable the user to enter a noun (place), verb, and number through three text fields (`UITextField`). The user may also enter or modify a template that contains the outline of the story to be generated. Because the template can be several lines long, we'll use a text view (`UITextView`) to present this information. A button press (`UIButton`) will trigger an action that generates the story and outputs the finished text in another text view, demonstrated in Figure 7.3.

Although not directly part of the input or output process, we'll also investigate how to implement the now-expected "touch the background to make the keyboard disappear" interface standard, along with a few other important points. In other words, pay attention!

FIGURE 7.3
The tutorial app
this hour will
use two types
of text input
objects.

We'll be naming this tutorial project FieldButtonFun. You may certainly use something more creative if you'd like.

Setting Up the Project

This project will use the same View-Based Application template as the previous hour. If it isn't already running, launch Xcode (Developer/Applications), and then choose File, New Project.

Select the iPhone OS Application project type, and then find and select the View-Based Application option in the Template list. Click Choose to continue, and then enter the project name, **FieldButtonFun**, and save the new project.

Xcode will set up a skeleton project for you. As before, we'll be focusing on the view, which has been created in FieldButtonFunViewController.xib, and the view controller class FieldButtonFunViewController.

Preparing the Outlets and Actions

This project contains a total of six input areas: Three text fields will be used to collect the place, verb, and number values. We'll be calling these thePlace, theVerb, and theNumber, respectively. The project also requires two text views: one to hold the editable story template, theTemplate; and the other to contain the output, theStory. Finally, a single button is used to trigger a method, createStory, which will create the story text.

> Yes, we'll be using a text view for output as well as input. Text views provide a built-in scrolling behavior and can be set to read-only, making them convenient for both collecting and displaying information. They do not, however, allow for rich text input or output. A single font style is all you get!

By the Way

Start by preparing the outlets and actions in the view controller's header file, FieldButtonFunViewController.h. Edit the file to contain the following:

```
 1: #import <UIKit/UIKit.h>
 2:
 3: @interface FieldButtonFunViewController : UIViewController {
 4:     IBOutlet UITextField *thePlace;
 5:     IBOutlet UITextField *theVerb;
 6:     IBOutlet UITextField *theNumber;
 7:     IBOutlet UITextView *theStory;
 8:     IBOutlet UITextView *theTemplate;
 9:     IBOutlet UIButton *generateStory;
10: }
11:
12: @property (retain,nonatomic) UITextField *thePlace;
13: @property (retain,nonatomic) UITextField *theVerb;
14: @property (retain,nonatomic) UITextField *theNumber;
15: @property (retain,nonatomic) UITextView *theStory;
16: @property (retain,nonatomic) UITextView *theTemplate;
17: @property (retain,nonatomic) UIButton *generateStory;
18:
19: -(IBAction)createStory:(id)sender;
20:
21: @end
```

Lines 4–9 create the outlets for each of the input elements, while lines 12–17 establish them as properties so that we can easily manipulate their contents. Line 19 declares a createStory method where we'll eventually implement the logic behind the application.

> If you're paying close attention, you may notice that we've declared an outlet and a property for the view's button, generateButton. As we mentioned earlier, typically buttons are used to trigger a method when a certain event takes place, so we don't usually need an outlet or property to manipulate them.
>
> In this example, however, we're going to programmatically alter the visual appearance of the button, so we need to be able to access the object, not just receive messages from it.

By the Way

After you've set up the outlets and actions, save the header file and open FieldButtonViewController.m. As you've learned, properties usually have corresponding @synthesize directives so that they can easily be accessed in code. Add the appropriate statements for all the properties defined in the header. Your additions should fall after the @implementation directive and look like this:

```
@synthesize thePlace;
@synthesize theVerb;
@synthesize theNumber;
@synthesize theStory;
@synthesize theTemplate;
@synthesize generateStory;
```

That should be all the setup we need for now. Let's turn our attention to creating the user interface.

In the previous hour, you learned that the MainWindow.xib is loaded when the application launches and that it will instantiate the view controller, which subsequently loads its view from the second XIB file in the project (in this case, FieldButtonFunViewController.xib). Locate the file in the project's Resources folder, and then double-click it to launch Interface Builder.

When Interface Builder has started, open the XIB file's document window (Window, Document), and then double-click the view icon to open the blank view for editing.

Adding Text Fields

Begin creating the user interface by adding three text fields to the top of the view. To add a field, open the Objects Library by choosing Tools, Library, and then locate the Text Field object (UITextField) and drag it into the view. Repeat this two more times for the other two fields.

Stack the fields on top of one another, leaving enough room so that the user can easily tap a field without hitting all of them. To help the user differentiate between the three fields, you'll want to add labels to the view as well. Click and drag the Label (UILabel) object from the Library into the view. Align three labels directly across from the three fields. Double-click the label within the view to set its text. I've labeled my fields Place, Verb, and Number, from top to bottom, as shown in Figure 7.4.

Editing Text Field Attributes

The fields that you've created are technically fine as is, but you can adjust their appearance and behavior to create a better user experience. To view the field attributes, click a field, and then press Command+1 (Tools, Attributes Inspector) to open the Attributes Inspector (see Figure 7.5).

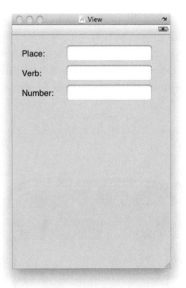

FIGURE 7.4
Add text fields and labels to differentiate between them.

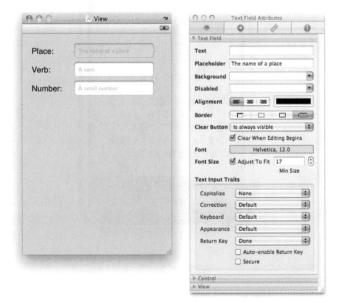

FIGURE 7.5
Editing a field's attributes can help create a better UI.

For example, you can use the Placeholder Text field to enter text that will appear in the background of the field until the user begins editing. This can be a helpful tip or an additional explanation of what the user should be entering.

You may also choose to activate the Clear button. The Clear button is a small X icon added to a field that the user can touch to quickly erase the contents. To add the Clear button, simply choose one of the visibility options from the pop-up menu; the functionality is added for free to your application! Note that you may also choose to automatically clear the field when the taps into it to start editing. Just enable the Clear When Editing Begins check box.

Add these features to the three fields within the view. Figure 7.6 shows how they will appear in the application.

FIGURE 7.6
Placeholder text can provide helpful cues to the user, while the Clear button makes it simple to remove a value from a field.

Did you Know?

Placeholder text also helps identify which field is which within the Interface Builder document window. It can make creating your connections much easier down the road!

In addition to these changes, attributes can adjust the text alignment, font and size, and other visual options. Part of the fun of working in Interface Builder is that you can explore the tools and make tweaks (and undo them) without having to edit your code.

Customizing the Keyboard Display with Text Input Traits

Probably the most important attributes that you can set for an input field are the "text input traits," or, simply, how the keyboard is going to be shown onscreen. Seven different traits are currently available:

Capitalize: Controls whether the iPhone will automatically capitalize words, sentences, or all the characters entered into a field.

Correction: If explicitly set to on or off, the input field will correct (on) or ignore (off) common spelling errors. If left to the defaults, it will inherit the behavior of the iPhone OS settings.

Keyboard: Sets a predefined keyboard for providing input. By default, the input keyboard lets you type letters, numbers, and symbols. Choosing the option Number Pad will only allow numbers to be entered. Similarly, using Email Address constrains the input to strings that look like email addresses. Seven different keyboard styles are available.

Appearance: Changes the appearance of the keyboard to look more like an alert view (which you'll learn about in a later hour).

Return Key: If the keyboard has a Return key, it is set to this label. Values include Done, Search, Next, Go, and so on.

Auto-Enable Return Key: Disables the Return key on the keyboard unless the user has entered at least a single character of input into the field.

Secure: Treats the field as a password, hiding each character as it is typed.

Of the three fields that we've added to the view, the Number field can definitely benefit from setting an input trait. With the Attributes Inspector still open, select the Number field in the view, and then choose the Number Pad option within the Keyboard pop-up menu (see Figure 7.7).

You may also want to alter the capitalization and correction options on the other two fields and set the Return key to Done. Again, all of this functionality is gained "for free." So, you can return to Interface Builder to experiment all you want later on.

Connecting to the Outlets

The first three fields of the view are now finished and ready to be connected to their variables back in Xcode. To connect to the outlets defined earlier, Control-drag from the File's Owner icon in the document window to the first field ("Place") either in the view window, or within the document window's view hierarchy. When prompted, choose thePlace from the pop-up list of outlets, as shown in Figure 7.8.

FIGURE 7.7
Choosing a key-
board type will
help constrain a
user's input.

FIGURE 7.8
Connect each
field to its corre-
sponding outlet.

Repeat the process for the Verb and Number fields, connecting them to the `theVerb`
and `theNumber` instance variable outlets. The primary input fields are connected.

Now we're ready to move on to the next element of the user interface: text views.

Copy and Paste

As part of iPhone OS 3.0, your text entry areas will automatically gain copy and paste without needing to change anything in your code. For advanced applications, you can override the protocol methods defined in `UIResponderStandardEditActions` to customize the copy, paste, and selection process.

Adding Text Views

Now that you know the ins and outs of text fields, let's move on to the two text views (`UITextView`) present in this project. Text views, for the most part, can be used just like text fields. You can access their contents the same way, and they support many of the same attributes as text fields, including text input traits.

To add a text view, find the Text View object (`UITextView`) and drag it into the view. This will add a block to the view, complete with Greeked text (Lorem ipsum...) that represents the input area. Using the resizing handles on the sizes of the block, you can shrink or expand the object to best fit the view. Because this project calls for two text views, drag two into the view and size them to fit underneath the existing three text fields.

As with the text fields, the views themselves don't convey much information about their purpose to the user. To clarify their use, add two text labels above each of the views, **Template** for the first, and **Story** for the second. Your view should now resemble Figure 7.9.

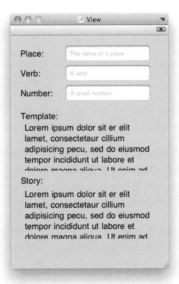

FIGURE 7.9
Add two text views with corresponding labels to the view.

Editing Text View Attributes

Text view attributes provide many of the same visual controls as text fields. Select a view, and then open the Attributes Inspector (Command+1) to see the available options, as shown in Figure 7.10.

FIGURE 7.10
Edit the attributes of each text view to prepare them for input and output.

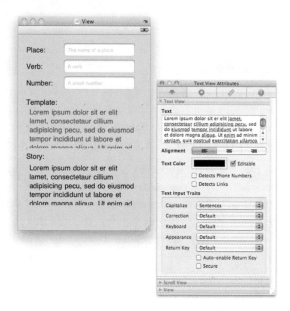

To start, we need to update the Text attribute to remove the initial Greeked text and provide our own content. For the top field, which will act as the template, select the content within the Text attribute of the Attributes Inspector, and then clear it. Enter the following text, which will be available within the application as the default:

```
The iPhone developers descended upon <place>.  They vowed to <verb> night and
day, until all <number> Palm Pre owners came to their senses. <place> would
never be the same again.
```

When we implement the logic behind this interface, the placeholders (<place>, <verb>, <number>) will be replaced with the user's input.

Next, select the "story" text view, and then again use the Attributes Inspector to clear the contents entirely. Because the contents of this text view will be generated automatically, we can leave the Text attribute blank. This view will also be a read-only view, so uncheck the Editable attribute.

In this example, to help provide some additional contrast between these two areas, I've set the background color of the template to a light red and the story to a light green. To do this in your copy, simply select the text view to stylize, and then click the Attributes Inspector's Background attribute to open a color chooser. Figure 7.11 shows our final text views.

FIGURE 7.11
When completed, the text views should differ in color, editability, and content.

Setting Scrolling Options

When editing the text view attributes, you'll notice that a range of options exist that are specifically related to its ability to scroll, as shown in Figure 7.12.

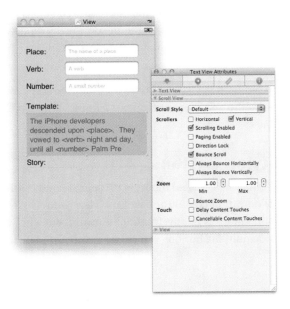

FIGURE 7.12
Scrolling regions have a number of attributes that can change their behavior.

Using these features, you can set the color of the scroll indicator (black or white), choose whether both horizontal and vertical scrolling are enabled, and even whether the scrolling area should have the rubber-band "bounce" effect when it reaches the ends of the scrollable content.

Data Detectors

New in iPhone OS 3.0 are data detectors. Data detectors automatically analyze the content within onscreen controls and provide helpful links based on what they find. Phone numbers, for example, can be touched to dial the phone; detected web addresses can be set to launch Safari when tapped by the user. All of this occurs without your application having to do a thing. No need to parse out strings that look like URLs or phone numbers. In fact, all you need to do is click a button.

To enable data detectors on a text view, select the view and return to the Attributes Inspector (Command+1). Within the Text View Attributes area, click the check boxes for Detects Phone Numbers to identify any sequence of numbers that looks like a phone number, or Detects Links to provide a clickable link for web and email addresses.

Data detectors are a great convenience for users, but *can* be overused. If you enable data detectors in your projects, be sure they make sense. For example, if you are calculating numbers and outputting them to the user, chances are you *don't* want the digits to be recognized as telephone numbers.

Connecting to the Outlets

Connect the text views to the theStory and theTemplate outlets you defined earlier. Control-drag from the File's Owner icon in the document window to the text view that contains the template. When prompted, choose theTemplate from the pop-up list of outlets (see Figure 7.13).

Repeat this for the second text view, this time choosing theStory for the outlet. You've just completed the text input and output features of the application. All that remains is a button!

Creating Styled Buttons

In the last hour's lesson, you created a button (UIButton) and connected it to the implementation of an action (IBAction) within a view controller. Nothing to it, right? Working with buttons is relatively straightforward, but what you may have noticed is that, by default, the buttons you create in Interface Builder are, well, kind of boring.

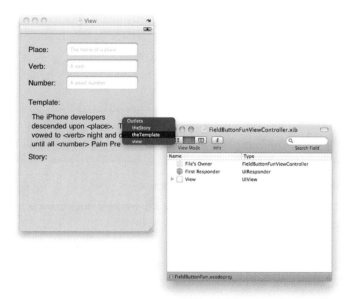

FIGURE 7.13
Connect each view to its corresponding outlet.

We need a single button in this project, so drag an instance of the Rounded Rect button (UIButton) from the Objects Library to the bottom of the view. Title the button **Generate Story**. The final view, with a default button, can be seen in Figure 7.14.

FIGURE 7.14
The default button styles are less than appealing.

While you're certainly welcome to use the standard buttons, you may want to explore what visual changes you can make in Interface Builder, and ultimately through code changes.

Editing Button Attributes

To edit a button's appearance, your first stop is, once again, the Attributes Inspector (Command+1). Using the Attributes Inspector, you can dramatically change the appearance of the button. Use the Type drop-down menu, shown in Figure 7.15, to choose common button types:

Rounded Rect: The default iPhone button style.

Detail Disclosure: An arrow button used to indicate additional information is available.

Info Light: An "i" icon, typically used to display additional information about an application or item. The "Light" version is intended for dark backgrounds.

Info Dark: The dark (light background) version of the Info Light button.

Add Contact: A + button, frequently used to indicate the addition of a contact to the address book.

Custom: A button that has no default appearance. Usually used with button images.

FIGURE 7.15
The Attributes Inspector gives several options for common button types, as well as a custom option.

In addition to choosing a button type, you can make the button interact with user touches, a concept known as changing state. For instance, by "default," a button is displayed unhighlighted within the view. When a user touches a button, it changes to a highlighted "on" state, showing that it has been touched.

Using the Attributes Inspector, you can use the State Configuration menu to change the button's title, background color, or even add a graphic image.

Setting Custom Button Images

To create custom iPhone buttons, you'll need to make custom images, including versions for the highlighted on state and the default off state. These can be any shape or size, but PNG format is recommended.

Once you've added these to the project through Xcode, you'll be able to select the image from the Image or Background drop-down menus in Interface Builder's button attributes. Using the Image menu sets an image that appears inside the button alongside the button title. This option allows you to decorate a button with an icon.

Using the Background menu sets an image that will be stretched to fill the entire background of the button. The option lets you create a custom image as the entire button, but you'll need to size your button exactly to match the image. If you don't, the image will be stretched and pixilated in your interface.

Another way to use custom button images that will correctly size to your text is through the code. We'll apply this technique to our project now.

Remember how we created an outlet for a button earlier in the project? We need the outlet so that we can manipulate the button in Xcode. Control-drag from the File's Owner icon in the document window in Interface Builder to the Generate Story button. Pick the generateStory outlet when prompted, as demonstrated in Figure 7.16.

Now, switch your attention to Xcode. Inside the FieldButtonFun directory is an Images folder with two Apple-created button templates: whiteButton.png and blueButton.png. Drag these image files into the Resources folder in Xcode, choosing to copy the resources, if necessary, as shown in Figure 7.17.

Within Xcode, open the FieldButtonFunViewController.m file and search for the method viewDidLoad, uncomment it by removing the /* */ comment markers that surround it.

FIGURE 7.16
We need to access the button properties from our application to manipulate its images.

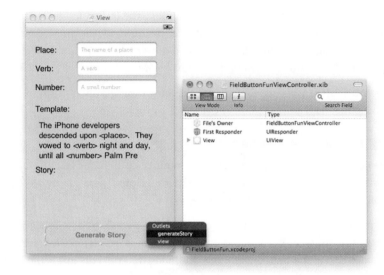

FIGURE 7.17
To use custom buttons, drag them into the Resources folder in Xcode, and choose to copy the resources if needed.

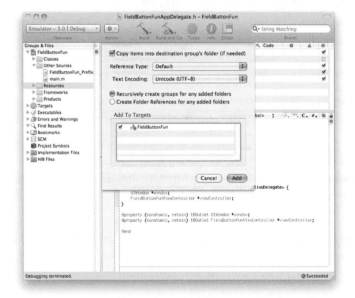

Implement the method using the following code:

```
1: - (void)viewDidLoad {
2:     UIImage *normalImage = [[UIImage imageNamed:@"whiteButton.png"]
3:                             stretchableImageWithLeftCapWidth:12.0
4:                             topCapHeight:0.0];
5:     [generateStory setBackgroundImage:normalImage forState:
➥UIControlStateNormal];
```

```
 6:        UIImage *pressedImage = [[UIImage imageNamed:@"blueButton.png"]
 7:                                 stretchableImageWithLeftCapWidth:12.0
 8:                                 topCapHeight:0.0];
 9:        [generateStory setBackgroundImage:pressedImage
10:                                 forState:UIControlStateHighlighted];
11:
12:        [super viewDidLoad];
13: }
```

In this code block, we're accomplishing several different things, all focused on providing the button instance (generateStory) with a reference to an image object (UIImage) that "knows" how it can be stretched.

> Why are we implementing this code in the viewDidLoad method? Because it is automatically invoked after the view is successfully instantiated from the XIB file. This gives us a convenient hook for making changes (in this case, adding button graphics) right as the view is being displayed onscreen.

Did you Know?

In lines 2–4 and 6–8, we first return an instance of an image from the image files that we added to the project resources. Then we define that image as being "stretchable." Let's break this down into the individual statements:

To create an instance of an image based on a named resource, we use the UIImage *class method* imagenamed, along with a string that contains the filename of the image resource. For example, this code fragment creates an instance of the "whiteButton.png" image:

```
[UIImage imageNamed:@"whiteButton.png"]
```

Next, we use the *instance method* stretchableImageWithLeftCapWidth: topCapHeight to return another new instance of the image, but this time with properties that define how it can be stretched. These properties are the left cap width and top cap width, which describe how many pixels in from the left or down from the top of the image should be ignored before reaching a 1-pixel-wide strip that can be stretched. For instance, if the left cap is set to 12, a vertical column 12 pixels wide is ignored during stretching, and then the 13th column is repeated however many times is necessary to stretch to the requested length. The top cap works the same way, but repeats a horizontal row to grow the image to the correct size vertically, as illustrated in Figure 7.18. If the left cap is set to zero, the image can't be stretched horizontally; similarly, if the top cap is zero, the image can't be stretched vertically.

FIGURE 7.18
The caps define
where, within an
image, stretch-
ing can occur.

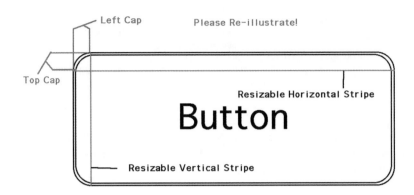

In this example, we use `stretchableImageWithLeftCapWidth:12.0`
`topCapHeight:0.0` to force horizontal stretching to occur at the 13th vertical column of pixels in, and to disable any vertical stretching. The `UIImage` instance
returned is then assigned to the `normalImage` and `pressedImage` variables, corresponding to the default and highlighted button states.

Lines 5 and 9–10 use the `setBackgroundImage:forState` instance method of our
`UIButton` object (`generateStory`) to set the stretchable images `normalImage` and
`pressedImage` as the backgrounds for the predefined button states of
`UIControlStateNormal` (default) and `UIControlStateHighlighted` (highlighted).

This may seem a bit confusing, and I empathize. Apple has not provided these same
features directly in Interface Builder, despite their usefulness in almost any application with buttons. The good news is that there is no reason that you can't reuse this
same code repeatedly in your applications.

Within Xcode, click Build and Run to compile and run your application. The
Generate Story button should take on a new appearance (see Figure 7.19).

Remember that despite all of our efforts to make a pretty button, we still haven't
connected it to an action. Switch back to Interface Builder to make the connection.

Connecting to the Action

To connect the button to the previously declared `createStory` action method, select
the button object and open the Connections Inspector (Command+3) or choose
Tools, Connections Inspector. Drag from the circle beside Touch Up Inside to the
File's Owner icon in the Interface Builder document window.

When prompted for a method, choose `createStory`. The Connections Inspector
should update, showing both the outlet that references the button (`generateStory`)
and the `createStory` method, similar to Figure 7.20.

FIGURE 7.19
The end result is a shiny new button in the application.

FIGURE 7.20
The button should now be connected to an outlet and an action.

At long last, our button is done!

Hiding the Keyboard

Before completing the application by implementing the view controller logic to construct the story, we need to look at a "problem" that is inherent to applications with character entry: keyboards that won't go away! To see what we mean, switch back into Xcode and use Build and Run to launch the FieldButtonFun in the iPhone Simulator.

With your app up and running, click into a field. The keyboard appears. Now what? Click into another field, the keyboard changes to match the text input traits you set up, but it remains onscreen. Touch the word Done. Nothing happens! And, even if it did, what about the number pad that doesn't include a Done button? If you try to use this app, you'll also find a keyboard that sticks around and that covers up the Generate Story button, making it impossible to fully utilize the user interface. So, what's the problem?

In Hour 4, "Inside Cocoa Touch," we described "responders" as an object that processes input. The "first responder" is the first object that has a shot at handling user input. In the case of a text field or text view, when it gains first responder status, the keyboard is shown and will remain onscreen until the field gives up or "resigns" first responder status. What does this look like in code? For the field thePlace, we could resign first responder status and get rid of the keyboard with this line of code:

```
[thePlace resignFirstResponder]
```

Calling the `resignFirstResponder` method tells the input object to "give up" its claim to the input; as a result, the keyboard disappears.

Hiding with the Done Button

The most common trigger for hiding the keyboard in iPhone applications is through the Did End on Exit event of the field. This event occurs when the Done (or similar) keyboard button is pressed.

To add keyboard hiding to the FieldButtonFun application, switch to Xcode, and create the action declaration for a method `hideKeyboard` in FieldButtonViewController.h by adding the following line after the `createStory` IBAction:

```
-(IBAction)hideKeyboard:(id)sender;
```

Next, implement the `hideKeyboard` method within the FieldButtonFunViewController.m file by adding this code, immediately following the `@synthesize` directives:

```
-(IBAction) hideKeyboard:(id)sender {
      [thePlace resignFirstResponder];
      [theVerb resignFirstResponder];
      [theNumber resignFirstResponder];
      [theTemplate resignFirstResponder];
}
```

You might be asking yourself, isn't the sender variable the field that is generating the event? Couldn't we just resign the responder status of the sender? Yes! Absolutely! This would work just fine, but we're going to also need the hideKeyboard method to work when sender isn't necessarily the field. We'll explain this in a few minutes.

By the Way

To connect fields to hideKeyboard, open the FieldButtonFunViewController.xib file in Interface Builder, and then open the view window so that the current interface is visible. Select the Place field, and open the Connections Inspector (Command+3). Drag from the circle beside the Did End on Exit event to the File's Owner icon in the document window. Choose the hideKeyboard action when prompted, as shown in Figure 7.21.

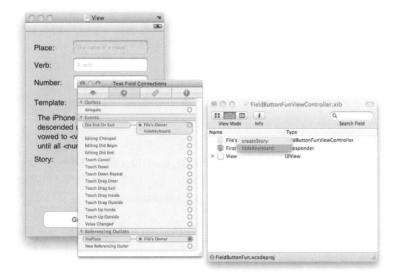

FIGURE 7.21
Connect each field to the hideKeyboard method.

Repeat this process for the Verb text field.

Unfortunately, the number input doesn't have a Done button, and the text view doesn't support the Did End on Exit event, so how do we hide the keyboard for these variations?

Hiding with a Background Touch

A popular iPhone interface convention is that if a keyboard is open and you touch the background (outside of a field), the keyboard disappears. This will be the approach we need to take for the number-input text field and the text view—and functionality that we need to add to all of the other fields to keep things consistent.

Wondering how we detect an event outside of a field? Nothing special: All we do is create a big invisible button that sits behind all of the other controls, and then attach it to the hideKeyboard method already written.

By the Way

> Note that in *this* case we won't know exactly *which* field is going to be the first responder when hideKeyboard is called, nor therefore the implementation that asks each possible input area to resign first responder status. If it isn't the first responder, it has no effect.

Within Interface Builder, access the Library (Tools, Library) and drag a new button (UIButton) from the Library into the view.

Because this button needs to be invisible, make sure it is selected, and then open the Attributes Inspector (Command+1) and set the type to Custom. Use the resizing handles to size the button to fill the entire view. With the button selected, choose Layout, Send to Back to position the button in the back of the interface.

To connect the button to the hideKeyboard method, it's easiest to use the Interface Builder document window. Expand the view hierarchy, select the custom button you created (it should be at the top of the view hierarchy list), then Control-drag from the button to the File's Owner icon. When prompted, choose the hideKeyboard method.

Save your work in Interface Builder and Xcode, and then use Build and Run to try running the application again. This time, when you click outside of a field or the text view, or use the Done button, the keyboard disappears!

Implementing the View Controller Logic

To finish off FieldButtonFun, we need to add the createStory method within the view controller (FieldButtonFunViewController). This method will search the template text for the <place>, <verb>, and <number> placeholders, and then replace them with the user's input, storing the results in the text view. We'll make use of the NSString instance method stringByReplacingOccurrencesOfString:WithString to do the heavy lifting. This method performs a search and replace on a given string.

For example, if the variable myString contains Hello town and you wanted to replace *town* with *world*, you might use the following:

```
myNewString=[myString stringByReplacingOccurrencesOfString:@"town"
WithString:@"world"];
```

In this case, our strings are the text properties of the text fields and text views (thePlace.text, theVerb.text, theNumber.text, theTemplate.text, and theStory.text).

Add this final method implementation to FieldButtonFunViewController.m after the @synthesize directives:

```
 1: -(IBAction) createStory:(id)sender {
 2:     theStory.text=[theTemplate.text
 3:                 stringByReplacingOccurrencesOfString:@"<place>"
 4:                 withString:thePlace.text];
 5:     theStory.text=[theStory.text
 6:                 stringByReplacingOccurrencesOfString:@"<verb>"
 7:                 withString:theVerb.text];
 8:     theStory.text=[theStory.text
 9:                 stringByReplacingOccurrencesOfString:@"<number>"
10:                 withString:theNumber.text];
11: }
```

Lines 2–4 replace the <place> placeholder in the template with the contents of the thePlace field, storing the results in the story text view. Lines 5–7 then update the story text view by replacing the <verb> placeholder with the appropriate user input. This is repeated again in lines 8–10 for the <number> placeholder. The end result is a completed story, output in the theStory text view.

Releasing the Objects

When you're done using an object in your applications, you should always release it to free up memory. This is good practice, even if the application is about to exit. In this application, we've retained six objects—each of the interface elements—that need to be released. Edit the dealloc method to release these now:

```
- (void)dealloc {
    [thePlace release];
    [theVerb release];
    [theNumber release];
    [theStory release];
    [theTemplate release];
    [generateStory release];
    [super dealloc];
}
```

Our application is finally complete!

Building the Application

To view and test the FieldButtonFun, click Build and Run in Xcode. Your finished app should look very similar to Figure 7.22, fancy button and all!

FIGURE 7.22
The finished application includes scrolling views, text editing, and a pretty button! What more could we want?

This project provided a starting point for looking through the different properties and attributes that can alter how objects look and behave within the iPhone interface. The take-away message: Don't assume anything about an object until you've reviewed how it can be configured.

Summary

This hour described the use of common input features as well as a few important output options. You learned that text fields and text views both enable the user to enter arbitrary input constrained by a variety of different virtual keyboards. Unlike text fields, however, text views can handle multiline input as well as scrolling, making them the choice for working with large amounts of text. We also covered the use of buttons and button states, including how buttons can be manipulated through code.

We'll continue to use the same techniques you used in this hour throughout the rest of the book, so don't be surprised when you see these elements again!

Q&A

Q. *Why can't I use a* `UILabel` *in place of a* `UITextView` *for multiline output?*

A. You certainly can! The text view, however, provides scrolling functionality "for free," whereas the label will display only the amount of text that fits within its bounds.

Q. *Why doesn't Apple just handle hiding text input keyboards for us?*

A. While I can imagine some circumstances where it would be nice if this were an automatic action, it isn't difficult to implement a method to hide the keyboard. This gives you total control over the application interface—something you'll grow to appreciate.

Q. *Are text views* (`UITextView`) *the only way to implement scrolling content on the iPhone?*

A. No! You'll learn about implementing general scrolling behavior in Hour 9, "Using Advanced Interface Controls."

Workshop

Quiz

1. What properties are needed to configure a stretchable image?

2. How do you get rid of an onscreen keyboard?

3. Are text views used for text input, or output?

Answers

1. The left cap and top cap values define what portion of an image can be stretched.

2. To clear the onscreen keyboard, you must send the `resignFirstResponder` message to the object that currently controls the keyboard (such as a text field).

3. Text views (`UITextView`) can be implemented as scrollable output areas or multi-line input fields. It's entirely up to you!

Activities

1. Expand the story creator with additional placeholders and word types. Use the same string manipulation functions described in this lesson to add the new functionality.

2. Modify the story creator to use a graphical button of your design. Either use an entirely graphical button, or the stretchable image approach described in this hour's tutorial.

Further Exploration

Throughout the next few hours, you'll be exploring a large number of user interface objects, so your next steps should be to concentrate on the features you've learned in this hour—specifically, the object properties, methods, and events that they respond to.

For text fields and text views, the base object mostly provides for customization of appearance. However, you may also implement a delegate (`UITextFieldDelegate`, `UITextViewDelegate`) that responds to changes in editing status, such as starting or ending editing. You'll learn more about implementing delegates in Hour 10, "Making Multivalue Choices with Pickers," but you can start looking ahead to the additional functionality that can be provided in your applications through the use of a delegate.

It's also important to keep in mind that although there are plenty of properties to explore for these objects, there are additional properties and methods that are inherited from their superclasses. All UI elements, for example, inherit from `UIControl`, `UIView`, and `UIResponder`, which bring additional features to the table, such as properties for manipulating size and location of the object's onscreen display, as well as customizing the copy and paste process (through the `UIResponderStandardEditActions` protocol). By accessing these lower-level methods, you can customize the object beyond what might be immediately obvious.

Apple Tutorials

Apple has provided a sample project that includes examples of almost all the available iPhone user interface controls: UICatalog (accessible via the Xcode documentation). This project also includes a wide variety of graphic samples, such as the button images used in this hour's tutorial. It's an excellent playground for experimenting with the iPhone UI.

HOUR 8

Handling Images, Animation, and Sliders

What You'll Learn in This Hour:

▶ The use of Sliders for user input
▶ Configuring and manipulating the slider input range
▶ How to add Image Views to your projects
▶ Ways of creating and controlling simple animations

The text input and output that we learned about in the last hour is certainly important, but the iPhone is known for its attractive graphics and "touchable" UI. In this hour, we'll expand our interface toolkit to include images, animation, and the very touchable slider control.

We'll be implementing an application to combine these new features along with simple logic to manipulate input data in a unique way. These new capabilities will help you build more interesting and interactive applications—and, of course, there's more to come in the next hour as well!

User Input and Output

When I first started developing for the iPhone, I was anxious to explore all that the interface had to offer. While application logic is always the most important part of an application, the way the interface works plays a big part in how well it will be received. The iPhone SDK's interface options give you the tools to express your application's functionality in fun and unique ways.

This hour introduces two very visual interface features—sliders for input, and image views for output.

Sliders

The first new interface component that we'll be using this hour is a slider (UISlider). Sliders are a convenient touch control that is used to visually set a point within a range of values. Huh? What?

Imagine that you want your user to be able to speed something up or slow it down. Asking the user to input timing values is unreasonable. Instead, you can present a slider, as seen in Figure 8.1, where they can touch and drag an indicator back and forth on a line. Behind the scenes, a value property is being set that your application can access and use to set the speed. No need for users to understand the behind-the-scene details or do anything more than drag with their finger.

FIGURE 8.1
Use a slider to collect a value from a range of numbers without requiring the user to type.

Sliders, like buttons, can react to events, or can be read passively like a text field. If you want the user's changes to a slider to immediately have an effect on your application, you'll need to have it trigger an action.

Image Views

Image views (UIImageView) are precisely what you'd think—they display images! They can be added to your application views and used to present information to the user. An instance of UIImageView can even be used to create a simple frame-based animation with controls for starting, stopping, and even setting the speed at which the animation is shown.

Creating and Managing Image Animations and Sliders

There's something about interface components that *move* that make users take notice. They're visually interesting, attract and keep attention, and, on the iPhone's touch screen, are fun to play with. In this hour's project, we'll be taking advantage of both of our new UI elements (and some old friends!) to create a user-controlled animation.

Implementation Overview

As mentioned earlier, image views can be used to display image file resources and show simple animations, while sliders provide a visual way to choose a value from a range. We'll combine these in an application we're calling ImageHop.

In ImageHop, we'll be creating a looping animation using a series of images and an image view instance (UIImageView). We'll allow the user to set the speed of the animation using a slider (UISlider). What will we be using as an animation? A hopping bunny. What will the user control? Hops per second, of course! The "hops" value set by the slider will be displayed in a label (UILabel). The user will also be able to stop or start the animation using a button (UIButton).

Figure 8.2 shows the completed application in use.

FIGURE 8.2
ImageHop uses an image view and a slider to create and control a simple animation.

There are two pieces of this project that we should discuss before getting too far into the implementation:

▶ First, image view animations are created using a series of images. We've provided a 20-frame animation with this project, but you're welcome to use your own images if you prefer.

▶ Second, while sliders enable users to visually enter a value from a range, there isn't much control over how that is accomplished. For example, the minimum value must be smaller than the maximum, and you can't control which dragging direction of the slider increases or decreases the result value. These limitations aren't show-stoppers; they just mean that there may be a bit of math (or experimentation) involved to get the behavior you want.

Setting Up the Project

Begin this project in the same way as the last. Launch Xcode (Developer/Applications), and then choose File, New Project.

Select the iPhone OS Application project type, and then find and select the View-Based Application option in the Template list on the right. Click Choose to continue, enter the project name **ImageHop**, and save the new project.

Adding the Animation Resources

This project makes use of 20 frames of animation stored as PNG files. The frames are included in the Images folder within the ImageHop project folder.

Because we know up front that we'll need these images, drag them into the Xcode project's Resources folder, being sure to choose the option to copy the resources if needed.

Preparing the Outlets and Actions

In this application, we need to provide outlets and actions for several objects.

For outlets, first we need the image view (UIImageView), which will contain the animation and be referenced through the variable imageView. The slider control (UISlider) will set the speed and will be connected via animationSpeed, while the speed value itself will be output in a label named hopsPerSecond (UILabel). A button (UIButton) will toggle the animation on and off and will be connected to an outlet toggleButton.

Why do we need an outlet for the button? Shouldn't it just be triggering an action to toggle the animation? Yes, the button could be implemented without an outlet, but by including an outlet for it, we have a convenient way of setting the button's title in the code. We can use this to change the button to read "Stop" when the image is animating, or "Start" when the animation has stopped.

For actions, we need only two: setSpeed will be the method called when the slider value has changed and the animation speed needs to be reset, and toggleAnimation will be used to start and stop the animation sequence.

Go ahead and define these outlets and actions as outlets and actions within ImageHopViewController.h. You'll also want to declare the four outlet variables as properties so that we can easily access them in the view controller code. The resulting header file should be very close to this:

```
 1: #import <UIKit/UIKit.h>
 2:
 3: @interface ImageHopViewController : UIViewController {
 4:     IBOutlet UIImageView *imageView;
 5:     IBOutlet UIButton *toggleButton;
 6:     IBOutlet UISlider *animationSpeed;
 7:     IBOutlet UILabel *hopsPerSecond;
 8: }
 9:
10: @property (retain,nonatomic) UIImageView *imageView;
11: @property (retain,nonatomic) UIButton *toggleButton;
12: @property (retain,nonatomic) UISlider *animationSpeed;
13: @property (retain,nonatomic) UILabel *hopsPerSecond;
14:
15: -(IBAction)toggleAnimation:(id)sender;
16: -(IBAction)setSpeed:(id)sender;
17:
18: @end
```

For all the properties you've defined in the header file, add a @synthesize directive in the ImageHopViewController.m implementation file. Your additions should fall after the @implementation line and look like this:

```
@synthesize toggleButton;
@synthesize imageView;
@synthesize animationSpeed;
@synthesize hopsPerSecond;
```

Make sure that both the ImageHopViewController header and implementation files have been saved, and then launch Interface Builder by double-clicking the ImageHopViewController.xib file within the project's Resources folder.

After it has loaded, switch to the document window (Window, Document), and double-click the view icon to open it and begin editing.

Adding an Image View

In this exercise, our view creation will begin with the most important object of the project: the image view (UIImageView). Open the Interface Builder Objects Library and drag an image view into the view window.

Because the view is has no images assigned, it will be represented by a light-gray rectangle. Use the resize handles on the rectangle to size it to fit in the upper two-thirds of the interface (see Figure 8.3).

FIGURE 8.3
Set the image view to fill the upper two-thirds of the iPhone interface.

Setting the Default Image

There are very few attributes for configuring the functionality of an image view. In fact, there is only one: the image that is going to be displayed. Select the image view and press Command+1 to open the Attributes Inspector (see Figure 8.4).

FIGURE 8.4
Set the image that will be shown in the view.

Using the Image drop-down menu, choose one of the image resources available. This will be the image that is shown before the animation runs, so using the first frame (frame-1.png) is a good choice.

By the Way

> What about the animation? Isn't this just a frame? Yes, if we don't do anything else, the image view will show a single static image. To display an animation, we need to create an array with all of the frames and supply it programmatically to the image view object. We're going to be doing this in a few minutes, so just hang in there!

The image view will update in Interface Builder to show the image resource that you've chosen.

Connecting to the Outlet

To display an animation, we need to access the object from the ImageHop view controller. Let's connect the image view to the `imageView` outlet that we created earlier.

Within the document window, Control-drag from the File's Owner icon to the image view icon in the document window, or to the graphical representation in the view window. When prompted for the outlet, choose `imageView`, as shown in Figure 8.5.

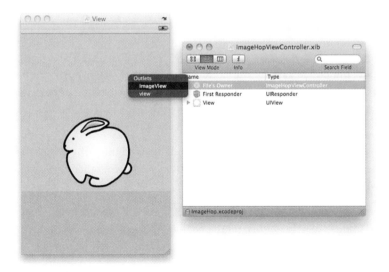

FIGURE 8.5
Connect the image view to an outlet so it can be easily accessed from code.

Now that the image view has been added, let's look at the code we need to add to change from a static image to an animation.

Animating the Image View

To truly customize an image view, we need to write some code. Animating images requires us to build an array of image objects (UIImage) and pass them to the image view. Where should we do this? As with the last project, the ViewDidLoad method of our view controller provides a convenient location for doing additional setup for the view, so that's what we'll use.

Switch back into Xcode, and open the view controller implementation file, ImageHopViewController.m. Find the ViewDidLoad method and uncomment it, and then add the following code to the method. Note that we've removed lines 7–20 to save space (they follow the same pattern as lines 4–6 and 21–23):

```
 1: - (void)viewDidLoad {
 2:     NSArray *hopAnimation;
 3:     hopAnimation=[[NSArray alloc] initWithObjects:
 4:                     [UIImage imageNamed:@"frame-1.png"],
 5:                     [UIImage imageNamed:@"frame-2.png"],
 6:                     [UIImage imageNamed:@"frame-3.png"],
 ...
21:                     [UIImage imageNamed:@"frame-18.png"],
22:                     [UIImage imageNamed:@"frame-19.png"],
23:                     [UIImage imageNamed:@"frame-20.png"],
24:                     nil
25:                     ];
26:     imageView.animationImages=hopAnimation;
27:     imageView.animationDuration=1;
28:     [hopAnimation release];
29:     [super viewDidLoad];
30: }
```

To configure the image view for animation, first an array (NSArray) variable is declared (line 2) called hopAnimation. Next, in line 3, the array is allocated and initialized via the NSArray instance method initWithObjects. This method takes a comma-separated list of objects, ending with nil, and returns an array.

The image objects (UIImage) are initialized and added to the array in lines 4–24. Remember that you'll need to fill in lines 7–20 on your own; otherwise, several frames will be missing from the animation!

Once an array is populated with image objects, it can be used to set up the animation of an image view. To do this, set the animationImages property of the image view (imageView) to the array. Line 6 accomplishes this for our example project.

Another image view property that we'll want to set right away is the animationDuration. This is the number of seconds it takes for a single cycle of the animation to be played. If the duration is *not* set, the playback rate will be 30 frames per second. To start, our animation will be set to play all the frames in 1 second, so line 27 sets the `imageView.animationDuration` to 1.

Finally, in line 28, we're finished with the `hopAnimation` array, so it can be released.

Starting and Stopping the Animation

A little later in this tutorial, we'll be adding controls to change the animation speed and to start/stop the animation loop. You've just learned how the `animationDuration` property can change the animation speed, but we'll need three more properties/methods to accomplish everything we want:

isAnimating   This property returns true if the image view is currently animating its contents.

startAnimating   Starts the animation.

stopAnimating   Stops the animation, if it is running.

If you run the application now, it will work, but only a static image will display. The image view does not start animating until the `startAnimating` method is called. We'll take care of that when implementing the view controller logic.

Adding a Slider

The next piece that our interface needs is the slider that will control the speed. Return to Interface Builder and the view, and then navigate to the Objects Library and drag the slider (`UISlider`) into the view, just under the image view. Using the resize handles on the slider, click and drag to size it to about two-thirds of the image view width, and align it with the right side of the image view. This leaves just enough room for a label to the left of the slider.

Because a slider has no visual indication of its purpose, it's a good idea to always label sliders so that your users will understand what they do. Drag a label object (`UILabel`) from the Library into your view. Double-click the text and set it to read **Speed:**. Position it so that it is aligned with the slider, as shown in Figure 8.6.

Setting the Slider Range Attributes

Sliders make their current setting available through a `value` property that we'll be accessing in the view controller. To change the range of values that can be returned, we'll need to edit the slider attributes. Click to select the slider in the view, and then open the Attributes Inspector (Command+1), as shown in Figure 8.7.

FIGURE 8.6
Add the slider and a corresponding label to the view.

FIGURE 8.7
Edit the slider's attributes to control the range of values it returns.

The Minimum, Maximum, and Initial fields should be changed to contain the smallest, largest, and starting values for the slider. For this project, use .25, 1.75, and 1.0, respectively.

Where Did These Min, Max, and Initial Values Come From?

This is a great question, and one that doesn't have a clearly defined answer. In this application, the slider represents the speed of the animation, which, as we've discussed, is set through the `animationDuration` property of the image view as the number of seconds it takes to show a full cycle of an animation.

Unfortunately, this means the *faster* animations would use smaller numbers and *slower* animations use larger numbers, which is the exact opposite of traditional user interfaces where "slow" is on the left and "fast" is on the right. Because of this, we need to reverse the scale. In other words, we want the big number (1.75) to appear when the slider is on the left side and the small number (.25) on the right.

To reverse the scale, we'll take the combined total of the minimum and maximum (1.75+0.25), and subtract the value returned by the slider from that total. For example, when the slider returns 1.75 at the top of the scale, we'll calculate a duration of 2 − 1.75, or 0.25. At the bottom of the scale, the calculation will be 2 − 0.25, or 1.75.

Our initial value will be 1.0, which falls directly in the middle of the scale.

Make sure the Continuous check box isn't checked. This option, when enabled, will have the control to generate a series of events as the user drags back and forth on the slider. When it isn't enabled, events are generated only when the user lifts his or her finger from the screen. For our application, this makes the most sense and is certainly the least resource-intensive option.

The slider can also be configured with images at the minimum and maximum sliders of the control. Use the Min Image and Max Image drop-downs to select a project image resource if you'd like to use this feature. (We're not using it in this project.)

Connecting to the Outlet

For convenient access to the slider, we created an outlet, `animationSpeed`, that we'll be using in the view controller. To connect the slider to the outlet, Control-drag from the File's Owner icon to the slider object in the view, or the slider icon in the document window. When prompted, choose the `animationSpeed` outlet.

By the Way

In case you're wondering, it's certainly possible to implement this application without an outlet for the slider. When the slider triggers an action, we could use the sender variable to reference the slider `value` property. That said, this approach will allow us to access the slider properties anywhere in the view controller, not just when the slider triggers an action.

Connecting to the Action

When the user drags the slider and releases their finger, the application should trigger the action method `setSpeed`. Create this connection by selecting the slider and then opening the Connections Inspector (Command+2).

Drag from the circle beside Touch Up Inside to the File's Owner icon in the document window. When prompted, choose to connect to the `setSpeed` action. Once complete, Connections Inspector should reflect this change, and show both the `setSpeed` and `animationSpeed` connections, as demonstrated in Figure 8.8.

FIGURE 8.8
When the user drags and releases the slider, the `setSpeed` method is called.

That completes the major parts of the UI, but there's still some cleanup work to do.

Finishing the Interface

The remaining components of the ImageHop application are interface features that you've used before, so we've saved them for last. We'll finish things up by adding a button to start and stop the animation, along with a readout of the speed of the animated rabbit in "hops per second."

Adding Labels

Start by dragging two labels (`UILabel`) to the view. The first label should be set to read **Hops per second:** and be located below the slider. Add the second label, which will be used as output of the actual speed value, to the right of the first label.

Change the output label to read **1.00 hps** (the speed that the animation will be starting out at). Using the Attributes Inspector (Command+1), set the text of the label to align right; this will keep the text from jumping around as the user changes the speed.

Finally, Control-drag from the File's Owner icon to the output label, and choose the hopsPerSecond outlet, as shown in Figure 8.9.

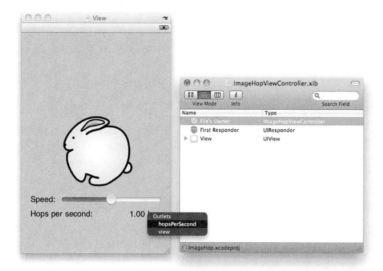

FIGURE 8.9
Connect the label that will be used to display the speed.

Adding the Hop Button

The last part of the ImageHop interface is the button (UIButton) that starts and stops the animation. Drag a new button from the Objects Library to the view, positioning it at the bottom center of the UI. Double-click the button to edit the title, and set it to **Hop!**

Like the slider, the hop button needs to be connected to an outlet (toggleButton) and an action (toggleAnimation). Control-drag from File's Owner icon in the document window to the button and choose the toggleButton outlet when prompted.

Next, select the button and open the Connection Inspector (Command+2). Within the inspector, click and drag from the circle beside the Touch Up Inside event to the File's Owner icon in the document window. Connect to the toggleAnimation action. Figure 8.10 shows the completed interface and button connections.

The application interface is finished. In the next section, we'll complete the application by writing the code for starting and stopping the animation and setting the speed.

FIGURE 8.10
Connect the
button to its
outlet and
action.

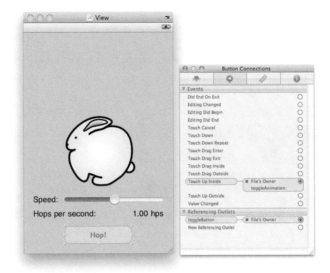

Implementing the View Controller Logic

The ImageHopViewController still needs a bit of work before we can call ImageHop done and finally view the animation. Two actions, toggleAnimation and setSpeed, need to be written. These methods will handle the user's interaction with the ImageHop application through the button and slider, respectively.

Starting and Stopping the Animation

When the user touches the Hop! button, the toggleAnimation method is called. This method should use the isAnimating property of the image view (imageView) to check to see whether an animation is running. If it isn't, the animation should start; otherwise, it should stop. To make sure the user interface makes sense, the button itself (toggleButton) should be altered to show the title Sit Still! if the animation is running, and Hop! when it isn't.

Add the following code to the ImageHopViewController implementation file, after the @synthesize directives:

```
1: -(IBAction) toggleAnimation:(id)sender {
2:     if (imageView.isAnimating) {
3:         [imageView stopAnimating];
4:         [toggleButton setTitle:@"Hop!" forState:UIControlStateNormal];
5:     } else {
6:         [imageView startAnimating];
7:         [toggleButton setTitle:@"Sit Still!" forState:UIControlStateNormal];
8:     }
9: }
```

Lines 2 and 5 provide the two different conditions that we need to work with. Lines 3 and 4 are executed if the animation is running, while lines 6 and 7 are executed if it isn't. In line 3 and line 6, the stopAnimating and startAnimating methods are called for the image view to start and stop the animation, respectively.

Lines 4 and 5 use the UIButton instance method setTitle:forState to set the button title to the string "Hop!" or "Sit Still!". These titles are set for the button state of UIControlStateNormal. As you learned earlier this hour, the "normal" state for a button is its default state, prior to any user event taking place.

Setting the Animation Speed

The slider triggers the setSpeed action after the user adjusts the slider control. This action must translate into several changes in the actual application: First, the speed of the animation (animationDuration) should change. Second, the animation should be started if it isn't already running. Third, the button (toggleButton) title should be updated to show the animation is running. Lastly, the speed should be displayed in the hopsPerSecond label.

Add this code to the view controller, and then let's review how it works:

```
 1: -(IBAction) setSpeed:(id)sender {
 2:     NSString *hopRateString;
 3:     imageView.animationDuration=2-animationSpeed.value;
 4:     [imageView startAnimating];
 5:     [toggleButton setTitle:@"Sit Still!"
 6:                     forState:UIControlStateNormal];
 7:     hopRateString=[[NSString alloc]
 8:                     initWithFormat:@"%1.2f hps",1/(2-animationSpeed.value)];
 9:     hopsPerSecond.text=hopRateString;
10:     [hopRateString release];
11: }
```

Because we'll need to format a string to display the speed, we kick things off by declaring an NSString reference, hopRateString, in line 2. In line 3, the image view's (imageView) animationDuration property is set to 2 minus the value of the slider (animationSpeed.value). This, if you recall, is necessary to reverse the scale so that faster is on the right and slower is on the left.

Line 4 uses the startAnimating method to start the animation running. Note that it is safe to use this method if the animation is already started, so we don't really need to check the state of the image view. Lines 5 and 6 set the button title to the string "Sit Still!" to reflect the animated state.

Lines 7 and 8 allocate and initialize the hopRateString instance that we declared in line 2. The string is initialized with a format of "1.2f", based on the calculation of 1 / (2 − animationSpeed.value). Let's break that down a bit further:

Remember that the speed of the animation is measured in seconds. The fastest speed we can set is 0.25 (a quarter of a second), meaning that the animation plays 4 times in 1 second (or "4 hops per second"). To calculate this in the application, we simply divide 1 by the chosen animation duration, or 1 / (2 − animationSpeed.value). Because this doesn't necessarily return a whole number, we use the initWithFormat method to create a string that holds a nicely formatted version of the result. The initWithFormat parameter string "1.2f hps" is shorthand for saying the number being formatted as a string is a floating-point value (f), and that there should always be one digit on the left of the decimal, and two digits on the right (1.2). The hps portion of the format is just the "hops per second" unit that we want to append to the end of the string. For example, if the equation returns a value of .5 (half a hop a second), the string stored in hopRateString is set to "0.50 hps".

In line 9, the output label (UILabel) in the interface is set to the hopRateString. Once finished with the string, line 10 releases it, freeing up the memory it was using.

By the Way

Don't worry if the math here is a bit befuddling. This is not critical to understanding Cocoa or iPhone development, it's just an annoying manipulation we needed to perform to get the values the way we wanted them. I strongly urge you to play with the slider values and calculations as much as you'd like so that you can get a better sense of what is happening here and what steps you might need to take to make the best use of slider ranges in your own applications.

Releasing the Objects

Our development efforts have resulted in four objects that should be released when we're finished: toggleButton, imageView, hopsPerSecond, and animationSpeed. Edit the dealloc method to release these now:

```
- (void)dealloc {
    [toggleButton release];
    [imageView release];
    [hopsPerSecond release];
    [animationSpeed release];
    [super dealloc];
}
```

Well done! You've just completed the app!

Building the Application

To try your hand at controlling an out-of-control bunny rabbit, click Build and Run in Xcode. After a few seconds, the finished ImageHop application will start, as shown in Figure 8.11.

FIGURE 8.11
Bouncing bun-
nies! What more
could we ask
for?

Although ImageHop isn't an application that you're likely to keep on your phone (for long), it did provide you with new tools for your iPhone application toolkit. The UIImageView class can easily add dynamic images to your programs, while UISlider offers a uniquely touchable input solution.

Summary

Users of highly visual devices demand highly visual interfaces. In this hour's lesson, we learned about the use of two visual elements that we can begin adding to our applications: Image Views and Sliders. Image Views provide a quick means of displaying images that you've added to your project—even using a sequence of images to create animation. Sliders can be used to collect user input from a continuous range of values. These new input/output methods start our exploration of iPhone interfaces that go beyond simple text and buttons.

The information you learned today, while not complex, will help pave the way for mega-rich touch-centric user interfaces.

Q&A

Q. *Is the* `UIImageView` *the only means of displaying animated movies?*

A. No. The iPhone SDK includes a wide range of options for playing back and even recording video files. The `UIImageView` is not meant to be used as a video playback mechanism.

Q. *Is there a vertical version of the slider control* (`UISlider`)?

A. Unfortunately, no. Only the horizontal slider is currently available in the iPhone SDK. If you want to use a vertical slider control, you'll need to implement your own.

Workshop

Quiz

1. What is one of the limitations of the slider control (`UISlider`)?

2. What is the default playback rate for an animation, prior to the `animationDuration` property being set?

3. What is the value of the `isAnimating` property in an instance of `UIImageView`?

Answers

1. The slider is limited in that the values must increase from left to right. This can be overcome, but not without programmatically manipulating the numbers.

2. By default, animation frames are shown at a rate of 30 frames per second.

3. The `isAnimating` property is set to `true` when the `UIImageView` instance is displaying an animation. When the animation is stopped (or not configured), the property is `false`.

Activities

1. Increase the range of speed options for the ImageHop animation example. Be sure to set the default location for the slider to rest in the middle.

2. Provide an alternative means of editing the speed by enabling the user to manually enter a number in addition to using the slider. The placeholder text of the field should default to the current slider value.

Further Exploration

Although many hours in this book focus on adding features to the user interface, it is important to start thinking about the application logic that will bring your user interface to life. As we experienced with our sample application, sometimes creativity is required to make things work the way we want.

Review the properties and methods for UISlider class and consider how you might use a slider in your own apps. Can you think of any situations where the slider values couldn't be used directly in your software? How might you apply application logic to map slider values to usable input? Programming is very much about problem solving—you'll rarely write something that doesn't have at least a few "gotchas" that need solved.

In addition to UISlider, you may want to review the documentation for UIImage. While we focused on UIImageView for displaying our image animation, the images themselves were objects of type UIImage. Image objects will come in handy for future interfaces that integrate graphics into the user controls themselves.

Apple Tutorials

UIImageView, UIImage, UISlider - UICatalog (accessible via the Xcode documentation). Once again, this project is a great place for exploring any and everything (including images, image views, and sliders) related to the iPhone interface.

HOUR 9

Using Advanced Interface Controls

What You'll Learn This Hour:

- ▶ How to use segmented controls (a.k.a. button bars)
- ▶ Ways of inputting Boolean values via switches
- ▶ How to include web content within your application
- ▶ The use of scrolling views to overcome iPhone screen limitations

After the last few hours' lessons, you now have a good understanding of the basic iPhone interface elements, but we've only just scratched the surface. The iPhone has additional user input features to help a user quickly choose between several predefined options. After all, there's no point in typing when a touch will suffice! This hour's lesson picks up where the last left off, providing you with hands-on experience with a new set of user input options that go beyond fields, buttons, and sliders.

In addition, we'll look at two new ways that you can present data to the user: via web and scrolling views. These features will make it possible to create applications that can extend beyond the hardware boundaries of the iPhone screen and include content from remote web servers.

User Input and Output (Continued)

When we set out to write this book, we originally dedicated one or two chapters to the iPhone interface "widgets" (fields, buttons, and so on). After we got started, however, it became apparent that for learning to develop on the iPhone, the interface was not something to gloss over. The iPhone interface options are what makes the iPhone so enjoyable to use, and what gives you, the developer, a truly rich canvas to work with. You'll still need to come up with ideas for what your application will *do*, but the interface can be the deciding factor in whether your vision "clicks" with its intended audience.

In the last two hours, you learned about fields, sliders, labels, and images as input and output options. In this lesson, you'll be exploring two new input options for handling discrete values, along with two new view types that extend the information you can display to web pages and beyond.

Switches

In most traditional desktop applications, the choice between something being "active" or "inactive" is made by checking or unchecking a check box, or by choosing between radio buttons. On the iPhone, Apple has chosen to abandon these options in favor of switches and segmented controls. Switches (UISwitch) present a simple on/off UI element that resembles a traditional physical toggle switch, as seen in Figure 9.1. Switches have very few configurable options and should be used for handling Boolean values.

FIGURE 9.1
Use switches to provide on/off input options to your user.

By the Way

Check boxes and radio buttons, while not part of the iPhone UI Library, can be created with the UIButton class using the button states and custom button images. Apple provides the flexibility to customize to your heart's content—but sticking with what a user expects to see on the iPhone screen is our recommendation.

To work with the switch, we'll make use of its Value Changed event to detect a toggle of the switch, then read its current value via the on property or the isOn instance method.

The value returned when checking a switch is a Boolean, meaning that we can compare it to TRUE or FALSE (or YES/NO) to determine its state, or evaluate the result directly in a conditional statement.

For example, to check if a switch mySwitch is turned on, we can use code similar to this:

```
if ([mySwitch isOn]) { <switch is on> } else { <switch is off> }
```

Segmented Controls

When user input needs to extend beyond just a Boolean value, a segmented control (UISegmentedControl) can be used. Segmented controls present a linear line of buttons (sometimes referred to as a button bar) where a single button can be active within the bar, as demonstrated in Figure 9.2.

FIGURE 9.2
Segmented controls combine multiple buttons into a single control.

Segmented controls, when used according to Apple's guidelines, result in a change in what the user is seeing onscreen. They are frequently used to choose between categories of information or to switch between the display of application screens, such as configuration and results screens. For simply choosing from a list of values where no immediate visual change takes place, the Picker object should be used instead. We'll be looking at this feature in the next hour.

> Apple recommends using segmented controls to update the information visible in a view. If the change, however, means altering *everything* onscreen then you are probably better off switching between multiple independent views using a toolbar or tab bar. We'll start looking at the multiview approach in Hour 12, "Creating Simple Multiview Applications with Toolbars."

By the Way

Handling interactions with a segmented control will be very similar to the toggle button. We'll be watching for the Value Changed event, and determining the currently selected button through the `selectedSegmentIndex`, which returns the number of the button chosen (starting with 0, from left to right).

We can combine the index with the object's instance method `titleForSegmentAtIndex` to work directly with the titles assigned to each segment. To retrieve the name of the currently selected button in a segmented control called mySegment, we could use the code fragment:

```
[mySegment titleForSegmentAtIndex: mySegment.selectedSegmentIndex]
```

We'll make use of this technique later in the lesson.

Web Views

In the previous iPhone applications that you've built, you've used the typical iPhone view: an instance of UIView to hold your controls, content, and images. This is the view you'll use most frequently in your apps, but it isn't the only view supported in the iPhone SDK. A web view, or `UIWebView`, provides advanced features that open up a whole new range of possibilities in your apps.

By the Way

In Hour 7's exercise, you did make use of another view type, `UITextView`, which provides basic text input and output, and straddles the line between an input mechanism and what we'll typically refer to as a "view."

Think of a web view as a borderless Safari window that you can add to your applications and control programmatically. You can present HTML, load web pages, and offer pinching and zooming gestures all "for free" using this class.

Supported Content Types

Web views can also be used to display a wide range of files, without needing to know anything about the file formats:

> HTML and CSS
>
> Word documents (.doc)
>
> Excel spreadsheets (.xls)
>
> Keynote presentations (.key.zip)
>
> Numbers spreadsheets (.numbers.zip)
>
> Pages documents (.pages.zip)
>
> PDF files (.pdf)
>
> PowerPoint presentations (.ppt)

You can add these files as resources to your project and display them within a web view, access them on remote servers, or read them from the iPhone's sandbox file storage (which you'll learn about in Hour 16, "Reading and Writing Data").

Loading Remote Content with `NSURL`, `NSURLRequest`, and `requestWithURL`

Web views implement a method called `requestWithURL` that you can use to load an arbitrary URL, but, unfortunately, you can't just pass it a string and expect it to work.

To load content into a web view, you'll frequently use `NSURL` and `NSURLRequest`. These two classes provide the ability to manipulate URLs and prepare them to be used as a request for a remote resource. You will first create an instance of an `NSURL` object, most frequently from a string. For example, to create an NSURL that stores the address for Apple, you could use the following:

```
NSURL *appleURL;
appleURL=[[NSURL alloc] initWithString:@"http://www.apple.com/"];
```

Once the NSURL object is created, you will need to create an NSURLRequest object that can be passed to a web view and loaded. To return an NSURLRequest from an NSURL object, we can use the NSURLRequest class method requestWithURL that, given an NSURL, returns the corresponding request object:

```
[NSURLRequest requestWithURL: appleURL]
```

Finally, this value would be passed to the requestWithURL method of the web view, which then takes over and handles loading the process. Putting all the pieces together, loading Apple's website into a web view called appleView would look like this:

```
NSURL *appleURL;
appleURL=[[NSURL alloc] initWithString:@"http://www.apple.com/"];
[appleView loadRequest:[NSURLRequest requestWithURL: appleURL]];
```

We'll be implementing web views in this hour's first project, so you'll have a chance to put this to use shortly.

Another way that you get content into your application is by loading HTML directly into a web view. For example, if you generate HTML content in a string called myHTML, you can use the loadHTMLString:baseURL method of a web view to load the HTML content and display it. Assuming a web view called htmlView, this might be written as follows:

```
[htmlView loadHTMLString:myHTML baseURL:nil]
```

Did you Know?

Scrolling Views

You've certainly used iPhone applications that display more information than what fits on a single screen; in these cases, what happens? Chances are, the application allows you to scroll to access additional content. Frequently, this is managed through a scrolling view, or UIScrollView. Scrolling views, as their name suggests, provide scrolling features and can display more than a single screen's worth of information.

Unfortunately, Apple has gone about halfway toward making scrolling views something that you can add to your projects in Interface Builder. You can add the view, but until you add a line of code to your application, it won't scroll! We'll close out this hour's lesson with a very quick example (a single line of code!) that will enable UIScrollView instances that you create in Interface Builder to scroll your content.

Using Switches, Segmented Controls, and Web Views

As you've probably noticed by now, we prefer to work on examples that *do* something. It's one thing to show a few lines of code in a chapter and say "this will do <blah>," but it's another to take a collection of features and combine them in a way that results in a working application. In some cases, the former approach is unavoidable, but this isn't one of them. Our first hands on example will make use of web views, a segmented control, and a toggle switch.

Implementation Overview

In this project, we'll be creating an application that displays flower photographs and flower information from the website FloraPhotographs.com. The application will enable a user to touch a flower color within a segmented control (UISegmentedControl), resulting in a flower of that color being fetched and displayed from the FloraPhotographs site in a web view (UIWebView). The user can then use a toggle switch (UISwitch) to show and hide a second web view that contains details about the flower being displayed. Finally, a standard button (UIButton) will enable the user to fetch another flower photo of the currently selected color from the site. The result should look very much like Figure 9.3.

FIGURE 9.3
The finished application will make use of a segmented control, a switch, and two web views.

Setting Up the Project

This project will, once again, use the View-Based Application template we're starting to love. If it isn't already running, launch Xcode (Developer/Applications), and then create a new project called **FlowerWeb**.

You should now be accustomed to what happens next. Xcode sets up the project and creates the default view in FlowerWebViewController.xib and a view controller class in `FlowerWebViewController`. We'll start with setting up the outlets and actions we need in the view controller.

Preparing the Outlets and Actions

To create the web-based image viewer, we'll need three outlets and two actions. The segmented control will be connecting to an outlet called `colorChoice`, because we'll be using it to choose which color is displayed. The web view that contains the flower will be connected to `flowerView`, and the associated details web view to `flowerDetailView`.

For the actions, the application must do two things: get and display a flower image, which we'll define as the action method `getFlower`; and toggle the flower details on and off, something we'll handle with a `toggleFlowerDetail` action.

Why Don't We Need an Outlet for the Switch?

By the Way

We don't need to include an outlet for the switch because we will be connecting its Value Changed event to the `toggleFlowerDetail` method. When the method is called, the `sender` parameter sent to the method will reference the switch, so we can just use `sender` to determine if the switch is on or off.

If we have more than one control using `toggleFlowerDetail`, it would be helpful to define outlets to differentiate between them, but in this case, `sender` will suffice.

Open the flowerWebViewController.h file in Xcode and create the IBOutlets for `colorChoice`, `flowerView`, and `flowerDetailView`. Then add the IBActions for `getFlower` and `toggleFlowerDetail`. Finally, add @property directives for the segmented control and both web views so that we can easily manipulate them in our code.

The completed header file should look very similar to this:

```
#import <UIKit/UIKit.h>

@interface FlowerWebViewController : UIViewController {
    IBOutlet UISegmentedControl *colorChoice;
```

```
        IBOutlet UIWebView *flowerView;
        IBOutlet UIWebView *flowerDetailView;
}

-(IBAction)getFlower:(id)sender;
-(IBAction)toggleFlowerDetail:(id)sender;

@property (nonatomic, retain) UISegmentedControl *colorChoice;
@property (nonatomic, retain) UIWebView *flowerView;
@property (nonatomic, retain) UIWebView *flowerDetailView;

@end
```

Save the header file and open the view controller implementation file (flowerWebViewController.m). Add matching @synthesize directives for each of the properties you declared in the header. These, as always, should be added after the @implementation directive:

```
@synthesize colorChoice;
@synthesize flowerDetailView;
@synthesize flowerView;
```

Now, let's build the user interface. Open the FlowerWebViewController.xib file in Interface Builder, and make sure that the view is open and visible. We'll begin by adding the segmented control.

Adding a Segmented Control

Add a segmented control to the user interface, by opening the Library (Tools, Library), finding the Segmented Control (UISegmentedControl) object, and dragging it into the view. Position the control near the top of the view, in the center. Because this control will ultimately be used to choose colors, click and drag a label (UILabel) into the view as well, position it above the segmented control, and change it to read **Choose a Flower Color**. Your view should now resemble Figure 9.4.

By default, the segmented control will have two segments, titled First and Second. You can double-click these titles and edit them directly in the view, but that won't quite get us what we need.

For this project, we need a control that has four segments, each labeled with a color: Red, Blue, Yellow, and Green. These are the colors that we can request from the FloraPhotographs website for displaying. Obviously, we need to add a few more segments to the control before all of the choices can be represented.

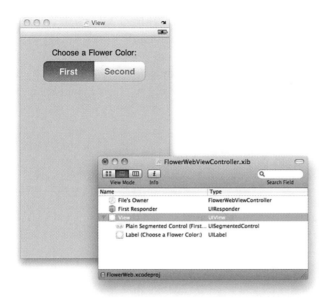

FIGURE 9.4
The default segmented control has two buttons, First and Second.

Adding and Configuring Segments

The number of segments displayed in the segmented control is configurable in the Attributes Inspector for the object. Select the control that you've added to the view, then press Command+1 to open the Attributes Inspector, demonstrated in Figure 9.5.

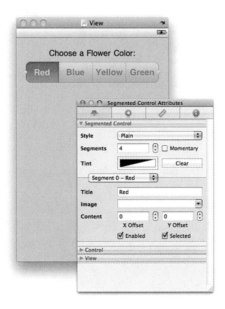

FIGURE 9.5
Use the Attributes Inspector for the segmented control to increase the number of segments displayed.

Using the Segments field, increase the number from 2 to 4. You should immediately see the new segments displayed. Notice that directly below where you set the number of segments in the inspector is a drop-down with entries for each segment you've added. You can choose a segment in this drop-down, and then specify its title in the Title field. You can even add images resources and have them displayed within each segment.

By the Way

> Note that the first segment is segment 0, the next is segment 1, and so on. It's important to keep this in mind when you're checking to see which segment is selected. The first segment is *not* segment 1, as you might assume.

Update the four segments in the control so that the colors Red, Blue, Yellow, and Green are represented.

Sizing the Control

Chances are, the control you've set up doesn't quite look right in the view. To size the control to aesthetically pleasing dimensions, use the selection handles on the sides of the control to stretch and shrink it appropriately. You can even optimize the size of individual segments using the Segmented Control Size options in the Size Inspector (Command+3), as shown in Figure 9.6.

FIGURE 9.6
You can use the Size Inspector to size each segment individually, if desired.

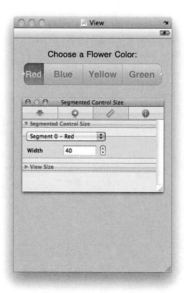

Choosing a Segment Control Appearance

In addition to the usual color options and controls available in Attributes Inspector, there are three variations of how the segmented control can be presented. Use the Style drop-down menu (visible in Figure 9.5) to choose between Plain, Bordered, and Bar. Figure 9.7 shows each of these.

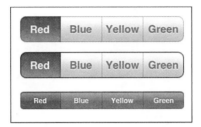

FIGURE 9.7
You can choose between three different presentation styles for your segmented control.

For this project, stick with Plain or Bordered. The segmented control should now have titles for all the colors and a corresponding label to help the user understand its purpose.

To finish things up for the segmented control, we need to connect it to the outlet we defined earlier (colorChoice) and make sure that it triggers the getFlower action method when a user switches between colors.

Connecting to the Outlet

To connect the segmented control to the colorChoice outlet, make sure the document window is visible, and then Control-drag from the File's Owner icon to either the visual representation of the control in the view, or to its icon in the document window, then release the mouse button. When prompted, choose the colorChoice outlet to finish the connection, as shown in Figure 9.8.

Connecting to the Action

Like other UI elements, the segmented control can react to *many* different touch events. Most frequently, however, you'll want to carry out an action when the user clicks a segment and switches to a new value (such as choosing a new color in this app). Thankfully, Apple has implemented a Value Changed event that does exactly what we want!

FIGURE 9.8
Connect the
segmented con-
trol to the
colorChoice
outlet so that
we can easily
access the
selected color
from within our
application.

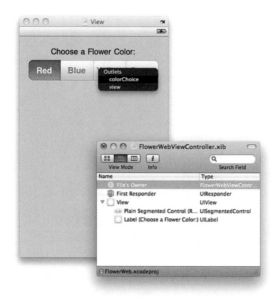

In our application, we want to load a new flower if the user switches colors. To do this, we need to create a connection from the Value Changed event to the getFlower action. Open the Connections Inspector by selecting the segmented control and then pressing Command+2. Drag from the circle beside Value Changed to the File's Owner icon in the document window, and release your mouse button. When prompted, choose the getFlower action method, as shown in Figure 9.9.

FIGURE 9.9
Connect from
the Value
Changed event
to the
getFlower
action.

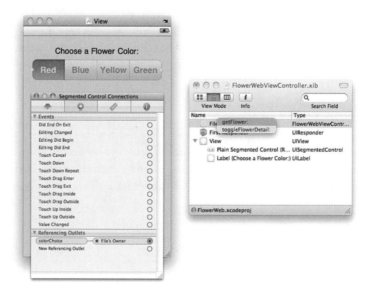

The segmented control is now wired into the interface and ready to go. Let's add our other interface objects, and then write the code to pull it together.

Adding a Switch

The switch that we'll use in our application has one role: to toggle a web view that displays details about the flower (flowerDetailView) on and off. Add the switch to the view by dragging the switch (UISwitch) object from the Library into the view. Position it along the right side of the screen, just under the segmented control.

As with the segmented control, providing some basic user instruction through an onscreen label can be helpful. Drag a label (UILabel) into the view and position it to the left of the switch. Change the text to read **Show Photo Details:**. Your view should now resemble Figure 9.10, but your switch will likely show up as "on."

FIGURE 9.10
Add a switch to toggle flower details on and off.

Setting the Default State

I know you're getting used to many of the different configuration options for the controls we use, but in this case, the switch has only a single option: whether the default state is on or off. The switch that you added to the view is set to "on;" we want to change it so that it is "off" by default.

To change the default state, select the switch and open the Attributes Inspector (Command+1). Using the State pop-up menu, change the default state to Off. That covers just about everything for buttons! We just need to connect it to an action and we can move on to the next element.

Connecting to the Action

The only time we're really interested in the switch is when its value changes, so, like the segmented control, we need to take advantage of the event Value Changed and connect that to the `toggleFlowerDetail` action method.

With the document window visible, select the switch, and then open the Connections Inspector (Command+2). Drag from the circle beside the Value Changed event to the File's Owner icon in the document window. When you release your mouse button, choose the `toggleFlowerDetail` action to complete the connection, as shown in Figure 9.11.

FIGURE 9.11
Connect the
Value Changed
event to the
`toggleFlower
Detail` action.

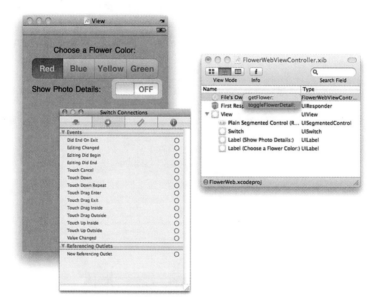

We're cruising now! Let's wrap this up by adding the web views that will show the flower and flower details, then the button that will let us load a new image whenever we want.

Adding the Web Views

The application that we're building relies on two different web views. One will display the flower image itself, while the other view (which can be toggled on and off) shows details about the image. The details view will be overlaid on top of the image itself, so let's start by adding the main view, `flowerView`.

To add a web view (UIWebView) to your application, locate it in the Library, and then simply drag it into your view. The web view will display a resizable rectangle that you can drag and position anywhere you'd like. Because this is the view that the flower image will be shown in, position it to fall about halfway down the screen, and then resize it so that it is the same width as the iPhone screen and so that it covers the lower portion of the view entirely.

Repeat this to add a second web view for the flower details (flowerDetailView). This time, size the view so that it is about one-third the height of the flower view, and locate it at the very bottom of the screen, over top of the flower view, as shown in Figure 9.12.

FIGURE 9.12
Add two web views (UIWebView) to your screen, and then position them as shown here.

Setting the Web View Attributes

Web views, surprisingly, have very few attributes that you can configure in Interface Builder, but what is available can be very important! To access the web view attributes, select one of the views you added, and then press Command+1 to open the Attributes Inspector (see Figure 9.13).

FIGURE 9.13
Configure how
the web view
will behave.

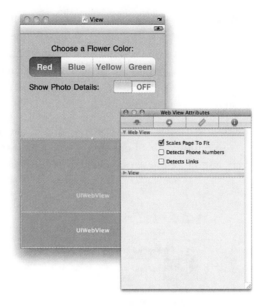

There are three options you can select: Scales Page to Fit, Detect Phone Numbers, and Detect Links. If Scales Page to Fit is selected, large pages will be scaled to fit in the size of the area you've defined. If the Detect options are used, the iPhone's data detectors go to work and will underline items that it has decided are phone numbers or additional web links.

For the main flower view, we absolutely want the images to be scaled to fit within the view. Select the web view, and then use the Properties Inspector to choose the Scales Page to Fit option.

For the second view, we do *not* want this to be set, so select the web view where the application will be showing the flower details and use the Attributes Inspector to ensure that no scaling will take place. You may also want to change the view attributes for the detail view to have an alpha value of around 0.65. This will create a nice translucency effect when the details are displayed on top of the photograph.

Watch Out!

> Scaling doesn't necessarily do what you'd expect for "small" web pages. If you display a page with only the text Hello World on it in a scaled web view, you might expect the text to be shown to fill the web view. Instead, the text will be *tiny*. The web view assumes that the text is part of a larger page, and scales it down rather than making it appear bigger.

Connecting to the Outlets

To prepare the two web views so that we can use them to display content, we need to connect them to the `flowerView` and `flowerDetailView` outlets created at the start of the project. To do this, Control-drag from the File's Owner icon in the document window to the web view in your view, or its icon in the document window. Release your mouse button, then, when prompted, choose the appropriate outlet.

For the larger view, connect to `flowerView`, as demonstrated in Figure 9.14. Repeat the process, connecting the smaller view to `flowerDetailView`.

FIGURE 9.14
Connect each web view to its corresponding outlet.

With the tough stuff out of the way, we just have one more finishing touch to put on the interface, then we're ready to code.

Finishing the Interface

The only piece that is missing from our interface is a button (`UIButton`) that we can use to manually trigger the `getFlower` method anytime we want. Without the button, we'd have to switch between colors using the segmented control if we wanted to see a new flower image. This button does nothing more than trigger an action (`getFlower`), something you've done repeatedly in the past few hours, so this should be a walk in the park for you by now.

Drag a button into the view, positioning it in the center of the screen, above the web views. Edit the button title to read **Get New Photo**, as shown in Figure 9.15.

FIGURE 9.15
The addition of the Get New Photo button finishes the user interface for FlowerWeb.

Finally, select the button and open the Connections Inspector (Command+2). Drag from the Touch Up Inside event to the File's Owner icon in the document window. When prompted choose the getFlower action, as shown in Figure 9.16.

FIGURE 9.16
Connect the Get New Photo button's Touch Up Inside event to the getFlower action.

The interface is complete! Switch back to Xcode and let's get to coding!

Implementing the View Controller Logic

There are two pieces of functionality that our view controller needs to implement via two action methods. The first `toggleFlowerDetail` will show and hide the `flowerDetailView` web view depending on whether the switch has been flipped on (show) or off (hide). The second method, `getFlower`, will load a flower image into the `flowerView` web view and details on that photograph into the `flowerDetailView` web view. We'll start with the easier of the two, `toggleFlowerDetail`.

Hiding and Showing the Detail Web View

A useful property of any object that inherits from `UIView` is that you can easily hide (or show) it within your iPhone application interfaces. Because almost everything you see onscreen inherits from this class, this means you can hide and show labels, buttons, fields, images, and yes, other views. To hide an object, all we need to do is set its Boolean property `hidden` to TRUE or YES (both have the same meaning). So, to hide the `flowerDetailView`, we'd write:

```
flowerDetailView.hidden=YES;
```

To show it again, we just reverse the process, setting the `hidden` property to FALSE or NO:

```
flowerDetailView.hidden=NO;
```

To implement the logic for the `toggleFlowerDetail:` method, we need to figure out what value the switch is currently set to. As mentioned earlier in the lesson, we can check the state of a toggle switch through the `isOn` method that returns a Boolean value of TRUE/YES if the switch is set to on, or FALSE/NO if it is off.

Because we don't have an outlet specifically set aside for the switch, we'll use the `sender` variable to access it in our method. When the `toggleFlowerDetail` action method is called, this variable is set to reference the object that invoked the action. In other words, the switch. So, to check to see if the switch is on, we can write:

```
If ([sender isOn]) { <switch is on> } else { <switch is off> }
```

Now, here's where we can get clever (you're feeling clever, right?). We want to hide and show the `flowerDetailView` using a Boolean value and we *get* a Boolean value from the switch's `isOn` method. This maps to two conditions:

▶ When [sender isOn] is YES, the view should *not* be hidden
   (flowerDetailView.hidden=NO)

▶ When [sender isOn] is NO, the view *should* be hidden
   (flowerDetailView.hidden=YES)

In other words, the state of the switch is the exact opposite of what we need to assign to the hidden property of the view. In C (and therefore Objective-C), to get the opposite of a Boolean value, we just put an exclamation mark in front (!). So all we need to do to hide or show flowerDetailView is to set the hidden property to ![sender isOn]. That's it! A single line of code!

Implement toggleFlowerDetail: in FlowerWeb right after the @synthesize directives. The full method should look a lot like this:

```
-(IBAction)toggleFlowerDetail:(id)sender{
        flowerDetailView.hidden=![sender isOn];
}
```

Loading and Displaying the Flower Image and Details

To fetch our flower images, we'll be making use of a feature provided by the Flora Photographs website for specifically this purpose. There are four steps we'll be following to interact with the website:

1. We'll get the chosen color from the segmented control.

2. We will generate a random number called a session ID so that florapho-tographs.com can track our request.

3. We will request the URL http://www.floraphotographs.com/showrandomi-phone.php?color=<color>&session=<session ID>, where <color> is the chosen color and <session ID> is the random number. This URL will return a flower photo.

4. We will request the URL http://www.floraphotographs.com/detaili-phone.php?session=<session ID>, where <session ID> is the same random number. This URL will return the details for the previously requested flower photo.

Let's go ahead and see what this looks like in code, and then discuss details behind the implementation. Add the getFlower code block following the toggleFlowerDetail method that you implemented:

```
 1: -(IBAction)getFlower:(id)sender {
 2:     NSURL *imageURL;
 3:     NSURL *detailURL;
 4:     NSString *imageURLString;
 5:     NSString *detailURLString;
 6:     NSString *color;
 7:     int sessionID;
 8:
 9:     color=[colorChoice titleForSegmentAtIndex:
10:         colorChoice.selectedSegmentIndex];
```

```
11:     sessionID=random()%10000;
12:
13:     imageURLString=[[NSString alloc] initWithFormat:
14:         @"http://www.floraphotographs.com/showrandomiphone.php?color=%@&session=%d"
15:                   ,color,sessionID];
16:     detailURLString=[[NSString alloc] initWithFormat:
17:                      @"http://www.floraphotographs.com/detailiphone.php?session=%d"
18:                   ,sessionID];
19:
20:     imageURL=[[NSURL alloc] initWithString:imageURLString];
21:     detailURL=[[NSURL alloc] initWithString:detailURLString];
22:
23:     [flowerView loadRequest:[NSURLRequest requestWithURL:imageURL]];
24:     [flowerDetailView loadRequest:[NSURLRequest requestWithURL:detailURL]];
25:
26:     flowerDetailView.backgroundColor=[UIColor clearColor];
27:
28:     [imageURLString release];
29:     [detailURLString release];
30:     [imageURL release];
31:     [detailURL release];
32: }
```

This is the most complicated code that you've written to date, but it's broken down into the individual pieces, so it's not difficult to understand:

Lines 2–7 declare the variables that we need to prepare our requests to the website. The first variables, imageURL and detailURL, are instances of NSURL that will contain the URLs that will be loaded into the flowerView and flowerDetailView web views. To create the NSURL objects, we'll need two strings, imageURLString and detailURLString, which we'll format with the special URLs that we presented earlier, including the color and sessionID values.

In lines 9–10, we retrieve the title of the selected segment in our instance of the segmented control: colorChoice. To do this, we use the object's instance method titleForSegmentAtIndex along with the object's selectedSegmentIndex property. The result, [colorChoice titleForSegmentAtIndex: colorChoice.selectedSegmentIndex], is stored in the string color and is ready to be used in the web request.

Line 11 generates a random number between 0 and 9999 and stores it in the integer sessionID.

Lines 13–18 prepare imageURLString and detailURLString with the URLs that we will be requesting. The strings are allocated, and then the initWithFormat method is used to store the website address along with the color and session ID. The color and session ID are substituted into the string using the formatting placeholders %@ and %d for strings and integers, respectively.

Lines 20–21 allocate and create the `imageURL` and `detailURL` NSURL objects using the `initWithString` class method and the two strings `imageURLString` and `detailURLString`.

Lines 23–24 use the `loadRequest` method of the `flowerView` and `flowerDetailView` web views to load the NSURLs `imageURL` and `detailURL`, respectively. When these lines are executed, the display updates the contents of the two views.

By the Way

Although we mentioned this earlier, remember that UIWebView's loadRequest method doesn't handle NSURL objects directly; it expects an NSURLRequest object instead. To work around this, we create and return NSURLRequest objects using the NSURLRequest class method requestWithURL and the imageURL and detailURL objects as parameters.

Line 26 is an extra nicety that we've thrown in. This sets the background of the `flowerDetailView` web view to a special color called `clearColor`. This, combined with the alpha channel value that you set earlier, will give the appearance of a nice translucent overlay of the details over the main image. You can comment out or remove this line to see the difference it creates.

Did you Know?

To create web views that blend with the rest of your interface, you'll want to keep clearColor in mind. By setting this color, you can make the background of your web pages translucent, meaning that the content displayed on the page will overlay any other content that you've added to your iPhone view.

Finally, Lines 28–31 release all the objects that we've allocated in the method. Since `getFlower` will potentially be called over and over, it's important that we release any memory that we might be using!

Fixing Up the Interface When the App Loads

Now that the `getFlower` method is implemented, you can run the application and everything should work—except that when the application starts, the two web views will be empty and the detail view will be visible, even though the toggle switch is set to off.

To fix this, we can start loading an image as soon as the app is up and running and set flowerDetailView.hidden to YES. Uncomment the viewDidLoad method and implement it as follows:

```
- (void)viewDidLoad {
    flowerDetailView.hidden=YES;
    [self getFlower:nil];
    [super viewDidLoad];
}
```

As expected, flowerDetailView.hidden=YES will hide the detail view. Using [self getFlower:nil], we can call the getFlower: method from within our instance of the view control (referenced as self) and start the process of loading a flower in the web view. The method getFlower: expects a parameter, so we pass it nil. (This value is never used in getFlower:, however, so there is no problem with providing nil.)

Releasing the Objects

As always, we need to finish things up by releasing the objects that we've kept around. Edit the dealloc method to release the segmented control and two web views now:

```
- (void)dealloc {
    [colorChoice release];
    [flowerDetailView release];
    [flowerView release];
    [super dealloc];
}
```

Building the Application

Test out the final version of the FlowerWeb application by clicking Build and Run in Xcode.

Notice that you can zoom in and out of the web view, and use your fingers to scroll around. These are all features that you get without any implementation cost when using the UIWebView class.

Congratulations! Another app under your belt!

Using Scrolling Views

After working through the projects in the past few hours, you might begin to notice something: We're running out of space in our interfaces. Things are starting to get cluttered.

One possible solution, as you learned earlier this hour, is to use the `hidden` property of UI objects to hide and show them in your applications. Unfortunately, when you're juggling a few dozen controls, this is pretty impractical. Another approach is to use multiple different views, something that you'll start learning about in Hour 12.

There is, however, a third way that we can fit more into a single view—by making it scroll. Using an instance of the `UIScrollView` class, you can add controls and interface elements out beyond the physical boundaries of the iPhone screen. Unfortunately, Apple provides access to this object in Interface Builder, but leaves out the ability to actually make it *work*.

Before closing out this hour, we want to show you how to start using very simple scrolling views in a mini-project.

Implementation Overview

When we say *simple*, we mean it. This project will consist of a scroll view (`UIScrollView`) with content added in Interface Builder that extends beyond the iPhone screen, as shown in Figure 9.17.

FIGURE 9.17
We're going to make a view. It will scroll.

To enable scrolling in the view, we need to define a property called `contentSize`, which describes how large the content is that needs to be scrolled. That's it.

Setting Up the Project

Begin by creating another View-Based Application. Name the new project **Scroller**. For this example, we're going to be adding the scroll view (`UIScrollView`) as a subview to the existing view (`UIView`) in ScrollerViewController.xib. This is a perfectly acceptable approach, but as you get more experienced with the tools, you may want to just replace the default view entirely.

Preparing the Outlet

There's only one thing we need to do programmatically in this project, and that's set a property on the scroll view object. To access the object, we need to create an outlet for it. Open ScrollerViewController.h and add an outlet for a `UIScrollView` instance called `theScroller`, and then declare it as a property. The finished header should read as follows:

```
#import <UIKit/UIKit.h>
@interface ScrollerViewController : UIViewController {
        IBOutlet UIScrollView *theScroller;
}
@property (nonatomic, retain) UIScrollView *theScroller;
@end
```

Update the `ScrollerViewController` implementation file (ScrollerViewController.m) with the corresponding `@synthesize` directive added after the `@implementation` directive:

```
@synthesize theScroller;
```

Now that we'll be able to easily access the scroll view, let's go ahead and add it in Interface Builder.

Adding a Scroll View

Open the ScrollerViewController.xib file in Interface Builder, making sure that the document window is open (Window Document) and the view is visible. Using the object Library (Tools, Library) drag an instance of a Scroll View into your view. Position the view however you'd like it to appear and place a label above it that reads Scrolling View (just in case you forget what we're building).

Did you Know?

The Text View (UITextView) you used in Hour 7, "Working with Text, Keyboards, and Buttons," is a specialized instance of a scrolling view. The same scrolling attributes that you can set for the text view can be applied for the scroll view, so you may want to refer to the previous hour for more configuration possibilities. Or just press Command+1 to bring up the Attributes Inspector and explore!

Adding Objects to the Scroll View

Now that your scroll view is included in the XIB file, you need to populate it with something! Frequently, objects are placed in scroll views by writing code that calculates their position. In Interface Builder, Apple *could* add the ability to visually position objects in a larger virtual scroll view canvas, but they haven't.

So, how do we get our buttons and other widgets onscreen? First, start by dragging everything that you want to present into the scroll view object. For this example, I've added six labels. You can use buttons, images, or anything else that you'd normally add to a view.

Once the objects are in the view, you have two options. First, you can select the object, then use the arrow keys to position the objects outside of the visible area of the view to "guesstimate" a position, or you can select each object in turn and use the Size Inspector (Command+3) to set their X and Y coordinates manually, as shown in Figure 9.18.

FIGURE 9.18
Use the Size Inspector to set the X and Y coordinates for each object.

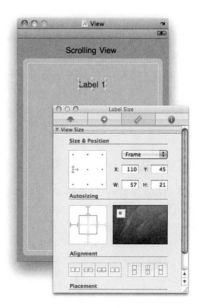

The coordinates of objects are relative to the view they are in. In this example, left corner of our scrolling view defines 0,0 (called the "origin point") for everything we add to it.

Did you Know?

To help you out, these are the X,Y coordinates left centers of my six labels:

Label 1   110,45

Label 2   110,125

Label 3   110,205

Label 4   110,290

Label 5   110,375

Label 6   110,460

As you can see from my final view, shown in Figure 9.19, the sixth label isn't visible, so we'll certainly need some scrolling if we're going to be able to view it!

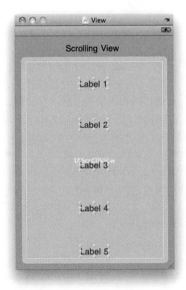

FIGURE 9.19
The final scrolling view, created with labels for content.

Connecting to the Outlet

To connect the scrolling view to theScroller outlet defined earlier, control drag from the File's Owner icon in the document window to the scroll view rectangle. When prompted, choose theScroller as your outlet, as shown in Figure 9.20.

FIGURE 9.20
We'll need to
access the
scroll view so
we can set its
`contentSize`
attribute. Create
the connection
to the
`theScroller`
outlet.

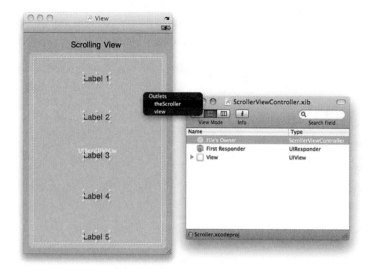

That finishes up our work in Interface Builder. Be sure to save the XIB file, and then switch back into Xcode.

Implementing Scrolling Behavior

For fun, try using Build and Run to run the application as it stands. It will compile and launch, but it doesn't scroll. In fact, it behaves just like we'd expect a typical *nonscrolling* view to behave. The reason for this is because we need to tell it the horizontal and vertical sizes of the region it is going to scroll. To do this, we need to set the `contentSize` attribute to a `CGSize` value. `CGSize` is just a simple C data structure that contains a height and a width, and we can easily make one using the `CGSizeMake(<width>,<height>)` function. For example, to tell our scroll view (`theScroller`) that it can scroll up to 280 pixels horizontally and 600 pixels vertically, we could type the following:

```
theScroller.contentSize=CGSizeMake(280,600);
```

Guess what? That isn't just what we *could* do, it's what we *will* do! Edit the ScrollerViewController.m file's `viewDidLoad` method to read as follows:

```
- (void)viewDidLoad {
    theScroller.contentSize=CGSizeMake(280,600);
    [super viewDidLoad];
}
```

> **Where Did You Get the Width and Height Values?**
>
> The width we used in this example is just the width of the scroll view itself. Why? Because we don't have any reason to scroll horizontally. The height is just a nice number we chose to illustrate that, yes, the view is scrolling. In other words, these are pretty arbitrary! You'll need to choose them to fit your own content in the way that works best for your application.

Releasing the Object

Edit the `dealloc` method to release the scroll view, and we're done:

```
- (void)dealloc {
    [theScroller release];
    [super dealloc];
}
```

Building the Application

The moment of truth has arrived. Does the single line of code make magic? Choose Build and Run, and then try scrolling around the view you created. Everything should work like a charm.

Yes, this was a quick and dirty project, but there seems to be a lack of information on getting started with `UIScrollView` and we thought it was important to run through a short tutorial. We hope this gives you new ideas on what you can do to create more feature-rich iPhone interfaces.

Summary

In this hour, you learned how to use two controls that enable applications to respond to user input beyond just a simple button press or a text field. The switch and segmented control, while limited in the options they can present, give a user a touch-friendly way of making decisions within your applications.

You also explored how to use web views to bring web content directly into your projects and how to tweak it so that it integrates into the overall iPhone user experience. This powerful class will quickly become one of your most trusted tools for displaying content.

Because we've reached a point in our development where things are starting to get a bit cramped, we closed out the hour with a quick introduction to the scroll view. You learned how, despite appearances, scroll views can be very easily added to apps.

Q&A

Q. *Why can't I visually lay out my scroll view in Interface Builder?*

A. Keep in mind that the iPhone interface development tools in Xcode are still quite new! Apple has been making steady improvements to Interface Builder to accommodate iPhone development, and I expect them to add this feature in the future.

Q. *You mentioned the `UIWebView` includes actions? What does that mean and how do I use them?*

A. This means that the object you drag into your view in Interface Builder is already capable of responding to actions (such as navigation actions) on its own—no code required. To use these, you would connect from the UI event that should trigger the action to your instance of the web view (as opposed to the File's Owner icon), and then choose the appropriate action from the pop-up window that appears.

Workshop

Quiz

1. What properties need to be set before a scroll view (`UIScrollView`) will scroll?

2. How do you get the opposite of a Boolean value?

3. What type of object does a web view expect as a parameter when loading a remote URL?

Answers

1. The `contentSize` property must be set for a scroll view before it will allow scrolling.

2. To negate a Boolean value, just prefix it with an exclamation point. `!TRUE`, for example, is the same as `FALSE`.

3. You typically use an `NSURLRequest` object to initiate a web request within a web view.

Activities

1. Create your own "mini" web browser by combining a text field, buttons, and a segmented control with a web view. Use the text field for URL entry, buttons for navigation, and hard-code some shortcuts for your favorite sites into the segmented control. To make the best use of space, you may want to overlay the controls on the web view, and then add a switch that hides or shows the controls when toggled.

2. Practice laying out a user interface within a scrollable view. Use graph paper to sketch the view and determine coordinates before laying it out in Interface Builder.

Further Exploration

Although useful, the segmented control (`UISegmentedControl`) and switch (`UISwitch`) classes are pretty easy to get the hang of. The best place to focus your attention for additional exploration is on the feature set provided by the `UIWebView` and `UIScrollView` classes.

As described at the start of this hour `UIWebView` can handle a large variety of content beyond what might be inferred by the "web" portion of its name. By learning more about `NSURL`, such as the `initFileURLWithPath:isDirectory` method, you'll be able to load files directly from your project resources. You can also take advantage of the web view's built-in actions, such as `goForward` and `goBack`, to add navigation functionality without a single line of code. One might even use a collection of html files to create a self-contained website within an iPhone application. In short, web views extend the traditional iPhone interface of your applications by bringing in HTML markup, JavaScript, and CSS—creating a very potent combination.

The `UIScrollView` class, on the other hand, gives us an important capability that is widely used in iPhone applications: touch scrolling. We briefly demonstrated this at the end of the hour, but there are additional features, such as pinching and zooming, that can be enabled by implementing the `UIScrollViewDelegate` protocol. We'll have our first look at building a class that conforms to a protocol in the next hour, so keep this in mind as you get more comfortable with the concepts.

Apple Tutorials

Segmented Controls, Switches, and Web Views – UICatalog (accessible via the Xcode developer documentation). Mentioned in the last hour's lesson, UICatalog shows virtually all the iPhone interface concepts in clearly defined examples.

Scrolling – ScrollViewSuite (accessible via the Xcode developer documentation). The ScrollViewSuite provides examples of just about everything you could ever want to do in a scroll view.

HOUR 10

Making Multivalue Choices with Pickers

What You'll Learn in This Hour:

▶ The types of Pickers available in the iPhone SDK

▶ How to implement the date picker object

▶ The capabilities offered by custom picker views

▶ The steps to implement the picker view protocols

▶ Ways to customize the display of a picker view

This hour marks a turning point in our lessons. With few exceptions, the past several hours presented iPhone interface components that you add to your applications. These typically involved accessing a few properties or trapping an event to execute an action. In this hour, the formula starts to change. We'll be exploring pickers—a unique UI element that both presents information to users *and* collects their input.

Unlike other components we've used, pickers aren't implemented through a single method; they require several. This means our example code is becoming a bit more complex, but nothing you can't handle! To make sure you're getting the information you need, we need to work a little faster and deviate from the simple project structure used in previous, simpler UI lessons.

Understanding Pickers

Because we're dedicating an entire hour to pickers (UIPickerView), you can probably surmise that they're not quite the same as the other UI objects that we've been using. Pickers are a unique feature of the iPhone. They present a series of multivalue options in a clever spinning interface—frequently compared to a slot machine. Rather than fruit or numbers, the segments, known as *components*, display rows of values that the user can choose from. The closest desktop equivalent is a set of pop-up menus. Figure 10.1 displays the standard date picker (`UIDatePicker`).

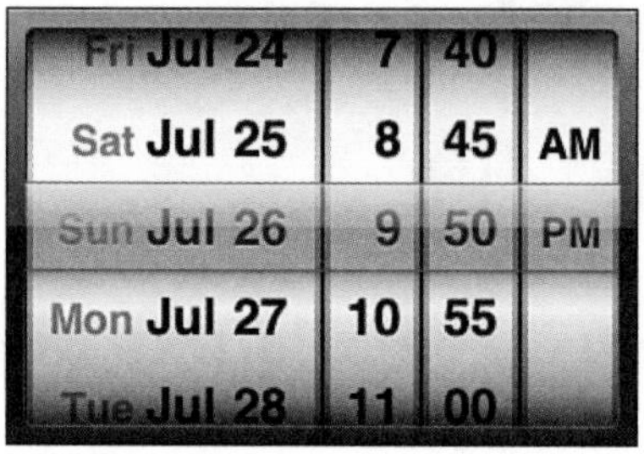

FIGURE 10.1
The picker offers a unique interface for choosing a sequence of different, but usually related, values.

Pickers should be used when a user needs to make a selection between multiple (usually related) values. They are frequently used for setting dates and times, but can be customized to handle just about any selection option that you can come up with.

By the Way

In Hour 9, "Using Advanced Interface Controls," you learned about the segmented control, which presents the user with multiple options in a single UI element. The segmented control, however, returns a single user selection to your application. A picker, on the other hand, can return several values from multiple user selections—all within a single interface.

Apple recognized that Pickers are a great option for choosing dates and times, so they've made them available in two different forms—date pickers, which are easy to implement and dedicated to handling dates and times; and custom picker views that can be configured to display as many components as rows as you'd like.

Date Pickers

The date picker (`UIDatePicker`), shown in Figure 10.1, is very similar to the other objects that we've been using over the past few hours. To use it, we'll add it to a view, wait for the user to interact with it, and then read its value. Instead of returning a string or integer, however, the date picker returns an `NSDate` object. The `NSDate` class is used to store and manipulate what Apple describes as a "single point in time" (in other words, a date and time).

To access the NSDate represented by a UIDatePicker instance, you'll make use of the date method. Pretty straightforward, don't you think? In our example project, we'll implement a date picker, and then retrieve the result, perform some date arithmetic, and display the results in a custom format.

Picker Views

Picker views (UIPickerView) are similar in appearance to date pickers, but have an almost entirely different implementation. In a picker view, the only thing that is defined for you is the overall behavior and general appearance of the control—the number of components and the content of each component are entirely up to you. Figure 10.2 demonstrates a picker view that includes two components with images and text displayed in their rows.

FIGURE 10.2
Picker views can be configured to display anything you'd like.

Unlike other controls, a picker view's appearance is not configured in Interface Builder's Attributes Inspector or via properties in code. Instead, we'll need to make sure we have a class that conforms to two protocols: UIPickerViewDelegate and UIPickerViewDataSource. I know it's been a while, so let's take a moment for a quick refresher.

Protocols

When I first started using Objective-C, I found the terminology painful. It seemed that no matter how easy a concept was to understand, it was surrounded with language that made it appear harder than it was. A protocol, in my opinion, is one of these things.

Protocols define a collection of methods that perform a task. To provide advanced functionality, some classes, such as UIPickerView, require you to implement methods defined in the protocol. Some methods are required, others are optional; it just depends on the features you need.

To make the full use of a `UIPickerView`, we'll just add some additional methods to one of our classes. In our sample application, we'll be using our view controller class for this purpose, but in larger projects it may be a completely separate class—the choice is entirely up to you. A class that implements a protocol is said to "conform" to that protocol.

We're going to be using protocols in the upcoming hours, so it's important that you get comfortable with the notion now.

The Picker View Data Source Protocol

There are two protocols required by `UIPickerView`. The first, the picker view data source protocol (`UIPickerViewDataSource`), includes methods that describe how much information the picker will be displaying:

> `numberOfComponentsInPickerView`: Returns the number of components (spinning segments) needed in the picker.

> `pickerView:numberOfRowsInComponent`: Given a specific component, this method is required to return the number of rows (different input values) in the component.

There's not much to it. As long as we create these two methods and return a meaningful number from each, we'll successfully conform to the picker view data source protocol. That leaves one protocol, the picker view delegate protocol, between us and a working picker view.

The Picker View Delegate Protocol

The delegate protocol (`UIPickerViewDelegate`) takes care of the real work in creating and using a picker. It is responsible for passing the appropriate data to the picker for display, and for determining when the user has made a choice. There are a few protocol methods we'll use to make the delegate work the way we want, but again, only two are required:

> `pickerView:titleForRow:forComponent`: Given a row number, this method must return the title for the row—that is, the string that should be displayed to the user.

> `pickerView:didSelectRow:inComponent`: This delegate method will be called when the user makes a selection in the picker view. The method will be passed a row number that corresponds to a user's choice, as well as the component that the user was last touching.

If you check the documentation for the `UIPickerViewDelegate` protocol, you'll notice that really *all* the delegate methods are optional—but unless we implement at least these two, the picker view isn't going to be able to display anything or respond to a user's selection.

By the Way

As you can see, implementing protocols isn't something terribly complicated—it just means that we need to implement a handful of methods to help a class, in this case a `UIPickerView`, work the way we want.

To get started with pickers, we'll first create a quick date picker example, and then move on to implementing a custom picker view and its associated protocols.

Using Date Pickers

Using the controls you currently know, there are probably half a dozen different ways that you might imagine creating a date entry screen on the iPhone. Buttons, segmented controls, text fields—all of these are potential possibilities, but none has the elegance and the inherent usability of a date picker. Let's put the picker to use.

Implementation Overview

This project, which we'll be calling DateCalc, will make use of a date picker (`UIDatePicker`) that, when set, will trigger an action that shows the difference in days between the chosen date and the current date. This will also make use of an `NSDate` object to store the result returned by the date picker, its instance method `timeIntervalSinceDate` to perform the calculation, and an `NSDateFormatter` object to format a date so that we can display it in a user-friendly manner via a single `UILabel`. Figure 10.3 shows the finished application.

Keep in mind that, despite its name, the `NSDate` class also stores the time. The application we create will take into account the time as well as the date when performing its calculation.

By the Way

Setting Up the Project

Start Xcode and create the DateCalc project using the View-Based Application template. Next, open the DateCalcViewController.h file and add an outlet and property declaration for the label (`UILabel`) that will display the difference between dates—`differenceResult`. Next, add an action called `showDate`. We'll be calling this when the user changes the value on the date picker.

FIGURE 10.3
The sample
application will
use a single
date picker and
a label as its
UI.

The (very simple) header file should read as follows:

```
#import <UIKit/UIKit.h>

@interface DateCalcViewController : UIViewController {
    IBOutlet UILabel *differenceResult;
}

@property (nonatomic, retain) UILabel *differenceResult;

-(IBAction)showDate:(id)sender;

@end
```

Switch to the implementation file (DateCalcViewController.m) and add a corresponding @synthesize directive for differenceResult, located after the @implementa-
tion line:

```
@synthesize differenceResult;
```

By the
Way

Notice that we don't have an outlet or property for the date picker itself? As with
the segmented control in the last hour, we'll just use the sender variable to reference the date picker within the showDate action method. Because nothing else is
calling the method, we know with certainty that sender will always be the picker.

Because we've got a pretty good handle on the project setup and you're probably sick of hearing us go on about it at the end of each project, let's take care of something we've done last, first: make sure we're properly releasing anything we've retained.

For this project, that's one object: `differenceResult`. Edit DateCalcViewController's dealloc method to read as follows:

```
- (void)dealloc {
    [differenceResult release];
    [super dealloc];
}
```

> Prior to this hour, we had always handled the final releases at the end of the project to make sure that it was a step you thought through prior to calling a project "done." Typically, I like to make sure that as soon as I've identified something that needs to be released, the release statement is written and added to the code. Obviously, you can work through whatever process is best for your coding style. Just make sure that you follow through and do it!

By the Way

Let's keep up the pace and move on to the UI and our date picker. After you've created the outlet and the action, save the file, and open DateCalcViewController.xib in Interface Builder.

Adding a Date Picker

Open the empty view in the DateCalcViewController.xib file, and then open the object Library (Tools, Library). Find the date picker (`UIDatePicker`) object and drag it into the view. You'll notice immediately that, unlike other UI elements we've used, the date picker takes up *a lot* of screen real estate. Typically, you'll need to hide your pickers when not in use, or use one of the multiview techniques we describe in Hour 12, "Creating Simple Multiview Applications with Toolbars," Hour 13, "Using Tab Bars to Manage Multiview Interfaces," and Hour 14, "Displaying and Navigating Data Using Table Views."

Position the date picker at the top of the screen, as seen in Figure 10.4. We'll be displaying the date calculations below it.

By default, the date picker displays a date and time, as demonstrated in our current view. As with other controls, the Attributes Inspector can customize how the date picker appears to the user.

FIGURE 10.4
Date pickers
use quite a bit
of screen
space.

Setting the Date Picker Attributes

Choose the date picker within the view, and then open the Attributes Inspector
(Command+1), shown in Figure 10.5.

FIGURE 10.5
Configure the
appearance of
the date picker
in the Attributes
Inspector.

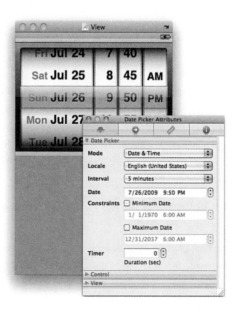

The picker can be configured to display in one of four different modes:

Date & Time: Shows options for choosing both a date and a time

Time: Shows only times

Date: Shows only dates

Timer: Displays a clock-like interface for choosing a duration

You can also set the locale for the picker, which determines the ordering of the different components, set the default date/time that is displayed, and set date/time constraints to help limit the user's choices.

For this project, leave the default settings as they are. We want the user to choose a date and a time that we'll use in our calculations.

> The "Date" attribute is automatically set to the date and time when you add the control to the view.

By the Way

Connecting to the Action

When the user interacts with the date picker, we want the showDate action method to be called. To create this connection, select the picker, and then open the Connections Inspector (Command+2).

Click and drag from the circle beside Value Changed to the File's Owner icon. When you release the mouse button, you'll be prompted for the action. Choose showDate, as demonstrated in Figure 10.6. This should be getting to be almost a reflex action by now!

> We've been making a point of using the Connections Inspector to create connections from objects that support many different events. This is always the safest way to know what connections you're creating, but it isn't the fastest. The picker (along with switches and segmented controls) will default to making connections using the Value Changed event if you Control-drag from the element to the File's Owner icon. You can use this shortcut if you feel comfortable with the process.

Did you Know?

FIGURE 10.6
Connect to the
showDate
action.

Finishing the Interface

Unlike some of our previous projects, the interfaces in this hour are pretty simple (so that we can focus on the picker itself). We'll wrap up our work in Interface Builder by adding a label to the view.

Add the Output Label

Use the Library to add a label (UILabel) with the title Choose a Date, positioned below the picker. This will be used for output in the application. For our implementation, we've used the Attributes Inspector to center the text, make it span four lines, set a font size of 20, and turn on word wrapping. Figure 10.7 shows the finished interface and attributes for the label.

Connecting to the Outlet

Connect the label to the outlet differenceResult by control dragging from the File's Owner icon to the UILabel within your view or in the document window. When prompted, choose the differenceResult outlet.

The interface is now complete. Save your work, and then switch back to Xcode for the implementation.

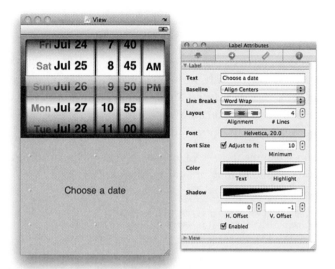

FIGURE 10.7
Finish up the
interface by
adding and
styling a label.

Implementing the View Controller Logic

As it turns out, the most difficult work that we still have in front of us with the date picker implementation is writing the showDate logic. To do what we've set out to (show the difference between today's date and the date in the picker), we need to be able to do several things:

- Get today's date
- Display a date and time
- Calculate the difference between two dates

Before writing showDate, let's look at the different methods and data types that we need to complete these tasks.

Getting the Date

To get the current date and store it in a NSDate object, all that we need to do is to allocate and initialize a new NSDate. When initialized, it automatically stores the current date! This means that a single line takes care of our first hurdle:

```
todaysDate=[[NSDate alloc] init];
```

Displaying a Date and Time

Unfortunately, displaying a date and time is a bit more tricky than *getting* the current date. Because we're going to be displaying the output in a label (UILabel), we already know *how* it is going to be shown on the screen, so the question is really, how do we format a string with a NSDate object?

Interestingly enough, there's a class to handle this for us! We'll create and initialize an NSDateFormatter object. Next, we use the object's setDateFormat to create a custom format using a pattern string. Finally, we apply that format to our date using another method of NSDateFormatter, stringFromDate—which, given an NSDate, returns a string in the format that we defined.

For example, if we assume that we've already stored an NSDate in a variable todaysDate, we can output in a format like "Month, Day, Year Hour:Minute:Second(AM or PM)" with these lines:

```
dateFormat = [[NSDateFormatter alloc] init];
[dateFormat setDateFormat:@"MMMM d, yyyy hh:mm:ssa"];
todaysDateString = [dateFormat stringFromDate:todaysDate];
```

First, the formatter object is allocated and initialized in a new object, dateFormat. Then the string @"MMMM d, YYYY hh:mm:ssa" is used as a formatting string to set the format internally in the object. Finally, a new string is returned and stored in todaysDateString by using the dateFormat object's instance method stringFromDate.

Where in the World Did That Date Format String Come From?

The strings that you can use to define date formats are defined by a Unicode standard that you can find here: http://unicode.org/reports/tr35/tr35-6.html#Date_Format_Patterns.

For this example, the patterns are interpreted as follows:

MMMM: The full name of the month

d: The day of the month, with no leading zero

YYYY: The full 4-digit year

hh: A two-digit hour (with leading zero if needed)

mm: Two digits representing the minute

ss: Two digits representing the second

a: a.m. or p.m.

Calculating the Difference Between Two Dates

The last thing that we need to understand is how to compute the difference between two dates. Instead of needing any complicated math, we can just use the timeIntervalSinceDate instance method in an NSDate object. This method returns the difference between two dates, in seconds. For example, if we have two NSDate objects, todaysDate and futureDate, we could calculate the time in seconds between them with this:

```
NSTimeInterval difference;
difference = [todaysDate timeIntervalSinceDate:futureDate];
```

Notice that we store the result in a variable of type NSTimeInterval. This isn't an object. Internally, it is just a double-precision floating-point number. Typically, this would be declared using the native C data type double, but Apple abstracts this from us by using a new type of NSTimeInterval so that we know exactly what to expect out of a date difference calculation.

> Note that if the timeIntervalSinceDate method is given a date *before* the object that is invoking the method (e.g., if futureDate were *before* todaysDate in the example), the difference returned is negative; otherwise, it is positive. To get rid of the negative sign, we'll be using the C function fabs(<float>) that, given a floating-point number, returns its absolute value.

By the Way

Implementing the Date Calculation and Display

Putting together all of these pieces, we should now be able to write the logic for the showDate method. Open the DateCalcViewController.m file in Xcode and add the following implementation for showDate method:

```
 1: -(IBAction)showDate:(id)sender {
 2:     NSDate *todaysDate;
 3:     NSString *differenceOutput;
 4:     NSString *todaysDateString;
 5:     NSDateFormatter *dateFormat;
 6:     NSTimeInterval difference;
 7:
 8:
 9:     todaysDate=[[NSDate alloc] init];
10:     difference = [todaysDate timeIntervalSinceDate:[sender date]] / 86400;
11:
12:     dateFormat = [[NSDateFormatter alloc] init];
13:     [dateFormat setDateFormat:@"MMMM d, yyyy hh:mm:ssa"];
14:     todaysDateString = [dateFormat stringFromDate:todaysDate];
15:
16:     differenceOutput=[[NSString alloc] initWithFormat:
17:             @"Difference between chosen date and today (%@) in days:
➥%1.2f",
18:                 todaysDateString,fabs(difference)];
19:     differenceResult.text=differenceOutput;
20:
21:     [todaysDate release];
22:     [dateFormat release];
23:     [differenceOutput release];
24: }
```

Much of this should look pretty familiar based on the preceding examples, but let's review the logic. First, in lines 2–6, we declare the variables we'll be using: `todaysDate` will store the current date, `differenceOutput` will be our final formatted string displayed to the user, `todaysDateString` will contain the formatted version of the current day's date, `dateFormat` will be our date formatting object, and `difference` is the double-precision floating-point number used to store the number of seconds between two dates.

Lines 9 and 10 do most of the work we set out to accomplish! In line 9, we allocate and initialize `todaysDate` as a new `NSDate` object. The `init` automatically stores the current date and time in the object.

In line 10, we use `timeIntervalSinceDate` to calculate the time, in seconds, between `todaysDate` and `[sender date]`. Remember that `sender` will be the date picker object, and the `date` method tells an instance of `UIDatePicker` to return its current date and time in an `NSDate` object, so this gives our method everything it needs to work with. The result is divided by `86400` and stored in the `difference` variable. Why 86400? This is the number of seconds in a day, so we will be able to display the number of days between dates, rather than seconds.

In lines 12–14, we create a new date formatter object (`NSDateFormatter`) and use it to format `todaysDate`, storing the results in the string `todaysDateString`.

Lines 16–18 format the final output string by allocating a new string (`differenceOutput`), and then initializing it with `initWithFormat`. The format string provided includes the message to be displayed to the user as well as the place-holders `%@` and `%1.2f`—representing a string and a floating-point number with a leading zero and two decimal places. These placeholders are replaced with the `todaysDateString` and the absolute value of the difference between the dates, `fabs(difference)`.

In line 19, the label we added to the view, `differenceResult`, is updated to display `differenceOutput`.

The last step is to clean up anything that we allocated in the method, which is accomplished in lines 21–23, where the strings and formatter object are released.

That's it! Use Build and Run to run and test your application. You've just implemented a date picker, learned how to perform some basic date arithmetic, and even formatted dates for output using date formatting strings. What could be better? Creating your own custom Picker with your own data, of course!

Implementing a Custom Picker View

In the lead-up to this project, we made it pretty clear that implementing your own picker view (UIPickerView) is going to be a bit different from other UI features you've added previously—including the date picker you just finished. This doesn't mean it will be *difficult*, just different. Because a picker view starts out empty and can contain anything we want, we need to provide it with data to display and describe how it should be displayed.

Implementation Overview

This project, named MatchPicker, will implement an instance of UIPickerView that presents two scrolling wheels of information: animal names and animal sounds. We'll use some simple logic to identify if an animal matches the correct sound and display a positive or negative response to the user. In short, a very easy matching game. Once we have the basics in place, we'll spruce things up by changing the animal names to actual pictures of the names. The final result that we're aiming for is shown in Figure 10.8.

FIGURE 10.8
We'll use a picker view to create a simple matching game.

Setting Up the Project

Since this a picker view that must conform to the UIPickerViewDataSource and UIPickerViewDelegate protocols, the setup we'll need to complete is just a teensy bit different from prior projects. Get started by opening Xcode and creating a View-Based Application named MatchPicker.

Conforming to a Protocol

To tell Xcode that one of our classes is going to conform to a protocol (or, in this case, multiple protocols), we need to edit the header file for the class and include the protocols in the @interface line.

For this project, we want our view controller (MatchPickerViewController) to conform to the UIPickerViewDataSource and UIPickerViewDelegate protocols. Open MatchPickerViewController.h and edit the @interface line to read as follows:

```
@interface MatchPickerViewController : UIViewController <UIPickerViewDataSource,
UIPickerViewDelegate> {
```

What we've done is add a comma-separated list of the name of the protocols we'll be implementing within the angle brackets <>. That (and writing the methods required by the protocols) is all we need to do to conform to a protocol. The rest of the project setup is pretty standard.

Adding Outlets but Not Actions

Amazingly, this project requires only two outlets, and *no* actions. The outlets will correspond to two labels (UILabel): lastAction will display the last action the user performed in the picker, and matchResult will be used to display feedback on whether the user successfully matched animal to sound.

So, why no action? Because the protocols we're conforming to define a method pickerView:didSelectRow:inComponent that will automatically be called when the user makes a selection. By adding the protocols to the @interface line, we've effectively added everything we'll need to connect to inside of Interface Builder.

Edit the MatchPickerViewController.h file to include outlets and property declarations for the lastAction and matchResult labels:

```
#import <UIKit/UIKit.h>

@interface MatchPickerViewController : UIViewController
                   <UIPickerViewDataSource, UIPickerViewDelegate> {
     IBOutlet UILabel *lastAction;
     IBOutlet UILabel *matchResult;
}

@property (nonatomic, retain) UILabel *lastAction;
@property (nonatomic, retain) UILabel *matchResult;

@end
```

Next, add the corresponding @synthesize lines to the implementation file (MatchPickerViewController.m) for each of the defined properties. These should be located after the @implementation directive:

```
@synthesize lastAction;
@synthesize matchResult;
```

Releasing the Objects

Edit the dealloc method in MatchPickerViewController.m to release the two labels we've retained. We'll need to revisit this with a few more edits later on, but, for now, the method should read:

```
- (void)dealloc {
    [lastAction release];
    [matchResult release];
    [super dealloc];
}
```

Make sure you've saved the view controller header and implementation files, and then let's turn our attention to hammering out the picker view interface with Interface Builder.

Adding a Picker View

Because the picker view is controlled mostly by the protocols we'll be implementing, there's surprisingly little to do in Interface Builder. Open the MatchPickerViewController.xib file, and make sure the view it contains is also open.

Using the Objects Library (Tools, Library), click and drag an instance of UIPickerView to the view, positioning it at the top of the iPhone interface. That's really all there is to it. If you open up the Attributes Inspector (Command+1), you'll notice that there is only a single attribute for the picker view—whether or not the selection indicator is present. You can turn this on or off, depending on how you feel it works with the aesthetics of your application. Figure 10.9 shows the picker added to the view, along with its available attributes.

When you add a UIPickerView to your view, it displays with a list of cities as the default contents. This won't change! Because the actual contents of the picker are determined by the code you write, you're not going to see the final result until you run the application.

By the Way

FIGURE 10.9
There's not much more to do be done with a picker view in Interface Builder beyond adding it to your view.

Connecting to the Data Source and Delegate Protocol Outlets

Remember that we didn't add any actions or outlets for the picker view to connect to, but we did declare that the `MatchPickerViewController` class we're writing will conform to the `UIPickerViewDataSource` and `UIPickerViewDelegate` protocols. Behind the scenes, this created the necessary outlets that the picker will need to connect to.

Control-drag from either the visual representation of the picker within your view or its icon in the document window to the File's Owner icon. When you release your mouse button, you'll be prompted to connect to either the Delegate or Data Source outlets, as shown in Figure 10.10. Choose the Delegate option to create the first connection.

After the delegate connection is made, repeat the exact same process, but this time choose Data Source. When both connections are in place, the picker is as "configured" as we can get it in Interface Builder. All the remaining work must take place in code.

Finishing the Interface

To complete the interface for the MatchPicker application, we need two labels (`UILabel`)—one for providing feedback of what the user just selected, another for showing whether the user successfully made a match. These labels will, in turn, connect to the `lastAction` and `matchResult` outlets, respectively.

FIGURE 10.10
Even though we didn't explicitly create any outlets, the view controller conforms to the picker's delegate and data source protocols and provides the appropriate connection points.

Adding the Output Labels

Drag two labels into the view, positioning one above the other. Change the title of the top label to read **Last Action** and the bottom label to read **Match Feedback**. In our sample project, we've also chosen to set the attributes so that both labels are centered and the Match Feedback label is larger (24 pt.) than the Last Action label, as shown in Figure 10.11.

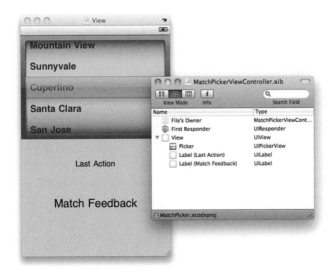

FIGURE 10.11
Add two labels to the view to handle output to the user.

Connecting the Outlets

Connect each of the labels to their corresponding outlets by Control-dragging from the File's Owner icon to each label and then choosing the `lastAction` and `matchResult` outlets, as appropriate. Figure 10.12 demonstrates the connection from the Match Feedback label to its `matchResult` outlet.

FIGURE 10.12
Make sure you remember to connect the two labels to their outlets!

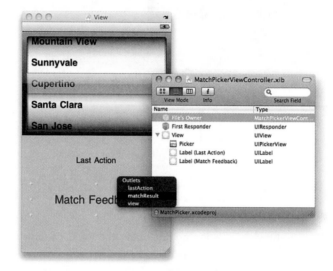

With that simple step, we're done with Interface Builder. All the work of actually customizing the appearance of the picker view must take place in Xcode.

Providing Data to the Picker

A big difference between the `UIPickerView` we're using now and other controls, such as the `UISegmentedControl`, is that what the control displays is determined entirely by the code we write. There is no "point and click" to edit the different components and values within Interface Builder. WYSIWYG isn't an option.

So, what information do we need to provide? Remember that the picker displays scrolling wheels called components. Within each component are any number of "rows" that display the values you want users to select. We'll need to provide the picker with data for each row in each component. For this example, we'll have one component with animal names and another with animal sounds.

Creating the Application Data Structures

Because the picker displays lists of information, it stands to reason that we'd want to store the data that they display as lists—a perfect job for an array! We'll create two arrays, animalNames and animalSounds, that contain all the information that the picker will display to the user.

We want these arrays to be available to everything in the MatchPickerViewController class, so we first need to add them to the @interface block within the view controller header file. Edit MatchPickerViewController.h to include two NSArrays (animalNames and animalSounds):

```
#import <UIKit/UIKit.h>

@interface MatchPickerViewController : UIViewController
                <UIPickerViewDataSource, UIPickerViewDelegate> {
    NSArray *animalNames;
    NSArray *animalSounds;
    IBOutlet UILabel *lastAction;
    IBOutlet UILabel *matchResult;
}

@property (nonatomic, retain) UILabel *lastAction;
@property (nonatomic, retain) UILabel *matchResult;

@end
```

These two arrays correspond to the components that we'll be displaying in the picker. Components are numbered starting at zero, left to right, so, assuming we want the names of the animals to be on the left and sounds on the right, component 0 will correspond to the animalNames array and component 1 to animalSounds.

Before going any further, take a few seconds to add the appropriate releases for these arrays within the dealloc method. The current version of the method should read as follows:

```
- (void)dealloc {
    [animalNames release];
    [animalSounds release];
    [lastAction release];
    [matchResult release];
    [super dealloc];
}
```

Populating the Data Structures

After the arrays have been declared, they need to be filled with data. The easiest place to do this is in the viewDidLoad method of the view controller

(MatchPickerViewController.m). Edit MatchPickerViewController.m by uncommenting the `viewDidLoad` method and adding the lines to allocate and initialize the arrays with a list of animals and sounds:

```
- (void)viewDidLoad {
    animalNames=[[NSArray alloc]initWithObjects:
      @"Mouse",@"Goose",@"Cat",@"Dog",@"Snake",@"Bear",@"Pig",nil];
    animalSounds=[[NSArray alloc]initWithObjects:
      @"Oink",@"Rawr",@"Ssss",@"Roof",@"Meow",@"Honk",@"Squeak",nil];
}
```

> `nil` is needed to denote the end of the array initialization list, so if it's missing, your application will almost certainly crash!

The arrays are initialized with a series of strings, but if you look closely, the strings don't match up! This is intentional. It wouldn't make sense to display the strings so that the animal name immediately matches the animal sound. Instead, element 0 of `animalNames` matches element 6 of `animalSounds`, `animalNames` element 1 matches `animalSounds` element 5, 2 matches 4, and so on. When it gets time to handle checking for a match between the components, we'll use this logic:

> *The total number of sounds, minus 1, minus the sound the user has chosen must be the same as the chosen animal.*

So, for a total of 7 sounds, where element 5 is chosen, we get $7 - 1 - 5 = 1$ (exactly the number we want). You're welcome to implement your own display and matching logic. This is just a quick way of "mixing things up" a bit for the purposes of this project.

To help simplify the application a bit, it would be nice if we could symbolically refer to "component 0" as the "animalComponent" and "component 1" as the "soundComponent." By defining a few constants at the start of our implementation file, we can do just that! Edit MatchPickerViewController.m and add these lines so that they precede the `#import` line:

```
#define componentCount 2
#define animalComponent 0
#define soundComponent 1
```

The first constant `componentCount` is just the number of components that we want to display in the picker, whereas the other two constants, `animalComponent` and `soundComponent`, can be used to refer to the different components in the picker without resorting to using their actual numbers.

What's Wrong with Referring to Something by its Number?

Absolutely nothing. The reason that it is helpful to use constants, however, is that if your design changes and you decide to change the order of the components or add another component, you can just change the numbering within the constants rather than each place they're used in the code. This will make a bit more sense in a few minutes as we start implementing the delegate and data source protocol methods.

Our application has everything it requires data-wise—it just needs the methods to get the data into the picker view.

Implementing the Picker Data Source Methods

Despite a promising sounding name, the picker data source methods (described by the UIPickerViewDataSource protocol) really only provide a small amount of information to the picker via these methods:

numberOfComponentsInPickerView: Returns the number of components the picker should display

pickerView:numberOfRowsInComponent: Returns the number of rows that the picker will be displaying within a given component

Let's start with component count. Edit MatchPickerViewController.m and add the following method to the file:

```
- (NSInteger)numberOfComponentsInPickerView:(UIPickerView *)pickerView {
    return componentCount;
}
```

We already defined a constant, componentCount, with the number of components we want to display (2), so the *entire* implementation of this method is just the line return componentCount.

The second method, pickerView:numberOfRowsInComponent, is expected to return the number of rows contained within a given component. We'll make use of the NSArray method count to return the number of items within the array that is going to make up the component. For example, to get back the number of names in the animalNames array, we can use this:

```
[animalNames count]
```

Implement it using the following code:

```
- (NSInteger)pickerView:(UIPickerView *)pickerView
           numberOfRowsInComponent:(NSInteger)component {
    if (component==animalComponent) {
        return [animalNames count];
    } else {
        return [animalSounds count];
    }
}
```

Here, we just compare the component variable provided when the picker calls the method to the animalComponent constant we declared earlier. If they are equal, we return a count of the names in animalNames. Otherwise, we return a count of the number of sounds in animalSounds.

Congratulations, you've just completed the methods required for conforming to the UIPickerViewDataSource protocol!

Populating the Picker Display

Where the data source protocol methods were responsible for defining *how many* items will appear in the picker, the UIPickerViewDelegate methods will define *what* items are shown, and how they are displayed. There's only a single method we really *need* before we can start looking at the results of our work: pickerView:titleForRow:forComponent. This method is called by the picker view to determine what text should be shown in a given component and row.

For example, if component 0 and row 0 are provided to the method as parameters, the method should return Mouse, because it is the first element of our animalNames array, which corresponds to component 0 in the picker.

This method requires the ability to retrieve a string from one of our arrays. The NSArray instance method objectAtIndex is exactly what we need. To retrieve row 5 from the animalSounds array we could use this:

```
[animalSounds objectAtIndex:5]
```

The pickerView:titleForRow:forComponent method provides us with both a row variable and a component variable, so we can implement it as follows:

```
- (NSString *)pickerView:(UIPickerView *)pickerView
           titleForRow:(NSInteger)row forComponent:(NSInteger)component {
    if (component==animalComponent) {
        return [animalNames objectAtIndex:row];
    } else {
        return [animalSounds objectAtIndex:row];
    }
}
```

The code first checks to see whether the supplied component variable is equal to the animalComponent constant that we configured, and then, if it is, returns the object (a string) from the specified row of the animalNames array. If component isn't equal to animalComponent, we can assume that we need to be looking at the animalSounds array and return a string from it, instead.

> Because we have just two components, we're making the assumption that if a method isn't referencing one, it must be referencing the other. Obviously if you have more than two components, you need a more complicated if-then-else structure, or a switch statement.

By the Way

After adding the method to MatchPickerViewController.m, save the file, and then choose Build and Run. The application will launch and show the picker view, complete with the contents of your two arrays, much like Figure 10.13.

FIGURE 10.13
The application should now run and show the customized picker view.

Notice that although the picker does work, choosing values has no effect—that's because we need to implement one more delegate method before our efforts will truly pay off.

Reacting to a Picker View Choice

For our application to respond to a user touching and changing the value within one of the picker components, we need to implement another method within the

UIPickerViewDelegate protocol: pickerView:didSelectRow:inComponent. This method is called when the user changes something in the picker view—as part of the parameters, we get back a reference to the picker itself, the row number that was selected and which component number it was in.

Do you see any problem with that? While the method certainly tells us when something was picked, and *what* was picked, it only gives us the value for the picker component that the user was changing. In other words, we'll get back the chosen animal name, but not the sound (or vice versa).

To access the value of *any* picker component at any time, we can use the UIPickerView instance method selectedRowInComponent. This returns the currently selected row in whatever component number we pass to it. If we have a reference to our picker in pickerView, for example, we could retrieve the selected animal name row like this:

```
[pickerView selectedRowInComponent:animalComponent]
```

By the Way

> It should now be obvious to you why it makes sense to use constants to keep track of the component numbers. Being able to use animalComponent or soundComponent directly in the code makes it much easier to read, and, long term, easier to maintain.

With all this information in hand, we're ready to write and review the pickerView:didSelectRow:inComponent method. Add the following code into MatchPickerViewController.m:

```
 1: - (void)pickerView:(UIPickerView *)pickerView didSelectRow:(NSInteger)row
 2:         inComponent:(NSInteger)component {
 3:     NSString *actionMessage;
 4:     NSString *matchMessage;
 5:     int selectedAnimal;
 6:     int selectedSound;
 7:     int matchedSound;
 8:
 9:     if (component==animalComponent) {
10:         actionMessage=[[NSString alloc]
11:                     initWithFormat:@"You selected the animal named '%@'",
12:                     [animalNames objectAtIndex:row]];
13:     } else {
14:         actionMessage=[[NSString alloc]
15:                     initWithFormat:@"You selected the animal sound '%@'",
16:                     [animalSounds objectAtIndex:row]];
17:     }
18:
19:     selectedAnimal=[pickerView selectedRowInComponent:animalComponent];
20:     selectedSound=[pickerView selectedRowInComponent:soundComponent];
```

```
21:
22:        matchedSound=([animalSounds count]-1)-
23:                    [pickerView selectedRowInComponent:soundComponent];
24:
25:        if (selectedAnimal==matchedSound) {
26:            matchMessage=[[NSString alloc] initWithFormat:@"Yes, a %@ does go '%@'!",
27:                            [animalNames objectAtIndex:selectedAnimal],
28:                            [animalSounds objectAtIndex:selectedSound]];
29:        } else {
30:            matchMessage=[[NSString alloc] initWithFormat:@"No, a %@ doesn't go '%@'!",
31:                            [animalNames objectAtIndex:selectedAnimal],
32:                            [animalSounds objectAtIndex:selectedSound]];
33:        }
34:
35:        lastAction.text=actionMessage;
36:        matchResult.text=matchMessage;
37:
38:        [matchMessage release];
39:        [actionMessage release];
40:
41: }
```

Lines 3–4 kick off the implementation by declaring two strings, actionMessage and matchMessage, which will be used to hold the contents of the messages that we'll be displaying to the user to view the labels in the interface.

Lines 5–7 define three integers (selectedAnimal, selectedSound, and matchedSound) that we'll be using to hold the currently selected animal and sound, and the "fixed" number of the currently selected sound. Recall that the sound and animal rows don't match up numerically? We'll use the matchSound variable to hold the results of the calculation that determines whether the sound the user has chosen matches the correct animal.

Lines 9–17 allocate and initialize a string, actionMessage, which describes what the user has done. If the component provided to the method is the animalComponent, the string will contain a message stating that they chose an animal. It will also identify the animal via the row variable and the animalNames array. If they choose a sound, the message and logic will be appropriate to that action instead. We're using the same techniques implemented earlier to populate the picker's display.

Lines 19–20 use the selectedRowInComponent method to retrieve the currently selected rows in the animal and sound components. The results are stored in the selectedAnimal and selectedSound variables, respectively.

Lines 22–23 work the magic of calculating if the chosen sound matches the chosen animal. The matchedSound value will equal the selectedAnimal value if the user has picked a match. You can refer to the earlier section "Populating the Data

Structures" for help understanding the math—it isn't critical in understanding the picker view itself.

Lines 25–33 compare `selectedAnimal` to `matchedSound`. If they are equal, the user has chosen correctly, and an appropriately congratulatory message is created and stored in the string `matchMessage`. If users make an incorrect choice, they're informed of the error with a slightly different message. In either case, the `matchMessage` string includes both the name of the animal and the sound so that users complete feedback about what they've selected.

Lines 35–36 output the `actionMessage` and `matchMessage` to the user by setting the `text` properties of the `lastAction` and `matchResult` labels.

Lines 38–39 release the two strings, `matchMessage` and `actionMessage`, allocated and initialized in the method.

Save your updated implementation file, and choose Build and Run. Scroll through the animals and sounds and make your choices. As you change the selection in the picker view, the messages should update accordingly, as Figure 10.14 shows.

FIGURE 10.14
Your application now reacts to changes in the picker view!

Done? Not just yet! When we started out, we promised that we'd be able to display images in the picker view, and we're not going to go back on our word!

Tweaking the Picker UI

Once you've got a working picker view, you can start using some of the optional `UIPickerViewDelegate` methods to dramatically alter its appearance. To close out this hour, for example, we'll change the picker to display icons of the animals rather than the animal names.

Adding the Image Resources and Data

We've supplied seven animal image PNG files inside the Animals folder of the Hour 10 MatchPicker project folder. Start by finding and dragging the image files into the Resources folder of your project in Xcode. When prompted, choose to copy the items if needed, as shown in Figure 10.15.

FIGURE 10.15
Copy the images to the project, if needed.

The `UIPickerView` can display any `UIView` or subclass of `UIView` within its components. To display an image, we'll need to add it to a view and make it available to the picker. Despite this sounding a bit daunting, we can create a new `UIImageView` instance and populate it with an image from our project resources using a single line:

```
[[UIImageView alloc] initWithImage:[UIImage imageNamed:<image name>]]
```

So, what do we do with these `UIImageViews` once we create them? The same thing we did with the animal names and animal sounds—we put them in an array. That way, we can simply pass the appropriate image view to the picker in the exact same way we were passing strings!

Start by updating the MatchPickerViewController.h file to declare an NSArray called animalImages. The final (for real!) header file should now read as follows:

```
#import <UIKit/UIKit.h>

@interface MatchPickerViewController : UIViewController
                    <UIPickerViewDataSource, UIPickerViewDelegate> {
    NSArray *animalNames;
    NSArray *animalSounds;
    NSArray *animalImages;
    IBOutlet UILabel *lastAction;
    IBOutlet UILabel *matchResult;
}
@property (nonatomic, retain) UILabel *lastAction;
@property (nonatomic, retain) UILabel *matchResult;

@end
```

Edit the viewDidLoad method within MatchPickerViewController.m to include the code to populate an array with seven image views corresponding to our animal PNG files. This code should be added following the allocation and initialization of the animalSounds or animalNames arrays:

```
animalImages=[[NSArray alloc]initWithObjects:
    [[UIImageView alloc] initWithImage:[UIImage imageNamed:@"mouse.png"]],
    [[UIImageView alloc] initWithImage:[UIImage imageNamed:@"goose.png"]],
    [[UIImageView alloc] initWithImage:[UIImage imageNamed:@"cat.png"]],
    [[UIImageView alloc] initWithImage:[UIImage imageNamed:@"dog.png"]],
    [[UIImageView alloc] initWithImage:[UIImage imageNamed:@"snake.png"]],
    [[UIImageView alloc] initWithImage:[UIImage imageNamed:@"bear.png"]],
    [[UIImageView alloc] initWithImage:[UIImage imageNamed:@"pig.png"]],
    nil
];
```

Next, update the dealloc method to release this new array when the application is finished with it:

```
- (void)dealloc {
    [animalNames release];
    [animalSounds release];
    [animalImages release];
    [lastAction release];
    [matchResult release];
    [super dealloc];
}
```

Using Views (with Images!) in a Picker View

Wouldn't it be great if we could just provide the image view to the picker in place of the animal name string in pickerView:titleForRow:forComponent and have it work? Guess what. It won't. Unfortunately, pickers operate in only one of two ways—either by displaying strings using the aforementioned method, or by displaying custom views using the method pickerView:viewForRow:forComponent:reusingView—but not a combination.

What this means for us is that if we want to display image views in the picker, everything else we want to show will have to be a subclass of UIView as well. The animal sounds are strings, so to display them, we need to create something that is a subclass of UIView that contains the necessary text. That "something" is a UILabel. By creating UILabels from the strings in the animalSounds array, we can successfully populate the picker with both images *and* text.

Begin by commenting out the pickerView:titleForRow:forComponent in MatchPickerViewController.m, by placing /* before the start, and */ after the end of the method. Alternatively, you can just delete the entire method (because we won't really need it again in this project).

Now, enter the following implementation of pickerView:viewForRow:forComponent:reusingView:

```
 1: - (UIView *)pickerView:(UIPickerView *)pickerView viewForRow:(NSInteger)row
 2:          forComponent:(NSInteger)component reusingView:(UIView *)view {
 3:     if (component==animalComponent) {
 4:         return [animalImages objectAtIndex:row];
 5:     } else {
 6:         UILabel *soundLabel;
 7:         soundLabel=[[UILabel alloc] initWithFrame:CGRectMake(0,0,100,32)];
 8:         [soundLabel autorelease];
 9:         soundLabel.backgroundColor=[UIColor clearColor];
10:         soundLabel.text=[animalSounds objectAtIndex:row];
11:         return soundLabel;
12:     }
13: }
```

In lines 3–4, we check to see if the component requested is the animal component, and if it is, we use the row parameter to return the appropriate UIImageView stored in the animalImages array. This is nearly identical to how we dealt with the strings earlier.

If the component parameter isn't referring to the animal component, then we need to return a UILabel with the appropriate referenced row from the animalSounds array. This is handled in lines 6–11.

In line 6, we declare a UILabel named soundLabel.

Line 7 allocates and initializes soundLabel with a frame using the initWithFrame method. Remember from earlier hours that views define a rectangular area for the content that is displayed on the iPhone screen. To create the label, we need to define the rectangle of its frame. The `CGRectMake` function takes starting x,y values and ending x,y values to define the height and width of a rectangle. In this example, we've defined a rectangle that spans 0 to 100 pixels horizontally and 0 to 32 pixels vertically.

Line 8 calls `autorelease` on the `soundLabel` object. This is a bit different from what we've done elsewhere. Why can't we just release `soundLabel` at the end of the method like everything else? The answer is that we have to return `soundLabel` so the picker can use it—so we can't just get rid of it. By using `autorelease`, we can hand off the object to the picker and relieve ourselves of the responsibility of releasing it.

Line 9 sets the background color attribute of the label to be transparent. As you learned with web views, `[UIColor clearColor]` returns a color object configured as transparent. If we leave this line out, the rectangle will not blend in with the background of the picker view.

Line 10 sets the text of the label to the string in of the specified row in `animalSounds`.

Finally, line 11 returns the `UILabel`—ready for display.

You can use Build and Run to run the application, but there's still going to be a slight issue: The rows aren't quite the right size to accommodate the images.

Changing Row Sizes

To control the width and height of the rows in the picker components, two additional delegate methods can be implemented:

> `pickerView:rowHeightForComponent:` Given a component number, this method should return the height, in pixels, of the row being displayed.
>
> `pickerView:widthForComponent:` Given a component number, this method returns the width of that component, in pixels.

For this example application, some trial and error led me to determine that the animal component should be 75 pixels wide, while the sound component looks best at around 150 pixels. Both components should use a constant row height of 55 pixels.

Translating this into code, implement `pickerView:rowHeightForComponent` as follows:

```
- (CGFloat)pickerView:(UIPickerView *)pickerView
          rowHeightForComponent:(NSInteger)component {
    return 55.0;
}
```

Similarly, `pickerView:widthForComponent` becomes this:

```
- (CGFloat)pickerView:(UIPickerView *)pickerView
widthForComponent:(NSInteger)component {
    if (component==animalComponent) {
        return 75.0;
    } else {
        return 150.0;
    }
}
```

With those small additions to MatchPickerViewController.m, the `UIPickerView` project is complete! You should now have a good understanding of how to create and customize Pickers as well as how to manage a user's interaction with them.

Summary

In this hour's lesson, you explored two classes, `UIDatePicker` and `UIPickerView`, that present the user with a list of choices ranging from dates to images. Despite being based on the same underlying technology, the implementation of these features is very different. The date picker works just like the other UI elements you've been using over the past few hours. The picker view, on the other hand, requires us to write methods that conform to the `UIPickerViewDelegate` and `UIPickerViewDataSource` protocols.

In writing the sample picker applications, you also had a chance to make use of `NSDate` methods for calculating the interval between dates, as well as `NSDateFormatter` for creating user-friendly strings from an instance of `NSDate`. Although not the topic of this lesson, these are powerful tools for working with dates and times and interacting with your users.

Workshop

Q&A

Q. *Why didn't you cover the timer mode of the* `UIDatePicker`*?*

A. The timer mode doesn't actually *implement* a timer; it's just a view that can display timer information. To implement a timer, you'll actually need to track the time and update the view accordingly—not something we can easily cover in the span of an hour.

Q. *Where did you get the method names and parameters for the* UIPickerView *protocols?*

A. The protocol methods that we implemented were taken directly from the Apple Xcode documentation for UIPickerViewDelegate and UIPickerViewDataSource. If you check the documentation, you can simply copy and paste from the method definitions into your code.

Q. *If we had to create a rectangle to define the frame of a* UILabel, *why didn't we do the same when creating the* UIImageView *objects?*

A. When a UIImageView is initialized with an NSImage, its frame is set to the dimensions of the image.

Quiz

1. An NSDate instance stores only a date. True or false?

2. Why doesn't a UIPickerView need to have an action defined for it?

3. Picker views can display images using the pickerView:titleForRow:forComponent method. True or false?

Answers

1. False. An instance of NSDate stores an "instant in time"—meaning a date *and* time.

2. By implementing the UIPickerViewDelegate methods and connecting the picker to the delegate, you gain the functionality of an action method automatically.

3. False. The pickerView:viewForRow:forComponent:reusingView method must be implemented to display images within a picker.

Activities

1. Update the dateCalc project so that the program automatically sets the picker to the current date when it is loaded. You'll need to use the setDate:animated method to implement this change.

2. Extend the MatchPicker project to give the appearance of the continuously scrolling/rotating components. You'll need to return a very large number of rows for each component, and then repeat the same rows over and over when they are requested. Rather than adding redundant data to the array, the best approach is to use a single array and map the row requests into the existing data in the array.

Further Exploration

As you learned in this lesson, `UIDatePicker` and `UIPickerView` objects are reasonably easy to use, and quite flexible in what they can do. There are a few interesting aspects of using these controls that we haven't looked at that you may want to explore on your own. First, both classes implement a means of programmatically selecting a value and animating the picker components so that they "spin" to reach the values you're selecting: `setDate:animated` and `selectRow:inComponent:animated`. If you've used applications that implement Pickers, chances are, you've seen this in action.

Another popular approach to implementing Pickers is creating components that appear to spin continuously—rather than reaching a start or stopping point. You may be surprised to learn that this is really just a programming trick. The most common way to implement this functionality is to use a picker view that simply repeats the same component rows over and over (thousands of times). This requires you to write the necessary logic in the delegate and data source protocol methods, but the overall effect is that the component rotates continuously.

While these are certainly areas for exploration to expand your knowledge of pickers, you may also want to take a closer look at the documentation for the `NSDate` class. The ability to manipulate dates can be a powerful capability in your applications.

Apple Tutorials

UIDatePicker, UIPickerView – UICatalog (accessible via the Xcode developer documentation). This great example code package includes samples of both the simple `UIDatePicker` and a full `UIPickerView` implementation.

Dates, Times, and Calendars – Date and Time Programming Guide for Cocoa (accessible via the Xcode developer documentation). This guide provides information on just about everything you could ever want to do with dates and times.

HOUR 11

Getting the User's Attention

What You'll Learn in This Hour

▶ Different types of iPhone notifications
▶ How to create alert views
▶ How to use action sheets to present options
▶ How to implement short sounds and vibrations

The iPhone presents developers with many opportunities for creating unique user interfaces, but certain elements must be consistent across all applications. When users need to be notified of an application event or make a critical decision, it is important that they be presented with interface elements that immediately make sense. In this hour, we look at several different ways an application can notify a user that *something* has happened. It's up to you to determine what that "something" is, but these are the tools you'll need to keep users of your apps "in the know."

Exploring User Notification Methods

Applications on the iPhone are user centered, which means they typically don't perform utility functions in the background or operate without an interface. They enable users to work with data, play games, communicate, or carry out dozens of other activities. (As Apple would say, "There's an app for that.") Despite the variation in activities, when an application needs to show a warning, provide feedback, or ask the user to make a decision, the iPhone does so in a common way. Cocoa Touch leverages three methods to gain your attention:

▶ UIAlertView
▶ UIActionSheet
▶ System Sound Services

This hour explains how you can implement these notification features into your iPhone application.

Prepping the Notification Project Files

To practice different classes and methods, we need to create a new project with buttons for activating the different styles of notifications. Open Xcode and create a new project based on the View-based Application iPhone template. Name the project **"GettingAttention."**

Within Xcode, open the GettingAttentionViewController.h file and add the following outlets and actions:

```
#import <UIKit/UIKit.h>

@interface GettingAttentionViewController : UIViewController {
    IBOutlet UILabel *statusMessage;
}

@property (retain, nonatomic) IBOutlet UILabel *statusMessage;

- (IBAction)doAlert:(id)sender;
- (IBAction)doActionSheet:(id)sender;
- (IBAction)doSound:(id)sender;
- (IBAction)doAlertSound:(id)sender;
- (IBAction)doVibration:(id)sender;

@end
```

The first outlet, `statusMessage`, will be implemented as a text label for providing simple feedback within the application. The five `actions` are methods that correspond to the different notification methods we'll be writing throughout the hour.

Next, edit the start of the GettingAttentionViewController.m file and add the following code after the existing `@implementation` line:

```
@synthesize statusMessage;

-(IBAction)doAlert:(id)sender {
}
-(IBAction)doActionSheet:(id)sender {
}
-(IBAction)doSound:(id)sender {
}
-(IBAction)doAlertSound:(id)sender {
}
-(IBAction)doVibration:(id)sender {
}
```

The @synthesize directive is used to create the getter/setter for the statusMessage text label. Next, five stub methods are defined for our actions. Finally, be sure to edit the dealloc method to release the statusMessage object:

```
- (void)dealloc {
    [statusMessage release];
    [super dealloc];
}
```

That completes the code skeleton that we'll be using throughout this hour. Now let's create the interface in Interface Builder and connect the outlets and actions.

Creating the Notification Project Interface

Open the GettingAttentionViewController XIB file in Interface Builder. We need to add five buttons and a text label to the empty view. You should be getting quite familiar with this process by now. Just follow these steps:

1. Double-click the View icon in the Documents window. This will open the empty view.

2. Add a button to the view by opening the library (Tools, Library), and dragging a Round Rect Button (IUButton) to the View window.

3. Continue adding buttons until you have a total of five within the view. Space them out evenly within the available vertical space, leaving room at the bottom for a label.

4. Change the button labels to correspond to the different notification types that we'll be using. Specifically, name the buttons (top to bottom) "**Alert Me!**", "**Lights, Camera, Action Sheet**", "**Play Sound**", "**Play Alert Sound**", and "**Vibrate Phone.**"

5. Drag a label (UILabel) from the library to the bottom of the view. Remove the default label text. The interface should resemble Figure 11.1.

Connecting the Outlets and Actions

The interface itself is finished, but we still need to make the connection to our properties and method stubs, as follows:

1. Select the first button (Alert Me!), and then press Command+2 to open the Connection Inspector.

FIGURE 11.1
Create an interface with five buttons and a label at the bottom.

2. From the Touch Up Inside connection point, click and drag to the File's Owner icon in the Document window.

3. When prompted, choose the doAlert: method from the list (see Figure 11.2).

FIGURE 11.2
Connect the buttons to the method stubs.

4. Repeat this pattern for the other four buttons. "Lights, Camera, Action Sheet" should connect to the doActionSheet: method, "Play Sound" to doSound:, "Play Alert Sound" to doAlertSound: and "Vibrate Phone" to doVibration:.

5. To connect the label, Control-drag from the File's Owner icon in the Document window to the label (either in the View window, or the View hierarchy in the Document window). Choose the `statusMessage` outlet to make the final connection, as demonstrated in Figure 11.3.

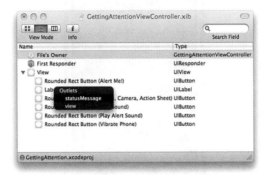

FIGURE 11.3
Connect the statusMessage outlet to the label in the view.

The framework for our test of notification is ready. We'll start by implementing an alert view.

Generating Alerts

Sometimes users need to be informed of changes when an application is running. More than just a change in the current view is required when an internal error event occurs (such as low-memory condition or a dropped network connection), for example, or upon completion of a long-running activity. Enter the `UIAlertView` class.

The `UIAlertView` class creates a simple modal alert window that presents a user with a message and a few option buttons (see Figure 11.4).

What Does *Modal* Mean?

Modal UI elements require the user to interact with them (usually push a button) before the user can do anything else. They are typically layered on top of other windows and block all other interface actions while visible.

FIGURE 11.4
Implement
UIAlertView to
display simple
messages to
the user.

Displaying a Simple Alert

In the preceding section, you created a simple project (GettingAttention) with several buttons that we'll use to activate the different notification events. The first button, "Alert Me!," should be connected to a method stub called doAlert in GettingAttentionViewController.m. In this first exercise, we write an implementation of doAlert that displays an alert message with a single button that the user can push to dismiss the dialog.

Edit GettingAttentionViewController.m and enter the following code for doAlert:

```
 1: -(IBAction)doAlert:(id)sender {
 2:     UIAlertView *alertDialog;
 3:     alertDialog = [[UIAlertView alloc]
 4:                        initWithTitle: @"Alert Button Selected"
 5:                        message:@"I need your attention NOW!"
 6:                        delegate: nil
 7:                        cancelButtonTitle: @"Ok"
 8:                        otherButtonTitles: nil];
 9:     [alertDialog show];
10:     [alertDialog release];
11: }
```

In lines 2 and 3, we declare and instantiate our instance of UIAlertView with a variable called alertDialog. As you can see, the convenient initialization method of the alert view does almost all the work for us. Let's review the parameters:

▶ `initWithTitle:` Initializes the view and sets the title that will appear at the top of the alert dialog box.

▶ `message:` Sets the string that will appear in the content area of the dialog box.

▶ `delegate:` Contains the object that will serve as the delegate to the alert. Initially, we don't need any actions to be performed after the user dismisses the alert, so we can set this to `nil`.

▶ `cancelButtonTitle:` Sets the string shown in the default button for the alert.

▶ `otherButtonTitles:` Adds an additional button to the alert. We're starting with a single-button alert, so this is set to `nil`.

After `alertDialog` has been initialized, the next step is to show it by using (surprise!) the show method, as shown in line 9. Finally, as soon as we're done with the alert, we can release it, as seen in line 10.

> If you prefer to set the alert message and buttons independently of the initialization, the `UIAlertView` class includes properties for setting the text labels (`message`, `title`) individually and methods for adding buttons (`addButtonWithTitle:`).

By the Way

Figure 11.5 shows the outcome of these settings.

FIGURE 11.5
In its simplest form, an alert view displays a message and button to dismiss it.

> An alert doesn't have to be a single-use object. If you're going to be using an alert repeatedly, create an instance when your view is loaded and show it as needed—but remember to release the object when you're finished using it!

Creating Multi-Option Alerts

An alert with a single button is easy to implement, because there is no additional logic to program. The user taps the button, the alert is dismissed, and execution continues as normal. If you need to add additional buttons, however, your application needs to be able to identify the button pressed and react appropriately.

In additional to the single-button alert that you just created, there are two additional configurations to learn. The difference between them is how many buttons you're asking the alert to display. A two-button alert places buttons side by side. When more than two buttons are added, the buttons are stacked, as you'll soon see.

Adding Buttons

Creating an alert with multiple buttons is simple: We just take advantage of the `otherButtonTitles` parameter of the initialization convenience method. Instead of setting to `nil`, provide a list of strings terminated by `nil` that should be used as the additional button names. The cancel button will always be displayed on the left in a two-button scenario or at the bottom of a longer button list.

> At most, an alert view can display five buttons (including the button designated as the "cancel" button) simultaneously. Attempting to add more may result in some very unusual onscreen effects, such as display of clipped/partial buttons.

For example, to expand the previous example to include two new buttons, the initialization can be changed as follows:

```
alertDialog = [[UIAlertView alloc]
                initWithTitle: @"Alert Button Selected"
                message:@"I need your attention NOW!"
                delegate: nil
                cancelButtonTitle: @"Ok"
                otherButtonTitles: @"Maybe Later", @"Never", nil];
```

Go ahead and build the updated project and test the result. Pressing the "Alert Me!" button should now open the alert view displayed in Figure 11.6.

Try pushing one of the buttons. The alert view is dismissed. Push another? The same thing happens. All the buttons do exactly the same thing—absolutely nothing. Although this behavior was fine with a single button, it's not going to be very useful with our current configuration.

FIGURE 11.6
Add additional buttons during initialization of the alert view.

Responding to a Button Choice

To identify the button that was pressed in a multi-option alert, an object in your application must conform to the UIAlertViewDelegate protocol and implement the alertView:clickedButtonAtIndex: method.

For this example, modify the GettingAttentionViewController.h header file to declare that our view controller class will be conforming to the necessary protocol. The interface should now read as follows:

```
@interface GettingAttentionViewController : UIViewController
<UIAlertViewDelegate> {
    IBOutlet UILabel *statusMessage;
}
```

Now, update the initialization code of the alert view in GettingAttentionViewController.m so that the delegate is pointed to the object that implements the UIAlertViewDelegate. Because this is the same object that is instantiating the alert, we can just use self:

```
    alertDialog = [[UIAlertView alloc]
                    initWithTitle: @"Alert Button Selected"
                    message:@"I need your attention NOW!"
                    delegate: self
                    cancelButtonTitle: @"Ok"
                    otherButtonTitles: @"Maybe Later", @"Never", nil];
```

The `alertView:clickedButtonAtIndex:` method that we write next will receive the index of the button that was pushed and give us the opportunity to act on it. To make this easier, we can take advantage of the `UIAlertView` instance method `buttonTitleAtIndex:`. This method will return the string title of a button from its index, eliminating the need to keep track of which index value corresponds to which button.

Add the following code to GettingAttentionViewController.m:

```
 1: - (void)alertView:(UIAlertView *)alertView
 2:     clickedButtonAtIndex:(NSInteger)buttonIndex {
 3:     NSString *buttonTitle=[alertView buttonTitleAtIndex:buttonIndex];
 4:     if ([buttonTitle isEqualToString:@"Maybe Later"]) {
 5:         statusMessage.text=@"Clicked 'Maybe Later'";
 6:     } else if ([buttonTitle isEqualToString:@"Never"]) {
 7:         statusMessage.text=@"Clicked 'Never'";
 8:     } else {
 9:         statusMessage.text=@"Clicked 'Ok'";
10:     }
11: }
```

To start, in line 3, `buttonTitle` is set to the title of the button that was clicked. Lines 4 through 10 test the value of `buttonTitle` against the names of the buttons that we initialized when creating the alert view. If a match is found, the `statusMessage` of the view is updated to something appropriate.

This is just one way to implement the button handler for your alert. In some cases (such as dynamically generated button labels), it may be more appropriate to work directly with the button index values. You may also want to consider defining constants for button labels.

Don't assume that application processing stops when the alert window is on the screen! Your code will continue to execute after you show the alert. You may even want to take advantage of this by using the `UIAlertView` instance method `dismissWithClickedButtonIndex:` to remove the alert from the screen if the user does not respond within a certain length of time.

Using Action Sheets

Alert views are used to display messages that indicate a change in state or a condition within an application that a user should acknowledge. There are times, however, when a user should be prompted to make a decision based on the result of an action. For example, if an application provides the option to share information with a friend, the user might be prompted for the method of sharing (such as sending an email, uploading a file, and so on). You can see this behavior when adding a bookmark in Safari, as shown in Figure 11.7. This interface element is called an **"action sheet"** and is an instance of the UIActionSheet class.

FIGURE 11.7
An action sheet provides multiple options based on the context in which an action is being carried out.

Action sheets are also used to confirm actions that are potentially destructive to data. In fact, they provide a separate bright-red button style to help draw a user's attention to potential deletion of data.

Displaying an Action Sheet

Action sheets are very similar to alerts in how they are initialized, modified, and ultimately, acted upon. However, unlike alerts, an action sheet can be associated with a given view, tab bar, or toolbar. When an action sheet appears onscreen, it is animated to show its relationship to one of these elements.

To create your first action sheet, we'll use the method stub doActionSheet created within the GettingAttentionViewController.m file. Recall that this method will be triggered by pushing the "Lights, Camera, Action Sheet" button. Add the following code to the doActionSheet method:

```
1: - (IBAction)doActionSheet:(id)sender {
2:     UIActionSheet *actionSheet;
3:     actionSheet=[[UIActionSheet alloc] initWithTitle:@"Available Actions"
4:                 delegate:self
5:                 cancelButtonTitle:@"Cancel"
6:                 destructiveButtonTitle:@"Destroy"
```

```
7:                     otherButtonTitles:@"Negotiate",@"Compromise",nil];
8:     [actionSheet showInView:self.view];
9: }
```

Lines 2 and 3 declare and instantiate an instance of `UIActionSheet` called `actionSheet`. Similar to the setup of an alert, the initialization convenience method takes care of nearly all the setup. The parameters are as follows:

▶ `initWithTitle`: Initializes the sheet with the specified title string.

▶ `delegate`: Contains the object that will serve as the delegate to the sheet. If this is set to `nil` (which we will do initially), the sheet will be displayed, but pressing a button will have no effect beyond dismissing the sheet.

▶ `cancelButtonTitle`: Set the string shown in the default button for the alert.

▶ `destructiveButtonTitle`: The title of the option that will result in information being lost. This button will be presented in bright red (a sharp contrast to the rest of the choices). If set to `nil`, no destructive button will be displayed.

▶ `otherButtonTitles`: Adds additional buttons to the sheet. In this example, we will have a total of four buttons (the cancel button, destructive button, and two "other" buttons).

In line 8, the action sheet is displayed in the current view controller's view (self.view) using the `UIActionSheet` `showInView:` method. Figure 11.8 shows the result.

FIGURE 11.8
Action sheets can include cancel and destructive buttons, as well as buttons for other options.

In iPhone OS 3.0, action sheets can take up to seven buttons (including cancel and the destructive button) while maintaining the standard layout. If you exceed seven, however, the display will automatically change into a scrolling table, as demonstrated in Figure 11.9. This gives you room to add as many options as you need.

By the Way

FIGURE 11.9
The action sheet automatically changes to a scrolling table when you exceed the available space.

Changing the Action Sheet Appearance

Based on what you've learned so far, you may have noticed that an action sheet is more configurable than the alert view. An action sheet defines three different types of buttons with three different appearances (cancel, destructive, other). Any of the button titles can be set to nil, and that button type will not be displayed in the sheet.

If you wish to add buttons to the action sheet outside of the initialization method, use the addButtonWithTitle: method. This could be handy if you generate the button names dynamically, for instance.

By the Way

You can also change how the sheet is drawn on the screen. In the example we're creating, the showInView: method is used to animate the opening of the sheet from the current controller's view. If you have an instance of a toolbar or a tab bar, you can use `showFromToolbar:` or `showFromTabBar:` to make the sheet appear to open from either of these user interface elements.

Perhaps more dramatically, an action sheet can take on different appearances if you set the `actionSheetStyle` property. For example, try adding the following line to the doActionSheet method:

```
actionSheet.actionSheetStyle=UIBarStyleBlackTranslucent;
```

This code draws the action sheet in a translucent black style. You can also use `UIActionSheetStyleAutomatic` to inherit the style of the view's toolbar (if any is set), or `UIActionSheetStyleBlackOpaque` for a shiny solid-black style.

Responding to Action Sheet Button Presses

As you've seen, there are more than a few similarities in how alert views and action sheets are set up. The similarities continue with how an action sheet reacts to a button press, for which we will follow almost the same steps as we did with an alert view.

First, we need to conform to a new protocol. Modify GettingAttentionViewController.h to include the `UIActionSheetDelegate` protocol:

```
@interface GettingAttentionViewController :
            UIViewController <UIAlertViewDelegate, UIActionSheetDelegate> {
    IBOutlet UILabel *statusMessage;
}
```

Next, to capture the click event, we need to implement the `actionSheet:clickedButtonAtIndex` method. As with `alertView:clickedButtonAtIndex:`, this method provides the button index that was pressed within the action sheet. Add the following code to GettingAttentionViewController.m:

```
 1: - (void)actionSheet:(UIActionSheet *)actionSheet
 2:     clickedButtonAtIndex:(NSInteger)buttonIndex {
 3:     NSString *buttonTitle=[actionSheet buttonTitleAtIndex:buttonIndex];
 4:     if ([buttonTitle isEqualToString:@"Destroy"]) {
 5:         statusMessage.text=@"Clicked 'Destroy'";
 6:     } else if ([buttonTitle isEqualToString:@"Negotiate"]) {
 7:         statusMessage.text=@"Clicked 'Negotiate'";
 8:     } else if ([buttonTitle isEqualToString:@"Compromise"]) {
 9:         statusMessage.text=@"Clicked 'Compromise'";
10:     } else {
11:         statusMessage.text=@"Clicked 'Cancel'";
12:     }
13: }
```

Now, we can use `buttonTitleAtIndex` (line 3) to get the titles used for the buttons based on the index provided. The rest of the code follows exactly the same pattern created earlier. Lines 4 through 12 test for the different button titles and update the view's status message to indicate what was chosen.

An Alternative Approach

Once again, we've chosen to match button presses based on the title of the onscreen button. If you're adding buttons dynamically, however, this might not be the best approach. The `addButtonWithTitle` method, for example, adds a button and returns the index of the button that was added. Similarly, the `cancelButtonIndex` and `destructiveButtonIndex` methods provide the indexes for the two specialized action sheet buttons.

By checking against these index values, you can write a version of the `actionSheet:clickedButtonAtIndex:` method that is not dependent on the title strings. The approach you take in your own applications should be based on what creates the most efficient and easy-to-maintain code.

Using Alert Sounds and Vibrations

Visual notifications are great for providing feedback to a user and getting critical input. Other senses, however, can be just as useful for getting a user's attention. Sounds, for example, play an important role on nearly every computer system (regardless of platform or purpose). They tell us when an error has occurred or an action has been completed. Sounds free a user's visual focus and still provide feedback about what an application is doing.

Vibrations take alerts one step further. When a device has the ability to vibrate, it can communicate with users even if they can't see or hear it. For the iPhone, vibration means that an app can notify users of events even when stowed in a pocket or resting on a nearby table. The best news of all? iPhone sounds and vibrations are both handled through the same simple code, so you'll be able to implement them relatively easily within your applications.

System Sound Services

To enable sound playback and vibration, we will take advantage of the System Sound Services C-style interface. System Sound Services provides an interface for playing back sounds that are 30 seconds or less in length. It supports a limited number of file formats (specifically CAF, AIF, and WAV files). The functions provide no manipulation of the sound, nor control of the volume, so you won't want to use System Sound Services to create the soundtrack for your latest and greatest iPhone game. In Hour 18, "Extending the Touch Interface," you'll be exploring additional media playback features of the iPhone OS.

Unlike most of the other development functionality we've discussed in this book, the System Sound Services functionality is not implemented as a class. Instead, you will be using more traditional C-style function calls to trigger playback.

We can invoke three different notifications using this API:

- ▶ **Sound**: A simple sound file is played back immediately. If the phone is muted, the user will hear nothing.

- ▶ **Alert**: Again, a sound file is played, but if the phone is muted and set to vibrate, the user is alerted through vibration.

- ▶ **Vibrate**: The phone is vibrated, regardless of any other settings.

Playing Sounds and Alerts

To play a sound file, you first need to make the file available as a resource to your iPhone application. Let's continue to expand the GettingAttention project to include sound playback:

1. With your project open in Xcode, return to the Finder and navigate to the "sounds" directory within this hour's project folder.

2. Drag the files soundeffect.wav and alertsound.wav into your Xcode project's Resources folder.

You should see the files listed as resources (see Figure 11.10).

FIGURE 11.10
Add the sound files as resources to your project.

Adding the AudioToolbox Framework

The AudioToolbox framework must be added to our project before we can use any of the playback functions. To add this framework, complete the following steps:

1. Right-click the Frameworks icon in Xcode and choose Add Existing.

2. Navigate to Developer/Platforms/iPhoneOS.platform/Developer/SDKs/ iPhoneOS3.0.sdk/System/Library/Frameworks, choose the AudioToolbox.framework, and then click Add.

3. Open the GettingAttentionViewController.h file and import the interface file necessary to access the sound functions (AudioToolbox/AudioToolbox.h). This should fall directly after the existing import line:

```
#import <AudioToolbox/AudioToolbox.h>
```

Creating and Playing System Sounds

With the prep work out of the way, we're ready to add some sounds to our project. The two functions that we'll need to use are AudioServicesCreateSystemSoundID and AudioServicesPlaySystemSound. We'll also need to declare a variable of the type SystemSoundID. This will represent the sound file that we are working with.

Edit GettingAttentionViewController.m and add the following implementation for the doSound method:

```
 1: -(IBAction)doSound:(id)sender {
 2:     SystemSoundID soundID;
 3:     NSString *soundFile = [[NSBundle mainBundle]
 4:                             pathForResource:@"soundeffect" ofType:@"wav"];
 5:
 6:     AudioServicesCreateSystemSoundID((CFURLRef)
 7:                             [NSURL fileURLWithPath:soundFile]
 8:                             , &soundID);
 9:     AudioServicesPlaySystemSound(soundID);
10: }
```

The code to play a system sound might look a bit alien after all the Objective-C we've been using. Let's take a look at the functional pieces.

Line 2 starts things off by declaring a variable, soundID, that we will use to refer to the sound file. (Note that this is *not* declared as a pointer, as pointers begin with a *!) Next, in line 3, we declare and assign a string (soundFile) to the path of the sound file "soundeffect.wav." This works by first using the NSBundle class method mainBundle to return an NSBundle object that corresponds to the directory containing the current application's executable binary. The NSBundle object's pathForResource:ofType: method is then used to identify the specific sound file by name and extension.

Once a path has been identified for the sound file, we must use the
`AudioServicesCreateSystemSoundID` function to create a `SystemSoundID` that will
represent this file for the functions that will actually play the sound. This function
takes two parameters: a `CFURLRef` object that points to the location of the file, and a
pointer to the `SystemSoundID` variable that we want to be set. For the first parameter, we use the `NSURL fileURLWithPath` class method to return an `NSURL` object from
the sound file path. We preface this with `(CFURLRef)` to cast the `NSURL` object to the
`CFURLRef` type expected by the system. The second parameter is satisfied by passing
`&soundID` to the function.

By the Way

> Recall that `&<variable>` returns a reference (pointer) to the named variable. This
> is rarely needed when working with the Objective-C classes, because nearly every-
> thing is already a pointer!

After `soundID` has been properly set up, all that remains is playing it. Pass the
`soundID` variable to the `AudioServicesPlaySystemSound` function, as shown in line
9, and we're in business.

Build and test the application. Pressing the "Play Sound" button should now playback the sound effect WAV file.

Playing Alert Sounds and Vibrations

The difference between an *"alert sound"* and a *"system sound"* is that an alert sound,
if muted, automatically triggers a phone vibration. The setup and use of an alert
sound is identical to a system sound. In fact, to implement the `doAlertSound`
method stub in GettingAttentionViewController.m, use the same code as the previous doSound method, substituting the sound file "alertsound.wav" and using the
function `AudioServicesPlayAlertSound` rather than
`AudioServicesPlaySystemSound`:

```
AudioServicesPlayAlertSound(soundID);
```

After implementing the new method, build and test the application. Pressing the
"Play Alert Sound" button will play the sound, and muting the phone will cause the
phone to vibrate when the button is pressed.

Vibrating the iPhone

For our grand finale, we'll implement the final method in our GettingAttention
application: `doVibration`. As you've already learned, the same System Sound
Services that enabled us to play sounds and alert sounds will also create vibrations.

The magic we need here is the kSystemSoundID_Vibrate constant. When this value is substituted for the SystemSoundID and AudioServicesPlaySystemSound is called, the phone vibrates. It's as simple as that! Implement the doVibration method as follows:

```
-(IBAction)doVibration:(id)sender {
    AudioServicesPlaySystemSound (kSystemSoundID_Vibrate);
}
```

That's all there is to it. You've now explored five different ways of getting a user's attention. These are techniques that you can use in any application to make sure that your user is aware of changes and can respond if needed.

Summary

In this hour, you learned about two types of modal dialogs that can be used to communicate information to an application user, as well as enable users to provide input at critical points in time. Alerts and action sheets have different appearances and uses, but very similar implementations. Unlike many of the UI components we've used in this book, these cannot be instantiated with a simple drag-n-drop in Interface Builder.

We also explored two nonvisual means of communicating with a user: sounds and vibrations. Using the System Sound Services (by way of the AudioToolbox framework), you can easily add short sound effects and vibrate the phone. Again, these have to be implemented in code, but in less than five lines, you can have your applications making noises and buzzing in your users' hands.

Q&A

Q: *Why aren't action sheets and alert views interchangeable?*

A: Technically, unless you're providing a large number of options to the user, you could use them interchangeably, but you'd be giving the user the wrong cues. Unlike alerts, action sheets animate and appear as part of the current view. The interface is trying to convey that the available actions are related to what is being displayed on the screen. An alert is not necessarily related to anything else on the display.

Q: *Can sounds be used in conjunction with alert views?*

A: Yes. Because alerts are frequently displayed without warning, there is no guarantee that the user is looking at the screen. Using an alert sound provides the best chance for getting the user's attention, either through an audible noise or an automatic vibration if the user's sound is muted.

Workshop

Quiz

1. Alert views are tied to a specific view. True or false?

2. Under iPhone OS 3.x, what happens when an action sheet exceeds the number of buttons that can be visible on the screen?

3. Vibrating the iPhone requires extensive and complicated coding. True or false?

4. System Sound Services supports playing back a wide variety of sound file formats, including MP3s. True or false?

Answers

1. False. Alert views are displayed outside the context of a view and are not tied to any other UI element.

2. The buttons are rendered using a table view. Users can scroll through pages of button options rather than being confined to a single screen.

3. False. Once the AudioToolbox Framework is loaded, a single function call is all it takes to give a phone the shakes.

4. False. System Sound Services supports only AIF, WAV, and CAF formats.

Activities

1. Rewrite either the alert view or action sheet handler to determine button presses using the button index values rather than the titles. This will help you prepare for projects where buttons may be generated and added to the view/sheet dynamically rather than during initialization.

2. Return to one or more of your earlier projects and add audio cues to the interface actions. Make switches click, buttons bing, and so on. Keep your sounds short, clear, and complementary to the actions that the users are performing.

Further Exploration

Your next step in making use of the notification methods discussed in this hour is to use them. Simple, but important, UI elements will help facilitate many of your critical user interactions. One topic that we didn't cover here was the ability for a developer to push notifications to the iPhone. Push notifications can display an alert, an application badge, or play a sound when a remote event occurs. This is discussed in Hour 21, "Interacting with Other Applications."

Even without push notifications, you might want to add numeric badges to your applications. These badges are visible when the application isn't running and can display any integer you'd like—most frequently, a count of items identified as "new" within the application (such as new news items, messages, events, and so on). To create application badges, look at the UIApplication class property applicationIconBadgeNumber. Setting this property to anything other than zero will create and display the badge.

Another area that you might like to explore is how to work with rich media (Hour 20). The audio playback functions discussed in this hour are intended for alert-type sounds only. If you're looking for more complete multimedia features, you'll need to tap into the AVFoundation framework, which gives you complete control over recording and playback features of the iPhone.

HOUR 12

Creating Simple Multiview Applications with Toolbars

What You'll Learn in This Hour:

▶ Why applications use multiple views and view controllers
▶ How to create a multiview application from scratch
▶ The role of toolbars in the iPhone UI
▶ Ways to customize the appearance of toolbar buttons

The iPhone SDK gives us plenty of capabilities for creating amazing applications with user interfaces that rival (and frequently surpass) desktop counterparts. What the iPhone lacks, however, are the multiple windows that traditional applications take advantage of. Instead of making everything visible onscreen in a window or tool palette, iPhone applications must be very conservative about what they display—showing only the tools needed at a given point in time. To that end, your applications may require multiple views and view controllers. Each view can contain its own information and interface, and, with a bit of programming, you can enable the user to easily switch between each view. This chapter explains the use of multiple views and introduces two new UI elements: toolbars and toolbar buttons.

Exploring Single Versus Multiview Applications

Cell phone applications were originally conceived as simple "calculator-like" widgets that enabled users to perform very limited tasks. Tip calculators and movie theater listings (just the times!) were the extent of the "world of information" that was at your fingertips. The lack of screen real estate, poor processing capability, and limited APIs prevented developers from writing applications that were more than simple novelties.

In the previous hours, the application frameworks that we've built have followed much the same approach as early mobile apps: present a screen with some controls, accept input, and produce output. These single-view applications use one view and one view controller. The controller may hide or show elements within the interface, but the majority of user interaction has been confined to the visible screen area. This is perfectly fine if that's all your application needs to do, but when Apple introduced the iPhone, they also introduced several new interface elements that made it possible for complex applications to be presented in a small space.

The iPhone gives developers the opportunity to segment their applications into multiple different views and view controllers. This keeps the UI clean and not overloaded and helps prevent the creation of "God classes" that attempt to perform every action under the sun. In our past examples, we've dealt with one view and one controller. By introducing multiple view controllers, we can create the mobile equivalent of a multiwindow desktop application. Information can be organized into logical groupings, and the user can easily switch between them.

In this hour, we explore multiview applications with "parallel" views. This means that the content of one view isn't directly dependent on another—there isn't any set order in which they should be displayed. In Hour 14, "Displaying and Navigating Data Using Table Views," we'll examine navigation view controllers, which present multiple views of related data arranged hierarchically.

Additional functionality usually implies additional complexity, and this isn't an exception. You've become accustomed to all of your coding being in a single class; this will change when building multiview applications. There won't be any real surprises in the code itself, but you'll need to start thinking a bit more about the application architecture and begin taking into consideration the additional outlets and connections you'll need to build if your view controllers need to communicate between one another.

Creating a Multiview Application

The project that we'll be building in this hour's lesson will create and manage multiple views from scratch. This will serve as an exercise to familiarize you with an approach to dealing with multiple views and introduce you to some new methods and properties, as well as the toolbar and toolbar button interface elements.

Implementation Overview

Much as a single-view application uses a view controller to direct the interactions of its interface elements, a multiview application needs a controller to help it switch between different views. In this implementation, we'll be creating a typical View-Based Application, but will be using the default view controller (UIViewController) to swap in and out three additional views, each with its own controller. The default controller will need to implement methods for clearing the current view and loading any of the other views (in any order, at any time).

In addition, our default view will be setting up a toolbar (UIToolbar). This interface element has a simple purpose: to provide quick access to common application functions via a row of buttons at the bottom of the screen. For switching between views, our toolbar will resemble Figure 12.1.

FIGURE 12.1
Toolbars provide quick access to common functions.

One interesting challenge that we'll need to overcome with this implementation is that while our main view will include the toolbar, it must be visible in all the other views, too. We'll need to display the views "under" the toolbar so that it isn't hidden as new views are shown or removed.

Setting Up the Project

To begin, start Xcode and create a new application called **MultipleViews** using the View-Based Application template. The layout of this template should be getting very familiar by now. The MainWindow.xib includes a view controller that loads its view from a second XIB file, MultipleViewsViewController.xib. This XIB file will hold the toolbar that serves as our interface for switching between views, as well as instances of three new view controllers that will ultimately manage three new views.

Adding Views and View Controllers

Each of the views that we will be switching between needs its own view controller and XIB file. Create three new UIViewController subclasses (File, New File, UIViewController subclass) named

> FirstViewController
>
> SecondViewController
>
> ThirdViewController

Be sure to check the "With XIB for User Interface" check box on the naming screen for each of the new classes that you create. When you've created the files, your Xcode Classes and Resources folders should resemble Figure 12.2.

FIGURE 12.2
Our first multi-view application will use a total of four views and view controllers.

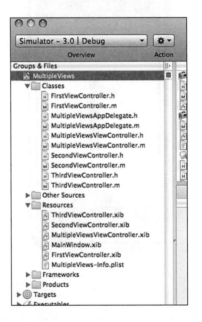

The goal of this project is to create a simple application that switches between independently controlled views. It is certainly possible that each of the views could share a view controller, but structurally it is a good practice to use separate controllers for views that do not serve the same function.

Prepping the View Content

To make sure that we know (visually) which view is which, open each of the three XIB files that correspond to the view controller classes in Interface Builder. For each view, drag a text label (UILabel) from the library (Tools, Library) into the view. Change the text of the label to **1** in FirstViewController.xib, **2** in SecondViewController.xib, and **3** in the ThirdViewController.xib file. In the sample files, for this project, we've also set the font size to 288 points for each label by using the Attribute Inspector (Command+1), as shown in Figure 12.3.

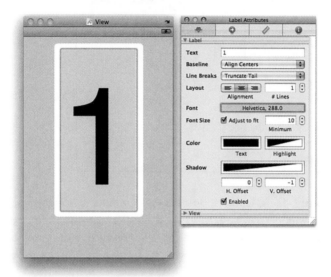

FIGURE 12.3
Add labels to each view so they can be easily identified.

Remember that we're going to be overlaying a toolbar on each of these views, so you don't have the entire screen real estate to work with. Although we can't see the toolbar just yet, we can simulate it for the purposes of laying out the view. To add a simulated toolbar to the view, select the view itself within the Interface Builder document window, and then press Command+1 to open the View Attributes Inspector. Choose Toolbar from the Bottom Bar Simulated User Interface Elements pop-up menu, demonstrated in Figure 12.4.

Instantiating the View Controllers

Your project should now contain content for each of the views and all of the view controller classes it needs to function. The classes, however, still need to be instantiated so that we have actual view controllers and view objects to use in the application.

Open the MultipleViewsViewController.xib in Interface Builder. This file contains the parent view that we will be using for the toolbar interface element, and it is also a logical place to add our other view controller instances.

FIGURE 12.4
Adding a simulated toolbar to the view can help with layout because the actual toolbar isn't visible.

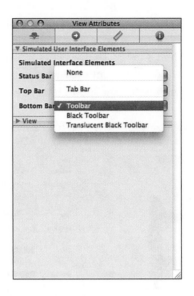

Using the library (Tools, Library), drag a view controller (UIViewController) into the document window. We want this view controller to be an instance of our FirstViewController class. With the controller selected, press Command+4 to open the Identity Inspector. Use the drop-down menu to choose FirstViewController (see Figure 12.5).

FIGURE 12.5
Update the view controllers to point to the classes you created earlier.

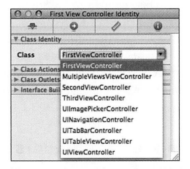

Next, the view controller must be updated to point to the correct XIB file (FileViewController.xib) for its view. Select the controller in the document window and press Command+1 to open the Attributes Inspector. Within the NIB Name drop-down menu, choose FirstViewController (see Figure 12.6).

Repeat these steps for the SecondViewController and ThirdViewController classes. (That is, a new view controller instance, set the class, and associate the view.) When finished, your MultipleViewsViewController.xib should look very similar to Figure 12.7.

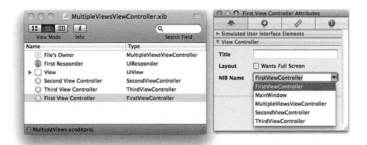

FIGURE 12.6
Associate every view controller with the appropriate XIB file.

FIGURE 12.7
Add three view controller instances to the XIB file.

With these changes, our project will build and instantiate the controllers, but there is still no way of displaying the different views. It's time to add the toolbar controls and code to make that happen!

Using a Toolbar to Switch Views

Toolbars (UIToolbar) are, comparatively speaking, one of the simpler user interface elements that you have at your disposal. A toolbar is implemented as a solid bar, usually at the bottom of the display, with buttons (UIBarButtonItem) that correspond to actions that can be performed in the current view. The buttons provide a single selector action, which works virtually identically to the typical Touch Up Inside event that you've encountered before.

The MultipleViews application that we're building now requires a single toolbar with buttons for each of the three views that we want to display. The toolbar itself will be added as a subview of the view in the MultipleViewsViewController.xib file.

Adding a Toolbar

If you haven't already, open the MultipleViewsViewController.xib file in Interface Builder. The view contained in this XIB file, as you know from previous View-Based Applications, is what will be added to the application's window when it first launches. Instead of providing all the onscreen content, however, we just want this view and its view controller to manage the toolbar and the user's interactions with it.

Open the view and, using the library objects (Tools, Library), drag an instance of a toolbar (UIToolbar) to the bottom of the view. You should now have an empty view with a single-button toolbar visible (see Figure 12.8).

FIGURE 12.8
Add a toolbar as a subview to the main view.

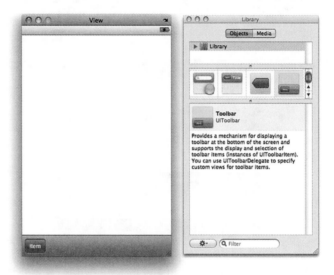

Adding and Editing Toolbar Buttons

The Interface Builder toolbar object includes, by default, a single button. However, we need three buttons for this project.

To add a button to the toolbar, return to the library and drag a bar button item (UIBarButton) to the toolbar. An insertion point will appear where the button will be added. Repeat this process until there are a total of three buttons (one for each view) in the toolbar.

Double-click the button's title to switch to an editable mode. Edit each button title to correspond to one of the views that needs to be displayed (that is, **First View**, **Second View**, **Third View**).

If you have difficulty selecting the buttons directly in the layout view, you may also select them using the document window and edit their titles by accessing the Attributes Inspector (Command+1).

After editing the titles, you may want to resize the buttons to create a uniform appearance in the toolbar. You can use the Size Inspector (Command+3) to adjust the width numerically, or just click and drag the resize handle that appears to the right of the currently selected button.

The end result should resemble Figure 12.9.

FIGURE 12.9
The final toolbar should contain three buttons with appropriate titles.

Bar button items do not have to be text-labeled buttons. Alternatively, you can set an image file to be used as the button representation in the Attributes Inspector.

By the Way

Adding Outlets and Actions

Now that all the interface elements are in place for the MultiViews application, we need to connect them to code. The MultiViewsViewController object will handle the switching of the views, so we need to edit the class to include outlets for each of the view controllers, as well as actions for each of the toolbar buttons, and a new method clearView that we'll use to clear the contents of the view as we switch between them.

Edit MultipleViewsViewController.h to reflect the following changes (in bold):

```
 1: #import <UIKit/UIKit.h>
 2:
 3: @class FirstViewController;
 4: @class SecondViewController;
 5: @class ThirdViewController;
 6:
 7: @interface MultipleViewsViewController : UIViewController {
 8:     IBOutlet FirstViewController *firstViewController;
 9:     IBOutlet SecondViewController *secondViewController;
10:     IBOutlet ThirdViewController *thirdViewController;
11: }
12:
13: @property (retain, nonatomic) FirstViewController *firstViewController;
```

```
14: @property (retain, nonatomic) SecondViewController *secondViewController;
15: @property (retain, nonatomic) ThirdViewController *thirdViewController;
16:
17: -(IBAction) loadSecondView:(id)sender;
18: -(IBAction) loadThirdView:(id)sender;
19: -(IBAction) loadFirstView:(id)sender;
20:
21: -(void) clearView;
22:
23: @end
```

Let's quickly run through what we've done here. Because this class needs to be aware of our other view controller classes, we first declare the view controller classes in lines 3 through 5.

Lines 8 through 10 create outlets for each of our view controller instances (firstViewController, secondViewController, and thirdViewController), because we'll need to access them to switch between views.

In lines 13 through 15, we declare these three instances as properties.

Lines 17 through 19 declare three methods for switching views and expose them as actions for Interface Builder (loadSecondView, loadThirdView, and loadFirstView).

Finally, on line 21, a new method, clearView, is declared. It will be used to remove the old content from our view when we switch to a new view.

Connecting Outlets and Actions

Save the changes you've made to MultiViewsViewController.h, and jump back into the MultiViewsViewController.xib file in Interface Builder. We can now make our final connections before writing the view switching code.

From the document window, Control-drag from the File's Owner icon to the instance of FirstViewController. When prompted for an outlet, choose firstViewController (see Figure 12.10).

FIGURE 12.10
Connect each view controller to its outlet within the MultipleViews ViewController class.

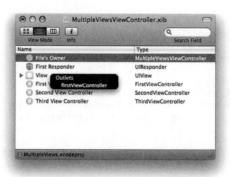

Repeat this process for the secondViewController and thirdViewController instances, choosing the appropriate outlet when prompted.

Next, expand the view and toolbar hierarchy to show the three bar button items that we added earlier. Control-drag from the First View button to the File's Owner icon. When prompted, choose the loadFirstView sent action (see Figure 12.11).

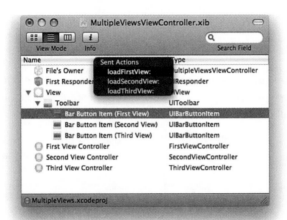

FIGURE 12.11
Connect each bar button item to the appropriate sent action.

Do the same for the two other buttons, connecting the Second View button to loadSecondView, and the third to loadThirdView. The interface connections are now complete and we can finish up the implementation of the view loading methods.

Implementing the View Switch Methods

To implement the view switching, we'll be making use of a UIView instance method called insertSubview:atIndex:. This method inserts a view as a subview of another view—just like creating a hierarchy of views within Interface Builder. By inserting a subview at an index of 0 into the view containing our toolbar, we will effectively "float" the toolbar view on top of the subview.

Begin the implementation by opening MultipleViewsViewController.m in Xcode. Import the headers from the three view controller classes so that we can properly access them in the code:

```
#import "MultipleViewsViewController.h"
#import "FirstViewController.h"
#import "SecondViewController.h"
#import "ThirdViewController.h"
```

Next, after the @implementation directive, use @synthesize to create the getters and setters for the view Controller instances (firstViewController, secondViewController, thirdViewController):

```
@synthesize firstViewController;
@synthesize secondViewController;
@synthesize thirdViewController;
```

Create the method to load the first view, loadFirstView, as follows:

```
-(IBAction) loadFirstView:(id)sender {
        [self.view insertSubview:firstViewController.view atIndex:0];
}
```

This single line of code uses the insertSubview:atIndex method of the MultiViewsViewController's view instance (which contains our toolbar!) to add a subview that will appear below it. That's all there is to it!

Following this pattern, implement the loadSecondView and loadThirdView methods to insert their respective view controller's views as subviews to the toolbar view.

By the Way

> If you're confused why "self.view" is the view containing the toolbar, look at the structure of the project and the XIB files. We're adding the loadView methods to the MultiViewsViewController class, so self refers to the instance of that class. The MultiViewsViewController has a single view with a toolbar that we added earlier, so self.view, within this context, is just a reference to that view.

After you've finished the view loading implementation, don't forget to release the view controllers in the dealloc method:

```
- (void)dealloc {
        [firstViewController release];
        [secondViewController release];
        [thirdViewController release];
    [super dealloc];
}
```

Setting a View When the Application Starts

If you try to run the application now, it should work, but it probably won't do quite what you may expect. When the application first starts, it loads the initial view containing the toolbar, but nothing else. Until a toolbar button is pressed, none of our three content views are visible. A much more user-friendly approach is to automatically load content as soon as the application starts.

To automatically switch to one of the views, we can simply use one of the loadView methods that we just defined.

Editing MultipleViewsViewController.m, implement the `viewDidLoad` method as follows:

```
- (void)viewDidLoad {
    [self loadFirstView:nil];
    [super viewDidLoad];
}
```

By calling the `loadFirstView` method upon successful loading of the view containing the toolbar, we ensure that some initial content is available for users without them first having to press any buttons.

By the Way

> Because `loadFirstView` is defined as requiring a parameter in its implementation, we must pass a parameter when using it here. Since the parameter (sender) is not used in the function, we can safely pass `nil` with no ill effects.

Clearing the Current View

Try building and executing the application again. This time, an initial view should load, but the application still won't perform correctly. You'll likely see sporadic behavior as you try to navigate between views, or the views will overlay on top of one another, creating an onscreen mess. The problem is that while we're adding subviews as the toolbar button is pressed, we're never removing them again! What we need to do to stabilize the application's behavior is to identify and remove the current subview each time the toolbar button is pressed.

When a view is added to another as a subview (its superview), a property called `superview` is set appropriately. In other words, when `firstViewController.view` is added as a subview to our toolbar view, its `superview` property is set to the toolbar view. If a view *hasn't* been added as a subview, the property is `nil`. So, how can this help us? Easily: By testing to see whether the `superview` property is set, we can identify which view has been made active, and then remove it when it's time to switch views. To remove a view from its superview, we can use the `removeFromSuperview` instance method.

Add the following `clearView` method in MultipleViewsViewController.m:

```
-(void) clearView {
    if (firstViewController.view.superview) {
        [firstViewController.view removeFromSuperview];
    } else if (secondViewController.view.superview) {
        [secondViewController.view removeFromSuperview];
    } else {
        [thirdViewController.view removeFromSuperview];
    }
}
```

In this implementation, we test for the existence of the `superview` property in all of the view controller's views, and if we find it, we use `removeFromSuperview` to remove the view.

All that remains is to add `clearView` so that it is called before any view is loaded. A completed version of the `loadFirstView` method becomes

```
-(IBAction) loadFirstView:(id)sender {
    [self clearView];
    [self.view insertSubview:firstViewController.view atIndex:0];
}
```

Make the same change to `loadSecondView` and `loadThirdView`, and then retest your application. It should now cleanly switch between the different views when you touch the toolbar buttons (see Figure 12.12).

FIGURE 12.12
Switch between views using the toolbar buttons.

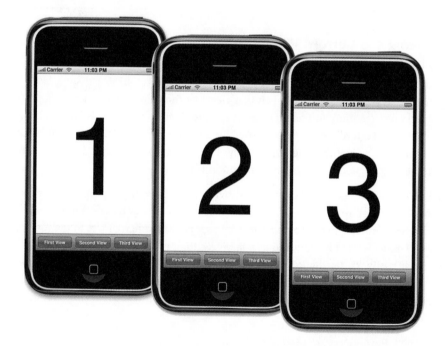

If this seemed overly cumbersome, don't fret. In the Hour 13 project, we'll implement multiple views using an object that gives us a lot of "free" functionality greatly simplifying the process of switching views.

Summary

In this hour, you learned how to create applications that extend beyond a single view and view controller. This will ultimately give you the ability to create a more involved and meaningful user experience. You also made use of the toolbar UI element (UIToolbar) to provide a simple button bar for common user activities within a view.

After being constrained to a single view in the past hours, multiple views should be a very liberating concept. You can start planning applications that span multiple screens and structuring your code accordingly.

Q&A

Q. *Why can't a single view (with appropriate hiding and showing of elements) do the same thing as multiple views?*

A. Technically, you could accomplish the same thing within a single view, but the complexity of maintaining your views, even with the drag-n-drop capabilities of Interface Builder, will quickly become overwhelming in more advanced applications.

Q. *Isn't there an easier way to do this?*

A. In the next hour, you'll learn about two classes that can greatly simplify the implementation of multiview applications. That said, loading and managing views manually can be helpful in applications with complex display requirements. You should now be able to create applications that use multiple views that are active simultaneously. One view could, for example, display changing data, while another handles user input. Just because it isn't easy doesn't mean it isn't worthwhile!

Workshop

Quiz

1. What message can we send to a view to ask it to remove itself from another view?

2. What image should you use in a toolbar for a "rewind" control?

3. What property is represented by the index value when adding a subview to an existing view?

Answers

1. The `removeFromSuperview` method will remove a view from its parent view.

2. Apple provides preset buttons for *many* common application activities. Just add a button bar item (`UIButtonBarItem`) and use the Interface Builder Attributes Inspector to set the identifier.

3. The index represents the "level" of the view in relation to other subviews. In other words, it determines whether or not the view falls in front of, or behind, other subviews.

Activities

1. Using the project that you created in this hour's tutorial as a starting point, update the views to provide functionality beyond simply displaying a label. You'll need to add actions and outlets to the proper view controllers for each view.

2. Consider a situation where input in one view needs to be used in another. How would you accomplish this? Try working with the views to enable data sharing between them. (Hint: we'll do this in the next hour's lesson, so don't spend too much time on it!)

Further Exploration

By now, you should have a good idea of how to implement multiple views and switch between them manually. There was quite a bit of information covered in this past hour, so I recommend reviewing the topics that we covered and spending some time in the Apple documentation reviewing the classes, the properties, and their methods. Inspecting the UI elements in Interface Builder will give you additional insight into how they can be integrated into your apps.

The toolbar (`UIToolbar`), for example, can be customized with image-based buttons rather than the round rectangles we used in the example. Apple provides a wide range of standard toolbar images/buttons covering everything from audio/video playback controls to a camera button for starting the built-in camera. If you have a set of actions that the user should be able to choose from within a view, implementing these with a toolbar will keep your screen free from clutter, and provide a convenient UI anchor that can be updated from view to view, or used across multiple views (as demonstrated in the example).

Apple Developer Tutorials:

Toolbars – AccelerometerGraph (accessible via the Xcode developer documentation). A simple example that uses a toolbar to choose between multiple functions within an application.

HOUR 13

Using Tab Bars to Manage Multiview Interfaces

What You'll Learn in This Hour:

▶ The purpose of tab bars and tab bar controllers
▶ How to add tab bars to your applications
▶ Configuration of graphical tab bar buttons
▶ Methods of enabling "inter-view" communication

One of the nice things about the iPhone is the level of functionality that you can get from some of the SDK classes without writing code yourself. As you've learned, implementing a multiview application requires quite a few steps—inserting subviews, clearing the contents of views, and dealing with other "overhead" activities. Wouldn't it be great if this is something we could have handled for us? With tab bars and tab bar controllers, it can be! In this hour, we'll learn how implementing multiview applications can be (almost) as easy as drag-n-drop.

Tab Bars and Tab Bar Controllers

Let's great straight to the point. It's important to know how to swap views and manually manage multiple views, but it's not something you should do if you can make use of existing code that does it for you.

Frequently, a more expeditious approach is to use a tab bar (UITabBar) and tab bar controller (UITabBarController). Tab bars provide a touchable graphical button bar where the user's options are represented by icons. The tab bar controller, on the other hand, makes sure that when one of the tab bar buttons is pressed, a view is swapped in and becomes active. This powerful combination handles the view switching process almost entirely on its own. You supply the views, define the interface, and it makes the magic. This frees you up to focus on application functionality, rather than interface details.

Tab bars are similar in appearance to toolbars, but are intended solely for working with multiple views rather than executing arbitrary commands. Figure 13.1 shows an example of the tab bar controller-based application you'll be building.

Building a Multiview Tab Bar Application

To get accustomed to using tab bars and tab bar controllers, we'll be creating an application for calculating areas and volumes. It will also provide a Summary view to show how many times the user has performed a calculation. This will help you understand how views, which are implemented largely independently, might exchange data.

Implementation Overview

This project will require you to create an instance of a tab bar and tab bar controller and, within that, instances of each of the three view controllers that we will be using for the calculations. You'll also add icons to the tab bar, giving it a professionally designed appearance. The views themselves will be in separate XIB files and will include a number of inputs and outputs. Figure 13.1 shows the sample application with tab bar that we'll be implementing in this example.

Setting Up the Project

As your applications become more complex, you'll want to start using more meaningful names for the classes and XIB files that you use in your projects. In this example, we're going to be implementing a tab bar controller, but we're *not* going to be using Apple's default tab bar template.

Apple's tab bar project template creates a two-view button bar with a view controller class called `FirstViewController`. The first view is contained in the MainWindow.xib and the second in SecondView.xib. The MainView.xib also contains view controller instances for both views.

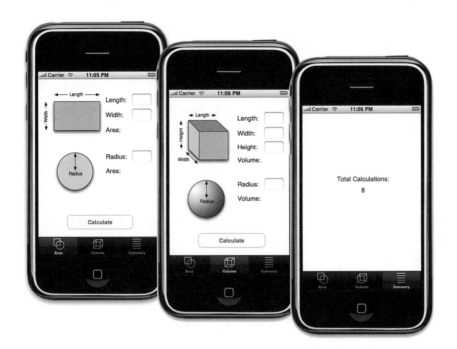

This, frankly, doesn't make much sense. If you're going to separate your content views into multiple XIB files, it should be consistent. This template gives us a tab bar implementation that is scattered and difficult to use. Instead, we're going to start from scratch with a simple Window-Based Application template.

Begin by creating a new project and choosing the Window-Based Application template. Name the project **TabbedConversion**.

Adding Additional View Controllers and Views

Our new application will provide three views, each corresponding to a different functional area: calculating area, calculating volume, and displaying a calculation summary. We'll name our view controller classes and corresponding XIB files based on the functions:

AreaViewController/AreaView.xib

VolumeViewController/VolumeView.xib

SummaryViewController/SummaryView.xib

Add the three new view controller classes (`UIViewController`) to the project; make sure that you've chosen to also add the XIB files for the new controllers.

Rename the newly created XIB files that will contain the view layouts to **AreaView**, **VolumeView**, and **SummaryView**. This will finish our initial setup for the view controller classes and XIBs, but we still need a tab bar controller object and instances of the three view controllers that will be managed by the tab bar.

Preparing the Application Delegate for the Tab Bar Controller

Open the TabbedConversionAppDelegate.h header in Xcode. Within the @interface directive, include an instance variable (tabBarController) and outlet for a tab bar controller (UITabBarController), as well as a declaration that we will conform to the UITabBarControllerDelegate protocol. (All the methods in this protocol are optional, meaning that we can have a fully functional tab bar without doing any additional coding!) Finally, declare tabBarController as a property. The final header should resemble this:

```
#import <UIKit/UIKit.h>

@interface TabbedConversionAppDelegate : NSObject
            <UIApplicationDelegate, UITabBarControllerDelegate> {
    UIWindow *window;
    IBOutlet UITabBarController *tabBarController;
}

@property (nonatomic, retain) IBOutlet UIWindow *window;
@property (nonatomic, retain) IBOutlet UITabBarController *tabBarController;

@end
```

Next, open TabbedConversionAppDelegate.m, and add the @synthesize directive for tabBarController to prepare our getters/setters for the property.

```
@synthesize tabBarController;
```

Update the applicationDidFinishLaunching method to add the view of the tabBarViewController instance to the window:

```
- (void)applicationDidFinishLaunching:(UIApplication *)application {
    [window addSubview:tabBarController.view];
}
```

Finally, make sure the tab bar controller is released in the dealloc method:

```
- (void)dealloc {
    [tabBarController release];
    [window release];
    [super dealloc];
}
```

This completes all the code additions that we need to make a tab bar controller function and switch views! Our next step is to instantiate an instance of the controller in the MainWindow.xib file along with the view controllers it will manage.

Adding a Tab Bar Controller

Open the MainWindow.xib file in Interface Builder. Because we started with a Window-Based Application, the file should be looking a bit sparse. We can fix that pretty quickly! Open the Library (Tools, Library) and drag a tab bar controller (UITabBarController) into the document window.

Before doing anything else, Control-drag from the Tabbed Conversion App Delegate icon to the new tab bar controller. Connect the controller instance to the tabBarController outlet (see Figure 13.2).

FIGURE 13.2
Connect the controller to its outlet.

Now, double-click the tab bar controller in the document window to preview what we're creating, and then expand the controller and the objects it contains. As you can see in Figure 13.4, Apple provides us with an initial setup for the tab bar controller. Nested in the controller is the tab bar itself (UITabBar), within which are two view controllers (UIViewController) and, within them, are tab bar items (UITabBarItem). In our project, we need a total of three view controllers: one for the area calculator, another for the volume calculations, and a third for a simple summary. In other words, the default controller is one view short from the three we need.

Adding New View Controllers and Tab Bar Items

There are two ways we can add a new view controller to the tab bar controller. We could drag a new view controller into the tab bar instance—this automatically creates the nested tab bar item—or we can use the Attributes Inspector for the tab bar controller object. The Attributes Inspector is my preferred approach, so that's what we'll use here. Select the Tab Bar Controller icon in the document window, and then press Command+1 to open the Attributes Inspector.

The inspector shows the different view controllers that are controlled by the tab bar, along with the titles of the individual tab bar items. To add a new controller (paired with a tab bar item), click the plus icon below the View Controllers list. This will create the third view controller instance that we need for the project. Now double-click the titles of each of the three view controllers and name them **Area**, **Volume**, and **Summary**, as seen in Figure 13.3.

FIGURE 13.3
You can add additional view controller instances along with tab bar items in the Attributes Inspector.

Adding Tab Bar Item Images

Looking at the preview of the tab bar, you can tell that something is missing: images. Each tab bar item can have an image that is displayed along with a title. The images are 32x32 pixels or smaller, and are automatically styled by the iPhone to appear in a monochromatic color scheme (regardless of what you choose). Simple line drawings turn out the best when creating your interface art.

For this project, there are three tab bar images included in the project's Images folder: Area.png, Volume.png, and Summary.png. Open Xcode and drag these files to the Resources folder for your project.

Switching back to Interface Builder and MainWindow.xib, use the document window to drill down to the individual tab bar items. Select the first item, titled Area, and open the Attributes Inspector (Command+1). Use the Image drop-down to choose Area.png (see Figure 13.4).

Repeat this step for the last two tab bar items, setting their images to Volume.png and Summary.png. As the images are set, the preview should update to show the new interface. If all is going according to plan, your display should resemble Figure 13.5.

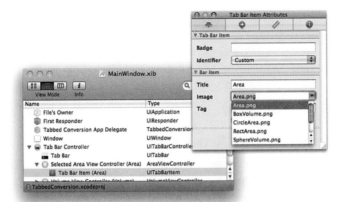

FIGURE 13.4
Update each tab bar item with the appropriate image resource.

FIGURE 13.5
Your finished tab bar should have three buttons, complete with images.

> Within the Tab Bar Item Attributes Inspector, there is an Identifier drop-down menu. This menu can be used to configure the tab bar item to one of several different standard types, such as "favorites" or "history." This will automatically set the title and a default image for the item.

Did you Know?

Configuring the View Controller Classes

The next step, before we start coding, is to set the view controller instances we've added to the tab bar controller so that they point to the AreaViewController, VolumeViewController, and SummaryViewController classes and their related views (AreaView, VolumeView, and SummaryView).

Select the first view controller icon in the MainWindow.xib (it should contain the Area tab bar item). Open the Identity Inspector (Command+4) and use the Class drop-down to choose AreaViewController. Without closing the inspector, switch to the attributes view (Command+1) and use the NIB Name drop-down to select the AreaView XIB. Set the view controller classes and NIBs for the other two view controller instances in the project.

Implementing the Area View

Although we haven't really written any code specific to switching views or managing view controllers, the TabbedConversion application can be built and executed and will happily switch views using the tab bar. No need for inserting subviews or clearing views. It just works!

We can now work with our view controller classes just as we would in any other application. The tab bar controller instance will take care of swapping the views when needed. We'll start with the area calculation view.

Adding Outlets and Actions

In the Area view, the application will calculate the area of a rectangle given the length and width, and the area of a circle, given the radius. We'll need UITextFields for each of these values, and two UILabel instances for the calculation results.

The view controller will need to access the instance of the SummaryViewController to increment a count of the calculations performed. It will provide calculate and hideKeyboard methods to perform the calculation and hide the input keyboard when the background is tapped, respectively. All told, we'll need six outlets and two actions. These are the naming conventions we've used in the sample project:

- ▶ rectWidth (UITextField): Field for entering the width of a rectangle

- ▶ rectLength (UITextField): Field for entering the length of a rectangle

- ▶ circleRadius (UITextField): Field for entering the radius of a circle

- ▶ rectResult (UILabel): The calculated area of the rectangle

- ▶ circleResult (UILabel): The calculated area of the circle

- ▶ summaryViewController (SummaryViewController): The instance of the Summary view

- ▶ calculate (method): Performs the area calculation

- ▶ hideKeyboard (method): Hides the onscreen keyboard

Got all that? Good! Within Xcode, open the AreaViewController.h header file and edit the contents to read as follows:

```
 1: #import <UIKit/UIKit.h>
 2: #import "SummaryViewController.h"
 3:
 4: @interface AreaViewController : UIViewController {
 5:     IBOutlet UITextField *rectWidth;
 6:     IBOutlet UITextField *rectLength;
 7:     IBOutlet UITextField *circleRadius;
 8:     IBOutlet UILabel *rectResult;
 9:     IBOutlet UILabel *circleResult;
10:     IBOutlet SummaryViewController *summaryViewController;
11: }
12:
13: @property (retain, nonatomic) UITextField *rectWidth;
14: @property (retain, nonatomic) UITextField *rectLength;
15: @property (retain, nonatomic) UITextField *circleRadius;
16: @property (retain, nonatomic) UILabel *rectResult;
17: @property (retain, nonatomic) UILabel *circleResult;
18:
19: -(IBAction)calculate:(id)sender;
20: -(IBAction)hideKeyboard:(id)sender;
21:
22: @end
```

We'll need to access a method within the `SummaryViewController` instance. So, in line 2, we import the header for the summary class. Lines 5 through 10 declare the outlets for the fields, labels, and Summary view controller. Lines 13 through 17 then declare these as properties. Finally, lines 19 and 20 declare two actions that we'll be triggering based on touch-up events in the interface.

Creating the View

Based solely on the code, you should be able to get a pretty good sense for what the view is going to look like. Figure 13.6 shows the finished view of our sample project.

Notice that we've included two images (`UIImageView`) in sample application view. These serve as cues for users so that they understand what is meant by length, width, radius, and so on (hey, you never know!). If you want to add these to your version of the application, drag the CircleArea.png and RectArea.png files to your Xcode Resources folder. You can also add the SphereVolume.png and BoxVolume.png images, which are used in the Volume view.

To create the view, open AreaView.xib, and begin by dragging three instances of `UITextField` to the view. Two should be grouped together for the length and width entry for a rectangle, the third will be for the radius. After you've added the fields to the view, select each and open the Attributes Inspector (Command+1). Set the text field traits so that the keyboard is set to a number pad (see Figure 13.7).

FIGURE 13.6
Create inputs,
outputs, and a
calculate but-
ton!

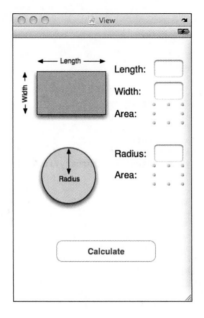

FIGURE 13.7
Because we
only need
numeric input,
set the key-
board to be a
number pad.

Drag instances of UILabel to the view and use them to label each of the fields.

The results of the area calculations need to be displayed near the entry fields, so add two additional UILabel instances to the view (one located near the fields for the rectangle, the other near the radius field). Double-click to edit and clear their contents, or set them to zero as the default. Use two more UILabels to create Area labels.

If you'd like to add the images to the view, add two image views from the library, positioning one beside the rectangle fields, the other beside the radius fields. Open the Attributes Inspector (Command+1) for each image view, and choose the RectArea.png or CircleArea.png images, as shown in Figure 13.8.

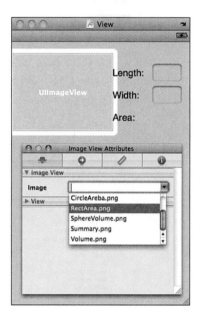

FIGURE 13.8
Add images to the interface to help the user understand the calculation taking place.

To finish the view, we need two buttons. Add the first button to the bottom of the view and title it **Calculate**. The second button will trap background touches and trigger the hideKeyboard method. Add a button that spans the entire background. Use the Layout menu to send it to the back, or drag its icon in the Interface Builder document window so that it falls at the top of the View hierarchy. Open the Attributes Inspector (Command+1) for the button, and choose Custom for the button type to make the button invisible (see Figure 13.9).

For a quick refresher on how we're going about hiding the keyboard, refer to Hour 7, "Working with Text, Keyboards, and Buttons."

FIGURE 13.9
Set a custom button type for the large background button.

When you're finished with the view layout, you'll have quite a few objects in the hierarchy. If you expand the document window, it should resemble what we've created in Figure 13.10.

FIGURE 13.10
There are quite a few objects in the view.

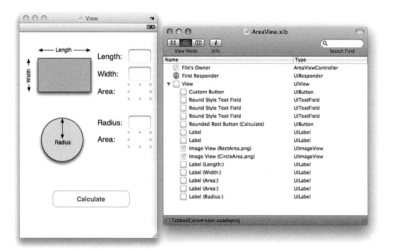

Connecting Outlets and Actions

After creating an appropriate user interface for the Area view, connect the objects to the instance variables that we defined earlier. Control-drag from the File's Owner icon to each of the three UITextField instances. When prompted, create the connection from the field to the correct variable.

Assign rectResult and circleResult by Control-dragging from the File's Owner icon to the two UILabels that will hold the results for the area calculations.

For the two buttons, Control-drag from the button to the File's Owner icon. Set calculate as the event for the calculate button, and hideKeyboard for the custom background button.

Implementing the Area Calculation Logic

We have our inputs, our outputs, and a trigger for the calculate method. Let's tie them together to finish up the Area view. Switch back to Xcode and edit the AreaViewController.m file.

Although it isn't quite necessary for a project this size, defining constants for commonly used values can be helpful in creating readable code. With this in mind, define a constant, Pi, near the top of the file. We'll use this in the calculation of the circle's area:

```
#define Pi 3.1415926
```

Next, after the @implementation directive, synthesize the getters/setters for all the properties defined in the header file:

```
@synthesize rectWidth;
@synthesize rectLength;
@synthesize rectResult;
@synthesize circleRadius;
@synthesize circleResult;
```

Now for the real work; implementing the calculate method. Add the following method definition to the class:

```
 1: -(IBAction)calculate:(id)sender {
 2:     float floatRectResult=[rectWidth.text floatValue]*
 3:             [rectLength.text floatValue];
 4:     float floatCircleResult=[circleRadius.text floatValue]*
 5:             [circleRadius.text floatValue]*Pi;
 6:     NSString *stringRectResult=[[NSString alloc]
 7:                             initWithFormat:@"%1.2f",floatRectResult];
 8:     NSString *stringCircleResult=[[NSString alloc]
 9:                             initWithFormat:@"%1.2f",floatCircleResult];
10:     rectResult.text=stringRectResult;
11:     circleResult.text=stringCircleResult;
12:     [stringRectResult release];
13:     [stringCircleResult release];
14:
15:     [summaryViewController updateTotal];
16: }
```

We're working with the assumption that you're comfortable with the equations for calculating the area of a rectangle (l*w) and a circle ($Pi*r^2$), but there are a few pieces of the code that might be unfamiliar. Lines 2–3 and 4–5 calculate the area for the rectangle and circle, respectively, and store the results in two new floating-point variables (floatRectResult, floatCircleResult). The calculations take advantage of the NSString class method floatValue to provide a floating-point number from the user's input.

By the Way

The `floatValue` method will return 0.0 if the user types in gibberish. This means we'll always have a valid calculation to perform, even if the user entered bad information.

Lines 6–7 and 8–9 allocate and initialize two strings to hold the formatted results. Using `initWithFormat` and the format `"%1.2f"` to create the strings, we ensure that there will always be at least one digit before the decimal, and two decimal places in the result.

Lines 10–13 set the results within the view, and then release the temporary strings. The last step, in line 15, uses an instance method of the `SummaryViewController`, `updateTotal`, to update the total number of calculations performed. Defining this method will be one of the last things we do this hour.

All in all, the calculation logic isn't difficult to understand. The only pieces missing are the implementation of `hideKeyboard` and releasing our objects in `dealloc`. Go ahead and define `hideKeyboard` as follows:

```
-(IBAction)hideKeyboard:(id)sender {
    [rectWidth resignFirstResponder];
    [rectLength resignFirstResponder];
    [circleRadius resignFirstResponder];
}
```

Wrap up the implementation of the Area view controller by editing `dealloc` to release the objects we used:

```
- (void)dealloc {
    [rectWidth release];
    [rectLength release];
    [circleRadius release];
    [rectResult release];
    [circleResult release];
    [super dealloc];
}
```

`AreaViewController` and `AreaView` are complete. Building the Volume view and view controller will follow a very similar process, so we'll move quickly through the next section.

Implementing the Volume View

In the Volume view, the application will accept input for the dimensions of a box (length, width, height) and a sphere (radius), and calculate the volume of the object based on these values. The interface elements will be largely identical to the Area view, but will require an additional field (height) for the box calculation. Begin the implementation by editing the `VolumeViewController` header.

Adding Outlets and Actions

With the exception of some terminology changes required by our switch from 2D to 3D, the outlets and actions that will be required in the Volume view should be very familiar:

▶ boxWidth (UITextField): Field for entering the width of a box

▶ boxLength (UITextField): Field for entering the length of a box

▶ boxHeight (UITextField): Field for entering the height of a box

▶ sphereRadius (UITextField): Field for entering the radius of a sphere

▶ boxResult (UILabel): The calculated area of the rectangle

▶ sphereResult (UILabel): The calculated area of the circle

▶ summaryViewController (SummaryViewController): The instance of the Summary view

▶ calculate (method): Performs the area calculation

▶ hideKeyboard (method): Hides the onscreen keyboard

Edit the VolumeViewController.h file to include the necessary outlets and actions for the view. When finished, your code should contain the following:

```
 1: #import <UIKit/UIKit.h>
 2: #import "SummaryViewController.h"
 3:
 4: @interface VolumeViewController : UIViewController {
 5:     IBOutlet UITextField *boxWidth;
 6:     IBOutlet UITextField *boxHeight;
 7:     IBOutlet UITextField *boxLength;
 8:     IBOutlet UITextField *sphereRadius;
 9:     IBOutlet UILabel *boxResult;
10:     IBOutlet UILabel *sphereResult;
11:     IBOutlet SummaryViewController *summaryViewController;
12: }
13:
14: @property (retain, nonatomic) UITextField *boxWidth;
15: @property (retain, nonatomic) UITextField *boxHeight;
16: @property (retain, nonatomic) UITextField *boxLength;
17: @property (retain, nonatomic) UITextField *sphereRadius;
18: @property (retain, nonatomic) UILabel *boxResult;
19: @property (retain, nonatomic) UILabel *sphereResult;
20:
21: -(IBAction)calculate:(id)sender;
22: -(IBAction)hideKeyboard:(id)sender;
23:
24: @end
```

Because of the similarity to the Area view, we won't go into detail on the individual lines. Let's move on to the Volume view itself.

Creating the View

Like the layout of the Area view, the Volume view will collect data, provide the user with a calculate button, and of course, display the results. Figure 13.11 shows our finished version of the view.

FIGURE 13.11
Once again, col-
lect data, calcu-
late, and pro-
vide the results!

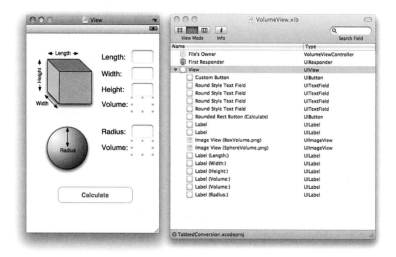

**By the
Way**

The Volume view includes images to help users identify the values that they will need to enter. If you didn't drag the SphereVolume.png and BoxVolume.png images to your Xcode resources when building the Area view, this would be a good time to add them!

Open VolumeView.xib in Interface Builder and drag four text fields to the view. For the volume calculations, three fields should be grouped for length, width, and height of the box. A single field is all that is required for the sphere. Be sure to set the field attributes so that the keyboard displayed is a number pad. Add labels to the view to identify each of the fields for the user.

Position two additional UILabel instances below the box/sphere input fields; these will be used for the output of the calculations. Be sure to clear the default contents of these labels, or set them to 0.

To add the images, drag to image views from the library to the view. Set the contents of the image views by opening the Attributes Inspector (Command+1) for each view and choosing the BoxVolume.png or SphereVolume.png images.

Finish the view by adding two buttons: the Calculate button at the bottom of the view, and the invisible button used to hide the keyboard. Remember to expand the "hide keyboard" button to fill the view, and send it to the back. Open the Attributes inspector (Command+1) for the button, and choose Custom for the button type to make the button invisible.

Connecting Outlets and Actions

Connect the fields, labels, and buttons in Interface Builder to the appropriate outlets that you created in the VolumeViewController.h file. Control-drag from the File's Owner icon in the document window to each of the input fields and output labels; choose the appropriate outlet when prompted.

To connect the button controls to the actions, Control-drag from the two UIButton instances to the File's Owner, choosing the fitting calculate and hideKeyboard method when prompted.

Implementing the Volume Calculation Logic

Switch back to Xcode and edit the VolumeViewController.m file. As before, define the Pi constant at the top of the file:

```
#define Pi 3.1415926
```

Next, use the @synthesize directive to create the getters and setters after the @implementation directive:

```
@synthesize boxWidth;
@synthesize boxHeight;
@synthesize boxLength;
@synthesize sphereRadius;
@synthesize boxResult;
@synthesize sphereResult;
```

Create and edit the calculate method to determine the volume of the two shapes. For the box, this is length*width*height, and for the sphere, $4/3*Pi*R^3$. Use the results to populate the boxResult and sphereResult labels in the view. Our implementation of this method is provided here:

```
-(IBAction)calculate:(id)sender {
    float floatBoxResult=[boxWidth.text floatValue]*
                        [boxLength.text floatValue]*[boxHeight.text floatValue];
    float floatSphereResult=(4/3)*Pi*[sphereRadius.text floatValue]*
                [sphereRadius.text floatValue]*[sphereRadius.text floatValue];
    NSString *stringBoxResult=[[NSString alloc]
                            initWithFormat:@"%1.2f",floatBoxResult];
    NSString *stringSphereResult=[[NSString alloc]
                                initWithFormat:@"%1.2f",floatSphereResult];
    boxResult.text=stringBoxResult;
```

```
    sphereResult.text=stringSphereResult;
    [stringBoxResult release];
    [stringSphereResult release];

    [summaryViewController updateTotal];
}
```

By the Way

> Because only the logic for the calculations has changed, you should refer to the
> Area view calculation for a detailed description of the methods used here.

Add the `hideKeyboard` method so that the user can dismiss the onscreen keyboard
by touching the background of the view:

```
-(IBAction)hideKeyboard:(id)sender {
    [boxWidth resignFirstResponder];
    [boxLength resignFirstResponder];
    [boxHeight resignFirstResponder];
    [sphereRadius resignFirstResponder];
}
```

And finally, release the objects in the `dealloc` method:

```
- (void)dealloc {
    [boxWidth release];
    [boxHeight release];
    [boxLength release];
    [sphereRadius release];
    [boxResult release];
    [sphereResult release];
    [super dealloc];
}
```

Implementing the Summary View

Of all the views, the Summary view is the easiest to implement. This view will provide a single count of the number of calculations performed—as determined by the
number of times the calculate button is pressed. Just a single outlet and a single
counter. No problem!

Adding the Outlet, Instance Variable, and Method

The `SummaryViewController` class will need a single outlet, `totalCalculations`,
that will be connected to a `UILabel` in the Summary view and used to display the
calculation summary to the user. It will also use a single integer value, `calcCount`,
to internally track the number of calculations performed.

Finally, the class will implement an instance method updateTotal that will update the calcCount value. Edit the SummaryViewController.h file to include these requirements:

```
#import <UIKit/UIKit.h>

@interface SummaryViewController : UIViewController {
    IBOutlet UILabel *totalCalculations;
    int calcCount;
}

@property (retain, nonatomic) UILabel *totalCalculations;

-(void) updateTotal;

@end
```

Creating the View and Connecting the Outlet

To create the Summary view, open the SummaryView.xib file in Interface Builder. As promised, this view is extremely easy to set up. Drag a UILabel object to the view. This will serve as the output of the total calculation count; so, set the default text of the label to 0.

Finish the view by adding another label with the text **Total Calculations:** positioned above or beside the output label. The result should be similar to the view pictured in Figure 13.12.

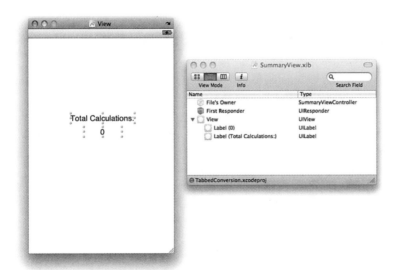

FIGURE 13.12
Add one label for the output value and one to serve as a description.

Connect the output label to the `totalCalculations` outlet by Control-dragging from the File's Owner icon to the `UILabel` instance within the Interface Builder document view.

Connecting the Area, Volume, and Summary Views

If you recall, the previous two views call the `updateTotal` method of the Summary view. For these views to have access to the `summaryViewController` instance variable, we must create two additional connections, this time in the MainWindow.xib file.

Open the MainWindow.xib document window and expand the Tab Bar Controller hierarchy. Control-drag from the Area view controller instance to the Summary view. Choose the `summaryViewController` outlet, as demonstrated in Figure 13.13.

FIGURE 13.13
Connect the Summary view controller to the Area and Volume view controllers.

Repeat this for the Volume view controller. The Area and Volume view controllers will now be able to successfully call the `updateTotal` method.

Implementing the Volume Calculation Logic

All that remains for the TabbedConversion project is implementing the logic to track the calculation total and update the Summary view. Let's open the SummaryViewController.m file and wrap this up! First use the `@synthesize` directive to create the getter/setter for the `totalCalculations` `UILabel`:

```
@synthesize totalCalculations;
```

Next, add the `updateTotal` method so that it will increment the `calcCount` variable when invoked:

```
-(void) updateTotal {
    calcCount++;
}
```

Now, the tough part. Notice that we don't display the new total in the updateTotal method? The reason for this is that until the view is displayed, there aren't any UILabel values to update. So if we try to update before the view is shown, the count will be wrong. Subsequent views *would* work, but initially the displayed result would be incorrect.

So, how do we get around this? The easiest way is to only update the view just before it is displayed onscreen. At that point, we have access to all the objects, so everything will be copacetic. Overriding the viewWillAppear method will provide us with the right hook into the display process. Implement the viewWillAppear method as follows:

```
- (void)viewWillAppear:(BOOL)animated {
    NSString *calcResult=[[NSString alloc] initWithFormat:@"%d",calcCount];
    totalCalculations.text=calcResult;
    [calcResult release];
    [super viewWillAppear:animated];
}
```

Nothing here should be a surprise. We format a temporary string using the calcCount variable, set the totalCalcuations (UILabel) "text" property to the string, release the string, and pass the method invocation up the chain.

The code isn't finished until the objects are released, so edit the dealloc method to release totalCalculations:

```
- (void)dealloc {
    [totalCalculations release];
    [super dealloc];
}
```

Congratulations! You just completed a tab bar–based multiview application with basic "inter-view" communication! Your experience working with multiple views will open up a whole new range of applications that you can develop. We'll look at more multiview goodness in Hour 14, where you'll learn how to use navigation controllers to build hierarchical views.

Summary

In this hour, we examined how a tab bar controller (UITabBarController) can handle much of the behind-the-scenes work of switching between parallel views automatically. Unlike the project in Hour 12, where we needed to manually load views and even manage the "index" of the view, all of this is handled for us with an instance of UITabBarController. Even better, tab bars look great! The graphical styling of the bar itself has the "flair" of the iPhone interface that we've grown to love.

With so much time freed up by the tab bar, we were able to implement a multiview calculator application that included a tab bar with images, multiple independent user interfaces, and inter-view communications. Quite an accomplishment for only an hour, don't you think?

Q&A

Q. *Can I use color tab bar buttons?*

A. No, not with Apple's default tab bar implementation. The tab bar buttons are tightly controlled and rendered as a gradient, regardless of what color choices you make when designing the button icons.

Q. *Can a tab bar be used for the same purpose as a toolbar?*

A. No. A tab bar should always be used to switch between similar views. This is its intended purpose within the Apple UI guidelines. A toolbar, however, can serve a more general role and be used to trigger any number of events that are relevant to the current state of the application.

Workshop

Quiz

1. How many methods of the `UITabBarControllerDelegate` protocol are required to implement to gain the view-switching functionality?

2. Why didn't we use Apple's tab bar template for our application tutorial?

3. What is one way that you can implement communications between multiple view controllers?

Answers

1. None! All of the `UITabBarControllerDelegate` protocol methods are optional.

2. The Apple template is inconsistent in structuring/naming the views and view controllers. We end up with a much better project structure if we build it ourselves.

3. View controllers, like any other objects, can communicate if you add the appropriate outlets and define the connections in Interface Builder.

Activities

1. Update the TabbedConversion application so that the Area and Volume views share user input data. In other words, when a user enters length, width, or radius in the Area view, the corresponding fields should be updated in the Volume view.

2. Create a new tab bar application using the provided Apple template. As mentioned earlier, this template seems to be at odds with itself in terms of the intended development direction. Even so, you can probably save yourself a few keystrokes if you learn to work around the initial configuration.

Further Exploration

The tab bar controller (`UITabBarController`) offers additional features beyond what we were able to cover here. If there are too many buttons to be displayed in a single tab bar, for example, the tab bar controller provides its own "more" view in the form of a navigation controller (which you'll learn about in the next hour). This enables you to expand the user's options beyond the buttons immediately visible onscreen. The `UITabBarControllerDelegate` protocol, which we conformed to, and the `UITabBarDelegate` can even implement optional methods to enable the user to customize the tab bar within the application. You can see this level of functionality within Apple's iPod application.

Another area that you will eventually want to review is the loading of multiple views/view controllers. In the project this hour and last, the view controllers were instantiated when the application was loaded. In small apps, this is fine, but in larger projects with more complex views, this can add to the load time and potentially uses memory for views the user may never select. To get around this, we can programmatically instantiate a view controller (something you'll see in Hour 14).

Apple Developer Tutorials:

Multiple views and tab bars – MoviePlayer (accessible via the Xcode developer documentation). This example demonstrates a complex multiview interface, including a tab bar controller.

HOUR 14

Displaying and Navigating Data Using Table Views

What You'll Learn in This Hour:

▶ The types of table views available in the iPhone OS

▶ How to implement a simple table view and controller

▶ Ways of adding more structure and impact to a table with sections and cell images

▶ How a navigation controller can be combined with a table view to create a hierarchy of views

So far, our explanation of iPhone development has included typical interface elements—fields, buttons, dialog boxes, views, and, of course, a variety of output mechanisms. However, what's missing is the ability to present categorized information in a structured manner. Everywhere you look (websites, books, applications on your computer), you see methods for displaying information in an attractive and orderly manner. The iPhone, given the limited screen real estate, has its own convention to display this type of information. To display structured information on the iPhone, you will use a table view. This UI element, coupled with a navigation controller, gives a clean, easy-to-understand toolset for building applications that display information by categories and subcategories.

Understanding Table Views

Let's begin by understanding what table views are and how they are used. Like the other views you've seen in this book, a table view holds information. A table view's appearance, however, is slightly counterintuitive. Rather than showing up as a true table (like an Excel worksheet), a table view displays a single list of cells onscreen. Each cell can be structured to contain multiple pieces of information, but is still a single unit. In addition, the cells can be broken into sections so that the clusters of information can be communicated visually. You might, for example, list computer models by manufacturers, or models of the Macintosh by year. Table views respond to touch events and allow the user to easily scroll up and down through long lists of information and select individual cells.

Types of Tables

There are two basic styles of table views: plain and grouped, demonstrated in Figure 14.1 and Figure 14.2, respectively. Plain tables lack the clear visual separation of sections of the grouped tables, but are frequently implemented with a touchable index (like the iPhone contact list). Because of this, they are sometimes called indexed tables. We will continue to refer to them by the names (plain/grouped) designated in Interface Builder.

FIGURE 14.1
Plain tables look like simple lists.

Implementation Overview

The skills needed to add table views to your projects are very similar to what you learned when working with pickers in Hour 9, "Implementing Advanced Multivalue Interfaces with Pickers." A table view is created by an instance of UITableView and classes that implement the UITableViewDataSource and UITableViewDelegate protocols to provide the data that the table will display. Specifically, the data source needs to provide information on the number of sections in the table and the number of rows in each section. The delegate handles creating the cells within the table and reacting to the user's selection.

FIGURE 14.2
Grouped tables
have empha-
sized sections.

Unlike the picker, where we implemented the required protocols within a standard
UIViewController, we'll be creating an instance of UITableViewController, which
conforms to both of the needed protocols. This simplifies our development and keeps
things as streamlined as possible. In a large project with complex data needs, you
may want to create one or more new classes specifically for handling the data.

Let's go ahead and get started.

Building a Simple Table View Application

In our first example of a table view, we will build a simple sectioned table that displays a list of flowers grouped by color. Begin by creating a new Xcode iPhone project
named **FlowerColorTable** using the Window-Based Application template.

Prepping the View Controller

Next, we will be adding a new subclass of the UITableViewController class to the project to handle interactions with our table view. To do so, complete the following steps:

   1. Create a new file in Xcode.

   2. Within the New File dialog box, select Cocoa Touch Classes, Objective-C class,
      and then UITableViewController (see Figure 14.3).

FIGURE 14.3
Create the files
for implement-
ing a new sub-
class of
UITableView-
Controller.

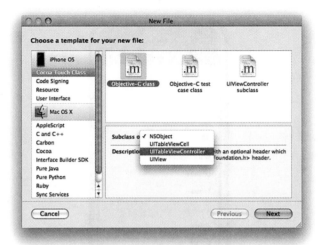

3. Click Next.

4. Type **FlowerTableViewController.m** as the filename, and be sure that Also Create 'FlowerTableViewController.h' is selected.

5. Finally, click the Finish button. The new subclass will be added to your project.

The FlowerTableViewController.m will include all the method stubs you need to get your table up and running quickly. In a few minutes, we'll add an instance of this new table view controller subclass to the MainWindow.xib file. This will create an instance of the `FlowerTableViewController` when the application launches.

Adding Outlets

Before we can make our connections in Interface Builder, we need to create an outlet for the application delegate to access the `FlowerTableViewController` that we're adding to the system.

Edit FlowerColorTableAppDelegate.h and add a class reference to `FlowerColorTableViewController` and an outlet for the instance of `FlowerViewController` that we will be creating; we'll call it **flowerColorTableViewController** for consistency.

The FlowerColorTableAppDelegate.h code should read as follows:

```
1: #import <UIKit/UIKit.h>
2:
3: @class FlowerColorTableViewController;
4:
5: @interface FlowerColorTableAppDelegate : NSObject <UIApplicationDelegate> {
6:     IBOutlet FlowerColorTableViewController *flowerColorTableViewController;
7:     UIWindow *window;
```

```
 8: }
 9:
10: @property (nonatomic, retain) IBOutlet UIWindow *window;
11:
12: @end
```

Lines 3 and 6 are the only additions to the app delegate header file.

Adding the View

Once the view controller has been instantiated, it will need to add its subview to the application window. Make these implementation changes within the FlowerColorTableAppDelegate class. Import FlowerClassTableViewController.h so that we can access the new view controller properties and methods, add the flowerColorTableViewController's view as a subview to the window, and release the view controller when finished. The completed FlowerColorTableAppDelegate.m should resemble the following:

```
 1: #import "FlowerColorTableAppDelegate.h"
 2: #import "FlowerColorTableViewController.h"
 3:
 4: @implementation FlowerColorTableAppDelegate
 5:
 6: @synthesize window;
 7:
 8: - (void)applicationDidFinishLaunching:(UIApplication *)application {
 9:
10:     // Override point for customization after application launch
11:     [window addSubview:flowerColorTableViewController.view];
12:     [window makeKeyAndVisible];
13: }
14:
15:
16: - (void)dealloc {
17:     [flowerColorTableViewController release];
18:     [window release];
19:     [super dealloc];
20: }
21:
22:
23: @end
```

With the initial coding finished up, it's time to open Interface Builder and add an instance of the FlowerColorTableViewController class we've created.

Adding a Table View and View Controller Instance

Double-click the MainWindow.xib file to open it within Interface Builder. Open the Library, and drag the Table View Controller icon into the MainWindow.xib file. This adds an instance of UITableViewController to your project, but that's not quite what we need! The FlowerTableViewController class is our subclass of

UITableViewController, and that's what we want to instantiate and use in the application.

By the Way

> The TableViewController instance that you just added includes an instance of a table view, so this is the only object needed in Interface Builder.

Select the Table View Controller icon in the XIB file, and open the Identity Inspector (Command+4). Edit the class identity to read **FlowerTableViewController**, as shown in Figure 14.4.

FIGURE 14.4
Update the class identity to **FlowerTable-ViewController** within the Identity Inspector.

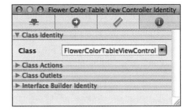

The application will now instantiate our table view controller when it launches, but the controller still isn't connected to anything. To connect to the flowerColorTableViewController IBOutlet created earlier, Control-drag from Flower Color Table App Delegate to the Flower Color Table View Controller icon. When the Outlets pop-up window appears, choose flowerColorTableViewController (see Figure 14.5).

FIGURE 14.5
Connect the application dele-gate to the flowerColor-TableView-Controller.

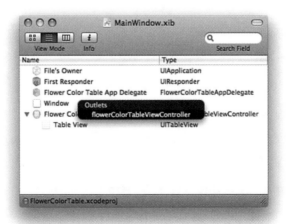

All the connections are in place for the table view controller and a table view. Switch back to Xcode, and click Build and Go to test the application. An empty table will appear. It's empty, but it's a table! Next step? Data!

Providing Data to the Table View

With all the structural work out of the way, the table is ready to display something. As mentioned earlier, implementing the required methods for the UITableViewDataSource and UITableViewDelegate protocols is very similar to creating a picker. For this example, we're going to create a table that lists flowers divided into sections by color.

Creating Sample Data

To keep things simple, we'll only consider two colors: red and blue. We'll populate two arrays (redFlowers, blueFlowers) with a few appropriate flower names.

Begin by updating FlowerColorTableViewController.h to include the two NSMutableArrays we'll be using:

```
@interface FlowerColorTableViewController : UITableViewController {
    NSMutableArray *redFlowers;
    NSMutableArray *blueFlowers;
}
```

Turning to the implementation in FlowerColorTableViewController.m, find the viewDidLoad method and uncomment it. We will implement this method so that we have a convenient place to populate the arrays. Edit the code to add in initialization of the redFlowers and blueFlowers arrays with five flowers each:

```
- (void)viewDidLoad {
    [super viewDidLoad];
    redFlowers = [[NSMutableArray alloc]
                    initWithObjects:@"Gerbera",@"Peony",@"Rose",@"Poppy",nil];
    blueFlowers = [[NSMutableArray alloc]
                    initWithObjects:@"Hyacinth",@"Hydrangea",@"Sea Holly",
                    @"Phlox",@"Iris",nil];
}
```

As always, make sure that you release the two arrays when finished. Edit the dealloc method to read as follows:

```
- (void)dealloc {
    [redFlowers release];
    [blueFlowers release];
    [super dealloc];
}
```

As a last step, add constants that we can use to refer to our color sections. At the top of FlowerColorTableViewController.m, enter the following constant definitions:

```
#define sectionCount 2
#define redSection 0
#define blueSection 1
```

The first constant, `sectionCount`, is the number of sections that will be displayed in the table. Because we're implementing red and blue flower lists, this value is 2. The next constant, `redSection`, denotes that the listing of red flowers in the table will be shown first (section 0), while the third and final constant, `blueSection`, identifies that the blue section of flowers will appear second (section 1).

Implementing the Table View Controller Data Source Methods

Our application now has the data it needs to create a table, but it doesn't yet "understand" how to get that data into the table view itself. Thankfully, the methods that a table requires to display information are easy to understand, and, more important, easy to implement. Because this example includes sections, we need to include these two methods in FlowerColorViewController.m as part of the `UITableViewDataSource` protocol:

> `numberofSectionsInTableView:`　Returns the number of sections within a given table.

> `tableView:tableViewnumberOfRowsInSection:`　Returns the number of rows in a section.

The number of sections has already been defined in the constant `sectionCount`, so implementing the first method requires nothing more than returning this constant.

```
- (NSInteger)numberOfSectionsInTableView:(UITableView *)tableView
{
        return sectionCount;
}
```

The second method requires us to return the number of rows (cells) that will be displayed in a given section. Because the rows in each section will be filled with the strings in the `redFlowers` and `blueFlowers` arrays, we can return the count of elements in each array using the `count` method.

Use a `switch` statement along with the `redSection` and `blueSection` constants that were defined earlier to return the appropriate counts for each of the two arrays. The final implementation should look very similar to the following:

```
- (NSInteger)tableView:(UITableView *)tableView
            numberOfRowsInSection:(NSInteger)section
{
        switch (section) {
                case redSection:
                        return [redFlowers count];
                case blueSection:
                        return [blueFlowers count];
                default:
                        return 0;
        }
}
```

> Even though it is impossible for our application to reach a section other than red or blue, it is still good practice to provide a default case to the `switch` statement. This ensures that even if we haven't properly identified all of our potential cases, it will still be caught by the default case.

By the Way

That wraps up what needs to be provided to satisfy the `UITableViewDataSource` protocol. However, as you've seen, these methods don't provide the actual data that will be visible in the table cells.

Populating the Section Headings and Cells

At long last, we've reached the methods that actually make our table display something! This project will be implementing the following methods required to conform to the `UITableViewDelegate` protocol. These methods do the "heavy lifting" in the application:

`tableView:titleForHeaderInSection:` Returns a string to be used as the title for a given section number.

`tableView:cellForRowAtIndexPath:` Returns a cell (UITableViewCell) object for a given table section and row.

> The methods required for working with table views frequently use an `NSIndexPath` object to communicate row and section information. When dealing with an incoming `IndexPath` object in your table methods, you can use the accessors `IndexPath.section` and `IndexPath.row` to get to the current section and row.

By the Way

For the first method implementation, you can turn again to the defined constants and a `switch` statement to very easily return an appropriate string for a given section number:

```
- (NSString *)tableView:(UITableView *)tableView
           titleForHeaderInSection:(NSInteger)section {
    switch (section) {
        case redSection:
            return @"Red";
        case blueSection:
            return @"Blue";
        default:
            return @"Unknown";
    }
}
```

The second method is a bit more complex. The `tableView:cellForRowAtIndexPath` method must create and return a properly formatted `UITableViewCell`.

What makes this process interesting is that as cells move on and off the screen, we don't want to keep releasing and reallocating memory. We also don't want to allocate memory for every single cell that the table could display. So, what is the alternative? To reuse cells that are no longer needed to generate the current display. The good news is that Apple has already set up methods and a process for this to occur automatically.

Take a close look at the method stub for `tableView:cellForRowIndexPath`, specifically, this snippet:

```
UITableViewCell *cell = (UITableViewCell*)[tableView
                         dequeueReusableCellWithIdentifier:CellIdentifier];
    if(cell == nil)
    {
        cell = [[[UITableViewCell alloc]
                initWithFrame:CGRectZero
                reuseIdentifier:CellIdentifier] autorelease];
    }
```

This code attempts to use the `dequeueReusableCellWithIdentifier` `UITableView` method to find a cell that has already been allocated but that is ready to be reused. In the event that an appropriate cell can't be found (such as the first time the table view loads its cells), a new cell is allocated and initialized. You shouldn't have any reason to change this prewritten logic for most Table-Based Applications.

After a cell object has been appropriately allocated, the method must format the cell for the `indexPath` object provided. In other words, we must make sure that for whatever section is specified in `indexPath.section` and whatever row is passed in `indexPath.row`, the cell object is given the necessary label.

To set a cell's label to a given string, first use `textLabel` to return the `UILabel` object for the cell, then the `setText` method to update the label. For example:

```
[[cell textLabel]setText: @"My Cell Label"]
```

Because we don't want to set a static string for the cell labels and our labels are stored in arrays, we need to retrieve the appropriate label string from the array, and then pass it to `setText`. Remember that the individual cell row that we need to return will be provided by `indexPath.row`, so we can use that to index into our array. To retrieve the current text label for a member of the `redFlowers` array, we can use the following:

```
[redFlowers objectAtIndex:indexPath.row]
```

These two lines can be combined into a single statement that sets the cell label text to the current row of the `redFlowers` array:

```
[[cell textLabel] setText:[redFlowers objectAtIndex:indexPath.row]]
```

This is good, but not quite the solution to all our problems. We need to account for both the redFlowers and blueFlowers arrays and display each within the appropriate section. Once again, we'll turn to the switch statement to make this happen, this time using indexPath.section to determine whether the cell should be set to a member of the redFlowers array or the blueFlowers array.

Your final code should be an addition to the existing tableView:cellForRowAtIndexPath method stub similar to lines 15–27:

```
 1: - (UITableViewCell *)tableView:(UITableView *)tableView
 2:            cellForRowAtIndexPath:(NSIndexPath *)indexPath
 3: {
 4:     static NSString *CellIdentifier = @"Cell";
 5:
 6:     UITableViewCell *cell = (UITableViewCell*)[tableView
 7:                         dequeueReusableCellWithIdentifier:CellIdentifier];
 8:     if(cell == nil)
 9:     {
10:         cell = [[[UITableViewCell alloc]
11:                 initWithFrame:CGRectZero
12:                 reuseIdentifier:CellIdentifier] autorelease];
13:     }
14:
15:     switch (indexPath.section) {
16:         case redSection:
17:             [[cell textLabel]
18:              setText:[redFlowers objectAtIndex:indexPath.row]];
19:             break;
20:         case blueSection:
21:             [[cell textLabel]
22:              setText:[blueFlowers objectAtIndex:indexPath.row]];
23:             break;
24:         default:
25:             [[cell textLabel]
26:              setText:@"Unknown"];
27:     }
28:     return cell;
29: }
```

The moment you've been waiting for has arrived! You should now be able to launch your application and view the result (see Figure 14.6). Congratulations, you've just implemented a table view from scratch!

Reacting to a Row Touch Event

A table that displays information is all fine and dandy, but it would be nice if the user had a means of interacting with it. Unlike other UI elements where we'd need to define an action and make connections in Interface Builders, we can add some basic interactivity to the FlowerColorTable application by implementing another method from the UITableViewDelegate: tableView:didSelectRowAtIndexPath. This method is called when a table row has been touched by the user. The key to identifying the specific row and section that was selected is indexPath, an instance of NSIndexPath.

FIGURE 14.6
You should now have a working table view application, albeit a bit light on functionality.

How you react to a row selection event is up to you. For the sake of this example, we're going to use `UIAlertView` to display a message. The implementation should look very familiar by this point:

```
 1: - (void)tableView:(UITableView *)tableView
 2:         didSelectRowAtIndexPath:(NSIndexPath *)indexPath {
 3:     UIAlertView *showSelection;
 4:     NSString    *flowerMessage;
 5:     switch (indexPath.section) {
 6:         case redSection:
 7:             flowerMessage=[[NSString alloc]
 8:                             initWithFormat:
 9:                             @"You chose the red flower - %@",
10:                             [redFlowers objectAtIndex: indexPath.row]];
11:             break;
12:         case blueSection:
13:             flowerMessage=[[NSString alloc]
14:                             initWithFormat:
15:                             @"You chose the blue flower - %@",
16:                             [blueFlowers objectAtIndex: indexPath.row]];
17:             break;
18:         default:
19:             flowerMessage=[[NSString alloc]
20:                             initWithFormat:
21:                             @"I have no idea what you chose!?"];
22:             break;
23:     }
24:
25:     showSelection = [[UIAlertView alloc]
26:                         initWithTitle: @"Flower Selected"
27:                         message:flowerMessage
28:                         delegate: nil
29:                         cancelButtonTitle: @"Ok"
```

```
30:                           otherButtonTitles: nil];
31:     [showSelection show];
32:     [showSelection release];
33:     [flowerMessage release];
34: }
```

Lines 3–4 declare flowerMessage and showSelection variables that will be used for the message string shown to the user and the UIAlertView instance that will display the message, respectively.

Lines 5–23 use a switch statement with indexPath.section to determine which flower array our selection comes from and the indexPath.row value to identify the specific element of the array that was chosen. A string (flowerMessage) is allocated and formatted to contain the value of the selection.

Lines 25–31 create and display an alert view instance (showSelection) containing the message string (flowerMessage).

Lines 32–33 release the instance of the alert view and the message string.

After implementing this function, build and test the application again. Touch a row and review the result. The application will now display an alert box, seen in Figure 14.7, with the results of your selection.

FIGURE 14.7
The application now reacts to row selection and identifies the item that was selected.

Understanding Navigation-Based Applications

Tables are a great tool for displaying information in lists and enabling a user to choose from the list. However, tables are rarely used on their own in an iPhone application. More frequently, they are used in conjunction with a navigation controller. Navigation controllers provide a simple means for a user to "drill down" through multiple views of data, as well as to return to where they started.

You might recognize navigation controllers from many other applications on the iPhone, such as the Contacts application, where a group of individuals can be chosen, then a specific person, and, finally, individual contact details. At any time, the user can click a button at the top of the view to return to the previous level of detail, as demonstrated in Figure 14.8.

FIGURE 14.8
Navigation controllers enable simple drill-down interfaces within an application.

The implementation of a navigation controller is surprisingly simple. As a developer, the navigation controller frees you up to focus on writing application functionality. When you want a new view to appear, you simply "push" its view controller onto the navigation controller's stack. The new controller is instantiated and added to the stack, and the previous controller gets pushed further down the stack. When (and if) it is time to go back, the navigation controller "pops" the current view off the stack, unloading it. The previous view controller then moves to the top of the stack, becomes active again, and the user can navigate to another item.

> If you haven't encountered stacks before, don't worry; you'll catch on quickly. Imagine creating a stack of papers on your desk. To add a page to the stack, you "push" it onto the stack. You may only remove the top page at any time, by "popping" it off. The more pages you push onto the stack of paper, the more you'll have to "pop" off to get back to the first page.
>
> A navigation controller does exactly this, but with view controllers/views rather than pieces of paper.

Creating a Navigation-Based Multiview Application

With a basic understanding of table controllers under our belt, we can move on to building an application that combines a table view with a navigation view. In the last example, we created a table view controller and went through all the steps of adding its view to the Window-Based Application template. This time, we're going to take a shortcut and use a handy Apple-created template.

Preparing the Project

This example uses what we know about tables to create a list of flowers, by color, including images for each row. It will also enable the user to touch a specific flower and drill down to a detail view. The detail view itself will load the content of a Wikipedia article for the identified flower.

We will be using a combination of `NSMutableDictionaries` and `NSMutableArrays` to store our data in a more easy-to-maintain format. In Hour 15, "Storing Application Preferences," you'll be learning about persistent data storage, which will simplify the use of data even more in your future projects.

Time to code!

Instead of starting with the Window-Based Application template, start Xcode and create a new project using the Navigation-Based Application template. If you want to follow along exactly with what we're doing, name the project **FlowerInfoNavigator**.

The Navigation-Based Application template does all the hard work of setting up a navigation controller and an initial table-based view. This is the "heart and soul" of many navigation-based applications and gives us a great starting point for adding functionality.

After creating the new project, click the Classes folder and review the contents. You should see header and implementation files for the application delegate (FlowerInfoNavigatorAppDelegate) and a subclass of UITableViewController called RootViewController. We will be supplementing this by creating a new detail view controller shortly.

Exploring the XIB files reveals an interesting hierarchy, as shown in Figure 14.9.

FIGURE 14.9
The MainWindow.xib contains a navigation controller along with a table controller for the root-level table view.

The MainWindow.xib file contains all the usual components, but also a navigation controller (UINavigationController) with navigation bar (UINavigationBar). The controller provides the functionality to push and pop other view controllers, while the UINavigationBar instance creates the horizontal bar that will contain our UI elements for navigating through views.

Inside the navigation controller is the instance of the Root View Controller (a subclass of UITableViewController). This is the top-level controller that is pushed onto the navigation controller. A user cannot navigate back beyond this controller. (Note that the table view itself is loaded RootViewController.xib.)

Finally, within the Root View Controller is a navigation item (UINavigationItem), which we will use to display a title in the navigation bar.

Feel free to build the app and try it out. Even though we're starting with an empty template, you'll still be able to see the navigation bar and the root table view.

Providing Data to the Application

In the previous table implementation project, we used multiple arrays and `switch` statements to differentiate between the different sections of flowers. This time around, however, we need to track the flower sections, names, image resources, and the detail URL that will be displayed.

Creating the Application Data Structures

What the application needs to store is quite a bit of data for simple arrays. Instead, we'll make use of an `NSMutableArray` of `NSMutableDictionaries` to hold the specific attributes of each flower and a separate array to hold the names of each section. We'll index into each based on the current section/row being displayed, so no more `switch` statements!

To begin, edit RootViewController.h to read as follows:

```
@interface RootViewController : UITableViewController {
    NSMutableArray *flowerData;
    NSMutableArray *flowerSections;
}

-(void) createFlowerData;

@end
```

We've added two `NSMutableArrays`: `flowerData` and `flowerSection`. These will hold our flower and section information, respectively. We've also declared a method `createFlowerData`, which will be used to add the data to the arrays.

Next, open the RootViewController.m implementation file and add the following `createFlowerData` method:

```
 1: - (void)createFlowerData {
 2:
 3:     NSMutableArray *redFlowers;
 4:     NSMutableArray *blueFlowers;
 5:
 6:     flowerSections=[[NSMutableArray alloc] initWithObjects:
 7:                     @"Red Flowers",@"Blue Flowers",nil];
 8:
 9:     redFlowers=[[NSMutableArray alloc] init];
10:     blueFlowers=[[NSMutableArray alloc] init];
11:
12:     [redFlowers addObject:[[NSMutableDictionary alloc]
13:                     initWithObjectsAndKeys:@"Poppy",@"name",
14:                     @"poppy.png",@"picture",
15:                     @"http://en.wikipedia.org/wiki/Poppy",@"url",nil]];
16:     [redFlowers addObject:[[NSMutableDictionary alloc]
17:                     initWithObjectsAndKeys:@"Tulip",@"name",
18:                     @"tulip.png",@"picture",
```

```
19:                              @"http://en.wikipedia.org/wiki/Tulip",@"url",nil]];
20:
21:     [blueFlowers addObject:[[NSMutableDictionary alloc]
22:                       initWithObjectsAndKeys:@"Hyacinth",@"name",
23:                       @"hyacinth.png",@"picture",
24:                      @"http://en.wikipedia.org/wiki/Hyacinth_(flower)",
25:                       @"url",nil]];
26:     [blueFlowers addObject:[[NSMutableDictionary alloc]
27:                       initWithObjectsAndKeys:@"Hydrangea",@"name",
28:                       @"hydrangea.png",@"picture",
29:                       @"http://en.wikipedia.org/wiki/Hydrangea",
30:                       @"url",nil]];
31:
32:     flowerData=[[NSMutableArray alloc] initWithObjects:
33:              redFlowers,blueFlowers,nil];
34:
35:     [redFlowers release];
36:     [blueFlowers release];
37: }
```

Don't worry if you don't understand what you're seeing; an explanation is definitely in order! The createFlowerData method creates two arrays: flowerData and flowerSections.

The flowerSections array is allocated and initialized in lines 6–7. The section names are added to the array so that their indexes can be referenced by section number. For example, Red Flowers is added first, so it is accessed by index (and section number!) 0, Blue Flowers is added second and will be accessed through index 1. When we want to get the label for a section, we'll just reference it as [flowerSections objectAtIndex:section].

The flowerData structure is a bit more complicated. As with the flowerSections array, we want to be able to access information by section. We also want to be able to store multiple flowers per section, and multiple pieces of data per flower. So, how can we get this done?

First, let's concentrate on the individual flower data within each section. Lines 3–4 define two NSMutableArrays: redFlowers and blueFlowers. These need to be populated with each flower. Lines 12–30 do just that; the code allocates and initializes an NSMutableDictionary with key/value pairs for the flower's name (name), image file (picture), and Wikipedia reference (url) and inserts it into each of the two arrays.

Wait a second, doesn't this leave us with two arrays when we wanted to consolidate all of the data into one? Yes, but we're not done. Lines 32–33 create the final flowerData NSMutableArray using the redFlowers and blueFlowers arrays. What this means for our application is that we can reference the red flower array as [flowerData objectAtIndex:0] and [flowerData objectAtIndex:1] (corresponding, as we wanted, to the appropriate table sections).

Finally, lines 35–36 release the temporary `redFlowers` and `blueFlowers` arrays. The end result will be a structure in memory that resembles Figure 14.10.

flowerData (NSMutableArray)				
Index	**NSMutableArray**			
0	**Red Flowers**			
	Index	**NSMutableDictionary**		
	0	**Name**	**Picture**	**URL**
		Poppy	poppy.png	http://en.wikipedia.org/wiki/Poppy
	1	**Name**	**Picture**	**URL**
		Tulip	tulip.png	http://en.wikipedia.org/wiki/Tulip
1	**Blue Flowers**			
	Index	**NSMutableDictionary**		
	0	**Name**	**Picture**	**URL**
		Hyacinth	hyacinth.png	http://en.wikipedia.org/wiki/Hyacinth_(flower)
	1	**Name**	**Picture**	**URL**
		Hydrangea	hydrangea.png	http://en.wikipedia.org/wiki/Hydrangea

FIGURE 14.10
The data structure that will populate our table view.

By the Way

The data that we included in the listing of the `createFlowerData` method is a small subset of what is used in the actual project files. If you would like to use the full dataset in your code, you can copy it from the Hour 14 project files, or add it manually to the method using these values:

Red Flowers

Name	Picture	URL
Gerbera	gerbera.png	http://en.wikipedia.org/wiki/Gerbera
Peony	peony.png	http://en.wikipedia.org/wiki/Peony
Rose	rose.png	http://en.wikipedia.org/wiki/Rose
Hollyhock	hollyhock.png	http://en.wikipedia.org/wiki/Hollyhock
Straw Flower	strawflower.png	http://en.wikipedia.org/wiki/Strawflower

Blue Flowers

Name	Picture	URL
Sea Holly	seaholly.png	http://en.wikipedia.org/wiki/Sea_holly
Grape Hyacinth	grapehyacinth.png	http://en.wikipedia.org/wiki/Grape_hyacinth
Phlox	phlox.png	http://en.wikipedia.org/wiki/Phlox
Pin Cushion Flower	pincushionflower.png	http://en.wikipedia.org/wiki/Scabious
Iris	iris.png	http://en.wikipedia.org/wiki/Iris_(plant)

Populating the Data Structures

The `createFlowerData` method is now ready for use. We can call it from within the `RootViewController`'s `viewDidLoad` method. Because an instance of the `RootViewController` class is calling one of its own methods, it is invoked as `[self createFlowerData]`:

```
- (void)viewDidLoad {
    [self createFlowerData];
    [super viewDidLoad];
}
```

Remember, we need to release the `flowerData` and `flowerSections` when we're done with them. Be sure to add the appropriate releases to the `dealloc` method:

```
- (void)dealloc {
    [flowerData release];
    [flowerSections release];
    [super dealloc];
}
```

Adding the Image Resources

As you probably noticed when entering the data structures, the application references images that will be placed alongside the flower names in the table. In the project files provided online, find the Flowers folder, select all the images, and drag them into your Xcode resources folder for the project. If you want to use your own graphics, size them at 100x75 pixels, and make sure the names of the images stored with the `picture` NSMutableDictionary key match what you add to your project.

Creating a Detail View

The next task in developing the application is building the detail view and view controller. This view has a very simple purpose: It displays a URL in an instance of a `UIWebView`. We automatically gain the ability to navigate back to the previous view through the project's navigation controller, so we can focus solely on designing this view.

Creating a New View Controller

Begin by creating a new view controller called **FlowerDetailViewController** using the `UIViewController` subclass, as follows:

1. In Xcode, choose File, New File, then UIViewController subclass.

2. Be sure to click the With XIB for our user interface.

3. Click Next.

4. Make sure that Also Create FlowerDetailViewController.m is selected.

5. Click Finish.

The implementation, header, and associated XIB for the new view controller will be added to the project.

Adding Outlets and Properties

The objects that we'll need to manipulate within the new detail view are very simple. There will need to be an outlet for accessing the UIWebView instance that we'll be adding to the XIB in a bit, as well as a place for storing and accessing the URL that the web view will display. We'll call these detailWebView and detailURL, respectively. Edit the FlowerDetailViewController header as follows:

```
#import <UIKit/UIKit.h>

@interface FlowerDetailViewController : UIViewController {
        IBOutlet UIWebView *detailWebView;
        NSURL    *detailURL;
}

@property (nonatomic, retain) NSURL *detailURL;
@property (nonatomic, retain) UIWebView *detailWebView;

@end
```

With these definitions out of the way, we can now implement the FlowerDetailViewController itself.

Implementing the Detail View Controller

Surprisingly, the implementation of FlowerDetailViewController is perhaps the easiest undertaking we have in this hour. When the view is loaded, the UIWebView instance (detailWebView) should be instructed to load the web address stored within the NSURL object (detailURL).

You might remember from Hour 9, "Using Advanced Interface Controls," that loading a web page in a web view is accomplished with the loadRequest method. This method takes an NSURLRequest object as its input parameter. Because we only have an NSURL (detailURL), we also need to use the NSURLRequest class method requestWithURL to return the appropriate object type. A single line of code takes care of all of this:

```
[detailWebView loadRequest:[NSURLRequest requestWithURL:detailURL]]
```

Add this to the `viewDidLoad` method in FlowerDetailViewController.m:

```
- (void)viewDidLoad {
    [detailWebView loadRequest:[NSURLRequest requestWithURL:detailURL]];
    [super viewDidLoad];
}
```

Last, but not least, release the `detailWebView` and `detailURL` objects in the `dealloc` method:

```
- (void)dealloc {
    [detailWebView release];
    [detailURL release];
    [super dealloc];
}
```

Adding the Web View in Interface Builder

Open the FlowerDetailViewController.xib in Interface Builder. You should see a single view in the document window. We *could* replace this view entirely with a web view, but by implementing the web view as a subview, we leave ourselves a canvas for expanding the view's interface elements in the future.

Add a web view by opening the library (Tools, Library) and dragging a web view object into the existing View icon. It should now appear as a subview within the view (see Figure 14.11).

FIGURE 14.11
Add a web view object as a subview of the existing view.

Connect the web view to the `detailWebView` outlet by Control-dragging from the File's Owner icon to the Web View icon in the document window. When prompted, choose the `detailWebView` outlet, as demonstrated in Figure 14.12.

FIGURE 14.12
Connect the file's owner to the `detailWebView` outlet.

Congratulations, the detail view is now finished! All that remains is providing data to the root view table controller and invoking the detail view through the navigation controller.

By default, the web view does not scale pages to fit the iPhone screen. You can quickly change this behavior by selecting the web view instance in Interface Builder, then opening the web view Attributes Inspector (Command+1). Check the Scale Page to Fit option in the Web View Settings group.

Did you Know?

Implementing the Root View Table Controller

In the project template we're working with, Apple has provided a table view controller called `RootViewController` for us to build off of.

Even though we're using a navigation controller, very little changes between how we implemented our initial table view controller and how we will be building this one. Once again, we need to satisfy the appropriate data source and delegate protocols to provide an interface to our data. We also need to react to a row touch to drill down to our detail view.

The biggest change to the implementation will be how we access our data. Because we've built a somewhat complex structure of arrays of dictionaries, we need to make absolutely sure we're referencing the data that we intend to be.

Creating the Table View Data Source Methods

Rather than completely rehashing the implementation details, let's just review how we can return the needed information to the various methods.

As with the previous example, start by implementing the data source methods within RootViewController.m. Remember, these methods (numberOfSectionsInTableView, and tableView:numberOfRowsInSection) must return the number of sections and the rows within each section, respectively.

To return the number of sections, we will simply need the count of the elements in the flowerSections array:

```
[flowerSections count]
```

Retrieving the number of rows within a given section is only slightly more difficult. Because the flowerData array contains an array for each section, we must first access the appropriate array for the section, and then return its count:

```
[[flowerData objectAtIndex:section] count]
```

Edit the appropriate methods in RootViewController.m so that they return these values.

Populating the Cells and Sections with Text and Images

The final mind-bending hurdle that we need to deal with is how to provide actual content to the table view so that the end result looks similar to Figure 14.13.

FIGURE 14.13
The view we're attempting to create includes sections, images, and an indicator to show that a cell can be selected.

As before, this is handled through the `tableView:cellForRowAtIndexPath` and `tableView:titleforHeaderInSection` methods, but unlike the previous example, we need to dig down into our data structures to retrieve the correct results.

Let's begin with the easy part first: providing the label for a given section via the `tableView:titleforHeaderInSection` method. To do this, the application should index into the `flowerSections` array by the section value, and return the string at that location:

```
[flowerSections objectAtIndex:section]
```

No problem! Implement this within the method now.

Next, we need to tackle `tableView:cellForRowAtIndexPath`. Recall that we will be setting the cell's label using an approach like this:

```
[[cell textLabel]setText:@"My Cell Label"]
```

In addition to the label, however, we also need to set an image that will be displayed alongside the label in the cell. Doing this is very similar to setting the label:

```
[[cell imageView] setImage:[UIImage imageNamed:@"MyPicture.png"]]
```

To use our own labels and images, however, things get a bit more complicated. Let's quickly review the three-level hierarchy of our `flowerData` structure:

flowerData(NSMutableArray)→NSMutableArray→NSMutableDictionary

The first level, the top `flowerData` array, corresponds to the sections within the table. The second level, another array contained within the `flowerData` array, corresponds to the rows within the section, and, finally, the NSMutableDictionary provides the individual pieces of information about each row. Refer back to Figure 14.10 if you're still having trouble picturing how information is organized.

So, how do we get to the individual pieces of data that are three layers deep? By first using the section value to return the right array, and then, from that, using the row value to return the right dictionary, and then finally, using a key to return the correct value from the dictionary.

For example, to get the value that corresponds to the `"name"` key for a given section and row, we can write the following:

```
[[[flowerData objectAtIndex:indexPath.section] objectAtIndex: indexPath.row]
objectForKey:@"name"]
```

Likewise, we can return the image file with this:

```
[[[[flowerData objectAtIndex:indexPath.section] objectAtIndex: indexPath.row]
objectForKey:@"picture"]
```

Substituting these values into the statements needed to set the cell label and image, we get the following:

```
[[cell textLabel] setText:[[[flowerData objectAtIndex:indexPath.section]
objectAtIndex: indexPath.row] objectForKey:@"name"]]
```

and

```
[[cell imageView] setImage:[UIImage imageNamed:[[[flowerData
objectAtIndex:indexPath.section] objectAtIndex: indexPath.row]
objectForKey:@"picture"]]]
```

Add these lines to the `tableView:cellForRowAtIndexPath` method, before the statement that returns the cell.

As a final decoration, the cell should display an arrow on the right side to show that it can be touched to drill down to a detail view. This UI element is called a "disclosure indicator" and can be added simply by setting the `accessoryType` property for the cell object:

```
cell.accessoryType=UITableViewCellAccessoryDisclosureIndicator
```

Add this line after your code to set the cell text and image. The table display setup is now complete!

> We've intentionally left out the full method implementations in this section because, with the exception of how values are accessed, the code is nearly identical to the previous example. Remember that you can always review the full implementations in the hour's project files.

Of course, the table doesn't yet understand how to respond to an event and display the detail view, but we'll wrap up those details next.

Handling Navigation Events

In the previous example application, we handled a touch event with the `tableView:didSelectRowAtIndexPath` method and displayed an alert to the user. This time, our implementation will need to create an instance of the `FlowerDetailViewController` and set its `detailURL` property to the URL that we want the view to display. Finally, the new view controller must be pushed onto the navigation controller stack.

Putting all of these pieces together, the result looks like this:

```
 1: - (void)tableView:(UITableView *)tableView
 2:          didSelectRowAtIndexPath:(NSIndexPath *)indexPath {
 3:
 4:        FlowerDetailViewController *flowerDetailViewController =
 5:            [[FlowerDetailViewController alloc] initWithNibName:
 6:             @"FlowerDetailViewController" bundle:nil];
 7:        flowerDetailViewController.detailURL=
 8:            [[NSURL alloc] initWithString:
 9:            [[[flowerData objectAtIndex:indexPath.section] objectAtIndex:
10:                indexPath.row] objectForKey:@"url"]];
11:        flowerDetailViewController.title=
12:            [[[flowerData objectAtIndex:indexPath.section] objectAtIndex:
13:                indexPath.row] objectForKey:@"name"];
14:        [self.navigationController pushViewController:
15:            flowerDetailViewController animated:YES];
16:        [flowerDetailViewController release];
17: }
```

> The navigationController instance that we're using in this code was created by the application template and is defined in the MainWindow.xib and Application Delegate files. You don't need to write any code at all to initialize or allocate it.

By the Way

Lines 4–6 allocate an instance of the FlowerDetailViewController and load the FlowerDetailViewController.xib file. Lines 7–8 set the detailURL property of the new detail view controller to the value of the dictionary key for the selected cell's section and row.

The detail view controller instance, flowerDetailViewController, is now prepped and ready to be displayed. In lines 11–13, it is pushed on the navigation controller stack. Setting the animated parameter to "YES" implements a smooth sliding action onscreen.

> You might be wondering: If we push a view controller onto the stack, shouldn't we have to pop it back off somewhere? The answer is *no*. Although there are methods available within the UINavigationController class that can be used to pop the view controllers off the stack, you get this basic functionality for free. As you push view controllers onto the navigation controller, the controller will automatically update the navigation bar to display a back button that is set to the title of the previous view controller. When the user touches this button, the top view controller is automatically popped off.

By the Way

Tweaking the UI

Before we can call this application "done," we need to make a few tweaks to the interface. First, if you've run the app already, you know that the table view row just isn't large enough to accommodate the images that were provided. Second, we need to set a title to be displayed in the navigation bar for the initial table view. This title will then be used to create the label in the "back" button on the subsequent detail view.

Changing the Row Size

To update the height of the rows in the table, open the XIB file that defines the table view (RootViewController.xib) in Interface Builder. Open the document window and make sure that the Table View icon is selected. Press Command+3 to open the Size Inspector window. Update the row height size to at least 100 (pixels), as shown in Figure 14.14.

FIGURE 14.14
Update the row height to fit the size of the images that will be displayed.

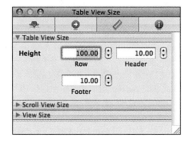

Setting the Table Style

So far, both tables we've created use the "plain" style. To change to the more rounded "grouped" style, within the RootViewController.xib, select the Table View icon, and open the Attributes Inspector. Use the Style drop-down menu to switch between the Plain and Grouped options.

If you set sizing information for one style of table, then change the style, your previous size selections will be lost.

Setting a Navigation Bar Title

The title that appears in the navigation bar usually comes from a few different places. If a UINavigationItem object exists in a view controller, the title property of that object will appear as the label in the center of the navigation bar. If no UINavigationItem exists within the view controller, the controller's title property is used as the navigation bar's center label.

In this example application, the MainWindow.xib contains an instance of the table view controller (RootViewController) and a UINavigationItem. To set a title that will appear in the navigation bar when the table view is present (and also in the back button of the detail view), open the MainWindow.xib and select the Navigation Item from the document window. With the item selected, press Command+1 to open the Attributes Inspector. Enter an appropriate title into the Title field, such as **Flower List**.

The application is now complete! If you've followed along with the example, your final result should look very much like the views shown in Figure 14.15.

FIGURE 14.15
The final application displays a graphical list of flowers and drills down to a Wikipedia article on each.

Summary

This hour introduced one of the most important iPhone interface elements—the table view—along with the associated table view controller. Table views enable users to sort through large amounts of information in an orderly manner. We covered how table cells are populated, including text and images, as well as the mechanism by which cell selection occurs.

We also explored the role of navigation controllers in managing a hierarchy of different views, making drill-down functionality simple.

Coming away from this chapter, you should feel comfortable working with tables in your applications and building basic drill-down apps using a navigation controller.

Q&A

Q. *What is the most efficient way to provide data to a table?*

A. You've almost certainly come to the conclusion that there has *got* to be a better way to provide data to complex views rather than manually defining all the data within the application itself. Starting in Hour 15, you'll learn about persistent data and how it can be used within applications. This will become the preferred way of working with large amounts of information as you move forward.

Q. *Can a table row have more than a single cell?*

A. No, but a customized cell can be defined that presents information in a more flexible manner than the default cell. As described in the "Further Exploration" section, custom cells can be defined in Interface Builder through the UITableViewCell class.

Q. *Do navigation controllers have to be used with tables?*

A. No. A navigation controller can push and pop any view controller and associated view. Tables, however, are commonly associated with navigation controllers because of the drill-down functionality that can be created.

Workshop

Quiz

1. When working with the NSIndexPath object in the table view controller methods, which two properties will come in handy?

2. Which two protocols, both conformed to by the UITableViewController class, are required for a table view to be displayed?

3. Where does the title for a navigation bar come from?

Answers

1. The section property will identify the section within the table, while the row property refers to the specific cell inside of that section.

2. A table view requires methods defined within the UITableViewDataSource and UITableViewDelegate protocols in order to display information.

3. If a view controller contains a navigation item (UINavigationItem), the title property of the navigation item will be used. If it doesn't, the view controller's title property will be substituted instead.

Activities

1. In the navigation-based application, the navigation bar does not display a title on the detail view. Update the application so that the detail view shows the name of the selected flower in the navigation bar of the detail view. You can use code very similar to what sets the detailURL property of the view.

2. A navigation controller can handle much more than two views in its stack. Use what you've learned about navigation controllers to create a three-level (or more) hierarchy of views.

3. Use Interface Builder to create and customize an instance of the UITableViewCell class.

Further Exploration

Table views are useful, but substantially complex beasts. In the span of an hour, you've learned how to create a table view from scratch within an application, and how to use a table view alongside a navigation controller. These are important first steps, but they're not the "whole story."

To continue your experience in working with tables, I suggest focusing on a few important enhancements.

The first is expanding what you can do with table cells. Review the property list for UITableViewCell. In addition to the TextLabel and ImageView properties, you can make numerous other customizations—including setting backgrounds, detail labels, and much, much more. In fact, if the default table cell options do not provide everything you need, Interface Builder supports visual customization of table cells by creating a customized instance of UITableViewCell.

Once you have a handle on the presentation of the table views, you can increase their functionality by implementing a few additional methods in your table view controller. Read the reference for UITableViewController, UITableViewDataSource, and UITableViewDelegate. You can quickly enable editing functionality for your table by implementing a handful of additional methods. You'll need to spend some time thinking of what editing controls you want to use and what the intended result will be, but the basic functionality of deleting, reordering, and inserting rows (along with the associated graphic controls you're used to seeing in iPhone applications) will come along "for free" as you implement the methods.

Apple Tutorials

Customizing table cells and views – TableViewSuite (accessible via the Xcode developer documentation). The TableViewSuite tutorial is an excellent look at how table views can be customized to suit a particular application.

Editing table cells – EditableDetailView (accessible via the Xcode developer documentation). The EditableDetailView tutorial implements row editing, including inserting, reordering, and deleting, within a table view.

HOUR 15

Storing Application Preferences

What You'll Learn in This Hour

▶ Good design principles for using application preferences

▶ How to store application preferences and read them later

▶ How to edit application preferences from within your application

▶ How to expose your application's preferences to the Settings application

Most substantial applications, whether on the computer or the iPhone, allow users to customize their operation to their own needs and desires. You have probably cursed an application before, only to later find a setting that removes the unholy annoyance, and you probably have a favorite application that you've customized to your exact needs, so that it fits like a well-worn glove. In this hour, we show you how your application can use application preferences to allow the user to customize its behavior.

> *Application preferences* is Apple's chosen term, but you may be more familiar with other terms such as settings, user defaults, user preferences, or options. These are all essentially the same concept.

By the Way

Design Considerations

The dominant design aesthetic of iPhone applications is for simple, single-purpose applications that start fast and do one task quickly and efficiently. Being fun, clever, and beautiful is an expected bonus. How do application preferences fit into this design view?

You want to limit the number of application preferences by creating opinionated software. There might be three valid ways to accomplish a task, but your application should have an opinion on the one best way to accomplish it, and then should implement this one approach in such a polished and intuitive fashion that your users instantly agree it's the best way. Leave the other two approaches for someone else's application. It may seem counterintuitive, but there is a much bigger market for opinionated software than for applications that try to please everyone.

This might seem like odd advice to find in a chapter about application preferences, but I'm not suggesting that you avoid preferences altogether. There are some very important roles for application preferences. Use preferences for the choices your users must make, rather than for all the choices they could possibly make. For example, if you are connecting to the application programming interface (API) of a third-party web application on behalf of your user, and the user must provide credentials to access the service, this is something the user must do, not just something users might want to do differently, and so it is a perfect case for storing as an application preference.

Another strong consideration for creating an application preference is when a preference can streamline the use of your application; for example, when users can record their default inputs or interests so that they don't have to make the same selections repeatedly. You want user preferences that reduce the amount of onscreen typing and taps that it takes to achieve the user's goal for using your application.

Once you've decided a preference is warranted, you have an additional decision to make. How will you expose the preference to the user? One option is to make the preference implicit based on what the user does while using the application. An example of an implicitly set preference is returning to the last state of the application. For example, suppose a user flips a toggle to see details. When the user next uses the application, the same toggle should be flipped and showing details.

Another option is to expose your application's preference in Apple's Settings application (see Figure 15.1). Settings is an application built in to the iPhone. It provides a single place to customize the iPhone. Everything from the hardware, built-in applications from Apple, and third-party applications can be customized from the Settings application.

A settings bundle lets you declare the user preferences of your application so that the Settings application can provide the user interface for editing those preferences. There is less coding for you to do if you let Settings handle your application's preferences, but less coding is not always the dominant consideration. A preference that is set once and rarely changes, such as the username and password for a web service, is ideal for configuring in Settings. In contrast, an option that the user might change with each use of your application, such as the difficulty level in a game, is not appropriate for Settings.

FIGURE 15.1
The Settings
application.

Users will be annoyed if they have to repeatedly exit your application, launch
Settings to change the preference, and then relaunch your application. Decide
whether each preference belongs in the Settings application or in your own application, but it's generally not a good idea to put them in both.

**Watch
Out!**

Also keep in mind that the user interface that Settings can provide for editing your
application preferences is limited. If a preference requires a custom interface component or custom validation code, it can't be set in Settings and it must be set from
within your application.

For the rest of this chapter, we don't strictly heed every aspect of this design advice
because we are creating an application whose main purpose is to teach us about
application preferences rather than to be an example of excellent product design.
But first, we will look at examples of some applications that do get it right.

Case Studies

The following case studies provide examples of appropriate use of application preferences. The case studies include examples from Apple as well as from an application developed by a third party.

Apple Applications

Weather and Stocks are two of the built-in applications from Apple. Both are Utility applications, meaning they have an information icon that when tapped causes an animation transition to a flipside view that exposes the application's preferences (see Figure 15.2).

Weather allows you to maintain a list of cities whose weather you have an interest in and lets you choose between the Fahrenheit and Celsius scales. This illustrates two of our design principles brilliantly. By letting the user persist the cities of interest, the user's interaction with Weather is made faster and simpler. Weather launches right to the display of weather information from a relevant city, and seeing weather for somewhere else becomes a simple matter of flicking left or right to select another city from the configured list. The scale of the temperature is something the user simply must select in any weather application, so it makes sense to have as a preference.

The Stocks application works much the same way as Weather. Users can select the market indexes and securities they are interested in so that only those show in the display. A three-way toggle between percent change, price, and market capitalization allows the user to choose how to make use of the limited real estate next to each security. The application preferences for Stocks keeps the application simple, fast, intuitive, and ideally fit for its single purpose.

FIGURE 15.2
Application preferences on the flipside views of Weather and Stocks.

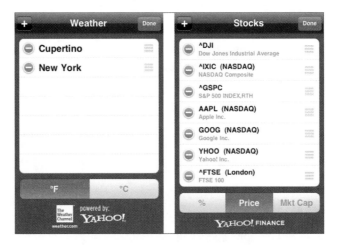

Maps is arguably the most complex application that ships with the iPhone. It can locate you through cellular triangulation, WiFi hot spot proximity or the iPhone's GPS hardware. It can show you maps and satellite views of most anyplace in the world, and can find places by their street addresses and provides step-by-step directions for walking, driving, or public transportation.

Despite all of this rich functionality, Maps has just two preferences. You tap the page-flip icon in the bottom right to peel back the map. This exposes some application functionality (dropping a new pin to mark a location) and the only two preferences (see Figure 15.3). The first preference lets you hide or show traffic data on the map, and the second preference lets you toggle between different types of maps. Obviously, users need to be able to change these settings for each use of the application depending on what they are trying to do at that moment, and having to exit Maps and launch the Settings application would be annoying.

FIGURE 15.3
Preferences in the Maps application.

We've already seen how Stocks lets users allocate limited screen real estate to the information that is most relevant to them. Another example of this type of customization is picking the items to have closest at hand on a toolbar.

Toolbar item customization is a common practice in Mac and Windows desktop applications, and it translates well to the iPhone. An example of this is in the YouTube application. The YouTube application has 10 possible toolbar items, but the toolbar has room for only four. The rest of the items end up being an extra tap away behind the More item. The YouTube application lets users pick the four items they use the most frequently to be on the toolbar (see Figure 15.4), making the application just a little faster and more enjoyable.

FIGURE 15.4
Toolbar cus-
tomization in
the YouTube
application.

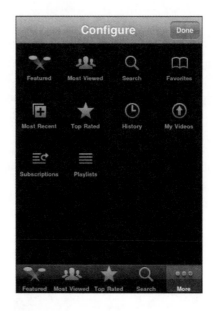

ESPN ScoreCenter

The ESPN ScoreCenter application provides scores and news from the world of sports. ESPN ScoreCenter has a design aesthetic very reminiscent of the Apple applications we just looked at. It launches quickly and shows an interesting bit of trivia while it downloads information from the network. It then shows scores and news from the last sport the user looked at, potentially providing the information wanted from the application without the user making any selection at all.

The application preferences for ESPN ScoreCenter are all about streamlining the use of the application. Users can pick the sports and teams that they follow so that the information presented is more tailored to their interests and is delivered more quickly, with fewer interactions (see Figure 15.5). There are no preferences you can change about how the application behaves, but because it can be tailored to your own particular sports interests, ESPN ScoreCenter feels like one of the more configurable applications on the iPhone.

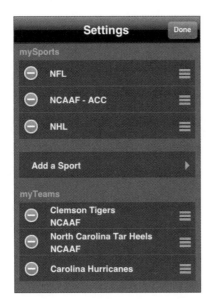

FIGURE 15.5
ESPN
ScoreCenter
settings.

Reading and Writing User Defaults

Application preferences is Apple's name for the overall preference system by which applications can customize themselves for the user. The application preferences system takes care of the low-level tasks of persisting preferences to the device, keeping each application's preferences separate from other applications' preferences, and backing up application preferences to the computer via iTunes so that users won't lose their preferences in case the device needs to be restored. Your interaction with the application preferences system is through an easy-to-use API that consists mainly of the NSUserDefaults singleton class.

The NSUserDefaults class works similarly to the NSDictionary class. The main differences are that NSUserDefaults is a singleton and is more limited in the types of objects it can store. All the preferences for your application are stored as key/value pairs in the NSUserDefaults singleton.

A *singleton* is just an instance of the Singleton pattern, and a *pattern* in programming is just a common way of doing something. The Singleton pattern is fairly common in the iPhone SDK, and it is a technique used to ensure that there is only one instance (object) of a particular class. In the iPhone SDK, it is most often used to represent a service provided to your program by the hardware or operating system.

Did you
Know?

Implicit Preferences

In our first example, we will create a (now infamous) flashlight application. The application will have an on/off switch and will shine a light from the screen when it is on. A slider will control the brightness level of the light. We will use preferences to return the flashlight to the last state the user left it in.

Add the Outlets and Action

Create a new View-Based Application in Xcode and call it **Flashlight**. Click the FlashlightViewController.h file in the Classes group and add outlets for our on/off switch, brightness slider, and light source. Add an action called setLightSourceAlpha that will respond when toggling the switch or sliding the brightness control. The FlashlightViewController.h file should read as shown in Listing 15.1.

LISTING 15.1

```
#import <UIKit/UIKit.h>

@interface FlashlightViewController : UIViewController {

    IBOutlet UIView *lightSource;
    IBOutlet UISwitch *toggleSwitch;
    IBOutlet UISlider *brightnessSlider;

}

@property (nonatomic, retain) UIView *lightSource;
@property (nonatomic, retain) UISwitch *toggleSwitch;
@property (nonatomic, retain) UISlider *brightnessSlider;

-(IBAction) setLightSourceAlphaValue;

@end
```

Lay Out the UI

Now we'll lay out the Flashlight application's user interface, as follows:

1. Open Interface Builder by double-clicking the FlashlightViewController.xib file in the Resources group.

2. In Interface Builder, click the empty view and open the Attribute Inspector (Command+1).

3. Set the background color of the view to black.

4. Open the Library (Shift+Command+L).

5. Search the Library for "switch" and drag a UISwitch onto the bottom left of the view.

6. Search the Library for "slider" and drag a UISlider to the bottom right of the view.

7. Size the slider to take up all the horizontal space not used by the switch.

8. Finally, search the library for "view" and add a UIView to the top portion of the view. Size it so that it is full width and takes up all the vertical space above the switch and slider. Your view should now look like Figure 15.6.

FIGURE 15.6
The Flashlight UI in Interface Builder.

Connect the Outlets and Action

The code we will write to operate the flashlight and deal with the application preferences will need access to the switch, slider, and light source. Right-click the File's Owner icon and connect the lightSource IBOutlet to the UIView, the toggleSwitch IBOutlet to the UISwitch, and the brightnessSlider IBOutlet to the UISlider by clicking the circle next to each outlet and dragging to the corresponding control on the interface.

In addition to being able to access the three controls, our code needs to respond to changes in the toggle state of the switch and changes in the position of the slider.

Connect the `setLightSourceAlphaValue` IBAction to the `UISwitch` by click-dragging from the circle next to the `setLightSourceAlphaValue` Received Action and dragging to the `UISwitch`. Select Value Changed from the pop-up menu. Repeat this step again and connect the same `setLightSourceAlphaValue` Received Action to the Value Changed event of the `UISlider` (see Figure 15.7). Save the XIB file and return to Xcode.

FIGURE 15.7
Connecting the slide action to the `UISlider`.

Adjust the Flashlight and Write the User Defaults

When the user toggles the flashlight on or off and adjusts the brightness level, the application will respond by adjusting the alpha property of the `lightSource` view. The alpha property of a view controls the transparency of the view, with 0.0 being completely transparent and 100.0 being completely translucent. The `lightSource` view is white, and is on top of the black background. When the `lightSource` view is more transparent, more of the black will be showing through and the flashlight will be darker. When we want to turn the light off, we just set the alpha property to 0.0 so that none of the white background of the `lightSource` view will be showing.

To make the flashlight work, we can add this code to the FlashlightViewController.m file in the Classes group:

```
@synthesize lightSource;
@synthesize toggleSwitch;
```

```
@synthesize brightnessSlider;

-(IBAction) setLightSourceAlphaValue {
      if (toggleSwitch.on) {
            lightSource.alpha = brightnessSlider.value;
      } else {
            lightSource.alpha = 0.0;
      }
}

- (void)dealloc {
      [lightSource release];
      [toggleSwitch release];
      [brightnessSlider release];
   [super dealloc];
}
```

The slider value property returns a float between 0 and 100, which happens to also be the value we need to set the alpha property on the lightSource view, so this is already enough code to make the flashlight work. You can run the project yourself and see. (Would you pay $0.99 for this?)

We don't just want the flashlight to work; we want it to return to its last state when the user uses the flashlight application again later. We'll store the on/off state and the brightness level as implicit preferences. First we need two constants to be the keys for these preferences. Add these constants to the top of the FlashlightViewController.h file in the Classes group:

```
#define kOnOffToggle @"onOff"
#define kBrightnessLevel @"brightness"
```

Then we will persist the two values of the keys in the viewWillDisappear event of the FlashlightViewController. We will get the NSUserDefault singleton using the standardUserDefaults method and then use the setBool and setFloat methods. Because NSUserDefaults is a singleton, we are not creating it and are not responsible for managing its memory.

Add a viewWillDisappear method to the FlashLightViewController.m file in the Classes group:

```
-(void) viewWillDisappear:(BOOL)animated {

      NSUserDefaults *userDefaults = [NSUserDefaults standardUserDefaults];
      [userDefaults setBool:toggleSwitch.on forKey:kOnOffToggle];
      [userDefaults setFloat:brightnessSlider.value forKey:kBrightnessLevel];

      [super viewWillDisappear:animated];
}
```

By the Way

Our code now saves the values for our two keys, but where do they go? The idea here is that we don't have to know because we are using the NSUserDefaults API to shield us from this level of detail and to allow Apple to change how defaults are handled in future versions of the iPhone OS.

It can still be useful to know, however, and the answer is that our preferences are stored in a plist file. If you are an experienced Mac user you may already be familiar with plists, which are used for Mac applications, too. When running on a device, the plist will be local to the device, but when we run our application in the iPhone Simulator, the simulator uses our computer's hard drive for storage, making it easy for us to peek inside the plist.

Run the Flashlight application in the iPhone Simulator, and then use Finder to navigate to /Users/<your username>/Library/Application Support/iPhone Simulator/User/Applications. The directories in Applications are generated globally unique IDs, but it should be easy to find the directory for Flashlight by looking for the most recent Data Modified. You'll see Flashlight.app in the most recently modified directory, and you'll see the com.yourcompany.Flashlight.plist inside the ./Library/Preferences subdirectory. This is a regular Mac plist file, and so when you double-click it, it will open with the Property List Editor application and show you the two preferences for Flashlight.

Read the User Defaults

Now our application is writing out the state of the two controls anytime our view disappears (for this application, essentially when the application closes). So, to complete the desired behavior, we need to do the opposite and read in and use the preferences for the state of the two controls anytime our flashlight view appears (essentially when the application launches). For this, we will use the viewDidLoad method, which is provided for us by Xcode as a commented-out stub, and the floatForKey and boolForKey methods of NSUserDefaults. Uncomment viewDidLoad and get the NSUserDefaults singleton in the same way as before, but this time we will set the value of the controls from the value returned from the preference rather than the other way around. In the FlashlightViewController.m file in the Classes group, modify viewDidLoad as follows:

```
// Implement viewDidLoad to do additional setup after loading the view,
typically from a nib.
- (void)viewDidLoad {

        NSUserDefaults *userDefaults = [NSUserDefaults standardUserDefaults];

        brightnessSlider.value = [userDefaults floatForKey:kBrightnessLevel];
        toggleSwitch.on = [userDefaults boolForKey:kOnOffToggle];
        if ([userDefaults boolForKey: kOnOffToggle]) {
                lightSource.alpha = [userDefaults floatForKey:kBrightnessLevel];
          } else {
                lightSource.alpha = 0.0;
```

```
    }
    [super viewDidLoad];
}
```

That's all there is to it. All we need now is a snazzy application icon and we too can make millions in the iTunes Store with our Flashlight application (see Figure 15.8).

FIGURE 15.8
Flashlight application in action.

While we are waiting for the cash to pour in, let's look at an application where the user takes more direct control of the application's preferences.

System Settings

One option to consider for providing application preferences is to use the Settings application. You do this by creating and editing a settings bundle for your application in Xcode rather than by writing code and designing a UI, so this is a very fast and easy option.

For our second application of the hour, we'll create ReturnMe, an application that tells someone who finds a lost device how to return it to its owner. The Settings application will be used to edit the contact information of the owner and to select a picture to evoke the finder's sympathy.

Add the Outlets and Images

Create a new Utility application in Xcode called **ReturnMe**. The Utility Application template wires in a flipside view for setting application preferences; but don't worry about this flipside view just yet, we'll set that up later in the hour. Initially, we'll focus on the main view and the settings bundle.

The main view is the view that is initially displayed. We want to provide the finder of the lost device with a sympathy-invoking picture and the owner's name, email address, and alternative phone number (not the owner's iPhone number!). Each of these items will be configurable as an application preference, so we'll need outlets to set the values of a UIImageView and three UILabels. Click the MainViewController.h file in the Classes group and add outlets and properties for each control. The MainViewController.h file should look like Listing 15.2.

LISTING 15.2

```
#import "FlipsideViewController.h"

@interface MainViewController : UIViewController
<FlipsideViewControllerDelegate> {

     IBOutlet UIImageView *picture;
     IBOutlet UILabel *name;
     IBOutlet UILabel *email;
     IBOutlet UILabel *phone;
}

@property (nonatomic, retain) UIImageView *picture;
@property (nonatomic, retain) UILabel *name;
@property (nonatomic, retain) UILabel *email;
@property (nonatomic, retain) UILabel *phone;

- (IBAction)showInfo;

@end
```

We want a few images that will help goad our Good Samaritan into returning the lost device. Right-click ReturnMe in the Groups & Files tree in Xcode and select Add, New Group. Name the group **Images**. Drag the rat.jpg, dog.jpg, and hamster.jpg files from the book's ReturnMe source code project into the Images group. When you drag the images into Xcode, make sure you click the option to copy them into the destination group's folder so that copies of the images will be placed in your Xcode project's directory.

Lay Out the UI

Now let's lay out the ReturnMe application's UI, as follows:

1. Open Interface Builder by double-clicking the MainView.xib file in the Resources group.

2. In Interface Builder, open the Library (Shift+Command+L) and search the Library for "label."

3. Drag three UILabels onto the view.

4. Click each label and open the Attribute Inspector (Command+1) and set the text to a default value of your choosing for name, email, and phone number.

5. Open the Library (Shift+Command+L) and search it for "image."

6. Drag a UIImageView to the view.

7. Size the image view to take up the majority of the space. Click the image view and open the Attribute Inspector (Command+1).

8. Set the mode to be Scale to Fill, and pick one of the fuzzy animal images you added to the Xcode project from the Image drop-down.

9. Add some additional labels to explain the purpose of the application and labels that explain each preference value (name, email, and phone number).

Try to make an attractive and compelling UI. This is a chance to have a little fun and stretch your UI design muscles. As long as you have the three labels and the image view in your UI (see Figure 15.9), you can design the rest as you see fit. Have fun with it!

Create the Settings Bundle

Create a new settings bundle in Xcode by selecting File, New File from the menu and selecting Settings Bundle from the Resources group in the sidebar (see Figure 15.10). Keep the default name of Settings.bundle when you create it. Drag the newly created settings bundle into the Resources group if it does not get created there.

The file that controls how our ReturnMe application will appear in the Settings application is the Root.plist file in the settings bundle. We can edit this file with the Property List Editor that is built in to Xcode. We will add preference types to it (see Table 15.1) that will be read and interpreted by the Settings application to provide the UI to set our application's preferences.

FIGURE 15.9
ReturnMe application's main view in Interface Builder.

FIGURE 15.10
Settings bundle in Xcode's New File dialog.

TABLE 15.1 Preference Types

Type	Key	Description
Text field	PSTextFieldSpecifier	Editable text string
Toggle switch	PSToggleSwitchSpecifier	On/off toggle button
Slider	PSSliderSpecifier	Slider across a range of values

TABLE 15.1   Continued

Type	Key	Description
Multivalue	PSMultiValueSpecifier	Drop-down value picker
Title	PSTitleValueSpecifier	Read-only text string
Group	PSGroupSpecifier	Title for a logical group of preferences
Child pane	PSChildPaneSpecifier	Child preferences page

The ReturnMe preferences will be grouped into three groups: Sympathy Image, Contact Information, and About. The Sympathy Image group will contain a multi-value preference to pick one of the images, the Contact Information group will contain three text fields, and the About group will link to a child page with three read-only titles.

Expand the Settings.bundle in Xcode and click the Root.plist file. You'll see a table of three columns: Key, Type, and Value. Expand the PreferencesSpecifiers property in the table and you'll see a series of four dictionary properties. These are provided by Xcode as samples, and each of them will be interpreted by Settings as a preference. You will follow the simple schema in the *Settings Application Schema Reference* in the iPhone Reference Library to set all the required properties, and some of the optional properties, of each preference.

Expand the first dictionary property under PreferenceSpecifiers called Item 1, and you'll see that its Type is PSGroupSpecifier. This is the correct Type to define a preference group, but change the Title property to **Sympathy Image** by clicking it and typing the new title. Expand the second item and you'll see that its Type is PSTextFieldSpecifier. Our Sympathy Image will be selected as a multivalue, not a text field, so change the Type to **PSMultiValueSpecifier**. Change the Title to **Image Name**, the Key to **picture**, and the DefaultValue to **Hamster**. The remaining four keys under Item 2 apply to text fields only, so delete them by selecting them and pressing the Delete key.

The values for a multivalue picker come from two arrays, an array of item names and an array of item values. In our case, the name and value arrays will be the same, but we still must provide both of them. To add another property under DefaultValue, click the plus sign at the end of the row (see Figure 15.11) to add another property at the same level.

FIGURE 15.11
Add another
property in
Xcode's
Property List
Editor.

Key	Type	Value
▼ Root	Dictionary	(2 items)
StringsTable	String	Root
▼ PreferenceSpecifiers	Array	(4 items)
▼ Item 1	Dictionary	(2 items)
Type	String	PSGroupSpecifier
Title	String	Group
▼ Item 2	Dictionary	(4 items)
Type	String	PSMultiValueSpecifier
Title	String	Image Name
Key	String	picture
DefaultValue	String	Hamster
▶ Item 3	Dictionary	(4 items)
▶ Item 4	Dictionary	(7 items)

The new item will have the default name of New Item, so change that to **Values**.
The Type column defaults to String, so change it to **Array**. Each of the three possible
image names needs a property under the Values property. Expand the Values item's
disclosure triangle and notice that the plus sign at the end of the row changes to an
icon with three lines (see Figure 15.12). This icon adds child properties, rather than
properties at the same level. Click the icon three times to add properties that'll be
called Item 1, Item 2, and Item 3.

FIGURE 15.12
Add child items
in Xcode's
Property List
Editor.

DefaultValue	String	Hamster
▼ Values	Array	(3 items)
Item 1	String	
Item 2	String	
Item 3	String	

Change the Value of the three new child properties to **Dog**, **Hamster**, and **Rat**.
Repeat this step to add a peer of Values called **Titles**. Titles is also an Array type and
has the same three String type children with the same values.

FIGURE 15.13
The completed
image selector
preference in
Xcode's
Property List
Editor.

Key	Type	Value
▼ Root	Dictionary	(2 items)
StringsTable	String	Root
▼ PreferenceSpecifiers	Array	(4 items)
▶ Item 1	Dictionary	(2 items)
▼ Item 2	Dictionary	(6 items)
Type	String	PSMultiValueSpecifier
Title	String	Image Name
Key	String	picture
DefaultValue	String	Hamster
▼ Values	Array	(3 items)
Item 1	String	Dog
Item 2	String	Hamster
Item 3	String	Rat
▼ Titles	Array	(3 items)
Item 1	String	Dog
Item 2	String	Hamster
Item 3	String	Rat
▶ Item 3	Dictionary	(4 items)
▶ Item 4	Dictionary	(7 items)

The third property in our plist PreferenceSpecifiers should be a PSGroupSpecifier with a title of **Contact Information**. Change the Type and Title of Item 3 and remove the extra items. The fourth property is the name preference. Change the Type to **PSTextFieldSpecifier**, the Key to **name**, and the DefaultValue to **Your Name** with a Type of String. The final three items are String types that are optional parameters that set up the keyboard for text entry. Set the keys to **KeyboardType**, **AutocapitalizationType**, and **AutocorrectionType**, and the values to **Alphabet**, **Words**, and **No**, respectively.

You can test your settings so far by saving the plist, building and running the ReadMe application in the iPhone Simulator, exiting the application with the Home button, and then running the Settings application in the simulator. You should see a Settings selection for the ReturnMe application and settings for the Sympathy Image and Name (see Figure 15.14).

Add two more PSTextFieldSpecifier preferences to the plist, one for Email and one for Phone Number. Make them like the Name preference, but use the keys of **email** and **phone** and change the KeyboardTypes to **EmailAddress** and **NumberPad**.

The final preference is About, and it opens a child preference pane. Below the Phone preference item, add an About PSGroupSpecifier property, and under the group add a property with a Type of PSChildPaneSpecifier, a Title of **About**, and a String property with a Key of **File** and a Value of **About**. The child pane element assumes the value of File exists as another plist in the settings bundle. In our case, this is a file called About.plist.

The easiest way to create this second plist file in the settings bundle is by copying the Root.plist file we already have. Right-click the Root.plist file in Xcode and select the Open with Finder menu option. This opens the plist in the external Property List Editor. Select File, Save As and change the name to **About.plist** before clicking Save. Xcode won't immediately notice that your settings bundle has a new plist file. Collapse and expand Settings.bundle to refresh the contents.

Edit About.plist to have one group property titled About ReturnMe and three PSTitleSpecifier properties for Version, Copyright, and Website. PSTitleSpecifier properties have four properties: Type, Title, Key, and DefaultValue. If you have any difficulties setting up your plist files, compare your preferences UI to Figure 15.14 and your plists to the plists in the settings bundle in the book's source code to see where you might have made a misstep.

FIGURE 15.14
ReturnMe's set-
tings in the
Settings
Application.

Create the Preference Keys

We have four preferences we want to retrieve from the preferences database: the
selected image and the device owner's name, email, and alternate phone number.
Add a key constant for each of these to the top of the FlipsideViewController.h file in
the Flipside View group in Xcode:

```
#define kName @"name"
#define kEmail @"email"
#define kPhone @"phone"
#define kReward @"reward"
#define kPicture @"picture"
```

The `FlipsideViewController` is a good spot for these constants because it is
imported by the `MainViewController` and because we will need to use these constants from the flipside view when we look at setting preferences from within the
application.

Use the Preferences

We have now bundled up our preferences so that they can be set by the Settings
application, but our ReturnMe application also has to be modified to use the preferences. We do this in the MainViewController.m file's `viewDidLoad` event. Here we
will call a helper method we write called `setValuesFromPreferences`. Our code to
use the preference values with the `NSserDefaults` API looks no different from the
Flashlight application. It doesn't matter if our application wrote the preference values or if the Settings application did; we can simply treat `NSUserDefaults` like a
dictionary and ask for objects by their key.

We provided default values in the settings bundle, but it's possible the user just installed ReturnMe and has not run the Settings application. We should provide the same default settings programmatically to cover this case, and we can do that by providing a dictionary of default preference keys and values to the NSUserDefaults registerDefaults method. Add the following to the MainViewController.m file in the Main View group in Xcode:

```
@synthesize picture;
@synthesize name;
@synthesize email;
@synthesize phone;

- (NSDictionary *)initialDefaults {
    NSArray *keys = [[[NSArray alloc] initWithObjects:
                        kPicture, kName, kEmail, kPhone, nil] autorelease];
    NSArray *values = [[[NSArray alloc] initWithObjects:
                        @"Hamster", @"Your Name", @"you@yours.com",
                        @"(555)555-1212", nil] autorelease];
    return [[[NSDictionary alloc] initWithObjects: values
                            forKeys: keys] autorelease];
}

-(void)setValuesFromPreferences {

    NSUserDefaults *userDefaults = [NSUserDefaults standardUserDefaults];
    [userDefaults registerDefaults: [self initialDefaults]];
    NSString *picturePreference = [userDefaults stringForKey:kPicture];
    if ([picturePreference isEqualToString:@"Rat"]) {
        picture.image = [UIImage imageNamed:@"rat.jpg"];
    } else if ([picturePreference isEqualToString:@"Dog"]) {
        picture.image = [UIImage imageNamed:@"dog.jpg"];
    } else {
        picture.image = [UIImage imageNamed:@"hamster.jpg"];
    }

    name.text = [userDefaults stringForKey:kName];
    email.text = [userDefaults stringForKey:kEmail];
    phone.text = [userDefaults stringForKey:kPhone];

}

// Implement viewDidLoad to do additional setup after loading the view,
// typically from a nib.
 - (void)viewDidLoad {
    [self setValuesFromPreferences];
    [super viewDidLoad];
}

- (void)dealloc {
    [picture release];
    [name release];
    [email release];
    [phone release];
    [super dealloc];
}
```

Build and run the modified ReturnMe application and switch back and forth between the Settings application and the ReturnMe application. You can see that with very little code on our part we were able to provide a sophisticated interface to configure our application. The Settings application's plist schema provides a fairly complete way to describe the preference needs of our application.

In-Application Preferences

An owner's contact information and preference for big-eyed, furry mammals doesn't change that often, so the Settings application is the right place for these preferences. But let's suppose these preferences were something a user would want to change more often; you can see how leaving the application and launching the Settings application could be annoying. Next we'll use the ReturnMe application's flipside to set some of the preferences from within the application itself.

Add the `TableViewDelegate` and `TableViewDataSource`

The flipside view of our application is accessed by tapping the *i* icon on the main view. Luckily there is nothing we need to do to make this animated magic happen; all the required steps for that have been provided by the Utility application Xcode template. Apple recommends that the flipside of a Utility application should consist of a table view in grouped mode. Rather than having a `TableViewController` for the table view, we will use the `FlipsideViewController` as the table view's delegate and data source. If we didn't, `FlipsideViewController` would have very little to do in our application and might get sad.

Our `FlipsideViewController` will implement the table view's delegate and data source protocols and will have two `Array` properties for storing the preference names and `UITextFields` that will edit the preference's values. Modify the FlipsideViewController.h in the Flipside View group to read as shown in Listing 15.3.

LISTING 15.3

```
#define kName @"name"
#define kEmail @"email"
#define kPhone @"phone"
#define kReward @"reward"
#define kPicture @"picture"

@protocol FlipsideViewControllerDelegate;

@interface FlipsideViewController : UIViewController
    <UITableViewDelegate, UITableViewDataSource> {

        id <FlipsideViewControllerDelegate> delegate;

    NSArray *preferenceNames;
```

LISTING 15.3   Continued

```
        NSArray *preferenceObjects;
}

@property (nonatomic, assign) id <FlipsideViewControllerDelegate> delegate;
@property (nonatomic, assign) NSArray *preferenceNames;
@property (nonatomic, assign) NSArray *preferenceObjects;

- (IBAction)done;

@end

@protocol FlipsideViewControllerDelegate
- (void)flipsideViewControllerDidFinish:(FlipsideViewController *)controller;
@end
```

Lay Out the UI and Connect the `TableView` **Data Source and Delegate**

Now we'll lay out the Flashlight application's flipside user interface, as follows:

1. Open the FlipsideView.xib file in Interface Builder by double-clicking it in the Resources group in Xcode.

2. Click the navigation item at the top of the view, open it in the Attribute Inspector (Command+1), and change the title to **Return Me**.

3. Open the Library (Shift+Command+L) and search for "table."

4. Drag a `TableView` onto the view.

5. Right-click the table view and click-drag from the circle next to the Data Source icon and Delegate Outlets icon to the File's Owner icon. This establishes the `FlipsideViewController` as the data source for the preferences that we'll be editing in the table view.

6. Save the XIB and return to Xcode.

Implement the `TableView` **Data Source Protocol**

Open the FlipsideViewController.m file in the Flipside View group in Xcode. At this point, we already know how to do everything we need to do in the flipside view controller. Following what we learned in Hour 14, "Displaying and Navigating Data Using Table Views," we will implement the `UITableViewDataSource` protocol. As data for the table, we have an array of title strings and an array of `UITextFields` that we set up in the `viewDidLoad` event. The `UITextFields` are added as subviews to the table cell's content view.

FIGURE 15.15
The flipside
view in Interface
Builder.

Notice that the initial values for the UITextFields are set in the viewDidLoad event by reading the preference's current value from the NSUserDefaults singleton. Also notice that we use the existing done action from the Utility application Xcode template to store the preference values back into the user defaults database once the user clicks Done to flip back to the main view. Update the FlipsideViewController.m file as shown in Listing 15.4.

LISTING 15.4

```
#import "FlipsideViewController.h"

@implementation FlipsideViewController

@synthesize delegate;
@synthesize preferenceNames;
@synthesize preferenceObjects;

#pragma mark -
#pragma mark UITableViewDataSource

- (NSInteger)numberOfSectionsInTableView:(UITableView *)tableView {
    return 1;
}

- (NSString *) tableView:(UITableView *)table
 titleForHeaderInSection:(NSInteger)section {
    return @"Settings";
}

- (NSInteger)tableView:(UITableView *)tableView
 numberOfRowsInSection:(NSInteger)section {
    return preferenceNames.count;
```

LISTING 15.4   Continued

```objc
}

- (UITableViewCell *)tableView:(UITableView *)tableView
        cellForRowAtIndexPath:(NSIndexPath *)indexPath {

    static NSString *identifier = @"ReturnMe";
    UITableViewCell *preference = [tableView
        dequeueReusableCellWithIdentifier:identifier];
    if (preference == nil) {
        preference = [[[UITableViewCell alloc]
                     initWithStyle: UITableViewCellStyleDefault
                   reuseIdentifier:identifier] autorelease];
    }

    preference.textLabel.text = [preferenceNames objectAtIndex:indexPath.row];
    [preference.contentView
        addSubview:[preferenceObjects objectAtIndex:indexPath.row]];
    return preference;
}

#pragma mark -

- (void)viewDidLoad {

    [super viewDidLoad];
    self.view.backgroundColor = [UIColor viewFlipsideBackgroundColor];

    preferenceNames = [[NSArray alloc] initWithObjects:
        @"Your Name", @"Email Address", @"Phone Number", nil];

    NSUserDefaults *userDefaults = [NSUserDefaults standardUserDefaults];

    UITextField *name = [[[UITextField alloc]
        initWithFrame: CGRectMake(150.0, 11.0, 150.0, 30.0)] autorelease];
    name.text = [userDefaults stringForKey:kName];

    UITextField *email = [[[UITextField alloc]
        initWithFrame: CGRectMake(150.0, 11.0, 150.0, 30.0)] autorelease];
    email.text = [userDefaults stringForKey:kEmail];

    UITextField *phone = [[[UITextField alloc]
        initWithFrame: CGRectMake(150.0, 11.0, 150.0, 30.0)] autorelease];
    phone.text = [userDefaults stringForKey:kPhone];

    preferenceObjects = [[NSArray alloc] initWithObjects:
                            name, email, phone, nil];

}

- (IBAction)done {

    NSUserDefaults *userDefaults = [NSUserDefaults standardUserDefaults];

    // Save each preference
    [userDefaults setObject:
     [[preferenceObjects objectAtIndex:0] text]
```

LISTING 15.4 Continued

```
    forKey:kName];
    [userDefaults setObject:
    [[preferenceObjects objectAtIndex:1] text]
    forKey:kEmail];
    [userDefaults setObject:
    [[preferenceObjects objectAtIndex:2] text]
                    forKey:kPhone];

    [self.delegate flipsideViewControllerDidFinish:self];
}


/*
// Override to allow orientations other than the default portrait orientation.

(BOOL)shouldAutorotateToInterfaceOrientation:(UIInterfaceOrientation)interfaceOr
ientation {
// Return YES for supported orientations
return (interfaceOrientation == UIInterfaceOrientationPortrait);
}
*/

- (void)didReceiveMemoryWarning {
    // Releases the view if it doesn't have a superview.
    [super didReceiveMemoryWarning];

    // Release any cached data, images, etc that aren't in use.
}

- (void)viewDidUnload {
    // Release any retained subviews of the main view.
    // e.g. self.myOutlet = nil;
}


- (void)dealloc {
    [preferenceNames release];
    [preferenceObjects release];
    [super dealloc];
}

@end
```

Now run the Remember Me application and flip the view (see Figure 15.16) to try out the in-application preferences.

FIGURE 15.16
The flipside view in action.

Summary

In this hour, you've developed two fairly complete iPhone applications, and along the way you've learned three different ways of using the application preferences system to configure your application. You captured the user's implicit preferences with the Flashlight application, and you allowed the ReturnMe application to be explicitly configured from the Settings application and from a custom in-application UI. You also learned some important design principles that should keep you from getting carried away with too many preferences and should guide you in putting preferences in the right location.

This hour explored a lot of ground, and you have covered the topic of application preferences fairly exhaustively. At this point, you should be ready for any user-customization needs you encounter while developing your own applications.

Q&A

Q. *What about games? How should game preferences be handled?*

A. Games are about providing the player with an immersive experience. Leaving that experience to go to the Settings application or to interact with a stodgy table view is not going to keep the player immersed. You want users to set up the game to their liking while still remaining in the game's world, with the music and graphical style of the game as part of the customization experience. For games, feel free to use the `NSUserDefaults` API, but provide a custom, in-game experience for the UI.

Workshop

Quiz

1. What is a singleton? What important singleton did we use in this hour's applications?

2. What is a plist file?

Answers

1. A singleton is a class that should only ever have one object instantiated from it. The singleton we used in this hour was the `NSUserDefaults` `standardUserDefaults` singleton.

2. A plist file is an XML property list file used to store the user's settings for a given application. Plist files can be edited from within Xcode and externally to Xcode with the Property List Editor application.

Activities

1. If you think through the life cycle of the Flashlight application, you may realize there is a circumstance we didn't account for. It's possible that the Flashlight application has never been run before and so has no stored user preferences. To try this scenario, select Reset Content and Settings from the iPhone Simulator menu, and then build and launch the Flashlight application in the simulator. With no prior settings, it defaults to off, with the brightness turned all the way down. This is the exact opposite of what we would like to default to the first time Flashlight is run. Apply the technique we used in the Remember Me application to fix this and default the flashlight's initial state to on and 100% brightness.

2. Not everyone will return a lost iPhone just because he feels sorry for the hamster. Add a reward preference to the ReturnMe application. Default the preference to $50 and allow the user to change the value in both the in-application preferences and from the Settings application.

Further Exploration

There is not much about preferences that you have not been exposed to at this point. My main advice is to gain some more experience in working with preferences by going back to previous hours and adding sensible preferences to some of the example applications you have already worked on. The Application Preferences system is well documented by Apple and you should take some time to read through it.

Apple Guides

Application Preferences in the iPhone Application Programming is a tutorial-style guide to the various parts of the Application Preference system.

Setting Application Schema References in the iPhone Reference Library is an indispensable guide to the required and optional properties for the preferences in your plist files that will be edited by the Settings application.

HOUR 16

Reading and Writing Data

What You'll Learn in This Hour:

▶ Application sandbox restrictions
▶ Data storage locations
▶ Object archiving
▶ Data persistence with Core Data

Up to this point, the applications we've built have not allowed the user to create and store a lot of new data. Quite a few types of iPhone applications, however, do need to store a substantial amount of new information. Consider some of Apple's applications, such as Notes and Contacts. These are data management applications whose main function is to reliably store and retrieve data for the user. Where does this data go when the application is not running? Just like with a desktop application, iPhone applications persist their data to the file system.

In this hour, we look at some restrictions placed on an application's access to the file system, and then we explore the two main options you should consider for persisting data to the file system: object archiving and Core Data.

> **By the Way**
>
> Data management is a core foundation of programming, so it's not surprising that there are many other ways for iPhone applications to persist data to the file system besides object archiving and Core Data. The options range from C file-handling functions to low-level Core Foundation and Cocoa application programming interfaces (APIs) to property lists and direct access to SQLite databases. Each of these alternatives has its pros and cons, but with object archiving for the simple cases and Core Data for more extensive data management needs, you will be well covered in most situations. These two persistence mechanisms are recommended approaches to persisting data on the iPhone, and they are the two that we focus on for this hour.

Application Sandbox

In creating the iPhone SDK, Apple introduced a wide range of restrictions designed to protect users from malicious applications harming their devices. The restrictions are collectively known as the application sandbox. Any application you create with the iPhone SDK exists in a sandbox. There is no opting out of the sandbox and no way to get an exemption from the sandbox's restrictions.

Some of these restrictions affect how application data is stored and what data can be accessed. Each application is given a directory on the device's file system, and applications are restricted to reading and writing files in their own directory. This means a poorly behaved application can, at worst, wipe out its own data, but not the data of any other application, such as photo albums, contacts, or Flight Control high scores.

It also turns out that this restriction is not terribly limiting. The information from Apple's applications, such as contacts, calendars, and the photo and music libraries, is for the most part already exposed through APIs in the iPhone SDK. (For more information, see Hour 20, "Working with Rich Media," and Hour 21 "Interacting with Other Applications.")

Watch Out!

> With each version of the iPhone SDK, Apple has been steadily ramping up what you can't do because of the application sandbox, but parts of the sandbox are still enforced via policy rather than as technical restrictions. Just because you find a location on the file system where it is possible to read or write files outside the application sandbox doesn't mean you should. Violating the application sandbox is one of the surest ways to get your application rejected from the iTunes Store.

Storage Locations for Application Data

Within an application's directory, four locations are provided specifically for storing the application's data: the Library/Preferences, Library/Caches, Documents, and tmp directories.

Did you Know?

> When you run an application in the iPhone Simulator, the application's directory exists on your Mac in /Users/<your user>/Library/Applications Support/iPhone Simulator/User/Applications. There are any number of applications in this directory, each with a directory named after a unique ApplicationID (a series of characters with dashes) that is provided by Xcode. The easiest way to find the directory of the current application you are running in the iPhone Simulator is to look for the most recently modified application directory. Take a few minutes now to look through the directory of a couple applications from previous hours.

You encountered the Library/Preferences directory already in Hour 15, "Storing Application Preferences," and as you learned in that hour, it's not typical to read and write to the Preferences directory directly. Instead, you use the NSUserDefaults API. The Library/Caches, Documents, and tmp directories are, however, intended for direct file manipulation. The main difference between them is the intended lifetime of the files in each directory.

The Documents directory is the main location for storing application data. It is backed up to the computer when the device is synced with iTunes, so it is important to store any data users would be upset to lose in the Documents directory.

The Library/Caches directory is used to cache data retrieved from the network or from any computationally expensive calculation. Files in Library/Caches persist between launches of the application, and caching data in the Library/Caches directory can be an important technique used to improve the performance of an application.

Lastly, any data you want to store outside of the device's limited volatile memory, but that you do not need to persist between launches of the application, belongs in the tmp directory. The tmp directory is a more transient version of Library/Caches; think of it as a scratch pad for the application.

> Applications are responsible for cleaning up all the files they write, even those written to Library/Caches or tmp. Applications are sharing the limited file system space (typically 4 to 32GB) on the device. The space an application's files take up is not available for music, podcasts, photos, and other applications. Be judicious in what you choose to persistently store and be sure to clean up any temporary files created during the lifetime of the application.

Watch Out!

File Paths

Every file in an iPhone file system has a path, which is the name of its exact location on the file system. For an application to read or write a file in its sandbox, it needs to specify the full path of the file.

Core Foundation provides a C function called NSSearchPathForDirectoriesInDomains that returns the path to the application's Documents or Library/Caches directory. Asking for other directories from this function can return multiple directories, so the result of the function call is an NSArray object. When this function is used to get the path to the Documents or Library/Caches directory it returns exactly one NSString in the array, and the NSString of the path is extracted from the array using NSArray's objectAtIndex method with an index of 0.

NSString provides a method for joining two path fragments together called stringByAppendingPathComponent. By putting the result of a call to NSSearchPathForDirectoriesInDomains together with a specific filename, it is possible to get a string that represents a full path to a file in the application's Documents or Library/Caches directory.

Suppose, for example, your next blockbuster iPhone application calculates the first 100,000 digits of pi, and you want the application to write the digits out to a cache file so that they won't need to be calculated again. To get the full path to this file's location, you need to first get the path to the Library/Caches directory and then append the specific filename to it.

```
NSString *cacheDir =
    [NSSearchPathForDirectoriesInDomains(NSCachesDirectory,
                                NSUserDomainMask, YES) objectAtIndex: 0];
NSString *piFile = [cacheDir stringByAppendingPathComponent:@"American.pi"];
```

To get a path to a file in the Documents directory, use the same approach but with NSDocumentDirectory as the first argument to NSSearchPathForDirectoriesInDomains:

```
NSString *docDir =
        [NSSearchPathForDirectoriesInDomains(NSDocumentDirectory,
        NSUserDomainMask, YES) objectAtIndex: 0];
NSString *scoreFile = [docDir stringByAppendingPathComponent:@"HighScores.txt"];
```

Core Foundation provides another C function called NSTemporaryDirectory that returns the path of the application's tmp directory. As before, this can be used to get a full path to a file:

```
NSString *scratchFile =
        [NSTemporaryDirectory() stringByAppendingPathComponent:@"Scratch.data"];
```

FlashCards Application

As our example application for this hour, we'll be creating a flash card application. The application shows the user one card at a time, initially hiding the answer, and then lets users indicate whether they got the answer right or not. It keeps track of how many times users answer each card right or wrong, and users can create new flash cards and delete existing flash cards. Initially, we'll put the UI and mechanics of the game together without any data persistence. Each time you run the application, you'll need to create the cards all over again. Then we'll look at how to persist the user-created flash cards between application launches, first using object archiving and then using Core Data.

Create the FlashCard Class

Create a new View-Based Application in Xcode and call it **FlashCards**. As you'd suspect with an object-oriented flash card application, the first thing that's needed is a class that represents flash cards. Create a new class by selecting File, New File and then the Objective-C class template. Call the new file **FlashCard.m**, and be sure the Also Create FlashCard.h check box is selected.

A flash card object needs to keep track of four distinct pieces of information: the question, the correct answer, how often the user knew the correct answer, and how often the user got it wrong. Create NSString properties for the question and answer, NSUInteger properties for the right and wrong counters, and create a custom initializer that accepts the question and answer as arguments (see Listing 16.1).

LISTING 16.1

```
#import <Foundation/Foundation.h>

@interface FlashCard : NSObject {

    NSString *question;
    NSString *answer;
    NSUInteger rightCount;
    NSUInteger wrongCount;

}

@property (nonatomic, retain) NSString *question;
@property (nonatomic, retain) NSString *answer;
@property (nonatomic, assign) NSUInteger rightCount;
@property (nonatomic, assign) NSUInteger wrongCount;

- (id)initWithQuestion:(NSString *)thisQuestion answer:(NSString *)thisAnswer;

@end
```

To implement the FlashCard class, synthesize the four properties and implement the initializer as in Listing 16.2.

LISTING 16.2

```
#import "FlashCard.h"

@implementation FlashCard

@synthesize question, answer, rightCount, wrongCount;

- (id)initWithQuestion:(NSString *)thisQuestion answer:(NSString *)thisAnswer {

    if (self = [super init]) {
        self.question = thisQuestion;
        self.answer = thisAnswer;
```

LISTING 16.2 Continued

```
        self.rightCount = 0;
        self.wrongCount = 0;
    }
    return self;
}

@end
```

Add the Outlets and Actions

Click the FlashCardsViewController.h file in the Classes group and import the FlashCard class. Add outlets for five different labels: a count of the total cards, a count of how many times the current card has been answered rightly and how many times wrongly, and the current question and answer. The view controller also needs outlets for four buttons: delete, mark right, mark wrong, and next action buttons. There is also some state of the application to track in the controller. Add an NSMutable array property that will hold all the flash card objects, a counter property that tracks which flash card is currently being displayed, and a read-only property that uses the counter and the array to return the currently displayed flash card object. After you've added the outlets and properties, your FlashCardsViewController.h file should look like Listing 16.3.

LISTING 16.3

```
#import <UIKit/UIKit.h>
#import "FlashCard.h"

@interface FlashCardsViewController : UIViewController {

    IBOutlet UILabel *cardCount;
    IBOutlet UILabel *wrongCount;
    IBOutlet UILabel *rightCount;
    IBOutlet UILabel *question;
    IBOutlet UILabel *answer;
    IBOutlet UIBarButtonItem *deleteButton;
    IBOutlet UIBarButtonItem *rightButton;
    IBOutlet UIBarButtonItem *wrongButton;
    IBOutlet UIBarButtonItem *actionButton;
    NSMutableArray *flashCards;
    NSUInteger currentCardCounter;
    FlashCard *currentCard;
}

@property (nonatomic, retain) UILabel *cardCount;
@property (nonatomic, retain) UILabel *wrongCount;
@property (nonatomic, retain) UILabel *rightCount;
@property (nonatomic, retain) UILabel *question;
@property (nonatomic, retain) UILabel *answer;
@property (nonatomic, retain) UIBarButtonItem *deleteButton;
```

LISTING 16.3   Continued

```
@property (nonatomic, retain) UIBarButtonItem *rightButton;
@property (nonatomic, retain) UIBarButtonItem *wrongButton;
@property (nonatomic, retain) UIBarButtonItem *actionButton;
@property (nonatomic, retain) NSMutableArray *flashCards;
@property (nonatomic, assign) NSUInteger currentCardCounter;
@property (nonatomic, readonly) FlashCard *currentCard;

@end
```

Before we leave the view controller header and design the UI, let's consider the user's actions. Users will add and delete flash cards, press the next action button to expose the flash card's answer or flip to the next card, and they will mark whether they knew the correct answer or not. Each of these five actions will be connected to the buttons of our UI, so create five actions below the properties in the FlashCardsViewController.h file:

```
-(IBAction) markWrong;
-(IBAction) markRight;
-(IBAction) nextAction;
-(IBAction) addCard;
-(IBAction) deleteCard;
```

Lay Out the UI and Connect the Outlets and Actions

Open Interface Builder by double-clicking the FlashCardsViewController.xib file in the Resources group. Then complete the following steps to lay out the UI and connect the outlets and actions:

1. Click the empty view, open the Attribute Inspector (Command+1), and then click the Background attribute's color picker and change the color to white.

2. Open the Library (Shift+Command+L) and search for "toolbar."

3. Drag a toolbar to the very top of the view and another to the very bottom of the view.

4. Click the Item button in the top toolbar three times until just the button is selected, open the Attribute Inspector (Command+1), and choose Add from the Identifier Properties drop-down list.

5. Click the Item button in the bottom toolbar three times until just the button is selected, open the Attribute Inspector (Command+1), and change the Title attribute to **Right**.

6. Open the Library (Shift+Command+L) and search for "button."

7. Drag one Bar Button item to the top toolbar and two Bar Button items to the bottom toolbar.

8. Click the new button in the top toolbar three times until just the button is selected, open the Attribute Inspector (Command+1), and choose Trash from the Identifier Properties drop-down list.

9. Click the middle button in the bottom toolbar three times until just the button is selected, open the Attribute Inspector (Command+1), and change the Title attribute to **Wrong**.

10. Click the rightmost button in the bottom toolbar three times until just the button is selected, open the Attribute Inspector (Command+1), and choose Action from the Identifier Properties drop-down list. The view should now look like Figure 16.1.

FIGURE 16.1
Add the toolbars to the UI.

11. Open the Library (Shift+Command+L) and search for "space."

12. Drag a Flexible Space Bar Button item from the library search results to the leftmost position in the top toolbar.

13. Drag a Fixed Space Bar Button item to the leftmost position in the bottom toolbar.

14. Drag a Flexible Space Bar Button item to the position between the Wrong and Action button in the bottom toolbar.

15. Drag the right handle on the Fixed Space Bar Button item on the bottom toolbar to the right until the Right and Wrong buttons are centered horizontally
in the toolbar. The view should now look like Figure 16.2.

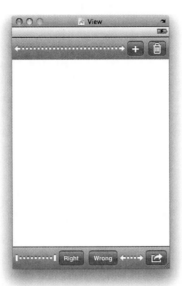

FIGURE 16.2
Lay out the tool-
bars.

16. Open the Library (Shift+Command+L) and search for "label."

17. Drag a label to the left alignment guide on the top toolbar. Size the label to be
as wide as the entire toolbar up to the Add button.

18. Click the new label, open the Attribute Inspector (Command+1), and change
the Text attribute to **100 of 200**. This label will tell users which card they are
on and how many cards they've created in total.

19. Drag four labels onto the view between the two toolbars.

20. Position one of the labels just under the top toolbar and against the left alignment guide. Size the label wider to about the midpoint of the view. Click the
label, open the Attribute Inspector (Command+1), and change the Text attribute to **Right: 0**. Click the Color attribute's color picker and change the text
color to green.

21. Position another one of the labels just under the top toolbar and against the
right alignment guide. Size the label wider to about the midpoint of the view.
Click the label, open the Attribute Inspector (Command+1), and change the
Layout attribute to Right Alignment, and change the Text attribute to **Wrong:
0**. Click the Color attribute's color picker and change the text color to red.

22. Position the third label just under the right and wrong labels and against the left alignment guide. Size the label wider to reach all the way to the right alignment guide. Size the label taller to reach about the midpoint of the view. Click the label, open the Attribute Inspector (Command+1), and change the Layout attribute to center alignment, and change the Text attribute to **Question?**.

23. Position the final label just under the question label and against the left alignment guide. Size the label wider to reach all the way to the right alignment guide. Size the label taller to reach the bottom toolbar. Click the label, open the Attribute Inspector (Command+1), and change the Layout attribute to Center Alignment, and change the Text attribute to **Answer**. The view should now look like Figure 16.3.

FIGURE 16.3
Lay out the labels.

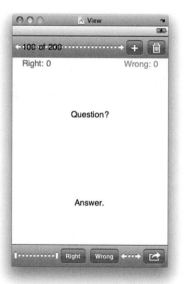

24. Open the NIB and right-click the File's Owner icon. Connect the four button outlets (delete, right, wrong, and action) to the respective buttons in the view. Connect the five actions (addCard, deleteCard, markRight, markWrong, and nextAction) to the respective buttons in the view.

25. Connect the five label outlets (question, answer, cardCount, rightCount, and wrongCount) to the respective labels in the view as in Figure 16.4. Save the XIB file, quit Interface Builder, and return to Xcode.

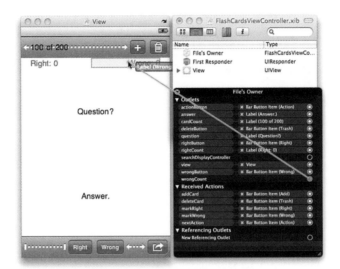

FIGURE 16.4
Connect the labels.

Add Another View Controller

We now have the complete view for using the flash cards, but users also need to be able to create new cards. When users press the Add button in the top toolbar, we'll show them another view to capture the question and answer for the new flash card. This new view will have its own controller and NIB.

Select the Classes group and then select File, New File, and then the UIViewController subclass template. Make sure the With XIB for User Interface check box is selected and click the Next button. Name the controller **CreateCardViewController.m**, make sure the Also Create CreateCardViewController.h check box is selected, and click the Finish button. Drag the new CreateCardController.xib file from the Classes group to the Resources group to keep the project tidy.

Add the Outlets and Actions

The new view controller needs outlets to access the two text fields that'll be on the view that will contain the question and answer the user typed. It also needs a delegate to call back to the FlashCardsViewController object when the user wants to save a new card or just dismiss the view. There will be an action for each of the user's two options: save and cancel.

Click the CreateCardViewController.h file in the Classes group. Add a CreateCardDelegate protocol with two methods: didCancelCardCreation and didCreateCardWithQuestion:answer. Both arguments to the second method are

NSString objects. Add the save and cancel actions and add an outlet and property for the question and answer text fields and a property for the CreateCardDelegate. After you've added the delegate, outlets, actions, and properties, your CreateCardViewController.h file should look like Listing 16.4.

LISTING 16.4

```
#import <UIKit/UIKit.h>

@protocol CreateCardDelegate <NSObject>

-(void) didCancelCardCreation;
-(void) didCreateCardWithQuestion:(NSString *)question
                          answer:(NSString *)answer;

@end

@interface CreateCardViewController : UIViewController {

    IBOutlet UITextField *question;
    IBOutlet UITextField *answer;
    id cardDelegate;
}

@property (nonatomic, retain) UITextField *question;
@property (nonatomic, retain) UITextField *answer;
@property (nonatomic, assign) id<CreateCardDelegate> cardDelegate;

-(IBAction) save;
-(IBAction) cancel;

@end
```

Lay Out the UI and Connect the Outlets and Actions

Open Interface Builder by double-clicking the CreateCardViewController.xib file in the Resources group. Then complete the following steps to lay out the UI and connect the outlets and actions:

1. Open the Library (Shift+Command+L) and search for "toolbar."

2. Drag a toolbar to the very top of the view.

3. Click the Item button in the top toolbar three times until just the button is selected, open the Attribute Inspector (Command+1), and choose Save from the Identifier Properties drop-down list.

4. Open the Library (Shift+Command+L) and search for "button."

5. Drag one Bar Button item to the top toolbar.

6. Click the new button in the top toolbar three times until just the button is selected, open the Attribute Inspector (Command+1), and choose Cancel from the Identifier Properties drop-down list.

7. Open the Library (Shift+Command+L) and search for "space."

8. Drag a Flexible Space Bar Button item to the leftmost position in the top toolbar.

9. Open the Library (Shift+Command+L) and search for "text."

10. Drag two text fields onto the view below the toolbar.

11. Position one of the text fields under the top toolbar and against the left alignment guide. Size the label wider to the right alignment guide. Click the text field, open the Attribute Inspector (Command+1), and change the Text attribute to **Question?**, change the alignment to centered, change the Border attribute to the leftmost style, and change the Correction Text Input Traits attribute to No. Open the Size Inspector (Command+3) and change the height to 74 pixels.

12. Position the second text field under the first and against the left alignment guide. Size the label wider to the right alignment guide. Click the text field, open the Attribute Inspector (Command+1), and change the Text attribute to **Answer.**, change the alignment to centered, change the Border attribute to the leftmost style, and change the Correction Text Input Traits attribute to No. Open the Size Inspector (Command+3) and change the height to 74 pixels. Your UI should now look like Figure 16.5.

FIGURE 16.5
The create card UI.

13. Open the NIB and right-click the File's Owner icon. Connect the two label outlets, question and answer, to the respective labels.

14. Connect the two actions, cancel and save, to the respective buttons in the view. Save the XIB file, quit Interface Builder, and return to Xcode.

Implement the Application's Mechanics

At this point, we've defined a flash card model and two complete views, one for creating flash cards and one for using them. All that remains to have a basic flash card application is to implement the two controllers.

Show Cards and Capture Results

The class header for the FlashCardsViewController provides a roadmap for the implementation. It tells us we have to synthesize 11 properties and implement 5 actions. Click the CreateCardViewController.m file in the Classes group, add code to synthesize the properties, and release all of them that were retained (all of them except the currentCardCounter) in dealloc:

```
@synthesize cardCount, wrongCount, rightCount;
@synthesize question, answer;
@synthesize deleteButton, rightButton, wrongButton, actionButton;
@synthesize flashCards;
@synthesize currentCardCounter;

- (void)dealloc {
    [cardCount release];
    [wrongCount release];
    [rightCount release];
    [question release];
    [answer release];
    [deleteButton release];
    [rightButton release];
    [wrongButton release];
    [actionButton release];
    [flashCards release];
    [super dealloc];
}
```

You may have noticed that we defined 12 properties in the class definition but we only synthesized 11. That's because we need to manually implement the getter for the read-only currentCard property. To implement this property and get the current flash card, we use the currentCardCounter as the index into the flashCards array, checking to be sure the array isn't empty:

```
-(FlashCard *) currentCard {
    if (self.currentCardCounter < 0) {
        return nil;
```

```
    }
    FlashCard *flashCard = [self.flashCards
                            objectAtIndex:self.currentCardCounter];
    return flashCard;
}
```

We've now created all 12 properties of our view controller, so let's start using them to implement the controller. When the view is first loaded, we won't have any flash cards yet, so we need to make sure the UI behaves properly with no flash cards. Consider for a moment that it's possible to get back to this same state of having no cards when the user deletes the last flash card. So it's best to handle the case of no flash cards in the normal flow of the application. Add a method to view controller called showNextCard, and make it able to handle populating the UI in each of the three interesting cases: when there are no flash cards, when there is a next flash card in the array, and when there is not a next flash card in the array and so we need to loop back to the beginning of the array of flash cards:

```
-(void)showNextCard {
    self.rightButton.enabled = NO;
    self.wrongButton.enabled = NO;

    NSUInteger numberOfCards = [self.flashCards count];

    if (numberOfCards == 0) {
        // UI State for no cards
        self.question.text = @"";
        self.answer.text = @"";
        self.cardCount.text = @"Add a flash card to get Started";
        self.wrongCount.text = @"";
        self.rightCount.text = @"";
        self.deleteButton.enabled = NO;
        self.actionButton.enabled = NO;
    } else {
        self.currentCardCounter += 1;
        if (self.currentCardCounter >= numberOfCards) {
            // Loop back to the first card
            self.currentCardCounter = 0;
        }
        self.cardCount.text =
            [NSString stringWithFormat:@"%i of %i",
            (self.currentCardCounter + 1), numberOfCards];
        self.question.text = self.currentCard.question;
        self.answer.hidden = YES;
        self.answer.text = self.currentCard.answer;
        [self updateRightWrongCounters];
        self.deleteButton.enabled = YES;
        self.actionButton.enabled = YES;
    }
}
```

Because the showNextCard method can set up the UI, even when we have no cards, handling the initial load of the view is straightforward. We just need to create and initialize the array that will hold the flash cards and then call the showNextCard method. Uncomment the viewDidLoad method of the controller and modify it as follows:

```
// Implement viewDidLoad to do additional setup after loading the view,
typically from a nib.
- (void)viewDidLoad {
    self.flashCards = [[NSMutableArray alloc] init];
    self.currentCardCounter = -1;
    [self showNextCard];
    [super viewDidLoad];
}
```

The showNextCard method uses outlets to set values on the labels in the UI, and to enable and disable the buttons as appropriate. Careful readers will have noticed that it also called a method we haven't written yet, updateRightWrongCounters. This method should provide the right text to the labels based on the counters in the current flash card. Add the method to the view controller:

```
- (void) updateRightWrongCounters {
    self.wrongCount.text =
        [NSString stringWithFormat:@"Wrong: %i",
        self.currentCard.wrongCount];
    self.rightCount.text =
        [NSString stringWithFormat:@"Right: %i",
        self.currentCard.rightCount];
}
```

Update the FlashCardViewsController.h file in the Classes group with the two methods we just defined:

```
-(void)showNextCard;
-(void)updateRightWrongCounters;
```

There are three user actions for progressing through the set of flash cards: nextAction, markWrong, and markRight. nextAction first reveals the answer and enables the Right and Wrong buttons, and the second time nextAction is used on a card it advances to the next card:

```
- (IBAction) nextAction {
    if (self.answer.hidden) {
        self.answer.hidden = NO;
        self.rightButton.enabled = YES;
        self.wrongButton.enabled = YES;
    } else {
        [self showNextCard];
    }
}
```

The markWrong and markRight actions increment the counter for the flash card by one. They also handle disabling the button that was pressed so that the user doesn't increment twice for the same card, and they allow the user to change his mind by decrementing the previously incremented counter:

```
- (IBAction) markWrong {

    // Update the flash card
    self.currentCard.wrongCount += 1;
    if (!self.rightButton.enabled) {
        // They had previously marked the card right
        self.currentCard.rightCount -= 1;
    }
    // Update the UI
    self.wrongButton.enabled = NO;
    self.rightButton.enabled = YES;
    [self updateRightWrongCounters];
}

- (IBAction) markRight {

    // Update the flash card
    self.currentCard.rightCount += 1;
    if (!self.wrongButton.enabled) {
        // They had previously marked the card right
        self.currentCard.wrongCount -= 1;
    }
    // Update the UI
    self.wrongButton.enabled = YES;
    self.rightButton.enabled = NO;
    [self updateRightWrongCounters];
}
```

Create New Cards

We previously created a separate view and view controller to interact with the user and create a new card. Add a statement to the FlashCardsViewController.h file to import the second view controller:

```
#import "CreateCardViewController.h"
```

The addCard action that is called when the user touches the Add button instantiates an instance of our CreateCardViewController and turns control over to it with UIView's presentModalViewController:animated method. Add the action to the FlashCardsViewController.m file as follows:

```
- (IBAction) addCard {

    // Show the create card view
    CreateCardViewController *cardCreator =
        [[CreateCardViewController alloc] init];
        cardCreator.cardDelegate = self;
```

```
[self presentModalViewController:cardCreator animated:YES];
[cardCreator release];
}
```

The addCard IBAction will now show our second view, but we still need to imple-
ment the controller for this view. The class header we created for
CreateCardViewController tells us we have to synthesize three properties and
implement the two actions. The actions simply need to call back to the
CardCreateDelegate when the user presses the Save or Cancel buttons. Click the
CreateCardViewController.m file in the Classes group and update the file as in
Listing 16.5.

LISTING 16.5

```
#import "CreateCardViewController.h"

@implementation CreateCardViewController

@synthesize cardDelegate;
@synthesize question, answer;

-(IBAction) save {
    [self.cardDelegate  didCreateCardWithQuestion: question.text
                                            answer: answer.text];
}

-(IBAction) cancel {
    [self.cardDelegate didCancelCardCreation];
}

- (void)didReceiveMemoryWarning {
        // Releases the view if it doesn't have a superview.
    [super didReceiveMemoryWarning];

        // Release any cached data, images, etc that aren't in use.
}

- (void)viewDidUnload {
        // Release any retained subviews of the main view.
        // e.g. self.myOutlet = nil;
}

- (void)dealloc {
    [question release];
    [answer release];
    [super dealloc];
}

@end
```

Now we need to implement the card delegate in the FlashCardsViewController. If
the callback indicates the user canceled, then we need to dismiss only the modal

view. When the delegate indicates a new card needs to be saved, we also must create a new FlashCard instance. After we create it, we need to insert the new flash card into the array of cards at the current spot or at the end of the array if we are on the last card. Then we show the next card in the array (which will always be the new card we just added). Click the FlashCardsViewController.m file in the Classes group and add the following two methods to implement the CreateCardDelegate protocol:

```
#pragma mark -
#pragma mark CreateCardDelegate

-(void) didCancelCardCreation {
    [self dismissModalViewControllerAnimated:YES];
}

-(void) didCreateCardWithQuestion:(NSString *)thisQuestion
                           answer:(NSString *)thisAnswer {

    // Add the new card as the next card
    FlashCard *newCard = [[FlashCard alloc]initWithQuestion: thisQuestion
                                                     answer:thisAnswer];
    if (self.currentCardCounter >= [self.flashCards count]) {
        [self.flashCards addObject:newCard];
    } else {
        [self.flashCards insertObject:newCard
                              atIndex:(self.currentCardCounter + 1)];
    }

    // Show the new card
    [self showNextCard];
    [self dismissModalViewControllerAnimated:YES];

}

#pragma mark -
```

Click the FlashCardsViewController.h file in the Classes group and modify the class's definition to indicate that we've implemented the CreateCardDelegate protocol:

```
#import <UIKit/UIKit.h>
#import "FlashCard.h"
#import "CreateCardViewController.h"

@interface FlashCardsViewController : UIViewController <CreateCardDelegate> {
```

Delete Cards

Because we wrote our showNextCard method to be flexible, deleting a card is just a matter of deleting the current card from the array and showing the next card with showNextCard. showNextCard can handle any of the circumstances that may result from this, such as there being no cards in the array or needing to loop back to the beginning of the array:

```
- (IBAction) deleteCard {
    [self.flashCards removeObjectAtIndex:currentCardCounter];
    [self showNextCard];
}
```

We've now put together a working flash card application that is not too shabby (see Figure 16.6). At this point, the FlashCards application does have one fatal flaw: When the application terminates, all the flash cards the user painstakingly created are gone! In the next two sections, we rectify this using object archiving and Core Data for data persistence.

FIGURE 16.6
The FlashCards application in action.

Object Archiving

A running iPhone application has a vast number of objects in memory. These objects are interlinked to one another with references in such a way that if you were to visualize the relationships, they would appear like a tangled spider web. This web of all the objects in an application and all the references between the objects is called an object graph.

A running iPhone application is not much more than the program itself (which is always the same, at least until the user installs an update) and the unique object graph that is the result of all the activity that has occurred in the running of the application up to that point. One approach to storing an application's data (so that it is available when the application is launched again in the future) is to take the object graph, or a subset of it, and store the object graph on the file system. The next time the program runs, it can read the graph of objects from the file system back into memory and pick up where it left off, executing the same program with the same object graph.

Most object-oriented development environments have a serialization mechanism that is used to stream a graph of objects out of memory and onto a file system and then back into memory again at a later time. Object archiving is the Cocoa version of this process. There are two main parts to object archiving: NSCoder and NSCoding. An NSCoder object can archive (encode and decode) any object that conforms to the NSCoding protocol. Apple supplies NSCoder for most data types, and any custom objects we want to archive implement the NSCoding protocol. We are in luck because the NSCoding protocol consists of just two methods: initWithCoder and encodeWithCoder.

Archiving FlashCard Objects

Let's start with encodeWithCoder. The purpose of encodeWithCoder is to encode all the instance variables of an object that should be stored during archival. To implement encodeWithCoder, decide which instance variables will be encoded and which instance variables, if any, will be transient (not encoded). Each instance variable you encode must be a scalar type (a number) or must be an object that implements NSCoding. This means all the instance variables you're likely to have in your custom objects can be encoded because the vast majority of Cocoa Touch and Core Foundation objects implement NSCoding. On the iPhone, NSCoder uses keyed encoding, so you provide a key for each instance variable you encode. Here is what encoding looks like for our FlashCard class:

```
- (void)encodeWithCoder:(NSCoder *)encoder {

    [encoder encodeObject:self.question forKey:kQuestion];
    [encoder encodeObject:self.answer forKey:kAnswer];
    [encoder encodeInt:self.rightCount forKey:kRightCount];
    [encoder encodeInt:self.wrongCount forKey:kWrongCount];

}
```

Notice that we used the encodeObject:forKey method for NSStrings and you'd use the same for any other objects. For integers, we used encodeInt:forKey. You can check the API reference documentation of NSCoder for the complete list, but a few others you should be familiar with are encodeBool:forKey and encodeDouble:forKey and encodeBytes:forKey. You'll need these for dealing with Booleans, floating-point numbers, and data.

The opposite of encoding is decoding, and for that part of the protocol there is the initWithCoder method. Like encodeWithCoder, initWithCoder is keyed, but rather than providing NSCoder an instance variable for a key, you provide a key and are returned an instance variable. For our FlashCard class, decoding works like this:

```
- (id)initWithCoder:(NSCoder *)decoder {

    if (self = [super init]) {
        self.question = [decoder decodeObjectForKey:kQuestion];
        self.answer = [decoder decodeObjectForKey:kAnswer];
        self.rightCount = [decoder decodeIntForKey:kRightCount];
        self.wrongCount = [decoder decodeIntForKey:kWrongCount];
    }
    return self;

}
```

The four keys we used are defined as constants in the FlashCard.h header file:

```
#define kQuestion @"Question"
#define kAnswer @"Answer"
#define kRightCount @"RightCount"
#define kWrongCount @"WrongCount"
```

The last step is to update the class definition in the FlashCard.h header file to indicate that FlashCard implements the NSCoding protocol:

```
@interface FlashCard : NSObject <NSCoding> {
```

Our FlashCard class is now archivable, and an object graph that includes FlashCard object instances can be persisted to and from the file system using object archiving.

Archiving in the FlashCards Application

To fix the fatal flaw in the FlashCards application, we need to store all the flash cards on the file system. Now, because FlashCard implements the NSCoding protocol, each individual flash card is archivable. Remember that object archiving is based on the notion of storing an object graph and we are not looking to store each flash card in an individual file (although we certainly could if we wanted to). We want one object graph with references to all of our flash cards so that we can archive it into a single file.

It turns out that the FlashCards application already has such an object graph in memory in the form of the FlashCardsViewController's NSMuteableArray property called flashCards. The flashCards array has a reference to every flash card the user has defined, and so it forms the root of an object graph that contains all the flash cards. An NSMuteableArray, like all the Cocoa data structures, implements NSCoding, so we have a ready-made solution for archiving an object graph containing all the flash cards.

We need a location for the file that'll store the flash cards. We'd like the flash cards to be safely backed up each time the user syncs her device with iTunes, so we'll put the file in the application's Documents directory. We can call the file anything; object archiving doesn't put any restrictions on the filename or extension. Let's call it **FlashCards.dat**. We'll need the full path to this file both when we store the flash cards to the file system and when we read them from the file system, so let's write a simple helper function that returns the path to the file. Open the FlashCardsViewController.m file in the Classes group and add the following method:

```
-(NSString *)archivePath {
    NSString *docDir =
        [NSSearchPathForDirectoriesInDomains(NSDocumentDirectory,
        NSUserDomainMask, YES) objectAtIndex: 0];
    return [docDir stringByAppendingPathComponent:@"FlashCards.dat"];
}
```

We need to archive the array of flash cards to the file before the application terminates and then unarchive the array of flash cards from the file when the application starts. To write an archive to a file, use the archiveRootObject:toFile method of NSKeyedArchiver. We'll want to do this when the FlashCardsAppDelegate receives the applicationWillTerminate event, so define a method in the FlashCardsViewController.m file that FlashCardsAppDelegate can call to archive the flash cards:

```
-(void)archiveFlashCards {
    [NSKeyedArchiver archiveRootObject:flashCards toFile:[self archivePath]];
}
```

Add the new method to the FlashCardsViewController.h file:

```
-(void)archiveFlashCards;
```

Open the FlashCardsAppDelegate.m file and add the applicationWillTerminate that will call the archiveFlashCards method of the FlashCardsViewController:

```
- (void)applicationWillTerminate:(UIApplication *)application {
    [viewController archiveFlashCards];
}
```

Each time our application terminates, whatever flash cards are in the array will be written out to the FlashCards.dat file in the Documents directory. On startup, we need to read the archive of the array from the file. To unarchive an object graph, use the unarchiveObjectWithFile method of NSKeyedUnarchiver. It's possible this is the first time the application has ever been run and there won't yet be a FlashCards.dat file. In this case, unarchiveObjectWithFile returns nil and we can simply create a new, empty array like we did before the FlashCards application had data persistence. Update the viewDidLoad method of the FlashCardsViewController.m file as follows:

```
// Implement viewDidLoad to do additional setup after loading the view,
typically from a nib.
- (void)viewDidLoad {
    self.flashCards = [NSKeyedUnarchiver
                        unarchiveObjectWithFile:[self archivePath]];
    self.currentCardCounter = -1;
    if (self.flashCards == nil) {
        self.flashCards = [[NSMutableArray alloc] init];
    }
    [self showNextCard];
    [super viewDidLoad];
}
```

That's all there is to it. Once the model objects of an application all implement NSCoding, object archiving is a simple and easy process. With just a few lines of code, we were able to persist the flash cards to the file system.

Because of this simplicity, there is no reason for many applications to ever use anything more complicated than object archiving. Yet advanced frameworks, such as Core Data, have been created for handling object persistence in applications with complex data requirements. One justification for these other frameworks is efficiency and performance as the amount of data an application manages grows. With object archiving, an application may have to write an entire object graph of tens of thousands of objects to the file system just because one property of one object changed. Dealing with large graphs of objects in an efficient way is a key function of Core Data, which we look at next.

Watch Out!

In our example of object archiving, we read and wrote just one file to the file system. This was appropriate for this FlashCards application, but it is not always the best approach when using object archiving. For example, if we were to extend the FlashCards application to allow the user to create different decks of flash cards for learning different topics, it would probably make more sense to write each deck of flash cards to its own file. Another consideration when deciding how many files to use for object archiving is how large the object graph is and how often it changes. An application with a small number of frequently changing objects and a much larger number of bigger objects that rarely change is better off segmenting these two into separate object graphs that are stored in separate files.

Core Data

Core Data is a framework that provides management and persistence for in-memory application object graphs. Core Data attempts to solve many of the challenges that face other, simpler forms of object persistence such as object archiving. Some of the challenging areas Core Data focuses on are multilevel undo management, data validation, data consistency across independent data assessors, efficient (that is, indexed) filtering, sorting and searching of object graphs, and persistence to a variety of data repositories.

Core Data is such a large topic that entire books have been written on the subject, and we are only going to scratch at the surface of what's available. The goal of this section is to give you a quick taste of Core Data to see whether it is something you would like to learn more about. I also hope to give you a positive first experience with Core Data by showing how the FlashCards application can be easily made to use Core Data for storage.

Core Data can be a divisive topic among developers who otherwise see eye to eye. These strong differences of opinion can usually be traced back to positive or negative first impressions of Core Data. All too often, a developer's first impression of Core Data is negative because he or she is thrust immediately into the deep end of a very deep pool. Consider this section your quick lap around the shallow end.

From Whence It Came

In the beginning (the early 1970s), there was SQL. SQL, pronounced either see-quel or es - que - el, is an acronym for Structured Query Language and is a standard vocabulary for working with relational databases. Despite its name, SQL does more than just querying; it handles the four basic functions of data management called CRUD (create, read, update, and delete).

In the early 1990s, when object-oriented programming languages such as Smalltalk, C++, and Objective-C began to make serious inroads into commercial development, there was a focus on the so-called impedance mismatch between objects in running programs and persistent relational data on the file system. A lot of the developer productivity that was gained from using object-oriented languages was immediately lost writing repetitive and error-prone objects to relational data transformations.

Two approaches to solving this mismatch were developed: the object-oriented database and the object-relational mapping framework. Eventually, the latter approach carried the day, and today most commercial software development is done in an object-oriented language with data persistence to a relational database via an object-relational mapping framework. An object-relational mapping (ORM or OR/M) framework handles the tedium of converting data back and forth between objects in the application and relational data in the database.

Core Data has its origins in these early days and is itself an object-relational mapping framework. As an ORM framework, one of the things Core Data does is provide a wrapper around SQL and relational databases that enables an application to take advantage of the benefits of a database while avoiding direct exposure to SQL. On the iPhone, Core Data wraps the SQLite database and is an alternative to using SQL and the SQLite APIs directly.

Just Enough Core Data

There are really only three Core Data concepts to understand before you can grasp the big picture: the managed object context, the managed object, and the managed object model.

The *managed object context* is the working subset of persistent objects that are being used by the application at a given point in time. The managed object context contains an object graph (or many disconnected object graphs). Changes to objects in the managed object context are noticed by Core Data so that when the application calls save on the managed object context, these changes are persisted to the database.

A *managed object* is simply any object being managed by Core Data in a managed object context. Managed objects can be added and removed from the object graph in the managed object context and this results in Core Data performing inserts and deletes from the database. Changes to attributes and relationships of managed objects result in Core Data performing update operations on the database.

The *managed object model* is the object-relational schema. It is the description of the entities that will be persisted via Core Data. An entity is a model of a managed object that contains only the parts of the object that Core Data will be persisting. Two different things are modeled in an entity: the object attributes (such as the question, answers, and counters of `FlashCard`) that should be persisted, and relationships to other entities that should be stored to form a persistent object graph.

A simplified diagram of Core Data is provided in Figure 16.7. The persistence stack depicted in the diagram shows the parts of Core Data that interact with a data repository, such as SQLite. As an application developer, it is rare to need to use the parts of the persistence stack directly, so we won't be discussing them in this book.

Just know that Core Data is like an iceberg with a large amount of the infrastructure quietly working away for you under the surface.

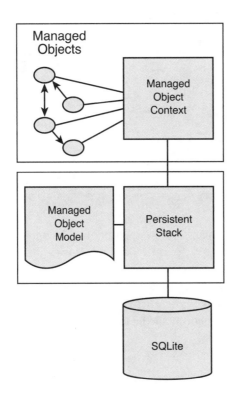

FIGURE 16.7
An application developer's perspective of Core Data.

A Core Data FlashCards Application

It's possible to add Core Data persistence into an existing application, but Xcode provides Core Data application templates that provide valuable boilerplate code that is tedious to re-create. So instead of adding Core Data to our existing FlashCards application, we are going to start a new application with a template.

Create a new Window-Based Application in Xcode and be sure to check the Use Core Data for storage check box (see Figure 16.8). Call the project **FlashCardsCoreData**.

The Navigation-Based Application template also has the Use Core Data for storage check box. If the data you want to persist is hierarchical in nature, and will be displayed with table views and a navigation controller (see Hour 14, "Displaying and Navigating Data Using Table Views") this is the application template you'll want to use.

By the Way

FIGURE 16.8
Create a
Window-Based
Application with
Core Data for
storage.

The first thing to notice about the new application is the application delegate. Open the FlashCardsCoreDataAppDelegate.h file in the Classes group and take a look. A Core Data application interacts with the managed object context through its application delegate, so the Xcode template has included additional properties and actions in the application delegate. These new additions are highlighted in bold in Listing 16.6, and most of them should be familiar to you from our discussion of Core Data in the previous section.

LISTING 16.6

```
@interface FlashCardsCoreDataAppDelegate : NSObject <UIApplicationDelegate> {

    NSManagedObjectModel *managedObjectModel;
    NSManagedObjectContext *managedObjectContext;
    NSPersistentStoreCoordinator *persistentStoreCoordinator;

    UIWindow *window;
}

- (IBAction)saveAction:sender;

@property (nonatomic, retain, readonly) NSManagedObjectModel
*managedObjectModel;
@property (nonatomic, retain, readonly) NSManagedObjectContext
*managedObjectContext;
@property (nonatomic, retain, readonly) NSPersistentStoreCoordinator
*persistentStoreCoordinator;

@property (nonatomic, readonly) NSString *applicationDocumentsDirectory;

@property (nonatomic, retain) IBOutlet UIWindow *window;

@end
```

Model the FlashCard **Entity**

A Core Data model, an .xcdatamodel file, is referred to as the managed object model. Think of the managed object model as the mapping between an object as it exists in Objective-C and an entity as it will be stored as rows in a database table in SQLite. Xcode provides a modeling tool to create this mapping. Click the FlashCardsCoreData.xcdatamodel file in the Resources group to open the data modeling tool (see Figure 16.9).

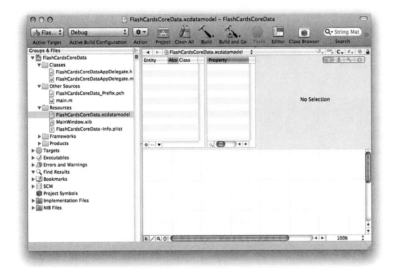

FIGURE 16.9
Data model
view in Xcode.

Complete the following steps to model the FlashCard entity:

1. Right-click the bottom view with the grid lines and select Add Entity from the context menu.

2. Change the entity name to **FlashCard** in the Name field of the selection editor (see Figure 16.10).

3. Right-click the entity and select Add Attribute from the context menu.

4. Change the attribute name to **question** in the Name field of the selection editor.

5. Change the attribute type to String in the Type drop-down menu of the selection editor.

6. Change the default value to **Question?** in the Default Value field of the selection editor.

7. Repeat steps 3 through 6 for an additional String attribute named **answer** with a default value of **Answer**.

FIGURE 16.10
Change the entity name.

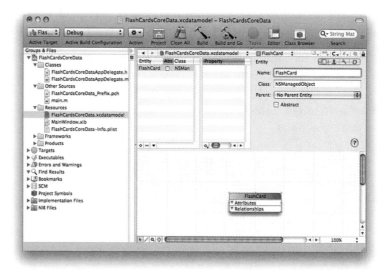

8. Right-click the entity and select Add Attribute from the context menu.

9. Change the attribute name to **rightCounter** in the Name field of the selection editor.

10. Change the attribute type to Integer 32 in the Type drop-down menu of the selection editor.

11. Change the default value to **0** in the Default Value field of the selection editor.

12. Repeat steps 8 through 11 for an additional Integer 32 attribute named **wrongCounter** with a default value of **0** (see Figure 16.11).

13. Save your changes to the model (Command+S).

Next we need to generate the Objective-C class for the FlashCard entity we just modeled. Click the Classes group and then select File, New File. Select the Managed Object class from the Cocoa Touch Class group (see Figure 16.12) and click the Next button twice.

FIGURE 16.11
Add attributes
to the entity.

FIGURE 16.12
Add a managed
object class.

Now Xcode reads the managed object model file and displays the list of modeled entities. We only modeled one entity, FlashCard, so select that entity and click the Finish button (see Figure 16.13).

FIGURE 16.13
Add a managed
object class.

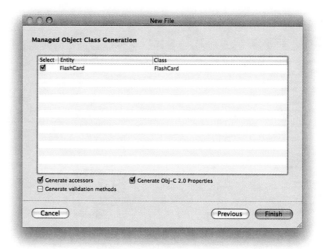

Open the generated FlashCard.h file in the Classes group. It looks very similar to the model classes we've been creating by hand up to this point with the exception of the CoreData.h import and the fact that the properties don't have corresponding instance variables (see Listing 16.7).

LISTING 16.7

```
#import <CoreData/CoreData.h>

@interface FlashCard :  NSManagedObject
{
}
@property (nonatomic, retain) NSString * answer;
@property (nonatomic, retain) NSString * question;
@property (nonatomic, retain) NSNumber * wrongCount;
@property (nonatomic, retain) NSNumber * rightCount;

@end
```

Open the generated FlashCard.m file in the Classes group and notice how tiny it is (see Listing 16.8). You are familiar with the use of @synthesize to tell the compiler to generate getters and setters for properties; the @dynamic construct tells the compiler not to worry about the missing property getters and setters because they will be provided by the superclass, NSManagedObject, at runtime.

LISTING 16.8

```
#import "FlashCard.h"

@implementation FlashCard

@dynamic answer;
@dynamic question;
@dynamic wrongCount;
@dynamic rightCount;

@end
```

Like before when we created a version of the FlashCard model that implemented the NSCoding protocol, we now have a flash card model object that can be persisted to the file system (this time to a SQLite database).

Copy and Update the NIBs and View Controllers

Next we need to copy over the NIBs and view controllers from the original FlashCards application. Open the FlashCards.xcodeproj file in Xcode and complete the following steps:

1. Click the FlashCardsViewController.h file in the Classes group. Hold the Command key and click the FlashCardsViewController.m file, the CreateCardsViewController.h file, and the CreateCardsViewController.m file so that they are all selected. Drag the four selected files into the Class group of the FlashCardsCoreData Xcode project. (You might need to resize the Xcode windows so that you can see the Classes group from both projects at the same time.)

2. The copy items dialog appears. Click the Copy Items into the Destination Group's Folder check box (see Figure 16.14), and then click the Add button.

FIGURE 16.14
Copy items from the FlashCards project to the FlashCardsCore-Data project.

3. Back in the FlashCards Xcode project, click the FlashCardsViewController.xib file in the Resources group. Hold the Command key and click the CreateCardViewController.xib file so that they are both selected. Drag the two selected files into the Resources group of the FlashCardsCoreData Xcode project. (You might need to resize the Xcode windows so that you can see the Classes group from both projects at the same time.)

4. The copy items dialog appears. Click the Copy Items into Destination Group's Folder check box, and then click the Add button.

5. Close the FlashCards Xcode project (Command-W).

Open the FlashCardsCoreDataAppDelegate.h file in the Classes group and add a property for the `FlashCardsViewController`. Update the file as in Listing 16.9.

LISTING 16.9

```
#import "FlashCardsViewController.h"

@interface FlashCardsCoreDataAppDelegate : NSObject <UIApplicationDelegate> {

    NSManagedObjectModel *managedObjectModel;
    NSManagedObjectContext *managedObjectContext;
    NSPersistentStoreCoordinator *persistentStoreCoordinator;

    UIWindow *window;
    FlashCardsViewController *viewController;
}

- (IBAction)saveAction:sender;

@property (nonatomic, retain, readonly) NSManagedObjectModel
*managedObjectModel;
@property (nonatomic, retain, readonly) NSManagedObjectContext
*managedObjectContext;
@property (nonatomic, retain, readonly) NSPersistentStoreCoordinator
*persistentStoreCoordinator;

@property (nonatomic, readonly) NSString *applicationDocumentsDirectory;

@property (nonatomic, retain) IBOutlet UIWindow *window;
@property (nonatomic, retain) IBOutlet FlashCardsViewController *viewController;

@end
```

Synthesize the `viewController` property by adding the following line to the FlashCardsCoreDataAppDelegate.m file:

```
@synthesize viewController;
```

Also update the dealloc method to release the viewController property:

```
- (void)dealloc {

    [managedObjectContext release];
    [managedObjectModel release];
    [persistentStoreCoordinator release];

    [viewController release];
    [window release];
    [super dealloc];
}
```

Now that the application delegate has a property for the FlashCardsViewController, we also need it to pass along the Core Data managed object context and display the controller's view when the application starts. Modify the applicationDidFinishLaunching method in the FlashCardsCoreDataAppDelegate.m file to set a managedObjectContext property on the controller and add the controller's view as a subview of the application's window:

```
- (void)applicationDidFinishLaunching:(UIApplication *)application {

    // Override point for customization after app launch
    viewController.managedObjectContext = [self managedObjectContext];
    [window addSubview:viewController.view];
    [window makeKeyAndVisible];
}
```

Open the FlashCardsViewController.h file and add the managed object context property:

```
#import <UIKit/UIKit.h>
#import "FlashCard.h"
#import "CreateCardViewController.h"

@interface FlashCardsViewController : UIViewController <CreateCardDelegate> {

    IBOutlet UILabel *cardCount;
    IBOutlet UILabel *wrongCount;
...snipped...
    NSUInteger currentCardCounter;
    FlashCard *currentCard;
    NSManagedObjectContext *managedObjectContext;
}

@property (nonatomic, retain) UILabel *cardCount;
@property (nonatomic, retain) UILabel *wrongCount;
...snipped...
@property (nonatomic, assign) NSUInteger currentCardCounter;
@property (nonatomic, readonly) FlashCard *currentCard;
@property (nonatomic, retain) NSManagedObjectContext *managedObjectContext;

-(IBAction) markWrong;
-(IBAction) markRight;
...snipped...
@end
```

Open the FlashCardsViewController.m file and synthesize the property:

```
@synthesize managedObjectContext;

- (void)dealloc {
    [cardCount release];
    [wrongCount release];
…snipped…
    [flashCards release];
    [managedObjectContext release];
    [super dealloc];
}
```

Double-click the MainWindow.xib file in the Resources group to launch Interface Builder and complete the following steps to connect the view controller outlet:

1. Open the Library (Shift+Command+L) and search for "view."

2. Drag a view controller to the NIB. Click the new view controller and open the Identity Inspector (Command+4). Choose FlashCardsViewController from the Class drop-down menu.

3. Right-click the FlashCardsCoreDataAppDelegate icon in the NIB and click and drag from the circle next to the viewController outlet to the FlashCardsViewController icon in the NIB. Save the XIB file, quit Interface Builder, and return to Xcode.

Update FlashCard **Persistence to Use Core Data**

For Core Data to persist flash card objects for us, we need to explicitly interact with Core Data's managed object context during four steps of the object life cycle: creating new objects, reading existing objects in from the database, saving updated objects, and deleting objects. We'll update the parts of the application that handle these four steps. Let's start with flash card creation.

Open the FlashCardsViewController.m file in the Classes group and look at the CreateCardDelegate protocol method called didCreateCardWithQuestion:answer. New flash cards are created with this line:

```
// Add the new card as the next card
    FlashCard *newCard = [[FlashCard alloc]initWithQuestion: thisQuestion
                                                    answer:thisAnswer];
```

To create a managed object in the managed object context, use the insertNewObjectForEntityForName:inManagedObjectContext method of NSEntityDescription. The first argument is an NSString with the name of the entity from the managed object model, and the second argument is a reference to

the managed object context. Update the didCreateCardWithQuestion:answer
method, adding new code and deleting the crossed-out lines, as follows:

```
-(void) didCreateCardWithQuestion:(NSString *)thisQuestion
                        answer:(NSString *)thisAnswer {

    // Add the new card as the next card
    FlashCard *newCard = [[FlashCard alloc]initWithQuestion: thisQuestion
                                              answer:thisAnswer];
    NSManagedObject *newCard = [NSEntityDescription
                                insertNewObjectForEntityForName:@"FlashCard"

inManagedObjectContext:self.managedObjectContext];
    newCard.question = thisQuestion;
    newCard.answer = thisAnswer;
    if (self.currentCardCounter >= [self.flashCards count]) {
        [self.flashCards addObject:newCard];
    } else {
        [self.flashCards insertObject:newCard
         atIndex:(self.currentCardCounter + 1)];
    }

    // Show the new card
    [self showNextCard];
    [self dismissModalViewControllerAnimated:YES];

}
```

To retrieve objects with a Core Data managed object context, use a fetch request,
which is an instance of the NSFetchRequest class. An NSEntityDescription is used
to specify the type of entity to be fetched. A fetch request can include constraints on
the values of the objects that will be returned in the request (for example, only flash
cards with a wrongCounter property greater than 5). A fetch request can also
include a sort descriptor that will determine the order in which the objects are
returned. The result of executing a fetch is an NSMutableArray of managed objects.
Update the viewDidLoad method of the FlashCardsViewController.m file as follows:

```
// Implement viewDidLoad to do additional setup after loading the view,
typically from a nib.
- (void)viewDidLoad {
    self.flashCards = [NSKeyedUnarchiver
                         unarchiveObjectWithFile:[self archivePath]];
    NSFetchRequest *request = [[NSFetchRequest alloc] init];
    NSEntityDescription *entity = [NSEntityDescription
➥entityForName:@"FlashCard"
                                    inManagedObjectContext:managedObjectContext];
    [request setEntity:entity];
    NSError *error;
    self.flashCards = [[managedObjectContext executeFetchRequest:request
                        error:&error] mutableCopy];
    [request release];

    self.currentCardCounter = -1;
    if (self.flashCards == nil) {
```

```
        self.flashCards = [[NSMutableArray alloc] init];
    }
    [self showNextCard];
    [super viewDidLoad];
}
```

In the original implementation of the FlashCard class, we used the data type NSUInteger for the rightCounter and wrongCounter. An NSUInteger is not actually an object, it's a defined name for a 32-bit or 64-bit scalar integer. When we modeled the FlashCard entity and generated a new FlashCard class, the generated code used a different type, NSNumber, for those two properties. An NSNumber is an object, so we can't read it or write it like a scalar integer. Update the updateRightWrongCounters, markWrong, and markRight methods of the FlashCardsViewController.m file as follows:

```
- (void) updateRightWrongCounters {
    self.wrongCount.text =
        [NSString stringWithFormat:@"Wrong: %i",
        self.currentCard.wrongCount];
        [self.currentCard.wrongCount intValue]];
    self.rightCount.text =
        [NSString stringWithFormat:@"Right: %i",
        self.currentCard.rightCount];
        [self.currentCard.rightCount intValue]];
}


- (IBAction) markWrong {

    // Update the flash card
    self.currentCard.wrongCount += 1;
    self.currentCard.wrongCount =
        [NSNumber numberWithInt:[self.currentCard.wrongCount intValue] + 1];
    if (!self.rightButton.enabled) {
        // They had previously marked the card right
        self.currentCard.rightCount -= 1;
        self.currentCard.rightCount =
            [NSNumber numberWithInt:[self.currentCard.rightCount intValue] - 1];
    }
    // Update the UI
    self.wrongButton.enabled = NO;
    self.rightButton.enabled = YES;
    [self updateRightWrongCounters];
}


- (IBAction) markRight {

    // Update the flash card
    self.currentCard.rightCount += 1;
    self.currentCard.rightCount =
        [NSNumber numberWithInt:[self.currentCard.rightCount intValue] + 1];
    if (!self.wrongButton.enabled) {
        // They had previously marked the card right
        self.currentCard.wrongCount -= 1;
```

```
        self.currentCard.wrongCount =
            [NSNumber numberWithInt:[self.currentCard.wrongCount intValue] - 1];
    }
    // Update the UI
    self.wrongButton.enabled = YES;
    self.rightButton.enabled = NO;
    [self updateRightWrongCounters];
}
```

The code that was included in the Core Data template for the application delegate calls save on the managed object context when the delegate receives the applicationWillTerminate notification. Click the FlashCardsCoreDataAppDelegate.m file and read through the applicationWillTerminate method. The managed object context tracks any changes to any managed objects associated with it. It can report whether there are any unsaved changes with hasChanges and can save them with save:

```
/**
 applicationWillTerminate: saves changes in the application's managed object
context before the application terminates.
 */
- (void)applicationWillTerminate:(UIApplication *)application {

    NSError *error;
    if (managedObjectContext != nil) {
        if ([managedObjectContext hasChanges]
➥&& ![managedObjectContext save:&error]) {
                    // Handle error
                    NSLog(@"Unresolved error %@, %@", error, [error userInfo]);
                    exit(-1);  // Fail
        }
    }
}
```

We don't have to do anything else in the FlashCards application to handle saving. We can clean up the two methods we previously used for saving by removing the archivePath and archiveFlashCards methods from the FlashCardsViewController.h file:

```
-(NSString *)archivePath;
-(void)archiveFlashCards;
```

Remove the implementation of these two methods from the FlashCardsViewController.m file:

```
-(NSString *)archivePath {
    NSString *docDir =
        [NSSearchPathForDirectoriesInDomains(NSDocumentDirectory,
            NSUserDomainMask, YES) objectAtIndex: 0];
    return [docDir stringByAppendingPathComponent:@"FlashCards.dat"];
}
```

```
- (void)archiveFlashCards {
    [NSKeyedArchiver archiveRootObject:flashCards toFile:[self archivePath]];
}
```

> In the previous section on object archiving, we specified the full path to the FlashCards.dat file in the application's Documents directory. We just removed that method, so where will the flash cards be stored using Core Data and SQLlite? The Core Data Xcode template provided a default location for the SQLite file in the application delegate implementation. Click the FlashCardsCoreDataAppDelegate.m file in the Classes group and read the `persistentStoreCoordinator` method. There you will find some familiar-looking code that uses NSString's `stringByAppendingPathComponent` method to append the filename FlashCardsCoreData.sqlite to the Documents directory location.

Deleting objects is also simple. Use the `deleteObject` method of NSManagedObjectContext and pass in the managed object you want to delete. Update the `deleteCard` action of FlashCardsViewController.m to add this extra step:

```
- (IBAction) deleteCard {
    FlashCard *cardToDelete = [self.flashCards
objectAtIndex:currentCardCounter];
    [self.flashCards removeObjectAtIndex:currentCardCounter];
    [managedObjectContext deleteObject:cardToDelete];
    [self showNextCard];
}
```

Build and run the FlashCards application and you will see that it persists the flash cards to the file system between invocations, this time to a SQLite database in the application's Documents directory. Despite all the complexity and powerful capabilities that lie under the surface, we were able to use the much more capable Core Data framework to store flash cards with just about the same amount of code as with object archiving. As the data management needs of our application grew, we could use additional features of Core Data to implement more sophisticated object persistence.

> One important feature of Core Data is persistence to different data repositories. The data repositories that Core Data supports on the iPhone are more limited than on the desktop, but there are two supported alternatives to the SQLite repository we are using in this hour. There is a binary file format and an in-memory implementation. You'll primarily be using the SQLite data repository because the binary file format has many of the same performance limitations on large data sets as object archiving, and the in-memory data repository doesn't provide any persistence between application invocations. These two alternatives exist for cases where you don't need any of the benefits of a relational database but you do want to take advantage of a feature of Core Data such as undo support or object schema versioning.

Summary

In this hour, we first looked at the application sandbox restrictions relating to reading and writing to the file system and then learned how to define the path to files that live inside the areas of the application sandbox designated for application data storage. We then developed a complete flash card application and added data persistence to it, first using object archiving and then using Core Data.

Q&A

Q. Can I use more than one entity type in a single SQLite database file?

A. Yes, the managed object model we used in this chapter was the simplest possible example, containing just one entity. A typical managed object model for a full-featured application will include many entities (which will map to different tables in SQLite) and relationships (references) between the entities that then form the runtime object graph. The good news is that the same easy-to-use, point-and-click operations in the Xcode data modeling tool can be used to create these more complex data models, and the majority of the model code is still generated for you by Xcode.

Q. How can I query the SQLite database to find exactly the objects I'm looking for?

A. You use an NSPredicate with an NSFetchRequest. The FlashCards application did not need to search the flash cards (it retrieved all the flash cards simultaneously), so we did not specify an NSPredicate on the NSFetchRequest. The most common way to use an NSPredicate is with a string that describes the matching objects the fetch request should return. (This string is similar to the WHERE clause of a SQL SELECT statement.) Some examples of predicate strings are

```
rightCounter == 0
wrongCounter >= 5
question contains[cd] "tempus"
```

Workshop

Quiz

1. What is the application sandbox?

2. What four directories in the application sandbox are designated for writing application data?

   3. To implement object archiving, an object must implement the `NSCopying` protocol. True or False?

Answers

   1. The application sandbox is the collective set of restrictions Apple places on third-party applications to protect the device and its data from accidentally or maliciously harmful operations.

   2. Documents, Library/Preferences, Library/Caches, and tmp.

   3. False, the `NSCoding` protocol must be implemented for an object to support object archiving. In fact, it is a good idea to implement the `NSCopying` protocol at the same time you implement the `NSCoding` protocol.

Activities

   1. If you work with the object archiving version and the Core Data version of the FlashCards application, you might notice a difference in their behavior. The order of the cards is preserved in the object archiving version, but in the Core Data version the flash card order is changed to the order the cards were created in after the application was restarted. This is because in the object archiving version, the array of flash cards itself is written out to the file system and read in when the application starts, but in the Core Data version, the array is created from the results of the `NSFetchRequest`. The default order for the fetch request is the order the objects were created in. What ways can you think of to preserve the flash card order in the Core Data version? Pick one approach and implement it so that the Core Data version preserves the flash card order.

   2. A user might want to have more than one deck of flash cards to cover different topics. Update the application to allow the user to create, delete, open, and close different decks of flash cards. Pick one of the two implementations, the object archiving or the Core Data version, to extend with this capability. If you extend the object archiving version, store each deck in a different file. Think about where you will store the deck name. If you decide to extend the Core Data version, model a `Deck` entity and create a relationship between the `Deck` and the `FlashCard` entities contained in the `Deck`. Add an attribute to the `Deck` to allow the user to provide a name.

Further Exploration

This hour has been an introduction to the rich field of data management. Many programmers have spent their entire career focused on just this one aspect of application design, and there is always more to learn when it comes to implementing robust, high-performance data management solutions. If you'd like to go further exploring object archiving, your next stop should be Apple's *Archives and Serializations Programming Guide for Cocoa.* The documentation around Core Data is more extensive, and there is even documentation about the available documentation in the form of Apple's *Core Data Overview.*

Apple has put together two tutorials that are especially helpful: the *Core Data Tutorial for iPhone OS* and *Creating a Managed Object Model with Xcode.* To get more information about querying with Core Data, which was only briefly mentioned in this hour, check out Apple's *Predicate Programming Guide.* Three other important Core Data topics you should be sure to research are undo support, schema versioning, and Cocoa bindings, which is an approach to using key value coding (KVC) in UIs to bind UI controls to Core Data values so that you can write less code (always a good thing).

HOUR 17

Building Rotatable and Resizable User Interfaces

What You'll Learn in This Hour:

▶ How to make an application "rotation aware"

▶ Ways of laying out an interface to enable automatic rotation

▶ Methods of tweaking interface elements' frames to fine-tune a layout

▶ How to swap views for landscape and portrait viewing

You can use almost every iPhone interface widget available, you can create multiple views and view controllers, add sounds and alerts, write files, and even manage application preferences—but until now, your applications have been missing a very important feature: rotatable interfaces. The ability to create interfaces that "look right" regardless of the iPhone's orientation is one of the key features that users expect in an application.

This hour's lesson explores three different ways of adding rotatable and resizable interfaces to your apps. You might be surprised to learn that *all* the apps you've built to-date can begin handling rotation with a single line of code!

Rotatable and Resizable Interfaces

Years ago, when I had my first Windows Mobile smartphone, I longed for an easy way to look at web content in landscape mode. There was a method for triggering a landscape view, but it was glitchy and cumbersome to use. The iPhone introduced the first consumer phone with on-the-fly interface rotation that feels natural and doesn't get in the way of what you're trying to do.

As you build your iPhone applications, consider how the user will be interfacing with the app. Does it make sense to force a portrait-only view? Should the view rotate to accommodate any of the possible orientations that phone may assume? The more flexibility you give users to adapt to their own preferred working style, the happier they'll be. Best of all, enabling rotation is a very simple process.

Enabling Interface Rotation

To allow your application's interface to rotate and resize, all that is required is a single method! When the iPhone wants to check to see whether it should rotate your interface, it sends the shouldAutorotateToInterfaceOrientation: message to your view controller, along with a parameter that indicates which orientation it wants to check.

Your implementation of shouldAutorotateToInterfaceOrientation: should compare the incoming parameter against the different orientation constants in the iPhone OS, returning TRUE (or YES) if you want to support that orientation.

You'll encounter four basic screen orientation constants:

Orientation	iPhone Orientation Constant
Portrait	UIInterfaceOrientationPortrait
Portrait upside-down	UIInterfaceOrientationPortraitUpsideDown
Landscape left	UIInterfaceOrientationLandscapeLeft
Landscape right	UIInterfaceOrientationLandscapeRight

For example, to allow your iPhone interface to rotate to either the portrait or landscape left orientations, you would implement shouldAutorotateToInterfaceOrientation: in your view controller like this:

```
- (BOOL)shouldAutorotateToInterfaceOrientation:
              (UIInterfaceOrientation)interfaceOrientation {
    return (interfaceOrientation == UIInterfaceOrientationPortrait ||
            interfaceOrientation == UIInterfaceOrientationLandscapeLeft);
}
```

The return statement handles everything! It returns the result of an expression comparing the incoming orientation parameter, interfaceOrientation, to UIInterfaceOrientationPortrait and UIInterfaceOrientationLandscapeLeft. If either comparison is true, TRUE is returned. If one of the other possible orientations is checked, the expression evaluates to FALSE. In other words, just by adding this simple method to your view controller, your application will automatically sense and rotate the screen for portrait or landscape left orientations!

Did you Know?

To enable *all* possible rotation scenarios, you can simply use `return YES;` as your implementation of `shouldAutorotateToInterfaceOrientation:`.

At this point, take a few minutes and go back to some of the earlier chapters, adding this method to your view controller code, returning YES for all orientations. Use Build and Run to test the applications in the iPhone Simulator or on your device.

Although some of the applications will probably look just fine, you'll notice that others, well... don't quite "work" in the different screen orientations, as shown in Figure 17.1.

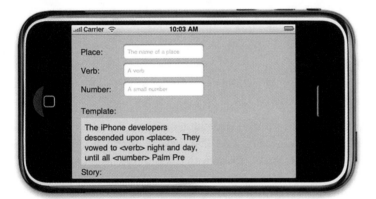

FIGURE 17.1
Allowing the screen to rotate doesn't mean your application will function perfectly in the new orientation!

Because the iPhone screen isn't square, it stands to reason that landscape and portrait views might not match up very well. Everything we've been building has been designed in portrait mode, so how can we create interfaces that look good in portrait or landscape mode? We obviously need to make some tweaks!

I Get "Rotatable", but What's with the "Resizable?"

When the iPhone rotates, the screen dimensions shift. You still have the same amount of usable space, but it is laid out differently. To make the best use of the available space, you can have your controls (buttons and so on) resize for the new orientation—thus the combination of "rotatable" *and* "resizable" when discussing screen rotation.

Designing Rotatable and Resizable Interfaces

In the remainder of this hour, we'll be exploring three different techniques for building interfaces that rotate and resize themselves appropriately when the user changes the iPhone's screen orientation. Before we get started, let's quickly review the different approaches and when you may want to use them.

Autorotating and Autoresizing

Interface Builder provides tools for describing how your interface should react when it is rotated. It is possible to define a single view in Interface Builder that positions and sizes itself appropriately when rotated, without writing a single line of code!

This should be the starting point for all interfaces. If you can successfully define portrait and landscape modes in single view in Interface Builder, your work is done.

Unfortunately, autorotating/autoresizing doesn't work well when there are many irregularly positioned interface elements. A single row of buttons? No problem! Half a dozen fields, switches, and images all mixed together? Probably not going to work.

Reframing

As you've learned, each iPhone UI element is defined by a rectangular area on the screen: its `frame` property.

To change the size or location of something in the view, you can redefine the `frame` using the Core Graphics C function `CGRectMake(x,y,width,height)`. `CGRectMake` accepts an x and y coordinate, along with a width and height, and returns a new frame value.

By defining new frames for everything in your view, you have complete control of each object's placement and size. Unfortunately, you need to keep track of the coordinate positions for each object. This isn't difficult, per se, but it can be frustrating when you want to shift an object up or down by a few pixels and suddenly find yourself needing to adjust the coordinates of every other object above or below it.

Swapping Views

A more dramatic approach to changing your view to accommodate different screen orientations is to use entirely different views for landscape and portrait layouts! When the user rotates the phone, the current view is replaced by another view that is laid out properly for the orientation.

This means that you can define two views in Interface Builder that look exactly the way you want, but it also means that you'll need to keep track of separate `IBOutlets` for each view! While it is certainly possible for elements in the views to invoke the same `IBActions`, they cannot share the same outlets, so you'll potentially need to keep track of twice as many UI widgets within a single view controller.

> To know *when* to change frames or swap views, you will be implementing the method `willRotateToInterfaceOrientation:toInterfaceOrientation:duration:` in your view controller. This method is called by the iPhone when it is about to change orientation.

By the Way

Creating Rotatable and Resizable Interfaces with Interface Builder

In the first of our three tutorial projects, we'll look at ways you can use the built-in tools in Interface Builder to control how your views "adapt" to being rotated. For simple views, these features provide everything you need to create orientation-aware apps.

We'll be using a label (UILabel) and a few buttons (UIButton) as our "study subjects" for this tutorial. Feel free to swap them out with other interface elements to see how rotation and resizing is handled across the iPhone object library.

Setting Up the Project

Begin by starting Xcode and creating a new application, **SimpleSpin**, using the Apple View-Based Application template. Although all our UI work will take place in Interface Builder, we still need to enable interface rotation with the `shouldAutorotateToInterfaceOrientation:` method.

Open the implementation file for the view controller (SimpleSpinViewController.m), and then find and uncomment `shouldAutorotateToInterfaceOrientation:`. Because we're not going to control the view programmatically at all, we'll go ahead and enable all possible iPhone screen orientations by returning YES from this method.

The finished method implementation should read as follows:

```
- (BOOL)shouldAutorotateToInterfaceOrientation:
        (UIInterfaceOrientation)interfaceOrientation {
    return YES;
}
```

Save the implementation file and switch to Interface Builder by opening the XIB file that defines the application's view: SimpleSpinViewController.xib. All the rest of our work for this example takes place in this file.

Building a Flexible Interface

Creating a rotatable and resizable interface starts out like building any other iPhone interface: Just drag and drop!

Using the Library (Tools, Library), drag a label (UILabel) and four buttons (UIButton) to the SimpleSpin view. Center the label at the top of the view and title it **SimpleSpin**. Name the buttons so you can tell them apart: **Button 1**, **Button 2**, **Button 3**, and **Button 4**. Position them below the label, as shown in Figure 17.2.

FIGURE 17.2
Build your rotatable application interface the same way you would any other application.

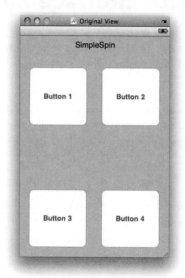

Testing Rotation

You've now built a simple application interface, just as you have in earlier lessons. To get an idea of what the interface looks like when rotated, click the curved arrow in the upper-right corner of the Interface Builder's view window (see Figure 17.3).

As you might expect, the reoriented view does not look "quite right." The reason is that objects you add to the view are, by default, "anchored" by their upper-left corner. This means that no matter what the screen orientation is, they'll keep the same distance from the top of the view to their top, and from left of the view to their left side. Objects also, by default, are not allowed to resize within the view. As a result, all elements have the exact same size in portrait or landscape orientations, even if they won't fit in the view.

To fix our problem and create an iPhone-worthy interface, we'll need to use the Size Inspector.

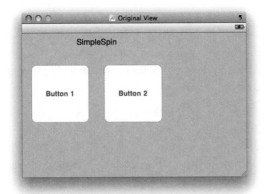

FIGURE 17.3
Use Interface
Builder to imme-
diately test the
effects of rotat-
ing the view.

Understanding Autosizing in the Size Inspector

As you've grown more experienced building iPhone applications, you've gotten accustomed to using the Interface Builder inspectors. The Attributes and Connections Inspectors have been extremely valuable in configuring the appearance and functionality of your application. The Size Inspector (Command+3), on the other hand, has remained largely on the sidelines, occasionally called on to set the coordinates of a control, but never used to enable functionality—until now.

The magic of autorotating and autoresizing views is managed entirely through the Size Inspector's Autosizing settings, shown in Figure 17.4. This deceptively simple "square in a square" interface provides everything you need to tell Interface Builder where to anchor your controls, and in which directions (horizontally or vertically) they can stretch.

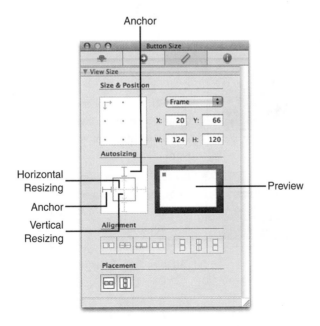

FIGURE 17.4
The Autosizing
settings control
anchor and size
properties for
any onscreen
object.

To understand how this works, imagine that the inner square represents one of your interface elements, and the outer square is the view that contains the element. The lines between the inner and outer square are the anchors. When clicked, they toggle between solid and dashed lines. Solid lines are anchors that are set. This means that those distances will be maintained when the interface rotates.

Within the inner square are two double-headed arrows, representing horizontal and vertical resizing. Clicking these arrows toggles between solid and dashed lines. Solid arrows indicate that the item is allowed to resize horizontally, vertically, or both. As mentioned earlier, by default, objects are anchored on their top and left, and are not allowed to resize. This configuration is visible in Figure 17.4.

Did you Know?

If you need a more "visual" means of understanding the autosizing controls, just look to the right of the two squares. The rectangle to the right shows an animated preview of what will happen to your control (represented as a red rectangle) when the view changes size around it. The easiest way to start understanding the relationship between anchors, resizing, and view size/orientation is to configure the anchors/resize-arrows, and then watch the preview to see the effect.

Applying Autosize Settings to the Interface

To modify our SimpleSpin interface with appropriate autosizing attributes, let's analyze what we want to have happen for each element and translate that into anchors and resizing information.

As we work through the list, select each of the interface elements, and then open the Size Inspector (Commnd+3) and configure their anchors and resizing attributes as described here:

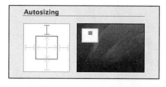

The "SimpleSpin" label: The label should float at the top center of the view. The distance between the top of the view and the label should be maintained. The size of the label should be maintained. (Anchor: Top, Resizing: None).

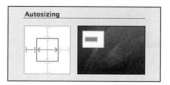

Button 1: The button should maintain the same distance between its left side and the left side of the view, but it should be allowed to float up and down as needed. It can resize horizontally to better fit a larger horizontal space. (Anchor: Left, Resizing: Horizontal).

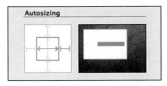

Button 2: The button should maintain the same distance between its right side and the right side of the view, but it should be allowed to float up and down as needed. It can resize horizontally to better fit a larger horizontal space. (Anchor: Right, Resizing: Horizontal).

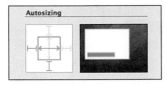

Button 3: The button should maintain the same distance between its left side and the left side of the view, as well as its bottom and the bottom of the view. It can resize horizontally to better fit a larger horizontal space. (Anchor: Left and Bottom, Resizing: Horizontal).

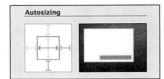

Button 4: The button should maintain the same distance between its right side and the right side of the view, as well as its bottom and the bottom of the view. It can resize horizontally to better fit a larger horizontal space. (Anchor: Right and Bottom, Resizing: Horizontal).

After you've worked through one or two of the UI objects, you'll realize that it took longer to describe what we needed to do, than to do it! Once the anchors and resize settings are in place, the application is ready for rotation! Click the rotate arrow in the Interface Builder's view window and review the result. Your view should now resize and resemble Figure 17.5.

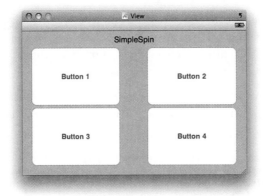

FIGURE 17.5
The finished view now properly positions itself when rotated into a landscape orientation.

You can, if you choose, save the SimpleSpinViewController.xib changes, and then return to Xcode and click Build and Run to test the application in the iPhone

Simulator or on your device. Because we haven't modified anything programmatically in the view, it should behave exactly the same as what you've seen in Interface Builder.

Reframing Controls on Rotation

In the previous example, you learned how Interface Builder can help quickly create interface layouts that look as good horizontally as they do vertically. Unfortunately, there are plenty of situations that Interface Builder can't quite accommodate. Irregularly spaced controls and tightly packed layouts will rarely work out the way you expect. You may also find yourself wanting to tweak the interface to look completely different—positioning objects that were at the top of the view down by the bottom, and so on.

In either of these cases, you'll likely want to consider reframing the controls to accommodate a rotated iPhone screen. The logic is simple: When the phone interface rotates, we'll identify which orientation it will be rotating *to*, and then set new `frame` properties for everything in the UI that we want to reposition or resize. You'll learn how to do this now.

Setting Up the Project

Unlike the previous example, we can't rely on Interface Builder for everything, so there will be a small amount of code in this tutorial. Once again, create a new View-Based Application project, named **Reframe**.

Adding Outlets and Properties

In this exercise, you'll be manually resizing and repositioning three UI elements: two buttons (`UIButton`), and one label (`UILabel`). Because we'll need to access these programmatically, we'll first edit the interface and implementation files to include outlets and properties for each of these objects.

Open the ReframeViewController.h file and edit it to include `IBOutlet` declarations and `@property` directives for `buttonOne`, `buttonTwo`, and `viewLabel`:

```
#import <UIKit/UIKit.h>

@interface ReframeViewController : UIViewController {
    IBOutlet UIButton *buttonOne;
    IBOutlet UIButton *buttonTwo;
    IBOutlet UILabel *viewLabel;
}

@property (nonatomic,retain) UIButton *buttonOne;
```

```
@property (nonatomic,retain) UIButton *buttonTwo;
@property (nonatomic,retain) UILabel *viewLabel;

@end
```

Save your changes, and then edit `ReframeViewController.m`, adding the appropriate `@synthesize` directives for `buttonOne`, `buttonTwo`, and `viewLabel`, immediately following the `@implementation` line:

```
@synthesize buttonOne;
@synthesize buttonTwo;
@synthesize viewLabel;
```

Releasing the Objects

Edit the `dealloc` method in ReframeViewController.m to release the label and button we've retained:

```
- (void)dealloc {
    [buttonOne release];
    [buttonTwo release];
    [viewLabel release];
    [super dealloc];
}
```

Enabling Rotation

Even when you aren't going to be taking advantage of the autoresizing/autorotating capabilities in Interface Builder, you must still enable rotation in the `shouldAutorotateToInterfaceOrientation:` method. Update ReframeViewController.m to include the implementation you added in the earlier lesson:

```
- (BOOL)shouldAutorotateToInterfaceOrientation:
        (UIInterfaceOrientation)interfaceOrientation {
    return YES;
}
```

With the exception of the logic to detect and handle the reframing of our interface elements, that finishes the setup of our application. Now, let's create the default view that will be displayed when the application first loads.

Creating the Interface

We've now reached the point in the project where the one big caveat of reframing becomes apparent: keeping track of interface coordinates and sizes. Although we have the opportunity to lay out the interface in Interface Builder, we need to note where all the different elements *are*. Why? Because each time the screen changes rotation, we'll be resetting their position in the view. There is no "return to default positions" method, so even the initial layout we create will have to be coded using x,y coordinates and sizes so that we can call it back up when needed. Let's begin.

Open the ReframeViewController.xib file and its view in Interface Builder.

Disabling Autoresizing

Before doing anything else, click within the view to select it, and then open the Attribute Inspector (Command+1). Within the View settings section, uncheck the Autoresize Subviews check box (see Figure 17.6).

FIGURE 17.6
Disabling autoresizing when manually resizing and positioning controls.

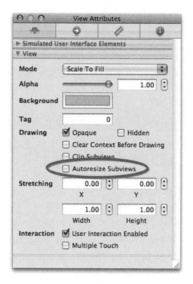

If you forget to disable the autoresize attribute in the view, your application code will manually resize/reposition the UI elements at the same time the iPhone OS tries to do it for you. The result can be a jumbled mess and several minutes of head scratching!

Laying Out the View... Once

Your next step is to lay out the view exactly as you would in any other app. Recall that we added outlets for two buttons and a label; using the Library, click and drag those elements into your view now. Title the label **Reframing** and position it at the top of the view. Set the button titles to **Button 1** and **Button 2**, and place them under the label. Your final layout should resemble Figure 17.7.

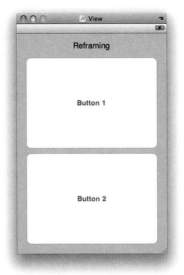

FIGURE 17.7
Start by laying out the view like a normal application.

When you have the layout you want, determine what the current frame attributes are for each of your objects. We can get this information from the Size Inspector.

Start by selecting the label and opening the Size Inspector (Command+3). Click the dot in the upper-right corner of the Size & Position settings to set the upper-right corner as the origin point for measuring coordinates. Next, make sure that the drop-down menu is set to Frame, as shown in Figure 17.8.

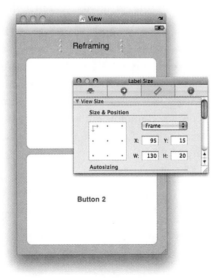

FIGURE 17.8
Configure the Size & Position settings to show the information you need to collect.

Now, write down the X, Y, W (width), and H (height) attributes for the label. This represents the frame property of the object within your view. Repeat this process for the two buttons. You should end up with a list of four values for each of your objects. Our frame values are listed here for comparison:

Label	X: 95.0, Y: 15.0, W: 130.0, H: 20.0
Button 1	X: 20.0, Y: 50.0, W: 280.0, H: 190.0
Button 2	X: 20.0, Y: 250.0, W: 280.0, H: 190.0

Before doing anything else, *save your view*! We'll be making some changes in the next section that you'll want to undo.

Did you Know?

> If you want to follow our example *exactly*, feel free to substitute the X, Y, W, and H values we've provided for the values of your objects in the Size Inspector. Doing this will resize and reposition your view elements to match ours!

Laying Out the View... Again

Your next step is to lay out the view exactly as you would in any other app. Wait a sec... this sounds very familiar. Why do we want to lay out the view again? The answer is simple. We've collected all the frame properties that we need to configure the portrait view, but we haven't yet defined where the label and buttons will be in the *landscape* view. To get this information, we lay the view out again, in landscape mode, collect all the location and size attributes, and then discard those changes.

The process is identical to what you've already done; the only difference is that you need to click the rotate arrow in Interface Builder to rotate the view. Once you've rotated the view, resize and reposition all the existing elements so that they look the way you want them to appear when in landscape orientation on your iPhone. Because we'll be setting the positions and sizes programmatically, the sky is the limit for how you arrange the display. To follow our example, stretch Button 1 across the top of the view and Button 2 across the button. Position the Reframing label in the middle, as shown in Figure 17.9.

As before, when the view is exactly as you want it to appear, use the Size Inspector (Command+3) to collect the x,y coordinates and height and width of all the UI elements. Our landscape frame values are provided here for comparison:

Label	X: 175.0, Y: 140.0, W: 130.0, H: 20.0
Button 1	X: 20.0, Y: 20.0, W: 440.0, H: 100.0
Button 2	X: 20.0, Y: 180.0, W: 440.0, H: 100.0

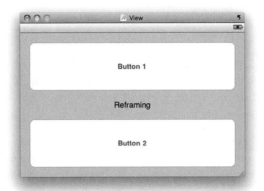

FIGURE 17.9
Lay the view out as you want it to appear in landscape mode.

When you've collected the landscape frame attributes, undo the changes by using Edit, Undo (Command+Z), or close ReframeViewController.xib (*not* saving the changes).

Connecting the Outlets

Before jumping back into Xcode to finish the implementation, we still need to connect the label and buttons to the outlets (viewLabel, buttonOne, and buttonTwo) that we added at the start of the project. Open ReframeViewController.xib again (if you closed it in the last step), and make sure that the view window and Document window are both visible onscreen.

Next, Control-drag from the File's Owner icon to the label and two buttons, choosing viewLabel, buttonOne, and buttonTwo as appropriate. Figure 17.10 demonstrates the connection from the Reframing label to the viewLabel outlet.

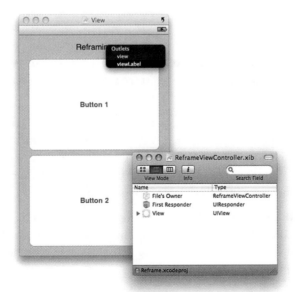

FIGURE 17.10
Finish up the interface by connecting the label and buttons to their corresponding outlets.

Save the XIB file and return to Xcode to finish up the project!

Implementing the Reframing Logic

Now that you've built the view and captured the values for the label and button frames in both portrait and landscape views, the only thing that remains is detecting when the iPhone is ready to rotate and reframing appropriately.

The willRotateToInterfaceOrientation:toInterfaceOrientation:duration: method is invoked automatically whenever the iPhone interface needs to rotate. We'll compare the toInterfaceOrientation parameter to the different iPhone orientation constants to identify whether we should be using the frames for a landscape or portrait view.

Open the ReframeViewController.m file in Xcode and add the following method:

```
 1: -(void)willRotateToInterfaceOrientation:
 2: (UIInterfaceOrientation)toInterfaceOrientation
 3:                                 duration:(NSTimeInterval)duration {
 4:
 5:     [super willRotateToInterfaceOrientation:toInterfaceOrientation
 6:                                     duration:duration];
 7:
 8:     if (toInterfaceOrientation == UIInterfaceOrientationLandscapeRight ||
 9:         toInterfaceOrientation == UIInterfaceOrientationLandscapeLeft) {
10:         viewLabel.frame=CGRectMake(175.0,140.0,130.0,20.0);
11:         buttonOne.frame=CGRectMake(20.0,20.0,440.0,100.0);
12:         buttonTwo.frame=CGRectMake(20.0,180.0,440.0,100.0);
13:     } else {
14:         viewLabel.frame=CGRectMake(95.0,15.0,130.0,20.0);
15:         buttonOne.frame=CGRectMake(20.0,50.0,280.0,190.0);
16:         buttonTwo.frame=CGRectMake(20.0,250.0,280.0,190.0);
17:     }
18: }
```

The logic is straightforward. To start, we need to make sure that any parent objects are notified that the view is about to rotate. So, in lines 5–6, we pass the same willRotateToInterfaceOrientation:toInterfaceOrientation:duration: message to the parent object super.

In lines 8–12 we compare the incoming parameter toInterfaceOrientation to the landscape orientation constants. If either of these match, we reframe the label and buttons to their landscape layouts by assigning the frame property to the output of the CGRectMake() function. The input to CGRectMake() is nothing more than the X,Y,W, and H values we collected earlier in Interface Builder.

Lines 13–16 handle the "other" orientation: portrait orientation. If the iPhone isn't rotated into a landscape orientation, the only other possibility is portrait. Again, the frame values that we assign are nothing more than the values identified using the Size Inspector in Interface Builder.

And, with this simple method, the Reframe project is now complete! You now have the capability of creating interfaces that rearrange themselves when users rotate their phone.

We still have one more approach to cover. In this final project, rather than rearranging a view in the landscape orientation, we'll replace the view altogether!

Swapping Views on Rotation

Some applications display entirely different user interfaces depending on the iPhone's orientation. The iPod application, for example, displays a scrolling list of songs in portrait mode, and a "flickable" Cover Flow view of albums when held in landscape. You too can create applications that dramatically alter their appearance by simply switching between views when the phone is rotated. Our last tutorial this hour will be short, sweet, and give you the flexibility to manage your landscape and portrait views all within the comfort of Interface Builder.

Setting Up the Project

Create a new project named **Swapper** using the View-Based Application template. Although this includes a single view already (which we'll use for the default portait display), we'll need to supplement it with a second landscape view.

Adding Outlets and Properties

This application won't implement any real user interface elements, but we will need to access two UIView instances programmatically.

Open the SwapperViewController.h file and edit it to include IBOutlet declarations and @property directives for portraitView, and landscapeView:

```
#import <UIKit/UIKit.h>

@interface ReframeViewController : UIViewController {
    IBOutlet UIView *portraitView;
    IBOutlet UIView *landscapeView;
}

@property (nonatomic,retain) UIView *portraitView;
@property (nonatomic,retain) UIView *landscapeView;

@end
```

You know the routine. Save your changes, and then edit the SwapperViewController.m implementation file, adding the appropriate @synthesize directives immediately following the @implementation line:

```
@synthesize portraitView;
@synthesize landscapeView;
```

Releasing the Objects

Edit the dealloc method in ReframeViewController.m to release the two views we've retained:

```
- (void)dealloc {
    [landscapeView release];
    [portraitView release];
    [super dealloc];
}
```

Enabling Rotation

Once more, for the iPhone to properly react when it changes orientation, we need to enable rotation. Unlike the previous two implementations of shouldAutorotateToInterfaceOrientation:, this time, we'll only allow rotation between the two landscape modes and upright portrait.

Update ReframeViewController.m to include this implementation:

```
- (BOOL)shouldAutorotateToInterfaceOrientation:
           (UIInterfaceOrientation)interfaceOrientation {
    return (interfaceOrientation == UIInterfaceOrientationPortrait ||
           interfaceOrientation == UIInterfaceOrientationLandscapeRight ||
           interfaceOrientation == UIInterfaceOrientationLandscapeLeft);
}
```

The incoming interfaceOrientation parameter is compared to the UIInterfaceOrientationPortrait, UIInterfaceOrientationLandscapeRight, and UIInterfaceOrientationLandscapeLeft. If it matches, rotation is allowed. As you might surmise, this covers all the possible orientations except upside-down portrait (UIInterfaceOrientationPortraitUpsideDown), which we'll disable this time around.

Adding a Degree to Radians Constant

Later in this exercise, we're going to need to call a special Core Graphics method to define how to rotate views. The method requires a value to be passed in radians rather than degrees. In other words, instead of saying we want to rotate the view 90 degrees, we have to tell it we want to rotate 1.57 radians. To help us handle the conversion, we will define a constant for the conversion factor. Multiplying degrees by the constant gets us the resulting value in radians.

To define the constant, add the following line after the #import line in
SwapperViewController.m:

```
#define deg2rad (3.1415926/180.0)
```

Creating the Interface

When swapping views, the sky is the limit for the design. You build them exactly as
you would in any other application. The only difference is that if you have multiple
views handled by a single view controller, you'll need to define outlets that encompass all the interface elements.

In this example, we'll just be demonstrating how to swap views, so our work in
Interface Builder will be quite simple.

Creating the Views

Open SwapperViewController.xib and drag a new instance of the UIView object from
the Library to the Document window. Don't put the UIView inside of the existing
view. It should be added as a new separate view within the XIB file, as seen in
Figure 17.11.

FIGURE 17.11
Add a second
view to the XIB
file.

Now, open each of the views and add a label to tell them apart. We've set the background color of each view to be different as well. You're welcome to add other controls and design the view as you see fit. Figure 17.12 shows our finished landscape
and portrait views.

Did you Know?

To differentiate between the two views within the Interface Builder document window, you can switch to icon view, and then edit the name of each view just like
you would in the Finder!

FIGURE 17.12
Edit the two
views so that
you can tell
them apart.

Connecting the Outlets

To finish up in Interface Builder, Control-drag from the File's Owner icon to each of the views. Connect the portrait view to the `portraitView` outlet, as shown in Figure 17.13, and the landscape view to `landscapeView`.

FIGURE 17.13
Connect the
views to their
corresponding
outlets.

Save the XIB file and return to Xcode to finish up the Swapper implementation.

Implementing the View-Swapping Logic

For the most part, swapping views is actually easier than the reframing logic that we had to implement in the last project—with one small exception. Even though we designed one of the views to be a landscape view, it doesn't "know" that it is supposed to be displayed in a landscape orientation. Before we can display it, we need to rotate it and define how big it is.

Understanding the View-Rotation Logic

Each time we change orientation, we'll go through three steps: swapping the view, rotating the view to the proper orientation through the `transform` property, and setting the view's origin and size via the `bounds` property.

For example, assume we're rotating to right landscape orientation:

1. First, we swap out the view by assigning `self.view`, which contains the current view of the view controller, to the `landscapeView` instance variable. If we left things at that, the view would properly switch, but it wouldn't be rotated into the landscape orientation. A landscape view displayed in a portrait orientation isn't a pretty thing! For example:

```
self.view=landscapeView;
```

2. Next, to deal with the rotation, we define the `transform` property of the view. This property determines how the view will be altered before it is displayed. To meet our needs, we'll have to rotate the view 90 degrees to the right (for landscape right), –90 degrees to the left (for landscape left), and 0 degrees for portrait. As luck would have it, the Core Graphics C function `CGAffineTransformMakeRotation()` accepts a rotation value in radians and provides an appropriate structure to the `transform` property to handle the rotation. For example:

```
self.view.transform=CGAffineTransformMakeRotation(deg2rad*(90));
```

> Note that we multiply the rotation in degrees (90, –90, and 0) by the constant deg2rad that we defined earlier so that `CGAffineTransformMakeRotation()` has the radian value it expects.
>
> **By the Way**

3. The final step is to set the `bounds` property of the view. The `bounds` define the origin point and size of the view after it undergoes the transformation. A portrait iPhone view has an original point of 0,0 and a width and height of 320 and 460. A landscape view has the same origin point (0,0), but a width of

480, and a height of 300. As with the `frame` property, we can set bounds using the results of `CGRectMake()`. For example:

```
self.view.bounds=CGRectMake(0.0,0.0,480.0,320.0);
```

What Happened to 320x480? Where Are the Missing 20 Pixels?

The missing 20 pixels are taken up by the iPhone status bar. When the phone is in portrait mode, the pixels come off of the large (480) dimension. In landscape orientation, however, the status bar eats up the space on the smaller (320) dimension.

Now that you understand the steps, let's take a look at the actual implementation.

Writing the View-Rotation Logic

As with the Reframing project, all this magic happens within a single method, `willRotateToInterfaceOrientation:toInterfaceOrientation:duration:`.

Open the SwapperViewController.m implementation file and implement the method like this:

```
 1: -(void)willRotateToInterfaceOrientation:
 2:             (UIInterfaceOrientation)toInterfaceOrientation
 3:             duration:(NSTimeInterval)duration {
 4:
 5:     [super willRotateToInterfaceOrientation:toInterfaceOrientation
 6:                                    duration:duration];
 7:
 8:     if (toInterfaceOrientation == UIInterfaceOrientationLandscapeRight) {
 9:         self.view=landscapeView;
10:         self.view.transform=CGAffineTransformMakeRotation(deg2rad*(90));
11:         self.view.bounds=CGRectMake(0.0,0.0,480.0,320.0);
12:     } else if (toInterfaceOrientation == UIInterfaceOrientationLandscapeLeft) {
13:         self.view=landscapeView;
14:         self.view.transform=CGAffineTransformMakeRotation(deg2rad*(-90));
15:         self.view.bounds=CGRectMake(0.0,0.0,480.0,320.0);
16:     } else {
17:         self.view=portraitView;
18:         self.view.transform=CGAffineTransformMakeRotation(0);
19:         self.view.bounds=CGRectMake(0.0,0.0,300.0,460.0);
20:     }
21: }
```

Lines 5–6 pass the interface rotation message up to the parent object so that it can react appropriately.

Lines 8–11 handle rotation to the right (landscape right). Lines 12–15 deal with rotation to the left (landscape left). Finally, lines 16–19 configure the view for the default orientation: portrait.

Save the implementation file, and then choose Build and Run to test the application. As you rotate the phone or the iPhone Simulator, your views should be swapped in and out appropriately.

> Although we used an if-then-else statement in this example, you could easily use a `switch` structure instead. The `toInterfaceOrientation` parameter and orientation constants are integer values, which means they can be evaluated directly in a `switch` statement.

Did you Know?

Summary

The iPhone is all about the user experience: a touchable display, intuitive controls, and now, rotatable interfaces. Using the techniques described in this hour's lesson, you can adapt to almost any type of rotation scenario. To handle simple interface size changes, for example, you can take advantage of the autosizing attributes in Interface Builder. For more complex changes, however, you might want to redefine the `frame` properties for your onscreen elements, giving you complete control over their size and placement. Finally, for the ultimate in flexibility, you can create multiple different views and swap them as the phone rotates.

By implementing rotation-aware applications, you enable your users to use their phone in the way that feels most comfortable to them.

Q&A

Q. *Why don't many applications implement the upside-down portrait mode?*

A. Although there is no problem implementing the upside-down portrait orientation using the approaches described in this hour, it isn't necessarily recommended. When the iPhone is upside-down, the Home button and sensors are not in the "normal" location. If a call comes in or the user needs to interact with the phone's controls, he or she will need to rotate the phone 180 degrees, a somewhat complicated action to perform with one hand.

Q. *I implemented the first exercise, but the buttons overlapped one another. What did I do wrong?*

A. Probably nothing! Make sure that your anchors are set correctly, and then try shifting the buttons up or down a bit in the view. Nothing in Interface Builder prevents elements from overlapping. Chances are, you just need to tweak the positions and try again.

Workshop

Quiz

1. The iPhone interface can rotate through three different orientations. True or false?

2. How does an application communicate which rotation orientations it supports?

3. What was the purpose of the deg2rad constant that we defined in the final exercise?

Answers

1. False. There are four primary interface orientations: landscape right, landscape left, portrait, and upside-down portrait.

2. By implementing the shouldAutorotateToInterfaceOrientation: method in the view controller, the application identifies which of the four orientations it will operate in.

3. We defined the deg2rad constant to give us an easy way to convert degrees to radians for the Core Graphics C function CGAffineTransformMakeRotation().

Activities

1. Edit the Swapper example so that each view presents and processes user input. Keep in mind that because both views are handled by a single view controller you'll need to add all the outlets and actions for *both views* to the view controller interface and implementation files.

2. Return to an earlier lesson and revise the interface to support multiple different orientations. Use any of the techniques described in this hour's exercises for the implementation.

Further Exploration

Although we covered several different ways of working with rotation in the iPhone interface, you may want to explore additional features outside of this hour's lesson. Using the Xcode documentation tool, review the UIView instance methods. You'll see that there are additional methods that you can implement, such as willAnimateRotationToInterfaceOrientation:duration:, which is used to set up a single-step animated rotation sequence. Even more advanced transitions can be accomplished with the willAnimateFirstHalfOfRotationToInterfaceOrientation:duration: and willAnimateSecondHalfOfRotationFromInterfaceOrientation:duration: methods, which implement a two-stage animated rotation process.

In short, there is more to learn about how to smoothly change from one interface layout to another. This hour gave you the basics to begin implementation, but as your needs grow, there are additional rotation capabilities in the SDK just waiting to be tapped.

HOUR 18

Extending the Touch Interface

What You'll Learn in This Hour:

▶ The multitouch gesture architecture
▶ How to detect taps
▶ How to detect swipes
▶ How to detect pinches
▶ How to use the built-in shake gesture

The buzz around the iPhone is now focused on the App Store and the innovation in third-party applications. When the iPhone was originally launched, however, there was no iPhone SDK for third-party developers, and the majority of the buzz was around the high-definition (163 pixels per inch) multitouch screen. The screen was unique at the time in mass-market consumer electronics because it could detect multiple fingers at once.

A multitouch screen allows applications to use a wide variety of natural finger gestures for operations that would otherwise be hidden behind layers of menus, buttons, and text. From the very first time you use a pinch to zoom in and out on a photo, map, or web page, you realize that's exactly the right interface for zooming. Nothing is more human than manipulating the environment with your fingers.

The iPhone interface controls you have become familiar with so far provide built-in events that can trigger your application to perform actions. In addition to these built-in controls, the UIEvent and UITouch APIs of the iPhone SDK make it possible for developers to create their own multitouch interfaces that extend beyond simple buttons, text fields, and sliders. This hour shows how you can respond to touch actions and gestures.

*Watch
   Out!*

> For most applications in this book, using the iPhone Simulator is perfectly accept-
> able, but the simulator cannot re-create all the gestures you can create with your
> fingers. For this hour, be sure to have a physical device that is provisioned for
> development. To run this hour's applications on your device, follow the steps in
> Hour 1, "Preparing Your System and iPhone for Development."

Multitouch Gesture Architecture

The multitouch gesture architecture is based on the concept of a responder chain.
The system generates instances of the UIEvent class to indicate that some user interaction with the hardware occurred, and a chain of responder objects are given a
chance to respond. Each UIEvent is a distinct gesture or gesture in progress (for
example, a double tap, a two-fingered swipe, or a pinch). Each UIEvent is received
along with the parts that made up the gesture. A swipe event, for example, might
be made up of a finger touching the screen, moving across the screen, and lifting off
the screen. These parts, one part per finger, are instances of the UITouch class.

A responder chain is a series of linked responder objects. Each responder is an implementation of UIResponder. The first link in the chain is known as the first responder. As you might suspect, the first responder is the responder that gets the first crack
at responding to the event. If a particular responder in the chain cannot fully
respond to the event, the responder can pass the event up the chain to the next
responder. Each responder decides what the event means to it, if and how it will
respond to the event, and if the event is fully consumed or if it should be passed up
the chain to the next responder for further handling.

A responder chain is not circular; it has both a beginning and an end. At the end of
the responder chain is the application's UIWindow instance and finally the application's instance of UIApplication.

UIApplication is the last responder to get a chance to handle the event. It's not
unusual for an event to pass through the entire chain and not elicit any response.
This is normal and does not cause any problems.

You may be wondering how the responder chain is put together. What determines
the chain's order? The responder chain mimics the view hierarchy, starting at the
lowest subview that is the origin of the event (determined by a hit test) and passing
up the view hierarchy all the way to the UIWindow and UIApplication. For each
view in the view hierarchy, two responders are added to the chain. First the view
itself has a chance to respond, and then the view's controller. If both responders forward the event, the next responder in the chain is the view's parent and the parent's
controller, and so on up the chain.

Responding to Events

To start using multitouch events in your application, you need to insert your own code into the responder chain by implementing any of the four touch methods in UIResponder. UIView and UIViewController are instances of UIResponder, and they provide default implementations of these four methods for you. Your custom view or view controller can override the methods you are interested in receiving:

```
- (void)touchesBegan:(NSSet *)touches withEvent:(UIEvent *)event
- (void)touchesMoved:(NSSet *)touches withEvent:(UIEvent *)event
- (void)touchesEnded:(NSSet *)touches withEvent:(UIEvent *)event
- (void)touchesCancelled:(NSSet *)touches withEvent:(UIEvent *)event
```

By implementing any of these four methods, you start receiving events that are relevant to your view or view controller. The next step is to understand the event you received so that you can do something interesting as a result. The two arguments you'll receive for any of these methods are a set of UITouch objects and a UIEvent object. You'll mostly be interested in the touches because they contain the details about the gesture. The UIEvent is used to gain access to the broader context of what occurred. The event provides a timestamp in case you need to determine the temporal relation of the current event to others that have occurred, and it has the ability to filter the touches to only the touches that occurred within a particular view rather than all the touches that made up the event.

Each UITouch in the NSSet of touches you receive has a phase, location, view in which the touch occurred, timestamp, and tap count. Whereas most of these UITouch properties are self-explanatory, the phase and location properties could use a little explanation.

The phase of a touch is a UITouchPhase constant that tells you what happened during the touch (see Table 18.1).

TABLE 18.1   The Possible Values of UITouchPhase

UITouchPhaseBegan	A finger for the event touched the screen.
UITouchPhaseMoved	A finger for the event moved on the screen.
UITouchPhaseStationary	A finger for the event paused on the screen.
UITouchPhaseEnd	A finger for the event was lifted from the screen.
UITouchPhaseCancelled	Something happened to abort the gesture (an incoming phone call, for example).

The location of a touch is an x, y coordinate offset relative to the view in which the touch occurred. If you need to know the location where the touch happened, it is crucial to understand the relative nature of the location of each touch. The touch's location property is not a coordinate of the touch on the entire window or screen. Figure 18.1 illustrates this for four different touches: A, B, C and D. Notice that even though each touch is further right and down in the absolute x and y coordinates for the whole screen, and would therefore receive a higher x and y coordinate value, the actual location coordinates for each touch are relative to the view they occurred in.

FIGURE 18.1
Relative location of touches.

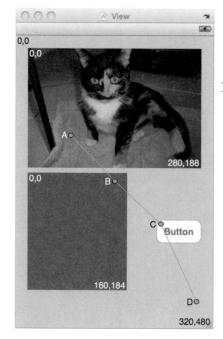

During this hour we are going to create a Simon Says game that asks players to complete a gesture and then determines whether they successfully completed it. We'll start by asking the user to tap the screen, and then we'll go on to add swipes, pinches, and shakes.

Detecting Taps

The iPhone keeps track of the taps that occur against the screen and delivers a single tap event to the responder chain with a count of the number of taps that occurred. You are familiar with the distinction between a single and a double mouse click in a traditional desktop application, and the iPhone will likewise report single and double taps. (It will also report triple, quadruple, quintuple, and more taps, although I don't recommend you include any of those gestures in your UI!) First, let's create the simple interface for our game.

Add the Outlet

Create a new View-Based Application in Xcode and call it **SimonSays**. Our game needs a way for Simon to ask the user to perform a gesture and we'll use a label for that. Click the SimonSaysViewController.h file in the Classes group and add an outlet property for an instruction label. The SimonSaysViewController.h file should read as shown in Listing 18.1.

LISTING 18.1

```
#import <UIKit/UIKit.h>

@interface SimonSaysViewController : UIViewController {
    IBOutlet UILabel *instructionLabel;
}

@property (nonatomic, retain) UILabel *instructionLabel;

@end
```

Lay Out the UI and Connect the Outlets

Open Interface Builder by double-clicking the SimonSaysViewController.xib file in the Resources group. Then complete the following steps to lay out the UI and connect the outlets:

1. Open the Library (Shift+Command+L) and search for "label."

2. Drag a label to the top of the view to the edge of the sizing guidelines. Expand the size of the label to the edge sizing guidelines on each side of the view.

3. Open the Attribute Inspector for the label (Command+1).

4. Click the center button of the Layout Alignment attribute to center the label's text.

5. Click the Font attribute and change the font size to 18 points.

6. Click the view to show its properties in the Attribute Inspector. Click the Multiple Touch check box so that the view will receive multitouch events.

7. Right-click the File's Owner in the NIB and connect the instructionLabel IBOutlet to the label by click-dragging from the circle next to the outlet to the label.

Your view should now look like Figure 18.2. Save the XIB file and return to Xcode.

FIGURE 18.2
Simon says,
"Lay out the UI."

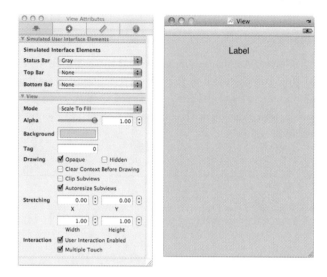

Simon Says, "Write Some Code"

Now that we have an interface that consists of a custom view and a label, the next thing our Simon Says game needs is a virtual Simon. Our Simon is really just an ordered collection of instructions to give the player. For each instruction from Simon, we need to be able to compare the player's gesture to what Simon said. Our game must be able to make Simon's instruction clear to the player and also to the responder code that will be checking for a matching gesture from the player. Let's create a minimal Instruction class that can accomplish both those goals.

Our game's Simon will issue four types of instructions: tap, swipe, pinch, and shake; so we need a type property for the instruction. Let's create an enumerated type called InstructionType and a property of the instruction called type. For most of these instructions, they'll be a numeric modifier, such as tap three times or swipe with four fingers, so we'll also need a modifier property on our Instruction. Finally, our Instruction needs an initializer to create instruction instances and a description method to provide a humanized version of the instruction that the player will understand:

1. Create a new Objective-C class in the Classes group by selecting the Classes group and then the File, New File (Command+N) menu item.

2. In the New File dialog, pick the Objective-C class template from the Cocoa Touch Class group.

3. Name the class **Instruction.m** and be sure the Also Create Instruction.h check box is checked.

4. Create the enumerated type and the two properties and methods by modifying Instruction.h, as shown in Listing 18.2.

LISTING 18.2

```
typedef enum {
    InstructionTypeTap,
    InstructionTypeSwipe,
    InstructionTypePinch,
    InstructionTypeShake
} InstructionType;

@interface Instruction : NSObject {

    InstructionType type;
    NSUInteger modifier; // # of taps or fingers, pinch type
}

@property(nonatomic,readonly) InstructionType type;
@property(nonatomic,readonly) NSUInteger modifier;

-(Instruction *)initWithType:(InstructionType)type
modifier:(NSUInteger)modifier;
-(NSString *)description;

@end
```

5. Next, synthesize the two properties and implement the initializer and description methods in the Instruction.m file as shown in Listing 18.3.

LISTING 18.3

```
#import "Instruction.h"

@implementation Instruction

@synthesize type;
@synthesize modifier;

-(Instruction *)initWithType:(InstructionType)thisType
                    modifier:(NSUInteger)thisModifier {

    self = [super init];

    type = thisType;
    modifier = thisModifier;

    return self;
}
```

LISTING 18.3   Continued

```
-(NSString *)description {

    NSString *description = nil;
    if (type == InstructionTypeTap) {
        description = [NSString stringWithFormat:@"Simon says tap %i times.",
modifier];
    }
    return description;
}

@end
```

We now have a representation of instructions from Simon that the responder will be able to understand through the type and count properties and that the player will understand by reading the description in the label we created earlier.

As the next step in completing our game, let's use our view's controller to get Simon ordering the user to perform a tap gesture of between two and five taps. (We'll make an exception to the no triple, quadruple, or quintuple taps recommendation because the difficulty in performing those gestures is actually part of the game.) We'll need to hold onto a randomized collection of instructions from Simon and keep track of which instruction is currently being given. An NSMutableArray and NSUInteger can accomplish those two tasks nicely. We'll call these **instructions** and **currentInstructionsCounter**, respectively.

The only other thing we'll keep track of is the last time a user successfully completed a gesture. Why track this? Primarily to see that it is easy to make temporal adjustments when responding to multitouch events, but also to be sure that a player doesn't get credit for overzealous tapping. This can happen when an extra tap turns a successful two-tap gesture into a successful three-tap gesture after a lucky ordering of the instructions.

Open the SimonSaysController.h file in the Classes group and make the modifications shown in Listing 18.4.

LISTING 18.4

```
#import <UIKit/UIKit.h>
#import "Instruction.h"

@interface SimonSaysViewController : UIViewController {

    IBOutlet UILabel *instructionLabel;

    NSMutableArray *instructions;
    NSUInteger currentInstructionCounter;
```

LISTING 18.4   Continued

```
    NSTimeInterval lastSuccess;
}

@property (nonatomic, retain) UILabel *instructionLabel;
@property (nonatomic, retain) NSMutableArray *instructions;

- (NSMutableArray *)randomizeInstructions:(int)howMany;
- (Instruction *)currentInstruction;
- (void)nextInstruction;
- (BOOL)tooSoon:(UIEvent *)event;

@end
```

The SimonSaysController.h file that we just modified gives us a roadmap of what we need to do in SimonSaysController.m to implement our game. We only have two properties: the Simon Says label, and the `NSMutableArray` of instructions from Simon. We can synthesize them so that the getters and setters are created for us and release them when we are done, as follows:

```
@synthesize instructionLabel;
@synthesize instructions;

- (void)dealloc {
    [instructionLabel release];
    [instructions release];
    [super dealloc];
}
```

We need to initialize the state of our game when the view loads from the NIB, so let's uncomment the `viewDidLoad` method of the SimonSaysController.m file and initialize the `lastSuccess` timestamp and the `currentInstructionCounter` to 0. We are only interested in how long ago our last success was if it was too recent, so a time of 0 is good for our initial `lastSuccess` value.

Our view controller has the helper method we defined, `randomizeInstructions:howMany`, that will return a `NSMutableArray` containing as many randomized instructions as we want. Let's ask for 100 instructions. Finally, we get the game started for the player by giving the first instruction with our `nextInstruction` method. The final `viewDidLoad` method should look like this:

```
- (void)viewDidLoad {

    lastSuccess = 0;
    currentInstructionCounter = 0;
    instructions = [self randomizeInstructions: 100];
    [self nextInstruction];

    [super viewDidLoad];
}
```

To implement `randomizeInstructions:howMany` let's start with an unrandomized `NSArray` of instructions created with our `Instruction` initializer. We create one `Instruction` for tap counts two through five. We can then loop through `howMany` times and pick an instruction at random, filling up our `NSMutableArray` of randomized instructions, and returning the filled array when we finish the loop:

```
-(NSMutableArray *)randomizeInstructions:(int)howMany {

    // Create an array of each instruction Simon knows
    NSArray *initialInstructions = [[NSArray alloc]initWithObjects:
    [[Instruction alloc]initWithType:InstructionTypeTap modifier:2],
    [[Instruction alloc]initWithType:InstructionTypeTap modifier:3],
    [[Instruction alloc]initWithType:InstructionTypeTap modifier:4],
    [[Instruction alloc]initWithType:InstructionTypeTap modifier:5],
    nil];

    instructions = [[NSMutableArray alloc]initWithCapacity:howMany];

    for (int i=0;i < howMany; i++) {
        // Add a random instruction
        [instructions addObject:
            [initialInstructions objectAtIndex: (arc4random() % 4)]];
    }
    return instructions;
}
```

`currentInstruction` and `nextInstruction` methods are fairly easy to implement. `currentInstruction` simply returns the `Instruction` at the current offset into the randomized `NSMutableArray` of instructions. `nextInstruction` increments our instruction counter and updates the label on the view so that the player knows what gesture to make for the new instruction. `nextInstruction` also must check whether the player has finished playing through the 100 instructions so that it can reset the counter back to the beginning:

```
- (Instruction *)currentInstruction {
    return [instructions objectAtIndex:(currentInstructionCounter - 1)];
}

- (void)nextInstruction {

    currentInstructionCounter += 1;

    // Loop back if we reached the last instruction
    if (currentInstructionCounter > [instructions count]) {
        currentInstructionCounter = 1;
    }

    // Instruct the user about the next action
    instructionLabel.text =
        [[self currentInstruction]description];

}
```

Now we come to the real heart of our game, the override of the UIResponder touchesEnded:touches:withEvent method that allows our view controller to act as a responder in the responder chain and receive events. In our responder, we want to understand the user gestures and determine whether they did what Simon asked of them. The first thing we do though is check the last time they did what Simon said, and make sure that at least three quarters of a second have passed. This is enough time to be sure that a lucky extra tap isn't counted.

In the tooSoon:event method, we just take the timestamp of the current event and subtract the timestamp of the last successful event and make sure the difference isn't less than 0.75. NSTimeIntervals are floating-point numbers; the whole number part represents seconds and the decimal part fractions of a second.

Assuming it's not too soon after the last successful gesture, we retrieve Simon's current instruction and then check that there is only one UITouch in the set of touches we were given. We can take advantage of the fact that the tap is the only touch gesture that can be made from just one touch, and a tap is also never more than one touch. (Remember, a multitap UIEvent does not come with multiple touches, but rather with one touch that has a tapCount greater than one.)

If the touch's tapCount matches the modifier on Simon's Instruction, the user has completed the requested gesture and they are rewarded with a pleasing green UIView backgroundColor and another request from Simon. If the tapCount doesn't match the modifier, the user gets an angry red-colored view.

Modify SimonSaysController.m in the Classes group to read as shown in Listing 18.5.

LISTING 18.5

```
#import "SimonSaysViewController.h"
#include <stdlib.h>

@implementation SimonSaysViewController

@synthesize instructionLabel;
@synthesize instructions;

- (Instruction *)currentInstruction {
    return [instructions objectAtIndex:(currentInstructionCounter - 1)];
}

- (void)nextInstruction {

    currentInstructionCounter += 1;

    // Loop back if we reached the last instruction
    if (currentInstructionCounter > [instructions count]) {
        currentInstructionCounter = 1;
```

LISTING 18.5   Continued

```
        }

        // Instruct the user about the next action
        instructionLabel.text =
            [[self currentInstruction]description];

}

-(NSMutableArray *)randomizeInstructions:(int)howMany {

        // Create an array of each instruction Simon knows
        NSArray *initialInstructions = [[NSArray alloc]initWithObjects:
         [[Instruction alloc]initWithType:InstructionTypeTap modifier:2],
         [[Instruction alloc]initWithType:InstructionTypeTap modifier:3],
         [[Instruction alloc]initWithType:InstructionTypeTap modifier:4],
         [[Instruction alloc]initWithType:InstructionTypeTap modifier:5],
         nil];

        instructions = [[NSMutableArray alloc]initWithCapacity:howMany];

        for (int i=0;i < howMany; i++) {
            // Add a random instruction
            [instructions addObject:
                [initialInstructions objectAtIndex: (arc4random() % 4)]];
        }
        return instructions;
}

- (BOOL) tooSoon:(UIEvent *)event {

        if (event.timestamp - lastSuccess < 0.75) {
            return YES;
        }
        return NO;
}

#pragma mark -
#pragma mark UIResponder

- (void)touchesEnded:(NSSet *)touches withEvent:(UIEvent *)event {

        // Don't count events that happen too soon after the last one
        if ([self tooSoon:event]) {
            return;
        }

        BOOL success = NO; // Assume the user is wrong!

        // Find out what Simon said
        Instruction *simonSaid = [self currentInstruction];

        if (simonSaid.type == InstructionTypeTap && touches.count == 1) {
            // If only 1 touch, the UIEvent must be a tap

            UITouch *touch = [touches anyObject];
            if (simonSaid.modifier == touch.tapCount) {
```

LISTING 18.5 Continued

```
            success = YES;
        }
    }

    if (success) {
        lastSuccess = event.timestamp; // Store the timestamp of this event
        self.view.backgroundColor = [UIColor greenColor];
        [self nextInstruction]; // Simon speaks again
    } else {
        self.view.backgroundColor = [UIColor redColor];
    }
}

#pragma mark -

/*
// The designated initializer. Override to perform setup that is required before
the view is loaded.
- (id)initWithNibName:(NSString *)nibNameOrNil bundle:(NSBundle *)nibBundleOrNil
{
    if (self = [super initWithNibName:nibNameOrNil bundle:nibBundleOrNil]) {
        // Custom initialization
    }
    return self;
}
*/

/*
// Implement loadView to create a view hierarchy programmatically, without using
a nib.
- (void)loadView {
}
*/

// Implement viewDidLoad to do additional setup after loading the view,
typically from a nib.
- (void)viewDidLoad {

    lastSuccess = 0;
    currentInstructionCounter = 0;
    instructions = [self randomizeInstructions: 100];
    [self nextInstruction];

    [super viewDidLoad];
}

/*
// Override to allow orientations other than the default portrait orientation.
-
(BOOL)shouldAutorotateToInterfaceOrientation:(UIInterfaceOrientation)interfaceOr
ientation {
    // Return YES for supported orientations
    return (interfaceOrientation == UIInterfaceOrientationPortrait);
}
*/
```

LISTING 18.5   Continued

```
- (void)didReceiveMemoryWarning {
      // Releases the view if it doesn't have a superview.
    [super didReceiveMemoryWarning];

      // Release any cached data, images, etc that aren't in use.
}

- (void)viewDidUnload {
      // Release any retained subviews of the main view.
      // e.g. self.myOutlet = nil;
}


- (void)dealloc {
    [instructionLabel release];
    [instructions release];
    [super dealloc];
}

@end
```

You can see our version of Simon Says in Figure 18.3. With only taps implemented, it's not very fun to play yet, but all the groundwork has been completed, and the additional gestures can now be easily added.

FIGURE 18.3
A monotonous version of Simon Says in action.

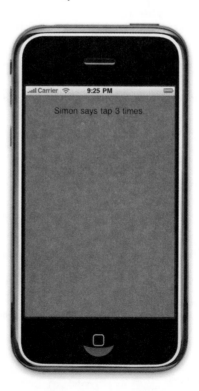

Detecting Swipes

We have one gesture, the tap, out of the way, and we have the plumbing for our basic Simon Says game. Now let's make the game a little more interesting by adding swipes for between one and four fingers.

Update the Game

The Instruction class can almost accommodate the addition of swipes unchanged. We do need to add handling of the swipe to the description method. Update the description method of the Instruction.m file as follows:

```
-(NSString *)description {

    NSString *description = nil;
    switch(type) {
        case InstructionTypeTap:
            description =
                [NSString stringWithFormat:@"Simon says tap %i times.", modifier];
            break;
        case InstructionTypeSwipe:
            if (modifier == 1) {
                description =
                    [NSString stringWithFormat:@"Simon says swipe with 1 finger."];
            } else {
                description =
                    [NSString stringWithFormat:@"Simon says swipe with %i fingers.",
                     modifier];
            }
            break;
    }
    return description;
}
```

The only other change we need to make to the game mechanics is to add the four swipe instructions to our initial unrandomized NSArray of instructions and increase the size of the random number by four. Modify the randomizeInstructions:howMany method in the SimonSaysViewController.m file as follows:

```
-(NSMutableArray *)randomizeInstructions:(int)howMany {

    // Create an array of each instruction Simon knows
    NSArray *initialInstructions = [[NSArray alloc]initWithObjects:
    [[Instruction alloc]initWithType:InstructionTypeTap modifier:2],
    [[Instruction alloc]initWithType:InstructionTypeTap modifier:3],
    [[Instruction alloc]initWithType:InstructionTypeTap modifier:4],
    [[Instruction alloc]initWithType:InstructionTypeTap modifier:5],
    [[Instruction alloc]initWithType:InstructionTypeSwipe modifier:1],
    [[Instruction alloc]initWithType:InstructionTypeSwipe modifier:2],
```

```
    [[Instruction alloc]initWithType:InstructionTypeSwipe modifier:3],
    [[Instruction alloc]initWithType:InstructionTypeSwipe modifier:4],
    nil];

    instructions = [[NSMutableArray alloc]initWithCapacity:howMany];

    for (int i=0;i < howMany; i++) {
        // Add a random instruction
        [instructions addObject:
            [initialInstructions objectAtIndex: (arc4random() % 8)]];
    }
    return instructions;
}
```

Identify Swipes

Unlike the tap gesture, which really only required one UIResponder method, the
swipe gesture is more involved and lasts longer. A swipe starts with a
touchesBegan:touches:withEvent when the finger or fingers first touch the screen.
Your responder will then see a series of touchesMoved:touches:withEvent calls as
users drag their finger or fingers across the screen. And finally, when any finger lifts
off the screen, there will be a touchesEnded:touches:withEvent.

Often it will be important to involve each of these UIResponder methods in your
handling of the swipe event. You may need to note the beginning location or view
of the swipe. You may have to calculate how far, how fast, or how straight the swipe
progresses as the fingers move, and then you might need to look at where the swipe
ended.

Things are just a bit simpler for our Simon Says game. We can ignore the
touchesBegan:touches:withEvent and pick up the swipe already in progress by
overriding the touchesMoved:touches:withEvent method. Like with the tap gesture, we should check that we aren't swiping too soon after the last successful gesture, and then we can just compare the finger count (number of UITouch instances)
to the requested count in Simon's instruction; if there is a match, we record the fact
that we saw a good swipe in progress in the controller's goodSwipe property. We
don't need to do anything else to confirm the nature of the swipe because we don't
care how far, fast, or straight the swipe was.

Update the SimonSaysController.h header file to include the goodSwipe property, as
shown in Listing 18.6.

LISTING 18.6

```
#import <UIKit/UIKit.h>
#import "Instruction.h"

@interface SimonSaysViewController : UIViewController {

    IBOutlet UILabel *instructionLabel;

    NSMutableArray *instructions;
    NSUInteger currentInstructionCounter;
    NSTimeInterval lastSuccess;
    BOOL goodSwipe;
}

@property (nonatomic, retain) UILabel *instructionLabel;
@property (nonatomic, retain) NSMutableArray *instructions;
@property (nonatomic, assign) BOOL goodSwipe;

- (NSMutableArray *)randomizeInstructions:(int)howMany;
- (Instruction *)currentInstruction;
- (void)nextInstruction;
- (BOOL)tooSoon:(UIEvent *)event;

@end
```

Update the SimonSaysController.m file to synthesize the property, as follows:

```
@synthesize goodSwipe;
```

Add the new touchesMoved:touches:withEvent method to the SimonSaysController.m file:

```
- (void)touchesMoved:(NSSet *)touches withEvent:(UIEvent *)event {

    // Don't count events that happen too soon after the last one
    if ([self tooSoon:event]) {
        return;
    }

    // Find out what Simon said
    Instruction *simonSaid = [self currentInstruction];

    if (touches.count == simonSaid.modifier) {
        goodSwipe = true;
    }
}
```

All we've done so far is noted that we did indeed witness a swipe with the right number of fingers while it was in progress, but we haven't marked Simon's instruction as completed until the touchesEnded:touches:withEvent. Here we can check if Simon's current instruction is for a swipe, and if it is, we can ignore handling taps, because they won't satisfy Simon anyway. Assuming Simon is asking for a swipe, then at this point we've already recorded if we've seen a swipe with the correct number of fingers, and so we can check the goodSwipe property. Be sure to reset the goodSwipe property after we give players credit for their swipe. Update the touchesEnded:touches:withEvent method of the SimonSaysViewController.m file as follows:

```
- (void)touchesEnded:(NSSet *)touches withEvent:(UIEvent *)event {

    // Don't count events that happen too soon after the last one
    if ([self tooSoon:event]) {
        return;
    }

    BOOL success = NO; // Assume the user is wrong!

    // Find out what Simon said
    Instruction *simonSaid = [self currentInstruction];
    if (simonSaid.type == InstructionTypeSwipe && goodSwipe == YES) {
        goodSwipe = NO;
        success = YES;
    } else if (simonSaid.type == InstructionTypeTap && touches.count == 1) {
        // If only 1 touch, the UIEvent must be a tap

        UITouch *touch = [touches anyObject];
        if (simonSaid.modifier == touch.tapCount) {
            success = YES;
        }
    }

    if (success) {
        lastSuccess = event.timestamp; // Store the timestamp of this event
        self.view.backgroundColor = [UIColor greenColor];
        [self nextInstruction]; // Simon speaks again
    } else {
        self.view.backgroundColor = [UIColor redColor];
    }
}
```

Adding swipes wasn't too hard, and already our little game is much more enjoyable. Give it a try yourself, and when you come back we'll add pinches.

Detecting Pinches

Our Simon Says game can now detect taps and swipes. There is just one more multi-touch gesture we need to account for, the two-finger pinch. A pinch comes in two varieties; the normal pinch starts with 2 fingers wider apart and ends with them closer to each other. There is also the opposite motion, which starts with the fingers together and spreads them apart. We'll call this second gesture "pinch apart." You are probably most familiar with these two gestures as zoom out and zoom in respectively, since that is the predominant use of these gestures in both Apple and third-party iPhone applications. Apple has used the pinch and pinch apart to zoom Web pages in Mobile Safari, maps in Maps, and images in the various Apple applications.

Update the Game

We'll use the instruction's `modifier` property for Simon to distinguish between the pinch and the pinch apart. Let's add a constant and an enumerated type to the Instruction.h file:

```
#define PINCH_DISTANCE 75
typedef enum {
    Pinch = 0,
    PinchApart = 1
} PinchType;
```

The `Instruction` class just needs an extension to the `description` method to accommodate pinches. Update the method in the Instruction.m file:

```
-(NSString *)description {

    NSString *description = nil;
    switch(type) {
        case InstructionTypeTap:
            description =
                [NSString stringWithFormat:@"Simon says tap %i times.",
➥modifier];
            break;
        case InstructionTypeSwipe:
            if (modifier == 1) {
                description =
                [NSString stringWithFormat:@"Simon says swipe with 1 finger."];
            } else {
                description =
                [NSString stringWithFormat:@"Simon says swipe with %i fingers.",
                 modifier];
            }
            break;
        case InstructionTypePinch:
            if (modifier == Pinch) {
                description = @"Simon says pinch.";
            } else {
                description = @"Simon says pinch apart.";
            }
            break;
    }
    return description;
}
```

Now we can add the pinch instructions to our initial unrandomized `NSArray` of instructions, and increase the size of the random number by two. Modify the randomizeInstructions:howMany method in the SimonSaysViewController.m file as follows:

```
-(NSMutableArray *)randomizeInstructions:(int)howMany {

    // Create an array of each instruction Simon knows
    NSArray *initialInstructions = [[NSArray alloc]initWithObjects:
    [[Instruction alloc]initWithType:InstructionTypeTap modifier:2],
    [[Instruction alloc]initWithType:InstructionTypeTap modifier:3],
    [[Instruction alloc]initWithType:InstructionTypeTap modifier:4],
    [[Instruction alloc]initWithType:InstructionTypeTap modifier:5],
    [[Instruction alloc]initWithType:InstructionTypeSwipe modifier:1],
    [[Instruction alloc]initWithType:InstructionTypeSwipe modifier:2],
    [[Instruction alloc]initWithType:InstructionTypeSwipe modifier:3],
    [[Instruction alloc]initWithType:InstructionTypeSwipe modifier:4],
    [[Instruction alloc]initWithType:InstructionTypePinch modifier:Pinch],
    [[Instruction alloc]initWithType:InstructionTypePinch modifier:PinchApart],
    nil];

    instructions = [[NSMutableArray alloc]initWithCapacity:howMany];

    for (int i=0;i < howMany; i++) {
        // Add a random instruction
        [instructions addObject:
            [initialInstructions objectAtIndex: (arc4random() % 10)]];
    }
    return instructions;
}
```

Identify Pinches

To detect a pinch, there are two main factors: We need to be sure there are only two fingers (two UITouch instances) involved in the gesture, and we need to be sure that the distance between the two fingers narrows or widens. The change in distance between the fingers is important: so we can determine whether the gesture is a pinch or a pinch apart, and so we can distinguish between a pinch and a two-finger swipe. The distance between the two fingers in a two-finger swipe will stay fairly constant, whereas there will be a significant change in the distance for a pinch gesture.

We need to keep track of the initial distance between the two fingers and the new distance, so we'll do that with two properties of type CGFloat. It will also be handy to have a reusable method to calculate the distance between two fingers. We can define the two properties and the method in the SimonSaysViewController.h file, as shown in Listing 18.7.

LISTING 18.7

```
#import <UIKit/UIKit.h>
#import "Instruction.h"

@interface SimonSaysViewController : UIViewController {

    IBOutlet UILabel *instructionLabel;

    NSMutableArray *instructions;
    NSUInteger currentInstructionCounter;
    NSTimeInterval lastSuccess;
    BOOL goodSwipe;
    CGFloat initialFingerDistance;
    CGFloat currentFingerDistance;
}

@property (nonatomic, retain) UILabel *instructionLabel;
@property (nonatomic, retain) NSMutableArray *instructions;
@property (nonatomic, assign) BOOL goodSwipe;
@property (nonatomic, assign) CGFloat initialFingerDistance;
@property (nonatomic, assign) CGFloat currentFingerDistance;

- (NSMutableArray *)randomizeInstructions:(int)howMany;
- (Instruction *)currentInstruction;
- (void)nextInstruction;
- (BOOL)tooSoon:(UIEvent *)event;
- (CGFloat)fingerDistance:(NSSet *)touches;

@end
```

To properly identify the pinch gesture, we need to store the initial distance between the two fingers so that we can check how the distance has changed at the end of the gesture. Let's synthesize the properties in the SimonSaysController.m file:

```
@synthesize initialFingerDistance;
@synthesize currentFingerDistance;
```

We calculate the distance between the fingers in SimonSaysViewController.m by using the two CGPoint instances we get by calling the locationInView method of the UITouch for each touch. With a bit of basic geometry, we can figure out how far apart the fingers are:

```
- (CGFloat)fingerDistance:(NSSet *)touches {

    CGFloat distance = 0.0;

    if (touches.count == 2) {

        NSArray *fingerTouches = [touches allObjects];

        UITouch *finger1 = [fingerTouches objectAtIndex:0];
        UITouch *finger2 = [fingerTouches objectAtIndex:1];
```

```
        CGPoint finger1Point = [finger1 locationInView:self.view];
        CGPoint finger2Point = [finger2 locationInView:self.view];

        // Use the distance formula: http://en.wikipedia.org/wiki/Distance
        CGFloat x = finger1Point.x - finger2Point.x;
        CGFloat y = finger1Point.y - finger2Point.y;
        distance = sqrt((x*x) + (y*y));
    }
    return distance;
}
```

We need to store the current distance in the `currentFingerDistance` property, and if we haven't already stored a value for the `initialFingerDistance` property, we store the distance there, too. Update the `touchesMoved:touches:withEvent` method of the SimonSaysViewController.m file:

```
- (void)touchesMoved:(NSSet *)touches withEvent:(UIEvent *)event {

    // Don't count events that happen too soon after the last one
    if ([self tooSoon:event]) {
        return;
    }

    // Find out what Simon said
    Instruction *simonSaid = [self currentInstruction];

    if (simonSaid.type == InstructionTypeSwipe &&
        touches.count == simonSaid.modifier) {
        goodSwipe = true;
    } else if (simonSaid.type == InstructionTypePinch &&
               touches.count == 2) {
        currentFingerDistance = [self fingerDistance:touches];
        if (initialFingerDistance == 0.0) {
            initialFingerDistance = currentFingerDistance;
        }
    }
}
```

Now, the two important pieces of information for determining a pinch, the starting distance of the fingers and the current distance of the fingers, are available to our controller, so all that remains to do when the gesture completes is to determine whether players pinched how Simon told them to pinch. A pinch apart widens the distance between the fingers, and a regular pinch lessens the distance. The `modifier` property of the current `Instruction` from Simon lets us know which it should be. Update the `touchesEnded:touches:withEvent` method of the SimonSaysViewController.m file as follows:

```
- (void)touchesEnded:(NSSet *)touches withEvent:(UIEvent *)event {

    // Don't count events that happen too soon after the last one
    if ([self tooSoon:event]) {
```

```
        return;
    }

    BOOL success = NO; // Assume the user is wrong!

    // Find out what Simon said
    Instruction *simonSaid = [self currentInstruction];
    if (simonSaid.type == InstructionTypeSwipe && goodSwipe == YES) {

        goodSwipe = NO;
        success = YES;

    } else if (simonSaid.type == InstructionTypePinch &&
               initialFingerDistance != 0.0 && currentFingerDistance != 0.0) {

        CGFloat distance = 0.0;
        // Reverse the calculation when looking for a pinch or pinch apart
        if(simonSaid.modifier == Pinch) {
            // A pinch makes the distance smaller
            distance = initialFingerDistance - currentFingerDistance;
        }
        else { // Pinch Apart
            // A pinch makes the distance greater
            distance = currentFingerDistance - initialFingerDistance;
        }
        if (distance > PINCH_DISTANCE) {
            initialFingerDistance = 0.0;
            currentFingerDistance = 0.0;
            success = YES;
        }
    } else if (simonSaid.type == InstructionTypeTap && touches.count == 1) {
        // If only 1 touch, the UIEvent must be a tap

        UITouch *touch = [touches anyObject];
        if (simonSaid.modifier == touch.tapCount) {
            success = YES;
        }
    }

    if (success) {
        lastSuccess = event.timestamp; // Store the timestamp of this event
        self.view.backgroundColor = [UIColor greenColor];
        [self nextInstruction]; // Simon speaks
    } else {
        self.view.backgroundColor = [UIColor redColor];
    }
}
```

Our Simon Says game can now detect all three common types of multitouch gestures: the tap, swipe, and pinch. Next we'll add a new type of gesture introduced in iPhone OS 3.0, the shake.

Using the Shake Gesture

We have saved the easiest gesture for last. The shake gesture is currently the only type of motion event, and motion events are simpler to deal with than touch events. You participate in the response chain for motion events in the same way, by overriding methods of UIResponder in your view or view controller. But whereas touch events come with a NSSet of UITouch objects that must be interpreted to determine what gesture is happening, a motion event provides a subtype that tells you exactly the gesture that is being performed. Let's add the only motion event, the shake, to our Simon Says game.

Update the Game

This is now routine: Add a description for the new shake gesture, add the new Instruction for the shake gesture to the unrandomized array, and increment the random number request by one. Update the description method of the Instruction.m file to have a description for the shake gesture:

```
-(NSString *)description {

    NSString *description = nil;
    switch(type) {
        case InstructionTypeTap:
            description =
                [NSString stringWithFormat:@"Simon says tap %i times.",
➥modifier];
            break;
        case InstructionTypeSwipe:
            if (modifier == 1) {
                description =
                [NSString stringWithFormat:@"Simon says swipe with 1 finger."];
            } else {
                description =
                [NSString stringWithFormat:@"Simon says swipe with %i fingers.",
                 modifier];
            }
            break;
        case InstructionTypePinch:
            if (modifier == Pinch) {
                description = @"Simon says pinch.";
            } else {
                description = @"Simon says pinch apart.";
            }
            break;
        case InstructionTypeShake:
            description = @"Simon says shake, shake shake.";
            break;
    }
    return description;
}
```

Update the `randomizeInstructions:howMany` method of the
SimonSaysViewController.m file to include the new gesture:

```
-(NSMutableArray *)randomizeInstructions:(int)howMany {

    // Create an array of each instruction Simon knows
    NSArray *initialInstructions = [[NSArray alloc]initWithObjects:
     /*[[Instruction alloc]initWithType:InstructionTypeTap modifier:2],
     [[Instruction alloc]initWithType:InstructionTypeTap modifier:3],
     [[Instruction alloc]initWithType:InstructionTypeTap modifier:4],
     [[Instruction alloc]initWithType:InstructionTypeTap modifier:5],
     [[Instruction alloc]initWithType:InstructionTypeSwipe modifier:1],
     [[Instruction alloc]initWithType:InstructionTypeSwipe modifier:2],
     [[Instruction alloc]initWithType:InstructionTypeSwipe modifier:3],
     [[Instruction alloc]initWithType:InstructionTypeSwipe modifier:4],*/
     [[Instruction alloc]initWithType:InstructionTypePinch modifier:Pinch],
     [[Instruction alloc]initWithType:InstructionTypePinch modifier:PinchApart],
     [[Instruction alloc]initWithType:InstructionTypeShake modifier:-1],
     nil];

    instructions = [[NSMutableArray alloc]initWithCapacity:howMany];

    for (int i=0;i < howMany; i++) {
        // Add a random instruction
        [instructions addObject:
            [initialInstructions objectAtIndex: (arc4random() % 11)]];
    }
    return instructions;
}
```

Detecting Shakes

We have only used the `timestamp` property of the `UIEvent` instance we are passed
in the `UIResponder`, but the `UIEvent` also has type and subtype properties.
Currently in the SDK, there are only two types and one subtype defined. Up to this
point, all the events we have been responding to have been of type
`UIEventTypeTouches` and subtype `UIEventSubtypeNone`. There is an additional
type called `UIEventTypeMotion`, and it has the possible subtype of
`UIEventSubtypeMotionShake`.

> By extending `UIEvent` to include shake gestures, Apple has removed the burden
> of each developer having to write his or her own shake detection using the
> accelerometer primitives. Send your thank you card to Cupertino. You can imagine
> Apple continuing to extend `UIEvent` in future iPhone OS SDK releases to include
> subtypes for touch gestures, such as vertical, horizontal, and diagonal swipes, and
> possibly more complex gestures such as a Z or a figure 8. By including predefined
> gestures in the SDK, Apple removes some tedious coding, which is good for devel-
> opers, and at the same time standardizes the gesture across different applica-
> tions, which is a win for users.

By the Way

If we want to receive events of the UIEventTypeMotion type, our view or view controller must be the first responder in the responder chain and must override one or more of the three UIResponder motion event methods:

- (void)motionBegan:(UIEventSubtype)*motion* withEvent:(UIEvent *)*event*
- (void)motionEnded:(UIEventSubtype)*motion* withEvent:(UIEvent *)*event*
- (void)motionCancelled:(UIEventSubtype)*motion* withEvent:(UIEvent *)*event*

For the purposes of the Simon Says game, it's enough to override just the motionEnded:motion:withEvent, and as long as Simon was looking for a shake, then our response is to credit the player with the gesture. In our game, there is no way the player can get the shake wrong.

For our view controller to be a first responder, we have to allow it and then ask for it. Add the following to the SimonSaysViewController.m file:

```
- (BOOL)canBecomeFirstResponder {
    return YES; // For the shake event
}

- (void)viewDidAppear:(BOOL)animated {
    [self becomeFirstResponder];  // For the shake event
    [super viewDidAppear: animated];
}
```

Because there are now two spots in our code where a gesture can succeed or fail, in touchesEnded:touches:withEvent:event and in motionEnded:motion:withEvent:event, let's refactor the succeed/fail code into its own method called handleSuccess:success:withEvent. With that change and with the addition of the motion event handling, our final event handling code in the SimonSaysViewController.m file should read as follows:

```
-(void)handleSuccess:(BOOL)success withEvent:(UIEvent *)event {

    if (success) {
        lastSuccess = event.timestamp; // Store the timestamp of this event
        self.view.backgroundColor = [UIColor greenColor];
        [self nextInstruction]; // Simon speaks again
    } else {
        self.view.backgroundColor = [UIColor redColor];
    }
}


#pragma mark -
#pragma mark UIResponder

- (void)touchesMoved:(NSSet *)touches withEvent:(UIEvent *)event {

    // Don't count events that happen too soon after the last one
    if ([self tooSoon:event]) {
        return;
```

```
    }

    // Find out what Simon said
    Instruction *simonSaid = [self currentInstruction];

    if (simonSaid.type == InstructionTypeSwipe &&
        touches.count == simonSaid.modifier) {
        goodSwipe = true;
    } else if (simonSaid.type == InstructionTypePinch &&
                touches.count == 2) {
        currentFingerDistance = [self fingerDistance:touches];
        if (initialFingerDistance == 0.0) {
            initialFingerDistance = currentFingerDistance;
        }
    }
}

- (void)touchesEnded:(NSSet *)touches withEvent:(UIEvent *)event {

    // Don't count events that happen too soon after the last one
    if ([self tooSoon:event]) {
        return;
    }

    BOOL success = NO; // Assume the user is wrong!

    // Find out what Simon said
    Instruction *simonSaid = [self currentInstruction];

    if (simonSaid.type == InstructionTypeSwipe && goodSwipe == YES) {

        goodSwipe = NO;
        success = YES;

    } else if (simonSaid.type == InstructionTypePinch &&
                initialFingerDistance != 0.0 && currentFingerDistance != 0.0) {

        CGFloat distance = 0.0;
        // Reverse the calculation when looking for a pinch or pinch apart
        if(simonSaid.modifier == Pinch) {
            // A pinch makes the distance smaller
            distance = initialFingerDistance - currentFingerDistance;
        }
        else { // Pinch Apart
            // A pinch makes the distance greater
            distance = currentFingerDistance - initialFingerDistance;
        }
        if (distance > PINCH_DISTANCE) {
            initialFingerDistance = 0.0;
            currentFingerDistance = 0.0;
            success = YES;
        }

    } else if (simonSaid.type == InstructionTypeTap && touches.count == 1) {
        // If only 1 touch, the UIEvent must be a tap

        UITouch *touch = [touches anyObject];
        if (simonSaid.modifier == touch.tapCount) {
```

```
            success = YES;
        }

    }

    [self handleSuccess: success withEvent:event];

}

- (void)motionEnded:(UIEventSubtype)motion withEvent:(UIEvent *)event {

    BOOL success = NO; // Assume the user is wrong!

    // Find out what Simon said
    Instruction *simonSaid = [self currentInstruction];
    if (simonSaid.type == InstructionTypeShake &&
        motion == UIEventSubtypeMotionShake) {
        success = YES;
    }

    [self handleSuccess: success withEvent:event];

}
#pragma mark -
```

Now you can play the final version of Simon Says. When Simon asks you to perform the shake gesture, you can either shake your physical device or if you are using the iPhone Simulator, you can select the Hardware, Shake Gesture menu option. Now congratulate yourself for writing your first iPhone game!

Summary

In this hour, we've given the multitouch gesture architecture a good workout. We incorporated a responder object (our custom view's controller) into the responder chain, received touch events, and took the appropriate action based on the touch gesture being performed. Our Simon Says game can now detect all three common types of multitouch gestures: the tap, swipe, and pinch.

We also added a motion event to our game, the shake. There is much more to do before we have a complete children's game, but you can already play it for a couple of minutes without getting bored. That's not bad for just one hour of work.

Q&A

Q. *Can I track how multiple fingers are moving across the screen?*

A. No, the best you can do is write intelligent code that takes an educated guess. The UIResponder touch events you can override pass the UITouch objects to your method as an unordered set. It's up to your code to determine which UITouch instance corresponds to the particular fingers you have seen in the past. Because of this, gestures that require precision should be limited to just one finger.

Workshop

Quiz

1. What is a first responder?

2. What is always the last responder object in an iPhone application's responder chain?

3. To participate in a responder chain, you implement methods from what class?

4. The UITouch event provides a type to indicate a finger touch or a motion touch. True or false.

Answers

1. The first responder is the first event handler in the responder chain of event handlers. It gets the first shot at responding to an event, and can pass the event up the chain if the event cannot be fully dealt with.

2. The last responder in an iPhone application responder chain is always the singleton instance of UIApplication.

3. Responder objects implement the methods of the UIResponder class.

4. False. There is a type property that indicates a touch or motion event, but that property is part of UIEvent, not UITouch. A motion event has no UITouch objects!

Activities

1. There is another type of user interaction that would make a fun addition to the game. The UIDevice class provides access to the proximity sensor. Simon can direct the player, "Simon says smoosh your face." Players would respond by pushing the phone up to their face. Unlike the events we used, the UIDevice is passive and is not going to dispatch an event to the responder chain when the state of the proximity sensor changes. Think through how you will decide when to check the sensor. How will your code be active to check it, since normally your code is only responding to system events?

2. There are some significant limitations to the game as is. Choose some of them and make improvements. Here are some ideas:

   ▶ Simon always says, "Simon says," whereas in a normal version of the game sometimes the "Simon says" part is left off and the user is not supposed to do the requested gesture.

   ▶ Users are given an infinite amount of time to respond, which means they can be very careful in deciding to do the gesture or not. For the user to ever be tricked into doing what Simon didn't say, there should be a time limit on performing the gesture.

   ▶ There is no end to the game, and no score is kept. Keep track of how many gestures users get right and limit the number of times they can be wrong before the game ends.

   ▶ If Simon asks for a five-tap gesture, then a one-, two-, three-, and four-tap gesture are received as misses to Simon's request before the five-tap gesture is received. This doesn't affect this version of the game, but how would you fix this in a better version?

3. In addition to the basic swipe with different finger counts, a one-finger swipe in different shapes can be added to the game. This is only limited by the time you want to put into it and your imagination. Add one or two custom gestures such as, "Simon says draw a Z" and "Simon says draw an X." How will you deal with shapes that don't involve lifting and resetting the finger, such as the Z, and shapes that involve two separate swipes, such as the X?

Further Exploration

The predominant ground left to explore is the custom touch gesture. Beyond the tap, swipe, and pinch lay an infinite variety of other finger motions that could make sense for your application. In deciding whether a custom gesture is right for your application, focus on the gesture being a natural analog to something the user would do in the physical world.

We humans do a lot with our fingers, such as draw, write, play music, and more. Each of these possible gestures has been exploited to great effect in third-party applications. Explore the App Store to get a sense for what's been done with the multi-touch screen.

Apple has put together a good guide to event handling and implementing gestures. See the "Event Handling" section of the *iPhone Application Programming Guide* for more information.

HOUR 19

Sensing Movement with Accelerometer Input

What You'll Learn in This Hour

▶ How to determine the device's orientation

▶ How to measure tilt

▶ How to measure movement

The Nintendo Wii introduced motion sensing as an effective input technique for mainstream consumer electronics. Apple applied this technology to great success with the iPhone and iPod Touch. Apple's devices are equipped with an accelerometer that can be used to determine the orientation, movement, and tilt of the device. With the iPhone's accelerometer, a user can control applications by simply adjusting the physical orientation of the device and moving it in space.

This innovative and natural input mechanism is exposed to third-party applications in the iPhone OS SDK. In Hour 18, "Extending the Touch Interface," you've already seen how the accelerometer provides the shake gesture. Now you will learn how to take direct readings from the accelerometer. For all the magic an accelerometer-aware application appears to exhibit, you will see that using the accelerometer is surprisingly simple.

An accelerometer measures acceleration relative to a free fall. Meaning that if you dropped your phone into a sustained free fall, say off the Empire State Building, its accelerometer would measure 0g on the way down. (Just trust us, don't try this out.) The accelerometer of an iPhone sitting on a desk, on the other hand, measures 1g along the axis it is resting on.

Watch
Out!

For most applications in this book, using the iPhone Simulator is perfectly acceptable, but the simulator does not simulate the accelerometer hardware. So for this
chapter, you'll want to be sure to have a physical device provisioned for development. To run this hour's applications on your device, follow the steps in Hour 2,
"Introduction to Xcode and the iPhone Simulator."

Accelerometer Background

An accelerometer uses a unit of measure called a g, which is short for gravity. 1g is
the force pulling down on something resting at sea level on Earth (9.8
meters/second^2). You don't normally notice the feeling of 1g (that is until you trip
and fall, and then 1g hurts pretty bad). You are familiar with g-forces higher and
lower than 1g if you've ever ridden on a roller coaster. The pull that pins you to
your seat at the bottom of the roller coaster loop is a g-force greater than 1, and the
feeling of floating up out of your seat at the top of a coaster loop is negative g-force
at work.

The measurement of the 1g pull of Earth's gravity on the device while it's at rest is
how the iPhone's accelerometer can be used to measure the orientation of the
phone. The accelerometer provides a measurement along three axes, called x, y, and
z (see Figure 19.1).

FIGURE 19.1
The three meas-
urable axes.

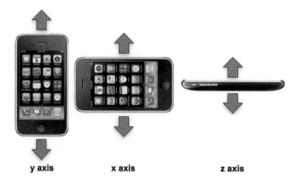

y axis   x axis   z axis

Depending on how your phone is resting, the 1g of gravity will be pulling differently
on the three possible axes. If your device is standing straight up on one of its edges
or is flat on its back or on its screen, the entire 1g will be measured on one axis.
If the device is tilted at an angle, the 1g will be spread across multiple axes (see
Figure 19.2).

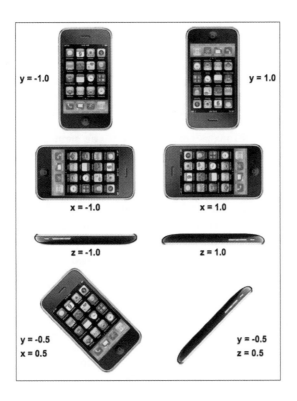

FIGURE 19.2
The 1g of force on an iPhone at rest.

Accelerometer API

You work with the accelerometer through the UIAccelerometer singleton. The UIAccelerometer defines a protocol, the UIAccelerometerDelegateProtocol, which you implement to receive measurements from the accelerometer. Your delegate receives updates as frequently as you request to receive them (up to the limit of 100 updates per second).

You need to decide how often your application can benefit from receiving accelerometer updates. You should decide this by experimenting with different update values until you come up with an optimal frequency. Receiving more updates than your application can benefit from can have some negative consequences. Your application will use more system resources processing all the unneeded accelerometer updates, which might negatively impact the performance of the other parts of your application and can certainly affect the battery life of the device. Because you'll probably want fairly frequent updates so that your application responds smoothly, you should take some time to optimize the performance of your UIAccelerometer delegate's code and to make sure it does not allocate and free a lot of memory.

Setting up your application to use the accelerometer is a simple three-step process of retrieving the singleton, registering your delegate, and requesting updates at a specific interval:

```
UIAccelerometer *accelerometer = [UIAccelerometer sharedAccelerometer];
accelerometer.delegate = self;
accelerometer.updateInterval = 0.1; // 10 times per second
```

The UIAccelerometerDelegateProtocol has just one method, accelerometer:didAccelerate. accelerometer:didAccelerate provides the UIAccelerometer singleton and a UIAcceleration object as arguments. The UIAcceleration object has properties for the current reading on each of the three axes and provides a timestamp with the time the reading was taken. This interface to the accelerometer readings is very simple, so the only tricky part in implementing this delegate is making your application respond appropriately to the accelerometer readings. This often involves aggregating numerous separate readings into a single application response. For getting your application to respond naturally, there is no substitute for extensive experimentation.

By the Way

In Hour 13, "Using Tab Bars to Manage Multiview Interfaces," we explained what a singleton is and we said that when services of the device's hardware are provided to your application, they are often provided as singletons. Because there is only one accelerometer in the device, it makes sense that it is accessed as a singleton. Multiple instances of accelerometer objects existing in your application wouldn't add any extra value and would have the added complexity of managing their memory and lifetime, both of which are avoided with a singleton.

Watch Out!

You may have wondered why a timestamp is included in the UIAcceleration object. The answer is that accelerometer readings aren't timed precisely. The frequency interval is a maximum frequency. Your delegate won't get called more often than the interval that you request, but it's not the case that it will be called exactly as many times as you request, or that each call will be equally spaced out in time. Depending on what you are trying to accomplish with reading the accelerometer, the timestamp may come in very handy because you may need to determine how long it's been since you received the prior reading.

Sensing Orientation

As our first introduction to using the accelerometer, we'll create the Orientation application. Orientation won't be wowing users, it's simply going to say which of six possible orientations the iPhone is currently in. The Orientation application will detect standing-up, upside-down, left-side, right-side, face-down, and face-up orientations.

Add the Outlet

Create a new View-Based Application in Xcode and call it **Orientation**. Click the OrientationViewController.h file in the Classes group and add an outlet property for an orientation label. Also indicate that this controller will be implementing the `UIAccelerometerDelegate` protocol. The OrientationViewController.h file should read as shown in Listing 19.1.

LISTING 19.1

```
#import <UIKit/UIKit.h>

@interface OrientationViewController : UIViewController
    <UIAccelerometerDelegate> {

    IBOutlet UILabel *orientation;

}

@property (nonatomic, retain) UILabel *orientation;

@end
```

Lay Out the UI and Connect the Outlet

Orientation's UI is simple (and very stylish), just a yellow text label in a field of black, which we construct as follows:

1. Open Interface Builder by double-clicking the OrientationViewController.xib file in the Resources group.

2. Click the empty view and open the Attributes Inspector (Command+1).

3. Click the Background attribute and change the view's background to black using the color picker.

4. Open the Library (Shift+Command+L) and search for "label."

5. Drag a label to the center of the view; expand the size the label to the edge sizing guidelines on each side of the view.

6. Click the label and open the Attributes Inspector (Command+1).

7. Click the Color attribute and change the label's text color to yellow.

8. Click the center button of the Layout Alignment attribute to center the label's text.

9. Click the Font attribute and change the font size to 36 points.

10. Click the Text attribute and change the label's text to **Face Up**.

Our UIAccelerometer delegate will need to be able to change the text of the label when the accelerometer indicates that the orientation of the device has changed. Connect the outlet we created earlier to the label. Right-click the File's Owner icon in the NIB and connect the orientation outlet to the label by click-dragging from the circle next to the outlet to the label. The view should look like Figure 19.3. Save the XIB file and return to Xcode.

FIGURE 19.3
The Orientation application's UI in Interface Builder.

Implement the UIAccelerometerDelegate

When our custom view is shown, we need to register our view controller as a UIAccelerometerDelegate. For this application, we don't need very many updates per second from the accelerometer. Two updates a second is frequent enough. We can set up the delegate and the interval in our controller's viewDidLoad method.

The only other thing needed to finish the Orientation application is to implement accelerometer:didAccelerate, which is the only method needed to fulfill the controller's responsibility as a UIAccelerometerDelegate. We use the x, y, and z properties of the UIAcceleration object to determine which axis has the most gravity pulling on it. Because we are trying to measure the device's orientation at rest, we can keep our delegate implementation simple by interpreting any reading of greater than 0.5 or less than –0.5 as meaning that axis has the most gravity. We can ignore the fact that if the phone were moving fast, more than one axis could have a high reading. Modify the OrientationViewController.m file in the Classes group to read as shown in Listing 19.2 and run the application (see Figure 19.4).

LISTING 19.2

```
#import "OrientationViewController.h"

@implementation OrientationViewController

@synthesize orientation;

#pragma mark -
#pragma mark UIAccelerometerDelegate

- (void)accelerometer:(UIAccelerometer *)accelerometer
        didAccelerate:(UIAcceleration *)acceleration {

    if (acceleration.x > 0.5) {
        orientation.text = @"Right Side";
    } else if (acceleration.x < -0.5) {
        orientation.text = @"Left Side";
    } else if (acceleration.y > 0.5) {
        orientation.text = @"Upside Down";
    } else if (acceleration.y < -0.5) {
        orientation.text = @"Standing Up";
    } else if (acceleration.z > 0.5) {
        orientation.text = @"Face Down";
    } else if (acceleration.z < -0.5) {
        orientation.text = @"Face Up";
    }

}

#pragma mark -

/*
// The designated initializer. Override to perform setup that is required before
the view is loaded.
- (id)initWithNibName:(NSString *)nibNameOrNil bundle:(NSBundle *)nibBundleOrNil
{
    if (self = [super initWithNibName:nibNameOrNil bundle:nibBundleOrNil]) {
        // Custom initialization
    }
    return self;
```

LISTING 19.2   Continued

```
}
*/

/*
// Implement loadView to create a view hierarchy programmatically, without using
a nib.
- (void)loadView {
}
*/

// Implement viewDidLoad to do additional setup after loading the view,
typically from a nib.
- (void)viewDidLoad {

    UIAccelerometer *accelerometer = [UIAccelerometer sharedAccelerometer];
    accelerometer.delegate = self;
    accelerometer.updateInterval = 0.5; // twice per second
    [super viewDidLoad];
}

/*
// Override to allow orientations other than the default portrait orientation.
- (BOOL)shouldAutorotateToInterfaceOrientation:(UIInterfaceOrientation)interface
Orientation {
    // Return YES for supported orientations
    return (interfaceOrientation == UIInterfaceOrientationPortrait);
}
*/

- (void)didReceiveMemoryWarning {
    // Releases the view if it doesn't have a superview.
    [super didReceiveMemoryWarning];

    // Release any cached data, images, etc that aren't in use.
}

- (void)viewDidUnload {
    // Release any retained subviews of the main view.
    // e.g. self.myOutlet = nil;
}


- (void)dealloc {
    [orientation release];
    [super dealloc];
}

@end
```

FIGURE 19.4
Orientation in action.

Detecting Tilt

In the Orientation application, we ignored the precise values coming from the accelerometer and instead just looked for the axis getting the dominant amount of gravity to make an all-or-nothing orientation decision. The gradations between these orientations, such as the device being somewhere between its left side and straight up and down, are often interesting to an application.

Imagine you are going to create a car racing game where the device acts as the steering wheel when tilted left and right and the gas and brake pedals when tilted forward and back. It is very helpful to know how far the player has turned the wheel and how hard the user is pushing the pedals to know how to make the game respond.

In this next example application, ColorTilt, we take a solid color and make it progressively more transparent as the user tilts the device left or right. It's not as exciting as a car racing game, but it is something we can accomplish in an hour, and everything learned here will apply when you get down to writing that next great iPhone application.

Add the Outlet

Create a new View-Based Application in Xcode and call it **ColorTilt**. Click the ColorViewController.h file in the Classes group and add an outlet property for the view; call it **colorView**. Indicate that this controller will be implementing the UIAccelerometerDelegate protocol. The ColorViewController.h file should read as shown in Listing 19.3.

LISTING 19.3

```
#import <UIKit/UIKit.h>

@interface ColorTiltViewController : UIViewController
    <UIAccelerometerDelegate> {
    IBOutlet UIView *colorView;
    }

@property (nonatomic, retain) UIView *colorView;

@end
```

Lay Out the UI and Connect the Outlet

Now we'll lay out the UI and connect the outlet for the ColorTilt application, as follows:

1. Open Interface Builder by double-clicking the ColorTiltViewController.xib file in the Resources group.

2. Click the empty view and open the Attributes Inspector (Command+1).

3. Click the Background attribute and change the view's background to green using the color picker.

4. Right-click the File's Owner icon and click-drag the circle to the right of the colorView IBOutlet to the view, as shown in Figure 19.5.

5. Save the XIB file and return to Xcode.

FIGURE 19.5
Connecting the colorView IBOutlet.

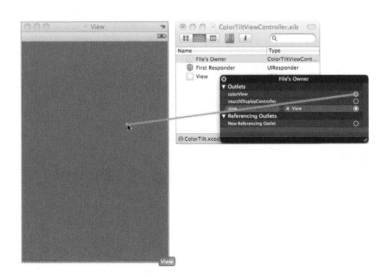

Implement the UIAccelerometerDelegate

Reading the exact tilt of the device results in an even simpler
UIAccelerometerDelegate than for the Orientation example because in this case
we are only going to pay attention to the x-axis. The closer the x-axis is to being on
edge (a reading of 1.0 or –1.0), the more solid (1.0 alpha) we'll make the color. The
closer the x-axis reading is to 0, the more transparent (0.0 alpha) the color.

We can use the accelerometer value directly as the alpha with just two bits of data
cleansing. We check to make sure a bump or jerk on the device hasn't resulted in an
x-axis reading greater than 1.0, and we use the C function fabs() to get the
absolute value of the reading, because for this example we don't care whether the
device is tilting left edge or right.

Set up the UIAccelerometerDelegate in the same manner as before, but this time
ask for an accelerometer reading 10 times a second. Modify the
ColorTiltViewController.m file in the Classes group to read as shown in Listing 19.4.

LISTING 19.4

```
#import "ColorTiltViewController.h"

@implementation ColorTiltViewController

@synthesize colorView;

#pragma mark -
#pragma mark UIAccelerometerDelegate

- (void)accelerometer:(UIAccelerometer *)accelerometer
        didAccelerate:(UIAcceleration *)acceleration {

    UIAccelerationValue value = fabs(acceleration.x);
    if (value > 1.0) { value = 1.0;}
    colorView.alpha = value;

}
#pragma mark -

/*
// The designated initializer. Override to perform setup that is required before
the view is loaded.
- (id)initWithNibName:(NSString *)nibNameOrNil bundle:(NSBundle *)nibBundleOrNil
{
    if (self = [super initWithNibName:nibNameOrNil bundle:nibBundleOrNil]) {
        // Custom initialization
    }
    return self;
}
*/

/*
```

LISTING 19.4   Continued

```
// Implement loadView to create a view hierarchy programmatically, without using
a nib.
- (void)loadView {
}
*/


// Implement viewDidLoad to do additional setup after loading the view,
typically from a nib.
- (void)viewDidLoad {

    UIAccelerometer *accelerometer = [UIAccelerometer sharedAccelerometer];
    accelerometer.delegate = self;
    accelerometer.updateInterval = 0.1; // 10 times per second

    [super viewDidLoad];
}

/*
// Override to allow orientations other than the default portrait orientation.
- (BOOL)shouldAutorotateToInterfaceOrientation:(UIInterfaceOrientation)interface
Orientation {
    // Return YES for supported orientations
    return (interfaceOrientation == UIInterfaceOrientationPortrait);
}
*/

- (void)didReceiveMemoryWarning {
    // Releases the view if it doesn't have a superview.
    [super didReceiveMemoryWarning];

    // Release any cached data, images, etc that aren't in use.
}

- (void)viewDidUnload {
    // Release any retained subviews of the main view.
    // e.g. self.myOutlet = nil;
}


- (void)dealloc {
    [colorView release];
    [super dealloc];
}

@end
```

FIGURE 19.6
ColorTilt in
action.

Detecting Movement

So far, we have used the accelerometer to detect the orientation and tilt of the device. In both cases, we relied on gravity acting differently on the three axes.

The accelerometer can also be used to sense movement. One way to do this is to look for g-forces greater than 1g. This is good for detecting quick, strong movements. A more subtle approach is to implement a filter to calculate the difference between gravity and the force the accelerometer is measuring. The measured difference is the subtle movements of the device through space.

Let's expand on the ColorTilt example application by allowing the user to change the color with a sudden movement in any one of six directions. Before setting the alpha of the color based on the tilt, we'll check for a large acceleration along one of the axes. If we detect one, we'll change the view's background color. Modify the ColorTiltViewController.m file in the Class group as follows:

```objc
- (void)setBaseColor:(UIAcceleration *)acceleration {

    if (acceleration.x > 1.3) {
        colorView.backgroundColor = [UIColor greenColor];
    } else if (acceleration.x < -1.3) {
        colorView.backgroundColor = [UIColor orangeColor];
    } else if (acceleration.y > 1.3) {
        colorView.backgroundColor = [UIColor redColor];
    } else if (acceleration.y < -1.3) {
        colorView.backgroundColor = [UIColor blueColor];
    } else if (acceleration.z > 1.3) {
        colorView.backgroundColor = [UIColor yellowColor];
    } else if (acceleration.z < -1.3) {
        colorView.backgroundColor = [UIColor purpleColor];
    }
}

#pragma mark -
#pragma mark UIAccelerometerDelegate
```

```
- (void)accelerometer:(UIAccelerometer *)accelerometer
        didAccelerate:(UIAcceleration *)acceleration {

    [self setBaseColor:acceleration];

    UIAccelerationValue value = fabs(acceleration.x);
    if (value > 1.0) { value = 1.0;}
    colorView.alpha = value;

}
#pragma mark -
```

A little experimentation shows that +/–1.3g is a good measure of an abrupt movement. Try it out yourself with a few different values and you may decide another
value is better.

Summary

At this point, you know all the mechanics of working with the accelerometer. You
used the shake gesture in Hour 18, and in this hour you took direct readings to
interpret the orientation, tilt, and movement of the device. You understand how to
access the UIAccelerometer singleton, how to write a UIAccelerometerDelegate,
and how to interpret the measurements from the UIAcceleration object.

Workshop

Quiz

1. Why is a timestamp provided to your delegate with the accelerometer reading? What might you use this timestamp for?

2. Should you drop your phone off the Empire State Building to test the
   accelerometer?

Answers

1. Accelerometer readings don't come at precisely regular intervals. The timestamp can be used to determine how long it's been since the last reading so
   that the application can take the appropriate amount of action that takes into
   account the interval of time that has elapsed.

2. No.

Activities

1. When the Orientation application is in use, the label stays put and the text changes. This means that for three of the six orientations (upside down, left side, and right side) the text itself is also upside down or on its side. Fix this by changing not just the label text but also the orientation of the label so that the text always reads normally for the user looking at the screen. Be sure to adjust the label back to its original orientation when the orientation is standing up, face down, or face up.

2. In the final version of the ColorTilt application, sudden movement is used to change the view's color. You may have noticed that it can sometimes be difficult to get the desired color. This is because the accelerometer provides a reading for the deceleration of the device after your sudden movement. So what often happens is that ColorTilt switches the color from the force of the deceleration immediately after switching it to the desired color from the force of the acceleration. Add a delay to the ColorTilt application so that the color can be switched at most once every second. This will make switching to the desired color easier because the acceleration will change the color but the deceleration will be ignored.

3. A high-pass filter that cancels out the effect of gravity is often used to process accelerometer readings to detect slower and subtler movements in space. Modify the ColorTilt application to keep an average reading of gravity over time and to change colors on subtle movements beyond the gravitational average rather than on abrupt jerks. Does this result in a better user experience for ColorTilt? Think about when you would want to use each approach.

Further Exploration

Your challenge now is to use accelerometer readings to implement subtler and more natural interfaces than those in the two applications we created in this hour.

The next step to building effective accelerometer interfaces for your applications is to dust off your old math, physics, and electronics texts and take a quick refresher course.

The simplest and most basic equations from electronics and Newtonian physics are all that is needed to create compelling interfaces. In electronics, a low-pass filter removes abrupt signals over a cutoff value, providing smooth changes in the baseline signal. This is good for detecting smooth movements and tilts of the device and ignoring bumps and the occasional odd, spiked reading from the accelerometer. A high-pass filter does the opposite and detects only abrupt changes; this is good for removing the effect of gravity and detecting only purposeful movements, even when they occur along the axes that gravity is acting upon.

Once you have the right signal interpretation in place, there is one more requirement for your interface to feel natural to your users. It must react like the physical and analog world of mass, force, and momentum, and not like the digital and binary world of 1s and 0s. The key to simulating the physical world in the digital is just some basic seventeenth-century physics.

Wikipedia Entries

Low-pass filter: http://en.wikipedia.org/wiki/Low-pass_filter

High-pass filter: http://en.wikipedia.org/wiki/High-pass_filter

Momentum: http://en.wikipedia.org/wiki/Momentum

Newton's laws of motion:
http://en.wikipedia.org/wiki/Newton's_laws_of_motion

HOUR 20

Working with Rich Media

What You'll Learn in This Hour:

▶ How to play full-motion video from local or remote (streaming) files

▶ Ways of recording and playing back audio files on your iPhone

▶ How to access the built-in iPod library from within your applications

▶ Methods of retrieving and displaying information about currently playing media items

Each year, a new iPhone comes out, and each year I find myself standing in line to snatch one up. Is it the new amazing features? Not so much. In fact, my primary motivation is to keep expanding my storage space to keep up with an ever-growing media library. Sounds, podcasts, movies, TV shows—I keep them all on my iPhone. When the original 8GB iPhone came out, I assumed that I'd never run out of space. Today, to fit everything under 32GB, I've just started having to cut back on my sync list.

There's no denying that the iPhone is a compelling platform for rich media playback. To make things even better, Apple provides a dizzying array of Cocoa classes that will help you add media to your own applications. This hour's lesson walks you through a few different features that you may want to consider including in your development efforts.

Exploring the Rich Media Frameworks

In Hour 11, "Getting the User's Attention," we introduced you to System Sound Services for playing back short (30 second) sound files. This is great for alert sounds and similar applications, but hardly taps the potential of the iPhone. This hour takes things a bit further, giving you full playback capabilities, and even audio recording within your own applications.

To accomplish this, we'll be using two new frameworks: the Media Player and AV Foundation frameworks. These two frameworks encompass more than a dozen new classes. Although we won't be able to cover everything in this hour, we'll give you a good idea of what's possible and how to get started.

Media Player Framework

The Media Player framework is used for playing back video and audio from either local or remote resources. It can be used to call up the iPod interface from your application, select songs, and manage playback. This is the framework that provides integration with all the built-in media features that your phone has to offer. We'll be making use of five different classes in our sample code:

- ▶ **MPMoviePlayerController**: Allows playback of a piece of media, either located on the iPhone file system or through a remote URL. The player controller can provide a GUI for scrubbing through video, pausing, fast forwarding, or rewinding.

- ▶ **MPMediaPickerController**: Presents the user with an interface for choosing media to play. You can filter the files displayed by the media picker or allow selection of any file from the media library.

- ▶ **MPMediaItem**: A single piece of media, such as a song.

- ▶ **MPMediaItemCollection**: Represents a collection of media items that will be used for playback. An instance of MPMediaPickerController returns an instance of MPMediaItemCollection that can be used directly with the next class—the music player controller.

- ▶ **MPMusicPlayerController**: Handles the playback of media items and media item collections. Unlike the movie player controller, the music player works "behind the scenes"—allowing playback from anywhere in your application, regardless of what is displayed on the screen.

Of course, many dozens of methods are available in each of these classes. We'll be using a few simple features for starting and stopping playback, but there is an amazing amount of additional functionality that can be added to your applications with only a limited amount of coding involved.

AV Foundation Framework

While the Media Player framework is great for all your general media playback needs, Apple recommends the AV Foundation framework for most audio playback functions that exceed the 30 seconds allowed by System Sound Services. In addition, the AV Foundation framework offers audio recording features, making it possible to record new sound files directly in your application. This might sound like a complex programming task, but we'll do exactly that in our sample application.

You need just two new classes to add audio playback and recording to your apps:

▶ **AVAudioRecorder**: Records audio (in a variety of different formats) to memory or a local file on the iPhone. The recording process can even continue while other functions are running in your application.

▶ **AVAudioPlayer**: Plays back audio files of any length. Using this class, you can implement game soundtracks or other complex audio applications. You have complete control over the playback, including the ability to layer multiple sounds on top of one another.

As you can see, there's quite a lot to cover, so let's get started using the Media Player and AV Foundation frameworks in a real iPhone application.

Preparing the Media Playground Application

Much like our tutorial in Hour 11, this hour's exercise will be less about creating a real-world application and more about building a playground for testing out the rich media classes. We'll start by creating an application skeleton with outlets and actions, and then fill them in to implement the features we've been discussing.

There will be three main components to the application. First, a video player that plays an MPEG-4 video file when a button is pressed; video scaling will be controlled by a toggle switch. Second, we'll create an audio recorder with playback features. Third, we'll be adding the ability to choose songs from the iPhone's iPod library and start or pause playback. The title of the currently playing song will also be displayed onscreen.

Setting Up the Project Files

Begin by creating a new View-based Application project in Xcode. Name the new project **MediaPlayground**.

Within Xcode, open the MediaPlaygroundViewController.h file and update the file to contain the following #import directives, outlets, actions, and properties:

```
#import <UIKit/UIKit.h>
#import <MediaPlayer/MediaPlayer.h>
#import <AVFoundation/AVFoundation.h>
#import <CoreAudio/CoreAudioTypes.h>

@interface MediaPlaygroundViewController : UIViewController
    <MPMediaPickerControllerDelegate,AVAudioPlayerDelegate> {
        IBOutlet UISwitch *toggleScaling;
        IBOutlet UIButton *recordButton;
        IBOutlet UIButton *ipodPlayButton;
        IBOutlet UILabel *nowPlaying;
        AVAudioRecorder *soundRecorder;
        MPMusicPlayerController *musicPlayer;
}

-(IBAction)playMedia:(id)sender;
-(IBAction)recordAudio:(id)sender;
-(IBAction)playAudio:(id)sender;
-(IBAction)chooseiPod:(id)sender;
-(IBAction)playiPod:(id)sender;

@property (nonatomic,retain) UISwitch *toggleScaling;
@property (nonatomic,retain) UIButton *recordButton;
@property (nonatomic, retain) UIButton *ipodPlayButton;
@property (nonatomic, retain) UILabel *nowPlaying;
@property (nonatomic, retain) AVAudioRecorder *soundRecorder;
@property (nonatomic, retain) MPMusicPlayerController *musicPlayer;

@end
```

Most of this code should look familiar to you. We're defining several outlets, actions, and properties for interface elements, as well as declaring the instances variables soundRecorder and musicPlayer that will implement our audio recorder and iPod music player, respectively.

There are also a few setup additions here that you may not recognize. First, we need to import three header files so that we can access the classes and methods in the Media Player and AV Foundation frameworks. The CoreAudioTypes.h file is required so that we can specify a file format for recording audio.

You'll also notice that we've declared that MediaPlaygroundViewController class must conform to the MPMediaPickerControllerDelegate and AVAudioPlayerDelegate protocols. These protocols will help us detect when the user has finished choosing media and when an audio file is done playing.

After you've finished the interface file, save your changes and open the view controller implementation file, MediaPlaygroundViewController.m. Edit the file to

include the following @synthesize directives and method stubs after the @imple-
mentation line:

```
@synthesize toggleScaling;
@synthesize soundRecorder;
@synthesize recordButton;
@synthesize musicPlayer;
@synthesize ipodPlayButton;
@synthesize nowPlaying;
```

Finally, for everything that we've retained, be sure to add an appropriate release
line within the view controller's dealloc method:

```
- (void)dealloc {
    [toggleScaling release];
    [soundRecorder release];
    [recordButton release];
    [musicPlayer release];
    [ipodPlayButton release];
    [nowPlaying release];
    [super dealloc];
}
```

Now, we'll take a few minutes to configure the interface XIB file, and then explore
the classes and methods that can (literally) make our apps sing.

Creating the Media Playground Interface

Open the MediaPlaygroundViewController.xib file in Interface Builder and begin
designing the view. This application will have a total of five buttons (UIButton), one
switch (UISwitch), and two labels (UILabel).

Position the first button near the top of the view, along with the switch. This combination of controls will be used to play back a movie file and enable or disable scaling of the movie. Title the button **Play Movie**, and add a label beside the switch
that reads **Scale Movie:** to help convey its function.

In the center of the view, add two more buttons, the first, **Record Audio**, will trigger
audio recording in the AV Foundation framework, and the second, **Play Audio**, will
play whatever has been recorded.

Add the last two buttons near the bottom of the view. The first button should be
titled **Choose iPod Music** and the second **Play iPod Music**. Finally, add a label
below these two buttons that reads **No Song Playing**. This will be updated dynamically to show the title of the currently playing song.

Figure 20.1 shows the final interface layout.

FIGURE 20.1
Create an inter-
face for the
three different
functions we'll
be implement-
ing.

Connecting the Outlets and Actions

Finish up the interface work by connecting the buttons and label to the corresponding outlets and actions that were defined earlier. For reference, the connections that
you should be creating are listed in Table 20.1. Be aware that some UI elements
need to connect to both an action *and* an outlet so that we can easily modify their
properties in the application.

TABLE 20.1   Interface Elements and Actions

Element Name (Type)	Outlet/Action	Purpose
Play Movie (`UIButton`)	Action: `playMedia:`	Initiates playback in an embedded movie player, displaying a video file.
On/Off Switch (`UISwitch`)	Outlet: `toggleScaling`	Toggles a property of the movie player, scaling or presenting the video full size.
Record Audio (`UIButton`)	Action: `recordAudio:` Outlet: `recordButton:`	Starts and stops audio recording.
Play Audio (`UIButton`)	Action: `playAudio:`	Plays the currently recorded audio sample.
Choose iPod Music (`UIButton`)	Action: `chooseiPod:`	Opens a dialog displaying the user's music library for creating a playlist.

TABLE 20.1   Continued

Element Name (Type)	Outlet/Action	Purpose
Play iPod Music (`UIButton`)	Action: `playiPod:` Outlet: `ipodPlayButton`	Plays or pauses the current playlist.
No Song Playing (`UILabel`)	Outlet: `nowPlaying`	Displays the title of the currently playing song (if any).

After creating all the connections to and from the File Owner's icon, save and close the XIB file. We've now created the basic skeleton for all the media capabilities we'll be adding in the rest of the exercise.

Using the Movie Player

The Media Player framework provides access to the built-in media playback capabilities of the iPhone. Everything you typically see when playing video or audio—the scrubber control, fast forward/rewind, play, pause—all of these features come "for free" within the classes provided by the Media Player.

In this exercise, we'll be making use of the `MPMoviePlayerController` class. There are only two methods between us and movie playback bliss::

> `initWithContentURL:`   Provided with an `NSURL` object, this method initializes the movie player and prepares it for playback.
>
> `play`   Begins playing the selected movie file.

Because the movie controller itself implements controls for controlling playback, we don't need to implement additional features ourselves. If we wanted to, however, there are many other methods, including `stop`, that we could call on to control playback.

In addition to using instance methods to control playback, we'll also make use of the `scalingMode` property to toggle between two available scaling modes: `MPMovieScalingModeAspectFit`, which best fits the movie (maintaining the aspect ratio) to the iPhone screen; and `MPMovieScalingModeNone`, which plays the movie back full size.

Did you Know?

These are only a few of the dozens of methods and properties available for the movie player. You can get pointers to additional resources in the "Further Exploration" section at the end of this lesson.

Adding the Media Player Framework

To use the MPMoviePlayerController class (and the MPMusicPlayerController we'll be implementing a bit later), we must first add the Media Player framework to the project. To do this, right-click the Frameworks folder icon in Xcode, and choose Add Existing. If you see the Media Player framework listed in the dialog box presented, choose it and click Add. Otherwise, click Add Other and navigate to Developer/Platforms/iPhoneOS.platform/Developer/SDKs/iPhoneOS3.0.sdk/System/ Library/Frameworks and choose the MediaPlayer.framework, and then click Add.

> Typically, you also need to add a corresponding import line in your header file (#import <MediaPlayer/MediaPlayer.h>), but because we already added this during the application setup, you should be good to go!

Adding Media Files

As you might have noticed earlier when we listed the methods we would be using, initializing an instance of MPMoviePlayerController is performed by passing in an NSURL object. This means that if you pass in a URL for a media file hosted on a web server, as long as it is a supported format, it will work!

> ### What Are the Supported Formats?
>
> Officially, Apple supports the following codecs: H.264 Baseline Profile 3, MPEG-4 Part 2 video in .mov, .m4v, .mpv, or .mp4 containers. On the audio side, AAC-LC, and MP3 formats are supported.
>
> This is the complete list of audio formats supported by the iPhone:
>
> > AAC (16 to 320Kbps)
> >
> > AIFF
> >
> > AAC Protected (MP4 from iTunes Store)
> >
> > MP3 (16 to 320Kbps)
> >
> > MP3 VBR
> >
> > Audible (formats 2–4)
> >
> > Apple Lossless
> >
> > WAV
>
> Interestingly enough, while this lesson was being written, it was discovered that the iPhone 3GS was capable of playing back full 1080p H.264 video files using Apple's built-in movie player. What this means for the future of media on the iPhone platform, we can only guess... but it's probably something big!

For this example, however, we've chosen to include a local media file so that we can easily test the functionality. Locate the movie.m4v file included in the MediaPlayground project folder and drag it into your Xcode resources group so that we can access it directly in the application.

Implementing Movie Playback

To add movie playback to the MediaPlayground application, we need to implement the playMedia: method that we built a button for in Interface Builder. Let's add the method, and then walk through how it works.

Add the following code to the MediaPlaygroundViewController.m file:

```
 1: -(IBAction)playMedia:(id)sender {
 2:     NSString *movieFile;
 3:     MPMoviePlayerController *moviePlayer;
 4:
 5:     movieFile = [[NSBundle mainBundle]
 6:                 pathForResource:@"movie" ofType:@"m4v"];
 7:     moviePlayer = [[MPMoviePlayerController alloc]
 8:                 initWithContentURL: [NSURL fileURLWithPath: movieFile]];
 9:
10:     if ([toggleScaling isOn]) {
11:         moviePlayer.scalingMode=MPMovieScalingModeAspectFit;
12:     } else {
13:         moviePlayer.scalingMode=MPMovieScalingModeNone;
14:     }
15:
16:     [[NSNotificationCenter defaultCenter] addObserver:self
17:                 selector:@selector(playMediaFinished:)
18:                 name:MPMoviePlayerPlaybackDidFinishNotification
19:                 object:moviePlayer];
20:
21:     [moviePlayer play];
22: }
```

Things start off simple enough. Line 2 declares a string movieFile that will hold the path to the movie file we added in the previous step. Next, we declare the moviePlayer, a reference to an instance of MPMoviePlayerController.

Next, lines 5–6 grab and store the path of the movie.m4v file in the movieFile variable.

Lines 7–8 allocate and initialize the moviePlayer itself using an NSURL instance that contains the path from movieFile. Believe it or not, this is most of the "heavy lifting" of the movie playback method! Once we've completed this line, we could (if we wanted) immediately called the play method on the moviePlayer object and see the movie play! We've chosen to add an additional feature instead.

Lines 10–14 check to see whether the toggle switch (`toggleScaling`) is turned "on" using the `UISwitch` instance method `isOn`. If the switch *is* on, the `scalingMode` property of the `moviePlayer` is set to the `MPMovieScallingModeAspectFit` constant—scaling the movie to fit correctly in the player. If the switch is off, scaling is disabled entirely using the `MPMovieScalingModeNone` constant.

Finally, playback is started using the `play` method in line 21.

Notice anything missing? We've conveniently skipped over lines 16–19. These lines add a notification for the movie player that will help us identify when the movie has stopped playing.

Receiving a Notification

There is a teensy-weensy problem with implementing the `MPMoviePlayerController` as we've done here. If we attempt to `release` the movie player after the `play` line, the application will crash. If we attempt to `autorelease` the player, the same thing happens! So, how in the world can we get rid of the player?

The key is that we need to wait until the movie is no longer playing. To do that, we use the `NSNotificationCenter` class to register an "observer" that will watch for a specific notification message from the `mediaPlayer` object, and then call a method of our choosing when it receives the notification.

The `MPMoviePlayerController` sends the `MPMoviePlayerPlaybackDidFinishNotification` when it has finished playing a piece of media. In lines 16–19 we register that notification for our `mediaPlayer` object and ask the notification center to invoke the `playMediaFinished:` method when it receives the notification. Put simply, when the movie player is finished playing the movie (or the user stops playback), the `playMediaFinished:` method is called.

Implementing the `playMediaFinished:` method allows us to clean up once we're done with the movie player!

Handling Cleanup

To clean up after the movie playback has finished, we need to release the `mediaPlayer` object. Add the `playMediaFinished:` method to the MPMoviePlayerController.m file, as follows:

```
1: -(void)playMediaFinished:(NSNotification*)theNotification
2: {
3:     MPMoviePlayerController *moviePlayer=[theNotification object];
4:
```

```
5:      [[NSNotificationCenter defaultCenter] removeObserver:self
6:                 name:MPMoviePlayerPlaybackDidFinishNotification
7:                 object:moviePlayer];
8:
9:      [moviePlayer release];
10: }
```

There are three things that need to happen in this method. First, in lines 3–4, we assign the local `moviePlayer` variable to the object that is passed in from the notification. This is the same object that we were using when we initiated the `play` method in `playMedia`, it just arrived in this method by way of a notification, so we need to call the `object` method on the notification to access it again.

In lines 5–6, we tell the notification center that it can stop looking for the `MPMoviePlayerPlaybackDidFinishNotification` notification. Because we're going to be releasing the movie player object, there's no point in keeping it around.

Finally, in line 9, we can `release` the movie player!

Movie playback is now available in the application, as demonstrated in Figure 20.2. Choose Build and Run in Xcode, press the Play Movie button and sit back and enjoy the show!

FIGURE 20.2
The application will now play the video file when Play Movie is touched.

Creating and Playing Audio Recordings

In the second part of the tutorial, we'll be adding audio recording and playback to the application. Unlike the movie player, we'll be using classes within the AV Foundation framework to implement these features. As you'll learn, there's very little coding that needs to be done to make this work!

For the recorder, we'll use the AVAudioRecorder class and these methods:

> initWithURL:settings:error: Provided with an NSURL instance pointing to a local file, and NSDictionary containing a few settings, this method returns an instance of a recorder, ready to use.
>
> record   Begins recording.
>
> stop   Ends the recording session.

Not coincidentally, the playback feature, an instance of AVAudioPlayer, uses some very similar methods:

> initWithContentsOfURL:error: Creates an audio player object that can be used to play back the contents of the file pointed to by an NSURL object.
>
> play   Plays back the audio.

When you were entering the contents of the MediaPlayground.h file a bit earlier, you may have noticed that we slipped in a protocol: AVAudioPlayerDelegate. By conforming to this protocol, we can implement the method audioPlayerDidFinishPlaying:successfully:, which will automatically be invoked when our audio player finishes playing back the recording. No notifications needed this time around!

Adding the AV Foundation Framework

To use the AVAudioPlayer and AVAudioRecorder classes, we must add the AV Foundation framework to the project. Right-click the Frameworks folder in Xcode, and choose Add Existing. If you see the AV Foundation framework listed, choose it and click Add. Otherwise, click Add Other and navigate to Developer/Platforms/iPhoneOS.platform/Developer/SDKs/iPhoneOS3.0.sdk/System/Library/Frameworks, select the AVFoundation.framework, and then click Add.

> Remember, the framework also requires a corresponding import line in your header file (#import <AVFoundation/AVFoundation.h>) to access the classes and methods. We added this earlier when setting up the project.

Implementing Audio Recording

To add audio recording, we need to create the recordAudio: method, but before we do, let's think through this a bit. What happens when we initiate a recording? In this application, recording will continue until we press the button again.

To implement this functionality, the "recorder" object itself must persist between calls to the recordAudio: method. We'll make sure this happens by using the soundRecorder instance variable in the MediaPlaygroundViewController class (declared in the project setup) to hold the AVAudioRecorder object. By setting the object up in the viewDidLoad method, it will be available anywhere and anytime we need it. Edit MediaPlaygroundViewController.m and add the following code to viewDidLoad:

```
 1: - (void)viewDidLoad {
 2:      NSString *tempDir;
 3:      NSURL *soundFile;
 4:      NSDictionary *soundSetting;
 5:
 6:      tempDir=NSTemporaryDirectory();
 7:      soundFile=[NSURL fileURLWithPath:
 8:                   [tempDir stringByAppendingString:@"sound.caf"]];
 9:
10:      soundSetting = [NSDictionary dictionaryWithObjectsAndKeys:
11:            [NSNumber numberWithFloat: 44100.0],AVSampleRateKey,
12:            [NSNumber numberWithInt: kAudioFormatMPEG4AAC],AVFormatIDKey,
13:            [NSNumber numberWithInt: 2],AVNumberOfChannelsKey,
14:         [NSNumber numberWithInt: AVAudioQualityHigh],AVEncoderAudioQualityKey,
15:              nil];
16:
17:      soundRecorder = [[AVAudioRecorder alloc] initWithURL: soundFile
18:                                      settings: soundSetting
19:                                      error: nil];
20:
21:
22:      [super viewDidLoad];
23: }
```

Beginning with the basics, lines 2–3 declare a string, tempDir, that will hold the iPhone temporary directory (which we'll need to store a sound recording), a URL, soundFile, which will point to the sound file itself, and soundSetting, a dictionary that will hold several settings needed to tell the recorder how it should be recording.

In line 6, we use NSTemporaryDirectory() to grab and store the temporary directory path where your application can store its sound find.

Lines 7 and 8 concatenate "sound.caf" onto the end of the temporary directory. This string is then used to initialize a new instance of NSURL, which is stored in the soundFile variable.

Lines 10–14 create an NSDictionary object that contains keys and values for configuring the format of the sound being recorded. Unless you're familiar with audio recording, many of these might be pretty foreign sounding. Here's the 30-second summary:

AVSampleRateKey   The number of audio samples the recorder will take per second.

AVFormatIDKey   The recording format for the audio.

AVNumberofChannelsKey   The number of audio channels in the recording. Stereo audio, for example, has two channels.

AVEncoderAudioQualityKey   A quality setting for the encoder.

By the Way

To learn more about the different settings, what they mean, and what the possible options are, read the AVAudioRecorder Class Reference (scroll to the "Constants" section) in the Xcode developer documentation utility.

Watch Out!

The audio format specified in the settings is defined in the CoreAudioTypes.h file. Because the settings reference an audio type by name, you must import this file: (#import <CoreAudio/CoreAudioTypes.h>).

Again, this was completed in the initial project setup, so no need to make any changes now.

Finally, in lines 17–19, the audio recorder, soundRecorder, is initialized with the soundFile URL and the settings stored in the soundSettings dictionary. We pass nil to the error parameter because we don't (for this example) care whether an error occurs. If we did experience an error, it would be returned in a value passed to this parameter.

Now that soundRecorder is allocated and initialized, all that we need to do is implement recordAudio: so that the record and stop methods are invoked as needed. To make things interesting, we'll have the recordButton change its title between Record Audio and Stop Recording when pressed.

Add the following code to MediaPlaygroundViewController.m:

```
-(IBAction)recordAudio:(id)sender {
    if ([recordButton.titleLabel.text isEqualToString:@"Record Audio"]) {
        [soundRecorder record];
        [recordButton setTitle:@"Stop Recording"
                      forState:UIControlStateNormal];
    } else {
        [soundRecorder stop];
        [recordButton setTitle:@"Record Audio"
                      forState:UIControlStateNormal];
    }
}
```

The method first checks the title of the recordButton variable. If it is set to Record Audio, the method uses [soundRecorder record] to start recording, and then sets the recordButton title to Stop Recording. If the title *doesn't* read Record Audio, then we're already in the process of making a recording. In this case, we use [soundRecorder stop] to end the recording and set the button title back to Record Audio.

That's it for recording! Let's implement playback so that we can actually *hear* what we've recorded!

Implementing Audio Playback

To play back the audio that we recorded, we'll simply create an instance of the AVAudioPlayer class, point it at the sound file we created with the recorder, and then call the play method. We'll also add the method audioPlayerDidFinishPlaying:successfully: defined by the AVAudioPlayerDelegate protocol so that we've got a convenient place to release the audio player object.

Start by adding the playAudio: method to MediaPlaygroundViewController.m:

```
 1: -(IBAction)playAudio:(id)sender {
 2:     NSURL *soundFile;
 3:     NSString *tempDir;
 4:     AVAudioPlayer *audioPlayer;
 5:
 6:     tempDir=NSTemporaryDirectory();
 7:     soundFile=[NSURL fileURLWithPath:
 8:                 [tempDir stringByAppendingString:@"sound.caf"]];
 9:
10:     audioPlayer = [[AVAudioPlayer alloc]
11:                     initWithContentsOfURL:soundFile error:nil];
12:
13:     [audioPlayer setDelegate:self];
14:     [audioPlayer play];
15: }
```

In lines 2–3, we define variables for holding the iPhone application's temporary directory and a URL for the sound file—exactly the same as the record.

Line 4 declares the audioPlayer instance of AVAudioPlayer.

Lines 6–8 should look very familiar, as, once again, they grab and store the temporary directory, and then use it to initialize an NSURL object, soundFile, that points to the sound.caf file we've recorded.

In lines 10 and 11, the audio player, audioPlayer is allocated and initialized with the contents of soundFile.

Line 13 is a bit out of the ordinary, but nothing too strange. The setDelegate method is called with the parameter of self. This tells the audioPlayer instance that it can look in the view controller object (MediaPlaygroundViewController) for its AVAudioPlayerDelegate protocol methods.

Line 14 initiates playback using the play method.

Handling Cleanup

To handle releasing the AVAudioPlayer instance once it has finished playing, we need to implement the protocol method audioPlayerDidFinishPlaying:success-fully:. Add the following method code to the view controller implementation file:

```
(void)audioPlayerDidFinishPlaying:
(AVAudioPlayer *)player successfully:(BOOL)flag {
    [player release];
}
```

We get a reference to the player we allocated via the incoming player parameter, so we just send it the release message and we're done!

Choose Build and Run in Xcode to test recording and playback. Press Record Audio to begin recording. Talk, sing, or yell at your iPhone. Touch Stop Recording, as shown in Figure 20.3, to end the recording. Finally, press the Play Audio button to initiate playback.

FIGURE 20.3
Record and play back audio!

It's time to move on to the final part of this hour's exercise: accessing the iPod library and playing content from the library.

Accessing and Playing the iPod Library

When Apple opened the iPhone SDK for development, they didn't initially provide a method for accessing the iPod library. This led to applications implementing their own libraries for background music, and a less-than-ideal experience for the end user.

With the release of iPhone OS 3.0, developers can now directly access the iPod library and play any of the available music files. Best of all, this is amazingly simple to implement!

First, you'll be using the `MPMediaPickerController` class to choose the music to play. There's only a single method we'll be calling from this class:

> `initWithMediaTypes:` Initializes the media picker and filters the files that are available in the picker.

We'll configure its behavior with a handful of properties that can be set on the object:

`prompt`	A string that is displayed to the user when choosing songs.
`allowsPickingMultipleItems`	Configures whether the user can choose one or more sound files.

Like the `AVAudioPlayer`, we're going to conform to the `MPMediaPickerControllerDelegate` protocol so that we can react when the user chooses a playlist. The method that we'll be adding as part of the protocol is `mediaPicker:didPickMediaItems:`.

To play back the audio, we'll take advantage of the `MPMusicPlayerController` class, which can use the playlist returned by the media picker. To control starting and pausing the playback, we'll use four methods:

`iPodMusicPlayer`	This class method initializes the music player as an "iPod" music player, capable of accessing the iPod music library.
`setQueueWithItemCollection`	Sets the playback queue using a playlist (`MPMediaItemCollection`) object returned by the media picker.
`play`	Starts playing music.
`pause`	Pauses the music playback.

As you can see, once you get the hang of one of the media classes, the others start to seem very "familiar," using similar initialization and playback control methods.

> The iPod music playback features require the same Media Player framework we added previously for the MPMoviePlayerController class. If you skipped that section, return to the "Adding the Media Player Framework" section, earlier in this hour.

Implementing the Media Picker

The media picker behaves a bit differently from other objects you may have encountered when working through the sample exercises. To use a media picker, we'll first initialize and configure the behavior of the picker, and then add the picker to our iPhone view. When the user is done with the picker, we'll add the playlist it returns to the music player, and dismiss the view of the picker.

For all of these steps to fall into place, we must already have an instance of the music player so that we can hand off the playlist. Recall that we declared an instance variable musicPlayer for the MediaPlaygroundViewController class. We'll go ahead and initialize this variable in the MediaPlaygroundViewController.m viewDidLoad method. Add the following line to the method now:

```
musicPlayer=[MPMusicPlayerController iPodMusicPlayer];
```

With that in place, our instance of the music player is ready, so we can proceed with coding the chooseiPod: method to display the media picker.

Update the MediaPlaygroundViewController implementation file with this new method:

```
 1: -(IBAction)chooseiPod:(id)sender {
 2:     MPMediaPickerController *musicPicker;
 3:
 4:     [musicPlayer stop];
 5:     nowPlaying.text=@"No Song Playing";
 6:     [ipodPlayButton setTitle:@"Play iPod Music"
 7:                     forState:UIControlStateNormal];
 8:
 9:     musicPicker = [[MPMediaPickerController alloc]
10:                     initWithMediaTypes: MPMediaTypeMusic];
11:
12:     musicPicker.prompt = @"Choose Songs to Play" ;
13:     musicPicker.allowsPickingMultipleItems = YES;
14:     musicPicker.delegate = self;
15:
16:     [self presentModalViewController:musicPicker animated:YES];
17:
18:     [musicPicker release];
19: }
```

First, line 2 declares the instance of MPMediaPickerController, musicPicker.

Next, line 4–7 make sure that when the picker is called, the music player will stop playing its current song, the nowPlaying label in the interface is set to the default string No Song Playing, and the playback button is set to read Play iPod Music. These lines aren't necessary, but they keep our interface from being out of sync with what is really going on in the application.

Lines 9–10 allocate and initialize the media picker controller instance. It is initialized with a constant, MPMediaTypeMusic, that defines the type of files the user will be allowed to choose with the picker. You can provide any of five values listed here:

MPMediaTypeMusic	Music files
MPMediaTypePodcast	Podcasts
MPMediaTypeAudioBook	Audio books
MPMediaTypeAnyAudio	Any audio type
MPMediaTypeAny	Any media type

In lines 12 and 13, we set properties for the music picker. The prompt property sets a message displayed to the user when the picker is onscreen. The allowsPickingMultipleItems property is set to a Boolean value (YES or NO) to configure whether the user can select one or more media files.

Line 14, as with the similar AVAudioRecorder property, configures the musicPicker object to look in the MediaPlaygroundViewController for the MPMediaPickerControllerDelegate protocol methods.

Finally, line 16 uses a UIViewController method, presentModalViewController, to add the MPMusicPlayerController instance musicPicker to the current view. This effectively displays the picker onscreen.

Dismissing and Cleaning Up the Media Picker

To get the playlist that is returned by media picker (an object called MPMediaItemCollection) and clean up after ourselves, we'll add the mediaPicker:didPickMediaItems: protocol method to our growing implementation:

```
1: - (void)mediaPicker: (MPMediaPickerController *)mediaPicker
2:          didPickMediaItems:(MPMediaItemCollection *)mediaItemCollection {
3:     [musicPlayer setQueueWithItemCollection: mediaItemCollection];
4:     [self dismissModalViewControllerAnimated:YES];
5:     [mediaPicker release];
6: }
```

When the user is finished picking songs in the media picker, this method is called and passed the chosen items in a MPMediaItemCollection object, mediaItemCollection. The music player instance, musicPlayer, is subsequently configured with the playlist via the setQueueWithItemCollection: method.

To clean things up, the UIViewController method dismissModalViewControllerAnimated: is called to remove the picker from the display, and then the media picker object is released.

> ### How Does the View Controller Know What Modal View to Remove?
>
> Modal views, like the media picker view, require user interaction and "own" the view while they are being displayed. This means that there will only be a single modal view added at a time. There is no need to track the media picker specifically; we just need to dismiss the current modal view controller, which *has* to be the media picker.

Congratulations! You're almost done! The media picker feature is now implemented, so our only remaining task is to add the music player and make sure the corresponding song titles are displayed.

Implementing the Music Player

Because the musicPlayer object was created in the viewDidLoad method of the view controller (see the start of "Implementing the Media Picker"), and the music player's playlist was set in mediaPicker:didPickMediaItems:, the only real work that the playiPod: method must handle is starting and pausing playback.

To spice things up a bit, we'll try to be a bit clever—toggling the ipodPlayButton title between Play iPod Music (the default) and Pause iPod Music as needed. As a final touch, we'll access a property of musicPlayer MPMusicPlayerController object called nowPlayingItem. This property is an object of type MPMediaItem, which, in turn, contains a string property called MPMediaItemPropertyTitle that is set to the name of the currently playing media file, if available.

> To grab the title from musicPlayer.nowPlayingItem, we'll use a MPMediaItem instance method valueForProperty:.
>
> For example: [musicPlayer.nowPlayingItem valueForProperty: MPMediaItemPropertyTitle]
>
> If you attempt to use musicPlayer.nowPlayingItem. MPMediaItemPropertyTitle, it will fail. You *must* use the valueForProperty: method to retrieve the title or other MPMediaItem properties.

When we put all this together, the implementation of playiPod: becomes

```
 1: -(IBAction)playiPod:(id)sender {
 2:     if ([ipodPlayButton.titleLabel.text isEqualToString:@"Play iPod Music"]) {
 3:         [musicPlayer play];
 4:         [ipodPlayButton setTitle:@"Pause iPod Music"
 5:                         forState:UIControlStateNormal];
 6:         nowPlaying.text=[musicPlayer.nowPlayingItem
 7:                         valueForProperty:MPMediaItemPropertyTitle];
 8:     } else {
 9:         [musicPlayer pause];
10:         [ipodPlayButton setTitle:@"Play iPod Music"
11:                         forState:UIControlStateNormal];
12:         nowPlaying.text=@"No Song Playing";
13:     }
14: }
```

Line 2 checks to see whether the ipodPlayButton title is set to Play iPod Music. If it is, line 3 starts playback, lines 4–5 reset the button to read Pause iPod Music, and lines 6–7 set the nowPlaying label to the title of the current audio track.

If the ipodPlayButton title is *not* Play iPod Music (line 8), the music is paused, the button title is reset to Play iPod Music, and the onscreen label is changed to display No Song Playing.

After completing the method implementation, save the MediaPlaygroundViewController.m file and choose Build and Run to test the application. Pressing the Choose iPod Music button will open a media picker, as shown in Figure 20.4.

FIGURE 20.4
The media picker enables browsing the iPhone's iPod music library.

After you've created a playlist, press the Done button in the media picker, and then touch Play iPod Music to begin playing the sounds you've chosen. The title of the current song is displayed at the bottom of the interface (see Figure 20.5).

FIGURE 20.5
The onscreen label displays the title of the currently playing song.

There was quite a bit covered in this hour's lesson, but consider the capabilities you've uncovered. Your projects can now tie into the same media capabilities that Apple uses in their own iPhone apps—delivering rich multimedia to your users with a relatively minimal amount of coding.

Summary

It's hard to believe, but in the span of an hour, you've learned about seven new media classes, two protocols, and a handful of class methods and properties. These will provide much of the functionality you need to create applications that handle rich media. The AV Foundation framework gives us a simple method for recording and playing back high-quality audio streams. The Media Player framework, on the other hand, handles streaming audio and video and can even tap into the existing resources stored in the iPod library on the iPhone.

Because there are many more methods available in the Media Player framework, I recommend spending additional time reviewing the Xcode documentation if you are at all interested in building multimedia iPhone applications.

Q&A

Q. *How do I make the decision between using* MPMusicPlayerController *versus* AVAudioPlayer *for sound playback in my applications?*

A. Use the AVAudioPlayer for audio that you include in your application bundle. Use the MPMusicPlayerController for playing files from the iPod library. Although the MPMusicPlayerController is capable of playing back local files, its primary purpose is integrating with the existing iPod media.

Q. *If I implement the* MPMediaPickerController *and the user doesn't pick any songs, is there a way to detect this?*

A. Yes! You can implement the method mediaPickerDidCancel: (part of the MPMediaPickerControllerDelegate protocol). This method would then be called if the user dismisses the picker without choosing a song.

Workshop

Quiz

1. What class can be used to implement a high-quality audio recorder?

2. What property and associated class represent the current piece of media being played by an instance of MPMusicPlayerController?

3. What do we take advantage of to determine whether a MPMoviePlayerController object has finished playing a file?

Answers

1. The AVAudioRecorder class enables developers to quickly and easily add audio recording capabilities to their applications.

2. The nowPlaying property of the MPMusicPlayerController is an instance of the MPMediaItem class. This class contains a number of read-only properties, including title, artist, and even album artwork.

3. To determine when a movie has finished playback, the MPMoviePlayerPlaybackDidFinishNotification notification can be registered and a custom method called. We use this approach to release the media player object cleanly in our example code.

Activities

1. Return to an earlier application, adding an instance of AVAudioPlayer that plays a looping background soundtrack. You'll need to use the same classes and methods described in this hour's lesson, as well as the numberOfLoops property.

2. Implement the mediaPickerDidCancel: delegate method and display additional MPMediaItem properties for the currently playing song, and thus improve the usability of today's MPMediaPickerController/MPMusicPlayerController example by detecting whether the user dismissed the media picker.

Further Exploration

We touched on only a few of the configuration options available for the MPMoviePlayerController, MPMusicPlayerController, AVAudioPlayer, and MPMediaPickerController classes—but far more customization is possible if you dig through the documentation.

The MPMoviePlayerController class, for example, offers the movieControlMode property for configuring the onscreen controls for when the movie is playing. You can also programmatically "scrub" through the movie, by setting the playback starting point with the initialPlaybackTime property. As mentioned (but not demonstrated) in this lesson, this class can even play back a media file hosted on a remote URL—including streaming media.

Custom settings on AVAudioPlayer can help you create background sounds and music with properties such as numberOfLoops to set looping of the audio playback and volume for controlling volume dynamically. You can even enable and control advanced audio metering, monitoring the audio power in decibels for a given sound channel.

For those interested in going a step further, you may also want to review the documents "OpenGL ES Programming Guide for iPhone," "Introduction to Core Animation Programming Guide," and "Core Audio Overview." These Apple tutorials will introduce you to the 3D, animation, and advanced audio capabilities available in the iPhone OS.

As always, the Apple Xcode documentation utility provides an excellent place for exploring classes and finding associated sample code.

Apple Tutorials

Getting Started with Audio & Video (accessible through the Xcode documentation): This introduction to the iPhone A/V capabilities will help you understand what classes to use for what purposes. It also links to a variety of sample applications demonstrating the media features.

AddMusic (accessible through the Xcode documentation): Demonstrates the use of the `MPMediaPickerController` and the `MPMediaPickerControllerDelegate` protocol as well as playback via the `MPMusicPlayerController` class.

MoviePlayer (accessible through the Xcode documentation): Explores the full range of features in the `MPMoviePlayerController` class, including custom overlaps, control customization, and loading movies over a network URL.

HOUR 21

Interacting with Other Applications

What You'll Learn in This Hour:

▶ How to access the iPhone Image Library and built-in camera
▶ How to create and send email with the Mail application
▶ How to access the Address Book

In previous hours, you learned how your applications can interact with various parts of the iPhone hardware and software. In the preceding hour, for example, you accessed the iPhone's iTunes Music Library. In Hour 19, "Sensing Movement with Accelerometer Input," you used the iPhone's accelerometer. It is typical of a full-featured iPhone application to leverage these unique capabilities of the iPhone hardware and software that Apple has made accessible with the iPhone SDK. Beyond what you have learned already, the iPhone applications you develop can take advantage of some additional built-in capabilities.

Getting Images from the iPhone Image Library and Camera

The iPhone SDK does a good job of abstracting how a photo gets from the iPhone into your application. The `UIImagePickerController` provides a standardized interface to allow a user to select a picture for use in your application. The best part of `UIImagePickerController` is that whether the user-selected image comes from an Image Library synced from iPhoto, from the camera roll of previously taken pictures, or from the user snapping a new photo with the camera, your application uses the same simple `UIImagePickerController` class and delegate.

It is important to understand that the `UIImagePickerController` is a modal navigation controller class, and when you use it, the iPhone SDK provides the UI for your application and interacts with the user. Your application acts as a delegate while temporarily stepping out of the way and letting the user interact with the system-supplied interfaces for browsing photos or taking a new picture.

By the Way

Modal is just a fancy way of saying that something takes control of the user interaction. A modal window, dialog, or interface interrupts the normal use of the application, forcing the user to interact with it before returning to where the user was in the application's UI. If you've ever had your typing interrupted midsentence by a pop-up dialog that wouldn't go away until you dealt with it, you know what modal means.

By the Way

The iPhone SDK does not provide direct access to the iPhone's camera, to the photos in the user's camera roll, or to the synced iPhoto libraries. And because of how the application sandbox works, you cannot find the photos on the file system and access them that way either. You might find this a frustrating limitation at times, but instead we have the sophisticated and polished interfaces that Apple has provided in the SDK to enable a user to select a photo. As a further benefit, users of your application don't have to learn anything new. They use the same familiar Photo Library, camera roll, and camera UIs from within your application.

The `UIImagePickerController` provides three types of image pickers, which are defined by their source type:

> **`UIImagePickerControllerSourceTypePhotoLibrary`** (synced iPhoto library)
>
> **`UIImagePickerControllerSourceTypeSavedPhotosAlbum`** (camera roll of saved photos)
>
> **`UIImagePickerControllerSourceTypeCamera`** (new snapshot from the camera)

It is important that you ask whether the device can handle the source type before attempting to use it. Today, the only limitation is that an iPod Touch does not have a camera and so is limited to the Photo Library source. Today's iPhones can use all three source types (see Figure 21.1). Get in the habit of asking if the source type is available and your code will continue to function as Apple adds new devices and source types.

FIGURE 21.1
The interface to
a Photo Library,
camera roll, and
camera snap-
shot (left to
right).

Photo Grabber Implementation

In our example of using the UIImagePickerController, we build a simple application that has a set of three buttons, one for each source type (library, saved, new).
Users will push one of the buttons to choose how they want to select a photo, select
the photo itself, and then they will see the photo they selected in the application. If
they have a device, such as an iPod Touch, that doesn't support all the sources, the
corresponding button is disabled.

Add the Outlets and Actions

Begin by creating a new Xcode iPhone project named **Photo Grabber** using the
Utility Application template. Click MainViewController.h in the Classes group, and
add IBOutlets and IBActions for the three buttons and add an IBOutlet for an
image view to display the image. While we are here, we will also indicate that we
implement the UIImagePickerControllerDelegate and
UINavigationControllerDelegate protocol because our MainViewController will
be the delegate for our image picker, and these are the protocols it requires of its delegate. Modify the MainViewController.h file to read as follows:

LISTING 21.1

```
#import "FlipsideViewController.h"

@interface MainViewController : UIViewController
        <FlipsideViewControllerDelegate,
        UIImagePickerControllerDelegate,
        UINavigationControllerDelegate> {

        IBOutlet UIButton *iPhoto;
        IBOutlet UIButton *cameraRoll;
        IBOutlet UIButton *camera;
        IBOutlet UIImageView *photo;
}
```

LISTING 21.1   Continued

```
@property (nonatomic, retain) UIButton *iPhoto;
@property (nonatomic, retain) UIButton *cameraRoll;
@property (nonatomic, retain) UIButton *camera;
@property (nonatomic, retain) UIImageView *photo;

- (IBAction)showInfo;

- (IBAction)iPhotoPressed:(id)sender;
- (IBAction)cameraRollPressed:(id)sender;
- (IBAction)cameraPressed:(id)sender;

@end
```

Lay Out the UI

To lay out the Photo Grabber UI, complete the following steps:

1. Open Interface Builder by double-clicking the MainView.xib file in the Resources group.

2. Open the library (Shift+Command+L).

3. Search the library for Image, and drag a `UIImageView` control onto the view.

4. Size and position the `UIImageView` to take up all but the bottom quarter of the view.

5. With the `UIImageView` selected, open the Attribute Inspector (Command+1) and change the Mode attribute to Scale to Fill. This causes the `UIImageView` to scale the image to the size we have provided for the image view.

6. Open the library (Shift+Command+L) again and search for Button.

7. Drag three Rounded Rect UI Buttons onto the view below the `UIImageView`.

8. Label each button by clicking it, accessing the Attribute Inspector (Command+1), and providing a title for each: iPhoto, Camera Roll, and Camera. Your view should now look like Figure 21.2.

Each button needs to be disabled if the device does not support the source type. We need to be sure it is clear to the user that the button is disabled. Right now, each button will look exactly the same enabled or disabled.

To disable the iPhoto button (for example), just complete these steps:

1. Select the iPhoto button on the interface.

2. Open the Attribute Inspector (Command+1).

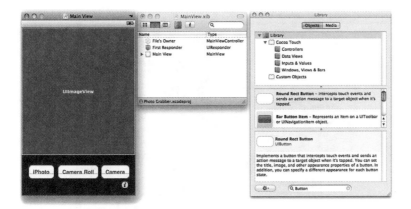

FIGURE 21.2
The user inter-
face of the
Photo Grabber
application.

3. Scroll to the bottom of the Attribute Inspector and uncheck the User Interaction Enabled check box.

This disables the iPhoto button, but notice that the button still looks exactly the same. To fix this, scroll to the top of the Inspector and select Disabled State Configuration in the drop down. We can now set the attributes of the button for its disabled state. We want to change the text color when the button is disabled. To do so, follow these steps:

1. Click the color picker for Text Color.

2. Select Developer from the pallete drop down in the color picker window.

3. Select the gray color labeled disabledControlTextColor.

Now the iPhoto button looks disabled (see Figure 21.3).

Repeat this color change for the disabled state of the other two buttons, and don't forget to recheck the check box to enable the iPhoto button.

Connect the Outlets and Actions

The code we are about to write needs to have access to the three buttons and the UIImageView and needs to respond to any of the buttons being pressed. To connect each of the three button outlets (IBOutlets), complete the following steps:

1. Right-click the File's Owner icon.

2. Click-drag from the circle next to each of the three UIButton outlets to the corresponding button on the interface.

FIGURE 21.3
Change the text
color for the dis-
abled state.

3. Repeat step 1 and 2 for each button, and then connect the photo outlet to the
   UIImageView as shown in Figure 21.4.

FIGURE 21.4
Connecting the
photo IBOutlet
to the
UIImageView.

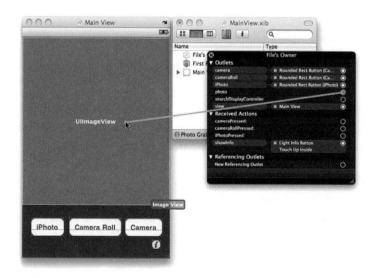

Next, you want to connect the three IBActions to the buttons, as follows:

1. Click-drag from the circle next to the Received Action to the corresponding button on the interface.

2. Select the Touch Down action from the pop-up menu (see Figure 21.5).

3. Save the XIB file and return to Xcode.

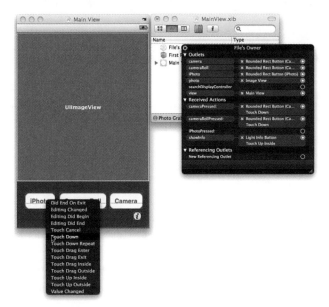

FIGURE 21.5
Selecting the Touch Down action for the iPhoto button.

Add the properties to the MainViewController.m file in the Classes group as follows:

```
@synthesize iPhoto;
@synthesize cameraRoll;
@synthesize camera;
@synthesize photo;

- (void)dealloc {
    [iPhoto release];
    [cameraRoll release];
    [camera release];
    [photo release];

    [super dealloc];
}
```

Disable the Buttons by Source Type

When our view is loaded, we will ask the UIImagePickerController whether the device supports each of the three input sources. If the input source is not supported,

we will use the outlet to the button to disable it using the enabled property. Modify
the `viewDidLoad` method of the MainViewController.m file to read as shown.

```
// Implement viewDidLoad to do additional setup after loading the view,
// typically from a nib.
- (void)viewDidLoad {
    [super viewDidLoad];

    if(![UIImagePickerController
        isSourceTypeAvailable:UIImagePickerControllerSourceTypePhotoLibrary]) {
        iPhoto.enabled = NO;
    }
    if(![UIImagePickerController

isSourceTypeAvailable:UIImagePickerControllerSourceTypeSavedPhotosAlbum]) {
                cameraRoll.enabled = NO;
    }
    if(![UIImagePickerController
        isSourceTypeAvailable:UIImagePickerControllerSourceTypeCamera]) {
        camera.enabled = NO;
    }
}
```

Grab the Image

When the user presses one of the three buttons, we respond in the `IBAction` method
by turning control over to the `UIImagePickerController` to interact with the user
and allow them to select a photo. We provide the image picker the source type that
corresponds to the button the user pressed so that it knows to provide the Photo
Library, camera roll, or camera interface. Add the following three methods to the
MainViewController.m file.

```
- (void)pickPhoto:(UIImagePickerControllerSourceType)sourceType {
    UIImagePickerController *picker = [[UIImagePickerController alloc] init];
    picker.delegate = self;
    picker.sourceType = sourceType;
    [self presentModalViewController:picker animated:YES];
    [picker release];
}

- (IBAction)iPhotoPressed:(id)sender {
    [self pickPhoto:UIImagePickerControllerSourceTypePhotoLibrary];
}

- (IBAction)cameraRollPressed:(id)sender {
    [self pickPhoto:UIImagePickerControllerSourceTypeSavedPhotosAlbum];
}

- (IBAction)cameraPressed:(id)sender {
    [self pickPhoto:UIImagePickerControllerSourceTypeCamera];
}
```

Display the Image

We've now told the image picker to display, and the user may have used the image picker's interface to select a photo (or may have canceled the operation). We'd like to pass the selected image to our UIImageView so that it can be displayed, but how do we find out what photo was selected, and how do we get it for use in our application?

Back when we were creating the IBActions and IBOutlets, we also implemented the UIImagePickerControllerDelegate protocol. At the time, we didn't implement either of the methods of this protocol; they are both optional. Now we must implement them so that we can get hold of the selected image and display it in our application. We also need to dismiss the image picker's control of the UI and return control of the user interaction to our own view.

> When a user takes a photo from the UIImagePickerController interface using the camera, the photo is not saved to the camera roll like it is when using the Camera application. It is up to your application to do something with the photo or it is gone forever.

Watch Out!

Implement the two UIImagePickerControllerDelegate protocol methods as shown. Build and run the project and go take a picture of a loved one (see Figure 21.6).

```
# pragma mark -
# pragma mark UIImagePickerControllerDelegate

// The picker does not dismiss itself; the client dismisses it in these
↪callbacks.
// The delegate will receive one or the other, but not both, depending on
↪whether the
// user confirms or cancels.
- (void)imagePickerController:(UIImagePickerController *)picker
            didFinishPickingImage:(UIImage *)image
                        editingInfo:(NSDictionary *)editingInfo {

        photo.image = image;
        [picker dismissModalViewControllerAnimated:YES];
}

- (void)imagePickerControllerDidCancel:(UIImagePickerController *)picker {
        [picker dismissModalViewControllerAnimated:YES];
}

# pragma mark -
```

FIGURE 21.6
Photo Grabber
displaying a
selected photo.

Creating and Sending Email

In the preceding section, you learned how to show a modal view controller supplied by the iPhone SDK to allow a user to use Apple's image picker interfaces to select a photo for your application. Showing a system-supplied modal view controller is a common pattern in the iPhone SDK, and the same approach is used in the Message UI framework to provide an interface for sending email.

Again, the iPhone SDK provides the UI for your application and interacts with the user to send the email. Your application provides the initial values for the email and then acts as a delegate while temporarily stepping out of the way and letting the user interact with the system-supplied interface for sending email. This is the same interface users use in the Mail application to send email, and so it will be familiar to them.

Similar to how the Photo Grabber application did not include any of the details of working with the iPhone's camera and database of photos, you do not need to include any of the details about the email service your user is using and how to interact with it to send an email. The iPhone SDK takes care of the details of sending email at the expense of some lower-level control of the process. The trade-off makes it very easy to send email from your application.

Email Feedback Implementation

In our example of using the Message UI framework, we will allow the user to email us feedback about our Photo Grabber application. The user will press a button to send feedback, and we will populate the fields of an email message to ourselves. The user can then use the interface provided by the `MFMailComposeViewController` to edit the email and send it.

Add the Message UI Framework

To add the Message UI Framework, follow these steps:

1. From within the Photo Grabber Xcode project, select the Photo Grabber target from the Targets group, right-click it, and select Get Info from the context menu.

2. Select the General tab, click the + button under the Linked Libraries list and pick the MessageUI.framework (see Figure 21.7).

3. Click the Add button to add it to your project.

4. Close the dialog and notice that the MessageUI.framework now appears in your project. Drag it to the Frameworks group to keep things tidy.

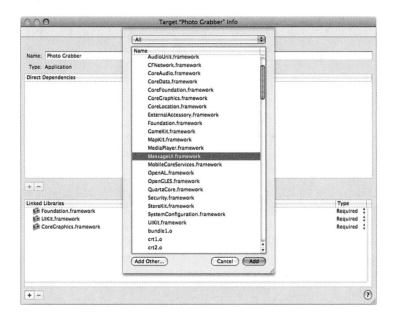

FIGURE 21.7
Add the Message UI framework to your project.

Add the Outlets and Actions

Open the Flipside View group and click the FlipSideViewController.h. Import the header for the Message UI framework and add the IBOutlet and IBAction for sending a feedback email. While we are here, we will also indicate that we implement the MFMailComposeViewControllerDelegate and UINavigationControllerDelegate protocols, because our FlipsideViewController will be the delegate for our email interface and it requires these protocols for its delegate. Modify the FlipsideViewController.h file to read as follows in Listing 21.2.

LISTING 21.2

```
#import <MessageUI/MessageUI.h>

@protocol FlipsideViewControllerDelegate;

@interface FlipsideViewController : UIViewController
      <MFMailComposeViewControllerDelegate,
      UINavigationControllerDelegate> {

      id <FlipsideViewControllerDelegate> delegate;

      IBOutlet UIBarButtonItem *feedback;
}

@property (nonatomic, assign) id <FlipsideViewControllerDelegate> delegate;
- (IBAction)done;

-(IBAction)sendFeedback:(id)sender;

@end

@protocol FlipsideViewControllerDelegate
- (void)flipsideViewControllerDidFinish:(FlipsideViewController *)controller;
@end
```

Lay Out the UI

We are creating the flipside of the Photo Grabber application. The flipside is a second view of iPhone Utility applications, accessed when the user clicks the Information icon of the main view, and animated with a flip transition. The majority of the screen on our flipside will be given over to an image promoting the application and the company producing it. A toolbar at the bottom will contain buttons for conducting various actions via email, including sending feedback about the application.

Let's start by creating an image to represent our Photo Grabber application. You can use the image provided in the Photo Grabber project or create your own (320x372 pixels). I recommend you create your own. Have some fun with it!

First, add your image to the Photo Grabber Xcode project, as follows:

1. Right-click Photo Grabber in the tree.

2. Select Add, New Group from the context menu and name the group **Images**.

3. Add your image by right-clicking the new Images group and selecting Add, Existing Files from the context menu.

4. Browse to your image and add it, and then check the Copy Items into the Destination Group's Folder check box.

Now open Interface Builder by double-clicking on the FlipsideView.xib file in the Resources group and lay out the UI with these steps:

1. Open the library (Shift+Command+L).

2. Search the library for Tool, and drag a UIToolBar control onto the bottom of the view.

3. Search the library for Image, and drag a UIImageView onto the view.

4. Size and position the UIImageView to take up all the space between the UINavigationBar at the top and the UIToolbar at the bottom.

5. Click the the UINavigationItem in the UINavigationBar at the top, open the Attribute Inspector, and change the title to **Photo Grabber**.

6. Click the UIImageView, open the Attribute Inspector, and select the image you added to Xcode from the image drop down.

7. Click the toolbar button, open the Attribute Inspector, and change the Title to **Feedback**. Your view should now look like Figure 21.8 (but with your own image).

Connect the Outlets and Actions

Before leaving Interface Builder, let's connect the IBOutlet and IBAction we created earlier to the Feedback button we just created. To do so, follow these steps:

1. Right-click the File's Owner icon.

2. Click-drag from the circle next to the feedback Outlet and the sendFeedback Received Action to the Feedback button (see Figure 21.9).

3. Save the XIB file and return to Xcode.

FIGURE 21.8
The user inter-
face of the
Photo Grabber
application's flip
view.

FIGURE 21.9
Connecting the
sendFeedback
action to the
button.

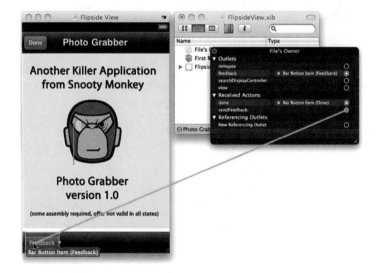

Disable the Feedback Button

Before attempting to send an email message, you should always check whether the
device is capable of doing so. Not all users configure their device to send and receive
email. Using the canSendMail of MFMailComposeViewController will tell us
whether the device is generally capable of sending email and if it has been configured to do so. It will not tell us if our message will be sent immediately. It's possible
that the user is not in range of a data network, or the device may be in airplane

mode. In this case, `canSendMail` will still tell us the device can send email, and the message will be safely stored in an outbox until the next time the device is connected to a network. If the test fails because the device is not configured to send email, we will disable the feedback button. Modify the `viewDidLoad` method of the FlipsideViewController.m file to read as follows:

```
- (void)viewDidLoad {
    [super viewDidLoad];
    self.view.backgroundColor = [UIColor viewFlipsideBackgroundColor];

    if (![MFMailComposeViewController canSendMail]) {
        feedback.enabled = NO;
    }
}
```

Send Feedback Email

All that is left to do now is to provide the `MFMailComposeViewController` with information about the email that we want to send and ask it to display the email interface to the user. Remember, the user is in control of the contents of the email and whether it gets sent. (They can cancel the email.) We are simply going to provide the initial default values of the email so that the user has less typing to do.

Like with the image picker, we also need to implement the view controller delegate to return control of the user interaction back to our own view with `dismissModalViewControllerAnimated` after the user has finished using the email interface. Add the following methods to the FlipsideViewController.m.

```
-(IBAction)sendFeedback:(id)sender {

    MFMailComposeViewController *mailer =
            [[MFMailComposeViewController alloc] init];
    mailer.delegate = self;

    [mailer setToRecipients: [NSArray arrayWithObject:
@"feedback@snootymonkey.com"]];
    [mailer setSubject:@"Feedback on Photo Grabber"];
    [mailer setMessageBody:
            @"<p>Hi Sean,</p><p>I have some feedback on Photo Grabber:</p>\
            <br><br><p>Thanks!</p>" isHTML: YES];

    [self presentModalViewController:mailer animated:YES];
    [mailer release];

}

# pragma mark -
# pragma mark MFMailComposeViewControllerDelegate
```

```
- (void)mailComposeController:(MFMailComposeViewController*)mailer
            didFinishWithResult:(MFMailComposeResult)result
                                      error:(NSError*)error {
        [mailer dismissModalViewControllerAnimated:YES];
}

# pragma mark -
```

Build and run the project. When you flip the view you'll see your promotional image and you can send a feedback email as in Figure 21.10.

FIGURE 21.10
Sending a feedback email from Photo Grabber.

Accessing the Address Book

The Address Book is a shared database of contact information that is available to any iPhone application. Having a common, shared set of contact information provides a better experience for the user than if every application managed its own separate list of contacts. With the shared Address Book, there is no need to add contacts multiple times for different applications, and updating a contact in one application makes the update available instantly in all the other applications.

The iPhone SDK provides comprehensive access to the Address Book database through two frameworks: the Address Book and the Address Book UI frameworks. With the Address Book framework, your application can access the Address Book and retrieve and update contact data and create new contacts. The Address Book framework is an older framework based on Core Foundation, which means the APIs and data structures of the Address Book framework are C rather than Objective-C. Don't let this scare you. As you'll see, the Address Book framework is still clean, simple, and easy to use, despite its C roots.

The Address Book UI framework is a newer set of user interfaces that wrap around the Address Book framework and provide a standard way for users to work with their contacts. You can use the Address Book UI framework's interfaces to allow users to browse, search, and select contacts from the Address Book, display and edit a selected contact's information, and create new contacts.

If you are considering storing contact information used in your application outside of the Address Book, *reconsider that decision*. There is almost no reason not to use the system Address Book if your application deals with contacts.

Watch Out!

Address Book Implementation

In our example of accessing the address book, we will allow users to pick a contact as their best friend from their Address Book. After they have picked their best friend, we will retrieve information from the Address Book about their friend and display it nicely on the screen.

Add the Address Book and Address Book UI Frameworks

Start by creating a new Xcode iPhone project named Best Friend using the View-based Application template, as follows:

1. From within the new Xcode project, select the Best Friend target from the Targets group, right-click it, and select Get Info from the context menu.

2. Select the General tab, click the + button under the Linked Libraries list, and pick both (Shift+left-click) the AddressBook.framework and AddressBookUI.framework (see Figure 21.11).

3. Click the Add button to add them to your project.

4. Close the dialog and notice that the AddressBook.framework and AddressBookUI.framework now appear in your project.

5. Drag them to the Frameworks group to keep things tidy.

FIGURE 21.11
Add the Address
Book and
Address Book
UI frameworks
to your project.

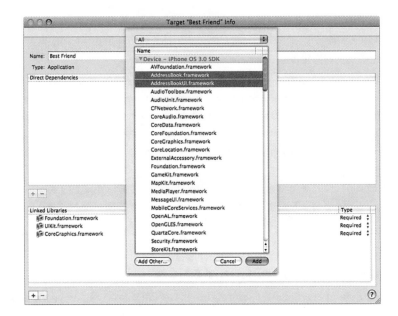

Add the Outlets and Actions

Click the Best_FriendViewController.h file in the Classes group and add IBOutlets
and IBActions for the *friend's name* label, and add an IBOutlet for an image view
to display the friend's picture.

While we are here, we will also import the headers for the Address Book and Address
Book UI frameworks and indicate that we implement the
ABPeoplePickerNavigationControllerDelegate protocol, because our
Best_FriendViewController will be the delegate for our Address Book people pick-
er, and this protocol is required of its delegate. Modify the
Best_FriendViewController.h file to read as shown in Listing 21.3.

LISTING 21.3

```
#import <UIKit/UIKit.h>
#import <AddressBook/AddressBook.h>
#import <AddressBookUI/AddressBookUI.h>

@interface Best_FriendViewController : UIViewController
        <ABPeoplePickerNavigationControllerDelegate> {

        IBOutlet UILabel *name;
        IBOutlet UIImageView *photo;
}

@property (nonatomic, retain) UILabel *name;
```

LISTING 21.3 Continued

```objc
@property (nonatomic, retain) UIImageView *photo;

- (IBAction)newBFF:(id)sender;

@end
```

Lay Out the UI

Lay out the Best Friend UI with these steps:

1. Open Interface Builder by double-clicking the Best_FriendViewController.xib file in the Resources group.

2. Open the library (Shift+Command+L).

3. Search the library for Image, and drag a `UIImageView` control onto the view.

4. Size and position the `UIImageView` to take up the center of the view.

5. With the `UIImageView` selected, open the Attribute Inspector (Command+1) and change the Mode attribute to Scale to Fill. This causes the `UIImageView` to scale the Address Book image to the size we have provided for the image view.

6. Open the Library (Shift+Command+L) again and search for Button.

7. Drag a Rounded Rect UI Button onto the bottom of the view.

8. Label the button by clicking it, accessing the Attribute Inspector (Command+1), and providing the title of **Pick a BFF**.

9. Search the library for Label and drag two `UILabel`s onto the view. Move one above the image view and the other below the `UIImageView` but above the button.

10. Set the properties of the top label by clicking it and opening the Attribute Inspector (Command+1).

11. Change the text to **My BFF**, change the color to white with the color picker, center align the text with the Layout Alignment property, and change the font to 30 pixels.

12. Resize the label so that the full label is shown with the larger font.

13. Click the bottom label to set its properties.

14. Set the text to empty, center align it, and set the font color to white.

15. Resize the bottom label to be the full width of the view up to the guidelines that appear when you get near the edge.

16. Then, change the view background to be black.

17. Click anywhere on the view that doesn't have another control and open the Attribute Inspector (Command+1).

18. And finally, choose the black color in the background property's color picker. Your view should now look like Figure 21.12.

FIGURE 21.12
The user interface of the Best Friend application.

Connect the Outlets and Actions

Before saving and closing Interface Builder, connect the outlets and action in the same way as we did in the other examples. Connect the name IBOutlet to the bottom label, the photo IBOutlet to the UIImageView, and the newBFF IBAction to the button. Save the XIB file and return to Xcode.

Pick the Best Friend

When the user clicks the Pick a BFF button, we want to show the Address Book Person Picker modal view controller, which will provide the user with the familiar interface from the Contacts application. Add the following IBAction method to the Best_FriendViewController.m file:

```
- (IBAction)newBFF:(id)sender {
    ABPeoplePickerNavigationController *picker =
            [[ABPeoplePickerNavigationController alloc] init];
    picker.peoplePickerDelegate = self;

    [self presentModalViewController:picker animated:YES];
    [picker release];
}
```

When the user picks a contact (see Figure 21.13), our controller, acting as the person picker's delegate, will be notified and given a chance to respond and tell the person picker if we want the user to continue on and have a chance to pick a specific property of the contact.

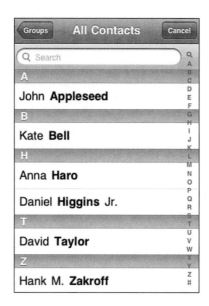

FIGURE 21.13
The ABPerson-PickerView-Controller running in the iPhone simulator has access to a default set of contacts.

For the Best Friend application, we need to know only the friend the user has selected; we don't want the user to go on and select or edit the contact's properties. So, we will respond to the peoplePickerNavigationContoller:peoplePicker:shouldContinueAfterSelectingPerson delegate method with NO. The only other thing our delegate responses need to do at this point is dismiss the person picker modal view controller to return control of the UI back to our Best_FriendView and its controller.

Add the following three methods to the Best_FriendViewController.m file to implement the ABPersonPickerViewControllerDelegate protocol.

```
# pragma mark -
# pragma mark ABPeoplePickerNavigationControllerDelegate

// Called after the user has pressed cancel
// The delegate is responsible for dismissing the peoplePicker
- (void)peoplePickerNavigationControllerDidCancel:
(ABPeoplePickerNavigationController *)peoplePicker {
     [self dismissModalViewControllerAnimated:YES];
}
```

```
// Called after a person has been selected by the user.
// Return YES if you want the person to be displayed.
// Return NO  to do nothing (the delegate is responsible for dismissing the
peoplePicker).
- (BOOL)peoplePickerNavigationController:
        (ABPeoplePickerNavigationController *)peoplePicker
          shouldContinueAfterSelectingPerson:(ABRecordRef)person {

        [self dismissModalViewControllerAnimated:YES];
          return NO;
}

// Called after a value has been selected by the user.
// Return YES if you want default action to be performed.
// Return NO to do nothing (the delegate is responsible for dismissing the
➥peoplePicker).
- (BOOL)peoplePickerNavigationController:
        (ABPeoplePickerNavigationController *)peoplePicker
          shouldContinueAfterSelectingPerson:(ABRecordRef)person
                                     property:(ABPropertyID)property

identifier:(ABMultiValueIdentifier)identifier {
        //We won't get to this delegate method
        [self dismissModalViewControllerAnimated:YES];
          return NO;
}

# pragma mark -
```

Display the Best Friend

If the user doesn't cancel the selection, the `peoplePickerNavigationContoller:`
`peoplePicker:shouldContinueAfterSelectingPerson:` delegate method will be
called, and with it we are passed the selected person as an `ABRecordRef`. An
ABRecordRef is part of the Address Book framework that we imported earlier.

We can use the C functions of the Address Book framework to read the data about
this person from the Address Book. For this example, we read two things: the person's first name, and the person's picture. We will check whether the person record
has a picture before attempting to read it.

Notice that we don't access the person's name or image as the native Cocoa objects
you might expect (namely, `NSString` and `UIImage`, respectively). Instead, the name
string and the photo are returned as Core Foundation C data, and we convert it
using the handy `ABRecordCopyValue` function from the Address Book framework
and the `imageWithData` method of `UIImage`.

Modify the delegate method in the BestFriend_ViewController.m file to read as
shown and build and run the project (see Figure 21.14).

```
// Called after a person has been selected by the user.
// Return YES if you want the person to be displayed.
// Return NO  to do nothing (the delegate is responsible for dismissing the
peoplePicker).
- (BOOL)peoplePickerNavigationController:
        (ABPeoplePickerNavigationController *)peoplePicker
          shouldContinueAfterSelectingPerson:(ABRecordRef)person {

        // Retrieve the friend's name from the address book person record
        NSString* bffName =
                (NSString *)ABRecordCopyValue(person, kABPersonFirstNameProperty);
        name.text = bffName;

        // Retrieve the friend's image from the address book person record
        // only if they have one
        if (ABPersonHasImageData(person)) {
                photo.image = [UIImage imageWithData:
                                (NSData *)ABPersonCopyImageData(person)];
        }

        [bffName release];
        [self dismissModalViewControllerAnimated:YES];
        return NO;
}
```

FIGURE 21.14
The Best Friend
application and
a great BFF.

Summary

In this hour, you learned how to allow the user to select images for your application from the device, how to send email messages, and how to interact with the Address Book. You've most likely recognized a pattern in these three interactions. The iPhone SDK provides a user interface in the form of a modal view controller, and your application sets up the view controller to behave as you want, turns control of the user experience over to the view controller, and then acts as a delegate to be notified when the interaction is complete. Now that you understand this pattern, you are prepared to take advantage of the other modal view controller UIs Apple provides in the iPhone SDK.

Q&A

Q. *Can I access the camera directly, provide my own interface to take a picture, and control the camera's focus and light settings?*

A. No, your interactions with the camera are only through the image picker view controller. There is a good reason for this. Besides making the SDK easier to use, this abstraction provides Apple the flexibility to make dramatic changes to the camera hardware and still have your application work without you needing to change anything.

Workshop

Quiz

1. Why is it so important to implement all the methods of the delegate protocols of the `UIImagePickerController`, the `MFMailComposeViewController`, and the `ABPersonPickerNavigationController`?

2. You should avoid the older Address Book framework and use the new Address Book UI framework instead. True or false?

Answers

1. You turn over control of the user interface to these view controllers with `presentModalViewController:animated`. You return control of the UI to your own view in the delegate protocol methods with `dismissModelViewControllerAnimated`. If you don't implement the delegates, you can never take back control, and your user will be stuck, unable to return to your application's views.

2. False. Although the Address Book UI framework provides user interfaces that save you a lot of time and provide familiarity to your users, you still work with C functions and data structures from the Address Book framework when using the interfaces in your application.

Activities

1. Apply what you learned in Hour 16, "Reading and Writing Data," and make the Best Friend application persist the name and photo of the selected friend so that the user doesn't need to repeat the selection each time the application is run.

2. Enhance the Best Friend application to have two additional buttons, one button to email your best friend and another to create your best friend as a new contact. For the latter part of this activity, read up on the `ABNewPersonViewController`. This activity is a great way to get more exposure to sending emails and using the Address Book.

Further Exploration

You've now learned most of what there is to know about picking images and sending email, but we haven't even scratched the surface of the Address Book and Address Book UI frameworks. In fact, the Address Book UI framework contains three additional modal view controllers. You can use the lower-level Address Book framework to create new contacts, set properties, and edit and delete contacts. Anything the Contacts application can do, you can do with the Address Book framework. For more detailed information about the use of these APIs, refer to the excellent guide from Apple iPhone Dev Center called the *Address Book Programming Guide for iPhone OS*.

You'll learn about a related topic in Hour 22, "Implementing Map and Location Services." In that hour, you'll learn that the functionality of the Maps application is available for your application's use through the MapKit framework.

HOUR 22

Implementing Map and Location Services

What You'll Learn in This Hour:

▶ Finding the device with Core Location
▶ Showing the way with Map Kit
▶ Orienting with the compass

In addition to being a cell phone, and a handy pocket computer, an iPhone is an amazing navigation device (see Figure 22.1). It's so proficient at this task it would give science fiction writers of 30 years ago a good shock. Having an iPhone is like having a whole store's worth of maps and guidebooks tucked away in your pocket or purse.

In this hour, we work with three navigation-related services of the iPhone SDK: Core Location, Map Kit, and the electromagnetic compass.

FIGURE 22.1
From left to right: directions from Apple's Maps application, restaurants from Tweakersoft's AroundMe application and GPS data from MotionX GPS.

By the Way

How does the iPhone's navigation magic work? The core operation of these services is called geolocation, which means figuring out where the phone is. The process of geolocation depends on the particular device. On the iPod Touch, geolocation works through WiFi triangulation. The iPod Touch queries a database of WiFi router locations and determines where you are by the strength of nearby WiFi routers. The results of this approach can be off by a fair bit, and it can't provide a location if there are no known WiFi hotspots nearby.

In addition to the WiFi geolocation of the iPod Touch, all iPhones can use cellular triangulation. Cellular triangulation works on the same principles as WiFi triangulation, but uses proximity to cellular towers instead of WiFi hotspots. The locations of cellular towers are better known, so this is a more reliable source of geolocation, especially where cell towers are plentiful. There are still plenty of spots in the world without cellular service or with so few towers that cellular triangulation can't operate.

Starting with the iPhone 3G, a satellite GPS receiver is part of the iPhone. GPS receivers work on the same theory of triangulation, but they use radio signals from orbiting satellites rather than signals from cellular towers or WiFi hotspots. While not completely immune to being blocked, particularly in tunnels or dense urban cityscapes, GPS is a much more reliable source of geolocation. With civilian GPS hardware like the iPhone, GPS is accurate to about 10 meters (about 30 feet). If you are interested in the engineering and math behind GPS technology, there is an excellent Wikipedia entry at http://en.wikipedia.org/wiki/Global_Positioning_System.

No form of geolocating, no matter how fine, can provide an orientation when at rest. To close this last gap, the iPhone GS includes a hardware compass that can be used by itself or can be used to orient a map showing a geolocated position.

Core Location

Core Location is a framework in the iPhone SDK that provides the location of the device. Depending on the device, any of three technologies can be used: GPS, cellular, or WiFi. GPS is the most accurate of these technologies, and will be used first by Core Location if GPS hardware is present. If the device does not have GPS hardware, or if obtaining the current location with GPS fails, Core Location falls back to cellular and then to WiFi.

Location Manager

Core Location is simple to understand and to use despite the powerful array of technologies behind it (some of it had to be launched into space on rockets!). Most of the functionality of Core Location is available from the Location Manager, which is an instance of the CLLocationManager class. You use the Location Manager to specify the frequency and accuracy of the location updates you are looking for, and to turn on and off receiving those updates.

To use a location manager, you create an instance of the manager, specify a location manager delegate that will receive location updates, and start the updating, like this:

```
CLLocationManager *locManager = [[CLLocationManager alloc] init];
locManager.delegate = self;
[locManager startUpdatingLocation];
```

When the application is done receiving updates (a single update is often sufficient), stop location updates with location manager's stopUpdatingLocation method.

Location Manager Delegate

The location manager delegate protocol defines the methods for receiving location updates. There are two methods in the delegate relating to location: locationManager:didUpdateToLocation:fromLocation and locationManager:didFailWithError.

The locationManager:didUpdateToLocation:fromLocation method's arguments are the location manager object instance and two CLLocation objects, one for the new location, and one for the previous location. The CLLocation instances provide a coordinate property that is a structure containing longitude and latitude expressed in CLLocationDegrees. CLLocationDegrees is just an alias for a floating-point number of type double.

We've already mentioned that different approaches to geolocating have different inherit accuracies, and that each approach may be more or less accurate depending on the number of points (satellites, cell towers, WiFi hotspots) it has available to use in its calculations. CLLocation passes this confidence measure along in the horizontalAccuracy property.

The location's accuracy is provided as a circle, and the true location could lie anywhere within that circle. The circle is defined by the coordinate property as the center of the circle, and the horizontalAccuracy property as the radius of the circle in meters. The larger the horizontalAccuracy property, the larger the circle defined by it will be, so the less confidence there is in the accuracy of the location. If the horizontalAccuracy property is negative, it is an indication that the coordinate is completely invalid and should be ignored.

In addition to longitude and latitude, each CLLocation provides altitude above or below sea level in meters. The altitude property is a CLLocationDistance, which is also just an alias for a floating-point number of type double. A positive number is an altitude above sea level, and a negative number is below sea level. There is another confidence factor, this one called `verticalAccuracy`, that indicates how accurate the altitude is. A positive `verticalAccuracy` indicates that the altitude could be off, plus or minus, by that many meters. A negative `verticalAccuracy` means the `altitude` is invalid.

An implementation of the location manager delegate's `locationManager:didUpdateToLocation:fromLocation` method that logs the longitude, latitude, and altitude would look like this:

```
- (void)locationManager:(CLLocationManager *)manager
    didUpdateToLocation:(CLLocation *)newLocation
           fromLocation:(CLLocation *)oldLocation {

    NSString *coordinateDesc = @"Not Available";
    NSString *altitudeDesc = @"Not Available";

    if (newLocation.horizontalAccuracy >= 0) {
        coordinateDesc = [NSString stringWithFormat:@"%f, %f +/- %f meters",
                        newLocation.coordinate.latitude,
                        newLocation.coordinate.longitude,
                        newLocation.horizontalAccuracy];
    }

    if (newLocation.verticalAccuracy >= 0) {
        altitudeDesc = [NSString stringWithFormat:@"%f +/- %f meters",
                        newLocation.altitude, newLocation.verticalAccuracy];
    }

    NSLog(@"Latitude/Longitude: %@   Altitude: %@", coordinateDesc,
        altitudeDesc);
}
```

The resulting log output looks like this:

```
Latitude/Longitude: 35.904392, -79.055735 +/- 76.356886 meters   Altitude:
28.000000 +/- 113.175757 meters
```

If the location manager delegate's `locationManager:didFailWithError` is called instead, it lets you know the device is unable to return location updates. A distinction is made as to the cause of the failure. If the user denies permission to the application, the error argument is `kCLErrorDenied`, if Core Location tries, but is unable to determine the location, the error is `kCLErrorLocationUnknown`, and if no source of trying to retrieve the location is available, the error is `kCLErrorNetwork`. Usually Core Location will continue to try to determine the location after an error, but after a user denial, it won't, and it is good form to stop the location manager with location manager's `stopUpdatingLocation` method and release the instance. Here is what an implementation of `locationManager:didFailWithError` might look like:

```
- (void)locationManager:(CLLocationManager *)manager
        didFailWithError:(NSError *)error {

    if (error.code == kCLErrorLocationUnknown) {
        NSLog(@"Currently unable to retrieve location.");
    } else if (error.code == kCLErrorNetwork) {
        NSLog(@"Network used to retrieve location is unavailable.");
    } else if (error.code == kCLErrorDenied) {
        NSLog(@"Permission to retrieve location is denied.");
        [locMan stopUpdatingLocation];
        [locMan release];
        locMan = nil;
    }

}
```

CLLocation also provides a property speed, which is based on comparing the current location with the prior location and comparing the time and distance variance between them. Given the rate at which Core Location updates, the speed property is not very accurate unless the rate of travel is fairly constant.

It is important to keep in mind that the location manager delegate will not immediately receive a location; it usually takes a number of seconds for the device to pinpoint the location, and the first time it is used by an application, Core Location first asks the user's permission (see Figure 22.2). You should have a design in place for what the application will do while waiting for an initial location, and what to do if location information is unavailable because the user didn't grant permission, or the geolocation process failed. A common strategy that works for many applications is to fall back to a user-entered ZIP code.

Location Accuracy and Update Filter

It is possible to tailor the accuracy of the location to the needs of the application. An application that only needs the user's country for example, does not need 10-meter accuracy from Core Location, and will get a much faster answer by asking for a more approximate location. This is done before you start the location updates by setting the location manager's desiredAccuracy property. desiredAccuracy is an enumerated type, CLLocationAccuracy. Five constants are available with varying levels of precision (with current consumer technology, the first two are the same): kCLLocationAccuracyBest, kCLLocationAccuracyNearestTenMeters, kCLLocationNearestHundredMeters, kCLLocationKilometer, kCLLocationAccuracyThreeKilometers.

FIGURE 22.2
Core Location
asks permission
to provide Now
Playing with
location data.

Once updates on a location manager are started, updates continue to come into the location manager delegate until they are stopped. You cannot control the frequency of these updates directly, but you can control it indirectly with location manager's `distanceFilter` property. The `distanceFilter` property is set before starting updates and it specifies the distance in meters the device must travel (horizontally, not vertically) before another update is sent to the delegate.

Starting the location manager with settings suitable for following a walker's progress on a long hike might look like this:

```
CLLocationManager *locManager = [[CLLocationManager alloc] init];
locManager.delegate = self;
locManager.desiredAccuracy = kCLLocationAccuracyHundredMeters;
locManager.distanceFilter = 200;
[locManager startUpdatingLocation];
```

**Watch
Out!**

Each of the three methods of locating the device, GPS, cellular, and WiFi, can put a serious drain on the device's battery. The more accurate an application asks the device to be in determining location, and the shorter the distance filter, the more battery the application will use. Be courteous of the device's battery life and only request location updates as accurately and as frequently as the application needs them. Stop location manager updates whenever possible to preserve the battery life of the device.

> The iPhone Simulator will provide just one location update and the location will be Apple HQ in Cupertino, California.

By the Way

A Core Location Application

My adopted hometown of Chapel Hill, North Carolina, is accurately described as the "southern part of heaven," and it's good to know how far you are from it at all times. I'm sure you agree that it would be useful to have an iPhone application for this. We're going to create a Core Location–powered application that keeps you informed of just how far away you are.

Add the Core Location Framework and Outlet

For the rest of this hour, we'll be working on a new application that uses the Core Location framework. Create a new View-Based Application in Xcode and call it **ChapelHill**. The Core Location framework isn't linked in by default, so we need to add it. Open the Targets group in Xcode and right-click on the ChapelHill target. Click the Get Info menu option, and the target info dialog will open. Click the General tab, and then click the plus button in the Linked Libraries table in the bottom half of the dialog. Select CoreLocation.framework in the list (see Figure 22.3), and then click the Add button. Close the dialog. Drag the CoreLocation.framework item to the Frameworks group to keep the project tidy.

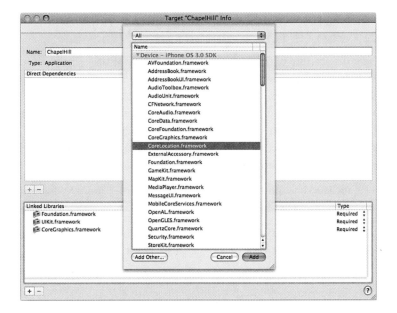

FIGURE 22.3
Add the Core Location framework to the project.

The ChapelHillViewController will serve as the location manager delegate, receiving location updates, and updating the user interface to reflect the new locations. Click the ChapelHillViewController.h file in the Classes group. Update the file by importing the Core Location header file, indicating that we'll be implementing the CLLocationManagerDelegate protocol, and adding properties for the location manager, a label with the distance to Chapel Hill, and two subviews, as in Listing 22.1.

LISTING 22.1

```
#import <UIKit/UIKit.h>
#import <CoreLocation/CoreLocation.h>

@interface ChapelHillViewController : UIViewController
    <CLLocationManagerDelegate> {

        CLLocationManager *locMan;
        IBOutlet UILabel *distanceLabel;
        IBOutlet UIView  *distanceView;
        IBOutlet UIView  *waitView;

}

@property (assign, nonatomic) CLLocationManager *locMan;
@property (retain, nonatomic) UILabel *distanceLabel;
@property (retain, nonatomic) UIView *distanceView;
@property (retain, nonatomic) UIView *waitView;

@end
```

Lay Out the UI and Connect the Outlets

We'll have a nice picture of the Old Well on the campus of UNC Chapel Hill as the application's background image. Right-click on the root level ChapelHill application icon in Xcode and select Add, New Group from the context menu. Name the new group **Images**. Drag the file old_well.png from the sample source code into the Images group and be sure to check the Copy items into destination group's folder check box in the copy dialog. (You can use any 320x480 image if you don't have the sample code from this chapter.)

Click the ChapelHillViewController.xib file in the Resources group to open Interface Builder, and then complete the following steps:

1. Open the Library (Shift+Command+L) and search for "image." Drag a UIImageView onto the view and center it so that it covers the entire view.

2. Click the image view and open the Attribute Inspector (Command+1). Select old_well.png from the drop-down list.

3. Open the Library (Shift+Command+L) and search for "uiview." Drag a `UIView` onto the image view. Size it to about 80 pixels high and up to the left, right, and bottom edge guidelines.

4. Click the `UIView` and open the Attribute Inspector (Command+1). Click the Background color well and set the background to black. Change the Alpha to 0.75.

5. Open the Library (Shift+Command+L) and search for "label." Drag a `UILabel` to the `UIView`. Size the label up to all 4 edge guidelines.

6. Click the label and open the Attribute Inspector (Command+1). Click the center Layout button. Change the Lines attribute to 2. Uncheck the Adjust to Fit check box for the Font Size attribute. Change the Text attribute to **Lots of miles to the Southern Part of Heaven**. Your view should look like Figure 22.4.

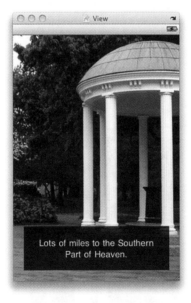

FIGURE 22.4
The ChapelHill UI.

7. Click on the semitransparent `UIView` and copy (Command+C) and paste (Command+V) the view. Drag the new copy of the view to be vertically centered in the image view.

8. Click the new copy of the view and open the Size Inspector (Command+3). Change the height to 77 pixels.

9. Click the label in the new view and open the Attribute Inspector (Command+1). Change the Text attribute to Checking the Distance and change the Lines attribute to 1. Resize the label so that it takes up approximately the right two-thirds of the semitransparent view.

10. Open the Library (Shift+Command+L) and search for "activity." Drag a UIActivityIndicatorView to the new semitransparent view. Follow the guides to properly align the activity indicator to the left of the label.

11. Click on the activity indicator and open the Attribute Inspector (Command+1). Check the check box on the Animated attribute.

12. Click on the original semitransparent UIView that says Lot's of Miles to... and open the Attribute Inspector (Command+1). Check the check box on the Hidden attribute. Your view should now look like Figure 22.5.

13. Open the NIB and right-click the File's Owner icon. Connect the three outlets: Click and drag from the circle next to the distanceLabel outlet to the Lots of Miles... label; click and drag from the distanceView outlet to the original semitransparent view; click and drag from the waitView outlet to the semitransparent view with the activity indicator. Save the XIB file and return to Xcode.

FIGURE 22.5
The final
ChapelHill UI.

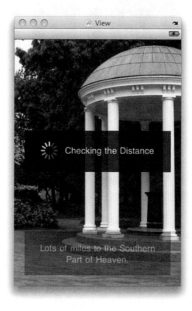

Implement the Location Manager Delegate

Based on the NIB we just laid out, the application will start up with a message and a spinner that let the user know we are waiting on the initial location reading from Core Location. We'll request this reading as soon as the view loads in the view controller's viewDidLoad method. As soon as the location manager delegate (which is also the view controller) gets a reading, we'll calculate the distance to Chapel Hill, update the label, hide the activity indicator view, and unhide the distance view.

Click on the ChapelHillViewController.m file in the Classes group. Synthesize the four properties we added to the ChapelHillViewController header file and release them in the dealloc method.

Uncomment the viewDidLoad method and instantiate a location manager with the view controller itself as the delegate and a desiredAccuracy of kCLLocationAccuracyThreeKilometers and a distanceFilter of 1,609 meters (1 mile). Start the updates with the startUpdatingLocation method. The implementation looks like this:

```
// Implement viewDidLoad to do additional setup after loading the view,
// typically from a nib.
- (void)viewDidLoad {
    [super viewDidLoad];

    locMan = [[CLLocationManager alloc] init];
    locMan.delegate = self;
    locMan.desiredAccuracy = kCLLocationAccuracyThreeKilometers;
    locMan.distanceFilter = 1609; // a mile
    [locMan startUpdatingLocation];

}
```

Now we need to implement the two methods of the location manager delegate protocol. We'll start with the error condition. In the case of an error getting the current location, we already have a default message in place in the distanceLabel, so we'll just remove the waitView with the activity monitor and show the distanceView. If the user denied access to Core Location updates, then we will also clean up the location manager request:

```
- (void)locationManager:(CLLocationManager *)manager
        didFailWithError:(NSError *)error {

    if (error.code == kCLErrorDenied) {
        // Turn of the location manager updates
        [manager stopUpdatingLocation];
        [locMan release];
        locMan = nil;
    }
    waitView.hidden = YES;
    distanceView.hidden = NO;

}
```

In the implementation of the other location manager delegate method, `locationManager:didUpdateToLocation:fromLocation`, we need a location in Chapel Hill that we can compare to the user's location. According to gpsvisualizer.com/geocode, the center of downtown Chapel Hill is at 35.9131501 latitude, –79.0557029 longitude. There is one more hidden gem for us in `CLLocation` that's important here. We don't need to write our own longitude/latitude distance calculations because we can compare two `CLLocation` instances with the `getDistanceFrom` method. We create a `CLLocation` instance for Chapel Hill and compare it to the instance we get from Core Location to get the distance in meters. We then convert the distance to miles, and if it's over 3 miles we show the distance, with a `NSNumberFormatter` used to add a comma if more than 1,000 miles (see Figure 22.6), and if the distance is less than 3 miles, we congratulate the user on his or her fine taste in locations. Listing 22.2 provides the complete implementation of the ChapelHillViewController.m file.

LISTING 22.2

```
#import "ChapelHillViewController.h"

#define kChapelHillLatitude 35.9131501
#define kChapelHillLongitude -79.0557029

@implementation ChapelHillViewController

@synthesize locMan;
@synthesize distanceLabel;
@synthesize distanceView;
@synthesize waitView;

// Implement viewDidLoad to do additional setup after loading the view,
typically from a nib.
- (void)viewDidLoad {
    [super viewDidLoad];

    locMan = [[CLLocationManager alloc] init];
    locMan.delegate = self;
    locMan.desiredAccuracy = kCLLocationAccuracyThreeKilometers;
    locMan.distanceFilter = 1609; // a mile
    [locMan startUpdatingLocation];

}

- (void)locationManager:(CLLocationManager *)manager
    didUpdateToLocation:(CLLocation *)newLocation
           fromLocation:(CLLocation *)oldLocation {

    if (newLocation.horizontalAccuracy >= 0) {

        CLLocation *chapelHill = [[[CLLocation alloc]
                             initWithLatitude:kChapelHillLatitude
                             longitude:kChapelHillLongitude] autorelease];
        CLLocationDistance delta = [chapelHill getDistanceFrom: newLocation];
```

LISTING 22.2 Continued

```
        long miles = (delta * 0.000621371) + 0.5; // meters to rounded miles
        if (miles < 3) {
            // Congratulate the user
            distanceLabel.text = @"Enjoy the\nSouthern Part of Heaven!";
        } else {
            NSNumberFormatter *commaDelimited = [[[NSNumberFormatter alloc]
                                            init] autorelease];
            [commaDelimited setNumberStyle:NSNumberFormatterDecimalStyle];
            distanceLabel.text = [NSString stringWithFormat:
                                @"%@ miles to the\nSouthern Part of Heaven",
                                [commaDelimited stringFromNumber:
                                [NSNumber numberWithLong:miles]]];
        }
        waitView.hidden = YES;
        distanceView.hidden = NO;
    }
}

- (void)locationManager:(CLLocationManager *)manager
        didFailWithError:(NSError *)error {

    if (error.code == kCLErrorDenied) {
        // Turn of the location manager updates
        [manager stopUpdatingLocation];
        [locMan release];
        locMan = nil;
    }
    waitView.hidden = YES;
    distanceView.hidden = NO;

}

- (void)didReceiveMemoryWarning {
        // Releases the view if it doesn't have a superview.
    [super didReceiveMemoryWarning];

        // Release any cached data, images, etc that aren't in use.
}

- (void)viewDidUnload {
        // Release any retained subviews of the main view.
        // e.g. self.myOutlet = nil;
}


- (void)dealloc {
    [locMan release];
    [distanceLabel release];
    [distanceView release];
    [waitView release];
    [super dealloc];
}

@end
```

FIGURE 22.6
The ChapelHill
application in
action showing
the distance
from Cupertino,
California, to
Chapel Hill,
North Carolina.

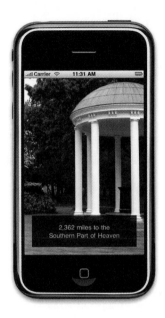

Map Kit

The obvious next step after learning the location of the device is to show a map of the immediate area, and to point out locations on the map that are relevant to the application. This is where Core Location's new companion framework, Map Kit, comes in. Map Kit enables you to embed a map into a view and provides all the map tiles (images) needed to display the map. It handles the scrolling, zooming, and loading of new map tiles as they are needed. Applications can use Map Kit to annotate locations on the map. Map Kit can also do reverse geocoding, which means getting place information (country, state, city, address) from coordinates.

Watch Out!

> Map Kit map tiles come from the Google Maps/Google Earth API. Even though you aren't making calls to this API directly, Map Kit is making those calls on your behalf, so use of the map data from Map Kit binds you and your application to the Google Maps/Google Earth API terms of service.

You can start using Map Kit with no code at all, just by adding the Map Kit framework to your project and an `MKMapView` instance to one of your views in Interface Builder. Once a map view is added, four attributes can be set within Interface Builder to further customize the view (see Figure 22.7). You can select between map, satellite, and hybrid modes; you can determine whether the map should use Core Location to center on the user's location; and you can control if the user should be allowed to interact with the map through swipes and pinches for scrolling and zooming.

FIGURE 22.7
A map view in
Interface
Builder's
Attribute
Inspector.

As an example of using the Map Kit, we are going to enhance the ChapelHill application for users that make it to Chapel Hill. Those users will have access to a map of the town that includes annotations for some interesting locations.

Add the Map Kit Framework and the Map View Controller

To add the Map Kit framework, open the Targets group in the ChapelHill Xcode project and right-click the ChapelHill target. Click the Get Info menu option and the target info dialog will open. Click the General tab, and then click the plus button in the Linked Libraries table in the bottom half of the dialog. Select MapKit.framework in the list (see Figure 22.3) and click the Add button. Close the dialog. Drag the MapKit.framework item to the Frameworks group to keep the project tidy.

Now that the Map Kit framework is linked into the project, we can use a map view. We'll create a new view, view controller, and NIB file for the map view. Right-click on the Classes group and select Add, New File from the context menu. In the New File dialog, select the Cocoa Touch group and the `UIViewController` subclass. Make sure the With XIB for User Interface check box is checked and click the Next button. Name the class **MapViewController.m** and make sure the Also Create "MapViewController.h" check box is checked. Click the Finish button, and then drag the MapViewController.xib file from the Classes group to the Resources group.

Show the Map View After a Delay

If the user is within 3 miles of downtown Chapel Hill, we will show the user the map of the town. We still want the user to see the congratulatory message, so we'll use an NSTimer to wait 2.5 seconds before showing the map. An NSTimer works by calling a selected method once the time has elapsed, so we'll have a method to start the timer called startMapViewSwitchTimer and another that gets called by the timer called mapViewSwitch. Add prototypes for both methods to the ChapelHillViewController.h file in the Classes group:

```
-(void)startMapViewSwitchTimer;
-(void)mapViewSwitch;
```

To show the map view, the ChapelHillViewController needs to know about the MapViewController, so add an import statement to the ChapelHillViewController.m file in the Classes group.

```
#import "MapViewController.h"
```

To invoke a specific method when the timer goes off, NSTimer needs a target, which is the object to invoke the method on, and a selector, a variable of type SEL, which has the signature (name and arguments) of the method to invoke. The selector for mapViewSwitch is simply the name of the method because the method takes no arguments. The other relevant arguments to NSTimer tell it how long to wait and to not repeat the timing cycle. Add the startMapViewSwitchTimer method to the ChapelHillViewController.m file in the Classes group:

```
-(void)startMapViewSwitchTimer {
    // Selector for a method matching mapViewSwitch
    SEL methodSelector = @selector(mapViewSwitch);

    // A 2 second timer that will call the mapViewSwitch method
    [NSTimer scheduledTimerWithTimeInterval:2.5
                             target:self
                           selector:methodSelector
                           userInfo:nil
                            repeats:NO];
}
```

To switch over to the map view when the timer elapses, we'll instantiate an instance of the MapViewController and use the presentModalViewController:animated method of UIViewController. Add the mapViewSwitch method to the ChapelHillViewController.m file in the Classes group:

```
-(void)mapViewSwitch {
    // Show the Map View
```

```
    MapViewController *mapViewController = [[MapViewController alloc] init];
        [self presentModalViewController:mapViewController animated:YES];
        [mapViewController release];
}
```

Once we switch to the map view, they'll be no returning to the original view (Chapel Hill is like Hotel California, you can never leave), so we can turn off location updates and release the location manager. Map Kit will handle location updates for us in the map view. Update the locationManager:didUpdateToLocation:fromLocation method as follows:

```
- (void)locationManager:(CLLocationManager *)manager
    didUpdateToLocation:(CLLocation *)newLocation
          fromLocation:(CLLocation *)oldLocation {

    if (newLocation.horizontalAccuracy >= 0) {

        CLLocation *chapelHill = [[[CLLocation alloc]
                                    initWithLatitude:kChapelHillLatitude
                                    longitude:kChapelHillLongitude] autorelease];
        CLLocationDistance delta = [chapelHill getDistanceFrom: newLocation];
        long miles = (delta * 0.000621371) + 0.5; // meters to rounded miles
        if (miles < 3) {
            // Turn of the location manager updates
            [manager stopUpdatingLocation];

            // Show the map view after a delay
            [self startMapViewSwitchTimer];

            // Congratulate the user
            distanceLabel.text = @"Enjoy the\nSouthern Part of Heaven!";
        } else {
            NSNumberFormatter *commaDelimited = [[[NSNumberFormatter alloc]
                                                   init] autorelease];
            [commaDelimited setNumberStyle:NSNumberFormatterDecimalStyle];
            distanceLabel.text = [NSString stringWithFormat:
                                    @"%@ miles to the\nSouthern Part of Heaven",
                                    [commaDelimited stringFromNumber:
                                    [NSNumber numberWithLong:miles]]];
        }
        waitView.hidden = YES;
        distanceView.hidden = NO;
    }
}
```

Import the Map Kit Framework and Add an Outlet

Now we need to set up the view and view controller for the map view. Click on the MapViewController.h file in the Classes group. Import the Map Kit header and add an outlet for an MKMapView, as shown in Listing 22.3.

LISTING 22.3

```
#import <UIKit/UIKit.h>
#import <MapKit/MapKit.h>

@interface MapViewController : UIViewController {

    IBOutlet MKMapView *map;

}

@property (retain, nonatomic) MKMapView *map;

@end
```

Lay Out the UI

Click on the MapViewController.xib file in the Resources group to open Interface Builder, and then complete the following steps:

1. Open the Library (Shift+Command+L) and search for "map." Drag a MKMapView onto the view and center it so that it covers the entire view.

2. Click the map view and open the Attribute Inspector (Command+1). Click the Show User's Location check box.

3. Open the NIB and right-click on the File's Owner icon. Click and drag from the map outlet to the map view. Save the XIB file and return to Xcode.

Go ahead and build and run the application at this point. Unless you are lucky enough to be in Chapel Hill, you'll need to change the miles < 3 conditional to something that will evaluate to true, so you can try out the map view we just added. What you'll see is that we aren't really showing a handy map of Chapel Hill as we intended (see Figure 22.8). We've added a map to the application with Interface Builder, but to really customize a map for an application's use, it does require some code.

Constrain the Map Dimensions

To get a map more like what we had in mind, we need to constrain the map so we aren't showing the whole world with a little blue dot for the state of North Carolina. We'll use Map Kit to scale the map down to a street-level view of Chapel Hill.

You constrain a map in Map Kit with an MKCoordinateRegion. To create an instance of MKCoordinateRegion, we'll use the Map Kit function called MKCoordinateRegionMakeWithDistance. As arguments, this function takes the coordinates of the center point and the span of the latitude and longitude.

FIGURE 22.8
This is not exactly the map we had in mind!

We want to center the map on the same longitude and latitude we used to calculate the distance to Chapel Hill. Move these two constants from the ChapelHillViewController.m file to the MapViewController.h file. The ChapelHillViewController class will still have access to the constants because it imports the MapViewController.h file.

For a span of at least 3 kilometers in any direction (so the user's location will be sure to appear on the map), the total span for both latitude and longitude is 6 kilometers. Uncomment the viewDidLoad method of the MapViewController.m file in the Classes group and constrain the map. The resulting map is much better (see Figure 22.9).

```
- (void)viewDidLoad {
    [super viewDidLoad];

    CLLocation *chapelHill = [[[CLLocation alloc]
                             initWithLatitude:kChapelHillLatitude
                             longitude:kChapelHillLongitude] autorelease];
    MKCoordinateRegion region =
        MKCoordinateRegionMakeWithDistance(chapelHill.coordinate,
        6000, 6000);
    [self.map setRegion:region animated:YES];
}
```

FIGURE 22.9
A constrained
map in the map
view.

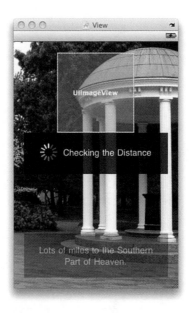

Add Map Annotations

Map annotations are made up of two distinct pieces: an annotation view overlaid at a particular coordinate location on the map, and a model with the data for the annotation. An annotation view is an instance of the MKAnnotationView class, which defines the MKAnnotation protocol. An annotation model implements the MKAnnotation protocol to provide the data (title, subtitle, coordinate location, and any custom properties) used to represent the annotation. The main benefit in this seemingly extra bit of indirection is that it allows the annotation model to be small and to use few resources, so there can be a lot of annotations on one map.

Creating a custom annotation, such as a hyperlink, an image, or a movie, involves creating a subclass of MKAnnotationView. Map Kit provides a subclass for us for one type of annotation, a pushpin. A pushpin annotation looks like a thumbtack stuck into the map (see Figure 22.1) and is implemented by the MKPinAnnotationView class. Adding annotations to a map view without implementing the mapView:viewForAnnotations method of the MKMapViewDelegate protocol and returning an MKAnnotationView results in the MKPinAnnotationView being used. This is exactly what we want for the ChapelHill application, which will use thumbtacks for annotations.

Map Kit provides us with half of the annotation implementation, the MKPinAnnotationView, but no default implementation of the MKAnnotation protocol is provided. We need to create one, as follows:

1. Right-click on the Classes group in Xcode and chose Add, New File from the context menu.

2. Click the Cocoa Touch Class group and the Objective-C class template, and then click the Next button.

3. Name the class **MapPin.h** and make sure the Also Create "MapPin.m" check box is checked.

4. Click the Finish button.

5. Click the MapPin.h file in the Classes group.

6. Update the class to import both Map Kit and Core Location frameworks and to implement the MKAnnotation protocol, which consists of three properties: coordinate, subtitle, and title.

7. In addition to the three properties, add an initializer that takes all three properties as arguments so that we can easily create new instances. The code looks like Listing 22.4.

LISTING 22.4

```
#import <Foundation/Foundation.h>
#import <MapKit/MapKit.h>
#import <CoreLocation/CoreLocation.h>

@interface MapPin : NSObject <MKAnnotation> {

    CLLocationCoordinate2D coordinate;
    NSString *subtitle;
    NSString *title;

}

@property (nonatomic, readonly) CLLocationCoordinate2D coordinate;
@property (nonatomic, readonly) NSString *title;
@property (nonatomic, readonly) NSString *subtitle;

-(id)initWithCoordinates:(CLLocationCoordinate2D)location
            placeName: placeName
         description:description;

@end
```

8. The implementation of the MapPin class is very simple; it synthesizes the three properties, sets their values in the initializer, and does the requisite memory management. Click the MapPin.m file in the Classes group and update it as shown in Listing 22.5.

LISTING 22.5

```
#import "MapPin.h"

@implementation MapPin

@synthesize coordinate;
@synthesize title;
@synthesize subtitle;

-(id)initWithCoordinates:(CLLocationCoordinate2D)location
              placeName: placeName
            description:description {

    self = [super init];
    if (self != nil) {
        coordinate = location;
        title = placeName;
        [title retain];
        subtitle = description;
        [subtitle retain];
    }
    return self;

}

-(void)dealloc {
    [title release];
    [subtitle release];
    [super dealloc];
}

@end
```

9. Now that we have both parts of the annotations, the last step is to actually add the annotations to the map view with its addAnnotation method. We can do this in the view controller's viewDidLoad method, the same place we constrained the view's region. We'll do it in a separate method that we'll call, so add a method definition to the MapViewController.h file in the Classes group:

   ```
   -(void)addAnnotations;
   ```

10. To implement the method, create coordinates from the latitude and longitude of the place and provide a title and a description. Longitude and latitude can be geocoded from an address using various online services such as the service at gpsvisualizer.com/geocode. The MKPinAnnotationView displays each annotation as a graphical thumbtack, and when the user touches it the title and subtitle are displayed (see Figure 22.10). The code to add six annotations to the map view looks like this:

```objc
-(void)addAnnotations {

    // Normally read the data for these from the file system or a Web service
    CLLocationCoordinate2D coordinate = {35.9077803, -79.0454936};
    MapPin *pin = [[MapPin alloc]initWithCoordinates:coordinate
                                           placeName:@"Keenan Stadium"
                                         description:@"Tar Heel Football"];
    [self.map addAnnotation:pin];
    [pin release];

    coordinate.latitude = 35.910777;
    coordinate.longitude = -79.048412;
    pin = [[MapPin alloc]initWithCoordinates:coordinate
                                   placeName:@"Davis Library"
                                 description:@"Main Campus Library"];
    [self.map addAnnotation:pin];
    [pin release];

    coordinate.latitude = 35.9131808;
    coordinate.longitude = -79.0557201;
    pin = [[MapPin alloc]initWithCoordinates:coordinate
                                  placeName:@"Spanky's"
                                description:@"Spanky's Restaurant"];
    [self.map addAnnotation:pin];
    [pin release];

    coordinate.latitude = 35.9639089;
    coordinate.longitude = -79.0567349;
    pin = [[MapPin alloc]initWithCoordinates:coordinate
                                  placeName:@"Sage"
                                description:@"Sage Vegetarian Cafe"];
    [self.map addAnnotation:pin];
    [pin release];

    coordinate.latitude = 35.914687;
    coordinate.longitude = -79.051539;
    pin = [[MapPin alloc]initWithCoordinates:coordinate
                                  placeName:@"Planetarium"
                        description:@"Morehead Planetarium & Science Center"];
    [self.map addAnnotation:pin];
    [pin release];

    coordinate.latitude = 35.9130572;
    coordinate.longitude = -79.055671;
    pin = [[MapPin alloc]initWithCoordinates:coordinate
                                  placeName:@"Art Museum"
                                description:@"Ackland Art Museum"];
    [self.map addAnnotation:pin];
    [pin release];

}
```

FIGURE 22.10
Annotations of points of interest on the zoomed-in map.

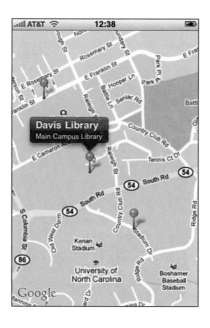

By the Way

For this example, we have hard-coded the annotations. A more complete application would probably load the coordinates and descriptions from the file system (see Hour 16, "Reading and Writing Data") so that annotations could be updated without changing code. Another option is to load the coordinates and descriptions from a web service so that they can be updated each time the application is run, without the user needing to download a new version of the application from the iTunes Store. The network service approach opens up the possibility for showing annotations for new events that come up after the application is published such as special events, recent car accidents, or homes for sale.

You probably expect me to say it's important to remember the steps we took to use Map Kit: We added a MKMapView to our view in Interface Builder, we set some attributes on the map view, and then we wrote some code to constrain the region and add some annotations. I won't say that, however, because to really appreciate Map Kit, it's more important to remember all the things that we didn't do. We never wrote code to use Core Location to show the user's position move across the map. We never wrote code to allow the user to pinch to zoom, or swipe to move the map. We never wrote code to make network requests to download map images, and we never did a single image manipulation or calculation using longitude or latitude. Map Kit and Core Location did all these things and more on our behalf. These are two truly powerful frameworks that put sophisticated, location-aware mapping software into the hands of every iPhone developer.

The Compass

The iPhone 3GS is the first iPhone OS device to include a magnetic compass. The compass is used in Apple's Compass application and in the Maps application (to orient the map to the direction you are facing). The compass can also be accessed programmatically with the iPhone SDK.

Location Manager and Location Manager Delegate

The location manager includes a `headingAvailable` property that indicates if the device is equipped with a magnetic compass. If the value is YES, you can use Core Location to retrieve heading information. Receiving heading events works very similarly to receiving location update events. To start receiving heading events, assign a location manager delegate, assign a filter for how frequently you want to receive updates (measured in degrees of change in heading), and call the `startUpdatingHeading` method on the location manager.

> There isn't one true north. Geographic north is fixed at the North Pole, and magnetic north is located hundreds of miles away and moves every day. A magnetic compass will always point to magnetic north, but some electronic compasses, like the one in the iPhone 3GS, can be programmed to point to geographic north instead. Usually, when we are dealing with maps and compasses together, geographic north is more useful. Make sure you understand the difference between geographic and magnetic north and know which one you need for your application. If you are going to use the heading relative to geographic north (the `trueHeading` property), request location updates as well as heading updates from the location manager or the `trueHeading` property won't be properly set.

Watch Out!

The location manager delegate protocol defines the methods for receiving heading updates. There are two methods in the delegate relating to headings: `locationManager:didUpdateHeading` and `locationManager:ShouldDisplayHeadingCalibration`.

The `locationManager:didUpdateHeading` method's argument is a `CLHeading` object. The `CLHeading` object makes the heading reading available with a set of properties: the `magneticHeading`, the `trueHeading` (see the Watch Out above), a `headingAccuracy` confidence measure, a `timestamp` of when the reading occurred, and an English language `description` that is more suitable for logging than showing to a user.

The locationManager:ShouldDisplayHeadingCalibration has the delegate return a YES or NO indicating if the location manager can display a calibration prompt to the user. The prompt asks the user to step away from any source of interference and to rotate the phone 360 degrees. The compass is always self-calibrating, and this prompt is just to help that process along after the compass receives wildly fluctuating readings. It's reasonable to implement this method to return NO if the calibration prompt would be annoying or distracting to the user at that point in the application, in the middle of data entry or game play for example.

> The iPhone Simulator will report that headings are available and it will provide just one heading update.

As an example of using the compass, we are going to enhance the ChapelHill application and provide the user with a left, right, or straight ahead arrow that will get them pointed toward Chapel Hill.

Add Outlets and Properties

To implement the new functionality, the ChapelHillViewController needs an outlet to a UIImageView to show the appropriate arrow, and needs a property to store the most recent location. We need to store the most recent location because we'll be doing a calculation on each heading update that uses the current location. During a header update, the location manager delegate receives only the new CLHeading and not a CLLocation. Click the ChapelHillViewController.h file in the Classes group and add an IBOutlet to a UIImageView, a property for the most recent CLLocation the controller received from location updates, and the method we will implement to calculate the heading to Chapel Hill called headingToLocation:current. Update the file as shown in Listing 22.6.

LISTING 22.6

```
#import <UIKit/UIKit.h>
#import <CoreLocation/CoreLocation.h>

@interface ChapelHillViewController : UIViewController
    <CLLocationManagerDelegate> {

        CLLocationManager *locMan;
        CLLocation *recentLocation;
        IBOutlet UILabel *distanceLabel;
        IBOutlet UIView  *distanceView;
        IBOutlet UIView  *waitView;
        IBOutlet UIImageView *directionArrow;

}
```

LISTING 22.6   Continued

```
@property (assign, nonatomic) CLLocationManager *locMan;
@property (retain, nonatomic) CLLocation *recentLocation;
@property (retain, nonatomic) UILabel *distanceLabel;
@property (retain, nonatomic) UIView *distanceView;
@property (retain, nonatomic) UIView *waitView;
@property (retain, nonatomic) UIView *directionArrow;

-(void)startMapViewSwitchTimer;
-(void)mapViewSwitch;

-(double)headingToLocation:(CLLocationCoordinate2D)desired
                  current:(CLLocationCoordinate2D)current;

@end
```

Click on the ChapelHillViewController.m file in the Classes group and synthesize the
two new properties and release them in the dealloc method.

Lay Out the UI and Add the Arrow Images

Click on the ChapelHillViewController.xib file in the Resources group to open
Interface Builder, and then complete the following steps:

1. Open the Library (Shift+Command+L) and search for "image." Drag a
   UIImageView onto the view.

2. Click the image view and open the Size Inspector (Command+3). Set the width
   (W) attribute to 150 pixels and the height (H) attribute to 150 pixels.

3. Open the Attribute Inspector (Command+1). Hide the image view by clicking
   the check box for the Hidden attribute.

4. Click the image view in the view and drag it to the top sizing guide and then
   center it horizontally. The image view should now be just above the view that
   contains the activity indicator. If these two views overlap, drag the view with
   the activity indicator down. The UI should now look like Figure 22.11.

5. Open the NIB and right-click the File's Owner icon. Click and drag from the
   directionArrow outlet to the image view. Save the XIB file and return to
   Xcode.

The sample source code for the ChapelHill application contains three arrow images:
arrow_up.png, arrow_right.png, and arrow_left.png. Drag these three images into
the Images group and be sure to check the Copy Items into Destination Group's
Folder check box in the copy dialog. (You can create your own 150x150 images for
the three arrows if you don't have the sample code from this chapter.)

FIGURE 22.11
ChapelHill appli-
cation UI in
Interface
Builder.

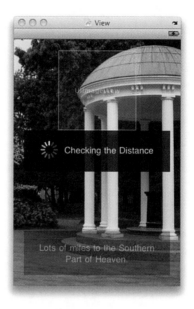

Request Heading Updates and Store the Current Location

Before asking for heading updates, check with the location manager to see whether heading updates are available. (The hardware compass is present on the device.) If heading updates aren't available, the arrow images will never be shown and the ChapelHill application works just as before. If headingAvailable returns YES, set the heading filter to 2 degrees of precision and start the updates with startUpdatingHeading. Modify the viewDidLoad method of the ChapelHillViewController.m file as follows:

```
- (void)viewDidLoad {
    [super viewDidLoad];

    locMan = [[CLLocationManager alloc] init];
    locMan.delegate = self;
    locMan.desiredAccuracy = kCLLocationAccuracyThreeKilometers;
    locMan.distanceFilter = 1609; // a mile
    [locMan startUpdatingLocation];
    if (locMan.headingAvailable) {
        locMan.headingFilter = 2; // 2 degrees
        [locMan startUpdatingHeading];
    }

}
```

As was previously mentioned, we now need to store the current location whenever we get an updated location from Core Location so that we can use the most recent

location in the heading calculations. Add a line to set the recentLocation property
we created to the newLocation in the locationManager:didUpdateLocation:
fromLocation method of the ChapelHillViewController.m file:

```
- (void)locationManager:(CLLocationManager *)manager
    didUpdateToLocation:(CLLocation *)newLocation
           fromLocation:(CLLocation *)oldLocation {

    if (newLocation.horizontalAccuracy >= 0) {

        // Store the location for use during heading updates
        self.recentLocation = newLocation;

        CLLocation *chapelHill = [[[CLLocation alloc]
                            initWithLatitude:kChapelHillLatitude
                            longitude:kChapelHillLongitude] autorelease];
        CLLocationDistance delta = [chapelHill getDistanceFrom: newLocation];
        long miles = (delta * 0.000621371) + 0.5; // meters to rounded miles
        if (miles < 3) {
            // Turn of the location manager updates
            [manager stopUpdatingLocation];
            [manager stopUpdatingHeading];

            // Show the map view after a delay
            [self startMapViewSwitchTimer];

            // Congratulate the user
            distanceLabel.text = @"Enjoy the\nSouthern Part of Heaven!";
        } else {
            NSNumberFormatter *commaDelimited = [[[NSNumberFormatter alloc]
                                            init] autorelease];
            [commaDelimited setNumberStyle:NSNumberFormatterDecimalStyle];
            distanceLabel.text = [NSString stringWithFormat:
                            @"%@ miles to the\nSouthern Part of Heaven",
                            [commaDelimited stringFromNumber:
                            [NSNumber numberWithLong:miles]]];
        }
        waitView.hidden = YES;
        distanceView.hidden = NO;
    }
}
```

Calculate the Heading to Chapel Hill

In the previous two sections, we were able to avoid doing calculations with latitude
and longitude. This time, it will require just a bit of computation on our part to get
a heading to Chapel Hill, and then to decide whether that heading is straight ahead
or requires the user to spin to the right or to the left.

Given two locations such as the user's current location and the location of Chapel
Hill, it is possible to use some basic geometry of the sphere to calculate the initial
heading the user would need to use to reach Chapel Hill. A search of the Internet

quickly finds the formula in pseudo-code (copied here in the comment), and from that pseudo-code we can easily implement the algorithm in Objective-C and provide the heading. Add the `headingToLocation:current` method in the ChapelHillViewController.m file as follows:

```
/*
 * According to Ask Dr. Math:
 * http://mathforum.org/library/drmath/view/55417.html
 * Reproduced with permission from Drexel University,
 * copyright 2009 by The Math Forum @ Drexel (http://mathforum.org/).
 * All rights reserved.
 *
 * y = sin(lon2-lon1)*cos(lat2)
 * x = cos(lat1)*sin(lat2)-sin(lat1)*cos(lat2)*cos(lon2-lon1)
 * if y > 0 then
 *    if x > 0 then tc1 = arctan(y/x)
 *    if x < 0 then tc1 = 180 - arctan(-y/x)
 *    if x = 0 then tc1 = 90
 * if y < 0 then
 *    if x > 0 then tc1 = -arctan(-y/x)
 *    if x < 0 then tc1 = arctan(y/x)-180
 *    if x = 0 then tc1 = 270
 *    if y = 0 then
 * if x > 0 then tc1 = 0
 *    if x < 0 then tc1 = 180
 *    if x = 0 then [the 2 points are the same]
 */
-(double)headingToLocation:(CLLocationCoordinate2D)desired
                  current:(CLLocationCoordinate2D)current {

    // Gather the variables needed by the heading algorithm
    double lat1 = current.latitude;
    double lat2 = desired.latitude;
    double lon1 = current.longitude;
    double lon2 = desired.longitude;
    double y = sin(lon2-lon1)*cos(lat2);
    double x = cos(lat1)*sin(lat2) - sin(lat1)*cos(lat2)*cos(lon2-lon1);

    double heading = -1;
    if (y > 0) {
        if (x > 0) heading = atan(y/x);
        else if (x < 0) heading = 180 - atan((-1 * y)/x);
        else heading = 90;
    } else if (y < 0) {
        if (x > 0) heading = -1 * atan((-1 * y)/x);
        else if (x < 0) heading = atan(y/x) - 180;
        else heading = 270;
    } else {
        if (x > 0) heading = 0;
        else heading = 180;
    }
    return heading;
}
```

The ChapelHillViewController class implements the
CLLocationManagerDelegate protocol, and as you learned above, one of the
optional methods of this protocol, locationManager:didUpdateHeading, provides
us heading updates anytime the heading changes by more degrees than the
headingFilter amount.

For each heading update our delegate receives, use the user's current location to calculate the heading to Chapel Hill, and then compare the desired heading to the
user's current heading, and finally display the correct arrow image: left, right, or
straight ahead.

For these heading calculations to be meaningful, we need to have the current location and some confidence in the accuracy of the reading of the user's current heading. Check these two conditions in an if statement before performing the heading
calculations. If this sanity check does not pass, just hide the directionArrow.

Because this heading to Chapel Hill feature is more of a novelty than a true source
of directions (unless you happen to be a bird or in an airplane), there is no need to
be overly precise. Use +/-10 degrees from the true heading to Chapel Hill as close
enough to display the straight ahead arrow. If the difference is greater than 10
degrees, display the left or right arrow based on whichever way would result in a
shorter turn to get to the desired heading. Implement the
locationManager:didUpdateHeading method in the ChapelHillViewController.m
file as follows:

```
- (void)locationManager:(CLLocationManager *)manager
       didUpdateHeading:(CLHeading *)newHeading {

   if (self.recentLocation != nil && newHeading.headingAccuracy >= 0) {
       CLLocation *chapelHill = [[[CLLocation alloc]
                                 initWithLatitude:kChapelHillLatitude
                                 longitude:kChapelHillLongitude] autorelease];
       double course = [self headingToLocation:chapelHill.coordinate
                                       current:recentLocation.coordinate];
       double delta = newHeading.trueHeading - course;
       if (abs(delta) <= 10) {
          directionArrow.image = [UIImage imageNamed:@"up_arrow.png"];
       } else {
          if (delta > 180) directionArrow.image =
                              [UIImage imageNamed:@"right_arrow.png"];
          else if (delta > 0) directionArrow.image =
              [UIImage imageNamed:@"left_arrow.png"];
          else if (delta > -180) directionArrow.image =
              [UIImage imageNamed:@"right_arrow.png"];
          else directionArrow.image = [UIImage imageNamed:@"left_arrow.png"];
       }
       directionArrow.hidden = NO;
   } else {
       directionArrow.hidden = YES;
   }

}
```

Build and run the project. If you have a device equipped with an electromagnetic compass, you can now spin around in your office chair and see the arrow images change to show you the heading to Chapel Hill. If you don't have a device with a compass, you can run the updated ChapelHill application in the iPhone Simulator and you will have an arrow pointing to the right as a result of the simulator's one simulated heading update (see Figure 22.12).

FIGURE 22.12
The completed ChapelHill application running in the iPhone Simulator.

Summary

In this hour, we worked with two powerful toolkits, Core Location and Map Kit. As we saw in the example application, these two toolkits are often used together to deliver the functionality of a location-aware iPhone application.

In the example application, we used the location manager to receive updates on the user's location and heading, we performed calculations on the distance and heading to a location, we showed a map of a particular spot, and put informative thumbtack annotations on the map. Pretty good work for just an hour!

Q&A

Q. *How can I show the user an address on the map, if I don't know the address ahead of time?*

A. The process of going from an address to map coordinates is called forward geolocation. In the examples in this chapter, we did the forward geolocating ahead of time and included the map coordinates in the application. Map Kit provides reverse geolocation (getting an address for coordinates), but forward geolocation capability is absent from the current implementation of Map Kit. There are web services available that you can use from your application to forward geolocate. A popular service with iPhone developers is at CloudMade.com.

Q. *Can I use Core Location and Map Kit to provide turn-by-turn directions in my application?*

A. Yes and no. You can use Core Location and Map Kit as part of a solution for turn-by-turn directions, and many developers do this, but they are not sufficiently functional on their own, and there are terms of services conditions that prohibit you from using the Google-provided map tiles in an application that provides turn-by-turn directions. In short, you'll need to license some additional data to provide this type of capability.

Workshop

Quiz

1. What are geolocation, forward geolocation, and reverse geolocation?

2. What can be done to limit the drain on battery life when using Core Location?

3. Explain the role of these important classes: `CLLocationManager`, `CLLocationManagerDelegate`, `CLLocation`, `MKMapKitView`, `MKAnnotationView`, `MKAnnotation`?

Answers

1. Geolocation is using network connectivity to identify the location of a mobile device. Forward geolocation is determining map coordinates from an address. Reverse geolocation is determining an address from map coordinates.

2. Use the `distanceFilter` and `headingFilter` properties of `CLLocationManager` to only get updates as frequently as your application can benefit from them. Use the `stopUpdatingLocation` and `stopUpdatingHeading` methods of `CLLocationManager` to stop receiving the updates as soon as you no longer need them.

3. A `CLLocationManager` instance provides the basis of the interaction with Core Location services. A location manager delegate, implementing the `CLLocationManegerDelegate` protocol, is set on the `CLLocationManager` instance, and that delegate receives location/heading updates. Location updates come in the form of a pair of `CLLocation` objects, one providing the coordinates of the previous location, and the other providing the coordinates of the new location. An `MKMapKitView` shows a map that the user can interact with. The map can include annotations, which implement the `MKAnnotation` protocol and are displayed with an `MKAnnotationView`.

Activities

1. Adopt the ChapelHill application to be a guide for your favorite spot in the world. At a minimum, you'll want to change all the text and images and map annotations, but also ask yourself whether the feature set is right for your particular place? What place-specific spin could you add to make the application better fit its location?

2. The thumbtack annotation may be in danger of becoming a little overused. Read up on the `MKAnnotationView` and provide an alternative view for your annotations. Maybe include a custom graphic or photographic image? Or use what you learned in Hour 20, "Working with Rich Media," to include a movie.

Further Exploration

The most significant part of these frameworks that we did not utilize is Map Kit's reverse geolocation functionality. You can learn about this capability in the "MapKit Framework Reference" in the iPhone Reference Library.

HOUR 23

Application Debugging and Optimization

What You'll Learn in this Hour:

▶ Debugging in Xcode
▶ Monitoring with Instruments
▶ Profiling with Shark

Despite our best efforts, no application is ever bug-free. The ability to find and eliminate bugs quickly is an essential skill.

This hour covers the debugging, tracing, and profiling tools included in the iPhone SDK. You'll learn how to use Xcode's debugger to find and correct errors. We also delve into the Instruments and Shark tools to profile an application's resource usage and performance. This potent combination of tools can help you deliver applications that run more efficiently and with fewer bugs.

> With the term *debugging*, it is assumed your project builds with no errors but then encounters an error or otherwise fails to work as designed when it's executed. If there is an error in your code that prevents it from building, then you are still coding, not debugging. The tools in this hour are for improving applications that build but then have errors or resource-utilization problems.

Watch Out!

Debugging in Xcode

Xcode brings together the five basic tools of the software developer's trade into a single application: the text editor, compiler, linker, debugger, and reference documentation. Xcode has debugging tools integrated within it, and so all your debugging activities can take place from within the now-familiar confines of Xcode.

Debugging with NSLog

The first, and most primitive, debugging tool in your Xcode arsenal is the humble NSLog function. Many a gnarly bug has been slain with just this function alone. At any point in your application, you can embed a call to NSLog to confirm the flow of your application into and out of methods or to check the current value of a variable. Any statement you log with NSLog is echoed to Xcode's Debugger Console. The Debugger Console appears when you run your application from Xcode. If it doesn't appear, or if you've closed the Debugger Console window, you can get it back at anytime with the Run, Console menu option or by pressing Command+Shift+R.

The NSLog function takes an NSString argument that can optionally contain string format specifiers. NSLog then takes a variable number of arguments that are inserted into the string at the location of the specifiers. This is colloquially known as "printf style" from the C printf function.

A string format specifier is nothing more than a percent sign (%) followed by one or two characters. The characters after the % sign indicate the type of the variable that will be displayed. You can get the full list of string format specifiers from the "String Format Specifier" section of the *String Programming Guide for Cocoa* in Xcode's Help. Three string format specifiers to learn and know are %i for integers (often used to debug loop counters and array offsets), %f for floats, and %@ for any Objective-C object, including NSString objects. Here are a few examples of typical NSLog function calls:

```
NSLog(@"Entering method");

int foo = 42;
float bar = 99.9;
NSLog(@"Value of foo: %i, Value of bar: %f", foo, bar);

NSString *name = [[NSString alloc]initWithString: @"Prince"];
NSDate *date = [NSDate distantPast];
NSLog(@"Value of name: %@, Value of date: %@", name, date);
[name release];
```

And here is what the output from these calls looks like in the Debugger Console:

```
2009-07-12 06:22:50.855 Logger[56095:20b] Entering method
2009-07-12 06:22:50.858 Logger[56095:20b] Value of foo: 42, Value of bar:
99.900002
2009-07-12 06:22:50.882 Logger[56095:20b] Value of name: Prince, Value of date:
0001-12-31
```

Did you Know?

When the %@ string format specifier is used with an Objective-C object, the object's description method is called. Many of Apple's classes include an implementation of description that is useful for debugging. If you need to debug your own objects with NSLog, you can implement description, which returns an NSString variable.

Watch Out!

As its name implies, the NSLog function is actually intended for logging, not debugging. In addition to printing the statements to Xcode's console, the statements are written out to a file on the file system. Logging to the file system is not what you're intending, it's just a side effect of using NSLog for debugging. It's easy to accidentally leave old NSLog statements in your code after you've finished debugging, which means your application is taking time to write out statements to the file system and is wasting space on the user's device. Search through your project and remove or comment old NSLog statements in your application before you build a release to distribute.

Building a Project for Debugging

NSLog is a good quick-and-dirty approach to debugging, but it is not the best tool for debugging more complex issues. It's often more productive to use a debugger, which is a tool that lets you examine a running program and inspect its state. It's been said that what separates true software development professionals from weekend hackers is the ability to proficiently use a debugger. If this statement is true, then you are in luck, because using Xcode's debugger is not hard.

Normally an application executes at computer speeds, which on an iPhone is millions of instructions per second. A debugger acts like the developer's brake, slowing the progress of the application down to human speeds and letting the developer control the progress of the program from one instruction to the next. At each step in the program, the developer can use the debugger to examine the values of the variables in the program to help determine what's gone wrong.

Debuggers work on the machine instructions that are compiled from an application's source code. With a source-level debugger, however, the compiler provides data to the debugger about which lines of source code generated which instructions. Using this data, the source-level debugger insulates the developer from the machine instructions generated by the compiler and lets the developer work with the source code he has written.

Xcode's debugger, called gdb (GNU Debugger), is a source-level debugger. The compiler doesn't always generate the data needed for source-level debugging. It can amount to a lot of data, and it provides no benefit to an application's users, so the data is not generated in a release build configuration. Before you can benefit from source-level debugging, you need to build your application in a debug build configuration that will generate the debug symbols.

By default, a new Xcode project comes with two build configurations, Debug and Release. The Debug build configuration includes debug symbols, whereas the Release build configuration does not. Whenever you are working on developing your application, it makes sense to use the Debug configuration so that you can drop into the debugger whenever you need to. Because Debug is usually the build configuration you want to work with, it's the default configuration, too. To switch back and forth between the Debug and Release configurations, use the Active Build Configuration drop-down menu (see Figure 23.1) or use the Project, Set Active Build Configuration, Debug menu option.

FIGURE 23.1
The Active Build Configuration drop-down menu.

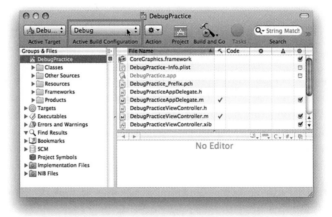

Watch Out!

Make sure you remember to use the Release build configuration when you create a version of your application for distribution. See Hour 24, "Distributing Applications Through the App Store," for details on preparing your application for distribution.

Setting Breakpoints and Stepping Through Code

Create a new Xcode project with the View-Based Application template and call it **DebuggerPractice**. Many of Xcode's debugging features are located in the gutter (see Figure 23.2), so it's important that it be displayed. The debugger frequently references source code line numbers, and it is helpful to have these displayed in the gutter. If you don't see the gutter or if your gutter is not displaying line numbers, open the Xcode, Preferences menu and check the Show Gutter and Show Line Numbers check boxes in the Text Editing tab (see Figure 23.3).

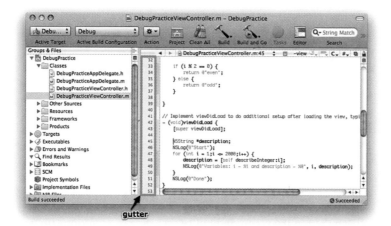

FIGURE 23.2
Xcode's gutter.

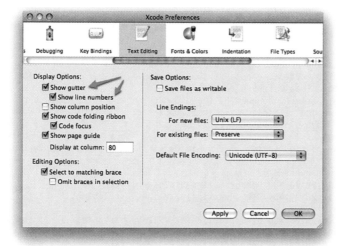

FIGURE 23.3
Show the gutter and line numbers in Xcode Preferences.

Open the DebugPracticeViewController.m file in the Classes group and uncomment the viewDidLoad method. Add a loop that uses NSLog to display the numbers between 1 and 10 in Xcode's Debugger Console. Add a describeInteger method with a conditional to return a string that describes the number as odd or even, as shown here:

```
-(NSString *)describeInteger:(int)i {

    if (i % 2 == 0) {
        return @"even";
```

```
    } else {
        return0 @"odd";
    }

}

// Implement viewDidLoad to do additional setup after loading the view,
typically from a NIB.
- (void)viewDidLoad {
    [super viewDidLoad];

    NSString *description;

    NSLog(@"Start");
    for (int i = 1;i <= 10;i++) {
        description = [self describeInteger:i];
        NSLog(@"Variables: i - %i and description - %@", i, description);
    }
    NSLog(@"Done");
}
```

Select Run, Debug from the menu and notice that the program starts up and brings us to our application's empty view. The output from our NSLog statements are in the Debugger Console. There is some extra, unbolded output in the Debugger Console from gdb, and a gdb prompt, but nothing else indicates that we are running in the debugger:

```
[Session started at 2009-07-12 10:27:58 -0400.]
GNU gdb 6.3.50-20050815 (Apple version gdb-966) (Tue Mar 10 02:43:13 UTC 2009)
Copyright 2004 Free Software Foundation, Inc.
GDB is free software, covered by the GNU General Public License, and you are
welcome to change it and/or distribute copies of it under certain conditions.
Type "show copying" to see the conditions.
There is absolutely no warranty for GDB.  Type "show warranty" for details.
This GDB was configured as "i386-apple-darwin".sharedlibrary apply-load-rules
all
Attaching to process 57871.
2009-07-12 10:28:00.433 DebugPractice[57871:20b] Start
2009-07-12 10:28:00.434 DebugPractice[57871:20b] Variables: i - 1 and
description - odd
2009-07-12 10:28:00.435 DebugPractice[57871:20b] Variables: i - 2 and
description - even
2009-07-12 10:28:00.435 DebugPractice[57871:20b] Variables: i - 3 and
description - odd
2009-07-12 10:28:00.436 DebugPractice[57871:20b] Variables: i - 4 and
description - even
2009-07-12 10:28:00.436 DebugPractice[57871:20b] Variables: i - 5 and
description - odd
2009-07-12 10:28:00.437 DebugPractice[57871:20b] Variables: i - 6 and
description - even
2009-07-12 10:28:00.437 DebugPractice[57871:20b] Variables: i - 7 and
description - odd
2009-07-12 10:28:00.437 DebugPractice[57871:20b] Variables: i - 8 and
description - even
2009-07-12 10:28:00.438 DebugPractice[57871:20b] Variables: i - 9 and
description - odd
```

```
2009-07-12 10:28:00.438 DebugPractice[57871:20b] Variables: i - 10 and
description - even
2009-07-12 10:28:00.439 DebugPractice[57871:20b] Done
(gdb)
```

The gdb debugger is running; we just haven't told it that we want it to do anything.
To use the debugger, we need to interrupt it and get its attention. Press Control+C in
the Debugger Console to start an interactive prompt with the debugger. Type **help** at
the prompt and press enter. You get a list of the topics you can get additional help
for. Type **help data** to see a list of debugger commands you can use for inspecting
application data. Try executing some of these commands. Some of what you'll find
is obscure, and all of it may not make sense at first, but take a little time to read the
help and explore gdb from the interactive prompt. You won't hurt anything by taking a guess and typing in what you think makes sense:

```
(gdb) help
List of classes of commands:

aliases -- Aliases of other commands
breakpoints -- Making program stop at certain points
data -- Examining data
files -- Specifying and examining files
internals -- Maintenance commands
obscure -- Obscure features
running -- Running the program
stack -- Examining the stack
status -- Status inquiries
support -- Support facilities
tracepoints -- Tracing of program execution without stopping the program
user-defined -- User-defined commands

Type "help" followed by a class name for a list of commands in that class.
Type "help" followed by command name for full documentation.
Command name abbreviations are allowed if unambiguous.
(gdb) help data
Examining data.

List of commands:

append -- Append target code/data to a local file
call -- Call a function in the program
delete display -- Cancel some expressions to be displayed when program stops
delete mem -- Delete memory region
disable display -- Disable some expressions to be displayed when program stops
disable mem -- Disable memory region
disassemble -- Disassemble a specified section of memory
display -- Print value of expression EXP each time the program stops
dump -- Dump target code/data to a local file
enable display -- Enable some expressions to be displayed when program stops
enable mem -- Enable memory region
inspect -- Same as "print" command
mem -- Define attributes for memory region
output -- Like "print" but don't put in value history and don't print newline
print -- Print value of expression EXP
```

```
print-object -- Ask an Objective-C object to print itself
printf -- Printf "printf format string"
ptype -- Print definition of type TYPE
restore -- Restore the contents of FILE to target memory
set -- Evaluate expression EXP and assign result to variable VAR
set variable -- Evaluate expression EXP and assign result to variable VAR
undisplay -- Cancel some expressions to be displayed when program stops
whatis -- Print data type of expression EXP
x -- Examine memory: x/FMT ADDRESS

Type "help" followed by command name for full documentation.
Command name abbreviations are allowed if unambiguous.
(gdb)
```

You can use gdb from the Debugger Console in this fashion, and some experienced
debuggers do, but this isn't the way you'll usually be interacting with the debugger.
Many of the important functions of gdb are accessible indirectly via Xcode. The
most common way to start interacting with the debugger is to set a breakpoint in
your application's source code.

Setting a Breakpoint

A breakpoint is an instruction to the debugger letting it know you want the program
execution to pause at that point. To set a breakpoint, click once in the gutter next to
the line where you want the application to pause. A breakpoint will appear as a
bright blue arrow (see Figure 23.4). Click the blue arrow to toggle the breakpoint off
and on. When the breakpoint is off, it is light blue and the debugger ignores it. To
remove a breakpoint, right-click it and select Remove Breakpoint from the context
menu.

FIGURE 23.4
Set a break-
point by clicking
in the gutter.

Let's create and use a breakpoint. Quit the execution of the application and click the gutter to set a breakpoint next to this line:

```
NSLog(@"Variables: i - %i and description - %@", i, description);
```

Click the Build and Run icon and notice that the application stops after printing just two log statements to the Debugger Console:

```
2009-07-12 10:19:39.933 DebugPractice[57829:20b] Start
2009-07-12 10:19:39.935 DebugPractice[57829:20b] Variables: i - 1 and
description - odd
```

The debugger has paused the execution of the application at our breakpoint (see Figure 23.5) and is awaiting further direction.

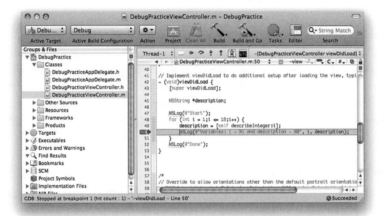

FIGURE 23.5
The debugger paused at a breakpoint.

Examining and Changing State

Now that the execution of the program is paused in the debugger, we can look at the value of any variables that are in scope. One of the easiest ways Xcode provides to examine variables is the debugger datatip. Simply hover over a variable in the source code of the paused method and Xcode will display a cascading pop-up menu (see Figure 23.6). The type, name, memory address, and value of the variable are displayed. Hover over the i loop counter and the description variable and look at the datatip. Notice that the datatip for i is just one level, but the datatip for the more complex NSString object has three levels. (Hover over the disclosure triangles to see the two additional levels.)

FIGURE 23.6
Datatip for the
description vari-
able.

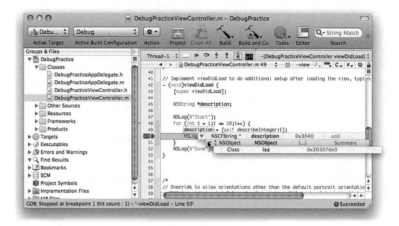

Datatips can also be used to change the value of a variable. Hover over the i variable and click the value. It is currently 2, but you can change it to 4 by typing **4** and
pressing Enter. The value in the running program is immediately changed, so this
trip through the loop will log to the console with a value of 4, and there won't be a
logged statement with a value of 2 or 3. To confirm that the program does execute
as if the i variable has a value of 4, we need to continue the execution of the program.

Stepping Through Code

By far, the most common debugging activity is watching the flow of your application and following what it does while it's running. To do this, you need to be able to
control the flow of execution, pausing at the interesting parts, and skipping over the
mundane.

The debugger provides four icons for controlling program execution (see
Figure 23.7):

▶ **Continue**: Resumes execution of the paused program, pausing again at the
next error or active breakpoint.

▶ **Step Over**: Steps to the next line of code in the same method.

▶ **Step Into**: Steps into the method that is being called. If a method isn't being
called on the current line of code, it acts like Step Over.

▶ **Step Out**: Steps out of the current method back to the caller of the current
method.

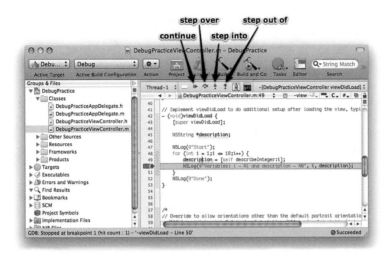

FIGURE 23.7
Program execution control icons.

Let's take a look at how each of these works to control the flow of our application. First click the Continue icon a couple of times. Control returns back to the same breakpoint each time you continue, but if you hover over the i and description variables, you'll see that i is incrementing and description is switching between even and odd.

Add a breakpoint to this line of code by clicking the gutter:

```
description = [self describeInteger:i];
```

Click the Continue icon again, and this time you'll see the program stops at the new breakpoint because it's the next breakpoint the program encounters. This breakpoint is on a line of source where we are calling the describeInteger method. If we want to see what's going on inside that method, we need to step into it. Click the Step Into icon, and the program stops on the first line of the describeInteger method (see Figure 23.8).

To step line by line through a method without entering any of the methods that might be called, use the step over task. Click the Step Over icon three times to step through the describeInteger method and return to the viewDidLoad method.

Click the Continue icon to return to the breakpoint on the describeInteger method, and click the Step Into icon to step into the method a second time. This time, rather than stepping all the way through describeInteger, click the Step Out icon, and you'll be stopped back at the line where the describeInteger method was called. The rest of the describeInteger method still executed, you just didn't watch each step of it. You are stopped where the program flow has just exited the describeInteger method.

FIGURE 23.8
Program execu-
tion after step-
ping into the
describe-
Integer
method.

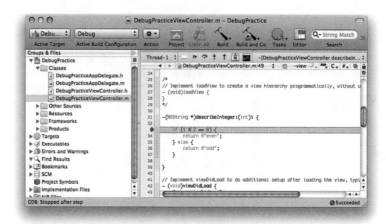

In addition to these four program control tasks, an important fifth option is hidden in the gutter. It's called Continue to Here. Continue to Here works on the line of code you select it on, and it works like a combination of the continue task and a temporary breakpoint. Program flow continues until it reaches an error, an active breakpoint, or it reaches the line of code you continued to.

To try this, right-click in the gutter next to this line:

```
NSLog(@"Done");
```

Click Continue to Here in the context menu (see Figure 23.9) and notice that we did-n't make it to the line of code we continued to; we stopped on one of the two existing breakpoints inside the for loop. Click each breakpoint once to make it inactive, and click Continue to Here on the gutter next to the final line of the method one more time. This time we make it to the end of the method. Inspect the i and description variables with the hover datatip and notice that description's value is even but i is no longer in scope and can't be inspected. The i variable was scoped only to the for loop, and now that we have exited the for loop, it no longer exists. You can now quit the application.

Setting a Watch Point

Let's suppose now that there is a tricky bug in your application that only occurs on the 1,000th time through the loop. You wouldn't want to put a breakpoint in the loop and have to click the continue icon 1,000 times! That's where a watchpoint comes in handy. A watchpoint is a conditional breakpoint; it doesn't stop execution every time, it only stops when a condition you define is true.

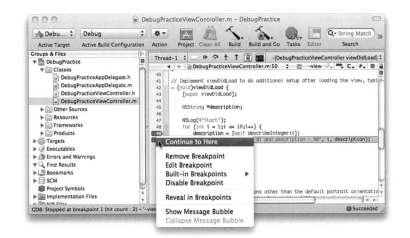

FIGURE 23.9
The Continue to
Here option of
the gutter con-
text menu.

To test this out, update the for loop to execute 2,000 times rather than 10 times:

```
// Implement viewDidLoad to do additional setup after loading the view,
typically from a nib.
- (void)viewDidLoad {
    [super viewDidLoad];

    NSString *description;

    NSLog(@"Start");
    for (int i = 1;i <= 2000;i++) {
        description = [self describeInteger:i];
        NSLog(@"Variables: i - %i and description - %@", i, description);
    }
    NSLog(@"Done");
}
```

Now let's set a watchpoint that'll stop execution when the loop counter is equal to 1,000. First, right-click the two existing breakpoints and remove them with the Remove Breakpoint option in the context menu. Add a normal breakpoint by clicking in the gutter next to this line:

```
NSLog(@"Start");
```

Right-click the gutter next to this line to add a watchpoint:

```
NSLog(@"Variables: i - %i and description - %@", i, description);
```

To add the watchpoint, click the Add & Edit Breakpoint menu option in the context menu. The Breakpoints Window will open and you'll see a table containing two breakpoints in the viewDidLoad method. There is a column called Condition. Click in the cell for this column in the second row and type **i == 1000** (see Figure 23.10).

FIGURE 23.10
Program execu-
tion after step-
ping into the
describe-
Integer
method.

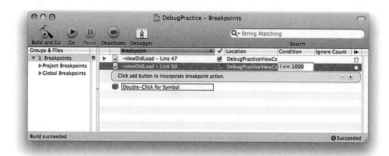

Click the Build and Run icon to execute the application. The program will stop at
the first breakpoint. Click the Continue icon and the application will go through the
loop 999 times before stopping on the watchpoint on the 1,000th trip through the
loop when the loop counter i is equal to 1,000. You can confirm this by looking at
the 999 log messages in the Debugger Console or by hovering over the i variable in
the source and looking at its value in the datatip.

Debugging in the Debugger View

We first looked at the debugger in the Debugger Console and since then we've been
debugging in the Text Editor window. There is also a window dedicated to debugging
that has some helpful benefits. With the application still paused on the 1,000th trip
through the loop, open the Debugger Window using the Run, Debugger menu
option (Shift+Command+Y).

The same options for controlling the program are present in this window, just with
much larger icons (see Figure 23.11). The window is divided into three panels. The
lower-middle panel is the same view we've been working with in the Text Editor and
so should be familiar. The upper-left panel is the application's call stack listed by
thread. A call stack is the list of all the subroutines (methods and functions) currently being executed.

Each method in the call stack has been called by the method below it. Notice that
the viewDidLoad method of our view controller is at the top of the stack and it was
called by the superclass's (UIViewController) view method. Also notice that two of
the methods, viewDidLoad and the app delegate's
applicationDidFinishLaunching, are listed in bold. The bold listing indicates the
debugger has source code symbols for those methods and can display them as
source. Click the row for the app delegate's applicationDidFinishLaunching
method and you'll see the code and you'll see that program execution is waiting for
this line of code to return from executing:

```
[window addSubview:viewController.view];
```

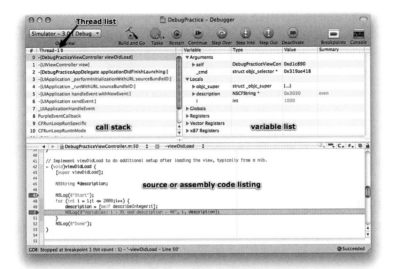

FIGURE 23.11
The Debugger
window.

The rows in the call stack that are not in bold are for methods where the debugger only has assembly language available. Click the row for the UIViewController's view method to see some assembly code. (Doesn't that make you thankful that we have the gdb source-level debugger?)

The upper-right panel contains the variable list. This is a list of all the variables that are in scope in the current method. Click back on the row in the call stack for the viewDidLoad method and you'll see that both the i and description variables we've been inspecting with datatips are listed in the variable list under the Locals disclosure (see Figure 23.11). The Locals designation means these variables are declared locally in the method. The other disclosure in the variable list that you'll be most interested in is the Arguments scope for variables that have been passed into the current method as arguments.

You've done enough now to start getting the hang of using the debugger. With just these few simple steps for controlling program flow and inspecting and changing program state, you are able to debug many of the issues you may run into.

Monitoring with Instruments

The next tool we'll look at is called Instruments. Instruments is used for profiling various aspects of an application, and helps you to understand the runtime behavior of the application and the iPhone OS.

Instruments is a flexible container for plug-ins (also known as instruments) that each record and display a different aspect of an application's behavior. You choose the instruments you want to use to capture the particular aspects of the application you want to examine. The user interface is modeled after timeline editors such as Apple's GarageBand and iMovie, with the different instruments forming a vertical list, and the time expanding horizontally left to right (see Figure 23.12).

Each execution of an application that is monitored by Instruments is called a run and contains all the traces collected by the various instruments. A trace document can contain the traces from multiple instruments across multiple runs. Typically you'll work with traces immediately, but you can also save trace documents and open them again later.

Tracing an Application

Let's take one common use for Instruments, memory leak detection, and walk through a scenario.

As a quick reminder, a memory leak occurs when memory is allocated by an application but never released. One of the instruments available in Instruments is a leak detector called Leaks. How does Leaks know when an application has leaked memory? It tracks all memory allocation by the application, and it tracks the pointers to that memory. At the point where an application no longer has a valid pointer to memory it has allocated, Leaks knows the application can never free the memory, and therefore a leak has occurred.

By the Way

> An application can simply use too much memory by never freeing the memory it allocates, even after it no longer needs it, but as long as a pointer to the memory exists in the application then there is at least the possibility that the application will free the memory, and so a leak does not yet exist. You'd use the Object Allocations instrument to detect this scenario of using too much memory without every actually leaking any. It's typical, when debugging memory issues, to use these two instruments together.

To test the Leaks instrument, we are going to purposely leak memory. Let's first trace the application as is to confirm there are no leaks yet. There are many ways to start a trace session with Instruments: You can run Instruments and have it launch the iPhone application on the device or in the simulator, or you can have Instruments attach to an already running application on the device or in the simulator.

By the Way

> Instruments.app is located in /Developer/Applications. You can launch it from there using Finder, or you can drag it to the Dock for quicker access.

For this scenario, we'll use a third and more straightforward method: launching Instruments from within Xcode. When launching Instruments from Xcode, we need to decide if we want to trace the application on the device or in the simulator. The device provides a much more accurate picture of how our application is going to perform and should be your default choice in most cases, but for the purposes of detecting leaks, the simulator works just fine, so let's trace from there.

Open the Debugger window with the Run, Debugger menu option (Shift+Command+Y) and use the Active SDK drop-down to target the iPhone Simulator. To launch the DebugPractice application in Instruments from Xcode, select Run, Start with Performance Tool, Leaks from the Xcode menu (see Figure 23.12).

FIGURE 23.12
Launching the application with Instruments tracing.

The Instruments application will launch, and it will start the DebugPractice application in the iPhone Simulator. Our boring gray application will display its boring gray interface in the simulator, and after the initial object allocations involved in getting the application started, displaying the UI, and iterating through our odd/even loop, there is no other activity for Instruments to trace.

When you are convinced of this, you can stop the application in the iPhone Simulator with the Home button. Notice that this also stops the trace session in Instruments. We've now completed one run in Instruments. Click the row for the Leaks instrument and you can see, as in Figure 23.13, that it has no leaks to report.

FIGURE 23.13
No leaks during
the first run.

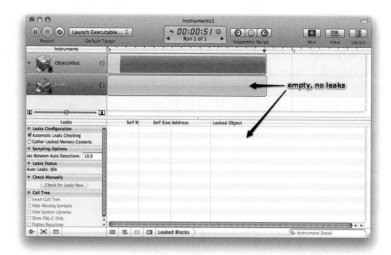

Now let's be nefarious and introduce a memory leak into the application. Allocate memory for a new string each time through the loop and let the pointer to the string go out of scope at the end of each loop iteration. Update the `viewDidLoad` method of the DebugPracticeViewController.m file as follows:

```
// Implement viewDidLoad to do additional setup after loading the view,
typically from a NIB.
- (void)viewDidLoad {
    [super viewDidLoad];

    NSString *description;

    NSLog(@"Start");
    for (int i = 1;i <= 2000;i++) {
        description = [self describeInteger:i];

        // Don't try this at home!
        NSString *status = [[NSString alloc]initWithUTF8String:"leaking"];

        NSLog(@"Variables: i - %i and description - %@ and status - %@",
            i, description, status);
    }
    NSLog(@"Done");
}
```

Now we are ready to give the application a second run. Because we last ran the application with Instruments, Xcode keeps that as the default. This time we can start the application with the Build and Run icon.

You can't use Xcode's gdb debugger and Instruments at the same time. Their use is mutually exclusive. When we run the DebugPractice application with Instruments tracing, breakpoints are ignored, and there is no output to the Debugger Console. Whereas Xcode's first option in the Run menu had been called Run, Go (Debug), after running with Instruments tracing, the default option becomes Run, Go (Leaks). To stop running with Instruments tracing and to go back to running in the debugger, use the Run, Debugger menu option.

Watch Out!

After about 10 seconds you'll see a red spike in the output of the leaks application (see Figure 23.14). This spike represents our leaking of 2,000 strings. After you see the spike you can stop the application with the iPhone Simulator's Home button.

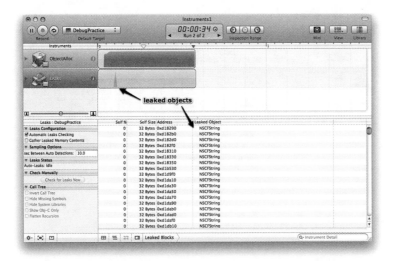

FIGURE 23.14
Oh no, in this run we are leaking like a sieve!

It didn't actually take 10 seconds for the DebugPractice application to leak the memory. This happened within the first second. The Leaks instrument is trying to keep out of the way of our application and is only sampling every 10 seconds; it was 10 seconds into the run before Leaks had its first chance to notice our leakage. We can increase or decrease the sample rate using the Sec. Between Auto Detections text box (see Figure 23.14). While the application is running, you can also force a check for leaks at any time by clicking the Check for Leaks Now button.

By the Way

Knowing we have leaked some objects is helpful, but unlike in this artificial case, we usually won't know where the leak is coming from. Remember that we said the Leaks instrument works by tracking all the application's memory allocations. The Leaks instrument knows where in the application we allocated the memory that was leaked.

Click the View drop-down list in the upper-right corner and select Extended Detail. This opens a new panel on the right of the Instruments application (see Figure 23.15). Now click the first leaked object in the list and you'll see a color-coded stack trace. The colors indicate the library that each method belongs to, and our application's code is purple. We can see that our application's DebugPracticeViewController's viewDidLoad method allocated the leaked NSString objects.

FIGURE 23.15
Details on the leak.

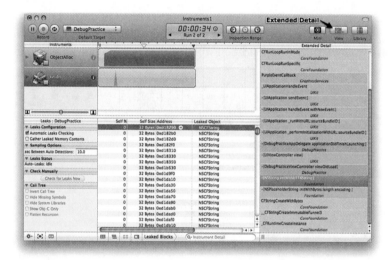

Available Instruments

Tracking down excess memory consumption and leaks is one use for Instruments, but it's really just the tip of the iceberg. There are other instruments besides Leak and Object Allocations that can quickly shed light on aspects of your application that would be difficult and very time-consuming to explore with just NSLog and the debugger. Not every instrument works with iPhone applications. Table 23.1 is a list of default instruments that are useful with iPhone applications. When you need one of these instruments, you add it to your trace document's instrumentation using the Library (see Figure 23.16), which is accessed from the Instrument's Window, Library menu option (Command+L).

FIGURE 23.16
Instruments
Library.

TABLE 23.1 Available Instruments

Activity Monitor	Monitors overall CPU, memory, disk, and network activity
CPU Sampler	Precise time-based sampling of CPU usage
Leaks	Detects memory leaks
Object Allocations	Measures memory usage by class
Core Data	Monitors Core Data activity and performance, including writes to the data repository and cache efficiency
File Activity	Monitors an application's interaction with the file system
UI Recorder	Captures and plays back UI events so that multiple runs can work with the exact same sequence of user interactions
Core Animation	Measures Core Animation graphics performance and the resulting CPU load
Open GL ES	Measures Open GL ES graphics performance and the resulting CPU load
System Usage	Monitors file, network and memory I/O use and duration for each method

Profiling with Shark

The last tool we'll look at in this hour is the Shark profiler. A profiler is a tool for better understanding application performance so that you know where to make targeted optimizations in the application. A profiler like Shark polls the application while it's running to see where it is spending time. The result of a profiling session with Shark is a report on which methods and lines of code your application is spending its time on. These lines of code and methods where you application is spending the bulk of its time are referred to as hot spots, and are where you should direct your optimization efforts.

Many iPhone applications are going to spend the bulk of their time waiting on user input or a network response, and will not benefit at all from optimization or from using a profiler. In fact, a classic sin of application development is premature optimization. Premature optimization is spending time improving the performance of your code before you know a particular section of code has a real and significant impact on the user's experience. A profiler can be a dangerous tool in this regard, because it tells you where your application is spending its time and there can be temptation to blindly optimize according to the profiler's results. Don't profile your application looking for slow spots. This is a mistake. Instead, find the slow spots by using your application as the user will use it, and then profile those slow spots to determine what's causing the slow down.

Attaching to Your Application

Using Shark for iPhone applications is a little tricky because to get data that has any value, you need to remotely profile the application running on the device. Profiling your application in the simulator usually doesn't make sense because the performance characteristics will be completely different.

Also, it can be especially tricky to use Shark to profile application startup time because Shark must attach to an already running application. To avoid this problem, let's go ahead and make a small adjustment to the DebugPractice application so that there will be something interesting happening after startup for Shark to profile. Add an IBOutlet called loopButton and an IBAction called loop to the DebugPracticeViewController.h file in the Classes group, as shown in Listing 23.1.

LISTING 23.1

```
#import <UIKit/UIKit.h>

@interface DebugPracticeViewController : UIViewController {

    IBOutlet UIButton *loopButton;

}

@property (nonatomic, retain) UIButton *loopButton;

-(IBAction)loop;

@end
```

In the DebugPracticeViewController.m file in the Classes group, synthesize the loopButton property and add a loop method that does the same thing as the non-leaking version of the loop from the viewDidLoad. Remove the for loop from viewDidLoad:

```
@synthesize loopButton;

// Implement viewDidLoad to do additional setup after loading the view,
typically from a nib.
- (void)viewDidLoad {
    [super viewDidLoad];

    NSString *description;

    NSLog(@"Start");
    for (int i = 1;i <= 2000;i++) {
        description = [self describeInteger:i];

        // Don't try this at home!
        NSString *status = [[NSString alloc]initWithUTF8String:"leaking"];

        NSLog(@"Variables: i - %i and description - %@ and status - %@",
            i, description, status);
    }
    NSLog(@"Done");
}

- (IBAction)loop {

    NSString *description;

    for (int i = 1;i <= 2000;i++) {
        description = [self describeInteger:i];
        NSLog(@"Variables: i - %i and description - %@", i, description);
    }

    [loopButton setTitleColor:[UIColor redColor]
        forState:UIControlStateNormal];
}
```

Perform the following steps to add the button to the view and connect the outlet and action for the button:

1. Double-click the DebugPracticeViewController.xib file in the Resources group to launch Interface Builder.

2. Open the Library (Shift+Command+L) and search for "button." Drag a UIButton to the center of the view.

3. Click the new button and open the Attribute Inspector (Command+1). Click the Title field and type **Loop**. Click the Text Color color picker well and select green.

4. Open the NIB window and right-click the File's Owner icon. Drag-click from the circle next to the loop Received Action to the button. Select Touch Down from the menu.

5. Drag-click from the circle next to the loopButton outlet to the button.

6. Your view should now look like Figure 23.17. Save the XIB file and return to Xcode.

FIGURE 23.17
The DebugPractice view in Interface Builder.

To use Shark to profile the modified DebugPractice application, follow these steps:

1. Set the Active SDK to the device with the Project, Set Active SDK, iPhone Device menu option.

2. Click the Build and Run icon to build the application and install it on the device. We want to run without gdb attached, so once the application starts, press the Home button on the device to stop it. Find the application on the device (it will have a completely white icon) and start it back up again. This time, leave it running on the device.

3. Use Finder to navigate to /Developer/Applications/Performance Tools and double-click the Shark.app application.

4. Once Shark starts up, make sure iPhone profiling is enabled by checking the Sampling, Network/iPhone Profiling menu option (Shift+Command+N).

5. Select the Control Network Profiling of Shared Computers radio button, and the devices you have connected to your Mac will appear.

6. Click the Use check box on the mobile device where the DebugPractice application is running. After a small delay, the Target column will populate with a list of the processes running on the device. "Everything" will be the initially selected value.

   Profiling everything running on the iPhone will result in a lot of data, and it will take a long time to gather and analyze it. We are just interested in data for the DebugPractice application, and so that's the only process we'll profile.

7. Click the Target drop-down menu for the device and select DebugPractice from the list (see Figure 23.18).

8. Press the Start button in the upper-left corner of the Shark UI, and Shark will start sampling where DebugPractice is spending its time.

9. Click the Loop button in the DebugPractice application on the device and wait until the button text turns red to let you know the loop is complete (20 to 30 seconds). Press the Stop button in the upper-left corner of the Shark UI. Shark will spend a couple of minutes or more analyzing the samples.

Shark data is computationally expensive to collect and analyze. If you sample 20 minutes of your application, prepare to wait a *long* time before you'll be able to see the results. Try to keep your shark samples small and focused and under a minute long.

Watch Out!

FIGURE 23.18
Connecting
Shark to a run-
ning application.

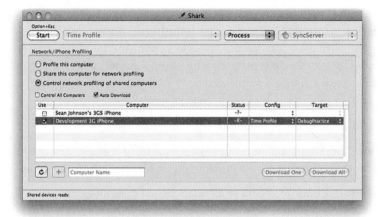

Understanding Profile Results

When Shark finishes analyzing the profile data, it displays the Session window (see
Figure 23.19). By default, data from the session is ordered by where the most time
was spent, which is called the Heavy (Bottom-Up) view. The heaviest methods are
often not your own code, but are code from the various frameworks that make up
the iPhone SDK such as UIKit and Core Foundation. It can also be hard to correlate
this view to any sense of how your application works, because the methods are
inverse of the normal call stack order; the sense of the program's flow of execution
can become lost.

FIGURE 23.19
Profile results in
the Heavy view.

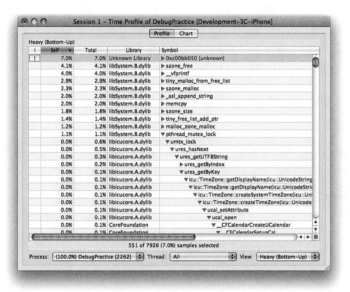

There is another view called Tree (Top-Down) that provides the call stack order of methods and will likely seem more familiar. Tree view starts with the application's main, then UIApplicationMain, and the tree progresses from there on into the methods of your application that you coded yourself and that you'll recognize (see Figure 23.20).

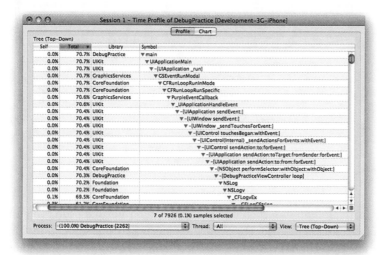

FIGURE 23.20
Profile results in the Tree view.

Finally, there is a Heavy and Tree view that stacks the Heavy view above the Tree view and let's you see both at the same time. Change the view with the View drop-down in the lower-right corner. At any point, you can look at a method's implementation by double-clicking the method name in the Symbol column. Like the debugger, Shark will show you the source of the method if it has the debug symbols for that method (see Figure 23.21) and will otherwise show the assembly code. Shark also has some built-in optimization tips that will display.

The key data point to consider in the Shark profile data is the total and self percentages for each of your methods. The Total column tells you approximately how much of the application's time (during the window of time that was profiled) was spent in that method, and the Self column tells you how much of the time was spent in the method itself rather than in the other methods that were called by the method.

The majority of the time, the methods you write yourself will have fairly small self percentages, because often the heavy computation in your application is done by the iPhone SDK frameworks on your behalf. Consider how a single line of your code can dismiss a complex model view with a flip transition and return to displaying the parent view. A huge amount of code in Core Animation and Quartz must then execute to make this one line of your code happen. Optimizing iPhone applications usually means changing your application to make a more informed use of the iPhone SDK, once you understand the expense of the operations you're asking be performed.

FIGURE 23.21
An optimization
hint from Shark.

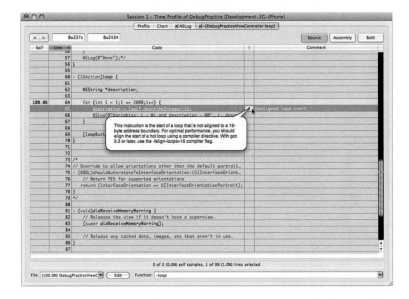

There is more art than science in profiling and optimizing, and I can't begin to tell you the exact way to proceed. The overall approach is to look through the Shark data for the things that surprise you the most. When writing your application, you have some sense of how it is going to perform. You expect certain operations you are calling to be expensive and others to be computationally cheap. When you find something in the data that breaks your mental model and surprises you, follow your nose and get to the bottom of it.

Remain patient and resist the urge to jump into optimizing. It's usually best to try a little test first to fake any optimization you are contemplating making. Make sure that if you succeeded in the optimization, there is a noticeable impact in the user experience of the application before you invest the time in implementing the optimization.

Summary

In this hour, we used three important tools of the iPhone SDK: Xcode's gdb debugger, the Instruments tracing tool, and the Shark profiler. It takes much longer than an hour to understand everything these powerful tools can do for you, but the goal has been to give you enough exposure to them that you recognize when you need the benefits of each of these tools. You also know enough to start using each tool and exploring further what it can do for you.

Workshop

Quiz

1. What is a breakpoint? What is a watchpoint?

2. Name some useful things you can monitor with Instruments.

3. Shark helps track down application performance problems when running in the iPhone Simulator. True or False?

Answers

1. A breakpoint tells the debugger to stop execution at the start of a particular line of source code so that the developer can inspect and possibly change the state of the running application and control and monitor the application's progress. A watchpoint is a conditional breakpoint that only stops execution if a specified condition is true.

2. Answers will vary. In this hour, we used Instruments to look at memory allocation and leakage. Read through Table 23.1 again if you couldn't remember any other uses.

3. False. You're really interested in using Shark to see how an application performs on the targeted device hardware. In most cases, applications will perform better in the simulator than on the actual device.

Activities

Use the File Activity and Core Data instruments to trace through the object archiving and Core Data versions of the FlashCards application from Hour 16, "Reading and Writing Data." What interesting things can you learn from tracing this application? What differences do you notice between the two versions of the application? Does this insight make you want to change anything about either implementation?

Further Exploration

Investing some time into becoming proficient with Xcode debugging, Instruments, and Shark can really pay off toward the end of a development project when you are trying to get a product release out the door, or when you are trying to quickly turn around a fix to an embarrassing bug or performance problem. In these cases, time is short and the stress level is high, so it's not the ideal circumstances to be learning these applications for the first time. Become comfortable with these tools now, and they'll provide a significant productivity boost when you need it the most.

To really start to master the iPhone SDK toolset, and to delve deeper into debugging, Instruments, and Shark, you should read Fritz Anderson's excellent book *Xcode 3 Unleashed.* If instead you want to focus in on just one of these tools, you can find Apple's *Xcode Debugging Guide, Instruments User Guide* and *Shark User Guide* in the iPhone Reference Library.

If you want to start interacting with the debugger directly, I recommend Richard Stallman's *Debugging with GDB: The GNU Source-Level Debugger* and Arnold Robbin's *GDB Pocket Reference.*

HOUR 24

Distributing Applications Through the App Store

What You'll Learn in This Hour:

▶ How to prepare and build a release version of your application for distribution

▶ The three different ways in which you can distribute an application

▶ Learn to market your application to let the whole world know how to get it

You've done it! Your application is built, tested, and ready for prime time. Now you need to decide how to deploy and market it. Tens of thousands of applications are available for download via Apple's iTunes App Store. The trick to success is to stand out from the crowd. This hour provides step-by-step instructions to submit your application and examines how to most effectively get your application to those who need it.

Did you Know?

Keep a close eye on how your app is managed in the App Store. If Apple makes changes, such as requiring support for the latest OS (as with the release of OS 3.0), ensure that you application supports the latest requirements. (Otherwise, you risk your application being dropped from the App Store.) Also, give Apple plenty of time to evaluate your updates. Typically, Apple takes about a week to evaluate an update or new submission before posting it to the App Store. Apple does continue to tweak and evaluate their process, but it is still far from perfect. Part of the problem is the massive number of new applications posted to the App Store each day. So, if Apple mandates specific changes, get to them fast.

Preparing an Application for the App Store

You're almost there: Your application has been developed and tested, and now you want to share it. However, before you can sell on the App Store, you must complete a few finishing touches.

Creating Artwork

Remember that admonition to never judge a book by its cover? Unfortunately, that sage advice doesn't apply to iPhone applications. Artwork for your application is important. People browsing the iTunes App Store are presented with thousands of applications. You need to have artwork that stands out from the crowd, as shown in Figure 24.1.

FIGURE 24.1
Artwork you submit with your app can help it stand out.

You have tight control over two pieces of artwork: the artwork used to present your application in your iTunes Applications library, and the icon used to present your application on your iPhone.

Open the Applications library in your copy of iTunes to see how iTunes artwork is used to visually identify applications (see Figure 24.2). Many companies extend their company brand to the colors, images, and treatment of their artwork used by their applications (for example, Weather.com, Pandora.com, and Facebook).

FIGURE 24.2
You can see iTunes artwork used by every application in your Applications library in your copy of iTunes.

Apple prefers that you create your artwork in the PNG file format. The final images should be 72 pixels per inch (ppi), with no transparency or layers. If you are using layers, you will want to create a "flat" version of your artwork for use with your application.

The artwork used in the iTunes Applications library is a specific 512x512 pixels in size, and the final exported PNG image must be named iTunesArtwork, with no file extension.

The icon that distinguishes your application on the iPhone also has specific restrictions. The file must be 57x57 pixels, with no transparency or layers. To help you identify the image, you may want to name the image icon.png. In the following exercise, you learn how to add these two different images to your project.

You can use any of the dozens of available image-editing tools to create the icons and iTunes artwork for your application. The PNG file format Apple prefers is a noncommercial file format that most image-editing tools now support. Two popular image-editing tools are Adobe PhotoShop and Fireworks. If your budget is tight, consider GIMP, an open source image-editing tool (www.gimp.org/macintosh). Alternative illustration tools include Acorn, Pixelmator, and Paintbrush. In other words, you have lots of choices.

By the Way

We use a simple Hello World project here to demonstrate how to add artwork to your application. You can follow these same steps for your own application:

1. Open the project HelloWorld for this hour. Included with the project are two PNG files that have been formatted for use as the iTunes artwork and as the default icon for your application.

2. Let's start by adding the iTunes artwork file to your project. In Xcode, select Project, Add to Project (Shift+Command+A) and choose the file named iTunesArtwork (see Figure 24.3).

FIGURE 24.3
iTunes artwork is shown as a file called iTunesArtwork in your project.

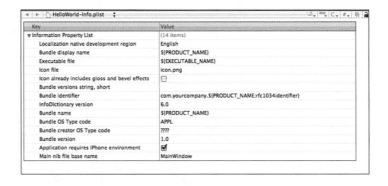

Key	Value
▼ Information Property List	(14 items)
Localization native development region	English
Bundle display name	${PRODUCT_NAME}
Executable file	${EXECUTABLE_NAME}
Icon file	icon.png
Icon already includes gloss and bevel effects	☐
Bundle versions string, short	
Bundle identifier	com.yourcompany.${PRODUCT_NAME:rfc1034identifier}
InfoDictionary version	6.0
Bundle name	${PRODUCT_NAME}
Bundle OS Type code	APPL
Bundle creator OS Type code	????
Bundle version	1.0
Application requires iPhone environment	☑
Main nib file base name	MainWindow

3. Repeat this process to add the icon file for the application. Select Project, Add to Project and choose the file named icon.png. The icon requires an additional modification of the plist (see Figure 24.4).

FIGURE 24.4
The plist allows you to associate the image that will be used for your icon and modify how that icon will be presented in your iPhone.

Key	Value
▼ Information Property List	(14 items)
Localization native development region	English
Bundle display name	${PRODUCT_NAME}
Executable file	${EXECUTABLE_NAME}
Icon file	icon.png
Icon already includes gloss and bevel effects	☐
Bundle versions string, short	
Bundle identifier	com.yourcompany.${PRODUCT_NAME:rfc1034identifier}
InfoDictionary version	6.0
Bundle name	${PRODUCT_NAME}
Bundle OS Type code	APPL
Bundle creator OS Type code	????
Bundle version	1.0
Application requires iPhone environment	☑
Main nib file base name	MainWindow

4. Open HelloWorld-Info.plist. Find the key labeled icon and add the value icon.png. By default, Apple will add glossy image treatment to the icon to keep it consistent with other icons as they appear on your iPhone. You can, however, override that by using a special key added to the plist called UIPrerenderedIcon.

5. Create a new key and enter **UIPrerenderedIcon** as the key value. The name will change to Icon Already Includes Gloss and Bevel Effects. Check the box to activate the feature. Save all your work.

6. Build your application and view it through your iPhone or the iPhone Simulator. When the application is running, your custom icon art represents your application, as shown in Figure 24.5.

FIGURE 24.5
Your application should have a design that makes it stand out from other icons on an iPhone.

Apple is continually increasing the number of applications you can run on your iPhone. Originally, the limit was 148, but OS 3.0 increased that number to 160, and this number will most likely increase further as customers demand more and more from their iPhones and iPod Touches. Therefore, spend the time necessary to create artwork that accurately and succinctly conveys what your application is all about. Remember, the icon size is only 57x57 pixels and shares space with as many as 20 other applications on any given screen.

Getting Your iPhone Distribution Certificate

The person responsible for submitting final applications to the iTunes store is called the team agent. For the team agent to be able to submit any solutions, he or she must have an approved iPhone Distribution Certificate. This section discusses how to obtain this certificate.

From the Applications folder on your Mac, launch the Keychain Access utility. You are going to request a certificate from a certificate authority (CA). To do this, you must change some of the settings in the Keychain Access utility (see Figure 24.6).

Select the Preferences menu, and then set Online Certificate Status Protocol (OSCP) and Certificate Revocation List (CRL) to Off.

FIGURE 24.6
Modifying the
settings for the
Keychain
Access utility.

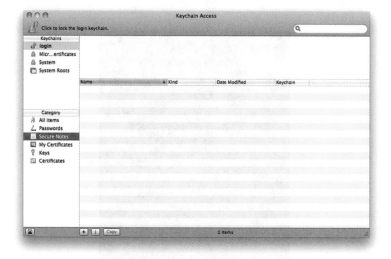

To request a new certificate, complete the following steps:

1. Choose Certificate Assistant, Request a Certificate from a Certificate Authority (see Figure 24.7).

2. Enter the team agent's email address and the name of your company as it appears in the iPhone Developer Program. You do not need a CA email address.

3. Save the data to disk and select Let Me Specify Key Pair Information.

FIGURE 24.7
Requesting a
new certificate
from a CA.

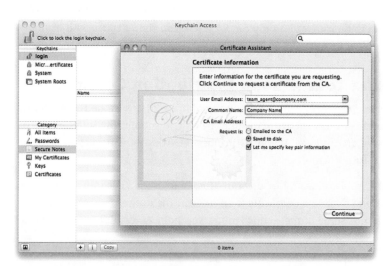

4. Choose Key Size and Algorithm. Select 2048 bits and RSA for the algorithm. Save the certificate as a CSR file to your desktop.

5. Navigate to http://developer.apple.com/iphone/manage/certificates/team/distribute.action in the iPhone Developer Program. Display the Distribution tab. All active certificates you have will be listed in the Distribution window. To obtain a certificate, select Request Certificate and upload the CSR file you just created.

6. After your certificate has been approved, you can download a CER file to your computer. The CER file is the iPhone Distribution Certificate associated with your computer. Install the CER file to your Keychain Access utility.

You should save your iPhone Distribution Certificate somewhere safe. The certificate ties your development environment directly to your solutions. Without the iPhone Distribution Certificate, you cannot deploy your applications. Best practice is to burn the certificate to a CD and store that CD somewhere safe.

You next need to create an iPhone Distribution Provisioning Profile, which allows you to associate your certificate with Apple with your application in Xcode:

1. In the iPhone Developer Program, choose Provisioning, Distribution (http://developer.apple.com/iphone/manage/provisioningprofiles/viewDistributionProfiles.action). Then click the New Profile button.

2. Choose whether the application will be uploaded to the App Store or will be deployed ad hoc.

3. Give your profile a meaningful name.

4. Double-check that the certificate is correct, and then select Submit. The profile is generated and can now be downloaded. The file you will download has the extension .mobileprovision. Save the .mobileprovision file to your desktop.

5. To install the profile, drag the .mobileprovision file onto either iTunes or Xcode in your dock.

Configuring a Project for Distribution

The final thing you need to do is to create a version of your application that you can submit to the App Store, as follows:

1. Open your project in Xcode. Double-click the name of the application in Xcode to open the Information panel. Display the Configurations tab (see Figure 24.8).

FIGURE 24.8
The Configurations pane.

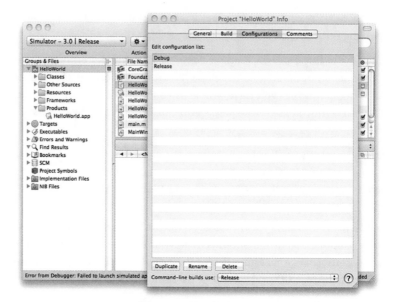

2. Select the Release configuration option, click the Duplicate button in the lower-left corner, and rename the new copy **Distribution**.

3. Select Target from the main project. Double-click the Target project name to open the Target Info window (see Figure 24.9). Display the Build tab, and select Distribution from the build options.

FIGURE 24.9
The Target Info pane.

4. You now need to associate your distribution certificate and provisioning profile with the build. From the Code Signing section, select Any iPhone Device, and choose your certificate from the drop-down list. Your certificate will be in bold, with your provisioning profile in gray. Without a valid certificate, you cannot upload your applications to the App Store.

5. Display the Properties tab so that you can enter the bundle identifier for your application (see Figure 24.10). The bundle identifier needs to be the same as your App ID you used to register with the Developer Portal. (An example of a bundle identifier is 123456789.com.yourcompany.yourappname.)

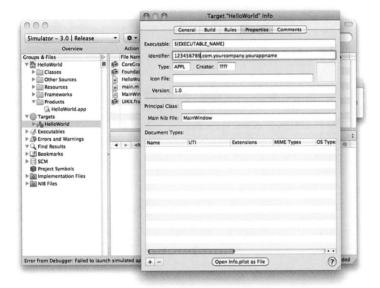

FIGURE 24.10
Creating a bundle identifier for your application.

6. Now you create an entitlement plist, a file that provides the code signing for the app, as shown in Figure 24.11. Choose New File, iPhone OS, Code Signing, Entitlements.

7. Most people name the entitlement file Entitlement.plist. The file is saved to the root of your application. The Entitlement.plist has one property called `get-task-allow`. Uncheck the Boolean value of this property, as shown in Figure 24.12.

8. Open the Target Info panel for your application. Display the Build tab and select Code Signing Entitlements from the Code Signing section. Type in **entitlements.plist** and save your work.

FIGURE 24.11
Creating an enti-
tlement plist.

FIGURE 24.12
The
Entitlement's
get-task-
allow property
must be
unchecked.

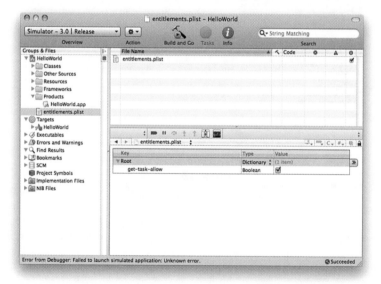

9. Now change the application's active configuration to Distribution and build your application. The final build will have the extension .app. Open the folder with the final build and compress the APP file. This document is now ready for submission to the App Store.

Submitting an Application for Approval

The Apple iTunes App Store is a dazzling success. Now duplicated by RIM, Palm, Nokia, and Microsoft, the iTunes App Store boasts more than 65,000 unique applications, 1.5 billion (that's with a *b*, not an *m*) downloads, and an audience of 40 million users.

The success of the App Store is built on making the user experience easy. For many people, the hardest part of running an application is installing it. With the iPhone App Store, Apple has introduced a one-click installation process that makes it easy to install any solution. In the App Store, users just click an application's price button to start the buying and installing process. The application's price display is red. Click that button and the wording on the button changes to Purchase. To actually purchase the application, you must click the button again and then enter your account password. That's it. After that, OS 3.0 does the rest.

This simple process enables every developer to easily deploy a solution and know that it will be installed correctly. In addition, the customer can apply updates to your application via a one-click download from the App Store app.

Apple is also upfront about the charges. Apple charges just one rate: 30% of the price of your application (or nothing if the app is given away for free). So, if you are selling an application for $2.99, 30% goes to Apple and 70% to you. In this case, you get $2.00 for each sale.

At first it might seem that Apple is gouging you of your profits; but if you have developed content for the Nintendo DS, Microsoft Xbox 360, or Sony PlayStation, you know that Apple's fee is reasonable. After all, it is Apple that is hosting the applications in their own server farms, managing the 40 million accounts, and giving you access to tools to effectively control how you sell your applications. Yes, the 30% cost is *very* reasonable.

Apple strives for transparency about how well your application is selling. In fact, they created iTunes Connect to help you manage your account. You can log in to the iTunes Connect site at https://itunesconnect.apple.com.

Uploading Your Application

When you have your accounts set up, you will want to start uploading your applications to the store (see Figure 24.13). Only a release version of your application can be uploaded. In iTunes Connect, click the Manage Your Applications link, and then start the process by clicking the Add New Application link.

FIGURE 24.13
Uploading an
application to
the App Store.

Select your default country and name, as shown in Figure 24.14.

FIGURE 24.14
Choose your
country and
business name.

Next, answer the export question.

The fourth screen asks you for all the information about the application:

▶ Application Name.

▶ Application Description (limit 4,000 characters; see Figure 24.15).

▶ Device Requirements. (Currently, you can choose iPhone only, iPhone and iPod [2nd Generation], and iPhone and iPod.)

▶ Primary Category. (There are 20 primary categories, including Games, Entertainment, Business, Books, and News. Some categories, such as Games, have subcategories to help organize the content more effectively.)

▶ Secondary Category. (You can choose a second category for your application.)

▶ Copyright (the person who owns the code).

▶ Version Number. (You can use your own schema for version number.)

▶ SKU Number (a unique identifier that you create). A simple way to create an SKU is to insert the date, such 08312009 for August 31, 2009. When you update the application, just apply a new date.

▶ Keywords. Keywords are used to help return results when a customer is searching for an application.

- Application URL. The application URL links to the application's website.
- Support URL. The support URL links to the support site for the application.
- Support Email Address.

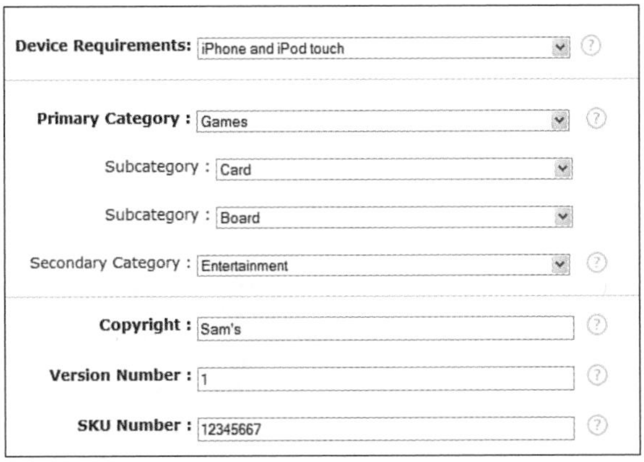

FIGURE 24.15
Accurately describe your application before submitting it.

With OS 3.0, Apple included a rating scheme that allows parents to control which applications their children download. You must complete this screen (see Figure 24.16). The age limit will change depending on how you rate your application. Make sure you rate the application correctly. During an internal process, Apple reviews how you score your application.

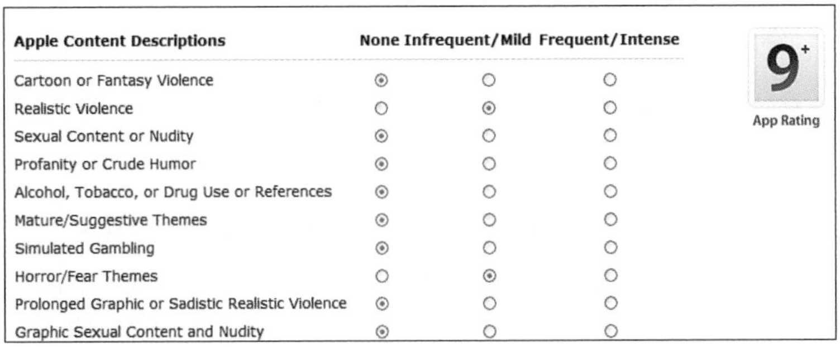

Apple Content Descriptions	None	Infrequent/Mild	Frequent/Intense
Cartoon or Fantasy Violence	⦿	○	○
Realistic Violence	○	⦿	○
Sexual Content or Nudity	⦿	○	○
Profanity or Crude Humor	⦿	○	○
Alcohol, Tobacco, or Drug Use or References	⦿	○	○
Mature/Suggestive Themes	⦿	○	○
Simulated Gambling	⦿	○	○
Horror/Fear Themes	○	⦿	○
Prolonged Graphic or Sadistic Realistic Violence	⦿	○	○
Graphic Sexual Content and Nudity	⦿	○	○

FIGURE 24.16
All applications must be scored using the rating tool.

Along with the iTunes artwork and application icon, you need to have a screen shot of the application. The screen shot promotes the application in iTunes. The screen shot should be 320x460 pixels, to allow the image to fit onto your screen when you view the image via the iPhone App Store. You can also have up to four additional screen shots to show different parts of the application, as shown in Figure 24.17.

FIGURE 24.17
You can easily
add artwork for
your application.

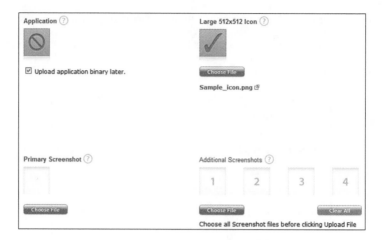

The Pricing screen lets you select when the application will go on sale and what pricing tier you prefer. Apple uses a pricing tier schema to help you manage the price of the application as it sells internationally (see Figure 24.18).

FIGURE 24.18
You can sell
your application
in any country
that supports
the App Store.

On a Review screen, you can double-check everything about your application before you submit it for Apple's approval.

Building a Store Inside of Your Application

New to OS 3.0 is a new feature called In App Purchases. The In App Purchases feature allows for an application to have a store within itself. For instance, if you develop a game with multiple levels, you can sell optional additional levels using the In App Purchases feature.

This feature provides significant benefits:

▶ Apple manages payment transactions, and so you don't have to worry about storing credit card data.

▶ Transactions with In App Purchases are quick and do not require customers to "register" to make a payment.

▶ For the customer, there is a level of comfort that the purchase will be secure because Apple is managing the transaction.

▶ Transactions are recorded on a single iTunes receipt and can be easily tracked by the customer.

▶ As with normal software purchases, the charge Apple applies to In App purchases is 30%.

You can leverage several different types of In App Purchases transactions. The most obvious is allowing a customer to purchase something, such as a new game level, directly inside your own store. Another transaction type is a subscription. Just as with purchasing a magazine subscription, an In App Purchase subscription will renew on a scheduled basis.

Applications that are downloaded for free from the iTunes App Store cannot use the In App Purchases feature. You must first sell the application. A good price point might be $0.99.

Did you Know?

In App Purchases transactions are managed through a new application programming interface (API) called the Store Kit. Fundamentally, the Store Kit API enables you to run the functionality of the iTunes App Store inside your own application, as shown in Figure 24.19. The new Manage Your In App Purchases option lets you see sales numbers specific to In App Purchases transactions.

At the end of the day, no matter how you deploy to the iTunes Store and whether or not you add functionality such as the Store Kit API, the largest audience your application can reach is via the iTunes App Store.

Apple claims that their review process for an application is completed in less than a week, but this is not always the case. What can help you is to be clear and honest about the content of your app, whether or not the application connects to the Internet, and whether your application features any violence. Apple also strictly prohibits pornographic applications.

By the Way

FIGURE 24.19
The workflow
used to manage
payments using
the Store Kit
API.

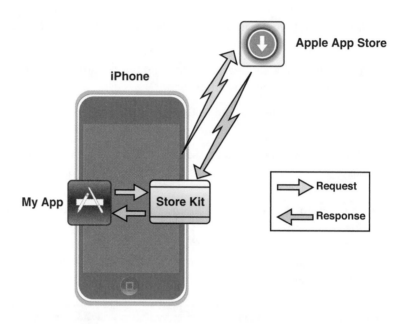

Promoting Your Application

You've done it. Your application is installed in the App Store. You have heard all the "rags to riches" stories of developers who have made tens of thousands from sales of apps, and now you are waiting for your pot of gold to arrive. But, you might be waiting for a while. Although you can make a lot of money from selling your application, you must be willing to expend a bit of effort.

To sell any piece of software, take advantage of all the traditional ways software has been sold in the past. In addition, we now have some seriously focused tools (and tactics) that can really help your sales, including the following:

- ▶ Use Apple's iTunes Connect to monitor/manage sales.
- ▶ Exploit websites and social networks.
- ▶ Update your application.
- ▶ Change your price.

Any or all of the "tools" listed here can help build interest and drive sales of your application.

Using iTunes Connect to Monitor/Manage Sales

iTunes Connect is the tool you use to upload and manage your applications in the App Store (see Figure 24.20). Via iTunes Connect, you can do the following:

▶ Manage and upload your applications to the App Store

▶ Assess sales/trends

▶ Review your contracts, tax, and banking information

▶ Download financial reports

▶ Manage users

▶ Include an internal Application Store in your application, which allows you to sell optional content for your app

▶ Request promotional codes

▶ Contact Apple support with any questions you may have

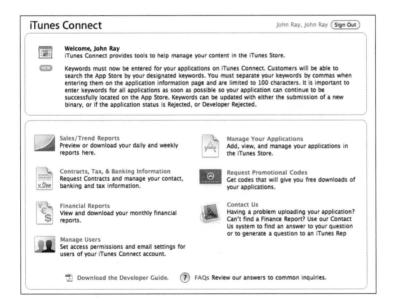

FIGURE 24.20
iTunes Connect tells you how your application is selling.

When you log in to iTunes Connect, ensure that your banking information is correct. After all, if you are selling something, you want to make sure that you are being paid.

Then, set up accounts for those persons in your company who need access to iTunes Connect. Three user types can access the iTunes Connect account in addition to the original person who set up the account (called the Legal account), as follows:

▶ The Admin account has the right to view, add, and delete additional accounts and manage the whole iTunes Connect environment.

▶ The Finance account gives the user access to financial reports and contracts, tax and banking information, and sales/trend reports modules.

▶ The Technical account allows the user to manage applications and manage users' modules.

Generally, you will add multiple accounts only if you have a large organization that requires different levels of access to the iTunes Connect service.

A feature that you will want to use to promote your applications is Request Promotional Codes. This feature, located on iTunes Connect (in the Request Promotional Codes section), allows you to send promo codes to users who can then download and use your application for free. The promotional code cannot be shared after it has been used. You can have up to 50 promotional codes for an application.

If you have a lot of applications for sale in a lot of countries, managing all the Apple-provided data can get confusing. However, a number of companies provide tools to sift through all the iTunes Connect data. Check out the Developer Tools section of Apple's website for the latest solutions (www.apple.com/downloads/macosx/development_tools/).

Arguably, the most important feature in iTunes Connect is Sales Trends Analysis. This tool tells you how your sales are going (by date and by country).

By the Way

One of the most popular applications sold via the App Store is Firemint's Flight Control. In an unusual move, Firemint released the sales numbers for their application. You can view the report at http://firemint.com/files/FlightControl-SalesNumbers.pdf.

Exploiting Websites and Social Networks

It might seem very turn of the millennia, but websites work well to advertise your applications. A website can be built very quickly using tools such as Adobe Dreamweaver, WordPress, Joomla, or even iWeb if you are pressed for resources.

The key is to build a website that's easy to view on any device (including via Mobile Safari on the iPhone). In addition, test your site on Windows and Mac computers.

As mentioned earlier, you must associate a website with your application during the submission process. Therefore, every application available via the iPhone App Store has a web address. Customers can use Mobile Safari, the iPhone's own web browser, to view your application's website.

Mobile Safari is one of the most advanced web browsers available, and therefore you can add many of the latest HTML tricks to your website. For instance, Mobile Safari supports HTML 5, and so you can add rich transition and animation effects to your website.

From your website, you can advertise and link back to applications you are selling in the App Store. You can find the URL for any application in the App Store by right-clicking the link inside of iTunes. The cryptic URL you are given will look something like this:

```
http://itunes.apple.com/WebObjects/MZStore.woa/wa/viewSoftware?id=306220440&mt=8
```

Add this link to your web page. When potential customers click it, they will be taken directly to the page in iTunes where they can purchase your application. Similarly, if a potential customer is using Mobile Safari and clicks a link to your app, Mobile Safari will close and the App Store app will open and go directly to your application.

The really long URL link is great to add to your own website, but it doesn't work if you want to use social networking sites such as Twitter and Facebook. Twitter, in particular, limits the number of characters you can type to 140, and thus prevents long URLs from being entered. To resolve this problem, use URL-shortening services such as bit.ly so that you can post a URL that has fewer than a dozen characters.

You can also build social networking directly into your application. Many social networking sites have their own API. For example, with Facebook's API, you can post the latest high score or challenge your Facebook friends to a game. Freeverse's Postman enables you to send custom postcards directly to Facebook, Twitter, or Tumblr.

In addition to social networks, you will also want to contact the editors of websites that cover iPhone applications. You can often get a boost in sales by working with these editors and getting a link to your app from their website. Good sites to contact and work with include the following:

▶ AppStoreApps.com

▶ 148apps.com

▶ AppCraver.com

▶ AppSafari.com

▶ AppleiPhoneApps.com

▶ iPhoneApplicationList.com

▶ NativeiPhoneApps.com

▶ iPhoneApps.co.uk

▶ Apptism.com

▶ AppShopper.com

▶ Apprater.com

When you contact these sites, be courteous and give the editors a promotional code for your application so that they can test it and write a review.

As you build your website, think about how web search engines such as Google and Bing see your site. There are lots of great websites that lay out the search engine optimization techniques. Adding search engine optimization to your site can increase the number of times the site is presented on a search engine results page.

In addition to relying on organic placement on a search engine results page, you can purchase paid advertising. The goal of paid advertising is to appear alongside results similar to your product. Google's paid advertising allows your results to show on both their Google.com website and through their affiliate sites.

Finally, add analytical tools such as Google Analytics to your website. These tools provide information about how people are using your website, how often they return, and how they came to your site.

Updating Your Application

Unlike traditional computer-based software, applying updates to iPhone applications is very easy, and you will find that your customers will have few problems updating their apps. There is a tactical benefit to releasing updates to an application on a regular, scheduled basis (see Figure 24.21):

▶ The first benefit is that customers think that they are getting something for free. The update is a bonus.

▶ The second benefit is that the update brings the user's attention back to the app. An update is an opportunity to rediscover an application.

▶ The final benefit is each update gets separate reviews in the App Store.

FIGURE 24.21
Updates are a great way to draw attention back to your application.

A final thought as you update your apps: Add good, descriptive explanations for the update. Frequently, developers list "bug fixes" as the only reason for the update. Although this is important to the developer and the users experiencing problems with the application, for the rest of your users it is not a very exciting update. A different approach is to add one or two new features with the bug fixes. This way a customer can get excited about installing the update and trying out a new feature.

Changing Your Price

How much should you charge for your application? This is a tough question for all developers and companies selling applications on the App Store. With hundreds of new applications being added each week, you can easily become lost in the melee.

A tactic that many developers adopt is to start selling at $4.99 and then, shortly after release, temporarily dropping the price by a couple of dollars for a specified period. The effect is to create a fire sale, and thus drive urgency to purchase.

Dropping your price can also increase the number of sales in the iTunes App Store. Your goal is to break into the Top 100. Often referred to as racing to the bottom, the result of dropping your price as far you can go is to devalue your product just to get to number 1. Companies such as Electronic Arts and 2K Games, however, recognize that you can make more profit by keeping your price higher and not hitting number 1. For instance, EA's Scrabble spent several weeks in the Top 10 without changing its price of $4.99. The Scrabble app did not sell as many units as the number 1 app, but at 5x the price, it most likely made more profit.

Ultimately, how you choose and manage the price for your application depends on your marketing plan.

Did you Know?

Traditional Marketing

There have never been so many ways in which you can spend your marketing dollars. Building websites, frequenting social networks, and spending money on Google advertising are new media solutions you can spend your money on. Interestingly, however, Apple has done a lot to help promote and validate traditional media.

The number one traditional media marketing spot you may want to look at is TV. Apple promotes apps through their own iPhone commercials, and you should, too (if possible). For example, Nationwide Insurance promotes their iPhone application in their TV commercials. Although Nationwide's television advertising may be costly, referencing the iPhone App helps reinforce their message of being a technology-savvy company. Television advertising can be too expensive for small companies, but if you are already using TV, there is no reason not to include advertising space for your iPhone apps.

Magazines are also good places to advertise niche apps (even though subscription numbers are falling for most magazines). For instance, if you have an application for finding the cheapest college textbooks, why not advertise in college magazines?

Finally, why not lease a billboard to advertise your app? Just because no one has done it yet doesn't mean it won't work.

Ultimately, you must leverage a marketing plan built of many different media to help promote your app. In the words of a wise man, in a forest you must find the tallest tree, climb to the top, and yell from the top of your lungs to be heard. And the Apple iTunes Store is a very crowded forest these days.

Other Distribution Methods

In addition to the App Store, Apple provides two other ways to distribute your application:

▶ Ad hoc deployment

▶ Enterprise delivery

Ad Hoc Deployment

Sometimes you do not want to deploy an application immediately to the App Store. Sometimes you just want to send it directly to some friends and coworkers to get feedback.

Ad hoc deployment allows you to package a release version of your application into a zip file and give it to whomever you want to via email, website download, or USB drive.

Packaging an application for ad hoc deployment is easy. After you have created a release build of your application in Xcode, right-click the Products folder and select Reveal in Finder to locate on your hard drive where the physical build files are located.

To create an ad hoc deployment, you must associate your Xcode build with iPhone Distribution Provisioning Profile configured for ad hoc deployment. The setup for an ad hoc version of the iPhone Distribution Provisioning Profile is the same one for an app that will be deployed to the iTunes store. The only difference is that you choose Ad Hoc as the distribution type.

Open the Build folder to see subfolders for each deployment type you have used in your project. The release version of your app will be located in a folder that starts with the word *release* (see Figure 24.22).

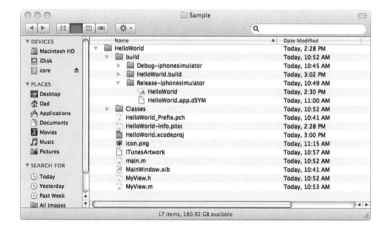

FIGURE 24.22
The final, release version of your app is located in a Release folder under Build.

Inside the Release folder are two files: a file with the extension .app, and a second file with the extension .app.dSYM. Copy both of the files into a zip file. Apple suggests that you use a specific naming convention for your zip file of *<application_name> for <user_name>.zip*. For example, you can name the zip file that uses the sample in this chapter **HelloWorld for Matthew David.zip**.

Those persons receiving the zip file just need to unpackage it and drag the APP file into their local copy of iTunes and sync with their iPhone or iPod Touch. That's it. You have now effectively distributed your application using the ad hoc deployment method.

> When you build a release version of an application, you do not include the debugging and tracking tools. Including them can make the final version of the application massive in size and can lead to performance issues. If they have been included, you can always remove them. Removing the debugging information does, however, make it difficult to track errors and crashes that users of the application may experience. The dSYM file is Xcode's answer to this problem.
>
> The dSYM file uses a technology called Debugging with Attributed Records Format (DWARF) that allows an application to send debugging information to the dSYM file while keeping its own file size small. The dSYM file logs user activity with the application. You can then analyze any data associated with a crash by looking at the dSYM file. This is important when a friend who is running your new game on her iPhone says, "Well, it just stopped working." The debugging information captured in the dSYM file may tell you that your friend received a call while using the application, which caused the application to crash. Now you know to add additional code to protect the application when a phone call is received.

Regarding the ad hoc process, be aware of the following caveats:

▶ Apple states that you are limited to only 50 people per release version of an app when you want to share the app ad hoc. Of course, there are ways around this limitation. You can change the version number each time you want to create an ad hoc deployment or even change the name of the application.

▶ The actual installation for users is more complex than they may be used to with the iTunes App Store.

▶ This method should be used only for early releases and testing of your application. The ad hoc deployment method can in no way reach the number of people you can reach using the iTunes App Store (unless, of course, you have 40+ million users' email addresses in your Contacts folder).

Enterprise Provisioning

Some of the most prolific users of iPhones are enterprises. Kraft Foods, for instance, is deploying more than 100 iPhones each and every month to employees. To take advantage of the enterprise deployment model...

▶ You must have an Enterprise subscription to Apple's Dev Center ($299/yr).

▶ Each custom application your company develops must be signed using your own digital certificate.

▶ An Enterprise Provisioning Profile must be created allowing authorized devices to install applications with your certificate.

▶ You then deploy your iPhone applications to authorized desktops.

Authorized users can drag and drop a deployed application into their iTunes and sync the next time they connect their iPhone to their computer. The process is the same for Mac, Windows XP, Vista, and Windows 7 versions of iTunes.

Summary

Over this past hour, you have learned how to submit your iPhone application to the App Store for publication.

So, you have prepared your app, you have deployed it, and now you have to let everyone know how to get it. Marketing can be the biggest challenge for any iPhone application developer. In this hour, you learned ways to leverage both traditional and "new" media to get your application noticed and sold.

Q&A

Q. *What type of applications are the most popular in the iTunes App Store?*

A. Currently, one-third of all applications published on the iPhone App Store are games. That's more than 20,000 games. You can choose to write a game for this popular group or review the other categories in the App Store and look for areas where there appears to be missing applications. Ultimately, a great solution will always sell as long as your customers know that it exists.

Q. *Should I only develop solutions for specific iPhones, such as the 3GS?*

A. The iPhone 3GS is, without doubt, the fastest iPhone Apple has released, with great new functionality such as a compass and video recording. You can choose to develop for the latest device if you want to. The downside is that by doing so you limit your potential sales by targeting only a specific audience.

Workshop

Quiz

1. What does *release* mean in the build process?

2. Where can you modify the settings for iPhone icons?

3. What is iTunes Connect?

Answers

1. When you have finished testing an application and are ready to deliver to the iTunes App Store, you must change the build process to Release. The release step will build a version of your application with the extension .app that will be sent to the iTunes App Store, to your enterprise App Store, or ad hoc via email.

2. The icon settings can be modified in the plist file. Add the setting `UIPrerenderedIcon` and set the option to `true`.

3. iTunes Connect is how you manage your application after you have uploaded it to the iTunes App Store.

Activities

1. Build a deployable version of your application and send it to some friends and have them test it on their iPhones. When you are sure the application is good to be published, submit it to the iTunes App Store.

2. Develop a marketing strategy and start letting people know that your application exists. Easy ways to promote your application include contacting iPhone fan sites and asking whether they can review your app, posting to forums, and updating your Facebook and Twitter accounts.

Index

Symbols

#import directive, 65

% (percent sign), string format specifiers, 604-605

@property directive, 63-64, 137

@synthesize directive, 66, 137

A

accelerometer, 501-503
- configuring, 504
- g-forces, 502
- movement, detecting, 513-514
- orientation, sensing, 505-507
- tilt, detecting, 509-512

accessibility attributes (IB), 119-120, 129

Accessibility Inspector, 121

accessing iPod library for MediaPlayground project, 533-534

action sheets
- appearance, changing, 285-286
- buttons, responding to, 286-287
- displaying, 283

actions, 125
- adding
  - Best Friend project, 560-562
  - DateCalc project, 245
  - FlashCards project, 404-405
  - MediaPlayground project, 522-523
  - to multiview applications, 303-304
  - Photo Grabber project, 546-549, 554-556
- connections
  - adding to multiview applications, 304-305
  - creating in IB, 126-128
- preparing
  - for FieldButtonFun project, 161-162

How can we make this index more useful? Email us at indexes@samspublishing.com

FREE Online Edition

Your purchase of **Sams Teach Yourself iPhone Application Development in 24 Hours** includes access to a free online edition for 45 days through the Safari Books Online subscription service. Nearly every Sams book is available online through Safari Books Online, along with more than 5,000 other technical books and videos from publishers such as Addison-Wesley Professional, Cisco Press, Exam Cram, IBM Press, O'Reilly, Prentice Hall, Que, and Sams.

SAFARI BOOKS ONLINE allows you to search for a specific answer, cut and paste code, download chapters, and stay current with emerging technologies.

Activate your FREE Online Edition at www.informit.com/safarifree

> **STEP 1:** Enter the coupon code: LWWHPXA.

> **STEP 2:** New Safari users, complete the brief registration form.
> Safari subscribers, just log in.

If you have difficulty registering on Safari or accessing the online edition, please e-mail customer-service@safaribooksonline.com

Addison Wesley

Adobe Press

ALPHA

Cisco Press

FT Press
FINANCIAL TIMES

IBM Press

lynda.com

Microsoft Press

New Riders

O'REILLY

Peachpit Press

PRENTICE HALL

QUE

Redbooks

SAS Publishing

Sun microsystems

WILEY